SUPPLEMENTARY LIVES IN SOME MANUSCRIPTS OF THE *GILTE LEGENDE*

EARLY ENGLISH TEXT SOCIETY

No. 315

2000

that kyght wilfride and bade hym with other
bischops to go and seke the place where this
holy kyng kenelme was beryed in colbage
in the wode of Clent and then place was
sone knowe bycause of the myracle that our
lorde shewith by the white cowe And when
the erchebisshop come to the place he lete ta
ke the holy bodi oute of the erthe with ful
gret solempnite and anone ther sprang ou
te of the same graue a fayre welle that is cal
lid seint kenelme is welle where many a cra
ture hath receyued helth that hath long tyme
be sike And when this holy bodi was take
oute of the graue ther fil gret striffe bytwe
ne Winchesterschire men and Glowcetschire
men who shulde haue this holy bodi And
then on that was a ful goode man yafe cou
seil that al the peple shulde lye downe and
slepe to reste them for the wedir was tho
right hote. And whiche of the .ij. schires that
god wolde that a wakyd first shulde take the
holy bodi and go ther they thercks and so it
happnd that the Abbot of wynchecombe and
as thei come vpon an hie hille a myle oute of
the seid abbey the seid abbey of wynchecom
be and as thei come vpon an hie hille a my
le oute of the seid abbey then were so sore a thur
ste that thei wiste not what to do And anone
thei made ther prayers to god and to this ho
ly kyng and the Abbot pight downe his croo
se in the erthe and anone ther sprang vp ȝ

SUPPLEMENTARY LIVES
IN SOME
MANUSCRIPTS OF THE
GILTE LEGENDE

EDITED BY

RICHARD HAMER AND VIDA RUSSELL

Published for

THE EARLY ENGLISH TEXT SOCIETY

by the

OXFORD UNIVERSITY PRESS

2000

OXFORD
UNIVERSITY PRESS

Great Clarendon Street, Oxford OX2 6DP

Oxford University Press is a department of the University of Oxford.
It furthers the University's aim of excellence in research, scholarship,
and education by publishing worldwide in

Oxford New York

Athens Auckland Bangkok Bogotá Buenos Aires Calcutta
Cape Town Chennai Dar es Salaam Delhi Florence Hong Kong Istanbul
Karachi Kuala Lumpur Madras Melbourne Mexico City Mumbai
Nairobi Paris São Paulo Singapore Taipei Tokyo Toronto Warsaw

and associated companies in Berlin Ibadan

Oxford is a registered trade mark of Oxford University Press

Published in the United States
by Oxford University Press Inc., New York

© Early English Text Society, 2000

British Library Cataloguing in Publication Data

Data available

Library of Congress Cataloging in Publication Data

Data applied for

ISBN 0-19-722313-3

1 3 5 7 9 10 8 6 4 2

Typeset by Joshua Associates Ltd., Oxford
Printed in Great Britain
on acid-free paper by
Print Wright Ltd., Ipswich

270.
92
SUP

03123227

PREFACE

This volume will be followed in due course by an edition of the complete original text of the *Gilte Legende*. It may seem irrational to publish supplementary material from a minority of the manuscripts before publishing the main text, but since this part of the work has been completed first, there seems to be no good reason to withhold it. The Introduction to this volume is therefore rather limited in scope, since it will make better sense to supply full descriptions of the manuscripts and similar matter in the General Introduction to the main legendary.

We are pleased to acknowledge permission to print the texts and to include plates from manuscripts in the British Library and Lambeth Palace Library, and also the text of one Life from a manuscript in the library of Trinity College, Dublin. We are grateful to the librarians and their staffs of the above libraries and also of the Bodleian Library, Oxford, Chetham's Library, Manchester, St John's College, Cambridge, Southwell Minster Library and the University Library, Durham, for access to manuscripts in their care and for much other help; to the authorities of the Bibliothèque Royale, Brussels, Cambridge University Library and the Beinecke Rare Books Library at Yale University for the provision of microfilms; and to the Inter-Library Loans Librarians of the Barr Smith Library of the University of Adelaide.

We also wish to thank the following individuals, who have given valuable and in some cases very substantial help: Professor Norman Blake, Miss Diane Bolton, Dr T. L. Burton, Dr Jane Cartwright, Professor Sir Henry Chadwick, Miss Lucy Davey, Miss Eileen Davies, Dr Ian Doyle, Dr Ralph Hanna III, Mrs Margaret Hosking, Professor Anne Hudson, Mrs J. Juchniewicz, Mrs Margaret Lewis, Professor Sherry L. Reames, Ms Larissa C. Tracy, Miss Margaret Weedon, Professor Gordon Whatley and Dr Christiania Whitehead. We are especially grateful to Dr H. L. Spencer for her patient and expert support during the final stages of preparation of this edition. Our greatest debt is to Professor Manfred Görlach, whose published work on these texts has been of major importance, and whose encouragement has been much appreciated.

CONTENTS

ABBREVIATIONS AND SHORT TITLES

Manuscripts containing texts edited in this edition are referred to by the following sigla:

A1	London, British Library, Additional MS 11565
A2	London, British Library, Additional MS 35298
B	Oxford, Bodleian Library, MS Eng. th. e. 17
C	Cambridge, University Library, MS Ll.v.18
Co	Durham, University Library, MS Cosin V.iv.4
J	Cambridge, St John's College, MS N.17 (250)
L	London, Lambeth Palace Library, MS 72
Lb	London, Lambeth Palace Library, MS 432
M	Manchester, Chetham's Library, MS 8009 (Görlach's C)
R	London, British Library, MS Royal 2.A.xviii
S	Southwell Minster, MS 7 (Görlach's S2)
T1	Dublin, Trinity College, MS 319
Y	New Haven, Yale, Beinecke Library, MS 317

Other MSS:

A	Oxford, Bodleian Library, MS Ashmole 43 (South English Legendary)
Br	Brussels, Bibliothèque Royale, MS 21003 (Latin Life of St Barbara)
P	Cambridge, Magdalene College, MS Pepys 2344 (South English Legendary)
Y	Oxford, Bodleian Library, MS Additional c.38 (South English Legendary)

Sigla for MSS of the *Liber Indulgentiarum* are listed at the beginning of the Notes to 4 'Pardon', p. 476 below.

The normal form of reference to printed works is by author's name followed by the date of publication in brackets; these references are expanded in the Select Bibliography, as are the abbreviated titles for frequently cited works which are given with other abbreviations in the following list.

Abbo	Abbo: *Life of St Edmund* in Winterbottom (1972)
Aelred	Aelred of Rievaulx, *Vita Edwardi Regis* from Twysden
ALL	Additional Lives
Anal.Boll.	*Analecta Bollandiana*
Bede, *HE*	Bede, *Historia Ecclesiastica Gentis Anglorum*, ed. B. Colgrave and R. A. B. Mynors (1969)
Butler	*Butler's Lives of the Saints*, ed. Thurston, Herbert and Attwater, Donald, 4 vols. (London, 1956)
Capgrave	*Ye Solace of Pilgrimes*, see Capgrave (1911)
Cuthbert	Colgrave, Bertram, ed., *Two Lives of Saint Cuthbert* (Cambridge, 1940), pp. 141–307
Early SEL	Horstmann, Carl, ed., *The Early South-English Legendary*, EETS os 87 (1887)
EETS os	Early English Text Society, Original Series
EStn	*Englische Studien*
Farmer	Farmer, David Hugh, comp., *The Oxford Dictionary of Saints* (3rd ed. Oxford, 1992)
GiL	*Gilte Legende*
GoL	Caxton's *Golden Legend*
Goscelin	Goscelin, *Vita S. Augustini* (1668)
IMEV	Brown, C. and Robbins, R. H., *The Index of Middle English Verse* (New York, 1943)
LALME	McIntosh, A., Samuels, M. L. and Benskin, M., *A Linguistic Atlas of Late Mediaeval English*, 4 vols. (Aberdeen, 1986)
LgA	*Legenda Aurea*, ed. Maggioni (1998)
LgAsupp.	Supplementary materials in *Legenda Aurea* ed. Graesse (1846 etc.), pp. 858–957
LSE	*Leeds Studies in English*
MÆ	*Medium Ævum*
MED	*The Middle English Dictionary*, ed. H. Kurath, S. M. Kuhn *et al.* (Ann Arbor, 1952–)
Memorials	Stubbs, *Memorials of St Dunstan* (1874)
Miraculi	*Miraculi Erkenwaldi*, in Whatley (1989)

MLN	*Modern Language Notes*
MMBL	Ker, N. R., *Medieval Manuscripts in British Libraries*, vols. 1–3, Ker, N. R. and Piper, A. J., vol.4, (Oxford, 1969–92)
NLA	*Nova Legenda Anglie*, see Horstmann (1901)
NM	*Neuphilologische Mitteilungen*
NS	New Series
NSB	*Navigatio Sancti Brendani Abbatis*, O'Meara (1978)
ODCC	Cross, F. L., and Livingstone, E. A., *The Oxford Dictionary of the Christian Church* (Oxford, 3rd ed. 1997)
OED	*The Oxford English Dictionary* (13 vols., Oxford, reissued 1933)
Osbert	Osbert, *La vie de S. Edouard le Confesseur*, ed. Bloch (1923)
Passio	*Passio sancti Eadwardi regis et martyris* in Fell (1971)
PL	*Patrologia Latina*, ed. J. P. Migne (Paris, 1841–)
PMLA	*Publications of the Modern Language Association of America*
Quadrilogus	Robertson, J. C., ed., *Materials for the History of Thomas Becket, archbishop of Canterbury*, *RS* 67 (1875–1885), IV, 266 ff.
RS	Rolls Series (London, 1858–1911)
SC	*A Summary Catalogue of Western Manuscripts in the Bodleian Library at Oxford* (Oxford, 1895–1953)
SEL	D'Evelyn, Charlotte and Mill, Anna J., *The South English Legendary*, 3 vols., EETS os 235, 236, 244 (1956, 1959)
Sp.E.	*Speculum Ecclesie*, ed. Forshaw (1973)
Stella Maris	*The Stella Maris of John of Garland*, Wilson (1946)
Tynmouth	John of Tynmouth, *De Sancto Erkenwaldi*, in *NLA* II.391–405 (Horstmann, 1901)
Vita	*Vita Erkenwaldi*, in Whatley (1989)
Vita B	*Vita B* (Frideswide), in Blair (1987)
Vita Kenelmi	*Vita et Miracula S. Kenelmi* in Love (1996), pp. 49–89

INTRODUCTION

1. THE TEXTS

Gilte Legende (hereafter *GiL*) is a close translation, with slight modifications of the contents, of Jean de Vignay's *Légende Dorée* of about 1333–40, which in turn is a close translation of Jacobus de Voragine's *Legenda Aurea*, completed about 1267.[1] It is given the title *Gilte Legende* in the colophon to Bodleian MS Douce 372, and this has now been generally adopted, as first suggested by Auvo Kurvinen.[2] Earlier it was referred to as *Golden Legend*, a title better reserved for Caxton's version.

GiL was 'drawen out of Frensshe into Englisshe' in 1438, according to the Douce colophon, and is extant in varying degrees of completeness in eight manuscripts. Three of these, BL MS Add. 11565 (A1), BL MS Add. 35298 (A2) and Lambeth Palace Library MS 72 (L), contain extra material, mostly in the form of additional Saints' Lives, the majority of which are shared by the three manuscripts concerned, except that some of the folios which contained these Lives are now missing from A1. We call this main group of twenty-one shared Lives *Additional Lives* (*ALL*)[3], to distinguish them from the other added matter in these three manuscripts.

It was common for supplementary material to be added to legendaries, and most frequently this consisted of Lives of interest to the institution, locality or nation of the new compiler, though sometimes other additions were made, such as Lives of more recent saints or accounts of other liturgical feasts; thus 'St Thomas Aquinas' and 'The Conception' were frequently added to the *Legenda Aurea* and its translations. For example, in about 1402 Jean Golein compiled a collection called *Festes Nouvelles*, consisting largely of Lives of French saints and apparently designed to be added to Vignay's *Légende Dorée*, and they are found at the end of ten of its surviving

---

[1] The edition of the Latin text by Graesse (1846), now superseded by Maggioni (1998), remains useful for its appendix of supplementary Lives. For a selection of de Vignay's original French version, see Hamer and Russell (1989), and for an edition of the whole of it as corrected by Jean Batallier and printed at Lyon in 1476, see Dunn-Lardeau (1997).

[2] Kurvinen (1959), p. 354.

[3] Görlach (1998), p. 74. He calls them *Additional Legends*; we have retained his abbreviation to *ALL*.

manuscripts. These manuscripts, however, are not all in the same part of the stemma of the *Légende Dorée*, so it appears that the *Festes Nouvelles* were transmitted laterally from a central copy, though in fact no separate manuscript copy of them is known to exist.[4]

The situation in the expanded *GiL* manuscripts is similar, in that the three manuscripts are not particularly close to each other in the stemma of the work as a whole; however in this case the *ALL* are not inserted at the end, nor even in the same place in each manuscript, nor have the compilers inserted them at their correct calendar dates, which, since the rest of *GiL* is in the order of the liturgical calendar, one might have expected. They must, therefore, have spread laterally, probably in the first place into lost exemplars of the extant manuscripts.

Most of the *ALL* are of English saints, and their main source is the *South English Legendary*, from which they have been deversified, except for 'Dorothy', which is from a prose source; but her Life is placed at the same point among the others in all three manuscripts, so it must be regarded as integral to the group. There are no other known instances of deversified lives from the *South English Legendary*, so it is likely these were created specially for addition to the *GiL*. None of them has been found in any other manuscript, except that six have been added to a manuscript of Mirk's *Festial*, Southwell Cathedral MS 7 (S). These additions to S are not derived from A1, A2, L or their immediate sources, as they share no distinctive variants with any of these three manuscripts. At the end of the *Festial*, S has two appendices, both in the hand of the scribe who wrote the *Festial* itself, the first consisting of an 'Ursula' (not the version in *GiL*), and a 'Catherine' similar to the one in *GiL*, but differing from it sufficiently to show that its source was external to that work.[5] The second appendix consists of the six *ALL*. Since nothing in these appendices comes from the original *GiL*, we do not regard S as containing selections from *GiL*, as Görlach does (1972, pp. 15–16; 1998, pp. 76–77), and, following him, Ker and Piper (*MMBL* 4, p. 351), and we prefer to reserve that title for the unexpanded 1438 English version.

The following is a list of the *ALL* as found in MSS A1, A2, L and S. * means the item is lost, or if attached to a folio reference that it is

---

[4] Hamer (1986).

[5] Nevanlinna, Saara and Taavitsainen, Irma, eds., *St Katherine of Alexandria: the late Middle English prose legend in Southwell Minster MS 7* (Cambridge, 1993).

incomplete. Presence in Caxton's *Golden Legend* (see below, p. xvii) is recorded by 'x' in the column headed C:

	A1	A2	L	S	C
6 Edmund of Abingdon	* (?)	73ra	212vb	194v	x
7 Bride	*	74va	216ra		
8 Edmund king & martyr	*	75ra	217va	199r	x
9 Frideswide	*	75rb	218ra		
10 Edward king & martyr	*	75vb	219rb	199v	x
11 Alphege	*	76ra	220rb		x
12 Augustine	*	76va			
13 Oswald Bishop	*	76vb	221rb	191r	
14 Dunstan	53ra*	77rb	222vb	193r	x
15 Aldhelm	53vb	77vb	224ra		x
16 Theophilus	54ra*	78ra	224vb		
17 Swithun	55ra	78va	227vb		x
18 Kenelm	55va	78vb	228va		x
19 Chad	56va	79va	230rb		
20 Cuthbert	56vb	79vb	230vb		x
21 Faith	57rb	80rb	231va	201r	
22 Dorothy	57vb	80va	232rb		x
25 Leger	58vb	81rb	233vb		
26 Brendan	59ra*	81va	202rb		x
27 Michael	177vb		234va		
28 Thomas of Canterbury	45vb*		237rb		x
Additional Lives end	61vb	84rb	251rb		

In its missing quire A1 doubtless had substantially the same items as the others; but according to Görlach's calculations (1998, p. 84) the missing folios could not quite have accommodated them all, and on the basis of their lengths he suggests that 'Edmund of Abingdon' may have been absent. It seems likely that A1 contained the *ALL* version of 'Augustine', which is in A2 and seems to be loosely based, at least in part, on the *South English Legendary*, rather than the longer version, 'Augustine 2', which is placed in L before the *ALL* and not in the A2 position. The precise source of 'Augustine 2' is not known (see p. 367 below), and it is the only one of L's individual additions that appears, in an adapted version, in Caxton's *Golden Legend* (*GoL*).

A longer version of 'Thomas of Canterbury', different from the one in *GiL*, appears in L, A1 (partly lost) and *GoL*. In L it is at the end of the *ALL* after a second account of 'Michael', the first 'Michael' being in its normal *GiL* position. In A1 this 'Michael 2' has been added to the end of the usual *GiL* 'Michael', and the longer 'Thomas of Canterbury' has been substituted for the normal version at its calendar place, where it is followed by the rest of the *ALL*. Since these are both derived in part from the *South English Legendary*, albeit with material from other unknown sources, they may be regarded as an integral part of the *ALL*. They were doubtless omitted from A2 to avoid duplication of Lives already apparently covered in *GiL*.

A close cognate version of the 'Dorothy' of the main group is found in London, British Library, MS Royal 2.A.xviii (R); Cambridge, University Library, MS Ll.v.18 (C); Manchester, Chetham's Library, MS 8009 (M); and Lambeth Palace Library MS 432 (Lb). Also, among a few manuscripts containing a small selection of Lives from *GiL* (but none of the *ALL)*, Trinity College, Dublin, MS 319 (T1), contains a 'Dorothy' broadly similar to that in the *ALL*, and an incomplete copy of this version is found in Oxford, Bodleian Library, MS Eng. th. e. 17 (*SC* 32217) (B). In this volume we supply all three versions, since the differences even between the first two are too great to be recorded satisfactorily in the apparatus.

Additions appearing in L alone consist of a Life of 'Jerome' (ff. 188va–202rb) different from that which appears in the normal *GiL*, a 'Barbara' (ff. 251rb–285vb), and 'The Three Kings of Cologne' (ff. 437rb–461rb). The latter is not included in the present volume, since its length and the number of surviving manuscripts suggest that it requires a new edition of its own. This 'Jerome' is also in New Haven, Yale University, Beinecke Library, MS 317 (Y); Cambridge, St John's College, MS N.17 (250) (J); and Lambeth Palace Library, MS 432 (Lb). There is another copy of 'Barbara' in Durham University Library, MS Cosin V.iv.4 (Co). It should here be noted that earlier accounts of L which report 'Cayme' (i.e. 'Cain') as an added item are mistaken, as it is in fact part of the preceding 'Life of Adam' made to look like a separate piece by being given a conspicuous heading.

A2's individual additions consist of Lives of two English saints and one Welsh, 'Edward the Confessor' (ff. 48ra–53ra), 'Winifred' (ff. 53ra–b), and 'Erkenwald' (ff. 53rb–57ra), which appear together, and *The Pardon of all þe chvrchis in Rome* (ff. 65rb–66vb), hereafter 'Pardon', which is tacked on to the *GiL* 'Peter the Apostle', where it immediately follows the concluding words: 'And also for he was gretter of dignite and was the furst in conuersion and helde furste the principalite of Rome.' At the end of *GiL* in A2 is added a treatise headed *Certein tretys that declarith whate the churche betokenyth and dyvers oper maters* (ff. 168vb–174vb), hereafter 'Tokens'. It follows straight on from the words *Deo gracias* after the end of 'Advent', which is the final *GiL* item in A2 (but not in the other manuscripts).

Apart from the lost exemplars of A1, A2 and L, another now lost manuscript of *GiL* once existed which contained these lives, or most of them. In the Prologue to his *Golden Legend*, Caxton wrote[6]:

I have submysed myself to translate into Englysshe the Legende of Sayntes which is callyd Legenda Aurea in Latyn, that is to say the Golden Legende. . . . Ageynst me here myght somme persones saye that thys Legende hath be translated tofore, and trouthe it is. But for as moche as I had by me a Legende in Frensshe, another in Latyn, and the thyrd in Englysshe whiche varyed in many and dyvers places, and also many hystoryes were in the other two bookes whiche were not in the Englysshe book, and therefore I have wryton one oute of the sayd thre bookes, which I have ordryd otherwyse than the sayd Englysshe Legende is whiche was so tofore made.

Caxton did indeed use three 'Legendes' as here described, and in his *Golden Legend* appear thirteen of the *ALL*, as well as the three Lives added only to A2, and, although Caxton somewhat modified them, they are clearly derived from the versions under discussion. There are enough similarities to show that Caxton's lost exemplar, designated C* by Görlach, was closer to A2 than to any other extant manuscript. For supporting evidence of this from another part of the work, Caxton has at the end of the *GiL* 'George' an additional passage which is also in A2 but in no other *GiL* manuscript. But A2 itself was not C*, as can be shown both by individual variants in the texts and by some variations in contents, including the printing by Caxton of the substituted longer version of 'Thomas of Canterbury' which is in A1 and L but not A2. It is also interesting that, as noted above, Caxton shares 'Augustine 2' with L, thus raising the question whether it was also in C*, or whether Caxton took it from some other source.[7]

The last expanded *GiL* manuscript for which there is evidence survives only in the form of a damaged leaf pasted into the binding of Paris B.N. MS nouv. acq. lat. 3175 (P*), consisting of part of the

---

[6] Cited from Blake (1973), pp. 89–90. The BL copy of *GoL* lacks this leaf. The most accessible version of the whole work (but in modernised spelling) is Ellis (1900).

[7] On this see Kurvinen (1959).

contents table of a Middle English legendary which was almost certainly a *GiL*.[8] What survives of this leaf shows that the contents of this legendary were in *GiL* rather than *GoL* order, and that it contained three saints who appear in the *ALL*, 'Dunstan', 'Swithun' and 'Kenelm', as well as the three added to A2. The *ALL*, if indeed they were the same versions, are inserted in their correct calendar positions, but the A2 group are not. Sauer calculates that there was room in the missing parts of the table for several more of the *ALL*, and indeed eight of them have calendar dates which would come within these parts, but that another eight, which would by date have been in the surviving part of the list, are absent. The list gives the folio numbers of the items, and Sauer notes that the space available for *Thomas of Canterbury* is sufficient for the longer *Additional* type as in A1 and L rather than the original *GiL* version retained in A2. Some of the *ALL* which appear in Caxton, 'Edmund of Abingdon', 'Edmund King', 'Aldhelm' and 'Brendan', are not in P* in their correct date positions, so presumably they were not there at all; in which case P* cannot have been C*. Sauer also observes: 'The absence of any exclusively *GoL* pieces speaks against a derivation from the *GoL*. It is hard to imagine a scribe copying from a *GoL* edition, omitting all French and some English saints, and ordering the remainder in traditional *GiL* fashion.' It seems therefore safe to regard this as having been another copy of *GiL*, but not C*, and not a copy from Caxton.

In his description of Gloucester Cathedral MS 12 (G), first identified by Görlach (1972, p. 27) as the first half of a *GiL*, N. R. Ker pointed out that a missing quire of twelve leaves contained the point at which the three extra lives are inserted in A2, and suggested that they might therefore have been in G.[9] This cannot, however, have been the case. At this point G lacks the end of 'Gervase and Protase' and the beginning of 'Alban'. The missing portions of these amount to 24 columns in BL MS Harley 4775 (H2), a *GiL* manuscript reasonably close to G and therefore suitable for comparison. The preceding quire in G fills $25\frac{3}{4}$ columns in H2, and the following one $26\frac{3}{4}$, but these slightly larger numbers are within the range one might expect from random variation of script size, etc.,

---

[8] This fragment came to the notice of Görlach too late to be included other than as a brief postscript in his earlier book, and it was studied and described by W. Sauer in his review of Görlach (1972) in *Anglia* 93 (1975), 247–250. See too Görlach (1998), pp. 83–4.

[9] *MMBL* 2, p. 945.

and the difference is certainly not enough to allow for inclusion of
any extra Lives.

Earlier work on *GiL*, including the *ALL*, and on Caxton's *Golden
Legend*, is summarised by Charlotte D'Evelyn.[10] Her account now
needs to be modified to some extent, especially in the light of
Görlach's subsequent work. Four manuscripts of *GiL* were known
to Carl Horstmann, but A1, A2 and L were not among them.[11] He did,
however, notice the presence in Caxton's *GoL* of English lives which
were neither in versions of the Latin or French, nor in the *GiL*
manuscripts he knew, and he suggested that the *South English
Legendary* was the source of some of them. A dissertation by Pierce
Butler, in which he studied the relationships of *GiL* to its French and
Latin predecessors and to *GoL*, was published in 1899.[12] It was an
enterprising work, but in the state of knowledge at the time it was too
big a subject for a thesis, and as a result it is in some respects confused
and confusing. Butler knew and discussed A1, but he became aware of
A2 and L only when his work was nearly completed, and supplied
descriptions in an appendix. Between 1944 and 1952 Sister Mary
Jeremy published a number of short articles clarifying the relationships between the various versions of the *Golden Legend* from the
Latin original to Caxton's, but added little about the additional
material.[13] In 1960 Auvo Kurvinen completed her Oxford doctoral
thesis consisting of a study and edition of the *GiL* 'Catherine', which
she chose because it differs significantly from the versions in the
French and Latin sources, and might therefore be expected to shed
light on the affiliations of the English manuscripts; and in a published
article she made a substantial contribution to explaining the relationship between the *GiL* and *GoL*, and demonstrated the closeness of
Caxton's English source to A2 (see above).[14] In 1972 Manfred Görlach
published a thorough study of the *ALL*, and discussed their relationship and that of the *GiL* to their predecessors and successors. He
confirmed Horstmann's insight that some of Caxton's English lives
were substantially derived from the *South English Legendary*, but

---

[10] C. D'Evelyn, 'Saints' Legends', in J. Burke Severs (ed.), *A Manual of the Writings in
Middle English 1050–1500*, vol. 2 (Hamden, Connecticut, 1970), 410–57, 553–649.

[11] C. Horstmann (ed.), 'Bokenham's *Mappula Angliae*,' *EStn* 10 (1887), 5.

[12] Pierce Butler, *Legenda Aurea—Légende Dorée—Golden Legend* (Baltimore, 1899).

[13] Those relevant to the *ALL* are: Sr Mary Jeremy, 'The English Prose Translation of
the *Legenda Aurea*,' *MLN* 59 (1944), 181–3; 'Caxton and the "Synfulle Wretche",' *Traditio*
4 (1946), 423–8

[14] Kurvinen (1960) and (1959).

showed that this happened by way of the *ALL*, and he described the process in detail, supplying a number of parallel passages. He also identified the *ALL* in S, which had previously been incorrectly referred to (e.g. in *IMEV*) as verse lives. This study appears in revised and corrected form incorporated in Görlach (1998).

If it is accepted that the *ALL* were compiled as a group to supplement *GiL*, there is no evidence as to who the compiler might have been. The compiler of *GiL* itself described himself in the Douce (MS 372) colophon as a 'synfulle wrecche', but no more is known about him. There is no reason to suppose that he himself later devised this supplement to his own work. Horstmann, not knowing of A1, A2 and L, suggested that the 'synfulle wrecche' might have been Osbern Bokenham, who stated in his *Mappula Angliae* that he had written a collection of saints' lives

compiled of legenda aurea and of oþer famous legendes. . . . Of seynt Cedde, seynt Felix, seynt Edwarde, seynt Oswalde, and many oþer seyntis of Englonde . . .

But since the English lives here named were not in the *GiL* manuscripts known to him, Horstmann felt obliged to withdraw this proposition. Sr Mary Jeremy revived it on the basis of the three expanded manuscripts, and it was virtually accepted by both Wolpers[15] and d'Evelyn, but convincingly refuted by Görlach (1998, pp. 133–35) as follows: there are, among the *ALL*, a 'Chad', 'Edward' and 'Oswald', though Bokenham's spelling of the former suggests that he was more probably referring to St Cedd; but his 'Felix' must be English, and therefore to be identified as 'Felix of Dunwich', who does not appear in any *GiL* manuscript. Two other Felixes are present, however, and Sr Jeremy suggested that one of these might be the English one; but this turns out on investigation not to be the case.

The sources for the texts edited in this volume, in so far as they have been identified, are recorded at the beginning of each item. The most important source is the *South English Legendary*, extant in 25 major manuscripts, 19 fragments and 18 miscellanies containing single items, as recorded by Görlach (1974) pp. viii–x. In this study he supplies a comprehensive survey of the manuscripts and their contents, and on pp. 51–63 works out their affiliations, demonstrating that the source of the *ALL* belonged to a group which he denominates 'P', which includes Cambridge, Magdalene

---

[15] T. Wolpers, *Die englischen Heiligenlegende des Mittelalters* (Tübingen, 1964).

ynn And then euer after he leuyd a fulle holye
lyfe and brought moche people to gode leuyng by
hys holye prechyng and gode ensample yeuyng
And after hys dethe he was translatyd ⁊ putte
m to a worshypfulle shryne m the towne of Dur-
hm Whereonne lorde shewyth manye a grete myracle for hys holye seruannt seynt Cuthbert
Wherefore onte lorde be prayssd worlde with
oute ende Amen

Here endith the lyf of Seynt Cuthbert
⁊ begynneth the lyfe of Seynt ffeyth.

Seynt ffeythe the holy virgyn became
Crysten m hyr yong auge ⁊ was right
holye of leuyng that hyr holynes spranq
fulle wyde And then the wyckyd tyrand ⁊ emperour Dioclesian ⁊ hys felowe maxymyan and
the wyckyd mstyce Dacyan thaye sworne the
dethe of alle Crysten people And alle abowte m to
dyuers londis thaye wente and distroyed alle the
Crysten men that thaye myght fynde And then
thaye came to the towne where thys holy virgyn
seynt ffeyth dwellyd And anone these wyckyd
tyrauntis men brought thys virgyn before Dioclesian ⁊ maxymyan ⁊ Dacyan the Iuge And whe
thaye so hyr thaye enquyred vpon hyr for an eyre
and seyde to hyr whate arte thue ⁊ then she made
the sygne of the crosse and she prayed onte lorde
to make hyr stedefast and strong m hys feythe
for to answere to hys pleasyng to Dacyan the
Iuge And then she sayde boldlye to the Iuge
am a Crysten woman and ffeyth is my name for
I am nothyng aferde of thye tormentis And yen
began Dacyan to entrete hyr wyth fayrenes

BL MS Add 35,298 f. 80ʳ

College, MS Pepys 2344 (P), and the fragmentary Oxford, Bodleian Library, MS Additional C. 38 (S.C. 30236) (Y). He concludes: 'A 'P' MS, similar to the existing MS Y, was the source of the additional prose legends included in three manuscripts of the *GiL* and in an appendix of a Mirk MS,' i.e. A1, A2, L and S.[16]

The stylistic and literary features of the *ALL* have been discussed by Wolpers in a general account of English medieval Saints' Lives, and more briefly by Görlach.[17] They mostly consist of a tendency to reduce the complexities of the *South English Legendary* to a simpler and more clearly factual form. Their style is generally very similar to that of the original *GiL*, so that, as Görlach puts it, with the exception of some 'French calques which make the *GiL* translation sound somewhat strange in places [and] are of course not found in the *ALL*,' the deversifier 'perfectly merge[d] his legends with the remainder of the corpus so that, had the *South English Legendary* texts been lost, it would have been next to impossible to detect the fact that the *ALL* came from different sources and are by a different author.'

2. THE MANUSCRIPTS

London, British Library, Additional MS 11565 (A1),parchment, late fifteenth-century, has 214 leaves measuring 425 × 310 mm, written space 305 × 205 mm, in double columns of 56 lines, with red headings, gold initials and blue paragraph marks. The three items in the manuscript are in one hand, and small marginal corrections may be by the same scribe. See Plate 1. It contains:

1. ff. 1r–30r, *Speculum vite Domini nostri Ihesu Christi* translated by Nicholas Love, incomplete at the beginning.

2. ff. 30r–33v, *A shorte tretise of the hiest and moste worthy sacrament of Cristis blessid bodi and the myracles therof*, incomplete at the end.

3. ff. 34r–214v, *Gilte Legende*, beginning *Here begynnyth the life of seyntes and this boke is called yn Latyn Legenda Sanctorum*, incomplete at the end, breaking off in 'Catherine', which is item 165 out of 179 of the original *GiL*. Original foliation from *j* to *CCxxj* for *GiL* reveals that forty leaves have been lost before the losses at the end. The

---

[16] See too Görlach (1998), pp. 74–5, 91–3.
[17] Wolpers, pp. 373–402; Görlach (1998), pp. 125–6.

surviving *ALL* are on ff. 53r–61v, and were originally preceded by a further six to eight *ALL*.

Descriptions: Kurvinen (1960), pp. 4–6b; Görlach (1998), pp. 84–85.

London, British Library, Additional MS 35298 (A2), parchment, late fifteenth-century, has 174 leaves in two hands, the first on ff. 1r–9v, the second on ff. 10r–end, measuring 420 × 300 mm, written space 315 × 240 mm, in double columns of 67–73 lines first hand and 70–83 second hand, with red headings, gold initials, alternate red and blue paragraph marks, and a full border on f. 2r. It was previously Ashburton Appendix 91. Original foliation j to Clxxiij starts on the present f. 2. See Plate 2. It contains:

1. ff. 2r–168v *Gilte Legende*.

2. ff. 168v–174v *Certein tretys that declarith whate the churche betokenyth and dyvers oper maters*, incomplete at the end. A table of contents in the second hand on both sides of f. 1 gives subject headings for this item as well as naming the *GiL* chapters.

Descriptions: Kurvinen (1960), pp. 9–10; Görlach (1998), pp. 82–83.

London, Lambeth Palace Library, MS 72 (L), parchment, late fifteenth-century, now has i + 420 + i leaves measuring 330 × 225 mm, written space 225 × 160 mm, in double columns of 42 lines, written in one hand throughout, with blue initials on a red background, alternate red and blue paragraph marks, and red chapter headings. L consists of a *Gilte Legende* augmented by *ALL* and other items which, with the exception of *The Three Kings of Cologne*, are the subject of this volume, but with 35 of the original *GiL* chapters omitted. In addition it has lost 40 leaves at the beginning (old foliation from xlj to CCCCxlij, but containing three mistakes, begins on f. 1) and starts in *GiL* chapter 23, 'Agnes'. Probably one leaf is lost at the end of the text, which is followed by an early table of contents which includes the missing first 22 chapters. See Plate 3.

Descriptions: James, M. R., *A descriptive catalogue of the manuscripts in the Library of Lambeth Palace: the Mediaeval Manuscripts* (Cambridge, 1932), pp. 116–17; Kurvinen (1960), pp. 73–74; Görlach (1998), p. 85.

See too Pickering, O. S., and O'Mara, V. M., *The Index of Middle English Prose, Handlist 13, Lambeth Palace Library* (Cambridge, 1999), pp. 3–13.

les ioye ⁊
...yth the
duftyn
begynneth
...ynt ieron
Brigytte /
...e was
...pers ftfe
...e bleffed
...te uj · 4ſo
...ta very
...e ⁊ power
...t ⁊ trulwis
and haue
a flowre
in the feld
...ayzed the
...taftyng
...lectacion
...t in alle
...nerse vn
...y ledyng
the wylle
...e more
...phete of
...of the
...grauuta
the mys
yous and
...zs And
...The

clemes / ¶A nother tyme owr
lady feyde to feynt Brygytte doughtʳ
haue mynde howe I tolde the that ʒe
rome was a lover of wyfdome
a folower of perfyte monkes And
an auctour and defender of trowthe
that gate the be hys merytes that
prayer that thowe fydift And nowe
I hadde to And faye to Ierome was a
trompe be whyche the holy goft fpake
he was alfo a flowne in flamed of
that fyr that come vpon me And
vpon the apoftles on pentecofte daye
And therfor bleffyd ar they that
thys trompe herith and folowe ther
after ¶Amen ¶There begynneth
the lyfe of Seynt Brandon Cap [iiij] ¶Cᴹ [iiij]
[S]eynt Brandon ye holy man
was a monke ⁊ borne in Ir
lond And ʒ he was abbot of
an houfe wher in were a thowfand
monkis And ʒ he led a fulle ftreyte
⁊ holy lyfe in grret penaunce ⁊ abfty
nenc And goynd his monkis fulle
vtuoufly ¶And pen w t a while
aftur come to hym an holy abbot ʒ
hight Beryn to bufhe of his welfare
⁊ ecfe of them to talke with other ⁊
fo to ioie in our lord ihu And then
feynt Brandon bygane to telle the
abbot Beryn of many wondris ʒ

Lambeth Palace Library MS 72 f. 202ʳ

Southwell Minster, MS 7, (S), paper, late fifteenth-century, has vi + 202 + iv leaves measuring 284 × 204 mm, written space 200 × 120 mm, 32–37 long lines, written in one secretary hand throughout. It contains:

1. ff. 1r–171v Mirk's *Festial*.

2. ff. 172r–202r Prose Lives of Saints Ursula and Katherine and six of the *ALL*.

Descriptions: Görlach (1998), pp. 86–87; *MMBL* 4, pp. 351–2; Wakelin, Martin F., 'The Manuscripts of John Mirk's *Festial*,' *LSE* NS 1 (1967), 93–118; Nevanlinna, Saara and Taavitsainen, Irma, *St Katherine of Alexandria: the late Middle English prose legend in Southwell Minster MS 7* (Cambridge, 1993), pp. 49–61; Pahta, Päivi, 'The Middle English prose legend of St Faith,' *NM* 94 (1993), 153–5.

Other manuscripts containing one or more of the items edited in this volume:

Cambridge, St John's College, MS N.17 (250), (J), parchment, 222 × 146 mm, 36 folios, 30 lines to the page, fifteenth-century, 'clearly written'. This manuscript, previously part of a larger one, contains only the Life of St Jerome, with the Prologue beginning on f.1r, a chapter list on ff. 2v–3r, and the Life on ff. 3v–35v.

Other sections of this manuscript are now Cambridge, St John's College MS N.16 (249), containing 'St John the Baptist' and 'St John the Evangelist'; Harvard, Houghton Library, MS Richardson 44, containing 'St Catherine of Alexandria'; and San Marino, Huntington Library, MS HM 115, containing Lydgate's *Life of our Lady*.

Description: James, M. R., *A descriptive catalogue of the manuscripts in the library of St John's College Cambridge* (Cambridge, 1913), pp. 285–6. See also Voigts, L. E., *A Handlist of Middle English in Harvard Manuscripts*, Harvard Library Bulletin Volume 33: Number 1, Winter (1985), pp. 64–66; Dutschke, C. W., *Guide to Medieval and Renaissance Manuscripts in the Huntington Library*, vol. 1 (San Marino, CA, 1989), pp. 152–3.

Cambridge, University Library, MS Ll.v.18, (C), small quarto on paper, 41 leaves, about 30 lines to the page, fifteenth-century.

1. ff. 1–24 *The Abbey of seint Spirite*, by Alcock, bishop of Ely.

2. ff. 25–28 *The lyff of the holy virgine Seynte Dorothea* (version 2).

3. f. 29r A short extract from 'Seynt Austyne' translated.

4. ff. 29v–41 John Lydgate, *The lyff of the holy virgine and martyr Seynt Margerete.*

Description: H. R. Luard in *A catalogue of the manuscripts preserved in the Library of the University of Cambridge, edited for the Syndics of the University Press*, vol. 4 (Cambridge, 1861), pp. 100–1.

Dublin, Trinity College, MS 319, (T1), parchment, late fifteenth-century, 96 leaves numbered 1–81, 81–95 measuring about 216 by 152 mm, in several hands with 25–36 lines to the page. The manuscript is in poor condition, several leaves are lost, and those that remain are bound in the wrong order. The correct order should be: 7–14, 5–6, 1–4, 15–40, 43–50, 41, 51–56, 42, 57–95. It came to Trinity College from the library of Archbishop Ussher in the late seventeenth century. As well as St Dorothy, (our 'Dorothy 3'), on ff. 2v–4v, 15r–16v, it contains the 'Catherine' edited by Kurvinen (see above p. xix) and 18 lives from the *GiL*.

Descriptions: Gerould, G. H., *Saints' Legends* (Boston, 1926), pp. 195–6; Kurvinen (1960), pp. 121–2.

Durham, University Library, MS Cosin V.iv.4, (Co), parchment, mid- or later fifteenth-century, ii (paper, s.xvii) + 78 + 2 (fragments of another manuscript), measuring 200 × 142 mm, written space 160 × 103 mm, 24–26 long lines, by two collaborating anglicana hands. It contains only *The Lyf and Passion of the blessed Virgyn and Martyr Seint Barbara.*

The only published account is that of Rud, Thomas, *Catalogi Veteres Librorum Ecclesiae Cathedralis Dunelm, Surtees Society* 7 (1834). We are indebted to Dr A. I. Doyle for the above short description.

London, British Library, MS Royal 2.A.xviii (Beauchamp Hours), (R), parchment, ff. 240, before 1399. On ff. 236r–240r has been added in a late fifteenth-century hand a Life of St Dorothy (version 2).

Descriptions: Warner, Sir George F. and Gilson, Julius P., *British Museum Catalogue of Westminster Manuscripts in the Old Royal and King's Collection, Vol. 1, Royal Mss I.A.i to II.E.xi.* (Oxford, 1921), pp. 32–33; Scott, Kathleen L., *Later Gothic Manuscripts 1390–1490, II Catalogue and Indexes*, A survey of manuscripts illuminated in the British Isles, vol. 6 (London, 1996), pp. 127–32.

London, Lambeth Palace Library, MS 432, (Lb), paper, 216 × 146 mm, ff. 1–95, 29 lines to page, fifteenth-century in a clear current hand. The manuscript contains nine items, of which article 1, ff. 1–37a, is the Life of St Jerome, and article 8, ff. 90–94v, the Life of St Dorothy (version 2). These two articles and article 9, *Miracles of the Virgin*, were printed by Carl Horstmann, 'Prosalegenden,' *Anglia* 3 (1880), 293–360.

Description: James, M. R., *A descriptive catalogue of the manuscripts in the Library of Lambeth Palace: the Mediaeval Manuscripts* (Cambridge, 1932), pp. 599–601.

See too Pickering, O. S., and O'Mara, V. M., *Handlist 13, Lambeth Palace Library*, pp. 31–33.

Manchester, Chetham's Library, MS 8009, (M), paper, late fifteenth-century, has v + 372 + v leaves measuring 262 × 190 mm, written space c. 190 mm high, 30–33 long lines. 'Dorothy' (version 2) is article 1 on ff. 1–2v in a secretary hand.

Descriptions: Kölbing, E., 'Vier Romanzen-Handschriften,' *Englische Studien*, vii (1884), 195–201; Kurvinen (1960), p. 77; *MMBL* 3, pp. 361–4; Guddatt-Figge, G., *Catalogue of manuscripts containing Middle English romances* (Munich, 1976), pp. 238–40.

See too Lester, G. A., *The Index of Middle English Prose, Handlist 2, John Rylands University Library of Manchester and Chetham's Library, Manchester* (Cambridge, 1985), pp. 86–89.

New Haven, Yale, Beinecke Rare Book Library, MS 317, (Y), paper, fifteenth- to sixteenth-century, has iii + 56 + ii leaves measuring 215 × 145 mm, written space 172 × 125 mm, c. 45 long lines, described by Barbara Shailor as 'written primarily by a single scribe in secretary script, with additions and corrections of s. xvi,' and 'compiled and copied at the end of the 15th or beginning of the 16th century in England.' The manuscript contains devotional writings in English and Latin, and 'Jerome' is article 5, ff. 5r–21v.

Description: Shailor, Barbara A., *Catalogue of Medieval and Renaissance Manuscripts in the Beinecke Rare Book Library Yale University, Volume II: MSS 251–500*, Medieval & Renaissance Texts and Studies 48 (Binghamton, NY, 1987), pp. 120–23.

Oxford, Bodleian Library, MS Eng. th. e. 17 (*SC* 32217), (B), 6 leaves measuring 221 × 155 mm, now consisting only of an incomplete copy of the version of 'Dorothy 3' found also in Dublin, Trinity College, MS 319 (T1, above). It is a fragment of a much larger manuscript of which MS Eng. th. e. 18, containing most of an apparently unique 'St Margaret', was also a part. They were previously Phillipps 10106 and 9227 respectively.

Description: Madan, Falconer and Craster, H. H. E., *A Summary Catalogue of Western Manuscripts in the Bodleian Library at Oxford*, vol. 6 (Oxford, 1924), p. 133.

See too Hanna III, Ralph, *The Index of Middle English Prose, Handlist 12, Smaller Bodleian collections* (Cambridge, 1997), pp. 11–12.

3. LANGUAGE

The language of most of the manuscripts is fairly typical of that to be found in works copied in the London area in the mid-fifteenth century, containing a mixture of forms variously suggestive of the midlands and the south-east. There is no external evidence for the place of origin of any of them.

The exception to this is S, which appears as LP80 in *LALME* 3, pp. 451–2, where it was assigned to Staffs, but was subsequently re-located in South Salop, *LALME* 4, p. 332 fn. This location is confirmed for 'Catherine', by Nevanlinna and Taavitsainen (1993), pp. 35–42, but with some instances of updating of spellings, some North Midland features, and a few East Midland and Southern forms. Pahta (1993) analysed the language for 'Faith', and again found dominant indications of South Salop, but no signs of the North or East Midland forms noted for 'Catherine'. Instead there are a number of forms which 'cannot be pinpointed to any particular one location with the help of *LALME*.' However, these can severally be located in the adjoining counties, in West Staffs, Northern Worcs and Herefordshire, though in two cases the nearest *LALME* sighting is in Warwickshire. It seems most probable that the South Salop forms are attributable to the scribe, but that to some extent he recorded spellings of his exemplars.

The *ALL* in S confirm these general findings. Most tellingly, the forms *won* 'one', *hure* 'their', *sye* 'saw' preterite singular, *þrou, þau,* are found in Salop among a limited number of other counties, while *hitt* and *yes* 'eyes' (also the more widespread *yen*) are found not in Salop but in adjoining counties.

SELECT BIBLIOGRAPHY

Aelred of Rievaulx, *Vita S. Edwardi Regis et Confessoris, PL* CXCV cols. 737–790, from Twysden, ed., *Historiae Anglicanae Scriptores* 10 (London, 1652).

Axon, W. E., 'A fifteenth-century Life of Dorothea,' *The Antiquary* 37 (1901), 53–55.

Baring-Gould, S. and Fisher, J., *The Lives of the British Saints* (London, 1907–13).

Barlow, Frank, 'The *Vita Ædwardi* (Book II); The Seven Sleepers: some further evidence and reflections,' *Speculum* 40 (1965), 385–97.

Barlow, Frank, ed. and trans., *Vita Ædwardi Regis qui apud Westmonasterium requiescit* (London, 1962).

Barlow, Frank, *The English Church 1000–1066* (London, 1963).

Barlow, Frank, *Edward the Confessor* (London, 1970).

Barlow, Frank, *Thomas Becket* (London, 1986).

Barthélemy, Charles, tr., *Rational ou Manuel des Divins Offices de Guillaume Durand*, vol. 1 (Paris, 1854).

Bede, *Historia Ecclesiastica Gentis Anglorum*, ed. B. Colgrave and R. A. B. Mynors (Oxford, 1969).

Bennett, J. A. W. and Smithers, G. V., eds., *Early Middle English Verse and Prose* (2nd ed. Oxford, 1968).

Bibliorum Sacrorum iuxta vulgatam Clementinam (nova ed. Milan, 1914).

Blair, John, 'Saint Frideswide Reconsidered,' *Oxoniensia* 52 (1987), 71–127.

Blake, N. F., ed., *Middle English Religious Prose* (London, 1972).

Blake, N. F., *Caxton's Own Prose* (London, 1973).

Bloch, Marc, ed., 'La vie de S. Edouard le Confesseur, par Osbert de Clare,' *Anal. Boll.* 41 (1923), 5–131.

Bond, Francis, *Westminster Abbey* (London, 1909).

Bond, Francis, *Dedications and Patron Saints of English Churches* (London, 1914).

Boyd, B., *The Middle English Miracles of the Virgin* (San Marino, CA, 1964).

Brewer, J. S., and Gairdner, J., eds., *Letters and Papers, Foreign and Domestic, of the Reign of Henry VIII 1509–1547*, 21 vols. (London, 1862–1910).

Brewyn, William, *A XVth Century Guide-Book to the Principal Churches of Rome*, ed. and trans. C. Eveleigh Woodruff (London, 1933, repr. NY 1980).

Brompton's *Chronicle*, see Twysden below.

Brown, P. A., *The Development of the Legend of Thomas Becket* (Philadelphia, 1930).

Butler, Pierce, *Legenda Aurea—Légende Dorée—Golden Legend* (Baltimore, 1899).

Capgrave, John, *Ye Solace of Pilgrimes*, ed. C. A. Mills (London, 1911).

Charlesworth, James H., ed., *The Old Testament Pseudepigrapha*, 2 vols. (London, 1985).

Colgrave, Bertram, *Two Lives of Saint Cuthbert* (Cambridge, 1940).

Cook, A. S., 'Sources of the Biography of Aldhelm,' *Transactions of the Connecticut Academy of Arts and Sciences*, 28 (1927), 273–93.

Cross, F. L. and Livingstone, E. A., eds., *Oxford Dictionary of the Christian Church* (3rd ed. Oxford, 1997).

Deanesly, Margaret, *The Pre-Conquest Church in England* (London, 1961).

De Gaiffier, Baudouin, 'La Légende Latine de Sainte Barbe par Jean de Wackerzeele,' *Anal. Boll.* 77 (1959), 5–41.

Derolez, Albert, 'A devotee of Saint Barbara in a Belgian beguinage (Marston MS 287),' *Yale University Library Gazette* 66 (1991), 197–218.

D'Evelyn, Charlotte and Mill, Anna J., *The South English Legendary*, 3 vols., EETS os 235, 236, 244 (1956, 1959).

D'Evelyn, Charlotte, 'Saints' Legends', in J. Burke Severs, ed., *A Manual of the Writings in Middle English 1050–1500*, vol. 2 (Hamden, Connecticut, 1970), 410–57, 553–649.

Douglas, D. C. and Greenaway, G. W., eds., *English Historical Documents, Vol. II, 1042–1189* (London, 1953).

Duggan, Anne J., 'The Lyell Version of the *Quadrilogus* life of St Thomas of Canterbury,' *Anal. Boll.* 112 (1994), 105–38.

Duggan, Anne J., *Thomas Becket: A Textual History of his Letters* (Oxford, 1980).

Dunbar, Agnes B. C., *A Dictionary of Saintly Women*, 2 vols. (London, 1904).

Dunn-Lardeau, Brenda, ed., *Jacques de Voragine, La Légende Dorée, Edition critique dans la révision de 1476 par Jean Batallier, d'après la traduction de Jean de Vignay (1333–1348) de la Legenda Aurea (c.1261–1266)* (Paris, 1997).

Durandus, Gulielmus, *Rationale divinorum officiorum*, ed. A. Davril and T. M. Thibodeau, vols. 1 and 2, Corpus Christianorum 140, 140a, Continuatio Mediaevalis (Turnhout, 1995 and 1998).

Ellis, F. S., ed., *The Golden Legend or Lives of the Saints as Englished by William Caxton*, 7 vols. (London, 1900).

Ellis, Roger, '"Flores ad fabricandam . . .coronam"', an investigation into the uses of the Revelations of St Bridget of Sweden in fifteenth-century England,' *MÆ* 51 (1982), 163–86.

Eve, Julian, *Horsham St Faith: a history* (Norwich, 1994).

Faricius, *Life of Aldhelm*, in J. A. Giles, ed., *Vitae Quorundum Anglo-Saxonum* (London, 1854, repr. NY, 1967), 119–52.

Farmer, David Hugh, comp., *The Oxford Dictionary of Saints* (3rd ed. Oxford, 1992).

Fell, Christine E., *Edward King and Martyr*, Leeds Texts and Monographs NS 3 (Leeds, 1971).

Fleetwood, Wiliam, *The Life and Miracles of St Wenefrede together with her Litanies with some historical observations made thereon* (2nd ed. London, 1713).

Forshaw, Helen P., ed., *Edmund of Abingdon: Speculum Religiosorum and Speculum Ecclesie* (London, 1973).

Gerould, G. H., *Saints' Legends* (Boston, 1926).

Görlach, Manfred, *The South English Legendary, Gilte Legende and Golden Legend* (Brunswick, 1972).

Görlach, Manfred, *The Textual Tradition of the South English Legendary*, Leeds Texts and Monographs, NS 6 (Leeds, 1974).

Görlach, Manfred, *Studies in Middle English Saints' Legends*, Anglistische Forschungen Band 257 (Heidelberg, 1998).

Goscelin, *Vita S. Augustini episcopi cantuariensis primi*, in J. Mabillon, ed. *Acta Sanctorum Ordinis S. Benedicti in sæculorum classes distributa sæculumni quod est ab anno christi D AD DC* (Paris, 1668), pp. 498–534.

Goymer, C.B., *A parallel text edition of the Middle English prose versions of the 'Mirror of St Edmund' based on the known complete MSS*. M.A. thesis (University of London, 1962).

Graesse, Th., ed., *Jacobi a Voragine Legenda Aurea vulgo Historia Lombardica dicta ad optimorum librorum fidem recensuit* (Dresden, 1846, 2nd Leipzig, 1850, 3rd Breslau, 1890, *reproductio phototypica* Osnabruck, 1969).

Gransden, Antonia, *Legends, Traditions and History in Medieval England* (London, 1992).

Hamer, Richard, 'Jean Golein's *Festes Nouvelles*: a Caxton source,' *MÆ* 55 (1986), 254–60.

Hamer, Richard and Russell, Vida, 'A critical edition of four chapters from the *Légende dorée*', *Mediaeval Studies* 51 (1989), 130–204.

Harper, John, *The Forms and Orders of Western Liturgy from the Tenth to the Eighteenth Century* (Oxford, 1991).

Henken, Elissa R., *Traditions of the Welsh Saints* (Cambridge, 1987).

Horstmann, Carl, ed., 'Prosalegenden,' *Anglia* 3 (1880), 293–360.

Horstmann, Carl, ed., *The Early South-English Legendary*, EETS os 87 (1887).

Horstmann, Carl, ed., 'Bokenham's *Mappula Angliae*,' *EStn* 10 (1887), 1–34.

Horstmann, Carl, ed., *Nova Legenda Anglie*, 2 vols. (Oxford, 1901).

Huelsen, Christian, *Le chiese di Roma nel medio evo: Cataloghi ed appunti* (Florence, 1927, repr. Hildesheim, 1975).

Humphreys, J., 'The story of St Kenelm and St Kenelm's church, Romsley,' *Studies in Worcestershire History* (1938), 209–16.

Jeremy, Sr Mary, 'The English Prose Translation of the *Legenda Aurea*,' *MLN* 59 (1944), 181–3.

Jeremy, Sr Mary, 'Caxton and the "Synfulle Wretche",' *Traditio* 4 (1946), 423–8.

Keiser, George R., 'Patronage and piety in Fifteenth-Century England: Margaret, Duchess of Clarence, Symon Wynter and Beinecke MS 317,' *Yale University Library Gazette* 60 (1985), 32–46.

Keiser, George R., 'St Jerome and the Brigittines: Visions of the afterlife in fifteenth-century England,' in William Daniel, ed., *England in the Fifteenth Century: Proceedings of the 1986 Harlaxton Symposium* (Woodbridge, 1987), 143–52.

Kelly, J. N. D., *Jerome, his life, writings and his controversies* (London, 1975).

Knowles, David, *The Monastic Order in England* (Cambridge, 1950).

Kurvinen, Auvo, 'Caxton's *Golden Legend* and the manuscripts of the *Gilte Legende*,' *NM* 60 (1959), 353–75.

Kurvinen, Auvo, ed., *The Life of St Catherine of Alexandria in Middle English Prose*, D. Phil. thesis (Oxford University, 1960).

Laȝamon, *Brut*, vol. 2, ed. G. L. Brook and R. F. Leslie, EETS os 277 (1978).

Lavery, Simon, 'The source of the St Brendan story in the *South English Legendary*,' *LSE*, NS 15 (1984), 21–32.

Lawrence, C. H., *St Edmund of Abingdon, A Study in Hagiography and History* (Oxford, 1960).

Lewis, C. S., *The Discarded Image: An Introduction to Medieval and Renaissance Literature* (Cambridge, 1964).

Lingley, Janice M., *The Legend of Saint Frideswide in Middle English*, MA thesis (University of Bristol, 1987}.

Love, Rosalind C., ed. and trans., *Three Eleventh-Century Anglo-Latin Saints' Lives, Vita S. Birini, Vita et Miracula S. Kenelmi, Vita S. Rumwoldi* (Oxford, 1996).

Maggioni, P. M., *Iacopo da Varazze: Legenda Aurea*, 2 vols. (Florence, 1998).

Moore, Grace Edna, *The Verse Life of Edward the Confessor* (Philadelphia, 1942).

Neale, J. H. and Webb, B., *The symbolism of churches and church ornaments, a translation of the 1st book of the Rationale divinorum officiorum* (London, 1843).

Neilson, George, *Caudatus Anglicus: a mediæval slander* (Edinburgh, 1896).

Nevanlinna, Saara and Taavitsainen, Irma, eds., *St Katherine of Alexandria: the late Middle English prose legend in Southwell Minster MS 7* (Cambridge, 1993).

O'Meara, John J., trans., *The Voyage of Saint Brendan: Journey to the Promised Land (Navigatio Sancti Brendani Abbatis)* (Dublin, 1978).

Pahta, Päivi, 'The Middle English prose legend of St Faith,' *NM* 94 (1993), 149–65.

Passmore, T. H., *The sacred vestments, an English rendering of the 3rd book of the Rationale divinorum officiorum* (London, 1899).

Pilkington, James, *The burnynge of Paules Church in London in the yeare of our Lord 1561 etc.* (London, 1563).

Raine, J., ed., *Historians of the Church of York*, RS 71, vols. 1 and 2 (London, 1874, 1886).

Rees, William Jenkins, *Lives of the Cambro-British Saints* (London, 1853).

Ridyard, Susan, *The Royal Saints of Anglo-Saxon England* (Cambridge, 1988).

Robert, prior of Shrewsbury, *The Admirable Life of Saint Wenefride, Virgin, Martyr, Abbesse*, English Recusant Literature 1558–1640, vol. 319 (Ilkley and London, 1976).

Robertson, J. C., ed., *Materials for the History of Thomas Becket, archbishop of Canterbury*, 7 vols., RS 67 (London, 1875–85).

Robinson, J. Armitage, *St Oswald and the Church of Worcester*, British Academy Supplemental Papers 5 (London, 1919).

Rossetti, W. M., 'Notes on "The Stacyons of Rome",' in Frederick J. Furnivall ed., *Political, Religious, and Love Poems*, EETS os 15 (1866), xxi–xlv.

Sadlek, Gregory M., 'The Archangel and the Cosmos: The inner logic of the *South English Legendary*'s "St Michael",' *Studies in Philology* 85 (1988), 177–91.

Sauer, W., Review of Görlach (1972) in *Anglia* 93 (1975), 247–50.

Selmer, Carl, 'The Vernacular Translations of the *Navigatio Sancti Brendani*: a Bibliographical Study,' *Mediaeval Studies* 18 (1956), 145–57.

Sinclair, William Macdonald, *Memorials of St Paul's Cathedral* (London, 1909).

Southern, R. W. 'The English origins of the "Miracles of the Virgin",' *Mediaeval and Renaissance Studies* 4 (1958), 176–216.

Stanley, Arthur P., *Historical Memorials of Westminster Abbey* (7th ed. London, 1890).

Stenton, F. M., *Anglo-Saxon England* (2nd ed. Oxford, 1947).

Stow, John, *A Survey of London*, ed. C. L. Kingsford, 2 vols. (Oxford, 1908).

Stubbs, William, ed., *Memorials of St Dunstan*, RS 63 (London, 1874).

Thompson, Anne B., 'Shaping a Saint's Life,' *MÆ* 63 (1994), 34–52.

Townsend, David, 'Anglo-Latin hagiography and the Norman transition,' *Exemplaria* 3 (1991), 385–433.

Tryon, Ruth Wilson, 'The miracles of Our Lady in Middle English verse,' *PMLA* 38 (1923), 308–88.

Twysden, Robert, ed., *Chronicle of John Brompton*, in *Historiae Anglicanae Scriptores* 10 (London, 1652), cols. 736–7.

Urry, William, *Canterbury under the Angevin Kings* (London, 1967).

Wace, *Le Roman de Brut de Wace*, ed. Ivor Arnold, vol. 2 (Paris, 1940).

West, S. E., 'A new site for the martyrdom of St Edmund?' *Proceedings of the Suffolk Institute of Archaeology and History* 35 (1981–4), 223–4.

Whatley, E. Gordon, *The Saint of London; the Life and Miracles of St Erkenwald* (Binghamton, NY, 1989).

Whatley, E. Gordon, 'A "symple wrecche" at work: The Life and Miracles of St Erkenwald in the *Gilte Legende*, BL Add. 35298,' in Brenda Dunn-Lardeau, ed., *Legenda Aurea: Sept Siècles de Diffusion* (Montreal & Paris, 1986).

Whitelock, Dorothy, Douglas, David C. and Tucker, Susie I., *The Anglo-Saxon Chronicle: a revised translation* (London, 1961).

Whitelock, Dorothy, 'Fact and Fiction in the legend of St Edmund,' *Proceedings of the Suffolk Institute of Archaeology* 31 (1970), 217–33.

Wilkins, D., ed., *Concilia Magnae Britanniae et Hiberniae*, 4 vols. (London, 1737).

William of Malmesbury, *De Gestis Pontificum Anglorum*, ed. N. E. S. A. Hamilton, RS 52 (London, 1870).

Wilson, Evelyn Faye, ed., *The Stella Maris of John of Garland* (Cambridge, Mass., 1946).

SELECT BIBLIOGRAPHY

Winterbottom, Michael, ed., *Three Lives of English Saints* (Toronto, 1972).

Wolf, Kirsten, 'The legend of St Dorothy: medieval vernacular renderings and their Latin sources,' *Anal. Boll.* 114 (1996), 41–72.

Wolf, Kirsten, ed., *The Icelandic Legend of Saint Dorothy* (Toronto, 1997).

Wolpers, T., *Die englischen Heiligenlegende des Mittelalters* (Tübingen, 1964).

EDITORIAL METHOD

The texts that follow are based on three manuscripts; items 1–13 on A2, items 14–22 and 25–26 on A1, and items 27–31 on L. In addition closely related versions of 'Dorothy' are edited from other manuscripts, 23 'Dorothy 2' from R, and 24 'Dorothy 3' from T1.

Given the somewhat diverse origins of the material in this volume, it seems sensible to present the *ALL* (as defined above, pp. xiii–xv) as one block, and also to keep together the extra items found only in A2 or only in L. It also seems desirable to keep together texts edited from the same base MS, and, since A1 lacks the beginning of the *ALL*, we start with the extra items from A2, following them by the *ALL* from A2 and A1, and concluding with the items specific to L. There are no strong reasons to prefer any of three manuscripts as base text, and we have on somewhat slender grounds decided on the order of priority A1, A2, L, according to availability. All are prone to inaccuracy, and A1 is perhaps the most conservative.

The intention is to present the texts as far as possible as they appear in the manuscripts, but with modernised punctuation, capitalisation, word-division and paragraph division.

Emendations are enclosed within square brackets [ ], and letters or words impossible to read in the manuscript within pointed brackets ⟨ ⟩. Marginal and interlinear corrections are printed in half brackets ⌐ ¬ with the details in the apparatus. When corrections in a different hand are used to emend the text, the hand is mentioned in the apparatus. The texts are rarely emended without support from the MSS, and the sources for emendations are given in the apparatus.

Abbreviations are expanded silently and follow scribal practice. *Ihu* is expanded to *Ihesu*, *Ihc* to *Ihesus*. A stroke through the descender of *p* is transcribed as *par/per/por* according to the scribe's own spelling practice where this is available, or to editorial discretion elsewhere, and final curls for plurals are treated similarly. Other strokes are treated as representative of scribal spelling only when there is a correlation between appearances of the word in question with or without such strokes. Thus, in L, where the scribe consistently spells *alle* with a final *-e* or with a stroke through *-ll*, the word is transcribed as *alle*. Macrons over medial and final indeterminate *u/n* are also treated according to scribal practice. Where scribal use of such strokes is inconsistent, they are ignored. The same treatment is given to a prominent upward curl on *-r* at the end of a line, and to the superscript curves over the final *p/pp* on forms of such words as *bishop*, *worship*, *lordship*.

In 31 'Barbara' there are 32 occurrences between ll. 173 and 1789 of *therefor* in L that are not in the Durham MS (Co). These have been omitted from the apparatus. Scribal *this* for modern *thus* is reproduced without comment. It is harder to decide what to do about words whose spellings look like scribal carelessness but are recorded by *MED* and *LALME*, and such forms as *wordely* ('worldly'), and *schyryne* ('shrine') have been allowed to stand.

The introductory remarks at the head of each Life are intended only to give enough information to clarify or correct inaccuracies in the texts. Specific problems are dealt with in the notes. Saints' Lives from medieval manuscripts should always be read with caution: names and dates were especially liable to scribal error or alteration, and stories were often elaborated on in transmission. For an accurate short account of any saint in this volume the standard reference work is Farmer (1992).

1 ST EDWARD THE CONFESSOR

St Edward the Confessor was the elder of the two sons of King Ethelred II and his second wife Emma, a Norman. He was born c. 1005 at Islip, Oxon, and was taken to Normandy in 1013 when the Danish Sweyn was acknowledged king of England. Edward and his brother Alfred remained with their uncle in Normandy when Emma returned to England to marry Cnut in 1017, but Edward returned to England in 1041 at the invitation of Harthacnut and was proclaimed king on Harthacnut's death in 1042. In 1045 he married Edith, daughter of Godwine of Wessex. They had no children. Edward died of a stroke in 1066.

There is no direct source for the Life that follows, but to some extent it depends on that by Aelred of Rievaulx, sometimes agreeing with it word for word, sometimes curtailing or omitting drastically.[1] Aelred's Life is based on that of Osbert of Clare.[2] There are also additions in our Life such as the account in ll. 15–16 of Ethelred's fouling the font, from William of Malmesbury (see note). Moore points out, however, that some passages omitted from the *PL* text appear in some MSS of Aelred and, lacking a critical edition, we cannot determine whether some seeming additions may have come from an as yet unedited MS.[3]

[1] The *Vita S. Edwardi Regis et Confessoris auctore Beato Aelredo* is printed in *PL* 195, cols 737–790, from Twysden (1652). Aelred re-wrote Osbert's Life 'in 1163, in time for the translation of Edward's body to a new tomb in the abbey after the papal canonization, and [this] is therefore the archetype for all later versions of the ecclesiastical legend.' Barlow (1970), p. xxiv.
[2] ed. Bloch (1923), pp. 64–131.   [3] Moore (1942), p. xliii.

Here endith the lyfe of Seinte Leon [pope] and begynneth
the lyfe of Seinte Edwarde kyng and confessour.

In olde tyme the reame of Ynglonde was gretely troublid with the
Danys, so that in many kyngis dayes þer cowde no peas be made but
contynually werre. And the Danys prevaylid ayenste Ynglonde and
thaye brought it vnder there subieccion, for there tyranny was so
grete and so cruelle that thaye sparid nothyng, but brente and 5
distroyed ouer alle. But at the laste it plesid almyghty God þat
this tyranny shulde cesse, and he ordeynid for Ynglonde a pesible
kyng that hight Edgar, in whos byrth angels were herde synge, that
saide pees shulde be in Ynglonde alle his lyfetyme, for þer was no
werre in Ynglond in alle his dayes. 10
  Seinte Edwarde the yonge kyng and martir reignid in this reame
but a lytle tyme, for his stepmoder did do slee hym in his yong age
for that she wolde make hir son Adilrede kyng after hym. And Seinte
Dunstone baptized this Adylred, and he prophecied of hym saying
that he shulde leve in grete trouble alle his dayes, for when Seinte 15
Dunstone cristenyd this Adilrede he fowlid in the fonte, the which
prophecy was fulfylled. In the begynnyng of his reyne the Danys
brente and distroyed a grete parte of þis londe, and this trouble
endurid manye yeris. And this Kyng Adilred weddid the doughter of
þe erle Goodwyn, vpon whom he begate a sone that was clepid 20
Edmonde Yronside. And after the deth of this saide queen he þan
weddid the doughter of Richard duke of Normandy the which hight
Emme, by whom he had .ij. sones, Alred and Seinte Edwarde kyng
and confessoure, of whom we purpose to speke nowe.
  When Kyng Adylred was falle in age he made a perlement to 25
knowe which of his .ij. sones that his people wolde haue to there
kyng after hym. And then by the provision of God thaye concludid
that Edwarde, which was yet in his moders wombe, shulde be þer
kyng, excludyng bothe Edmonde Yronside and Alred, which were
the kyngis sones also. And whan the kyng had consentid þereto, a 30
generalle wothe was made to perfourme the same in tyme comyng,
and after when this childe was bore then alle this londe was fulfylled
with grete ioye, trustyng to God to haue som grete benefete by hym

MS A2   *Rubric* pope] *erased* A2

in tyme comyng that were so mervelously kendelid with love to chese
35 hym kyng in his moders wombe.

But yet þe cruelte of the Danys was so grete that the kyng drad |
f. 48rb gretely to lese his sones, wherefore he sente the quene and his sones
bothe into Normandy, and toke his eldiste sone Edmonde with hym
into bateyle to fyght ayenst the Danys. The sorowe þat was than in
40 Ynglonde cowde no tonge telle, for moche people of Ynglonde
turnyd that tyme ayenst there owne kyng and did bothe brenne
and slee withoute pyte, lyke as the wyckid Danys did, and þay slewe
Seinte [Alphey] archiebisshop of Canterbury at Grenewyche. And
many other gode bisshoppis with preestis and other men of relygion
45 fledde into secrete placis into deserte and into wyldernes, and there
thaye prayed fulle devoutely to almyghty God for to haue very pees
in þis londe, but this werre endurid tylle the deth of Adilrede.

And so the prophecye of Seinte Dunstone was fulfylled, after
whom reignyd Edmonde Yronside in fulle grete trouble, for in his
50 dayes no man durste truste oþer ne opyn his herte to his neighboure,
for that tyme eche man appechid oþer of treson to the entent that he
myght haue his godis. And thaye that were not of power to ouercome
þer neighboure turnyd to the Danys ayenst þer owne neighbours,
and than by helpe of the Danys þei fulfylled there cursid entent, and
55 by this thaye causid many men to be slayne, som in there own howsis
and som in þe feeldis, and some in the stretis, that vnneth there
durste anye man appiere to bery them.

And in these dayes there was fulle grete extorcion and tyranny in
this londe done, and also grete [murther] and ouerpressyng of wyfis.
60 Wedows and maydens were ravisshid ayenste there wylle, and in this
grete persecucion the Ynglysh almost was distroyed and fulfylled
with fulle grete waylingis and clamours and grete desolacion ouer alle
holy Churche. For þei brent monasterijs and parissh churchis, and
thaye distroyed preestis and men of religions, and thaye causid many
65 one to fle into wyldernes, among whom the gode bysshop of
Wynchester, Brightwolde, fled into the abbey of Glastynbury,
where he daily besought almyghty God for þe pees of this reame
of Ynglond. Oure blessid lorde seyng his mekenes shewid to hym in
a vision whereby he was gretely comfortid, for in a nyght as he was in
70 his oratory and was made very wery in his prayers, sodenlye he felle
into a swete sclombre and sawe the glorious apostle of oure lorde,
Seinte Peter, with bright shynyng clothis appieryng in an high place

43 Alphey] Alpley A2   59 murther] muther A2

of dignyte, and with hym a semely yong man richely arayed in the clothyng of a kyng, whom Seinte Peter did consecrate and anoynte, and he commendid gretely his pure and chaste levyng, and it was 75 shewid to the bisshop many yeris þis kyng shulde reigne in this londe. And then this bisshop was gretely astonyd, and he askid of Seinte Peter to knowe the mystery of this vysion.

To whom Seynt Peter saide and beganne to telle hym the state of the reame, sayng that the wodenes of the Danys shulde cesse sone 80 after. And he tolde hym that alle this ponyshment was for the synnes of the people, and howe oure lorde wolde be mercyfulle to the people of Ynglond and purvey for a pesible kyng lyke Kyng Dauid, which shalle fynysh and brynge to nought alle the strenght and wodenes of his enemyes the Danys, in whose tyme shalle be plentye of pees 85 bothe to þe Churche and to the londe grete habundaunce of alle maner of cornes and frutis. And þe reame shalle be prosperus in alle thyngis, and the people shalle be of such condicions that alle other londis shalle bothe love them and drede them. The kyngis name shalle be clepid Edwarde, which shall rule alle maner þyngis to the 90 plesyng of God, and he shalle ende his lyfe gracyouslye in the love of almyghty God. And this bisshop awoke, he knelid ayen to prayer with shedying of teeris, and though that pees was not yet refourmed neuerþelese he thonkid almyghty God that he was certeyne þat he by Goddis grace shulde se it in his dayes, wherefore he wente abowte 95 and prechid to the people for to do penaunce, and oure lorde wolde yeve to vs mercy and peas and alle thyngis plentefulle.

And in this werre was the kyng slayne by treson, and he was buried at Glastynbury, and then bothe his sones were brought to Kyng Knoude the Dane to do with them whate þat he wolde, and 100 when he se them he myght not for pety sle them, but sente them ouer the se to be slayne þere, so that he myght reigne in Ynglonde pesibly when the rightfulle blode were distroyed. Notwithstondyng | thaye were preseruyd and kept alyfe, and thaye were conveyid to the f. 48ᵛᵃ emperoure of Rome, the which kepte þem tylle Seinte Edward was 105 made kyng of Ynglonde, and þen he lete mary the eldist of them to a cosyn of his because of the love that he had to Kyng Edward, þe which was vncle to them.

Now hath Kyng Knowde the rule of alle Ynglonde by stronge honde alle lawe and gode rule sette asyde, for in his dayes was fulle 110 moche trouble and robbery, with other grete oppressions and

78 this] *add* mystery of þis A2

importable chargis amonge the comynte, for he drad no man except the .ij. sones of the kyng that were than with the emperoure. Wherefore his counseyle wolde that he shulde wed the moder of
115 them, that was callid Emme, to make the more alyaunce betwene them. And sone after Alred desirid to go into Yngelonde to speke with his moder, and anone as he was come ouer þe se into this londe Erle Goodwyn came to hym and welcomyd hym, but anone after sotylly by treson he slewe hym or he came to the presence of his
120 moder, for whos deth Seinte Edwarde made grete sorowe.

And while this gode child Seinte Edwarde was in Normandy, he vsid a fulle gode lyfe, hauntyng oftetymes holy Churche. And he lovid fulle welle the felouship of holy men, and was ofte in the company of holy religious men and specially amonge holy monkis,
125 and he vsid ofte to praye, saying thus: 'Lo gode Lorde, I haue none helpe but the only. My freendis be gone fro me and thaye ben become myne aduersarijs. My fader is dede, my brethern beth slayne by treson, myne nevewis ben exiled, my moder is weddid to my moost enemy and I am lefte allone, and daily thaye seke the meanys
130 to sle me. But to the, Lorde, I am lefte pore. I beseke the, Lorde, to helpe me that am a faderlese childe, for thou somtyme holpist mervelously Edwyn and Oswolde, the which were exiled and ordeynid for to dye. Thou not only defendist þem fro deth, but also thou, gode Lorde, restoryst them ayen to þer owne kyngdoms. O
135 gode Lorde, I beseke the and praye þe to kepe me save and to brynge me into the kyngdom of my fader. Thou shalte be my God, and Seinte Peter þe apostle my patron, the reliques of whom by thy grace, Lord, I purpose to visite and to wurship in the same place where þaye nowe reste, if thou, Lorde, sende me lyfe, helth,
140 opertunyte and space.'

And when Kyng Knoude had reignid in Ynglond .xx. yere, havyng .ij. sones by the saide Emme, that is to saye Horolde and Hardeknoude, he died. And when his furste sone had be kyng .iiij. yere he exiled his owne moder, and he died sone after. And after
145 hym reigned his brother a lytle tyme and dyed as oure lorde had ordeynid, and þen was Ynglonde delyuerid from the grevous yoke of thraldom of the Danys. And then the lordis and the comyns of Ynglond remembrid the othe that thaye made in the perlement, and thaye swore that Edward, that was yet in his moders wombe, shulde
150 be made þer kyng. And þen anone thaye sente into Normandy for this childe Edward, and the lordis and the comyns recyuid hym with

grete gladnes, and then [the] archiebisshop of Canterbury, the archiebisshop of Yorke with oþer bisshops did consecrate and anoynte hym and crownyd hym kyng of this londe of Ynglonde.

O gode Lorde, whate ioy and gladnes was than in Yngelonde, for when the olde felicite of this londe was allemoost dispeyrid, than was kyndelid ayen by the comyng of the blessid kyng Seinte Edward. Then receyvid the comyn people rest and pees, and the lordis and the gentilmen reste and wurship, and holy Churche receyuid then alle his hole lybertees ayen. Than was the sonne lyfte vp and þe mone sette in his ordre, that is to saye preestis than shyned in wysedom and in holynes. The monasterijs florysshid by holy religion, the clergy yeafe lyght and prosperid in there office to the plesyng of God, the comyn people were contente and were fulle mery in there degre. And in this kyngis dayes þere was no venym that myght that tyme corrupte þe erthe with pestilence, and in the se was none outerage tempestis, and the londe fulle plentefulle of al maner of frutis, and in the clergye nothyng inordynate, and then among the comyn people was no grucchyng.

And the fame of this holy kyng Seynte | Edward sprange so mervelously aboute to oþer nacions that alle crysten kyngis desired to haue pees with hym. The kynge of Fraunce, that was nye of his kynne, made with hym a generalle pees, so that it myght be saide of hym as it was saide of Salomon, alle the kyngis of the erthe desirid to se his face and to here his wysedom, excepte only Denmarke, the which yet conspyred ayenst þis londe of Ynglonde. And whate felle þerof hit shal be declarid hereafter more opynly, for this holy Kyng Edwarde was euer fulle meke and vertues and neuer lyfte vp by veynglorye, but euer he remembrid the wordis of oure lorde that sayeth: 'I haue the sette prynce of þe people, but be not therefore lyfte vp in veynglorye, but be thou amonge them as one of them.'

He was amonge his householde men equalle and famylier, amonge preestis meke and debonayre, to his people amyable [and] cherefulle, to wrecchis and nedy men fulle of compassion and large of almesyevyng. He was also mervelous devoute in þe seruyce of God, and fulle besy to make ayen the churchis þat were distroyed by þe Danys, and in iugement fulle discrete, consideryng no mannys persone but only the weight of his cause as welle to the riche [as] to þe pore, and he had rychesse inough and his tresoure semyd comyn to alle pore men.

155

160

165

f. 48ᵛᵇ
171

175

180

185

190

152 the(1)] *om.* A2   183 and(2)] *om.* A2   188 as(2)] at A2

His wordis were sadde and discrete and medelid with myrth, spekyng ofte of Cryste Ihesu the secounde persone in Trynyte and of oure blessid lady his moder, spekyng somtyme sharpely as he sawe nede correctyng trespassours, gentylle and swete to gode men. He
195 was neuer inflate ne lyfte vp in pryde ne dishonestid by gloteny. He wolde not be compellid by wreth ne bowid by yefte. He dispisid alle riches above alle mennys reson. He was neuer sory for the lose of wordely gode and richesse nor the gladder for þe wynnyng thereof, so that alle men merveilid of þe sadnes of hym.

200 And aboute the kyng were dyuers covetouse men that tolde the kyng howe his tresoure wastid fast, that if the Danys came ayen he had not wherewith to defende hym. Wherefore thaye counceylid hym togeder and gadrid among his comyns, lyke as Kyng Knoude had gaderid of þe comynis dyuers tymes. A neyde was clepid than
205 the Danegelte in his tyme, and thaye counceylid Kyng Edward to do the same, but þat he saide naye and wolde not applye to þer councelle. And yet thaye cried vpon hym dayly, and when he se them so importune and laide so grete peryls, þen he saide at the laste to preve them: 'Lete vs se howe ye wolle do.'

210 And than thaye, heryng this of his owne mouthe, were right gladde, and anone thaye sente out commyssyons for to gadre it and sparid no contre, but made þem paye at the largist wyse. And when this monye was brought into the kyngis tresoure howse, then thaye brought the kyng theder to se it. The kyng stondyng fer therefro se the devylle in
215 lykenes of an ape foule defourmed syttyng vpon the tresoure, and sayde: 'Whate haue ye done and whate mony haue ye brought me? Forsothe þer shalle not one peny þerof be spente in myne vse. But I charge you for to delyuer to euery man his percels of mony ayen.' But þerto thaye were fulle lothe and saide that he myght spende it in dedis of charyte.
220 Then the kyng saide: 'God forbede that I shulde do spende the goodis of oþer men, for whate almes shulde I make with there goodis of pore widowis and orphalynis and of other pore labourers? Se ye not howe the devylle sittyth vpon the hepe of mony and makith grete ioye þat he hath take vs in his snare? I charge you in the peyne of deth that ye delyuer this
225 mony ayen there ye had it, euery peny.' Then thaye drad gretely and delyuerid þe mony ayen, and durste neuer after meove the kyng more in that mater nor in none other lyke that, so þat [in] alle Seinte Edwardis dayes there was neither taxe ne talage gaderid, which was grete ioye and gladnes to alle þe comyns of his londe.

227 in(2)] *om.* A2

In a time the kyng was syke and in his chambre there stode a   230
chiste opyn fulle of goold and syluer. And a clerke came into the
chambir wenyng þat the kyng had be aslepe, and he toke oute of that
chyste a grete som of mony and went his waye. And after hym there
came anoþer yong man and toke of the tresoure as moche as he
myght bere and fled faste anone, and within a lytle tyme after he | 235
came ayen and wolde haue takyn awey more. Than the kyng said: f. 49ra
'Forsothe, nowe thou arte vnwyse to come ayen, for thou haddyst
sufficiently inough afore, therefore be ware, if the tresourer come and
fynde the here, þou art lyke to dye. Wherefore yf thou love thye lyfe
fle faste awaye with that thou haste.'   240
    And anone after came the tresourer and founde the tresoure
borne awaye, and then he sought dyligently ouer alle for the thefe
þat stale it, and than þe kyng sawe the grete trouble and sorowe of
the tresourer. He askid hym the cause of his hevynes, and when he
tolde hym the kyng saide: 'Sorowe no more therefore, for para-   245
venture he that hath it hath more nede thereof than we.' And so
this younge [man] escapid and was neither chasid ne pursued after
therefore.
    When the reame was made alle sure and stedefast, the councelle of
the londe drewe them togeder tretyng of a mariage for the kyng. And   250
when it was mevid to the kyng he was than gretely astonyed, dredyng
to lese the tresoure of his virgynite, the which was kepte in a bretelle
and a fulle frayle vessele. And what that he shulde do or saye he
wyste not, for if he shulde obstynately denye it he drad leste his
avowe in chastite shulde be opynly knowen, and if he consentid   255
thereto he drad to lese his chastite. Wherefore he commendid
hymselfe onlye to God, saying these wordis, and saide: 'Gode
Lorde, thoue delyuerist somtyme .iij. childrenne from the flame of
the fyre in the chymney and furneyse of Chaldeis, and by gode
Ihesu, Ioseph escapid with the tytle of chastite fro þe wyfe of Pharao,   260
she pluckyng his mantelle fro hym, and so by the mercy of God he
escapid awaye. And by the vertue of oure lorde, Susan mervelously
escapid and ouercame the vnchaste preestis. Thurgh þy grace, Iudith
was preservid amonge the hoost of Holefernes and hir virgynyte not
hurte, but she slewe the tyraunte and escapid harmeles, and so was   265
delyuerid fro that grete myschefe. And above alle this, gode Lorde,
thou haste kepte my moost beste and swettist lady thy blessid moder
and woldist haue hir bothe wyfe and virgyn. Beholde on me thye

247 man] om. A2

servaunt and the sone of thye handemayde, that am in grete drede. I
270 lyfte vp myne herte to the, besechyng the that arte my Lorde, and
thye moder my swettiste lady, to helpe me nowe in this moost nede
that I maye so receyue the sacramente of wedlok that I falle not in
perylle of my chastite.'

And vnder this condicion in his herte he consentid to matrimonye.
275 þen was his councelle right glad, and sought for a mayde þat was
accordyng to his estate, and amonge alle the maydyns of this londe
Egide doughter of the erle Goodwyn was fownde the moost
accordyng to hym by hir vertues condicions. And hir fader made
grete meanys to the kyngis councelle for to brynge this mariage
280 abowte, whereby he came into the kyngis conseyte, and whate for his
grete myght and power he had his entente. And when þe maryage
was solempnyzed bothe he and the queen accordid togeder in þe
vowe of chastite, no man beryng witnes but God allone. þer was
betwene them a lovyng spoushed withoute bodely dede, chaste
285 clippyng withoute defloracion of virgynite. He was belovid of hir
and not broken, she was belovid of hym and not touchid. Afterwarde
dyuers of this londe grucchid ayenste hym because he had no frute to
reigne after hym, and som saide he had take a wyfe ayenst his wylle
by compulcion of a fals stok, and [for] that he wolde bryng forthe no
290 mo tyraundis he wolde not knowe his wyfe by generacion. Therefore
right fewe or none knewe the very trouthe as longe as he was in this
present lyfe, but the purety of his mynde was sufficient witnes of his
chastite.

In a Whitsondaye as the kyng werid his crowne at [Westmynster]
295 in his estate and knelid in his prayers before an auter of the Trynite,
praying for the tranquyllite and pees of his londe, in the levacion
tyme he felle into a soufte and a demure laughyng, so that his lordis
that were aboute hym merveylid gretely and durste saye nothyng to
hym tylle masse was done. Then one that was bolder than anoþer
300 enquyrid the cause of his laughyng, and then he fulle godely tolde
hym that the Danys had gaderid a grete power of people ayenste
Ynglonde and were takyng þer shippis, and as the kyng of Danys was
aboute to entre into a ship, sodenly his strenght was take aweye fro
hym and so he felle into the see betwene .ij. shippis and was
305 drownyd, so that by his deth the people of Denmarke and of
Ynglonde were delyuerid fro synne and perylle. Thaye heryng this

289 for] om. A2   294 Westmynster] Westmyster A2

merveilid gretely and sent into Denmarke to knowe the trouthe, and
when the messynger came home thaye fownde trewe alle that the
kyng had saide, and the kyng of | Denmarke was þe same tyme f. 49rb
drowned that he lough. This is the holynes of Seinte Edwarde that 310
causid alle nacyons to love Ynglond and to drede it.

The reame of Ynglond beyng in grete prosperite, the blessid kyng
Seinte Edward forgate not the promys of his iournaye that he had
made in Normandy to visite Seinte Peter at Rome, wherefore he lete
calle his lordis and his comyns to a councelle before hym, and then 315
he comenyd with his lordis of this promys made to Rome and of
other necessary maters also, and who shulde haue the guydyng of
this londe in his absence, and whate people shulde be convenyent for
to go wyth hym, and what mony were sufficient for hym and for his
men. And when his lordis and comyns herde this, thaye were fulle 320
hevy that he shulde departe fro them. And when Seynte Edward
knewe this he comfortid þem godely and saide: 'Lete euery man be
welwillid to do his diligence, for almyghty God is oure keper and
oure defender, and lyke as we haue had pees hiderto, so oure lorde of
his grete godenes wolle contynewe þe same pees in myne absence 325
and save vs from alle maner of peryls by his grete mercy and
godenes.'

And when thay herde the kyng saye thus and sawe nedis that he
wolle kepe his purpose, þen the people of this londe bothe grete and
smale were fulle of hevynes and besought hym at the reuerence of 330
God that he wolde sende to oure holy fader the pope to be assoyled
of that othe, or els to delaye it tylle another tyme. Then the kyng,
seyng the mornyng and the lamentacion of his people, that wepte and
wronge there hondis as though thaye had be faderlese and moderlese,
and wyste not whate to do, but stode this alle amasid, then the kyng, 335
seyng there grete sorowe, comfortid þem and grauntid them to abide
stylle with them. And then he ordeynid that þer shulde be sente
certeyne bisshops to oure holy fader the pope of Rome to aske of
hym councelle in this mater, howe he shulde be assoylid of his grete
avowe that he had made to visite Seinte Peter. And þen the kyng 340
sente to Rome the archiebisshop of Yorke, þe bisshop of Wynchester,
and .ij. abbottis, with other dyuers clerkis and laye men.

And when thaye came to Rome the pope had made that tyme a
grete congregacion of clerkis for dyuers grete maters belongyng to
holy Churche, and when þe pope herde of þer comyng he was right 345
glad and sente for them anone for to knowe the entent of there

comyng. And when thaye came into the presence of the pope and to
alle this wurshipfulle congregacioun, then the pope bade them telle
þe cause of þer comyng, and anone scylence was made. Thaye
350 expownyd the wylle, the vowe and the desire of þe kyng, the perylle
of the reame, the trouble, the drede and the brekyng of the pees, the
clamour of pore men, the teerys of orphalyns and of wedows, þe
petevous distruccion that the Danys had made late afore by þer
crueltye, and in whate ieopardy the londe myght stonde in if he were
355 absent. And when thaye had alle saide and declaryd whate devocion
the kyng had to visite þat holy place of Peter and Poule, then the
pope and his clergy merveylid gretely, and thaye yeafe laude and
praysing to almyghty God that he had sette so vertuous, so devoute
and so gracyous a prince in a corner of the worlde to encrese and
360 meynteyn by his wysedom and by his holynes the cristen feyth and
to the distruccion of heretykis and ponysshyng of evylle doers, and
thaye merveilid of the grete love and desire þat he had for to please
almyghty God, and howe dredeful he was to offende ayenste holy
Churche.
365 And when þe pope sawe whate love his people had to hym and
how sorowful thaye wolde be of his departyng, [he] merveilid
gretelye and thought verily that he was gretely belovid of almyghty
God and was with hym in alle his werkis, for thaye se in hym the
mekenes of Dauid, the chastite of Ioseph and the rychesse of
370 Salomon, and yet he set nought by his rychesse.
And then the pope, consideryng godely the perylle that myght
growe by the kyngis absence, sente hym a bulle sealid with led, in the
which he wrote a clere absolucion and assoyling the kyng from the
[bonde] of his avowe in the which he drad to haue falle in, and
375 ioyned hym in penaunce to yeve tho goodis that he had ordeynid for
his expencis to pore men, and either to arere a newe abbey of monkis
in the wurship of Seinte Peter or els to repayre an olde abbeye and to
endewe it sufficiently with lyfelode. And then the messyngers
receyuid the popis blessyng, and thaye returnyd ayen into Ynglonde
380 with there leters with fulle grete ioye and gladnes, and within shorte
tyme came to the kyngis presence to Westmynster. And when the
kyng herde howe thaye had sped he was fulle glad, and he thonkid
f. 49va oure lorde | fulle mekely þat he had his absolucion to be assoyled of
his avowe.

366 he] thaye A2   374 bonde] londe A2

There was a holy man, a recluse, in þe diocyse of Wurcetter that 385
knewe nothyng of the gouernaunce of the londe, nor of the
gouernaunce of the lordis and the comyns in the councelle at
Westmynster, nor of the message that was sente to Rome, to
whom Seinte Peter appierid in a nyght with grete light and saide
to hym: 'Kyng Edward hath sente to Rome to be assoyled of þe 390
avowe that he made whan he was beyonde the see, and he haþe grete
conscience because his councelle wolle not suffre hym to fulfylle it in
goyng his propre persone to Rome. Wherefore þou shalte wryte to
hym in my name and yeve hym knowlich that he is assoyled by myne
auctorite fro þe bonde of his avowe, and howe he shalle haue in 395
commaundement of the pope in the waye of penaunce to yeve such
godis as he hath ordeynid for his expencis to Rome for to yeve it to
pore men, and to arere a newe abbey in the wurship of Seinte Peter
or els to repayre an olde abbey and to endewe it with godis
sufficiently. By the same tokyn that he chase me somtyme to his 400
patron in Normandy, lete hym repayre the abbey clepid Thorney in
þe weste side of þe cyte of London, which somtyme I halowid
myselfe, and lete hym set therein monkis of gode conuersacion, for
from þat place shalle be a ladder strecchyng into hevyn and angels
assendyng and descendyng beryng vp to hevyn to oure lorde the 405
prayers of meke and devoute men. And to hym that assendith by that
ladder I shalle opyn the yeatis of paradise, as oure lorde hath
enioyned me by myne office, and I shalle lose them that ben
bounde and receyue them that be vnbounde. Also this that thou
haste herde of me thou shalte wryte it and sende it to Kyng Edward,' 410
which was then many a myle thens.

And the messynger þat came fro this anker or recluse, when he
came into the presence of the kyng with his letters, the same houre
the bisshops with other came fro Rome, and whan þe kyng had
receyuid the letters þat came fro Rome with grete reuerence and red 415
them, he thonkid God þat he was so clerely relesid of the bonde of
his avowe. And then he commaundid the letters of the recluse for to
be red, and when thaye were red and [he] sawe þat þay were
accordyng to the letters that came fro Rome, then he was fulle
glad and ioyfulle in his conscience and thonkid God and Seinte Peter 420
his patrone. And anone he disposid hym to fulfylle his penaunce, and
beganne for to repayre the abbey that he was assigned to by the
gloryous apostle Seinte Peter, and anone he beganne to distribute his

416 them] add and A2   418 he] om. A2

goodis largely to the pore, and also he losid Ynglonde of the tribute
425 þat was vsid yerely to be paide to the Danys for euermore.

In a tyme when the gode kynge Seinte Edwarde was at Westmynster, there came to hym a crepulle borne in Yrelonde which was
callid Gilemychel. And he had no fete, but went vpon his hondis and
knees, havyng in eyther honde a litle stole to go with. His leggis were
430 bente backewarde and clevid to his thyes and his toes grewe faste to
his buttockis. This crepulle entrid boldely into the kyngis paleys and
came to þe kyngis chambre dore, and one Hewlyn the kyngis
chambirleyn axid hym sherpely whate he did there. To whom þis
crepulle saide: 'Let me not, I praye the, for I muste nedis speke with
435 the kyng, for I haue be oute of this londe beyonde the se .vj. tymes to
visite reliques of the holye apostle Seinte Peter to þe entent for to be
helid, and Seinte Peter denyed me not, but bade me come into
Ynglonde and lete þe kyng bere me on his backe into the churche of
Seinte Peter, and then I shulde be made perfitly hole.' And it was
440 tolde to þe kyng by this Hewlyn, and when he herde it he had pety
on the pore man and he disdeynid not to bere this foule crepulle on
his backe into the church, for he supposid that Seinte Peter wolde
hele hym because that he had sought hym so ferre with grete
devocion.

445 And then the kyng fulle mekely toke hym vp, and when he was on
the kyngis backe he clippid þe kyng abowte the necke with his fowle
hondis and skabby armes, and then som that sawe the kyng so beryng
this crepulle lough hym to scorne and saide that he was illudid of the
crepylle. And manye that were welle disposyd wepte for ioye for þat
f. 49vb grete mekenes of the kyng, and thaye folowid after to se whate | wolde
451 befalle, and by the waye his senewis were recchid oute and the
kernels of þe bouchis of his face, and grete plentye of blode rane oute
of his scurvis vpon the kyngis clothis. And then one tolde þe kyng
that the crepul was made alle hole [and] he myght lete hym go on his
455 fete, but the kyng toke hede alwaye to the commaundement of Seint
Peter and bare hym vp to the hye auter, and þer he was set downe on
his feete, and than he felte himselfe made perfitly hole to go or ryde
wheder he wolde. But þe kyng wolde not discryve þis myracle vnto
himselfe, but yeafe hym a rewarde and bade hym go to Rome and
460 thonke God and his holy apostle Seinte Peter.

In the tyme of Kyng Adelberte, which reignid in Kente, and
Sexbert his nevewe, conuertid to the feyth of Ihesu Cryste by þe holy

454 and] *om.* A2

bisshop of Ynglond Seinte Austyn, this foresaide Adilbert dwellyng in London his chefe cyte made within þe walles a ryalle churche in the wurship of Seinte Poule, desyryng of Seinte Austyn that he wolde ordeyne a bisshop þat myght be a fader and a ruler of the cyte. And then Seinte Austyn purveyid a fulle discrete man of his owne felouship that came fro Rome with hym, that was Mellyte. The which kyng, not satisfied with that gode dede, thought to bylde another churche withoute þe wallis of the apostle Seinte Peter in the weste side of the cyte that nowe is callid Westmynster. And when it was fulle made he prayed þe bisshop Mellyte for to halowe it. And the nyght afore that he had purposid to haue halowid it on the next daye, Seinte Peter appierid to a fyssher in Temmys and bade hym set hym ouer fro Stangate to Westmynster. And he prayed þe fyssher to abide hym there tylle he came ayen, and he wolde quyte hym right welle for his laboure. And sone after, the fyssher sawe Seynte Peter entre into þe churche with a grete light, the which was newe made, the which light endurid stylle as longe as he was in the church. And within a certein space after, he came ayen and he askid the fyssher: 'Hast thoue any mete to ete?' And the fyssher sawe so grete light come oute of the churche with hym that he durste not for fere speke to hym. To whom Seinte Peter saide: 'Brother, drede the not, I am a man as thou arte. Haste thou take any fyssh?' And he saide: 'Naye, for Sir, I haue waytid on you alle this nyght while ye haue ben in the churche.' And then bothe þay entrid into the bote.

Than Seinte Peter commaundid hym to cast oute a nette, and whan it was done there came so grete a multitude of grete fysshis into the nette þat vnneth thaye myght take vp the nette for brekyng. And when thaye were caste on the lond, Seinte Peter devidid þe fyssh. And he toke the grettist and bade the fyssher bere them to Mellyte bisshop of London and take him þat and saye that Peter the apostylle sente it to hym. 'And telle hym that I haue halowid the church of Westmynster this nyght, and byd hym saye masse þere tomorow, and if he wolle not beleve þe, saye when he comyth theder he shalle fynde there tokyns sufficient, and I shalle be patron of that church and visite it often tymes and bere into the sight of almyghty God the prayers and devocion of true cristen people that praye in that place, and take thou þe remnaunde of the fyssh for thye laboure.' And then he vanysshid awaye. þan the fyssher, merveyling gretely of this sight that he had sene, erly by the morowe he wente to the bisshop Mellyte of London and toke hym the fysh that Seinte

465

470

475

480

485

490

495

500

Peter had sente hym, and tolde hym alle Seynt Peters sayingis by
ordre. But the bisshop wolde not beleve hym anone tylle he came to
505 Westmynster to se som tokyns for to put hym oute of doute, and
when he had openyd the churche dore and entrid in he founde a
crosse made of sonde fro that one side of the church to that other
with A B C of letters of Grewe. And he founde also .xij. crossis made
on the walles at dyuers placis of þe churche, and the endis of .xij.
510 candels almoost brente oute, and also he sawe the placys that were
anoyntid with holy oyle that were yette moyste and appierid newly
done. Than the bysshop belevid this þyng verily and saide masse that
same daye in the church, and he made there to the people a fulle
gloryous sermon, and therein he declarid this grete myracle opynly,
515 and the people yeafe laude and praysyng to God and to his glorious
f. 50ra apostel Seynte | Peter.

    And when Seinte Edward vnderstode þat this church of olde tyme
was halowid by Seinte Peter, and howe Seinte Peter had commaundid hym to repayre the same churche as the letter of the recluse
520 made very mencion, than after that he had fulle grete devocion to the
same place, and he did cast downe the olde werke, and he bylde it vp
newe as it appierith nowe to þis daye. And he endowid that
monastery wurshipfully with lyfelode and with iewels. And by that
tyme Pope Leo was dede and Pope Nycholas was after hym, and
525 then the kyng thought to yeve relacion to hym how he was enioynid
by Leo his predecessoure to repeyre a monastery of the gloryous
apostle Seinte Peter, and þen he sent Alured the archiebisshop of
Yorke with other clerkis to Rome for to enforme the pope þat he had
fulfyllid his penaunce, that is to saye bothe distribute his goodis to
530 pore men and also repeyrid a monastery of Seinte Peter, and that he
had by revelacion whate place that he shulde repayre, praying hym to
ratefye and to conferme the same that Pope Leo had do afore hym.
Then Pope Nicholas, consideryng the grete devocion and the treue
entente of this cristen kyng Seynt Edward, confermyd the bulle of
535 absolucion and ratefied the fundacion of the statutis of the same
monastery. And he yeafe also thereto grete previlegis, that whosoeuer
presumyd to take awaye any meveable or vnmeveable goodis or
wolde take awaye any man by strenght oute of that churche, or oute
of þe precyncte thereof, shulde be accursid by the auctoryte of Peter
540 and of Paule to be dampnyd with Iudas in helle euerlastyngly to lye
in payne. Then the messyngers returnyd ayen fro Rome with there
letters of confirmacion, and when the kyng sawe the grete bene-

volence of oure holy fader the pope and his favoure in gentilnes
gevyng to hym by wryting more previlegis and fredoms than he
desired, then he was fulle of gladnes and ioye and thonkid almyghty
God of alle his yeftis.

On a tyme the kyng was on þe churche of Seinte Peter at
Westmynster and was disposid in grete devocion as his custom
was to here masse. Erle Leofryke knelid behynde the kyng and sawe
with his bodely eyen oure lorde Ihesu Cryste betwene the preestis
hondis appieryng in the lykenes of the moost gloryous and moost
bewtevous persone that euer the kyng and he lokid vpon, the which
blessid the kyng with his right honde, and the kyng, that was gretely
comfortid with that sight, bowid downe his hed and with grete
devocion and mekenes he receyuid the blessyng of oure lorde. Then
the erle aroos vp to telle the kyng þereof, supposyng that the kyng
had not se it, but then he knewe the erles entent and bade hym:
'Stonde stylle, for that thou seyst I se.' And when masse was done
they talkid togeder of there vision, and thaye were mervelously
refresshid with the yeftis of the holye goost, and thaye myght not
welle speke for ioye and for wepyng. Then the kyng commaundid
Leofryke that this vision shulde neuer be vtterid ne opynly knowen
tylle þe tyme þat þaye shulde dye. And when this Leofryke shulde
hens passe he tolde it in confession to his gostely fader and made it to
be wryten, and þat wryting was leyde in a chyste amonge oþer
reliquys. And manye yeris after, when þaye were both dede, the
wryting was founde and rad, and then the holynes of the kyng was
knowe and his mekenes shewid, þat durst not for veynglory telle this
myracle while thaye levid.

There was a yong woman yovyn in mariage to a noble man, and
not longe after she had .ij. mysfortunes. Furste she was bareyne, and
also there rose vp vnder hir cheke manye foule bouchis and kyrnels
fulle of corrupte humors, þe which engendrid foule wormes and
made hir flessh to stynke, so that she was abhomynable and hatefulle
to hir husbonde and to alle hir frendis. And when she coude not be
helid by no medycyne, then she put alle hir hope and truste in
allemyghty God, and with many a bytter teer bothe daye and nyght
besought hym to lose hir fro that reprofe, or els take hir oute of this
worlde. And when she had long this contynued in prayer, she was
commaundid by a voyce in hir sleepe that she shulde go to þe holy
kyng Edward, and if he wolde waissh hir face with his hondis she
shulde be made hole. And when she awoke she made hir avowe to

seke the kyng in his paleys, and þen she came theder and made
meanys that the kyng myght haue knowyng of hir dreme, and when
585 the kyng vnderstode it he clepid hir to hym and saide: 'If God wolle
that I shulde waissh þy face I wolle not refuse it.' And then he callid
after water and with his owne hondis wissh hir face, and he wrong
oute the wormes and alle the foule blode oute of hir face and he bade
hir tary there .iij. or .iiij. dayes tylle þe skynne myght cover ayen hir
590 face, 'and then thanke God for þy delyueraunce.' And when she was
made perfitly hole and hir face fayre and bewtevous, then she felle
downe at the kyngis fete and she thonkid hym fulle mekely of hir
delyueraunce. But he forbade hir to yeve any praysing to hym
therefore, but bade hir: 'Yeve laude and praysing to God þerfore, |
f. 50ʳᵇ for he is the doer and not I.' Than she praid þe kyng that he wolde
596 praye to God that she myght haue a childe by hir husbonde, for she
had be fulle longe bareyne, and þen þe kyng promysed hir so for to
do, and then she was fulfylled with grete gladnes and wente home to
hir husbonde. And then she praysed and blessid the name of
600 almyghty God that by the meritis of Seinte Edward she was helid
of bothe hir dissesis.

Seint Poule he writeth that to som men þe holy goost yeuyth the
worde of wysdome, and to some cunnyng, and to som grace of
helyng and curyng, and þis moost cristen kyng Seint Edward had a
605 specialle grace above other in yevyng sight to the blyndid folkis.
There was a blynde man that was right welle knowen amonge þe
people, that herde a voyce in his sleep, that if he myght gete the
water that the kyng had waissh his hondis in he shulde waish his
eyen therewith, and than he shulde receyue his sight. Than the next
610 daye after, this blynde man wente to the kyngis paleys and tolde this
vision to the kyngis chambirleyne, and he tolde it to the kyng that if
he myght waish his eyen with the water þat he wysh his hondis in he
shulde haue his sight. Then the kyng saide, 'That myght welle be an
illusion or a dreme that be not alwaye true, for it hath not be seen
615 that the foule water of a synners hondis shulde yeve sight to blynde
men.' Then saide the chambirleyne that manye tymes dremes haue
be founde true, as the voyce that spake to Ioseph in a dreme and
saide: 'Take Mary with hir childe and fle into Egipte', the dreme of
Danyelle, the dreme of Pharao that Ioseph expounyd were founde
620 true. Than the kyng ouercome by mekenes and by innocencie went
into the churche in a solempne daye with a basyn of water, and he
commaundid þe blynde man to be brought to hym, and as he wyssh

the face of the blynde man his eyen were openyd and he sawe and
stode alle astonyd lokyng on þe people as he had then be newlye
come into this worlde. And then the people wepte for grete ioye to se 625
the holynes of the kyng, and thaye askid hym if he myght se clerely,
and he saide: 'Ye forsothe,' and then the kyng knelid downe before
the auter sayng this verse with grete mekenes and drede: '*Non nobis
Domine, non nobis sed nomini tuo da gloriam*,' that [is] to saye: Not to
vs Lorde, not to vs, but to the yeve glory. 630
    After this the holynes and fame of Seinte Edward sprang aboute,
so þat a citeseyne of Lincoln that had be blynde .iij. yere came to þe
kyngis paleys to haue of the water þat the kyng had waish his hondis
in, for he belevid that it wolde hele hym. And as he had gete of that
water of one of the kyngis chambirleyns, he wyssh his face and his 635
eyen therewith, and anone he myght se as welle as euer he myght,
and then he wente home with grete ioye, magnyfying God and
Seinte Edward that he had his sight ayen &c.
    In a tyme þer were gaderid togeder a felouship of werkemen to kut
downe trees to make with þe kyngis paleys at Bruham. And when 640
thaye were wery of laboure thaye laide them downe to slepe in the
shadowe, and a yong man of the felouship that hight Wylwyne, when
that he shulde ryse, he openyd his eyen and myght not se. And he
wyssh his face and rubbid his eyen, but he cowde not se. þen he was
fulle of hevynes, and then one of his felowis led hym home to his 645
howse and þer [he] bode blynde .xviij. yere.
    And at the laste þer came to hym a wurshipfulle woman to visite
hym and to comforte hym. And when she knewe howe he was made
blynde, then she bade hym be of gode chere, and saide if he wolde
visite .lx. churchis with gode deuocion and then desire to haue þe 650
water that the kyng had waish his hondis in and he to waish his eyen
withalle and þen he shulde be made hole. Then he was gretely
comfortid and gate hym a gyde and did after hyr councelle and
visitid .lx. churchis with gode deuocion, and then came to the kyngis
paleys crying for helpe. Then þei that herde hym bade hym leve his 655
crying, but alwaye he cryed more and more. And when the kyng
vnderstode it, then he clepid hym to hym and saide: 'Whye shulde I
not set to my hondis to helpe this pore man, though I be vnworthye,
and it plese God to releve hym and to yeue hym sight?' And leste he
shulde be founde inobedyent to God and also presumptevous, he 660
toke water and wyssh his eyen fulle mekelye of the blynde man, and

629 is] it A2   646 he] *om*. A2

anone he had his sight and se alle thyng clerely as welle as he did
euer afore.

    There was also a fayre myracle shewid of .iij. blynde men and the
665 .iiij.th had but one eye, þe which came to the kyngis paleys. And
f. 50ᵛᵃ then came one of the | kyngis men that had pety on them, and he gate
of the water that the kyng had waish his hondis in whan he helid that
other blynde man afore rehersid. And he brought this water to the
gate and tolde these pore men howe that the kyng a lytle afore had
670 helid a blynde man with the same water, and he saide if thaye wolde
weish there eyen þere with gode deuocion thaye myght be helid by
Goddis grace with the same water. And þen thaye knelid with grete
devocion and prayed this man to weish there eyen þerwith. And
when he had made a crosse with the water vpon eche of there eyen
675 and besought almyghty God to opyn þere eyes, not thurgh his
meritis but by the meritis of Seint Edward, anone the squames felle
fro þer eyes and thaye alle receyuid there perfite sight, and wente
there waye magnyfiing God of there sight yovyn to them by the
meritis of Seint Edward.

680   As the kyng in a tyme sate at the table with the queen and hir
fader Godewyn and sawe howe Horalde and Tostyne the .ij. sones of
Godewyn played afore hym, but at the laste þer game was turnyd
into ernest and þay beganne to fyght. And Harolde toke his brother
by the here and he caste hym to the erthe, and he felle vpon hym in
685 grete angre as he wolde haue strangelid hym, but he was lette. Than
the kyng askid of Goodwyn if he vnderstode anythyng thereby, and
he saide: 'Naye, forsoth.' Then the kyng saide: 'Ye shalle se in tyme
when thaye come to mannys state the one shalle slee that oþer if he
can, and Harolde that is the strenger shalle put his brother Tostyne
690 oute of this londe, and he shalle take vpon hym to be kyng of this
londe, and then shalle his brother Tostyne come ayen with the kyng
of Norwaye and holde a bateyle ayenste Harolde his brother in
Ynglonde, in the which bateyle bothe the kyng of Norweye and
Tostyne shal be slayne and alle there oste, saue a fewe that shalle
695 escape. And the same Harolde, other he shalle yeve hymselfe to
penaunce for the deth of his brother and so escape, or els he shalle be
putte oute of his kyngdom and dye wrecchidly.'

    The kyng was many tymes meovid and displesid with Goodwyne
for he mysvsid the kyngis power, and he attemptid the kyng in many
700 thyngis that were vnlefulle. And in alle that he myght he labourid to
brynge oute of conceyte the kyngis cosyns and freendis þat came

with hym oute of Normandy, to the entente that he myght haue alle
the rule aboute the kyng bothe inwarde and outewarde. And the
kyng, that vnderstode his falsenes, saide but lytle. But in a tyme as
the kyng sate at his dyner with dyuers lordis and gentils aboute hym, 705
one of hys seruauntis was allemoste falle downe in the flore as he
smote the one fote with the other, and yet the sadder fote savid alle
and kepte hym on his feete, the which was an occasion of talkyng to
the kyng and to his lordis, for þey lykened the .ij. feet to .ij. brethern,
that if one were ouerchargid that oþer wolde helpe hym and socoure 710
hym. Then sayde the kyng: 'So myght my brother haue ben an helpe
to me and a supporter in tyme of nede if he had not be betrayed of
Godewyne.' Then Godewyne heryng these wordis of þe kyngis
mouthe was sore adrad and saide: 'Sir, ye deme þat I shulde betraye
youre brother. I praye God this morcelle of brede maye choke me if I 715
consentid to his dethe.' Than the kyng blessid the brede and bade
hym ete it, and the morcelle abode stylle in his throte for alle that he
myght do tylle his breth was stoppid, and so he died wrecchydly.
And þen the kyng saide: 'Drawe the dogge and traytoure oute of my
presence, for nowe alle his falsehode and treson apperith.'   720
    In an Ester Day when oure gode Kyng Edwarde had receyuid oure
lorde Ihesu in fourme of brede with fulle grete reuerence, then he
wente to his dyner with his lordis aboute hym. And in the myddis of
the dyner, when þei were alle in sylence, he felle into a smylyng and
sone after into a sadnes, wherefore alle that were there merveylid 725
gretely, but none durste aske hym whate it mente. But after dyner
Duke Horalde folowyd hym into his chambre with a bisshop and an
abbot that were of his prevy councelle, and axid hym the cause of
that thyng. Then the kyng saide: 'When I remembrid at my dyner þe
grete benefytis of wurship and dignyte of metis and of drynkis, of 730
seruauntis araye and of alle the riches and of ryalte that I stode in at
that tyme, and I refferrid alle þat wurship to almyghty God as my
custome is, than oure lorde openyd my eyes and I sawe the .vij.
slepers lying in the hylle of Selyon besidis the cyte of Ephesym in the
same fourme and | maner as though I had ben there besidis them. f. 50ᵛᵇ
And I smyled when I se þem turne hem fro the right syde to þe lyfte 736
side, but when I vnderstode whate is signyfied by the saide turnyng I
had not cause to laugh but rather to morne. The turnyng signyfieth
that the prophecy of þe gospelle be fulfylled that sayeth: *Surget gens
contra gentem &c.*, that is to saye, people shalle ryse ayenst people 740
and one kyngdom ayenst another. Thaye haue layne manye yeris

vpon there right side and thaye shalle lye yet on þer lyfte side .lxx.
yere, in the which tyme shalle be grete bateyls, grete pestilence and
grete moreyn, grete erthquakis, grete hungre and grete derthe ouer
745 alle the worlde.'

And then thaye mervaylid to here þe kyng saye suche straunge
wordis, and thaye sente to þe emperoure to knowe yf þer were any
suche cyte and hylle in his londe in the which shulde .vij. men sleep.
Then the emperoure mervaylyng of this thyng sente to the same
750 hylle, and there þaye founde the cave and .vij. martirs slepyng þerin
as though thaye had be dede, lying on the lyfte sides euerych one.
And then the emperoure was gretely astonyed of that sight and
commendid gretely the holynes of Seynte Edward the kyng of
Ynglond which had the spiryte of prophecye. For after his deth
755 beganne grete insurreccions ouer alle þe worlde, for the paynyms
distroyed a grete parte of Sirie and thaye caste downe bothe
monasterijs and churchis, and whate by pestilence and by dynte of
swerde, stretis, townys and feeldis laye fulle of dede men. The
prynce of Grece was slayne, the emperoure of Rome was slayne, the
760 kyng of Ynglonde and þe kyng of Fraunce were slayne, and alle oþer
reames of the worlde gretely troubelid with dyuers dissesis.

When the blessid kyng Edward had levid many yeris and was falle
into grete age, by fortune he came rydyng by a churche in Essex
callid Claueryng, which was at þat tyme in halowyng and shulde be
765 dedicate in the wurship of God and Seynte Iohn the Euaungelyste,
whereof the kyng was right glad and light downe of his horse with
his meyne, purposyng to tary that he myght wurship in that place
almyghty God and his avowry Seynte Iohn the Evangelyst. And in
the procession tyme, a fayre olde man came to þe kyng and askid of
770 hym almes in þe wurship of God and Seinte Iohn the Evangelyste.
þen the kyng sought in his purse with his honde and cowde fynde
nothyng, and also his awmener was then absent, then he toke of the
rynge of his fyngur and with gode wylle he yeafe it to the pore man.
Then he thonkid hym lowlye and wente his waye.

775 And within certeyne yeris after .ij. pylgryms of Ynglonde wente to
the Holye Londe for to vysite holye placis þere. And as thaye had
loste þer waye and were gone fro there felouship and the nyght
comyng vpon them, wherefore thaye sorowid gretelye and wyste not
whate for to do, for thaye stode in drede to perish amonge wylde
780 beestis, at the laste thaye sawe a fayre companye of men arayed in
white clothyng with .ij. lyghtis borne afore them, and behynde them

þer came a fayre auncient man with white here for age. Then these pylgryms thought to folowe that lyght, and thaye drewe nye. Than this olde man askid þem whate thaye were and of whate region, and thaye saide thaye were pylgryms of Ynglonde and had loste there 785 felouship and there waye also. Then this olde man comfortid þem godely, and he brought them into a fayre cyte where was a fayre cenacle honestly arayed with alle maner of deyntees, and when thaye had welle refresshid them and restid there alle nyght, on the morowe this fayre olde man wente with them and brought them into there 790 right waye ayen. And he was right glad to here them talke of the welfare and holynes of there kyng Seynte Edwarde, and when he shulde departe fro þem, then he tolde them whate he was and saide: 'I am Iohn the Euangelyste, and telle ye Edward your kyng that I grete hym welle by the tokyn that he yeafe me the ryng with his 795 owne hondis at þe halowyng of my churche. Ye shalle take hym this ryng ayen and lete hym dispose his goodis, for within .vj. monethis he shalle be in the ioye of hevyn, where he shalle haue his rewarde for his chastite and for his gode levyng. And drede you not, for ye shalle spede right welle in youre iournaye and ye shalle come home 800 in shorte tyme safe and sownde.'

And whcn he had delyuerid them the rynge he departid fro them sodenlye and thaye came home sone after in safety, and then thaye did there message to the kyng and delyuerid hym the rynge and saide þat Seynte Iohn the Euaungelyst sente it hym. And as sone as he 805 herde that name he was fulfyllid with fulle grete gladnes, and for ioye he lete falle terris, yevyng laude | and thonkyng to almyghty God and f. 51ʳᵃ to Seynte Iohn his avowry that he wolde vouchesaufe for to yeue hym knowlych of his passyng hens.

Another tokyn he had of Seynte Iohn that tho .ij. pylgryms shulde 810 dye afore hym, the whych was provid trewe, for thaye levid not longe after. The kyng at Westmynster allemoost fynysshid and endid, hastid his werkeman to þe entent that he myght haue hit halowyd and to se masse do þerin or he died. And vpon Christismas Yevyn the kyng felle syke, wherefore the lordis and the gentyls were ful 815 hevy, for thaye had purposid to haue be fulle mery with hym alle þe Cristismasse, but alle þer myrth was turnyd into sorowe and hevynes. And on the Daye of the Ynnocentis the churche was halowid, and though þe kyng were right feble for sikenes, yet he was present the same daye hauyng right grete ioye in his soule, and 820 when alle was done and masse saide, he yeafe laude and praysing to almyghty God, and then he wente to his bed abydyng ayen the mercy of almyghty God.

And then were alle þe lordis, gentyls and comyns right sory and
825 fulle of hevynes when thaye vnderstode that the kyng myght not leve, remembryng whate welthe and prosperite the londe had ben in alle his dayes and whate ieopardy it was lyke to stonde in after his decesse. Than was alle thyngis commyttid to the quene, that he lovid specially, and she fulle diligently mynystrid to hym alle thyngis necessary. And
830 when he was brought so feble by sykenes that his naturalle hete was allemoost gone, he laye nye .ij. dayes in a transe as a man that had be ravisshid. And when he came to hymselfe ayen thaye that were aboute hym merveylid gretely, for thaye wende verily that he shulde no more haue spokyn, notwithstondyng after he spake with a hole spirite these
835 wordis: 'O thou mercyfulle God, þat arte infynyte almyghty, in whos power alle thyngis ben put which chaungist reames and empyres, if þo thyngis be true that thou haste shewid me, graunte me space and strenght to declare them to my people, that yf peraventure thaye yeve them to penaunce thaye maye haue grace and foryevenes.' Than
840 almyghty God yeafe hym a newe strenght þat passiþe alle mannys reson and that myght not be withoute myracle, for before that tyme he spake so softe that for febylnes he myght not welle be herde, and at that tyme he spake with an hole breest these wordis folowyng of þe vysion þat he se in his agonye.

845 'When I was yonge and dwellid in Normandy I lovid welle the feloushipp of gode men, for he that spake moost religiously and godely, with hym was I moost conuersaunt. And amonge the which ther were .ij. men that I drewe moche to for there honest conuersacion and for the holynes of the lyfe and for the swetnes of there
850 maners and for þer comfortable wordis, whom I sawe translatyd into hevyn, for many yeris agon thaye dyed. And nowe thaye haue appierid to me by the sufferaunce of God and shewid to me the state of my people and whate synnes reigne amonge them and whate vengeaunce shall be take on them for there synnes. Preestis haue
855 offendid, for thaye mynister the holy sacramentis with vnclene þoughtis and pollute hondis, and as an hirid man and not as a very shepeherde defende not þer shepe, and as for princis and gentyls thaye ben founde fals and vntrewe and felowis to feendis and thevys and rubbers of the cuntre which haue no drede to God ne to
860 his wurship, and true lawe is a burþyn to them and true lawe is had in dispite and very right also, and cruelnes is moche lovid. And the

prelatis also kepe not rightwysnes. Thaye correcte not there sogettis ne thay teche them ne informe them not as thaye shulde do, and therefore oure lorde hath nowe drawen owte his swerde of vengeaunce to smyte his people. This ponysshment shalle begynne within þis yere bothe by swerde and by fyre, wastyng this reame petevouslye. And then I beganne to sigh and to morne for the trouble that was comyng to my people and saide: "If thaye wolle be turnyd and do penaunce, shalle not thaye haue foryevenes and God shalle blesse them ayen?" And it was aunswerid to me: "The hertis of people be so indurate and so blyndid and there eeris be so grevid þat thaye wolle here of no correccion ne thaye be not mevid ne provokid by no benefetis that oure lorde yevith them." Then I askid if þere were any remedy that myght tempre the wrethe of God. To whom it was aunswerid in þese wordis: "A grene tre cutte from his stocke shalle be devidid from his propre rote the space of .iij. furlongis, and withoute mannys honde shalle turne ayen to his olde rote and take ayen his sape and florisshith and bryngith forth frute, and when this is done þere maye come remedy." And when | this was saide thaye were sodenly gone oute of my sight.'

There was aboute þe kyng þat tyme the quene, Duke Harolde, hir brother Robert keper of the paleyse, and Stigande that had defoulid his faders bed, for whilis bisshop Robert archiebysshop of Canterbury levid the saide Stigande put hym downe and came in by simony, wherefore he was suspendid of the pope. And afterwarde God toke vengeaunce vpon hym so that his bely brake and his bowels wente oute, and so he died wrecchidly. This Stygande yeafe no credence to the kyngis wordis, but dyscryvid it to the age and to the febylnes of the kyng, and he made it but a fantesye. But oþer þat were better avisid wepte and sorowid and wronge þer hondis and sente to oure holy fader the pope yevyng hym informacion of the saide vision, and oure holy fader þe pope wrote epystlis to Ynglond exhortyng the people to do penaunce, but his wrytyng profited not.

Then afterward, when Kyng Harolde had broke þe othe that he had made to Duke William and therefore he was slayne in bateyle, then thaye knewe welle that the prophecy of Seynte Edwarde was come, for then the lyberte of Ynglonde made an ende, and then came in bondship and thraldom. In that tyme alle Ynglonde was ouerturnyd and I vnderstonde Seinte Dunstone prophecied the same trouble comyng, and after a certeyne tyme he promysed comforte also, wherefore this vision maye be conuenyently expownyd in this wyse:

The declaracion of þe vysyon.

The tre signifyeth the reame of Ynglonde, whos grenes and fayrenes betokenyth riches, plentevousnys and wurship of Ynglond. The
905 wurship of whom alle þis wurship hath procedid is the true blode of the londe and of the crowne which descendid fro Alured, whom oure holy fader the pope crownyd and anoyntid kyng into the furste kynge of true lyne of Ynglonde vnto Kyng Edwarde by succession. The tre is cutte downe fro the stocke when the reame is devidid and
910 translatid fro one seede to another. The space of .iij. furlongis is the tyme of .iij. kyngis, that is to saye Harolde and William conquerour and Willyam his sone. The comyng ayen of the tre to the stocke withoute mannys helpe was when Kyng Harry the furste came into this reame not with mannys strenght but by very true love of his
915 comyns. He toke his sape and his very strenght when he weddid Molde, the doughter of þe nece of Seynte Edwarde, iunyng togeder the seede of Normandye and of Ynglonde and by the frute that came of þem made bothe one. The tree florysshid when of there seed spronge Molde that was emperes, and it brought forthe frute when of
920 hir spronge oure Harry like a daye sterre when bothe the people were ioyned togeder. If this exposicion displease any man, other lete hym expowne it better or els lete hym abyde a tyme vnto it be fulfylled, leste the prophecy of Seynte Edwarde be fownde contrary to the prophecye of Seinte Dunstone.

925   Of þe laste wordis that Seinte Edwarde spake.

This holy kyng Seinte Edwarde, knowyng that his houre drewe nygh, spake vnto them that stode wepyng aboute hym, and in comfortyng them saide: 'Forsothe if ye lovid me ye wolde ioye þat I shulde passe fro this worlde to the fader of hevyn, there to receyue
930 the ioye that is promysid to alle true cristen men. Put ye awaye youre wepyng and spede forth my iornaye with prayers, with holy psalmys and with almys dedis, for though myne enemy the feend maye not ouercome me in my feythe, yet þer is none fownde so perfite but he wolle assaye and attempte to lette hym or to fere hym.'
935   And then he betoke the quene to hir brother, commendyng hir gretely to his lordis, and declarid to þem hir pure chastyte, for she was to hym in opyn placis as his wyfe and in secrete placis as his suster, and he commaundid also that hir dowry shulde be made sure

to hir and stedefaste, and thaye that came with hym oute of Normandy shulde be put to there choyse whether thaye wolde 940 abyde stylle in Ynglonde, and to be indowid with lyfelode after there degre, or els to turne ayen into Normandy with a sufficient rewarde. And he chase hys place to be buryed in the church of Seinte Peter, the which he had byldid, and saide that he shulde not longe abide in this worlde. And when he behylde the quene and sawe hir 945 wepe and sigh amonge, then he saide to hir ofte tymes: 'My doughter, wepe ye not, for I shalle not dye, but I shalle leve and I shalle departe fro þe londe | of dethe and I beleve to se the godenes of f. 51ᵛᵃ God in the londe of lyfe.'

And than he set his mynde alle in God and yeafe hymselfe holly to 950 the feyth of the Churche in the hope and promyses of Cryste vnder the sacramentis of the Churche, and among these wordis of praysyngis he yeldid vp the spirite to God in the yere of oure lorde .Ml.lxvj. whan he had reignyd in this londe kyng .xxiij. yere and .vj. monthis and .xxvij.ti dayes in the .iiij.th daye of Ianyuere. 955 And as his cosyns and hys lovers stode aboute this holy body, when the spirite was paste thaye sawe a mervelous bewty and an hevynly sight in his face, and when thaye lokid on his nakid body thaye se it shyne with a mervelous brightnes. Then þaye vnderstode that almyghty God wolde shewe that myracle of brightnes for the clerenes 960 of his virginite. And then þei wrappid the holy body in pallys and buried it with grete reuerence and wurship, and thaye distribute almys largely to þe pore for hym. And many a wurshipfulle lorde bothe spiritualle and temporalle and fulle grete nombre of þe comyn people were presente at his burying, to do hym worship and 965 reuerence and to magnefie almyghty God for the grete benefettis shewid to hym and to the reame in his tyme while he reigned in this londe of Ynglond, wherefore the name of almyghty God be praysid worlde withoute ende. Amen.

The .viij.th daye after his burying þer came a crepulle to his 970 tombe to be holpyn of his grete dissese, which many tymes afore had receyuid almes of þe kyngis honde, and he had be waisshyn also of the kyngis owne hondis on Shere Thursdaye. Notwithstondyng the myracle of his curyng was prolongid by þe provysion of God and not shewid in his lyfe tyme, because oure lorde wolde that he which 975 shewid so many myraclis in his lyfetyme in curyng bothe the blynde and the lame shulde as welle shewe myraclis after his dethe. This crepulle was clepid Raffe, þe which was a Norman borne, and the

senewis of his hammys were clonkyn and stronkyn togeder that his
980 fete were drawen vp to his buttuckis that he myght not go nether on
his fete neither on his knees, but sate in an holowe vesselle in maner
of a basyn drawyng his bodye after hym with his hondis. And when
he came to the tombe, he besought almyghty God and the holye and
blessid Seinte Edwarde with devoute prayers in grete devocion that
985 he myght be helid and curid of his dissese which in his lyfe tyme had
moost levid by his almes. And when he had contynued a while in his
prayers, other people that had compasshion of hym prayed for hym
also, and at the laste he lyfte hymselfe vp and þen he felte his senewis
losid, and then he rose vp and stode on his feete and felte hymselfe
990 made perfitlye hoole for to do whate he shulde.

We haue red of the grete vertues that blessid kyng Edward had in
helyng blynde men whiles he levid, and that oure lorde hath not
withdrawe fro hym nowe after his dethe, as it is opynlye shewid by
this crepulle a fulle grete myracle. The .xxx.ti daye after his burying
995 there came a man to his tombe that had but one eye, ledyng after
hym .vj. blynde men. Eueryche of them hylde oþer by the skyrte and
alle þay prayed to God and to this holy Seynte Edwarde þat thaye
myght haue þer sight and to be delyuerid oute of that grete miseri
that thaye stode in, and moche people came theder to se whate
1000 shulde befalle of þis thyng. And when thaye se howe hertely these
blynde men prayed, then alle the people with pyte knelid downe fulle
devoutely and praied for them to God and to the holye seynte, and as
sone as thaye had endid þer prayers, alle thaye receyuid perfitly þer
sight. And then eche of þese men þat were blynde afore lokyd faste
1005 on eche other and thought this was a newe worlde with them. And
then thaye with fule grete ioye enquirid eche of oþer whether thaye
myght se, and eche saide: 'Ye, forsothe'. þen thaye alle knelid downe
and praysid almyghty God fulle hertely and his holye kyng Seynte
Edwarde that had heelid them, and then thaye wente home with
1010 grete gladnes eche into his owne cuntre.

Howe Harolde had the victory of þe kyng of Denmarke.

Whan Harolde the sone of Godewyne was founde fals in brekyng the
othe that he had made to Seinte Edwarde in vsurpyng the crowne,
the which he shulde haue kepte to William the cosyn of Seynte

1001 pyte] *add* and A2

Edwarde, therefore his enemyes aroos ayenste hym by the suffer- 1015
aunce of | God in the northe partye, for there came into this londe f. 51vb
Tostyne his brother with Harolde Harfage kyng of Norwaye with a
grete navy into the water of Humbir. And thaye aryvid vp besidis
Yorke, where the men of the cuntre wolde haue put hym of, but he
opteynid and slewe moche people of the Ynglysh men, and when 1020
that Kyng Harolde vnderstode it he gadrid a grete multitude of
people to withstonde hym. Than Seinte Edwarde appierid to an holy
abbot in a nyght as he was in his prayers, which was gretely aferde of
that sodeyn appieryng, but þen Seynt Edwarde comfortid hym
godely and bade hym: 'Go and telle Harolde that he shalle ouercome 1025
his enemyes the which intendid to distroye and consume this reame
of Ynglonde, and bid hym dred not, for I shalle guyde his oste, and
as for this tyme he shalle haue the victory, for y maye not suffre to se
the reame of Ynglond thus to be distroyed. And when thoue haste
tolde hym this he wolle beleve the [not], wherefore thoue shalte 1030
prove thy vision in this maner. Lete hym set his mynde on a thyng
and thynke that it plesith hym best, and thou shalte telle hym whate
he thynkyth, for almyghty God shalle yeue that by revelacion. Then
he shalle knowe welle that it comyth not of the but of almyghty God,
and then he shalle yeve credence to thye wordis.' 1035
On the morowe this gode abbot of Ramsey that was callid Alexi
wente to Kyng Harolde and tolde hym þis vysion, that he shulde
overcome his enemyes by the meritis of Seinte Edwarde, the which
appierid to hym in the nyght afore, and whan he thought it was but a
fantesye he made hym credible by the appieryng of þe prevy 1040
þoughtis of his herte, and þerby he was made bolde for to fyght
notwithstondyng he was syke at that tyme in pestylence and he had a
sore in his grynde. But then he went to þe bateyle and þere he slowe
Tostyne his brother and Harolde Harfage the kyng also, and right
fewe or none escapid alyfe fro the bateyle that came with Harolde 1045
Harfage and with Tostyne, wherefore the Ynglysh men thonkid God
and Seynte Edwarde of this grete victory.
In the monastery of Westmynster there was a fayre yonge man
that was blynde whom the monkis ordeynid to rynge the bellis. But
he had in custome dayly to visite the tombe of Seinte Edwarde with 1050
certein prayers, and in a tyme as he prayed þer he felle asleepe and
he herde a voyce that bade hym go and rynge to the laste houre. And
when he awoke he se Seynte Edwarde goyng fro hym arayed lyke a

1030 not] *om.* A2

kyng with a crowne on his hed, and he had a mervelous light aboute
1055 hym. And he behilde hym tille he came to the high auter, but then he
se hym no more nor the light, but he had his sight alwaye after tylle
his lyvis ende. And then he tolde the monkis in whate wyse he was
heelid, and then thaye thonkid God and Seynte Edwarde for this
grete myracle.

1060   Howe Seinte Wulstone was wrongfully deposid and after
          he was restoryd ayen.

Whan William Conqueroure had gotyn alle Ynglonde and had it
vnder his power, than he began for to medle with the Churche, and
he commaundid for to make a congregacion of the clergy at
1065 Westmynster, beyng that tyme present .ij. cardynals Iohn and
Peter and a bisshop that was callid Hermnyfride, a legate, of
whom Stigande that we spake of before was tho deposid and put
into perpetualle pryson. And at the laste his bowels felle out and in
his stede was chosyn Lamfranke, a wyse man and of mervelous
1070 cunnyng, in so moche that oure holye fader the pope whan he sawe
hym come he rose ayenste hym: 'I do this not for thye archiebis-
shopriche, for the grete tresoure of wysedome and cunnyng that is in
the therefore I do it.'
      Than there were some envyous men that had accusid Wulstane to
1075 the archiebisshop Lamfranke, puttyng on hym that he was not able
to be a bisshop, and þe kyng consentid also that he shulde be put
downe and that he shulde resigne to Lamfranke, the which tolde
Wulstane that alle the clergy were so agreid and þat he shulde
delyuer his staffe and his power to a man of gretter cunnyng. To
1080 whom Wulstane saide: 'Forsoth fader, I knowe welle that I am not
worthy to haue this dignyte nor am not sufficient to this grete
burthyn, for I knowe myne vncunnyng that tyme when the clergy
chase me thereto when oure holy fader the pope and gode Kyng
f. 52ʳᵃ Edwarde compellid me þerto, | and nowe while the councelle of the
1085 kyng wolle that I shalle resigne alleredy, but not to you but to hym
that compellid me þerto.' And with that saying departid fro the
archiebisshop and wente to the tombe of Seynte Edwarde with his
crosse in his honde, and he spake as he had be alyfe to the kyng and
saide: 'O thou holy and blessid kyng, þou knowist welle that I toke
1090 not this grete charge on me with my gode wylle tylle I was compellid
bothe by the and by oure holy fader the pope, but nowe we haue a

newe kyng and thaye make newe lawys and yeue [newe] sentence and
thaye repreve nowe bothe þe and me. Thaye repreve the of erroure
for that þu yeavist hit to me, an vnkunnyng man, and me of
presumpcion that I wolde consente to take it. That tyme thou 1095
myghtist be begyled for thou were but a fyel man, but nowe þu
arte ioynid to God. Wheder mayste thou nowe be disseyuid or not,
thou yeavist me this charge and to the I resigne it.' And with that he
fyxid his pastoralle staffe into the stone of his tombe and saide: 'Take
this and yeve it to whom thou wylte.' And the pastoralle staffe styked 1100
so faste in the stone that he myght not be take oute by mannys
honde. Then he did of the abite of a bisshop and stode amonge the
monkis in the same degre that he was afore or he was bisshop.

And when worde of this came to the congregacion that had
consentid to hys resignacion thaye mervelid gretely and stode as 1105
men alle dismayed, and som of them assaied to drawe oute þe staffe
previly, but thaye cowde not prevayle. And when the archiebisshop
Lamfranke had worde of this he wolde not beleve it, but commaundid Gunnulfe bisshop of Rochester to fette hym the pastoralle staffe
anone. And when he came to the tombe the strenght of hevyn that 1110
was in the stone prevaylid ayenste his strenght, for the more that he
drewe the faster it clevid to þe stone, whereof he was sore abasshid
and wente ayen to Lamfranke and tolde hym of that myracle. Then
were Lamfranke and the kyng astonyed, and thaye came to se this
thyng and felle to prayer, and after Lamfranke assayed with grete 1115
reuerence if he myght pulle oute þe staffe, but it wolde not remeove.
Then was the kyng and the archiebisshop sore aferde and repentid
them, and thaye askid foryevenes and lete seke oute Wulstan amonge
the monkis and brought hym to the kyng and to the archiebisshop,
which knelid to hym and askid hym foryevenes, and Wulstan vsyng 1120
his olde mekenes felle downe also and forbade them that thaye
shulde not do so to hym, but with gode wylle forgaue them, and he
prayed the archiebisshop fulle mekely to blesse hym. Than Lamfranke wente to this holye man Wulstane and saide to hym: 'Brother,
thye rightfulle symplenes was lytle sette by amonge vs, but oure 1125
lorde hath made thye rightwysnes opyn shynyng as a daye sterre. But
brother, we haue a cause to morne and sorowe, for we haue iugid the
[gode] evylle and the evylle gode. Oure iugement hath erryd, but
oure lorde hathe arerid the spirite of Seinte Edward, the which hath
made voyde alle oure sentencis, and thye symplenes is alowid before 1130

1092 newe(2)] nowe A2   1128 gode(1)] om. A2

God. Come hither to thye kyng and ouris, Seinte Edwarde. We suppose that he wolle resigne the pastoral staffe to the, which hath denyed it to vs.' Than Wulstan the seruaunte of God obeyed with alle reuerence to þe commaundement of the archiebisshop, and he
1135 wente to the auter where the staffe stode faste fyxid in þe stone, and þer he knelid downe and saide: 'O thou Edwarde my lorde, I am here thye seruaunt which submytte me to þy sentence that sumtymes yeavist me this staffe. What plesith the nowe? Whate wylte thou do? Whate discernyst forsothe? Thou hast savid thyne owne wurship and
1140 reseruyd thye dignyte and thou haste purgid myne innocencye. In shewyng thye magnyficence, if thyne olde sentence abide yet, yeve me ayen the pastoralle staffe, and if it be chaungid shewe vs hym to whom thou wylte yeve it.' When he had saide this he attemptid softelye with grete reuerence to pulle oute þe staff of þe stone, and
1145 anone he lete it go as though it had be fyxid in softe cleye. And when thaye that stode aboute hym se this grete myracle thaye wepte and
f. 52ʳᵇ lete falle teeris for ioye, and thaye axid hym also for | foryevenes, and thaye alle yeafe laude and praysyng to almyghty God and to the blessid and holy Seinte Edwarde, and euer after the kyng William
1150 lovid fulle welle his cosyn Seinte Edwarde and had grete devocion to visite his tombe, and after he did fulle grete coste in makyng of his shryne.

Howe his holye bodye was fownde incorrupte manye yeris after.

1155 After this myracle was shewid there was moche talkyng of his holynes, and the deuocion of the people encresid dayly more and more, so that þer were manye wurshipfulle persons that desired to se his holy body, for som saide that it laye incorrupte and som saide naye, and in this meke stryfe thaye gate lycence of the abbot Gylbert
1160 to se it. And when the daye was sette that this holye relyke shulde be shewid, there came theder manye a wurshypfulle man and wemen of religion, amonge whom came Gunnolfe bisshop of Rowchester, and this was done .xxxvj.ti yere after his burying that thaye openyd his tombe.
1165   And when the stone was remeovid thaye felte a mervelous swete savoure, that alle the churche was replete þerof, semyng that aromatike had be flowyd oute of þe tombe, and thaye founde the palle that laye nexte his holy body as hole and as fayre as it was when

he was buryed, wherefore thaye supposid to se merveylis. And whan
the palle was take awaye, thaye drewe forthe his armys, thaye movyd 1170
his fyngurs and his toes, and thaye were bowyng and hole as though
he had ben newly dede. And in his flessh þere was founde no
corrupcion, but it was fayre and fressh of coloure, purer and brighter
than glasse, whitter þan snowe, and it semyd as a body glorified. And
when thaye drad to opyn his face, Gunnolfe that was bolder than 1175
oþer with devocion vnbounde his hed, and the furste that appierid
was his fayre hore here of his berde. Then he thought to haue somme
of that heere for a relique, and with fere and reuerence pullid at his
berde, but he coude not prevayle, for thaye were as faste as when he
was alyfe. Than saide the abbot: 'Fadre, suffre hym to lye in reste 1180
and attempte not to mynysh þat þat oure lorde hath so longe
preseruyd and kepte hole.' Than the palle wherein the holy body
was wrappid was withholde and anoþer of the same valure was fette,
wherein the holy body was lappid and laide ayen into his tombe with
fulle grete reuerence and wurship, abydyng the grete resurreccion. 1185

How vengeaunce was shewid to a damselle that blasphemyd Seinte Edwarde.

In the cyte of London there was a noble matrone that was right
cunnyng in silke worke, which was commaundid to enbrowdre the
garnementis of the countesse of Gloucester, that was than fressh and 1190
yong and newlye weddid and wolde haue hir garmentis made in
shorte tyme. And when the festefulle daye of Seinte Edwarde drewe
nygh, this noble matrone was sore troubelid in hir mynde, for she
drad þe indignacion of that proude lady if hir garmentis shulde not
be redy, and she drad also to werke on the Daye of Seinte Edwarde, 1195
for it was bothe synfulle and perylous. Than she saide to a yong
damyselle þat was hir felowe and wrought with hir: 'Whate þynke ye
best nowe, oþer to displese this ladye or els this gode Seinte
Edwarde?' And she saide: 'Is not this Edwarde whom the chorles
of the cuntre wurshippith as he were a God?' And saide: 'Whate 1200
[haue] I to do with hym? I wolle no more wurship hym than a
chorylle if he were.' Than þis noble matrone was sore abasshid and
sore amevid with hir that she saide suche wordis of blasphemy to þis
holy seinte, and she alle tobete hir for to make hir be in pees, but she
of frowardnes blasphemyd hym more and more. And then sodenly 1205

1201 haue] *om.* A2

she was smetyn with a palsy, so that hir mouthe was drawyn to hir right ere, and also she had loste hir speche and she vomyd at the mouthe lyke a boore and she gnast hir tethe togeder mervelously and alle hir membris were sore ponysshid.

1210 And when this matrone sawe this, she was fulle hevy that she had bete hir while almyghty God had so punysshid hir, and she wepte fulle bitterly, and when it was knowyn in the cyte, hir neighboris came to hir, some to comforte hir and some to wonder vpon hir so lying. And then þere came a wurshipfulle man to visite hir, that 1215 counceylid hir to cary hir by water to the shryne of Seinte Edwarde if parauenture God wolde shewe any myracle for hir. And when it was done, moche people prayed for hir, but þey had not there entent anone but abode þer in prayers tylle mydnyght that Matyns beganne, f. 52ᵛᵃ and then thaye prayed | the monkys to praye for hir. And when thaye 1220 had do Matyns þaye came to þe shryne and prayed also for this dameselle, that laye þer in fulle grete trouble and turment. And when the holy monkis had prayed for hir a gode while, then this damyselle aroos vp alle hole and axid whye thaye wepte and made so moche sorowe, and when thaye se hir mouthe in his right place and alle hir 1225 membris restorid ayen, þaye were fulle ioyfulle and yeafe thankyngis to almyghtye God and to his holy kyng and confessoure Seint Edwarde.

Howe a monke was heelid of þe feuer quarten.

In þe abbey of Westmynster there was a vertues monke and a 1230 cunnyng that was callid Osberte. This monke was vexid with a stronge feuer and a fervent that is callid þe feuer quarten, and he had it fro þe monyth of Iuylle to Cristemasse, which had consumyd hym with intollerable payne, that he lokid lyke a drye ymage, wherefore he prayed almyghty God oþer to relese his peyne or els to take hym 1235 oute of this worlde. And on Cristismasse nyght he toke gode herte to hym and wente to Matyns as oþer did. And when he herde þe gospelle red, that made mencion howe a lytle childe was borne and yovyn to vs of the fader of hevyn, whos modir is a pure virgyn, then he considerid this gospelle with so grete devocion that his mynde was 1240 ravysshid and he was fulfyllid with so grete ioye that he felte no dissese in .ij. dayes after. And after .ij. dayes were past his feuer came ayen and vexid hym contynuallye tylle the festefulle daye of Seynte Edwarde came, which fallith on þe Evyn of þe Epyphanye,

and that daye in þe high masse tyme he came to the tombe of Seinte
Edward, where this monke laide hym downe prostrate as he wolde 1245
have died. Then whate waylyngis, what sighyngis and whate
sobbyngis was in þat sike body hit was pety to se. Than he brake
oute, saying these wordis: 'O thou my lorde and my kyng, howe
longe wylte thoue forgete me? Howe longe shalle I suffre this payne?
Howe longe wilte thoue turne thye face fro me? Where ben alle the 1250
grete myraclis that oure faders haue tolde vs done by þe in þer dayes?
þu hast holpe many straungers, but I that am þy seruaunte in thyne
owne churche thou forgetist, and shittist to me the dore of pyte.
Wolde God þat I myght dye, but alas I am norysshid forthe with
payne and maye not dye. My lyfe is sorowe to me, but it can haue 1255
none ende, and I desire dethe but I cannot haue hit. Whate shalle I
stryfe with the, but I beseche þe, gode kyng, lovable prynce and
swete patrone, meve thye bowels of mercy on me. If I be worthye to
haue helthe, yeue it me, or els lete me dye anone.'

And amonge these wordis, teeris and sobbyngis braste oute, that 1260
he myght not speke with his mouthe but with his affeccion. And
when masse was done he aroos vp from prayer alle hole, and þen he
felte alle his membris mervelously refresshid with a newe strenght.
And then he axid after mete and drynke, and when he felte hymselfe
that he had receyuid ayen his strenght, than he was gretely movid 1265
with devocion euery daye more and more to þat gloryous kyng Seinte
Edwarde, for by his merytis he was delyuerid fro his grete sykenes
and dissese.

Howe a knyght was helid of the feuer quarten.

The nexte yere folowyng, on þe same festfulle daye, one Geryne, a 1270
knyght, which was keper of the kyngis paleys, that had longe tyme
ben seke on the feuer quarten, he came to the shryne of Seinte
Edward with fulle grete devocion for to haue helthe and relese of his
peyne. And that same daye prechid þer the holye monke Osberte,
that was helid þer of the same sykenes that same daye .xij. monyth 1275
afore, and he was þat tyme pryoure of þe place and did þe office in
the churche. And when he had declarid the gospelle, then he
beganne to prayse Seynte Edwarde, commendyng gretely his chastite
and his grete mekenes, and he openyd his holy lyfe to the people.
And when thaye herde it, manye were mevid with teeris of 1280
compassion when thaye herde of his grete myraclis. And at the

laste he made a laude and a thonkyng to almyghty God and to hym
for his owne delyueraunce. And þer he tolde howe grevouslye he was
vexid and howe lowe he was brought with þe feuer quarten, and
1285 howe lightely he was helid by the merytis of Seynte Edward, and
Geryne the knyght herde this. He was gretely meovid with devocion
in these swete wordis, and þought þat he wolde not cesse of prayer |
f.52ᵛᵇ tylle he had remedye of his payne. And he abode þere stylle in his
prayers alle that daye and the nyght also tille Matyns were begunne
1290 on .xij. nyght, and then he prayd the monkys to praye for hym. And
when thaye had prayed for hym a gode while, than he felte hymsilfe
made perfitly hole, and then he with alle the people yeafe laude and
praysing to almyghty God and to the blessid Seinte Edwarde of his
delyueraunce.

1295   Howe a none was helid þer of the feuer quarten.

A religyous woman of Berkyng, that had leyne seke in the feuer
quarten .xij. monthis and she was nye consumyd awaye with payne,
this woman in a nyght whan hir susters wente to Matyns, felle
asleepe, and she dremyd that she rode into hir cuntre with hir
1300 meyne. And whan she came by Westmynster, a fayre olde man mette
hir and bade hir tarye and refresh hir, and whan he had so saide he
vanysshid awaye. Then she enquirid of hir meyne if thaye knewe that
man, and thaye saide naye. Than they mervelid whate it mente that
thaye shulde be refresshid þer when no man knewe them there,
1305 either to make þem chere either to refresh them with mete and
drynke. þan þer was one that spake anone and saide: 'There lyeth
Seinte Edwarde the holy kyng and confessoure, by whos meritis
many sike folke be made hole, wherefore I councelle you that ye go
þeder.'
1310   And with that she awoke and rose oute of hir bedde and wente to
hir oratory, and þer she beganne to saye hir .vij. psalmys and the
letanyes and besought almyghty God and Seinte Edwarde for helpe,
and she was right sory that she myght not visite the shryne of Seynte
Edwarde for to be delyuerid of hir grete sikenes. And then she saide:
1315 'Blessid Seinte Edwarde, if it please the, I knowe welle thoue maiste
make me hole here as welle as [if] I came to seke the at Westmynster
at thye shryne.' And when she felte hir grete paynes comyng vpon
hir, then she wolde entre into hir oratory as she myght and beseke

1316 if] om. A2

Seynte Edwarde to praye for hir, and þen she wolde begynne þe .vij. psalmys and the letanyes, and so she escapid hir peyne þe furste daye. And when .ij. dayes were paste and she felte hir payne comyng, by hir prayers and by the helpe of Seynte Edward she escapid that daye. And after this she felte neuer more of that sykenes, and then she was made perfitly hole by the grace of almyghtye God and by the merytis of Seinte Edwarde. And then she came to Westmynster sone after to thonke God and Seinte Edward of hir delyueraunce and to make opyn this myracle in what wyse she was made hole.

Howe a monke of Westmynster was helid of .iij. dyuers sykenes.

There was a devoute monke of Westmynster þat had in custome to saye euery daye .v. psalmes in the wurship of God and Seinte Edwarde, the which monke after was grevid with .iij. maner sikenes, for he had on his arme a congellacion of blode in maner of a postome. He had also in his breest such a streytenes þat vnneth he myght drawe his brethe, and he had also in his fote a mervelous swellyng and a grete, that he myght not go but with grete payne.

And when the yerely feest of Seynte Edwarde was halowid he sawe his brethern go to þe churche at mydnyght for to rynge the bellis, and he was right sory that he myght not do the same, notwithstondyng he paynid hymselfe and wente theder and saide the .vij. psalmys. And whan he had done and sawe his brethern rynge meryly he saide in his prayer to Seinte Edwarde: 'O thou my gode kyng, I beseke þe praye for me that I maye haue [strenght] to do as I se my brethern do, for I commytte me fully to thye myght and I beleve veryly þat þou wylte suffre me no lenger in this grete dissese.' And when he had made an ende of his prayers he roos vp and wente to the bellis for to rynge them, and anone the postume of his arme brake, and when the foule mater was oute, þen he felte hymselfe hole of that dissese.

Then his moost peyne was in his breest, and he wente ayen to prayer to yeve thonkyngis to God and to Seinte Edwarde of that delyueraunce of the postome, and he prayed þer fulle devoutely þat he myght be delyuerid of that dissese in his breest. And he aroos fro prayer and felte his herte made alle hole fro that sykenes that he had in his breste. Then he felte no dissese but on his fote, and when he

1343 strenght] strengh A2

came amonge his breþerne into the fraytoure he tolde them howe he
was delyuerid fro .ij. of his sykenes. And when thaye sawe hym thaye
mervelid gretely, and besought almyghty God and Seint Edward that
he myght be delyuerid of that dissese in his fote. And at nyght when
f. 53ra   he wente to his bed he put hymselfe | holly in þe meritis of Seinte
1360   Edward, and when he arose and felte no payne he put downe his
honde to his fote to fele howe hit was and he felte that the swellyng
was gone. He lepe out of his bed and tolde his brethern with fulle
grete ioye howe that he was made perfytly hole as euer he was. Then
1365   thaye alle were fulle glad and wente with hym to the churche to yeve
thonkyngis and praysingis to almyghty God and to his holy kyng
Seinte Edwarde for these myraclis and for his delyueraunce fro tho
.iij. sykenessis, wherefore God in his holy seruaunt be praysyd
worlde withoute ende. Amen.

1370   Here endith the lyfe of Seinte Edwarde kyng and confessoure and begynneth the lyfe of Seint Wenefride a holy
virgyn.

2 ST WINIFRED

St Winifred lived in the seventh century. We can be certain of nothing in the earliest (Latin) Life from the twelfth century, nor anything from later Lives. What is certain is that there was a pre-existing cult of St Winifred (Welsh *Gwenfrewi*) at a miraculous spring in Holywell when her relics were translated from Gwytherin to Shrewsbury in 1138.

Baring-Gould and Fisher give a full account of the two surviving Latin Lives, and edit *Buchedd Gwenfrewi* from National Library of Wales MS Llanstephan 34.[1] Middle Welsh Saints' Lives are usually translations, made from the thirteenth century onwards, of earlier Latin *vitae*. No translation of *Buchedd Gwenfrewi* exists, but elements of Winifred's legend from Welsh MSS and printed sources are analysed by Elissa R. Henken.[2]

It has yet to be substantiated that *Buchedd Gwenfrewi*, as has been widely asserted, derives from the twelfth-century Life by Robert of Shrewsbury, whose florid and prolix version, in Oxford, Bodleian MS Laud misc. 114, Cambridge, Trinity College MS O.4.43 and Brussels, Bibliothèque Royale MS 8072, provides all the elements for this English Life. It was translated into English twice, by Caxton (1485?) (STC 25852),[3] and by I.F (John Falconer?), a Jesuit, in 1635 (STC 21102).[4] The latter was reprinted with a long preface and much comment by William Fleetwood, bishop of St Asaph, who criticised I.F's translation, added miracles, and claimed that his own book was not a reprint of I.F.[5] In his preface, Fleetwood refers to and quotes from a prose Life of Winifred which appears in what he calls the English Legend, and at the end of his work appears the following footnote: 'Since the printing off a great Part of this Book, I have seen (by the Favour of Roger Gale, Esq; the worthy Son of a most learned Father, the late Dean of York) another MS Life of Wenefrede, which

---

[1] Baring-Gould & Fisher (1907–13) III, 185–196 and IV, 397–423.

[2] Henken (1987), pp. 141–51.

[3] ed. Horstmann (1880).

[4] Robert, prior of Shrewsbury, *The Admirable Life of Saint Wenefride, Virgin, Martyr, Abbesse*, English Recusant Literature 1558–1640, vol. 319 (Ilkley and London, 1976).

[5] *The Life and Miracles of St Wenefrede together with her Litanies with some historical observations made thereon*, second edition, printed for Sam. Buckley at the Dolphin in Little Britain, 1713.

was, I guess, taken out of Rob. Salop. but has none of his Preface, differs very much in many Places, is much shorter, and leaves off entirely at the Death of Theonia; as does the old English Legend, and this Life in verse which I guess to be about 400 years old.'[6] Fleetwood's very short quotation from what he calls the English Legend is identical with the Caxton version of lines 58–60 below. We have been unable to trace the verse Life he mentions.

[6] *ibid.*, p. 127.

Here endith the lyfe of Seinte Edwarde kyng and Confessoure and begynneth the lyfe of Seint Wenefride a holy
virgyn.

After that a holy man Beuno had do make many churchis and had
ordeynid the seruyce of God devoutely to be saide in them, then he
came to þe place of a fulle wurshipfulle man, his name was callid
Teuythe, the which [was] the sone of a noble senatoure clepid
Elyude, and he desirid that he wolde yeue hym as moche grownde 5
as he myght bylde a churche on to þe wurship of God. Then he
graunte hym his askyng with gode wylle, and then he lete make
thereon a fulle fayre churche to the which he, his wyfe and his
doughter Wenefryde resortid to dayly for to here devyne seruyce.
    And then was Wenefride sett to scole to this holy man Beuno and 10
he taught hir fulle diligently and he enformyd hir perfitlye in the
feythe of Ihesu Cryste. And this holy maide Wenefryde yeafe grete
credens to his wordis, and she was so enflamyd with his holy
doctryne that she purposid to forsake alle worldely plesauncis and
to serue almyghty God in mekenes and in chastite. 15
    And then it fortunyd vpon a Sonedaye she was dissesid, and she
abode at home to kepe hir faders howse while thaye were at churche,
to whom þer came a yonge man for to defoule hir. His name was
callid Cradok, the sone of þe [kyng] Alane. þe yong man was set
afyre by the feend in vnchaste loue ayenste this clene virgyn 20
Wenefride. And when she se hym she welcomyd hym godely,
desiryng to knowe þe cause of his comyng, and when she knewe
his corrupte entent she drad leste he wolde oppresse hir by strenght.
And then she feynid hirselfe for to go into hir chambre to araye
hirselfe in suche wyse that she myght plese hym better, and whan he 25
had grauntid hir, she sperryd the chambre dore to hir and fled
previly at a backe dore towarde the churche. And when this yonge
man had aspied hir he folowid hir with his swerde drawyn lyke a
wode man, and when he had ouertake hir he saide to hir these
wordis: 'Sumtyme I lovid and desirid the to my wyfe, but one thyng 30
telle me shortely, eiþer consent to me nowe or I shalle slee the with
this swerde.'
    Then this blessid mayden Wenefride thought þat she wolde not

MS A2   4 was] *om.* A2   19 kyng] *om.* A2

forsake the sone of the euerlastyng kyng for þe sone of a temperalle
35 kyng, and then she saide to hym sadly: 'I wolle not consente to the,
for I am ioyned to my spouse Ihesu Cryste, the which preseruyth and
kepith my virginyte, and truste thou verily þat I wolle not forsake
hym for alle thy manassyngis and thretyngis.' And when she had
saide this, the cursid tyraunte, fulle of malyce and of wrath, smote of
40 hir hed. And in the same place where hir hed felle to the grownde
þer spronge a fayre welle, the which into this daye heelyth and curith
manye dissesis, and in the bottom of the saide welle appiere stonys
alle blody which maye not be waish awaye with no crafte nor with no
laboure.

45   And when hir fadir and hir moder knewe it, thaye made fulle grete
sorowe and lamentacion for there doughter Wenefride, for þay had
no mo children. And when this holy man Beuno vnderstode this
dede and se whate hevynesse the fader and hir modir made for hir,
then he comfortid þem godely and brought them to the place where
50 she laye ded, and þer he made a sermon to the people declaryng hir
virginite and howe she had made a vowe to be a relygeous woman.
Wherefore he sette the hed ayen to the body, and he desirid the
people for to knele downe and praye devoutely that if it pleasid
almyghty God she myght haue hir lyfe ayen, not only to the comforte
f. 53rb of hir fader and moder, but to fulfylle the vowe of | religion. And
56 when thaye aros vp fro prayer, þis maide ros vp made alyf ayen by
the power of God, wherefore al the people praysid his holy name for
this grete myracle shewid for this holy virgyn Seinte Wenefride. And
as longe as she levid after, þere appierid aboute hir necke a rednesse
60 lyke a red silkyn threde in signe and tokyn of hir martirdome.

And the tyraunte that did slee hir had wyped his swerde on the
grasse and stode stylle þerbeside, and he had neither power to go
awaye nor to repente hym of that cursid dede. And then this holy
man Beuno reprevid hym, not only of that homycide but also that he
65 yeafe no reuerence to the Sabbot daye and to the grete power of God
þer shewid vpon this holy virgyn. And then this holy man saide to
hym: 'Whye hast thou no contricion for thy mysdede, wherefore I
beseche almyghty God to rewarde the after thy deseruyng.' And then
he felle downe dede to the grownde and his body was alle blacke and
70 sodenly borne awaye with feendis.

Than was this holy mayde Wenefride veylid and consecrate into
religion by þe hondis of this holy man Beuno, and he commaundid

71 consecrate] *add* and consecrate A2

hir to abide in the same churche that he had made, and there she
shulde dwelle .vij. yere to wurship and praynge God, and þer she
shulde geder togeder virgyns of honest conuersacion and þerto 75
informe þem in the lawes of God, and after these .vij. yere to go
to some other holy place. And when this holy man shulde departe fro
hir and go into Yrlonde, she folowid hym tille she came to the
foresaide welle, where thaye stode a long tyme euer talkyng of
hevynly thyngis, and at þe laste þis holye man saide: 'It is oure 80
lordis wylle that þou sende to me euery yere som tokyn and put it
into the streme of this welle, which shalle brynge it into the se, and
then by the purviaunce of God it shalle be conveyd ouer the see the
space of .l. myle to the place where I dwelle.' And when thaye were
departid she with hir virgyns made a chisiple of sylke worke, and the 85
nexte yere folowyng she wrappid it in a white mantylle and she put it
into the saide streme, and it was [brought] thurgh the wawis of the se
to the howse of this holy man Beuno.

This blessid virgyn Wenefride encresid fro daye to daye in grete
vertu and godenes and specially in talkyng of hevynly swetnes with 90
hir susters, that she meovid there hertis mervelously to devocion and
into the loue of almyghty God. And after .vij. yere were passid she
wente to a monastery callid Witheriacus, in which þer were bothe
men and wymen of vertues conversacion, and whan she had tolde hir
lyfe to the holye abbot Elerius he receyuid hir wurshipfully and 95
brought hir to his moder Theonie, a fulle blessid woman which had
the rule and the charge of alle the susters of that place. And whan
Theonie was decessid, this holy abbot Eleryus betoke to Wenefride
the cure and the charge of þe susters, but she refusid it as longe as
she myght, and after that she was compellid þerto. She levid fulle 100
vertuosly, but after that she levid a fulle vertues lyfe and more
strayter and harder, yeuyng gode ensample to alle hir susters. And
when she had contynued in the seruyce of God þer certeyn yeris, she
yeldid vp the spirite to God in the .v.th daye of Decembre.

Here endith the lyfe of Seinte Wenefryde and begynnyth 105
the lyfe of Seynte Erkenwolde.

87 brought] brough A2

3 ST ERKENWALD

St Erkenwald was consecrated as bishop of the East Saxons in 675. He came from a royal house and founded the monasteries of Chertsey and Barking, the latter for his sister Ethelburga. He died in 693.

The sources for this account of the life and miracles of St Erkenwald are the *Vita* and *Miraculi* of Arcoid, Canon of St Paul's,[1] the Latin Life of John of Tynmouth, *De Sancto Erkenwaldo Episcopo et Confessore*,[2] and some additions presumably from a London source. Their treatment in this Life is described by Gordon Whatley.[3]

[1] Whatley (1989).
[2] *NLA*, pp. 391–405.
[3] Whatley (1986).

Here endith the lyfe of Seinte Wenefryde and begynnyth
the lyfe of Seynte Erkenwolde.

In olde tyme when the kyngdom of Ynglond by the provysion of
God was holsomly brought to the gouernyng of one kyng which
before that tyme had be vnder the rule of .viij. kyngis, there was that
tyme a noble prince the which was callid Offa kyng of Este
Ynglonde, and though he were right noble yet he was a paynym. 5
And of this Offa kyng were begotyn .ij. noble seyntis, that is to saye
Erkenwolde and Alburgh, which were of right perfite lyfe. And
Erkenwolde was furste abbot of Chertesaye and after that bisshop of
London, and Alburgh his suster was his true felowe in gode werkis
and she was a woman of religion and by the provision of God she was 10
made abbas of Berkyng, which were norisshid in þer | yong age in that   f. 53ᵛᵃ
party of Ynglonde that nowe is namyd Lendeseye, in the castelle or
in the towne of Stalyngburgh, so namyd in olde tyme.

Forsothe Erkenwolde by the inspyracion of God was yovyn alle to
cristen religion in þe tyme [when] Seinte Austyne and Mellyte wyth 15
his oþer felouship were sente into Ynglonde by Seinte Gregory in
the yere of oure lorde .v.C.iiij.xx.xvj., and Albourgh his suster was
chosyn by the provision of God to be spouse to the euerlastyng kyng,
which toke baptym and was namyd Ethelburga. And as the roos
comyth oute of the sherpe brere, so this blessid virgyn came of the 20
stoke of paynyms and yeafe a swete odoure by vertues levyng to
almyghty God. To the which gode begynnyng, the wickid enemy
that is the feend, havyng grete envie to hir, sterid hir fader to so
grete tyranny and wrath that he entendid vtterly to distroye his
doughter, the which was grete merveile. And yet notwithstondyng 25
alle hyr faders cruelnes, the tender herte of the blessid virgyn abode
alwaye vnmeveable in hir gode purpose and kepte previlye hir
holynes fro the knowyng of hir fader.

And she vsid to resorte secretely to the chapelle wherin she had be
baptized, praying to almyghty God for helpe by many a sore sighyng 30
and grete affliccions that he wolde not suffre hir chastite to be
defowlid with carnalle corrupcion. And when she was come to
gretter age hir fader wolde haue maryed hir, but she refusid it

vtterly and lothid it as venym, and saide she wolde haue none other
35 spouse but Ihesu Cryste, whom she had chosyn in hir youthe. And
because she wolde not abide the daily intysingis of hir fader, she
forsoke bothe hir fader and hir cuntray and she was contente with
the feloushhip of one damyselle, the which folowid hir afterwarde
whan the fame of þe holy virgyn was made opyn in alle the parties of
40 Ynglonde. And Edwyne kyng of Northumbirlonde desirid hir to be
his wyfe, but Seinte Paulyne archiebisshop of Yorke yeafe hym his
aunswere that it was not lefulle a cristyn virgyn to be weddid to a
paynym, and so the blessid virgyn abode stylle vncorupte.

And then this holy childe Erkenwolde folowid the doctryne and
45 feyth of Seint Mellite the bisshop. And he profited so gretely in the
lawes of God that within shorte tyme he waxid right holy, that he
euer desired the riches of euerlastyng glory. And he put abak alle
worldely ioye and plesaunce, in so moche that when he was of gretter
age, than he chase rather to be in solytary placis to serue God in
50 contemplacion than to be among worldely curis and besynes. And
than sone after he bylde .ij. monasterys, one to hym and anoþer to
his suster Albourgh, and he ordeynid in bothe placis fulle gode rulis
and godly. And his monastery was in the cuntraye of Surry besid
Temse in a place callid Chertesey, and his susters monastery was in
55 the provynce of Saxonis in a place callid Berkyng. And Seinte
Erkenwolde conseilid his suster to put awaye with alle hir myght
alle worldly vanytees, and so he purposid to do hymselfe, and with
alle his power and strenght he occupied hymselfe in devyne
contemplacion. And he yeafe gladly of his worldely goodis to the
60 helpe of pore and nedy people, that came to hym by heritage, besidis
the godis that he spente in the byldyng of .ij. monasterys, that is to
saye Chertesey and Berkyng. And bothe the placis he endewid
sufficiauntly with lyfelode to the plesyng of God and to contynuance
of his seruyce to the helpe of crysten people.

65   And thus þis holy man Seinte Erkenwolde chaungid his erthly
heritage, his worldly dignyte and his grete patrimonies into the
heritage and lyfelode of holy Churche for to haue his heritage in
heuyn. And alle these grete expensis he did or he was callid to be
bysshop of London. And the holy Theodoure the archiebisshop of
70 Canterbury consecrate hym bisshop of London. And when this holy
virgyn Albourgh had kepte stedfastly hir virgynite contrary to
hir faders wylle, and after that she beganne to take vpon hir
grete labours as wacchyngis, fastyngis, goyng in pylgrymaige, this

tormentyng hir body by dyuerse [peynes] | for the loue of hir spouse   f. 53vb
Ihesu Cryste. And after she came to Berkyng by the guydyng of the   75
holy goost, and þere Seinte Erkenwolde ordeynid hir with other
virgyns to be alwaye occupied in the seruyce of God.

A myracle of the drawyng oute of the beem.

It happid on a tyme that the artificers that bylde the saide abbey of
Berkyng were ouerseen in takyng the mesure of a principalle beem,   80
for it was to shorte and wolde not accorde to his propre place,
wherefore thaye made moche sorowe. Than this holy man Seinte
Erkynwolde with his suster, seyng this mysfortune, toke this same
beme betwene there hondis, and thaye drewe it oute so that it had his
sufficient lenght proporcynate to the byldyng. The which myracle   85
was anone knowen opynly amonge alle the people.

And that tyme þer was no monastery of nonnys in al Ynglond,
wherefore Seinte Erkynwolde sente ouer the se for a devoute
religious woman clepid Hildelith, to whom Seinte Erkenwolde
betoke his suster for to be informyd and taught bothe in cunnyng   90
and in gode maners and in vertues doctrine, the which she conceyuid
lightlye and kepte it iustelye in hir mynde, in so moche that within
shorte tyme she excedid and passid alle hir felowes and also hir
maisters both in vertue and in cunnyng, and sone after she was made
abbas and chefe of alle the monastery.   95

Hit happid afterwarde that the bisshop of London decessid, whos
name was clepid Cedda. And by the consente of Kyng Sebbe and of
alle the people, this holye man of God Erkenwolde was chosyn
bysshop of London, alle worldely pompe and pryde forsaken. For
whatesoeuer he taught in worde he fulfyllid it in dede, for he was   100
perfite in wysedom, softe and discrete in worde, besy in prayer,
chaste of body, and alle hole yeve to Goddis lore, and he was plantid
in the rote of charyte. And afterwarde, when he had suffrid moche
tribulacion with manye gostely batels, he beganne to waxe right sike.
And then he commaundid for to make redy his chare, that he myght   105
ryde by the stretis of the cyte for to preche the worde of God,
wherefore it was kepte in custome longe tyme after of his disciplis
and of fulle many oþer to towche hym and kysse hym, and
whatesoeuer sykenes that thaye had thaye were anone delyuerid

74 peynes] *om.* A2

110 thereof and made perfitly hole. And when the chippys and paryngis
of his chare and of the sete þat he sate vpon was brought to the sike,
anone thaye receyuid helthe of body, thurgh the grete grace and
mercy of oure Lorde Ihesu Cryste and of his holy bisshop Seinte
Erkenwolde.

115   A myracle howe the chare wente on one whele and fylle
         not downe.

In a daye of somer, as this blessid Seinte Erkynwolde rode aboute in
his chare for to preche the worde of God, it fortunyd that the one
whele of the chare fylle of fro the axe tre, and yette the chare wente
120 forthe vpon the oþer whele withoute fallyng, for God was then the
guyde, þe which was grete merveyle to alle them that se it.
O merciable God and mervelous aboue alle thyng, to whom al
brute beestis be made meke and alle wode thyngis be made obedyent,
thou vouchesaufe to calle to thye mercye thye blessid seruaunt for to
125 make hym pertable of thyne excellent ioye, thou yeue vs grace by his
prayer, which knewe by revelacion that his soule shulde be losid
from the body by temporalle dethe, to be preseruyd fro alle maner
evylle and fro euerlastyng dethe.
When the blessid Seinte Erkynwolde, as oure Lorde Ihesu wolde,
130 came to Berkyng, he felle into a grete sykenes, in the which he endid
his temporalle lyfe. And in as moche as he knewe it before, he sente
for his seruauntis and suche as were drawyng to hym and he yeafe
them holsome and swete lessons and he blessid them with fulle gret
f. 54ra deuocion, and amonge þer hondis he yeldid vp þe spyrite | to
135 almyghty God, in whos passyng there was felte a mervelous swete
savoure as though alle the howse had be fulle of swete bawme.
The chanons of Poulis in London and the monkis of Cherteseye,
heryng that this holy man was departid to God, thaye came þeder
anone to haue this holy body with them. And þe nonnys, seyng that
140 the holy body shulde be take fro them, withstode it to þer power and
wolde not suffre it, and saide þat it was moost accordyng to his wylle
the body to be buryed þer in þer place in as moche as he was here
founder. The monkis of Cherteseye were of the contrary opynyon,
for thaye saide he was þer abbot and founder: 'And therefore we ben
145 come hider nowe to bryng hym to oure place, for he made oure
monastery furste for hymselfe and he was oure abbott, wherefore we
wolle haue hym.' Then the clergy with alle the people of London

aunswerid to bothe parties so beyng in stryfe and saide: 'Ye speke
alle in veyne, for neither of you shalle haue hym, for it is the vse and
the maner in alle cytees, as in Rome and alle oþer placis, that the 150
bisshop shalle be buryed and lye in his owne cyte where his see is.'
Furthermore, while these wordis were in sayng, the people of the
cyte ranne to the body and toke it vp and bere it towarde London.
And the monkis and the nonnys folowid after, sore wepyng, and
made grete lamentacion that so precyous a body shulde be take awaye 155
fro them.

And as thaye wente towarde London there fylle a fulle grete
tempeste of wynde and of water, so that when that thaye came to a
brydge thaye myght not passe for grete water, for the waye was
ouerflowyn and thaye had no bote, wherefore thaye were constreynid 160
to set downe this holye bodye. And then the monkis and the nonnys
saide to the men of the cyte: 'Se nowe howe youre iniury appierith
that ye haue done to vs for the body of the holy seinte. Ye se howe a
sodeyne tempest is fallyn vpon you by þe wylle of oure Lorde,
wherefore,' saide the nonnys, 'turne ye ayen and lete vs haue the 165
body, for it is shewid opynly þat it is Goddis wylle so to be.' And in
alle this grete tempestis the tapers that were bore aboute the holy
body wente not oute, but alway þaye were bright brennyng. And also
the nonnys saide that while he levid, 'Oure lorde shewid to hym by
revelacion that after his temporalle deth he shulde rest in oure 170
monastery, and ye ravynours dispoyle vs and take hym awaye
violently from vs, wherefore turne ye ayen and bryng hym to his
owne place that he was founder of, leste the vengeaunce and the
wreth of God falle on you.' Then the cytezyns of London, heryng
this, aunswerid and saide: 'Ye shalle vnderstonde that youre wordis 175
shalle not avayle you, for we ben neither ravenours nor theves, for we
take nothyng fro you but oure owne fader which hath ben oure
patron many yeris. Neiþer we dispoyle you ne robbe you, for we bere
hym to his owne cyte, and by hym we truste and hope þat we shalle
neuer falle into the daunger of oure enemyes. And ye shalle rather 180
bete downe the wallys of oure cyte than to haue awey oure patrone
fro vs.'

þan there was there presente a clerke that was longyng afore to
Seinte Erkenwolde by his lyfe. He, seyng the grete murmur of the
people and the stryfe, he wente vp into an hye place and commaun- 185
did alle the people to kepe silence, and when silence was made he
tolde them a grete commendacion of this vertu charite, counseylyng

and excyting bothe parties to kepe the same. And he saide it was not
sittyng ne accordyng so to mystrete that holy body by stronge and
190 violent hondis, 'but ye shulde beseke almyghty God with true
deuocion and with mekenes in herte for to shewe them som tokyn
by revelacion in whate place þis holy body shulde reste.' And then
alle the people consentid to his byddyng, and anone thaye knelid
downe alle and prayed fulle devoutely to God to knowe his wylle in
195 this mater. And the clergy saide the Letanye and the laye people
f. 54ʳᵇ knelid downe saying there *Pater noster* and þer *Aue | Maria* with
shedyng of terys, besechyng almyghty God to sese that stryfe
betwene them and to shewe them som tokyn by revelacion where
it plesid hym that this holy body shulde reste.

200   Howe the people se the water devide and a fayre path in
         the myddis.

The people beyng in prayer þaye sawe the water devide, as it did to
Moyses and to þe childryn of Ysrael goyng into the Londe of
Beheste, and as it did to Ely goyng into the mounte of rest þat
205 yeafe hym a drye pathe. So almyghty God yeafe a dry path to the
people of London for to convey this holy body thurgh the water
towarde the cyte. And then alle the people aroos vp fro prayer and
thankid almyghty God that he had shewid them that grete myracle to
þe comforte and grete ioye to them alle, and so with grete gladnes
210 and reuerence and by one assent toke vp the bere and bare it thurgh
the path, the water stondyng vpon euery side and alle the people
passing thurgh not wetyn there fete. And then thaye came to
Stratforde, and þer thaye sett downe the bere to reste them in a
fayre mede fulle of fayre flowris, that the grete multitude of people
215 myght passe by, and then the weder beganne for to wex fulle fayre
and clere after the tempest.

         Howe the tapers were light by myracle withoute any
         mannys honde.

And the tapers were made to brenne withoute puttyng to of fyre of
220 mannys honde. And thus it plesid oure lorde to multeply myraclis to
the honoure and wurship of this holy seinte, wherefore the people
were fulle of ioye and gladnes and yeafe laude and praysyng to God
for alle these grete myraclis shewid for his holy seruaunte Seinte

Erkenwolde. And then thaye toke vp this holye bodye and bare it
fulle reuerently to the cyte of London, and þer alle the cyte met with   225
this holy body and brought it to Poulis with grete ioye and mery
songe of praysing. And alle sike folkis that touchid his bere were
made anone perfitly hole of alle there sikenes, wherefore moche seke
people drewe dayly to his tombe and were made hole of alle there
sikenes by the mercy of God and by þe prayer of his holy bisshop   230
Seinte Erkenwolde.

A myracle of a yonge scoler.

There was dwellyng in a doctours house in London a scolemaister
which was callid Ellewyne, the which was a right gode man and a
cunnyng, and also of gode maners and of pyte and compassion that   235
he had. He wolde infourme childryn to the entente that thaye myght
be in tyme comyng pelers and berers vp of holy Churche. But there
was one childe amonge other that had plaide with his felowis and had
forgotyn his lesson. The tyme came on þe morowe that he shulde
reherse his lesson to the maister, and he drad gretely for he cowde it   240
not, and then he ranne awaye and came to Seinte Erkenwoldis
shryne. And there he founde a nonne in hir prayers, to whom this
childe with wepyng teeris saide: 'I praye you by the waye of pyte of
youre helpe and counceyle in this necessite,' and tolde hir shortely
the mater howe that he was pursuyd and durst not abide the crueltye   245
of his maister. And then she was meovid with mercy and compassion, and she counseylid hym to knele downe at the tombe of this
holye Seinte Erkenwolde and beseke hym mekely of helpe and to
sette his mynde sadly to almyghty God and to haue alwaye after a
singuler devocion to that holy seinte.   250
    This childe was fulle glad of this councelle and of the comforte of
this devoute nonne, and anone he fylle downe prostrate in prayer.
And whate inspiracion of cunnyng þat this chylde gate by the
merytis of this blessid Seinte Erkenwolde it passith mannys reson
to thynke, for when this childe was founde and brought of his   255
maister cruellye to scole there to be ponysshid, he cowde not only the
lesson that he had forgotyn, but he saide perfitly withoute the boke
suche thyngis as he neuer lernyd of erthely creature but by the
inspiracion of God. And when his maister herde this he merveylid
gretely and lefte his crueltye and for shame fled þe contray. And alle   260
his felowis, when thaye vnderstode how this myracle | was done,   f. 54ᵛᵃ

thaye had grete drede and yeafe thonkyngis to God and to Seinte
Erkynwolde and saide: 'Bretherne, lete vs not diffyne this myracle to
be done in veyne, for alle that is wryten of God is to oure doctryne.
265 For a contryte herte oure lorde shalle not dispise, lyke as the contrite
herte of the childe by the merytis of this blessid Seynte Erkenwolde
apese the wrathe of oure maister almyghty God.'

Of the payne and vengeaunce done to a man þat wolde not
halowe the feest of Seinte Erkenwolde.

270 There was in London a wrecchid man which of his owne wickydnes
and frowardnys disdeynid to halowe the feest of Seinte Erkenwolde.
And in the solempnyte of the same feest daye this vndevoute man of
his owne cursidnes brought a grete burthyn in his necke, and he
caste it downe ayenste the walle of þe churche wherein the relyques
275 of this blessid seinte restyn. And he did it in fulle grete dispite to
loke whate any man wolde saye to hym. And when the office of the
masse was done, a chanon of the same churche wente oute by fortune
and he founde this cursid man castyng downe his byrthyn. To whom
þe chanon saide in this wyse: 'Whate maner manne and of what
280 condicion arte thou, that lystyst not to kepe þe solempnyte of this
feest as oþer cristen people do? Hast thou no nede to his helpe, or
arte thou not welle with thyselfe? Remembryst thou welle whate
oure lorde sayeth: "He þat dispiseth anye of myne dispisith me." '
And he rehersid many ensamplis to hym and auctoritees of holy
285 scrypture. But þis frowarde man refusid alle his doctryne and wolde
not in no wyse be refourmyd, but sodenly brake oute in wordis of
reprefe and blasphemy, saying that þere were to many holy dayes
beside, though he kepte not þis feest to of Seinte Erkenwolde. 'For if
I lacke mete or drynke wolle youre Erkenwolde yeue it me? I myght
290 lightly dye for defaute if I shulde truste þerto. Ye that be preestis
and make so manye festfulle dayes and occupye youre lyfe in
ydulnes, kepe ye it if ye wylle, for I telle þe shortely I wolle not.'
And when this chanon sawe that he myght not by no exhortacion of
fayre speche ouercome hym and reforme hym to the Churche, then
295 he yeafe hym sharpe wordis and saide that he shulde be ponysshid by
the lawe, and bade hym beware leste oure lorde take vengeaunce on
hym for þe iniury that he had do to his holy seinte, the which fylle

   265 dispise] add and A2   266 Erkenwalde] add and A2

sone after, for whan he sawe the people drawyng abowte hym, the
which came for to wete whate þat mente, suche a fere sodenly toke
hym that he beganne to renne awaye as faste as he cowde, and in his 300
haste he ranne ayenste the sepulture of a ded man and felle downe
and neuer spake worde after, but this he endid his lyfe wrecchidly.

Than the people þat stode aboute mervaylid sore of þis thyng and
were in fulle grete fere. And there was a woman that was a frende of
this wrecchid man made moche sorowe and lamentacion for hym, 305
and she rehersid manye gode dedis that he had done for þe loue that
she had to hym, and with hir wayling beganne to stere the people to
haue compassion. Than a gode olde man, that vnderstode welle howe
this thyng was done by the vengeaunce of God and sawe that the
people cowde not vnderstonde it, then he enformyd them by 310
auctoryte of scripture howe oure lorde sayeth: 'Kepe ye myne holy
daye,' for he that doyth any seruyle werke in it his sowle shalle perish
in the myddis of the people: 'Wherefore vnderstonde ye veryly that it
is the vengeaunce of God, for he þat hath pollutyd the holy daye
with seruyle laboure and hath blasphemyd the gode lorde and his 315
holy seinte Erkenwolde oure patrone with his mouthe, he is not
worthye to be nombrid among true cristenne men, nor to be buryed
in cristen beryels.' And by the exhortacion of this olde man the
people were taught to kepe there holy daye, and then alle the people
with grete fere and drede yeafe thonkyngis to almyghty God and to 320
his holye seinte Erkenwolde, the which be praysid withoute ende.
Amen.

Howe a prisoner was delyuerid oute of prison and his
chaynes losid by myracle.

In | a tyme when the festfulle daye of Seinte Erkynwolde was f. 54vb
halowid, the bellys beyng ironge thurgh alle þe cyte as the custome 326
is, and moche people resortyng to the churche that the relyques of
this holy seynt restyn in, there was a prysoner which by the
commaundement of þe kynge was faste bounde in prisone with
stronge cheynes of yron. And when he vnderstode by inquyraunce 330
whate mente that grete sowne of bellis that he beyng in prison herde,
and that it was tolde hym that many notable myraclis were shewid
dayly at his tombe, for whye þer were blynde men made to se, defe
made to here, dombe men to speke and so euery sykenes or trouble
þat þei stode in by the merytis of this blessid seinte thaye were made 335

perfitly hole, than this prysoner hyryng this was right welle
comfortid and with a gode deliberacion set alle his mynde to God
and to this holye Seinte Erkynwolde, trustyng that by such deuocion
as God had yeue hym he myght be delyuerid by the merytis of Seint
340 Erkenwolde fro the perylle of dethe and of the ieopardy that he stode
in, and thought that as sone as he myght to breke oute of pryson and
visite the tombe of Seinte Erkenwolde.

But he euer drad gretely his kepers, for he wyste welle that if he
were take fleyng, his trouble and his peyne shulde be doublid. This
345 causid hym to be fulle sore aferde and troubelid within hymselfe, and
as a ship in grete tempest is cast towarde and frowarde with violence
of the wawis, so was the pore prysoner thurgh fere and sorowe that
he was in one while, and mevid with loue and deuocion anoþer
while, for to go oute to visite the tombe of holye Seinte Erkenwolde,
350 and thus the dred and fere hilde hym that he durst not go oute. Then
oure lorde allemyghty God, beholdyng these grete flowyng dowtis of
his prysoner, comfortid hym by his grace so that he knewe welle
hymselfe and iugid hymselfe worthye to suffre moche gretter payne
than he did, and if he were take he thought to suffre alle paciently for
355 his demerytis. And þus he commyttyd hymselfe to God, and with his
cheynes he came to the tombe where the holy reliques restyn of
Seinte Erkenwolde, and þer he fylle downe [on] his knees at the saide
tombe, saying these wordis: 'O thou mercyful God, that by the
merytis of this holy seinte haste yovyn refute, comforte and helpe to
360 synners and wrecchis, Lorde, thou lyghten my herte and my
vnderstondying to axe nothyng of þy mercy but þat that is necessary
to the helthe of my soule. Many thyngis I nede, but what I shulde
aske I wote not. I am sore bownde with cheynes which dayly turment
me sore, but I speke but lytle of the cheynes of synne wherein I am
365 bounde more sorer. Also I am sore turmentid with the fere of
temporalle dethe ayenst the kyng, but hiderto I neuer ferid the
ieopardy of the spiritualle dethe ayenst my moste souereyne lorde
kyng of hevyn. O gracious Lorde, haue pyte and mercy vpon me, for
to slowlye I haue highed to þe. I fare as a childe that wylle not lerne
370 withoute betyng. Nowe I come to the for to desire the losyng of my
body, which shulde haue come to the longe ago for to haue had the
[losyng of] my soule. O mercyfulle Lorde, I dare not for shame desire
the losyng of my body, which am so sore constreynid and bownde

357 on] one A2   371 losyng of] losyd A2

with the bondis of synne in my soule, but forsothe, Lorde, thou
knowyste whate profite shulde come to thye people and whate 375
reuerence and wurship shulde come to thye holy seinte Erkenwolde,
and if I by thye grace and by þe meritis of þy holye seinte were thus
mervelously delyuerid.'

And when this caytyfe had longe this contynued in his prayers and
moche people woundrid vpon hym, then his kepers had spyed that 380
he had brokyn the pryson and sought with grete dyligence for there
prysoner, promysyng fulle grete yeftis to hym that cowde telle where
he were, for thaye stode in grete fere ayenst the kynge for hym,
supposyng thaye shulde haue the same iugement that he shulde haue
had. Wherefore þei | ranne fulle faste aboute, and at the laste thaye f. 55ʳᵃ
were infourmyd that there prysoner was knelyng devoutely in his 386
prayers at the tombe of this blessid Seinte Erkenwolde amonge other
people. And then thaye were fulle gladde and thaye hastid þem fulle
faste theder, thynkyng verily for to ponysh hym more cruelly after
than þaye did before, and so thaye entrid boldely and proudely into 390
the churche and fownde hym there in his prayers. And as þay wolde
haue sette honde on hym, hys cheynes losid and fylle fro hym and
with a grete sowne alle tobrake so þat alle þat were there merveilid
gretely thereof. And when the bysshop vnderstode this thyng he
made a sermon to the people of this grete myracle, and he 395
commaundid that he shulde no more be put in pryson, but lete
hym go where he wolde. And then alle the people yeafe laude and
praysyng to almyghty God and to his holy seinte for his delyueraunce.

A myracle howe the body and þe shryne of Seynte 400
Erkenwolde was sauyd in the myddis of alle the fyre
when alle the churche was brente.

In þe tyme of Morys that was bisshop of London a mervelous fyre
was kyndelid in the cyte of London, which beganne att Ludgate and
brente contynually tylle it came to Algate, that was a pytevous and a 405
ferefulle sight to beholde. And it beganne in the nyght, the wynde
beyng in the west, the which fyre brente so cruelly that it made
pleyne to the erthe alle that he founde before hym, in so moche that
it neither sparid churchis ne towris but devourid them fervently. As
ye se that a smalle fyre consumyth anone stoble or towe, so this grete 410
fyre consumyd and wastid petevouslye fulle ryalle byldyngis bothe of

stone and of tre so cruelly and so hastely that thaye had no tyme to
remeve and for to saue þere goodis, but eche manne ranne aboute as
people fro themselfe, for it semyd as God wolde take vengeaunce and
415 distroye alle the cyte vtterly for the synnes that reynid therein. Then
the men of the cyte toke hokys and oþer instrumentis and temptid to
haue swagid the fyre as moche as thaye myght, but when thaye
cowde not prevayle thaye suffrid it to brenne and fled oute of the
cyte alle amasid and confusyd. And the wemen ranne oute of the cyte
420 in there here and thaye caste of þer heddis, and þen thaye cryed as
madde wymen and wysshid themselfe drownyd in the Temysse.

And amonge alle other byldyngis it was grete pety to se howe the
ryalle byldyngis of Poulis was devourid amonge oþer byldyngis, in þe
which the relyques of Seinte Erkenwolde reste. Thaye were alle
425 savid, for after the fyre was kyndelid in the saide churche there
myght no man entre in; the fyre brente so sore and so cruellye ouer
þer heddis vpon alle the hole roffe of the churche þat the vawte clove
asondre and felle downe, and the led aboue was alle molten and
ranne downe, and the grete beemys and the roffe felle downe halfe
430 brente and halfe vnbrente and laye benethe vpon þe pament, and it
yeafe so grete hete that it brake the glasse wyndowis. And þen the
people lokyd on and se the blessid Seinte Erkenwolde ouer his tombe
fyghtyng with þe fyre. His tombe was than not riche, for it was made
of tre and a clothe lying thereon, wherefore the people conceyuid
435 that oure lorde toke vengeaunce of the cyte because thaye suffrid
there holye fader and patrone to lye so vnreuerentlye. And as þaye
behilde thaye se a grete beeme halfe brennyng felle downe vpon the
tombe and laye þer brennyng tylle it was consumyd to coolis, and yet
the tombe by þe merytis of Seinte Erkenwolde was preseruyd and
440 kepte bothe fro brekyng with the falle of the grete beeme and also fro
brennyng, in so moche that the clothe that laye vpon the tombe was
nothyng brente with the fyre nor it had no savoure of the fyre.
Wherefore alle þe people with one assente knelid downe, and thaye
besought allemyghty God fulle mekely with alle þere hertis that lyke
445 as he had preseruyd his tombe of there holye fader harmeles, that he
f. 55ʳᵇ wolde haue pyte on them and save and | kepe the remnaunde of the
cyte, promysyng to amende there levyng by his grace and mercy and
to make there a wurshipfulle shryne in the wurship of hym and of his
holy seruaunte Seinte Erkenwolde.
450 And also thaye besought þere blessid patrone to praye for them so
that thaye myght be herde by his prayer, for thaye saide þer prayer

was vnworthye to be herde for þer wrecchid levyng, and þen thaye
rose vp fro prayer and set to there hondis and quenchid þe fyre by
Goddis myght anone, and so was the cyte delyuerid fro the outeragyous fyre by the merytis of the holy seinte Erkenwolde.   455

Alle this was done in tyme of Morys bisshop of this cyte of
London, the which beganne to bylde ayen the churche so grete and
large that men wente that it myght not haue ben endid. And when he
had made the shryne of Seynte Erkenwolde more wurshipfully and
richer than it was afore, then he endid his lyfe blessidly. And after   460
hym came bysshop Richarde, which was a right wurshipfulle man
and a noble, in whos tyme the saide churche was mervelouslye
encresid, for he did grete coste thereon and he sterid many oþer to
do the same, and after that he fylle into a fulle grete sikenes the
which hilde hym .v. yere, and in the ende thereof he slepte in oure   465
lorde.

Howe the drye honde of a woman was restored ayen.

There was a wurshipfulle woman that hight Benet which [had] .ij.
dyuers infirmytees, one [that] she was borne with a drye honde, that
fro hir yonge aige [neuer] encresid by noryshment but euer bode   470
stylle drye, and also she had þe collyke right stronglye and feruently.
And in .iiij. yere daye after the obyte of Seinte Erkenwolde, she
cessid not to praye for hir helthe, daylye vysitinge hys tombe, for she
had sought for helpe in many dyuers placis in visiting manye grete
pylgrymaigis and many holy seyntis, but it plesid almyghty God to   475
reserue hir to his holy and devoute confessoure Seinte Erkenwolde.

O thou holy Arkynwolde, that arte blessid among alle seyntis, for
Peter and Powle with many oþer seyntis refusid to yeue helth to this
woman because that þu shuldist appiere the more gloryous among
Ynglisshmen when thaye sawe the to yeve helthe and comforte to   480
this woman. For as it appierith afterwarde, when this woman
contynued in hir prayers besechyng mekely thye socoure and
helpe, the quycke blode refresshid so þe senewis of hir honde that
it was made anone lyke to hir oþer honde, apte and able to do
euerythynge with alle whate she wolde.   485

And when that she vnderstode that she was perfitly made hole,
then she yeafe thonkyngis to almyghty God and to his holy seruaunte

68 had] *om.* A2   469 that(1)] *om.* A2   470 neuer] neuerer A2

Seinte Erkynwolde, and in remembraunce of this gloryous myracle
she offrid vp þer an honde of wexe and forsoke the worlde and
490 became a nonne in the prouynce of Lugdune vpon the flode of Ligir
where she abode many yeris, and in hir laste dayes she returnyd ayen
to London for to yelde thonkyngis to hym that delyuerid hir and
holpe hir when she was in hir grete desese. And sone after she endid
hir lyfe pesibly.

495   How a weddid man was smetyn with a grete sikenes
             because he lettid his wyfe to offre certeine yeftis to þe
             repayring of the shryne of Seinte Erkenwolde.

When it plesid almyghty God that the shryne of Seinte Erkenwolde
shulde be ryally honourid with precyous stonys and with other
500 rychesse, and dyuers men were meovid to yefe of þere goodis thereto,
amonge alle þer was one þat had a fulle devoute woman to hys wyfe
the which had ordeynid a certein yefte for to offer to Seinte
Erkenwolde. And when hir husbonde vnderstode hir entente, he
rebukid hir sharpely and thretenyd hir so that she durst not nor myght
505 not perfourme hir entente. And in the night folowyng, hir wrecchid
husbonde was smetyn with a grevous sikenes in his reynes, þat
encresid daylye vpon hym so feruently that his phisicions dispayrid
of his lyfe. But Saynte Poule sayethe that an vnrightwis man shalle be
sauyd by a rightwys woman, and in the nyght folowyng Seinte
510 Erkenwolde appierid to the saide woman and bade hir take hir |
f. 55ᵛᵃ husbonde anone and brynge hym to his tombe and he shulde receyue
his helthe. And on the morne she ordeynid hym to be borne theder of
his seruauntis and leyde hym before þe shryne. And she prayed for
hym fulle devoutely, and anone oure lorde herde hir prayers by the
515 merytis of his holy confessoure Seinte Erkynwolde, and he was anone
made perfytly hole. And where as he came thedir by the helpe of
other, he wente home ayen afote by his owne strenght. And then he
amendid his lyfe, for before that he vsyd to do but fewe gode dedis of
charite, but after he waxe right large and plentevous and departid his
520 godis with þem that had nede in dedis of pite.

             Howe a childe was restorid to his sight.

In a tyme a wurshipfulle woman þat herde of these grete myraclis
broughte hir doughter þat was blynde to the churche where the

reliquys of þis holy [seinte] laye, and in the sight of moche people knelid downe and besought almyghty God with shedyng of hir teeris 525 that hir doughter myght receyue hir sight by the merytis of Seinte Erkenwolde, and with hir lamentable teeris she mevid oþer people to praye with hir. And as thaye were alle in þere prayer anone hir doughter receyuid ayen hir sight, wherefore alle the people yeafe thonkyngis and praysingis to almyghty God and to his holy and 530 gloryous confessoure Seinte Erkynwolde.

Howe a man was restorid not only of his sight but also he
was restorid ayen to alle his body strenghtis.

There was a noble yonge man that for certeyne causis came oute of Fraunce into Ynglonde, that hight William. And as he sate at his mete 535 amonge his men and oþer merchauntis in the howse of Amelyne and Breed his wyfe, which þo were gode and honest folks dredyng God, he was smyten with a ferefulle and a sodeyne sikenes that he appierid as halfe dede to alle them þat were aboute hym, which mervelid gretely of this soden afraye. And when thaye sawe none oþer helpe but that he 540 muste nedis dye, thaye bare hym into a chambre and layde hym vpon a bedde and sente for a preest which myght both comforte hym and þem in that sodeyne and dowtefulle case, which brought a crosse with hym to make hym remembre the passhion of oure lorde,and laborid to meove hym thereto wyth alle the meanys that he cowde; but he myght 545 not prevayle, for he had loste his heryng, his smellyng, his tastyng, and alle his bodely wyttis, in so moche þat whan thaye shewid hym the crosse, his eyes beyng opyn, he sawe nothyng þerof, nor he vnderstode nothynge that was saide to hym. And this he appierid as dede by the space of .iiij. daies, save a lytle breþyng that vnnethe myght be aspied 550 of anye man, in which tyme thaye made redy alle thyngis to his beryng with manye a sorowfulle teere, and wepte ful sore for hym.

And in alle this meane tyme there was none that cowde remembre of the grete benefettis and myraclis of this holy seinte Erkenwolde. And at the laste it came into the mynde of the preest, and then he 555 enformyd his felowis of the grete and notable myraclis that had ben done and shewid afore þat tyme in the wurship of God and of his holye confessoure Seint Erkenwold. Than a fulle devoute man of his felouship that lovid hym right welle made a vowe to vysite Seinte

524 seinte] sente A2

560 Erkenwolde, knelyng vpon his knees with moche people aboute hym,
besechyng almyghty God of his grete mercy and benevolence that he
wolde not only yeve to the syke his bodely strenght but also his
eyesight, þat he myght beholde and se the signe of the crosse þat
thaye hilde before his eyes. And then he toke .ij. eyes of waxe and
565 touchid the eyes of the dede man, and he arose vp in grete haste to
bere the saide eyes of waxe to the shryne of Seinte Erkenwolde.

And in the same tyme that the saide eyes were honge on the
shryne, þis sike man not only receyuid his sight, but also he was
restorid anone to the vse of alle his membris and was made perfitlye
570 hole. And then he and alle the people wente to þe tombe of this holye
seinte Erkenwolde and there thaye thonkid devoutely almyghty God,
f. 55vb and range alle | the bellys to the declaracion of this grete myracle,
wherefore praysyngis and thonkyngis be to almyghty God and his
holy and blessid confessoure Seinte Erkenwolde, worlde withoute
575 ende. Amen.

Howe anoþer sike man was curyd.

A sike man in a tyme that had longe tyme be ponysshid wyth manye
grevous sikenes came to the tombe of Seinte Erkynwolde, besechyng
devoutely to haue helthe, for his body was made fulle faynte and
580 feble with longe contynuaunce of his infirmitees. And whan he had
layne a while prostrate on the erthe in his prayers, than he felte
hymselfe made perfitly hole, and then he rose vp and thonkid God
with alle his herte and the blessid Seinte Erkynwolde.

Howe vengeaunce was takyn of one þat blasphemyd Seinte
585 Erkynwolde.

Not longe after, there was an argentere that vsid to visite the howse
where the case of tre for the shryne laye to be gylte and peyntid, to
the entente for to [talke] with his felowis which he had vsid of
custome to iangle with. His name was Eustace, which wolde be
590 dronke amoost euery daye, and then in his dronkennys he vsid to
swere manye grete othis and blasphemyd almyghty God and his
seyntis, for the fole wende that it had plesid his felowis welle to
swere suche othis. And so dayly that place was fulfylled with synfulle

588 talke] take A2

and with veyne talkyngis, for a mysrulid man nedith not to seke
longe for his felowe.   595
    And in a tyme as he layde his honde vpon the casse in spekyng
many foule and synfulle wordis, blasphemyng the name of almyghty
God, and in his dronkenes lyfte vp his honde and layde hym downe
in the case alonge and sayde: 'Lo, I am Seinte Erkenwolde, offre ye
yeftis to me and desire ye myne helpe, and peynte ye for me this   600
case, and laye ye vpon it syluer and golde.' These wordis and other
lyke þis vnhappy wrecche brought forthe with the mouthe of
blasphemye to the dirogacion of this holye seinte Erkenwolde,
wherefore immediately he was smetyn with a grete infyrmyte.
Then his felowis, dredyng the vengeaunce, caste hym oute and   605
bare hym home to his bedde. And whan he had longe tyme
contynued in his sikenes, his felowis mevid hym to aske foryeuenes
of his trespas, but the wrecche, obstynate in malice, refusid it and
wolde not aske mercye, wherefore he died wrecchidly.

    How a leche was helid of a dedly sikenes when alle   610
    phisicions lefte hym.

In the same tyme moche people were helid of dyuers sikenes, and
among alle other there was a noble yonge man that was welle lettrid
and had youyn hym to [laboure] and to studye in physike and in
surgery, which had youyn hym alle to þe delytis of the worlde. And   615
he levid after his owne lystis, but almyghty God of his grete mercy,
seyng and knowyng alle hid thyngis, wolde not suffre this yonge man
this wrecchidly to lese hymselfe, correctid hym fulle gentylly with a
sore sikenes in his lyuer so that he was amoste consumyd awaye. And
alle his lymmes feyntid and dyssoluyd, and where his truste was   620
before þat tyme in physike, yet his phisicions forsoke hym and thaye
counseylid hym for to dispose hym to dye.
    And when he was alone, he remembrid hym of his wrecchidnes
and howe he had longe levid in delytis, and then he repente hym
fulle sore and he askid God foryeuenes and made a faythfulle   625
promyse to God and to Seinte Erkenwolde that if he myght escape
that grevous sikenes he wolde chaunge his lyfe and leve vnder the
commaundementis of God. And also he remembrid hym of the grete
myraclis of this holy seinte, and he besought hym mekely to praye

614 laboure] labours A2

630 for hym, not only for his bodely helthe, but also for þe helthe of his
soule, for by lykelyhode he myght not long leve. And then he
commaundid his kepers for to brynge hym to Seinte Erkenwoldes
shryne, and þere he abode .iij. dayes in prayer, and he besought his
frendis to pray and to faste for hym, and at the .iij.de dayes ende he

635 was restorid and made alle hole. And the chanons met hym comyng
homwarde allone fro the churche, and þei merveylid whan thaye se
hym and askid hym howe the case was, and he tolde them euery dele
and in whate wyse he was restorid to his helthe. And then thaye
askid hym if he myght go welle, and then he saide as welle as euer he |

f. 56ʳᵃ did, blessid be God, and þat he was able to go or ryde whereeuer he
641 shulde, wherefore thaye alle yeafe thonkyngis to God and to Seinte
Erkenwolde of his helthe. And I, symple wrecche, that wrote furste
this myracle, sawe alle these myracles done.

And also in myne howse þer was a pore woman which soiernyd
645 with me, the which dayly and nyghtly cessid not to yeve laude and
praysinge to God and to Seinte Erkenwolde. And she tolde me that
as she knelid in hir prayers in the myddis of the nyght at the tombe
of Seinte Erkynwolde, there stode a candillestycke of tre before hir
and a candylle brennyng therein, and whan the waxe candylle was
650 wastid to the tree þen she styked the candylle a lytle hier, and when
it wastid ayen to the tre it went oute or she wyste it. And then she
herde a grete noyse aboute the tombe, wherefore she durst not abide
þer in þe derke, but she wente to a lampe and light the candylle ayen,
and as sone as the candylle was light the noyse was gone. And so it
655 fortunyd afterwarde as sone as there lackid light the noyse came
anone ayen. And she conceyuid that it was not syttyng to so
wurshipfulle a seinte to be withoute light, and so it was ordeinyd
that there was kepte alweye after that a light, as it accordith to so
holy a confessoure as he is.

660   Howe a violatour of the feest of Seinte Erkynwolde smote
        oute his owne eye and was restorid ayen by myracle.

In the feest of the deposicion of Seinte Erkenwolde þer was a man
þat dispisid to kepe and halowe that daye, and he wente to labour for
to tawe skynnes. And when oþer people se hym thaye wolde haue
665 refourmyd hym godely with softe and ientylle language, and tolde
hym that it was grete foly with so lytle wynnyng of þat pore crafte to
displese almyghty God and þat holye seinte that alle wel disposid

men wurship and halowe in that daye. And thaye saide that he owith
to be obedyente to the Churche, and not to holde no suche singuler
opynyons in frowardnes and in malice. And whan thaye had sterid 670
hym with manye gode exhortacions, then thaye conseylid hym to
leve his besynes and to go with them to þe churche of Seinte
Erkenwolde for to beseche almyghty God of foryeuenes, leste God
wolde take vengeaunce of hym for his cursidnes, and alle thaye
promysed hym to praye with hym. 675

But this symple wrecche wolde not be correctid by þer exhortacions, but scorned them and sette them at nought, and in grete angre
he toke his instrument and beganne to do his besynes. And as he
lyfte vp his instrument in grete haste he smote hymselfe in the eye,
and so he loste his eye. And then he was compellid by the peyne of 680
his eye to leve his werke and to halowe that daye with his neighboris.
Then he was brought to the churche of Seinte Erkynwolde, and then
this thyng was openyd to alle þe people, and when thaye se that
vengeaunce, then thaye drade gretely and mevid the synner to do
penaunce. And when thaye sawe hym sorowfulle and contrite for hys 685
synne, then alle the people prayed for hym and anone his eye was
restorid to hym ayen, wherefore thaye yeafe laude and praysingis to
almyghty God and to his holy confessoure for this grete myracle
shewid for this wreccid creature.

How a woman was restorid to hir sight. 690

A woman that dwellid nye to the churche of Seinte Erkenwolde had
be blynde many yeres, which was knowe right welle of alle the
people. And as she besought almyghty God for to helpe hir by the
merytis of the gloryous confessoure Seinte Erkynwolde, to whom she
had fulle grete devocion, and as she prayed þer fulle mekely, she had 695
anone hir sight and was made perfitly hole. Then the next Sondaye
after the people wente fulle many to se this woman that was knowen
fulle longe afore to be blynde. And then alle the people yeafe laude
and praysing to almyghty God and to his holy confessoure Seinte
Erkenwolde for this grete myracle. 700

697 people] *add* the people A2

Here folowith whate myraclis were shewid at his translacion.

There were a certein felouship of a monastery not fer fro the cyte of
London that were aboute to stele awaye the body of Seinte
f. 56rb Erkenwolde oute of his tombe by | nyght. And thaye boldely brake
706 vp the churche dore of Poulis and came to the quere dore and wolde
haue broke vp that also, but thaye made suche noyse þer that þe
keper of the churche awoke and cryed oute vpon them, but [he]
durste not go downe to them. Then this eville disposid felouship
710 demyd that by that crye the people wolde aryse for to distroye them
for þer felonye, and so thaye fled awaye in alle the haste at the same
dore where þay came in. And when thaye were gone the keper came
downe and range the bellys for to cause the people to come to hym.
And when the people came and se the dore so broken, and when
715 thaye had enquyred the cause, then thaye pursuyd after, but thaye
cowde not prevayle to ouertake þem. Then thaye came ayen and
wecchid alle that nyght, dredyng that thaye wolde make another
sawte to them, and on the morowe thaye thought to remeve this holy
body into a more wurshipfulle place. And theye ordeynid .viij.
720 wurshipfulle preestis to do that office previly, and at þe .iij.de
dayes ende, whan thaye had made redy the shryne of stone which
was wrought before fulle cunnyngly as it appierith nowe, the saide
preestis thought for to remeeve this holy body prevely, for yf the
people shulde knowe yt there shulde be to grete prese, and also the
725 prese of the people shulde lette them.

But allemyghty God, þat yeuyth wurship to alle his seintis in
mervelous wyse, wolde not suffre the translacion of his holy
confessour to be done so vnder couerte and hydly, but oure lorde
made it to be knowen opynly to alle the people the same houre that
730 thaye had ordeynid for to haue translate hym so previly, but the
people resortid theder wounderly faste. And when thaye came theder
and fownde the doris of the churche shette, anone with strenght
thaye lyfte þe dorys oute of the hokys and came in to do wurship and
reuerence to God and þer holy patrone and fader Seinte Erkynwolde.
735 Then these wurshipfulle preestis mervelid gretely of the soden
comyng in of the people, for thaye had tolde no creature thereof,
wherefore thaye knewe then that it was done by the provision of

708 he] þei A2   722 nowe] *add* And A2

God. And then thaye with fulle grete solempnyte and with ympnus and with songis of praysingis toke hym oute of a chiste of lede wherein this holy body had restid many yeris, and brought hym to a 740 more sure place and of more wurship, wherein this holy body restyth nowe.

And then a mervelous thyng felle, for when thaye wolde haue laide this chiste of led into the stonewerke, the chiste was to longe and the stonewerke to shorte, for the masons were disceyuid in as moche as 745 thaye toke no mesure þerof, for thaye thought that thaye had made it moche lenger than the chiste of ledde was. Then alle the people were fulle of sorowe and hevynesse and thought alle that grete cost but loste, and wyste not then whate was beste to do. And at the laste thaye felle to prayer, fulle mekely besechyng almyghty God and þere 750 holye fader Seinte Erkenwolde to be [relevid] of þer hevynes. And when thaye rose vp fro there prayers, thay founde the stonewerke large inough for to laye in the chiste of lede, for I myselfe that se this doyng cowde not put in my lytle fyngur betwene the chyste and the stonewerke, neither in the brede nor in þe lenght, wherefore we alle 755 were fulfylled with grete ioye and song this mery songe, *Te Deum laudamus &c.*

And it is founde that a lyke myracle was done at the tombe of Seinte Albourgh, which was his suster, and Bede wryteth in his storyes of Ynglonde þe same myracle to be done at the tombe of 760 Seinte Sebbe that was kynge of Ynglonde. And the holy body of Seinte Erkenwolde was translatid in the yere of oure lorde Ihesu a .Ml.C.xl. the .xvj.th daye of [ ].

Howe a chanon and a childe were bothe helid in the Daye of his Translacion. 765

In the Daye of his Translacion a chanon of the same churche wherein the reliquis of Seinte Erkenwolde reste nowe was grevously vexid with a feuer and cowde haue no remedy for to relese his peyne. Then he commaundid his seruantis to brynge hym to the shryne of this blessid confessoure | Seinte Erkenwolde, and when þaye had f. 56ᵛᵃ leyde hym þere fulle sore syke and had contynued there all the masse 771 tyme in his prayers, then he desirid the people fulle mekely that thaye wolde praye for hym that if it were expedient to hym for his

751 relevid] rvelid A2   763 [ ] *space in MS for date. anno ..millesimo centesimo quadragesimo, mense februario, die eiusdem mensis sextodecimo. Miraculi* C

soule helthe to receyue bodely helthe, that thereby the translacion of
775 þer holy fader and patrone myght þe more opynly be declarid and to
be wurshippid. And if it were not expedient to his soule helthe he
wolde not tempte almyghty God þerin, and þat condicion alle the
people prayed for hym that God thurgh the meritis of Seinte
Erkenwolde wolde sende hym helthe. And then almyghty God
780 made hym perfitly hole in the wurship of the translacion of his
holy confessoure, and then alle the people yeafe laude and praysyng
to God and to his holy seruaunt for this grete myracle.

Also þat same daye Theobalde, that was a chanon of Seinte
Martyns, had a childe with hym in his house that had leyne syke
785 halfe a yere and was nye dede. And whan thaye had do brought hym
of the powdre that came oute of the tree of his tombe and medlid it
with water and had yovyn it this sike childe to drynke, he was anone
made perfitly hole and myght go and renne whether he wolde.

790 Howe the gloryous confessoure Seinte Erkynwolde was
seen defendyng his churche fro the flame of fyre.

After this tyme of the translacion when it was halowid, a grete soden
fyre was kyndelid in the cyte of London, which thurgh his grete
fersnes had consumyd and wastid a grete parte of this cyte. And
when the grete flawme of fyre was aboute to descende vpon the
795 churche of Seinte Erkenwolde, he was sene of moche people arayed
lyke a bisshop stondyng an hye vpon the churche with a baner in hys
honde fyghtyng with the fyre, and so he savid and kepte his churche
fro alle peryls, so that the fyre durst not touche the churche in no
wyse.

800 And beside these myraclis and vertues that we haue seyn and
wryten þer ben many mo that we speke not of that wolde occupye
fulle longe tyme. And also I cannot suffise to expresse þem for the
grete nombre of them, wherefore oure lorde in his holy seruaunte be
blessid worlde withoute ende. Amen.

805 How a sike man was helid of a grete feuer.

There was a man that hight Baldewyn þat was an alene, and he came
fro beyonde the see and he was wel beknowen in London. And he
felle syke into a grevous feuer, and then he sought many phisicions
and medycynes, but he cowde fynde none helpe thereof.

And as he was led by fortune by the churche of Seinte Poulis and 810
herde grete melody of songe, þen he askid whate that mery songe
mente. And than it was tolde hym that that daye was a festefulle day
of Seinte Erkenwolde, and that causid þem to synge so meryly and so
swetely. Then he prayed his felowis to brynge hym to the shryne, for
there, he saide, he trustid for to be holpyn by the merytis of this 815
holye Seinte Erkenwolde. And when he came ayenst the quere he
was so wery and feynte that he sate downe to reste hym, and þer he
fylle into a slombre, and he thought that þer came to hym a bisshop
that semyd fulle wurshipfulle, and he was fulle ryally arayed *in
pontificalibus.* And he axid hym whate he wolde haue and whye he 820
came theder. And the sike man aunswerid and saide that he was
made so feynte and wery by his contynualle sikenes that he was
almoost dede, and that causid hym to come and seke the helpe of the
blessid confessoure [Seinte] Erkenwolde. Then saide this bisshop: 'I
am he, be it to the as thou wylle.' And then he touchid his hed 825
softely and he made the signe of the crosse bothe behynde and before
in his forehed and so wente his wey. And when this sike man awakyd
in the tyme of the gospelle saying, and his mynde was then flowyng
here and þer, then he beganne to crye loude and saide: 'Lorde haue
mercy on me and swage my payne and my sorowe.' And whan the | 830
gospelle was done he aroos vp by his owne strenght and wente to the f. 56ᵛᵇ
shryne and offrid þer fulle mekely. And when masse was done he
wente home alle hole and sownde.

And one of his felowis, that was sike also, herde of this myracle
and came theder fulle devoutely in the same houre and made his 835
prayers at the shryne of Seinte Erkenwolde, and anone he rose vp
and was made perfitly hole. And then alle the people yeafe laude and
praysinge to almyghty God and to his holy seruaunt for these grete
myraclis.

Howe a mayde was helid of a grete sikenes.   840

A mayde that was sore syke of the axys and had laye syke manye a
daye and she cowde not be holpyn by no medycyne, but she was
curid sone after by this meane. As she laye in hir bed and had
disposid hir for to dye, it happid þat she toke a lytle softe slepe, in
the which she had a vision that a fayre auncyent man appierid to hir 845

and saide: 'Thou hast had in tyme paste grete brennyng hete by the
temptacion of þe flesh, and thou arte nowe ponysshid for no dedly
synne that thou hast done, but for thou shuldist haue falle therein in
tyme comyng but for thye sikenes that thou hast nowe. And
850 therefore take gode hede fro hensforthe that thou chastice þy
flessh and make it subiecte and to obey to alle reson, and tomorowe
by the mornyng aryse and hye the to my sepulcre, for there thou
shalte be made alle hole.' And when she for fere durst not enquyre
his name and where his sepulcre was, than he tolde and wente fro
855 hir. And when this maide had tolde hir fader and hir moder this
vision, then thaye were right gladde and ioyfulle, and in the morowe
nexte brought þer doughter to the shryne of this holye confessoure
Seinte Erkenwolde, where she was helid and made perfitly hole,
wherefore alle the people yeafe laude and praysing to God and to his
860 holye confessoure Seinte Erkenwolde for this grete myracle.

How a peyntoure was correcte for he [wrought] on the
shryne vpon his festfulle daye.

We haue red of the ponyshment of dyuers that wolde not halowe þe
yerely feest of Seinte Erkynwolde, and amonge oþer there was a
865 peyntoure that hight Theodowyne, which had take vpon hym to
peynte the cheste and oþer þyngis of tree wherein the body of Seinte
Erkenwolde laye. And as the festfulle daye of Seinte Erkenwolde
drewe nye, which was the nexte yere after his dethe, and the saide
peynter had not alle fynysshyd his werke because of slouthe, he
870 shette the churche dore and layde his instrumentis on the auter and
thought to make an ende. Then grete multitude of people resortid to
the churche, and when thaye se the dore shytte, thaye bode stylle and
knockid fast, but þe saide peyntoure suffrid them to stonde stylle and
wolde not opyn the dore. Wherefore Seinte Erkenwolde was gretely
875 displesid, and he appierid to hym in the likenes of a bisshop and with
his pastoral staffe alle tobete hym. And when the people came in and
vnderstode this thyng and sawe hym lye as halfe dede, than thaye
merveylid gretely, and with wurship and drede offrid vp þer lightis
that thaye brought with them, and alle in prayers thaye kepte that
880 daye with grete solempnyte, and afterwarde the peyntoure recouerid
ayen, and by prayers of the people he was made alle hole.

861 wrought] wrough A2

Howe a lame mayde was made hole.

A cytezeyne of London that was endewid with grete ryches, his name was called Goslamis. He had a doughter which was fayre and bewtevous, but she haltid sore and myght not go vpright. And 885 many had desirid to wed hir, but hir haltyng euer lettid it, wherefore hyr fadir, hir modir and alle hir kynne were fulle hevye. And at the laste thaye thought best to set hir to scole, þat she myght be made a nonne in the monastery of Berkyng where she myght helpe by prayers bothe hirselfe and also hir frendis. And then she was take 890 vnto Dame Alwyne that was abbas of the saide monastery, and this mayde was euer fulle devoute in hir prayers | and she vsid to sytte in f. 57ra a derke place when she prayed byside the shryne of Seinte Albourgh, the which was the suster of Seinte Erkynwolde.

And in a nyght, as she had prayed fulle devoutely with meke teeris 895 of devocion, the blessid virgyn Seinte Alburgh appierid to hir as she was in a sclombre and saide to hir: 'Doughter, put awaye thye sorowe and hevynes, for thou shalte be holpyn in shorte tyme by the meritis of my brother Seinte Erkenwolde.' And when she was awakid she remembrid hir vision and tolde it on the morowe to hir susters, and 900 prayed them to praye for hir. Then she vsid fastyngis, wecchyngis and prayers, and within a lytle tyme after, as the nonnes were devoutly at there Matyns in the nyght tyme, Seint Erkenwolde appierid gloryously lyke an angelle to þe same nonne, that was in hir prayers knelyng in the saide derke place fulle devoutely besidis the shryne of 905 Seinte Alborgh, and he toke hir by the honde and saide: 'In the name of oure lorde Ihesu Cryste aryse, and like as Peter and Iohn helid þe crepulle and lyfte hym vp alle hole, so be thou hole.' And with that he lyfte hir vp, and then she brake vp with a crying voyce and saide: 'O moste holy fader Seinte Erkenwolde, haue mercy on me,' and there- 910 with the nonnes that were at Mattyns felte a mervelous swete savoure comyng fro the place where Seinte Erkenwolde appierid.

And as the nonnys lokid thederward thaye herde a grete noyse, as it had be the brekyng of a drye hedge, and then þaye arose and wente þeder to knowe whate this thyng mente. And when thaye came 915 theder thaye fownde there suster alle hole and stode vpright that before was euer lame and crokid, and then thaye alle were fulfylled with grete ioye and gladnes, and thaye anone beganne to prayse allemyghty God and his holy confessoure Seinte Erkenwolde with þis songe of praysinge, *Te Deum laudamus, te Dominum confitemur.* 920

Howe a deffe mayde was helid.

There was an husbondeman þat dwellid in the ferthist perties of the diocyse of London that had a doughter that was deffe and myght not here, and when that she cowde not be holpen by no medycyne, than
925 she was brought to the shryne of Seinte Erkynwolde. And as she had contynued in prayers a gode while she fylle aslepe, and when she woke ayen hir eeris were openyd and then she myght here perfitly. And also she had a foule scourfe vpon hir skyn that couerid a grete parte of hir body, the which felle awaye the same tyme, and then she
930 appierid as feyre as euer she was, and alle the people þat sawe this grete myracle then with one wylle yeafe laude and praysing to almyghty God and to his holy confessoure Seynte Erkenwolde.

Now, dere brethern, lete vs turne oure hertis to almyghty God and byseche hym that by the prayer of oure holy fader and patrone Seinte
935 Erkenwolde that he wolle gouerne vs so betwene welthe and aduersite þat we, beyng assoylid fro alle synne and vicis, maye be brought to the lyberte of hevynly ioye by Ihesus Cryste oure lorde, which levith and reignyth God by infynyte worldis. Amen.

Here endith the lyfe of Seinte Erkenwolde the hooly
940   bisshop and begynneth the lyfe of Seinte Albone and of
          Seinte Amphiabelle.

4 PARDON OF ALL THE CHURCHES OF ROME

This text is a translation of a *Liber Indulgentiarum*, a small MS book compiled for pilgrims to Rome in the Middle Ages, copies of which can be found in many European libraries. Christian Huelsen made a study of six of these MSS, one of which, Stuttgart, Staatsbibliothek Cod. hist. fol. 459, is very close to our text from A2.[1] Unfortunately, Huelsen chose to edit in full only his two Vatican MSS, dealing first with the '*nove chiese principali*' and then listing all the other churches, with MS sigils, in alphabetical order so that it is difficult to work out MS relationships. What can be said with certainty is that after the seven principal churches in A2 (which can be presumed to be the same as those in the Stuttgart MS) the numerical order as well as the textual descriptions of the churches in these two MSS agree.

Huelsen includes among the descriptions of the nine principal churches from the Vatican MSS the descriptions of the same churches from Florence, Biblioteca Riccardiana, Cod. 688, although there they appear scattered among the first fifteen entries, and there are some correspondences between these and A2. The Florence MS is also of interest because it lists a church of St Radegund, of which Huelsen says: '*Il solo codice Riccardiano dei Libri Indulgentiarum (scritto ad Avignone nel 1380–81) registra fra le chiese urbane, una della santa consorte di re Clotario. Essa è sconosciuta a tutte le fonti genuine.*'[2] This comment is quoted by subsequent authorities, so we may presume that no other mention of a church in Rome of St Radegund has been found.[3] A2 lists a church of Radegunde (l. 390) in place of the church of St Barbara occupying that position in the Stuttgart MS. The Florence MS lists a church of St Barbara immediately following that of Radegund.

Of all the churches listed in Huelsen's edition, six are shared only by Stuttgart and A2, and eight by Stuttgart, Florence and A2.

For a collection as varied as this volume, it has not been possible to make a detailed study of *Libri Indulgentiarum*. We have looked at John Capgrave's *Ye Solace of Pilgrimes*, ed. C. A. Mills (Oxford,

---

[1] Huelsen (1927), pp. xxi–xxv, 137–156, 521.

[2] *ibid.*, p. 521.

[3] e.g. Armellini (1942).

1911); *The Stacyons of Rome* in *Political, Religious and Love Poems,* ed. F. J. Furnivall, EETS OS 15 (1866); *The Stacions of Rome* ed. F. J. Furnivall, EETS OS 25 (1867); William Brewyn, *A XVth Century Guide-Book to the Principal Churches of Rome, compiled c. 1470,* trans. C. Eveleigh Woodruff (London, 1933); and Gregory Martin, *Roma Sancta (1581),* ed. G. B. Parks (Rome, 1969), but they have thrown light on only some of the puzzles in this text.

The pardon of al þe chvrchis in Rome.

In the cyte of Room ben .iiij.C.lxvij. parysh churchis, off the which
.vij. ben previlegid aboue alle other and thaye be of more pardon and
holynesse; amonge which the pryncypalle | churche is of Seinte Peter   f. 65ᵛᵃ
the Apostle, that is byldid in þe same place where he was crucified.
Thereto ben .xxx. steppis vppe, and as ofte as anye persone goyth vp   5
the steppis devoutlye and is oute of dedlye synne is graunte by Pope
Alysaunder in relesyng of penance inioyned that is not done .vij. yere
of pardon, and as moche in þe goyng downe of the saide steppis. And
in the same churche ben .j.C.x. auters, and when the Feest is there is
.xviij. yere of pardon at the lefte auter, and þer ben .vij. privilegid   10
þat haue more pardon at eche of tho auters, that is to saye the auter
of þe sudary of Cryste, the auter of oure ladye, the auter of Seint
Andrew þe Apostle, the auter of Seint Gregory by his sepulcre, the
auter of Seint Leon pope, where he hath grauntid to alle that visite
the auters with devoute prayers .vij. yere of pardon, and Seint   15
Syluester hath grauntid to alle þat pray devoutely at the auter of
Seinte Peter .xxviij. yeris and as manye lentis of penauncis inioyned,
and relese of the thryd parte of alle synnes.
    And Pope Gregory hath grauntid to alle that devoutelye comyth
and praye mekely at the high auter of Seint Peter pardon of alle   20
synnes þat be forgotyn, pardon of brekyng of vowys, and pardon of
the leying on hondis of fader and moder. The pardon þer is of .xlviij.
yere and as manye lentis, and fro the Assencion of oure lorde Ihesu
to the kalendis of August is euery daye .xiiij.Ml. yere of pardon, and
euery Holy Thursdaye .j.Ml. yere of pardon, and in alle the feestis of   25
Seinte Peter the Apostle .j.Ml. yere, and in the Assumpcion of Oure
Ladye and the oþer feestis of hir .j.Ml. yere, and in þe vtas of Seint
Martyn when þe same churche was halowid is .vij.Ml. yere of pardon
and as manye lentis, and foryevenes of þe thirde parte of alle synnes.
And as ofte as the sudary of oure lorde Ihesu Cryste is shewid to the   30
Romaynis thaye haue .iiij.Ml. yere of pardon, and other straungers
that drawe theder with devocion haue .ix.Ml. yere of pardon, and
theye that come over the see and ouer the mountaynes with devocion
theder haue .xij.Ml. yere of pardon and as manye lentis and the

MS A2   The title is in the margin in a different hand. The text follows without a
break from the Life of Peter Apostle, the last word of which is 'Room'.

35 .iij.de parte foryevyn of alle synnes, and in euery Lente alle these
pardons ben doublid.

And in the churche of Seint Poule withoute the yeatis of the cyte,
in the entryng of the churche where Seint Poulis hed was founde, is
euery daye .xlviij. yere of pardon and as manye lentis, and in the
40 feest of Seint Poule þere is a thousande yere of pardon, and in the
Conuercion of Seint Poule .j.C. yere of pardon and as manye lentis.
And in the Daye of Alle Innocentis is .xl. yere of pardon, and in the
vtas of Seint Martyn when the church was halowid is .vij.Ml. yere of
pardon and as many lentis and the thirde parte of alle synnes
45 foryevyn, and who that visiteth þe same churche of Seint Poule
euery Soneday of the yere shalle haue as moche foryevenes of synne
as though he went to Seint Iames in Spayne a pylgrymage.

And in the church of Seint Iohn Latran is euery daye .xlviij. yere
of pardon and as manye lentis and þe thirde parte of alle synnes
50 foryevyn, and Seynte Gregory and Seint Syluester, popis that
halowid þat churche, grantid þer so moche indulgence that it maye
not be nombrid of none man but allone of almyghty God, as Pope
Boneface sayeth that the indulgence of the churche of Seint Latran
maye not be nombryd but onlye of almyghty God. And he sayeth if
55 men knewe the indulgence þat be grauntid þer thaye wolde do
moche evylle, and the same Pope Boneface sayeth that who devoutely
comyth in the daye of þe halowyng of þat churche, where oure lorde
appierid in the sight of alle the Romayns, he shalle haue foryevenes
of alle synnes. And this daye fallyth on Seint Martyns Evyn, þat is
60 callid Seint Saluatours Daye. And in the same churche is a chambre
that is saide *sacristia*, and þere is the auter of Seint Iohn that he had
in wyldernesse. And þer is the table that oure lorde sopid at with his
disciplis on Shere Thursdaye when he gaue them þe sacrament. And
þer is the *archa* of the Olde Testament in which is the rodde of
65 Aaron and the .ij. tablis wherein is wryten þe .x. commaundementis
of oure lorde, and þerin is a goldyn potte fulle of angels mete and the
goldyn candelstyk and þe ornamentis of Aaron and brede of
proposicion of the temple of oure lorde. And alle these reliquys
brought Tytus and Vaspacyen fro Ierusalem, and þey brought þeder
70 the .iiij. brasyn pelers that stande at the high auter. |

f. 65ᵛᵇ   And in the same church ben .ij. vyals of the water and the blode
that ranne oute of oure lordis syde, and þer is the sudarye and the
clothe þat oure lorde wyped his discyplis fete with after the soper,
and there is parte of þe .v. lovis of barlye þat oure lorde fed with .v.

þousand people, and þer is the flesh of oure lorde that was cutte of 75
his body in his circumcision. And þer is the vayle of oure ladye, and
Zakaryes hed, and of the asshis and of the blode of Seint Iohn the
Baptist and the heyre that he weryd and the camels skyn þat he
weryd, and of the angels mete þat was founde in the grave of Seint
Iohn the Evaungelist. And there is the cote that the dede men were 80
reysid with after theye were poysonyd and dede, and þe vesselle that
Seynt Iohn the Evaungelist dranke venym in, and the sheerys that he
was shoryn with of [Domycyan] in scorne. And there is a certeyn
chapelle þat is callid *Sancta sanctorum*, and þer is a table of oure
savyoure where þe visaige of oure lorde was sene opynlye of the 85
people in the tyme of Seint Luke the Evangelist. And þer is þe hedis
of Peter and of Powle and manye oþer precious reliques, and þer is
euery daye .vij.Ml. yere of pardon. And Constantyne the emperoure,
after that he was baptized he saide: 'I shal do make here a churche
where I dwelle, wherefore I pray the graunte thye hooly blessyng to 90
alle that visite þis place devoutely,' and þen Seint Syluester
aunswerid to hym and saide: 'Oure lorde Ihesu Cryste, that haþe
clensid the of thye lepur, he of his hooly mercy and godenesse clense
alle them of there synnes that come mekelye to this place in enye
tyme of the yere. Amen. And we by the auctoryte of Peter and of 95
Powle and of oure power graunte fulle remyssyon of alle synnes.'

And in þe churche of Seint Marye the More in the high auter is
the bodye of Seinte Mathye the Apostle. And in þe auter collecteralye is the bodye of Seint Ierom the preest, and therein is parte of þe
lynnen clothis that oure lorde was wrappid in, and there is of the 100
holye crosse a parte, and þer is som of the clothyng of oure lorde
Ihesu, and þer is the arme of Seint Thomas þe Martyr, and ful many
oþer reliques ben þer, and there is euery daye .xlviij. yere of pardon
and as manye lentis. And in alle the feestis of oure ladye and the
Byrthe of Oure Lorde and in hys Resurreccion and the Feest of Seint 105
Laurence ben addid to .j.Ml. yere, and Pope Nycholas the .vij.th and
Pope Gregory þe .viij.th þat halowid this churche haue grauntid þer
.xiiij.Ml. yere of pardon, and fro the Assumpcion of Oure Ladye to
hir Natyuyte is grauntid þer euery daye .xiiij.Ml. and as manye lentis
and þe thirde parte of alle synnes foryevyn. 110

And in the churche of Seint Laurence withoute the wallys of the
cyte, where restyn the holy bodyes of Seint Laurence and of Seint
Stephyn þe holy martirs, at the high auter is .xlviij. yere of pardon

83 Domycyan] Domyan A2

and as manye lentis, and þer is a parte of þe hooly crosse, and there
115 is of the blode of Seint Thomas of Canterbury vpon a vestement, and
þer is one of the stoonys that Seint Stephyn was martyred with, and
þer is of the bowels of Seynte Andrewe þe Apostylle, and þer ben of
the rybbes of Seint Iulyan, and of the knee of Seint Andrewe the
Apostle a parte, and þer is of the water that oure lorde wysh his
120 disciplis fete with, and þer ben of the stonys þat Seint Iohn saide
masse in, and of the stonys where oure lady dyed in and where she
stode in hir prayer when oure lorde ascendid into hevyn. And þer is
the hed of Seynt Concorde the virgyn, and there is the arme of Seint
Stephyn, and þer is the lavatory that the angelle bare to Seint
125 Laurence with water when he was in prison, and þer is the stone that
he laye on when he was rostid on the yron gredeyron, and many oþer
reliques. And in the feest of them .j.C. yere and in the dedicacion of
them .iiij.C. yere, and Pope Pellagien that halowid þat churche hath
grauntid þer .iiij. tymes in the yere .viij.C. yere of pardon and as
130 manye lentis and the .iij.de parte of alle synnes foryevyn, alle the vtas
of them, and he that syngith there ones in the quarter shal delyuer
one soule oute of purgatory.

And in the churche of the Holy Crosse of Ierusalem þere is a
certein chambre vnder that churche closid, wherein is the body of
f. 66ra Seint Helyn, the which church Seint Syluester pope halowid | and he
136 clepid it Ierusalem, and in that auter is the corde that oure lorde was
bounde with when he was ledde to be crucyfied. And þer ben .ij.
cuppys, the one fulle of the blode of oure lorde, and þe other with
the mylke of oure ladye, and there is the sponge that was proferid
140 oure lorde to drynke fulle of oyselle and galle, and there be the naylis
that oure lorde was naylid with and a grete parte of the clothis of
Seinte Iohn the Baptyst, and þer the ⟨bawme⟩ of Ynnocent the
martir, and .ij. boonys of Peter and of Poule. And þer is euery
Sonedaye and euery Tewisdaye a .Ml. and .ij.C. yere of pardon, and
145 euery other daye of the weke .j.C.viij. yere of pardon. And in þe
same churche in þe high auter ben the bodies of Seint Anastace and
of Seint Cesarij martirs, and þer is a parte of the tree of the hooly
crosse, and þer is pardon .xlviij. yeris and as manye lentis. And in the
right side of the auter is the treen crosse of þe thefe þat was
150 conuertyd, and .ij. teth of Seint Blase the martir, and manye oþer
hooly bodies resten þer, and þer is .xiiij. yere of pardon; and above in
the auter is the tytil *Ihesus Nazarenus rex Iudeorum*, and þer is .vij.

142 *space for about eight letters in MS, perhaps* bawme. *See Note.*

yere of pardon. And Pope Stephyn, that lyeth in the saide chapelle callid Ierusalem, he graunte there playne remission of alle synnes.

And in the churche of Seinte Sebastian that shewid his bodye to Lucille [and] saide to [hyr]: 'My bodye hangyth in the eyre, where thou shalt fynde it.' There the angelle of God appierid to Gregory saying: 'In this place is verilye promysed foryevenes of alle synnes, and there is shynyng and euerlastyng light withoute ende of gladnes, þe which the hooly martir Sebastian deseruyd,' and Pope Pelagien grauntid þer .xlviij. yere of pardon. And in the same church is a pytte in the which were hydde the bodyes of Peter and Powle, and þer is as grete pardon as is at Seint Peters, and he that visitith that churche alle the Sonedayes in Maye there is playne remyssion of alle synnes, and fro Assencion of Oure Lorde to the kalendis of Auguste is euery daye þer .viiij.Ml. yere. And Pope Gregory, Pope Syluester, Pope Nycholas, Pope Alysaunder, Pope Pellagien and Pope Honorius haue youen and grauntyd eche of them a .Ml. yere of pardon, and þer lien buryed .xlvj. popes in that same churche, and eche of þem haue yeue there pardon þerto. And there ben the bodies of many hooly seyntis, and alle the bodies lye there of manye martirs, confessours and virgyns, of which nombre it were longe to telle, and in the churche is buryed Seint Kalixt the pope, where he hath grauntid playne remyssion of alle synnes.

And in the churche of Seint Peter *ad Vincula* there is playne remyssion of alle synnes by þe prayers of the doughter of Theodor the emperoure, the which brought Seint Peters chaynes from Ierusalem, and Pope Pellagien that halowid this saide church yeafe this pardon afore wryten. And in the churche of Vite and Modeste and Ceestence and Macello and manye other to the number of .v.Ml. were martired by Antonye the emperoure, and there is .j.C. yere of pardon and as many lentis, and the .iiij.th parte of alle synnes ben there foryovyn. And there is a place vnder the church that is halowid in the wurship of the apostlis, and there is euery daye a yere of pardon, and in the feest of anye apostle there is .iij.C. dayes of pardon.

And in the churche of Seint Martyn in the Hylles, where is buryed his body and the bodye of Seinte Syluester the pope, there is .viij.C. yere of pardon and as manye lentis. And in þe church of the .iiij. Crownyd Martirs is .xl. yere of pardon. And in the church of Seint Iulyan is .j.C. yere of pardon. And in the churche of Seint

155

160

165

170

175

180

185

190

156 and] *om.* A2   hyr] hym A2

Felice in Pyncis .j.Ml. yere of pardon. And in the churche of Seint
Vrcy .j.C. yere of pardon. And in the church of Seint Marcellyne
.j.Ml. yere of pardon. And in the churche of Seint Saturnyne is .j.C.
195 yere of pardon. And in the churche of Seint Marcellyne and Peter a
.Ml. yere of pardon. And in the churche of Seynt Ceryce and Iulycte
þer is foryevenes of the .iiij.th parte of alle synnes. And in the
churche of Iohn and Poule .j.Ml. yere of pardon. And in the churche
of Seinte Eustace, where he is buryed, his wyfe and þer .ij. chyldryn,
200 is a .Ml. yere of pardon.

   And in þe churche of Seint Bartylmewe, where he is buryed, and
also the body of Seint Paulyne, þer is a .Ml. yere of pardon. And in
þe church of Alle Hooly Angels is a .Ml. yere of pardon. And in the
churche of Seint Gregory is .iij.C. yere of pardon. And in the
f. 66ʳᵇ churche of Seint Austyn is a .Ml. yere of pardon. | And in the
206 churche of Seint Ierome a .Ml. yere of pardon. And in the churche of
Seinte Alexij, where his bodye is buryed, is a .Ml. yere of pardon.
And in the churche of Seint Saluatour de Thoure is a .Ml. yere of
pardon and .j.C.xl. dayes. And in the chapelle of .iiij. wellys, where
210 the hed of Seint Poule the doctoure was smete of, is a .Ml. yere of
pardon and as manye lentis. And in the churche of Seint Saluatour in
the waye of Seint Poule .j.C. yere of pardon. And in the churche of
Seint Syluester is .j.Ml. yere of pardon, and þer is parte of the hed of
Seint Iohn the Baptyst. And in the churche of Seint Iamys de
215 Syngnano is .j.Ml. yere of pardon and foryevenes of þe .iiij.th parte
of alle synnes, and there is the hed of Seint Iamys the Apostle. And
in the church of Seint Nycholas *de Carceribus* .j.C. yere of pardon
and as manye lentis. And in the churche of Seint Iames *in Portica* is
.iij.C. yere of pardon.
220   And in the hospytalle of Seint Nycholas is .j.C. yere of pardon.
And in the church of the Holy Goost is .vij. yere of pardon and
[foryeuenes] of the .vij.th parte of alle synnes. And in the church of
Seint Michael the Archaungel is a Ml. yere of pardon. And in the
churche of Seint Mathye is a .Ml. yere of pardon, and there is the
225 arme of Seint Christefir. And in the churche of Seint Celce is .j.C.
yere of pardon, and þer is one fote of Marye Magdalene and one
fyngur of Seinte Nycholas. And in the churche of Seint Symplicij
and Faustyn .v.Ml. yere of pardon.
   And in the churche of Seint Anastace in the waye of Seinte Poule
230 .j.Ml. yere of pardon, and þer is a chapelle halowid in the wurship of
   222 foryeuenes] foreuenes A2

oure ladye that is clepid *Scale Celi*, that is to saye þe ladder of hevyn, and þer Seint Bernard se a ladder that strecchid vp to hevyn, as he tellith in his legende. And yt is saide þat whosoeuer sayeth masse þer hymselfe or doyth do synge a masse there by anye oþer to praye for his gode frendis soule, anone that soule shalle be delyuerid oute of 235 purgatory. And in the churche of Seint Horose is .j.Ml. yere of pardon, and þer somtyme were þe scoolis of Room holden.

And in the churche of Seyint Port Latyn in the daye of þe feest and in oþer feestis of Seint Iohn, who that prayeth þer devoutlye shalle delyuer the soule of his frende that he prayeth for oute of the 240 paynes of purgatorye. And in þe churche of Seint Grysogon is a .C. yere of pardon. And in þe church of Seint Appollynar is a .C. yere of pardon. And in þe church of Seint Benet is .j.C. yere of pardon. And in þe churche of Seint Andrewe is a .Ml. yere of pardon. And in þe church of Seint Cosme and Damyan is .j.Ml. yere of pardon. And in 245 þe churche of Seint Symon and Iudee is .j.Ml. yere of pardon. And in þe chapelle that is callid *Domine quo vadis* þer ben the steppys of oure [lordis] fete sene, and þer is a .Ml. yere of pardon. And in the churche of Iohn and Poule is a .Ml. yere of pardon. And in the churche of Seynt Barnabe is .iij.C. yere of pardon. And in the 250 churche of Seint Liace is .j.Ml. yere of pardon. And in the churche of Seynte Marke is a .Ml. yere of pardon. And in the churche of Seint Pantalyon is .xlvj. yere of pardon. And in the churche of Seint Pancrace is .j.C. yere of pardon.

And in the churche þat is callid þe Rotunde of Oure Ladye the 255 .xiij. daye of Maij and in the Feest of Alle Seyntis there is playne remyssion of alle synnes, and in euery oþer daye is þer innumerable indulgence, the which churche bylde Agrippa after that he had ouercome þe Perses, but he made it furste in the wurship of Cybles the moder of false goddis and in the wurship of Neptymus the god, 260 of Mars, and of alle oþer fals goddis, and he namyd it Pantheon, and he made þer a goldyn ymage and put in the temple of Cybles, and he made a coueryng of brasse ouergylte to the same ymage and þer was an hole þerto where he prayed dayly to his goddis. But afterwarde Pope Boneface se this temple and the horrible nombre of 265 false goddis þat were within, and moche crysten people were hurte þer of the devyls, and then Boneface prayed the emperoure þat was tho crysten to yeve hym þat temple, and anone the emperour grauntid hym his desire. And then the pope the furste kalendis of

248 lordis] *om.* A2

270 Nouenebre with grete people of the cyte halowid that churche, and
he ordeinyd that euerye yere the pope shulde saye masse at þe high
auter in that daye, and there moche people vsid to be howselid and
in that daye kept þer feest of þe Natyuyte of Oure Lorde, the Feest
of Oure Ladye, and of Alle Seyntis, and in the daye folowyng thaye
275 do seruyce for the dede.

And in the churche of oure ladye that is callid *Ara Celi* þer
f. 66va Octavyan the emperoure se oure ladye, in hir armes | hir sone,
stondyng vpon an auter, and then he woundrid gretelye of that sight,
and then he herde a voyce fro hevyn that saide to hym: 'This auter of
280 hevyn is þe sone of God,' and anone he felle to the erthe and he
wurshipt Cryst, þat shulde come sone after to be borne of þe virgyn
Mary, and this vision he se in his chambre where is nowe made a
churche in the same place, and þer is .ij.Ml. yere of pardon.

And in the churche of Oure Ladye beyonde Tybre, where brake
285 oute a welle of oyle in the byrthe of Cryste, is .j.C. yere of pardon.
And in the churche of oure lady callyd *Mynorcya* is .j.Ml. yere of
pardon. And in the Newe churche of Oure Ladye is .v. yere of
pardon and in the Lente þer is .ij.C. yere of pardon. And in the
churche of oure ladye þat is callid *Transpadiun* þer ben .ij. pelers that
290 Peter and Poule were bounde to, and there is .iij.C. yere of pardon.
And in the churche of Oure Ladye in þe Feelde is .xl. yere of
pardon. And in the churche of oure ladye that is callid *in Portica* is an
hundryd yere of pardon. And in the churche of oure ladye that is
callid þe Pytte is .xl. yere of pardon. And in the church of oure ladye
295 that is callid *Passibola* is .vij. yere and as manye lentis of pardon. And
in the churche of Oure Lady vpon the Salte Water is .j.Ml. yere of
pardon and in the daye of the dedicacion is þer playne remyssion of
alle synnes. And in the churche of oure lady that is callid *de Populo*
.ij.C. yere of pardon. And in the churche of oure lady þat is callid
300 *Scala Greca* is euery daye þer .j.C. yere of pardon. And in the
chapelle of oure ladye that is callid *Libera nos a penis inferni* is þer
euery daye .xj.C. yere of pardon.

And in the churche of Seint Agnes is euery daye .xlvj. yere of
pardon and in hir feest is þer .ij.C. yere of pardon. And in the
305 churche of Seint Susanne is .iij.C. yere of pardon. And in the
churche of Seinte Sabyne þe wyfe of Seint Alexij þer is .ij.Ml. yere
of pardon. And in the churche of Seynte Potencyan is .j.Ml. yere of
pardon and as manye lentis. And in the churche of Seint Praxiede is
foryevenes of the .iiij.th parte of alle synnes, and there is þe peler þat

oure lorde was scorgid at and a fayre crosse of the tree of oure lorde 310
and manye oþer grete reliques.

And in the church of Seint Kateryn is .ij.C. yere of pardon. And
in þe churche of Seint Felicitas is .xl. yere of pardon. And in the
churche of Seint Helene is a .Ml. yere of pardon. And in the churche
of Seint Radegunde is .j.C. yere of pardon and as manye lentis. And 315
in the churche of Seynt Pernelle is .j.Ml. yere of pardon and as
manye lentis. And in the churche of Seint Elisabeth is .j.C. yere of
pardon. And in the churche of Seint Mary Magdelene is .j.C. yere of
pardon. And in the churche of Seint Iulyan is .iij.Ml. yere of pardon
and in þe tyme of Lente .v.Ml. yere of pardon. And in the churche of 320
Seint Agathe is xlviij. yere of pardon. And in þe churche of Seint
Margrete is ij.C. yere of pardon. And in the churche of Seint
Crystyne is .xl. yere of pardon. And in þe church where Seint
Peter was in prison is euery daye .j.Ml. yere of pardon and in euery
double feest byne graunte .iiij.Ml. yere of pardon. 325

And alle the pardons of the cyte of Rome in the Lente ben
doublid, and it is to knowe that if anye pylgryme dye by the waye
towarde Rome he is assoyled fro alle dedlye synne and fro alle oþer
synnes whatesoeuer thaye be, if he take his iournaye thederward
wyllyng to be reconsiled and in fulle purpose neuer to synne after to 330
his lyves ende.

In revelacionibus Sancte Birgitte.

And beleve verelye as deth þat þe indulgence of Rome is more afore
God than we knowe by any wrytyng, for thaye that seke suche
pardons with a perfyte and a meke herte he hath not only remyssion 335
of his synne but also he shalle haue euerlastyng ioye in the blysse of
hevyn, for though a man myght slee hymselfe a thousand tymes for
Goddis sake, he is not worthy therefore to haue the leest ioye that he
yevyth to his seyntys, for God yevith to vs alle thyngis frely of his
grace and godenes, and nothyng at alle of oure deservyng, and 340
though a man be not sufficient to leve here so longe and so manye
thousande yeres, neuerthelese for synnes withoute nombre we
deserue to haue turment and payne withoute nombre and infynyte,
the which is impossible for anye man to make dewe satisfaccion and
fulfylle in this lyfe. Therefore by pardons we ben losyd fro manye a 345
grevous payne and long enduryng, and thereby ben made and
chaungid into shorte peyne | or none after a mannys very gode f. 66vb

wylle and verye trust, and thaye that in perfite charyte and with
sorowfulle herte desire mekelye to haue such indulgencis and so
350 discesse oute of this worlde, they shulle not onlye be lousyd for alle
synnes and paynes for synne, 'for whye I God shalle yeve to my
seyntis and chosyn people that that þaye desyre, but I shalle for my
charite double my grace and glorye to them an hundredfolde.' Whate
thynkyst thou, man on erthe, that the sone of God shalle lye, þat
355 sayeth that man shalle yelde rekenyng in the daye of dome of the
leest ferthyng that euer he hath receyuid of God here on erthe? I saye
yee, forsothe, and more to, for he shal yelde a rekenyng at domys
daye of euery moment and of alle the mete and drynke that he hath
etyn in this worlde and howe he hath seruyd God therefore, and he
360 shalle yelde a rekenyng þere of euery worde and evyl þought that he
hath do here alle the dayes of his lyfe, but yf he waissh them awaye
here with very contrycion, shryfte and satisfaccion while he levith
here in this worlde. For oure lorde sayeth in the gospelle that .ij.
thyngis causith God to opyn hevyn to vs, that is if a man mekyth
365 hymselfe to God wylfully, and wolle gladlye foryeue trespasse done
to hym of his evyn crysten for Goddis loue. And if he fede the bodye
so that it be sogett to the soule and allewaye refreyne hym fro synne
and euer lete a man receyue mesurably mete and drynke and alle
other necessaryes here, that he yeve thonkyngis to God for them here
370 euery houre of his lyfe. Amen.

Here endith the lyfe of Seinte Peter the Apostle and of the
indulgence of alle the churchis in Rome and whate pardon
avayleth to man, and begynneth the Commemoracion of
Seint Poule the holye doctoure.

5 WHAT THE CHURCH BETOKENETH

This piece follows immediately after the scribal *Deo gratias* at the end of the *GiL* Advent in MS A2, and is in the same hand. It breaks off at the end of f. 174vb.

The first section, dealing with the 'Tokens of the Church', ll. 1–742, is a highly selective sequence of sentences or ideas, with little original material, from Durandus, *Rationale diuinorum officiorum* Books I-V.[1] The source for ll. 743–925, 980–1259 and 1327–1486 is a translation of Edmund of Abingdon's *Speculum Ecclesie* chapters 8–17 in the sequence 11, 8–10, 12–17.[2] In her collation of 17 MSS of the *Speculum*, Forshaw 'recorded a vast number of alternative readings which, where they are not the result of scribal error, add nothing of value to the basic text.'[3] We have therefore been unable to trace the Latin affiliations of this text, and C. B. Goymer's edition of Middle English translations provides insufficient evidence for any other connections.[4] The variations from both these editions seem to support Forshaw's statement that 'both Latin and French texts [of *Speculum Ecclesie*] were translated many times into English.'[5] That the text edited here is a copy, is shown by l. 817 reioyse (*possidebunt*), l. 990 envye (*inimicum*), and l. 1219 feyre (*quatuor*).

It may be that the author had seculars, rather than religious, in mind, as some references to the Divine Office are omitted and secular material added, such as 'but kepe to thyne owne wyfe if thou haue enye.' Also in one or two places the translator seems not to have been well acquainted with ritual or the Divine Office; see notes to ll. 211, 541, 565 below. It is a puzzle, therefore, to find retained ll. 1056–9, intended for a religious reader.

Interspersed with the material from *Speculum Ecclesie* are passages at ll. 810–56, 1100–1130 and 1298 to the end, covering topics that Archbishop Pecham, in the Constitutions of Lambeth, 1281, specified were to be taught four times a year.[6]

---

[1] Durandus (1995, 1998). See also the French translation by Barthélemy (1854); for English translations of Books I and III see Neale & Webb (1843) and Passmore (1899).
[2] Forshaw (1973). [3] *ibid.*, p. 14.
[4] Goymer (1962). [5] Forshaw (1973), p. 16.
[6] Wilkins (1737), II.54, *De ignorantia sacerdotum*.

Here folowith certein tretys that declarith whate the churche betokenyth and dyuers oþer maters.

The churche betokenyth .ij. thyngis, that is the place where the seruyce of God is saide and songe and þer is þe gadryng place togeder of alle true cristen people and þerin to serve God with one wylle in loue and charyte, for the churche is the specyalle place ordeynid for prayer.   5

Whate the wyndowis of glasse in þe churche betoken. It betokenyth the scripture of God that puttith awaye and defendith fro vs alle evils that noyen vs, and by hooly scripture oure myndis ben lightid with the grace of the hooly goost whan we praye in the churche devoutely. And also by þe glasse wyndowis is vnderstonde   10 oure .v. wyttis whereby we shulde kepe oute of oure soules al evils and vanytees, and by Goddis grace to kepe within vs mekelye loue and charite and oþer vertues.

Whate the churche doris betokyn. The dore of the churche is Cryste, for by hym we shal entre into the blysse of hevyn after this   15 lyfe if we kepe trulye his commaundementis here in this worlde, for by the dore we entre into þe churche to praye God to haue foryevenes of oure offencis, for þer, if we be repentaunt, Cryste that is þe very true dore wolle here vs and foryeve vs alle oure trespasse; for he sayethe in the gospelle: *Ego sum hostium, dicit*   20 *Dominus.* And by the dore, that is Cryste, alle gode thoughtis and offeryngis ben borne into the churche.

Whate the pelers in the churche betoken. The pelers betokyn the bysshops and doctours that maynten the feythe of hooly Churche by the doctrine of God *iuxta illud: sapiencia edificauit sibi Domum et*   25 *excidit columpnas septem,* for whye bisshoppis and doctours shulde be fulfylled with the .vij.foolde yeftis of the hoolye goost, so that oþer men maye take gode ensample by them.

Whate the pament of the churche betokenyth. The pamente signyfieth the grownde of oure feythe or fondament, and lyke as the   30

MS A2

pament is lowist vnder foot, that sygnyfieth oure affeccions; for by
charite and mekenes man is exaltid moost hie in the sight of God.
And also the pament betokenyth the pore people of Cryste in spirite,
for though þaye ben lowe, here whate sayeth Cryste of them: Blessid
35 be pore men in spirite, for the reame of hevyn is theris. And also the
pament signyfieth the comyn people that holye Churche is susteynid
by moost.

Whate betokyn the beemys of þe church. That betokenyth the
pryncis of this worlde and the prechours that kepe þe pees of hoolye
40 Churche, þat one in worde and þat other in dede, for al knyghthode
is made to maynteyn the right of hoolye Churche and to chastice
extorcioners that wolde oppresse the pore people.

Whate the pewis in the churche betokyn. The pewis of the
churche that men rest them in betokenyth contemplatyfe men in
45 whom oure lorde restith, for that is the hiest clerenesse of euerlastyng
lyfe that anye man maye haue in this lyfe. And lyke as we rest in the
f. 169ra pewys, right so in | the churche we shulde rest in mynde fro alle
worldelye besynesse, and onlye to entende to please God and to rest in
hym by holye meditacions; for the churche is the place of prayer as
50 oure lorde sayeth: *Domus mea domus oracionis vocabitur.*

Whate betokenyth the roffe of the churche. The roffe or the
coueryng of the churche betokenyth the prechours in hooly Churche
that liften vp the thoughtis of men into þe ioye of hevyn, and by
prechyng of the worde of God þe soule of man is made fayre with
55 manye vertues, and alle synne and malice is put oute by verye charite
quia caritas [operit] multitudinem peccatorum, that is to saye, charite
coueryth the multitude of synnes.

Whate betokenyth the chaunselle in the churche. The chaun-
celle is the hed of the churche and betokenyth the mekenes that
60 shulde be in the clergye and in the prelatis of the Churche, for the
hier þat þaye ben the more meker thaye owe to be, and the particion
betwene the queer and the book of the churche betokenyth that the
myndis of the spiritualte shulde be departid in especialle fro alle
erthelye thyngis, lyke as thaye be departid fro the laye people bodely
65 in tyme of Goddis seruyce.

    56 operit] cooperit A2

Whate the lightis of the tapers and lampis in þe churche betokenyth. The light in the churche betokenyth Criste, for he is the very light of alle the worlde as he sayeth hymselfe: *Ego sum lux mundi.* And the light betokenyth the apostlis and oþer hooly doctours, for by the hooly techyng of them, alle the people that ben vnder the lawe of hooly Church ben made light gostely in there sowlis by þere gode doctrine and by þer gode ensample yevyng; for þaye shulde be the light of the comyn people, as oure lorde sayeth: *Vos estis lux mundi et bonorum operum exempla.* And also the light in the churche betokenyth the .vij. yeftis of the hooly goost, the which lightith the blyndnesse of oure hertis in the derke nyght of this worlde, so that we be not ouercome of the feend. 70 75

Whate the crucyfyxe in the myddis of the churche betoke-nyth. The crucyfixe that is sette in the myddis of the churche betokenyth that, lyke as oure lorde died for oure redempcion in the myddis of the worlde, so we shulde haue euer Cryste in [lyke] remembraunce in the myddis of oure hertis, euer thankyng hym for the grete grace and godenes that he hath shewid to vs at alle tymes. And also he is set in the churche that we shulde ofte beholde whate payne and passhion he suffrid for vs to brynge vs oute of the feendis bondis. And for cause of that victory the crosse is set on hie, for we shulde alwaye dresse oure mynde vpwarde to God and remembre that we haue no grace but onlye of hym. 80 85

Wherefore come men and women to the churche. We come to the churche to aske God foryevenes of oure trespasse and synnes and to yeve laude and praysing to hym for alle his grace and godenes shewid to vs. And there we receyue the blessid bodye of oure lorde Ihesu Cryst to oure gostelye strenght and euerlastyng helthe, and þer is the bisshops power and the keyes of Seint Peter bothe to bynde and vnbynde. And þerfore whan thou comyst into the churche remembre wherefore thou comyst theder, for the churche is the house of God and the place of prayer; and þerfore than commytte the mekelye into the kepyng of God, withdrawyng thye mynde clene fro alle worldelye occupacions. And whan thou hast sett thye mynde stedefastlye in God, than begynne suche prayers as þou canst to the laude and praysyng of God, trustyng verelye to haue alle thyngis of 90 95 100

81 lyke] myke A2

hym þat ben profitable to þy soule, and þan, though worldely thyngis
come into thye mynde by the steryng of the develle, yet contynewe
forthe in thye prayer, for thou canst not lett suche wickid þoughtis to
105 come in thye mynde; but God alwaye except þy prayer after thye
furst entent, if thou haue very gode wyl to please hym and put alle
thye truste in hym and not in thyeselfe, for than thou shalte sone be
disseyuid; for þer is none euerlastyng helpe but onlye of God. And
therefore euer remembre this as ofte as thou comyst to þe churche.

110 **Whate betokenyth the coueryng of the auter with white
clothe.** The white coueryng of the auter betokenyth that oure
soules shulde be clothyd with the vertue of immortalite, and it
f. 169rb betokenyþe | oure soule whan it is made white with gode werkys.
And at alle tymes oure werkis shulde be white and clene, and moost
115 speciallye the busshops and the preestis that mynyster vpon the auter
the holye bodye of oure lorde Ihesu Cryste, þaye aught to be clene
fro synne and made white with good werkis to the gode ensample of
the laye people.

**Whye the ymage of oure lorde Ihesu Cryste and of other
120 seintis ben set in the churche.** It is to knowe that the ymage of
oure lorde Ihesu Cryste shulde be peyntid in the churche in .iij.
maner wyse conuenyentlye, that is as sittyng in his trone and
hongyng vpon the crosse and sittyng in his moders lappe. And
Adrian the pope sayeth that oure lorde shulde none other wyse be
125 peyntid in the newe lawe, though he were payntid like a lambe in the
wolde lawe, but if it be vnder the fote of the crosse, for he is the
lambe that takith awey the synne of the worlde. And alle oþer ymagis
ben sett in the churche as for a kalender to the laye people that be
not lernyd in scripture, for that movith them gretelye to deuocion of
130 the same seintis that thaye beholde. But thaye shulde not wurship
tho ymagis, but the holye seintis þat tho ymagis ben made after, and
so the curate shulde telle to the laye people.

Why the vayle is take or cutte doune afore Ester. For after the
passhion of oure lorde the olde lawe cessid, and than was the yeatis
135 of hevyn openyd and shewid to vs that þat was before helid and hyd
fro vs; and than God yeafe suche strenght to vs that the desiris of
oure flessh nor þe devyl nor the worlde shalle ouercome vs, if we wol
oure selfe aske helpe of God and trust not in oureselfe. And euery

Saturdaye in the Lent whan the seruyce of the Sonedaye comyth in,
than the vayle is put vp in a corner tylle the seruyce of the Sonedaye 140
be done, for þe Sonedaye betokenyth the resurreccion of oure lorde
whereby we shal haue euerlastyng ioye. For before hevyn was hyd
fro vs, and that signyfyeth the vayle, and also the helyng of Moyses
face fro the Iewis betokenyth the veyle. And the furst Sonedaye
signyfieth the ioye of oure furst faders in paradise, the .ij.de the ioye 145
of them in Noe is ship, the .iij.de that ioye þat the childryn of Israel
had vnder Ioseph, the .iiij.th the ioye that thaye had vnder Salamon
for þe grete pees in his dayes, the .v.th ioye when the people came
fro the captiuyte of Babilon, the .vj.th ioye that the disciplis had fro
the resurreccion tyl the assencion of oure lorde. And herefore the 150
veyle is not drawe in the seruyce tyme of these .vj. Sonedayes
aforesaide, for ioye of the resurreccion, whereby hevyn is openyd to
vs that was shytt fro vs before the space of .v.Ml. yere and more for
the synne of Adam and Eve.

Whye bellis ben ordeynid to ryng in the churche. For by the 155
ryngyng of bellis true cristen people ben callid togeders into the
churche to saye þer there deuocions in praysing of almyghty God
and in heryng devyne seruyce to the helthe of there soulis. And þerby
the frutis and the cornys on erthe ben savid and the power of the
gostelye enemyes is put fro them, and by the ryngyng of halowid bellis 160
thondryng, lightnyng and other tempestis ben put awaye fro vs. And
the bellis betokyn the prechyng of hooly doctours, for lyke as the bellis
calle the people to churche, so prechyng of hoolye doctours bryngith
true cristen people to hevyn by there holye meditacions in God.

Whate betokenyth the berying placis in the churche and in þe 165
churchyerde. For þer ben buryed the bodies of true cristen people,
there to rest and abide the comyng of oure lorde to the dome. And
than oure bodies shalle aryse fro dethe to lyfe as sekirlye as oure
lorde Ihesu Cryste rose from dethe to lyfe.

Whan the preest arayeth hym to go to masse, whate the 170
amyte betokenyth. Whan the preest hath waish hys hondis, than
he takith the amyte and couerith his hed therewith, and that
betokenyth the helthe that is grauntid to vs by very feithe, and
also it betokenyth þe chastite of the herte and of the bodye. And it
coueryth the breest, for there shulde be shynyng chastite within in 175

þe soule and withoute in the bodye by clennes of levyng. And also
the amyte representith the clothe that the Iewis couerid oure lordis
face with whan thaye bade hym go se who smote hym. And the .ij.
f. 169ᵛᵃ tapys of the amyte betokyn | the clene thoughtis and the gode wylle
180 that the preestis shulde haue to God in the seruyce of the masse.

Whate the awbe betokenyth. The awbe betokenyth the verry
clennes that shulde be in a preest and that he shulde not be desolate
of his levyng. And the awbe that couerith alle the bodye fro the ouer
parte to the neder parte, the ouer parte betokenyth oure hope that
185 comyth by grace from aboue and the neder parte betokenyth þe grace
that God yevith to vs by the sacramentis of the Churche. And also þe
awbe betokenyth the white shynyng clothe that oure lorde Ihesu
Criste had on in his transfiguracion, and alwaye þe clothis of Cryste
were clene and white, like as he is and was euer withoute synne and
190 did neuer synne. And the gurdylle that he is gurde with ouer the
awbe betokenyth that the preest shulde be contynent in his levyng.
And also the ouer parte and the nether parte of the awbe betoken
that God wolde thou shuldist do to thye neghboure as þou woldist be
do to thyeselfe. And the gurdille betokenyth the scorge that Pylate
195 smote Ihesu Cryste with.

Whate betokenyth the stoole. The stole betokenyth the yoke of
the commaundement that euery preest hath on his necke, þe whiche
he kyssith whan he puttith it aboute his necke and whan he takith it
fro his necke. He kyssith it also þat betokenyth his desire and his
200 assent that he hath to take the burthyn vpon hym for the loue of
God, and that he shulde neuer be brokyn by prosperite nor by
aduersite, but euer to thonke God mekelye and leve sobirly and
rightfullye to alle men in this worlde. And also the stole betokenyth
the corde that oure lorde was bounde with to the peler.

205 **Whate betokenyth the fanon and the manyplis.** The fanon on
the lyfte arme betokenyth that the preest shulde wake in gode werkis
and put fro hym alle werynesse and slouth in Goddis seruyce, and
thynke alwaye to be redye whate houre the sone of man shalle come;
and þerfore wake thou euer wyselye. The manyple on the lyfte arme
210 betokenyth the very feithe that he shulde haue to God in this lyfe,
and the manyple on the right arme betokenyth the corde þat the
Iewys drewe oure lorde with towarde his passhion.

Whate the chesiple betokenyth that he puttith on laste. The chesiple that the preest puttith ouer alle the other vestymentis betokenyth very charite, for withoute that the preest is but as brasse sownyng or þe betyng on the cymballe, *quia caritas operit multitudinem peccatorum et omnia leges et prophetares continent,* and so þe chesiple closith within hym alle other vestymentis. And the chesiple betokenyth the weddyng clothis that oure lorde spekith of in the gospelle: *Amice, quomodo huc intrasti non habens vestem nupcialem?* For withoute the vestyment of very charite no preest maye fulfylle his office to the plesyng of God, for that is the bonde that holdith alle vertues togeders, that comyth oute of a clene herte and oute of a gode consciens and oute of the feith not feynid. And also it betokenyth that the preest shulde haue verye loue to God and his neighbour, for in them .ij. hongith alle the lawe of God. And also the chesiple betokenyth the purpur vestyment that the knyghtis put aboute oure lorde in scorne.

Whate þe spryngyng of hooly water betokenyth. Furst the hooly water dryveth awaye alle wyckid and vnclene spiritis oute of alle placis where it is caste and oute of the hertis of true cristen people. And also holye water doith awaye alle venyalle synnes whan it is mekelye and devoutelye receyuid. And the halowyng of the hooly water euery Sondaye is blessid in the remembraunce of oure baptym, and we shulde cast it into euery place of oure howsis, and we shulde saye whan we caste it aboute: *Asperges me Domine, &c,* and than alle oure housis shalle be kepte oute of the power of alle wyckid spiritis. And therefore we shulde caste holye water vpon vs as ofte as we can haue it, for it doith aweye oure euery dayes venial synnes as ofte as we take it mekelye with charite.

Whate the goyng in procession betokenith and whate the crosse that is borne | before and the ryngyng of the bellys than betoken. Oure goyng in procession betokenyth the meke comyng fro hevyn of oure lorde for oure saluacion into þis worlde, and it betokenyth that if we folowe the crosse mekelye that than we shalle come into oure owne cuntraye after this lyfe, that is to the blysse of hevyn. And þerfore euery cristen man shulde folowe the procession with fulle grete deuocion and with fervent desire to folwe Cryste into oure heritage, and the crosse that is borne before the procession betokenyth the victory that we haue of þe feendis thereby

215

220

225

230

235

240

f. 169 vb

245

250

whan we put alle oure trust in God. And whan we folowe the crosse
mekelye, the feendis ben ouercome þerby and fle fro vs, for thaye
fere gretelye that signe of the crosse whan we folowe the crosse in
procession devoutelye; for that is the moost royalle signe of the kyng
255 of hevyn for oure defence ayenst the feendis power, for þei flee that
in alle placis. And as the bellis ryng ayenst þe kyng in alle cytees and
townes whan he passith by them, right so the bellys rynge in
procession tyme in the wurship of Ihesu Cryste the kyng of hevyn
whan he comyth with his crosse and with his baners of victorye. And
260 þese ben the .iiij. moost solempne processions in the yere, that is to
saye: the Purificacion of Oure Ladye, Palme Sonedaye, Ester Daye
and Ascencion Daye; for in the wurship of the Ascencion we go a
procession euery Sonedaye, for that was the laste procession that the
disciplis folowid after oure lorde Ihesu Cryste here in his manhode
265 on this erthe.

Whate þe *Confiteor* before masse betokenyth. The meke inclynyng
at the *Confiteor* of the preest betokenyth the meke comyng downe of
oure lorde fro hevyn to safe mankynde, and that a rightfulle man
shulde accuse hymselfe furste or he go to prayer; for if thou accuse
270 thyeselfe mekelye then God foryevith thye trespasse, *Dixi confitebor
et tu remisisti &c.* And also he desireth to be delyuerid fro temptacion
and for to be illumyned with the grace of God to fulfylle his office
worthelye, for if God yevith not vertue and grace he hath nothyng of
hymselfe worthye to offre to hym, and therefore he accusith hym to
275 God that he by his grace make hym worthye to do his office mekelye
and charitablye. And the knockyng on his breest betokenyth the
publican that saide: 'Lorde, be mercifulle to me, synner.' And so
shulde the preest do in lyke wyse. And the .iij. knockyngis on the
breest betokenyth the .iij. remedies for synne, that is contricion,
280 confession, and satisfaccion, for tho trulye done doith aweye alle
synne fro vs.

Whate betokenyth the smoke of the encense.   The encense
betokenyth meke and devoute prayers that the preest offerith to God
in the masse. By the sensour is signyfied the clene herte of the preest,
285 by the fyre þerin is signified fervent devocion to God, by the encense
meke prayer, and by the ship is signified holye Churche, for therein
moost specially holye prayers shulde be offrid to God; and the
vesselle that þaye bere the fyre into the churche signyfieth holye

prechours, that bare the fyre of charite and the holye exemplis of
seintis in there hertis, and thaye teche the true seruauntis the lawis of
God.

**Whate betokenyth that the preest kyssith the auter and
begynnyth þe office of the masse on the right side of the
auter, that is towarde the southe.** The kyssyng of the auter
betokenyth the pees that Cryste yeafe to bothe the people, that is to
saye, furst to þe Iewis and after to þe gentyles. For oure lorde came
downe fro hevyn onlye for the Iewis that were of the house of Israel,
and this is þe cause that þe preest begynneth the masse at þe southe
side of the auter; but after, for þer high pride and malice, oure lorde
forsoke the Iewis and toke the gentyles þat neuer he had shewid his
lawe to before, and than of them came cristen people; and that is the
cause that the gospelle is redde in the north side of the auter, for |
thaye receyuid furste the gospelle by the prechyng of the apostlis.
And in the tyme of Anticriste, whan Ennok and Hely shalle come
downe fro paradis and preche to þe Iewis the true lawe of Cryste,
whereby the Iewis shulle be conuertid to the feyth of Cryste and
abide alle the turmentis of Anticriste for Cristis loue; and that is the
cause that he comyth ayen to the southe side of the auter and endyth
his masse þer he beganne.

**Whate betokenythe þe *Kyrie leyson* and the *Christe leyson* in the
masse.** Thaye saye threes *Kyrie leyson,* and þat betokenyth the
Trynite þat we calle to haue mercy on vs, for *Kyrie leyson* is to saye:
'Oure lorde haue mercye on vs,' and *Criste leyson* is to saye: 'Criste
haue mercy on vs.' And also we seye .iij. tymes *Kyrie leyson* to the
fader and .iij. tymes *Christe leyson* to þe sone and .iij. tymes *Kyrie
leyson* to the hooly goost; and to the fader .iij. tymes, for the fader
and the hooly goost be onlye the same nature, and to the sone .iij.
tymes *Christe leyson* for in that persone he was made man to redeme
vs oute of the feendis power, but yet he is of þe same nature with
them.

Whate *Gloria in excelsis* betokenyth. Furst it betokenyth the birthe
of Cryste that þe angelle shewid to the sheperdis on Cristis masse
Daye by the morowe. He than stondyng in the myddis of þem taught
them to synge this hoolye ympne, for the angelle came fro the este to
Bethelem. And the preest whan he begynneth this hooly ympne

290

295

300

f. 170ra

305

310

315

320

325

302 for|] for| for A2

stondith afore the myddis of the auter, and that betokenyth that
Cryste was mediatour betwene vs and God; and he made pees
betwene God and vs and betwene angelle and vs and betwene man
and man, for man by inobedience offendid God his maker, and than
330 by his falle he lettid þe restoryng of angels. But whan Criste oure
verye pees came he than made pees betwene God, angelle, and man,
and so than very accorde was made that shalle laste euer, if we wolle
put alle oure truste in God and not in ouresilfe.

Whate betokenyth *Dominus vobiscum.* It betokenyth the gretyng
335 that oure lorde grete with his disciplis after his resurreccion, and
[Boaz] saide it also to his [repers] in the felde, and the angel saide it
to Gedion; and it is to saye: 'Oure lorde be with you.' And therefore
the Church hath ordeynid it to be saide .vij. tymes in the masse to
the people by the preest, and þat betokenyþe the .vij. yeftis of the
340 hooly goost. The furst salutacion betokenyth the spirite of wysedom
that oure lorde grete vs with at his comyng into this worlde. þe .ij.de
betokenyth the spirite of vnderstondyng, for þerfore he prechid to
teche vs. The thirde betokenyth þe spirite of conseile he offrid
hymselfe by his passhion to ayen by vs. The .iiij.th betokenyth the
345 spirite of strenght, for whan oure lorde hynge on the crosse he
ouercame þe devylle. The .v.th betokenyth the spirite of cunnyng,
for after his resurreccion he appierid to his disciplis to teche them his
lawis. The .vj.th betokenyth the spirite of pety that he had to
mankynde whan he lyfte vs aboue the skyes. The .vij.th betokenyth
350 the spirite of drede of oure lorde, for angels shulle quake whan Criste
comyth to þe dome to glorefye.

What the collet in the begynnyng of the masse betokenyth.
While the preste sayeth þe collet we shulde rest of praying and
attende to the preest and say: 'Amen' at the ende, for in þe presence
355 of þe maiestye of God and of his angels oure mynde and oure voyce
shulde accorde in one in very true sacrifice to God by mekenes; for a
meke and a contrite herte God shalle not dispise. And the preest in
his prayer desireth of God that alle gode thyngis maye be with vs and
alle evylle thyngis to be put fer fro vs. And euery prayer is dressid to
360 the fader and endid in þe name of the sone, for þer is none oþer waye
to hevyne but by hym; and therefore we shulde saye in the ende of

336 Boaz] Ruth A2   repers] kepers A2

oure prayer: *per Dominum nostrum Ihesum Christum filium tuum qui tecum viuat et regnat &c.*

Whate betokenyth þe epistle | in the masse. The epistle betokenyth the doctryne of þe apostlis. And the epistle shulde be saide in the right side of þe churche or in the myddis of the queer; and it betokenyth þe prechyng of Seint Iohn Baptist, for he prechid afore Criste lyke as the epistle is redde before the gospelle. And the epistle euer shulde be red the face towarde the auter þat signifieth Criste. And also the epistle betokenyth the lawe that was before the gospelle and as the shadowe is to the verry light. And the epistle shulde be redde vpon the lectrine withoute a clothe in the myddis of the quere, and the gospelle aboue the gryses by the auter vpon the lectryne on the clothe. And the epistlis were the letters that one holye apostle or disciple sent to anoþer to the edefying of the feith of Criste in the begynnyng of holye Churche &c.

Whate þe grayle betokenyth. The grayle betokenyth the penaunce that Iohn Baptist prechid of, for he saide: 'Doith penaunce and the kyngdom of hevyn is nye to you comyng.' And þe grayle betokenyth that after the prechyng of Iohn Baptist his disciplis folowid Criste; and also the grayle betokenyth that oure lorde forsoke the Iewis and toke the gentyles; and the grayle betokenyth the grete labour that man hath in this lyfe. And therefore the grayle is not saide in þe Ester woke and in the Whitson weke, for that betokenyth þe grete rest and ioye that we shalle haue in hevyn after þis life.

Whate betokenyth þe *Alleluya* saide after the grayle. *Alleluya* betokenyth þe grete ioye that we shalle haue in hevyn after this lyfe, if we kepe the commaundementis of God with mekenes and sobirnesse here while we leue in this troublis worlde. And *Alleluya* betokenyth þe vnspecable ioye that oure lorde hath ordeynid to þem þat loue hym in charite, and *Alleluya* is as moche to saye as: 'Lorde make me safe.' And also it betokenyth them that ioye in þe myraclis and in the godenes that God hath visite his people with. And *Alleluya* betokenyth contemplatife lyfe, and þerfore it shulde be radde nerer the auter than the responde that betokenyth actife lyfe.

Whate the tracte betokeniþe. The tracte betokenyth the tyme of mornyng, and þerfore *Alleluya* is not saide fro Septuagesime tyl

Ester Evyn. And þere is [as] grete dyuersite betwene *Alleluya* and the
tracte as is betwene gladnes and tribulacion, and as grete diuersite is
400 betwene the responde and the tracte as is betwene actyfe lyfe and
contemplatife lyfe. And þe tracte betokenyth the waylingis of holye
men that wolde be oute of this lyfe in hevyn.

Whate betokenyth þe sequence. The sequence betokenyth the
double stole of ioye þat holye seintis haue togeders in hevyn, and
405 þerfore the sequence is songe of alle in the quere so that eche shulde
haue verye charite with oþer and accorde togederis as brethern, for
suche songe pleasith God. And the sequence betokenyþe the grete
feest of euerlastyng lyfe þat we shalle knowe in hevyn, if that we leve
thankefulle to oure lorde God here in this lyfe, *vnde in primo: Beati*
410 *qui habitant in domo tua Domine in secula seculorum laudabunt te.*

Whate the gospelle betokenyth. Furst he that shalle rede the
gospelle shal take the boke and aske the blessyng of hym þat syngeth
the masse, and than he goith vp into the rode lofte or to the lectrine
at the north side of the auter, and þer he begynneþe the gospelle.
415 And than alle the people shalle stonde vp devoutelye and here the
wordis of oure lorde Ihesu Criste, for lyke as the hed is the moost
principalle membre of the bodye, right so is the gospelle the moost
principalle office of the masse. And the gospelle yeuyth euerlastyng
lyfe to men of gode wylle and of gode beleve. And the gospelle is red
420 in the northe partye of the auter so þat the hooly goost shulde put
oute þe colde malice of the devylle oute of oure soulis by his
brennyng loue and charite. And whan the gospelle is redde than
þe preest kyssith the boke, and that signyfieth the charite þat we
shoulde haue eche cristen man to other. And þan the preest sayeth:
f. 170ᵛᵃ *'Dominus vobiscum'*, þat is to saye: 'Oure lorde | be with you,' and alle
426 people shulde aunswere: 'Oure lorde be with the.'

Whye ben .iiij. euangelistis and no mo. For Cryste is God and
man, preest and kyng, and therefore the furst wrote of the godhed,
the .ij.de of the manhede, the .iij.de of þe preesthede of Criste, and
430 .iiij.th of his kyngdom.

Whate betokenyth the Crede in the masse. The Crede betokenyth þe verry feith that we shulde haue to God in oure hert to al

rightwysnes, and the confession with mouthe causith vs to haue euerlastyng helthe. And the *Credo* is saide with an hye voyce evyn after the gospelle, that we shulde verely beleve þe worde of God and **435** do thereafter to oure power and that euery cristen creature shulde kunne it, for withoute treu beleve and gode werkis no man maye be savid. But he that belevith in God that is in verry beleve to love God, he shal be savyd and by very beleve to go into hym and so to abide stylle in hym, for that do onlye God and feythfulle men and women; **440** for we euer shulde desire the gode thyngis of oure lorde in þe londe of levyng men, for that is euerlastyng lyfe to se God the fader *et quem misisti Christum Ihesum. Amen.*

Whate betokenyth *Sanctus* .iij. tymes. *Sanctus* betokenyth the holy felouship that we shalle haue with angels and archaungels and with **445** alle seyntis in hevyn, and that *Sanctus* is saide .iij. tymes that betokenyth the Trinite, that is the fader, the sone, and þe holy goost. And while *Sanctus* is songe we shulde stonde and bowe downe oure hedis mekelye to God, for that betokenyth the incarnacion of Ihesu Criste that is the very grounde of oure redempcion. And than **450** with the signe of the crosse we shulde merke vs, for þer by the crosse oure lorde ouercame the feend, and so shalle we by the signe of the crosse ouercome hym.

Whate betokenyth the brekyng of þe hoost in .iij. partis. The grettist parte of the hoost betokenyth the seintis that ben in hevyn, **455** and we shulde desire them to praye for vs; for thaye ben in euerlastyng ioye and passid oute of alle trouble. The .ij.de parte that lyeth on that betokenyth them that be in purgatory, for thaye haue nede of prayer and by oure prayer thaye maye the rather be delyuerid oute of þer grete peynes. The thirde parte that is in the **460** chalis betokenyth them that ben levyng here in this troublis worlde in wrecchidnes of synne and haue alle fulle grete nede of prayers, *vnde versus, Tres partes facte de Christi corpore, significat prima suam carnem sanctorumque, secunda sepultos, tercia viuentes, hoc est in sanguine tincta martirii calicem gustant in carne fideles.* **465**

Whate betokenyth þe yevyng of the paxe in the masse. The yevyng of þe paxe betokenyth that we shulde not onlye haue pees with oure mouthis but also in oure hertis to oure even cristen, and if we haue than verry charite we receyue the .vij.folde yeftis of the

470 holye goost; and than oure soulis ben þe templis of God, whan we
loue God aboue alle thyng and oure even cristen as oureselfe in alle
godenes. And whan we kysse the paxe we shulde enclyne mekelye
thereto, for charite is yoven þerby into oure hertis by the hooly
goost, and also the preest kyssith the paxe or he resceyue the hoost,
475 that we also shulde haue very pees eche with oþer so that we maye
worthelye receyue the sacrament spyrituallye with the preest.

Whye the paxe is not yevyn in the masse of requyem. For the
soulis of alle true cristen men that ben past oute of this worlde shulle
no more be troublid, but thaye shalle haue euerlastynglye rest in oure
480 lorde, and þerfore thaye haue no nede of the signe of accorde here in
this worlde. And also as for them that ben dampned oure pees here
cannot avayle them, for thaye bene sure of there payne euerlastynglye suche as þaye haue here deseruyd while þey levid. And the paxe
is not yovyn in the masse of requyem for we maye not comyn with
485 the dede, for thaye maye not aunswere to vs, and also for thaye ben
sure of suche pees as thaye shalle haue euerlastynglye is it gode or
evylle.

Whate betokenyth *Ite missa est*. *Ite missa est* is as moche to saye:
Go ye after Cryst and folowe we hym; for oure euerlastyng abydyng
f. 170vb is not here in | this worlde, but we shulde hye vs to hevyn that is oure
491 very contre by gode werkis doyng here in this lyfe. For by Criste
helle is broken and the yeatis of hevyn ben openyd, and þerfore we
shulde folowe Criste by very feyþe and gode werkis, for þer is none
oþer waye to hevyn but onlye by hym. And þerfore the quere and
495 alle the people yevyng þonkyngis to hym saye *Deo gracias*, that is to
saye: Thonkid be God for he yevith to vs alle grace and godenes.

Whate betokenith the blessyng after masse. The blessyng that is
yoven of the preest after masse to the people betokenyth þe sendyng
of the hooly goost to the apostlis on Whitsonedaye, so þat alle we
500 shulde receyve that blessyng mekelye whereby, if we be in charite,
we shalle resceiue the hooly goost and be fulfylled with alle grace and
godenesse. And that is þe blessyng of the hole Trinyte as it is saide in
the Psauter: *Benedicat nos Deus Deus noster, benedicat [nos] Deus et
metuant eum omnes fines terre.* And also this blessyng betokenyth þe

503 *nos*(2)] *om.* A2

blessyng that oure lorde shalle yeve to alle his chosyn people at þe 505
daye of dome, whan he shalle saye: *Venite benedicti patris mei percipite regnum &c*, that is to saye: Come ye þe blessid childryn of my fader and receyue ye þe euerlastyng kyngdom &c.

Whate betokenyth þe holye brede þat is yovin in the churche.
The yovyng of the hooly brede betokenyth the brekyng of the brede 510
to the .ij. disciplis that oure lorde brake in Emaus as he sate with them at the table and blessid þe brede, and after he brake it as evyn as it had be cut with a knyfe, and than he gave it to them. And the preest yevith holy brede to alle people to fede them, lyke as oure lorde blessid the .v. lovis in desert wherewith he fed .v.Ml. menne 515
and euery man was sufficientlye fulfylled. And by þe ensample of this men blesse þer mete or thaye go to dyner, if thaye done wysely, for we shulde blesse oure mete and oure drynke or we receyve into oure bodies þerof.

Whate betokenyth the Evynsonge that is saide in the churche. 520
The Evensonge betokenyth þe comyng of oure lorde whan he toke flesh and blode of the virgyn Mary, and at Evynsonge tyme oure lorde was take downe of the crosse, and att Evynsonge tyme oure lorde wesshe the fete of his discyplis, and at Evynsonge tyme oure lorde ordeynid þe holy sacrament of the auter that is Cristis flesh and 525
his blode. And for alle these grete thyngis and for manye moo þe church yeldith laude and praysyng to God at Evynsonge tyme. And thaye saye in the Evensonge .v. psalmys in þe wurship of the .v. woundis of oure lorde þat he suffrid for the redempcion of mankynde, and þerfore we shulde yeve to hym with alle oure .v. 530
wittis very laude and praysing for alle his benefettis.

Whate betokenyth Complyn that is saide in the churche.
Complyn begynneth *Conuerte nos &c*, and that betokenyth þat euery rightful man shulde be his owne accuser of his synnes to God and to his curate; for whan we saye *Conuerte nos* þan we desire 535
that oure synnes that we haue done before be take awaye fro vs, and whan we saye *Deus in adiutorium* than we desire that God wolle yeve vs grace to do gode werkis euer after to oure lyfes ende, for withoute his helpe we can do nothyng that gode is. And we saye .iiij. psalmys in Complyn so that we maye haue remyssion of alle synnes while the 540
soule is in þe bodye þat is made of the .iiij. elementis. And also we

saye the Crede in the Complyn, and þerin is conteynid alle oure
beleve. And if we saye oure Crede with very mekenesse and in
stedefast beleve into God, if it hap that we dye in that nyght we dye
545 than in confession and in þe feith of God; and þerfore euery cristen
creature shulde saye þe Crede with moost devocion or thaye slepe
anye nyght, for whan we lye downe we be not certein to leve tylle the
next daye; and þerfore remembre welle this.

Whate betokenyth the Matyns that ben saide in þe churche.
550 The Matyns betokenyth the penaunce enioyned to vs of oure curate
by the which we maye haue euerlastyng ioye and libertye. And
f. 171ʳᵃ Matyns betokenyth the tyme of | mercy and of grace that oure lorde
yevith to vs here into thende of the worlde, and in which tyme we
shulde euer prayse God for alle his yeftis yoven to vs. And the quyre
555 is devidid in .ij. partis for the one side syngith one verse and that
oþer side anoþer verse stondyng, and that betokenyth that we shulde
stonde stedefastlye in gode werkis and truste in God and that we
shalle ouercome alle the temptacions of the devylle, of the [worlde]
and of the flesh. And thaye synge *Te Deum laudamus* with an hie
560 voyce, and þat betokenyth if we leue welle here in this worlde, after
this lyfe we shalle come to the felowship of angels. And Seinte
Ambrose and Seint Austyn made *Te Deum laudamus* togeders, the
one saide *Te Deum laudamus* and þe oþer saide *Te Deum confitemur*,
and so thaye made þis ympne to the ende.

565 **Whate betokenyth þe Laudes in the Matyns.** The Laudis in
Matyns betokenyth þe resurreccion of oure lorde Ihesu Criste, and in
this tyme we shulde yeve laude and praysing to hym, for by his
resurreccion we ben savid and in that houre oure lorde made the
worlde and angels. And Laudis betokenyth if we worche gode werkis
570 here in this worlde, after þis lyfe we shalle be in þe felouship of
angels and prayse God withoute cessyng as thaye do. And þer ben
saide .viij. psalmys in Laudis, and that betokenyth .viij. persones þat
were savid in Noe is ship, and it betokenyth that by þe water of
baptym alle we ben savid like as the .viij. persones were savid by the
575 ship.

558 worlde] worde A2

Whate is the cause þat men ete fysh in alle fastyng dayes. The cause is for oure lorde neuer cursid the water, for whan alle levyng þyngis of this worlde were distroyed in Noe is flode save .viij. persons and a peyre of alle levyng bestis, than þe fisshis were not distroyed nor the water was not cursyd. For oure lorde purposid 580 after to save vs by the water of baptym and waish awaye þerby fro vs al oryginalle synne. And oure lorde cursid euery kynde of flesh þat was bred on the erthe, and þerfore we ete no flesh in fastyng dayes and oure lorde ete no flesh after his resurreccion; but he ete of a roost fysh and of an honyecombe. 585

Whate betokenith that alle the candils ben quenchid on the Wenysdaye Thursdaye and Fridaye afore Ester saue one candille. The tapers that ben quenchid betokenyth the .lxxij. disciples of oure lorde, for in his passhion tyme þere prechyng was nye quenchid for drede. And þe candille þat is not quenchid 590 betokenyth oure blessid ladye, for in hir the feyth abode vnquenchid, for she was euer stedefaste in the feith that Criste shulde rise fro deth to lyfe the .iij.de daye. But manye of the disciplis were feynte in the feithe, and þerfore þer candels ben quenchid eche after oþer; but by oure blessid lady al thaye were taught and lightid ayen, and þerfore 595 her candille that stondith hyest is not quenchid.

Whate betokenyth þe halowyng of the pascalle. Whan the pascalle shal be halowid al the fyre in þe churche shalle be quenchid and newe fyre shulde be smete oute of the stone, in tokyn þat in þe passhion of Criste the olde lawe [is] quenchid and the newe is lightid 600 and begunne in the resurreccion of Cryste, for he is þe very lyght of the worlde. And the waxe of þe taper betokenith Cristis manhode, the wyke þe soule, and þe light the godhede. And the light after the halowyng betokenyth Cristis new doctrine of the Newe Testament, that is: *Mandatum novum do vobis ut diligatis invicem.* This he saide to 605 his disciplis: 'I yeve to you a newe commaundement, that ye loue togeders in charite as I haue louyd you.' And the .v. graynes of frankencense on þe taper betokyn the oynement that the women brought to anoynt þe .v. woundis of Criste that he had on the crosse &c. 610

600 is] *om.* A2

Whate betokenyth the halowyng of the fonte. By the sacrament

f. 171ʳᵇ of baptym we be wasshyn | and clensid fro originalle synne. Furst in
þe halowyng of the water the preest prayeth to the fader, and by
Cryste he besekith the hooly goost by his godenes to descende into
615 the water of the fonte. And also the preest prayeth and he desireth
the people to praye that he by the grace of God maye make that
holye sacrament, for withoute his grace and helpe he cannot do it.
And the preest crieth with an high voyce for the helpe of God, and
than he puttith the taper into the water, and that betokenyth the
620 comyng downe of the hooly goost in the likenes of a douue whan
Ihon baptized Criste. And than alle the people shulde lifte vp þer
mynde mekelye to almyghty God, that there hertis maye be
enlumyned of his grace, so that we maye be kepte oute of the
power of the feend so that he neuer ouercome vs in no temptacion.

625 **How we shulde ete no maner mete on Ester Daye but if it
were blessid of the preest.** For in that daye the feend is moost
besye to disceyve vs and to bryng vs ayen into oure olde synnes, and
therefore in some cuntrayes the people bryng alle þe mete that thaye
shalle ete þat daye into the porche of the churche to be blessid of the
630 preest or thaye eete it. And also we shulde at alle tymes blesse oure
metis and oure drinkis or we resceyue enye þerof into oure bodies.
For Seint Gregory tellith in his *Dialogis* that a nonne went into hir
gardyn and ete letewse or she blessid it, and þe devylle sate on the
letewse and so she resceyuid the devylle therewith that longe tyme
635 after vexid hir ful sore. And also .ij. maydyns in the cyte of Bononye
ete of a pomegarnet vnblessid and anone þaye were vexid with .ij.
feendis; and manye moo suche ensamplis men maye fynde in
wryting, and therefore lete vs at alle tymes blesse oure metis and
drinkis or we resceyve them.

640   Seynt Austyn sayeth whan we come before þe sacrament in the
church we shulde knele downe mekely and saye oure *Pater noster* or
els this prayer: *Deus propicius esto michi peccatori*, that is to saye, God
be mercifulle to me, synner and be thou my keper alle the dayes of
my lyfe; or els this prayer: *Qui me plasmasti miserere mei Deus &c*,
645 that is to saye, Thou God that madist me haue mercye on me. And
this prayer was taught to a comyn woman that was a grete synner,
but by the meke saying of þis prayer knelyng before the sacrament
she was receyuid to grace and had foryevenes of hir synnes.

The .x. commaundementis of God.

The furst commaundement is: Thou shalte not wurship no straunge 650
goddis but thou shalte wurship thye lorde God that made the to his
ymage and lykenes. And thou shalte serue hym allone and wurship
hym by mekenes and rightfulle feith, and thou shalte serue hym by
gode werkis and mekenes and to wurship hym feythfullye that made
of nought bothe angels, man, hevyn and erthe, and alle þe gode 655
thyngis that be þerin. And thou owist to beleve stedefastely as deth
that the fader and the sone and the hooly goost is one God alone.
And here thou owist to remembre whether þou hast feithfully
wurshipt thye lorde God and seruid hym above alle thyngis, and
wheder thou hast kepte thye beheest to God and perfourmyd thye 660
penaunce enioyned to the, and whether thou hast holde feithfullye to
hym that thou behightist in thye cristendom takyng. And euery
creature aught to loue God aboue alle thyng and to wurship hym
with alle his herte, with alle his mynde and with alle his soule, and
thou shalte loue þy even cristen in alle godenes as thyeselfe. 665

The .ij.de commaundement is this: Thou shalte not take the
name of God in vayne. For no man shalle take the name of his lorde God
in veyn in sweryng, but as oure saviour Ihesu Cryste sayeth in the
gospelle: 'Your worde owith to be "Ye, ye, naye, naye," withoute
othe in as moche as in you is.' Neuerþelese wel a man maye swere 670
trulye to the kyng and to other men so that þe trouth be euer savid
and kept and falsenes be dampned, and this is to be done in rightfulle
dome | and very trouth. But euery lesyng and falsenes and nedeles f. 171ᵛᵃ
sweryng, al these ben forbodyn in this commaundement, for oure
lorde is the waye [of] trouthe and lyfe. 675

The .iij.de commaundement is this: Haue thou mynde to halowe
þe holye daye, that is, thou shalte halowe them in reste of body and
soule in euery holye daye ordeynid by holye Churche. For euerye
man is bounde to kepe the holye daye and the feestis ordeynid in the
Newe Testament, þat ben the Sonedayes and oþer high feestis of 680
God and oure ladye and of alle seyntis þat ben ordeynid by holye
Churche to be halowid. And if þou wolte kepe trulye thyne holye
daye, loke thou rise vp erlye oute of thye bed and spare not neither
for colde nor slepe nor for no fleshlye luste, for the more that it
grevyth þy slouggishe flesh to aryse fro thye bed, so moche more þou 685

675 of] *om.* A2

shalte plese God and helpe thye soule. And than þou shalte go to the
churche and beseche almyghty God to light þy soule with his grace
and godenes, so that thou mayste saye thye seruyce or prayers to the
plesyng of hym and to the helpe of thyne owne soule, and that þou
690 beleve verelye that al grace and godenes comyth onlye of God and
not of thyeselfe. And if thou be of power, yeve almesse to the nedye
with gode wylle and withoute longe tarying for the loue of God, and
loke thou truste verelye to haue thye mede of hym þerfore, for after
thye gode wylle and verry truste shalle be thye rewarde of God. And
695 loke thou haunte but lytle tauernes nor none oþer veyne sportis nor
suspecious placis, for þerof comyth evyl happes and somtyme dedely
synnes. But thou shalte visite the pore and nedy and bedrede people,
bothe to helpe them with thye goodis and with thye gode conseile if
thou be of abilite, and els helpe them with thye gode wylle, and praye
700 to God to helpe them and the bothe.

The .iiij.th commaundement is: Thou shalte honour and wurship thye fader and thy moder, and also thye gostelye fader and al oþer
that be sett in hier degre than thou arte, and praye God that thaye
maye kepe there charge to the plesyng of God and to the helpe of þer
705 owne soulis and of alle them that thaye haue charge of. And thou
shalte with verye mekenes and gode wylle obey to thye fleshly fader
and moder in al thyngis that ben plesyng to God and to helpe þem
with thye worldely goodis in þer nede, and also to praye for them
that God wolle kepe them in gode lyfe to þer lyfes ende. And he that
710 so doith shalle haue longe lyfe vpon erthe, and after this lyfe to haue
euerlastyng lyfe in the blysse of hevyn.

The .v.th commaundement is: Thou shalte not slee no man
neither gostelye nor bodelye, for þer ben manye maner of mansleyn-
gis bothe of honde, tonge and on soule. Mansleyng of honde is whan
715 one man sleith anoþer with his hondis, and also whan a man settith
hys evyn cristen wrongfullye in pryson than he puttith hym in the
place of dethe and he is a mansleer, for he sleith his owne soule. And
mansleyng of tonge is in .ij. maners, that is by tysyng, eggyng or
commaundyng. Forsoth mansleyng of herte is also in [.ij.] maners,
720 þat is whan .j. man coveitith or desireth the dethe of a man, or whan
he suffrith a man to dye for defaute and it lyeth in his power to helpe
hym if he wolde.

The .vj.th commaundement is: Thou shalte do no lechery, for it
is worthye and rightfulle that he that desireth to haue lyfe withoute

719 .ij.] .iij. A2

corrupcion in the ioye of hevyn that he kepe his bodye here clene 725
withoute corrupcion of his flesh in this worlde, both in thye bodye
and in thye soule to absteyne the fro alle the occasions of synne.

The .vij.th commaundement is: Thou shalte do no thefte; and
that is rightfulle, for he that wolle kepe and not lese the life of anoþer
man, he shulde not take awaye tho thyngis þat shulde susteyne his 730
lyfe and the lyfes of them that ben vnder his rule and gydyng.

The .viij.th commaundement is: Thou shalte not saye nor bere
no false witnesse | ayenst thye neighbour to sle hym, noye hym or hurte f. 171vb
hym by anye maner meane; and that is rightfulle, that he þat wole
not by hymselfe or by enye other hurte or harme his neighbour, but 735
to do to hym as thou woldist be do to.

The .ix.th commaundement is: Thou shalte not coveyte the wyfe
of thye neghbour, nor handemayde, nor lowe dameselle, nor none
oþer woman, but kepe the to thyne owne wyfe if thou haue enye.
And also that no woman in lyke wyse coveyte no man with fleshlye 740
love, that is to knowe hym fleshlye oute of the sacrament of
matrimonye.

The .x.th commaundement is: Thou shalte not coveyte the
þyngis of thye neighbour, that is thou shalte not coveit nor take fro
hym wrongfullye none of his worldely goodis neiþer his gostelye godis. 745
And þese .ij. laste commaundementis accorden to the oþer .ij. before,
that is thou shalt not do no lecherye, nor thou shalte do no thefte, for
he that hath evylle wylle and evylle entent in his herte maye not
absteyne hymselfe longe fro evylle werke. And þerfore if thou wolte
not do lecherye in dede than thou, man, coveyte no woman with 750
evylle entent of hert and þou, woman, coveyte no man with evylle
entente of hert. And if þou wilte not stele, than loke þou coveyte not
in thyne hert oþer mennys thyngis wrongfullye.

These ben the .x. commaundementis that God yeafe to Moyses in
þe Mounte of Synaye, of the which .iij. the furst perteyne to the loue 755
of God and the oþer .vij. perteyn to the love of oureselfe and of oure
neighbours. *Deo gracias.*

The .vij. dedely synnes: pryde, envye, wrath, slouth,
covetyse, glotenye, and lecherye.

Pride is an vnresonable love of a mannys owne excellence or highnes 760
in high beryng ayenst his even cristen, of the which come alle these
.vij. vicis or synnes, þat is inobedience ayenst God and ayenst thye

souerayne, that is to leve vndo that þou arte bodyn to do and to do
that þou arte forbodyn. The .ij.de spice is boost, whan a man
765 avauntith hymselfe and is proude of þe gode which he hath of
another or is proude of þe evyl which he hath of hymselfe. The
.iij.de spice is ypocrici, whan a man feyneth hymselfe to haue goodis
that he hath not of hymselfe or hidith evils that he hath of hymselfe.
The .iiij.th spice is dispite that he hath to his even cristen, whan he
770 discresith the godis or þe godenes of hym so that he hymsilfe myght
appiere þe better and richer. The .v.th spice is arrogaunce, whan he
makith comparison betwene his owne evils and oþer folkis evils so
that his evils myght appiere the lesse. The .vj. spice is vnshamefastenesse, whan a man hath no shame for opyn evylle. þe .vij. spice is
775 elacion eiþer hie beryng, whan a man makith ioye of his owne evils.

And þer ben .iij. þyngis in especial that makith a man proude. The
furst ben the goodis of kynde, as strenght, feyrnes, wytte and noble
of kynne, the .ij.de ben goodis of grace as cunnyng, vertue, gode
fame, thanke of men eiþer grace to worldelye love and dignite, the
780 .iij.de ben temperalle goodis as lyfelode, clothyng, house, rentis and
grete possessions, and plente of worldely catelle and grete honour of
the worlde.

Envye is ioye of anoþer mannys hurte and harme and he is
sorowfulle of his welfare and prosperite, and þis maye be in herte by
785 turment and in the mouthe by bacbyting, or in werke by withdrawyng of his goodis bodelye or gostelye or by tysing of evyl by
other.

Of wrathe there comyth forthe chidingis, stryves and bolnyngis of
the herte and shrewde wordis, disdeyn and blasphemye.

790 **Of slouthe** or sorowe comyth forthe malice or rancour of the soule
and dispeyre of mercy and necligent in the commaundementis of
God and rennyng aboute of mynde or thought aboute vnlefulle
thyngis.

Of covetyse þer comyth forth forsweryngis, vnrest, violence and
795 hardenesse of herte and dispeyre of the mercye of God.

Of glotenye comyth vnsittyng gladness, meche speche | and feble
vnderstondyng and nye alle maner of evils.

Of lechery comyth forthe blyndenesse of synne, vnstablenesse of
prayer, fersenes, hastynes, hedynesse and lofe of hymsilfe and
800 haterede of God, dispeyre of this present worlde, horror, hydousnes
and dispeyre of the worlde that is to comyng.

These ben the .vij. dedely synnes for whye thaye ben wel saide dedlye, for .iij. the furst robbe the wrecchid synner and thaye take hym prysoner, the .iiij.th betith the synner, þe .v.th castith hym downe, the .vj.th disceyvith hym and the .vij.th dryveth hym into 805 thraldom. For whye pride takiþe man awaye fro God, envye takith fro hym his neigboure, wrathe takith awaye a man fro hymselfe, covetyse castiþe hym downe, glotenye disceyvith hym, and lechery puttyth a man in moost vylest thraldome.

The .vij. vertues of the gospelle ayenst the .vij. dedelye 810
synnes.

Ayenste these .vij. vices oure lorde puttith .vij. remedies in þe gospel, the which ben þese .vij. vertues folowyng in this maner. Blessid ben pore men in spirite, for the rewme of hevyn is thers, and this is ayenst pryde that takith awaye God fro a man. Blessid be 815 mylde men that ben softe and esye to there even cristen, for thaye shulle reioyse the londe þat is euerlastyng and the blysse of hevyn, and this is ayenst envye that takith awaye from a man his neighboure. Blessid ben thaye that morne for there trespasse, for þei shalle be comfortid, and this is ayenst wrathe þat takith awaye a man fro 820 hymselfe. Blessid ben mercifulle men that do mercye to other men, for thaye shalle gete mercye that is of God, and this is ayenste covetice men þat haue neiþer petye nor mercye of no man. Blessid ben thaye þat hunger and thirst rightwisnes, for thaye shulle be fulfylled with the grace of God, and this is ayenst slouthe or 825 necligence in Goddis seruyce. Blessid ben thaye that be of clene herte, for thaye shalle se God, and this is ayenst glotenye that thynkith euer of fleshlynes and superfluite. Blessid ben thaye that ben pesible to there neighbours, for thaye shalle be clepid the sones of God, and this is ayenst lecherye for whye a lecherous man maye 830 neuer haue pees nor reste in his soule.

And also ayenst pride a man owith to haue very mekenes bothe in hert, in wordis and in alle his werkis. Ayenst envye he owith to haue ioye of euerye mannys gode welfare and to be sorowfulle of his dissese and evylle fare, and he owith to haue loue and charite to 835 euery creature and hate nothyng that God made. Ayenst wrathe he owith to haue pacience myldenesse or sobyrnesse. Ayenst slouthe he owith to haue swiftenesse and strenght of bodye and of soule to besye hym in the seruyce of God and in other gode werkis to þe helpe of thyne even cristen. Ayenst covetice he owith to haue largenesse, so 840

that he yeve of his godis to the pore and nedye folke with verye gode wylle as moche as he maye, and to trust feithfullye in God to haue his mede in hevyn þerfore. But loke thou neuer trust in thyeselfe, for than thou shalte be disceyuid. Ayenst glotenye thou owist to haue
845 mesure in etyng and drynkyng in thyesilfe, and moost be ware of drynke, for whye by ouermoche drynke manye fayre yong men and maydens haue perisshid and lost there virginite, and in lyke wyse manye men and women haue loste þer chastite and þaye haue falle into the dropsye, the feuers, the gowte, the postym, the akyng of
850 tethe and into manye oþer diuerse sykenes that comyth by super-fluite of drynke. Ayenst lechery þou owist to be chaste of bodye and soule, in speche and dede, and euer to rule so thye flesh that it be soget to the soule. And these .vij. vertues ben remedies ayenst the.vij. dedely synnes, and þerfore take hede wysely of these
855 remedies ayenst the .vij. dedlye sikenes that brynge a man sone to euerlastyng perdicion withoute amendyng &c.

The .vij. yeftis of the holye goost.

Nowe comyth the moost souerayne leche and yevith his medycyns and curyth a man of the .vij. sikenes, and he confermyth þe man in
860 þo .vij. vertues by the yeftis of the holye goost that ben these: the
f. 172rb spirite of wysedom and of vnderstondyng, | the spirite of councelle and of gostelye strenght, the spirite of cunnyng and of petye and the spirite of drede of the lorde.
By these .vij. yeftis oure lorde techith a man whate is nedefulle to
865 hym in actife lyfe and in contemplatife lyfe. And take þou gode hede howe euerye man owith to forsake alle evylle and to do gode by Goddis helpe, for that techith vs the spirite of drede of the lorde. And for to do gode to oure evyn cristen, þat techith vs the spirite of petye. And þer ben .ij. thyngis that lettyn ofte a man to do welle, that
870 is prosperite and aduersite of þis worlde, for prosperite disceyvith a man by flateryng oþer softenes, and aduersite by hardnesse. þerfore þou owist to dispyse the prosperite of this worlde lest þou be disceyuid, and the spirite of cunnyng techith vs this. And thou owist to suffre stronglye alle the aduersitees of this worlde leste þou
875 be ouercome bi them, and þe spirite of gostelye strenght techith vs þis. And these .iiij. yeftis suffysin to actyfe lyfe, and the .iij. oþer yeftis perteyn to contemplatife lyfe.
For þer be .iij. maner of contemplacions, one is in creaturis, and

this the spirite of vnderstondyng techith vs. And the .ij.de contemplacion is in hooly scripture, for þer thou maiste se whate thou 880
owist to do and whate þou owist to forsake, and the spirite of
councelle techith vs this. And þe .iij.de contemplacion is in God, and
the spirite of wysedom techith vs this. Se thou nowe howe besye
oure lorde Ihesu Criste is aboute oure helthe.

> The .iij. vertues, feith, hope and charite, and the .iiij. 885
> vertues, prudence, rightwisnes, temperaunce and goostly
> strenght.

The .x. commaundementis and these .vij. vertues bene one and the
same mater, but this is the dyuersite: that the .x. commaundementis
techith vs howe we owe to do and þese .vij. vertues teche vs the 890
maner of doyng. The furste .iij. vertues, faythe, hope and charite,
ordeyne vs howe we owith to lyve as to God. And the oþer .iiij.
vertues teche vs howe we shulde ordeyn oure lyfe in this worlde, so
that thaye maye lede vs to the ioyes of hevyn for oure gode wylle to
God and for the helpe of oure even cristen. 895
For alle we bene made to one ende, that is to knowe God, to haue
God and to loue God. But .iij. thyngis ben nedefulle to hym that
wolde come to a gode ende. One is that we knowe wheder that we
shulde go and that we desire feruentlye for to come theder, and also
that we hope stedefastlye to come theder. For it is grete folye to a 900
man for to begynne a werke that he maye not ende.
And also if anye man wolde do welle he muste haue these .iij.
thyngis, that is knowyng, power and wylle, that is to saye that he can
do welle and that he maye do welle and that he wolle do welle. But
for we haue none of these vertues of ouresilfe, therefore God yeafe vs 905
feithe to fulfylle that defawte of oure knowyng, and hope to fulfylle
the defaute of oure power, and charite to ordeyne oure wylle bothe to
the one and to the oder. For feyth ordeynith vs to God þe sone to
whom wysedom is approprid, hope ordeynith vs to God the fader to
whom power is appropried, and loue and charyte is appropried to 910
God the holy gost to whom godenes is appropried.
And þerfore feithe makith vs to haue the knowyng of God, and
that knowyng shewith to vs that God hymsilfe is wonderfulle
liberalle and fre of yeftis þat yevith to vs of his goodis largelye
euery daye and euery houre in suche maner. And of this knowyng 915
comyth hope. Of þe same knowyng that sayeth to vs that God is

moost souerenly gode comyth the .iij.de vertue, that is charite ether love, for whye euery creature kyndely louyth þat is god.

The .xij. articlis of the feithe.

920 Here thou shalte know which ben the .xij. articlis of the feith and the .vij. sacramentis. **The furst article of þe feith** is this: thou shalte beleve that the fader and the sone and the hooly goost is one God and .iij. persones; and that the same God that is on in beyng and .iij. in persones is and was withoute begynnyng and shalle be withoute
925 ende; and that the fader in his sone made of nought al thyngis bothe
f.172ᵛᵃ hevyn, erthe, þe | se and alle thyngis that ben in tho.

The .ij.de article is this: that the sone of God was made man and toke verry flessh and blode of the virgyn Marye, and very God and very man was borne of the same virgin Marye.

930 **The .iij.de article is þis**: that the same Ihesu Cryste, the sone of God and of the blessid virgyn Marye, suffrid peyne, was crucified, dede and buryed honestlye. He suffrid his passhion frelye and withoute enye gylte of synne, and of his owne gode wylle that he shulde ayen bye vs fro captyuite or prysonyng of helle. And his soule
935 with the godhed went downe to hellis while the bodye dwellid in the sepulcre and drewe oute with it the soulis that had done here his wylle in erthe.

The .iiij.th article is this: that the same Ihesu Cryste, very God and very man, roos ayen fro ded men in flesh glorified, and appierid
940 ofte to Mary Magdaleyn and to his apostlis and disciplis, and he spake and ete with them of a rostid fyssh and of an honyecombe, and by his rysing ayen we shalle ryse ayen fro deth to lyfe with the same bodye þat we haue nowe in this worlde.

The .v.th article is this: that the same Ihesu Criste, very God and
945 very man, styed into hevyns, and by hym we shalle stye to hevyn if we ben take oute of this worlde withoute dedely synne. And he sent the holye goost fro hevyn to his apostlis, and in the daye of dome he shalle come in his manhede fro hevyn to deme þe quyck and the dede men that shalle than resceyue eche after his werkis.

924 persones] *add* and A2

The .vij. articlis [that] sewe these ben the .vij. sacramentis 950
of holye Churche that ben remedies ayenst oryginalle
synne, dedlye synnes and venyal synnes.

The furst sacrament of hooly Churche is baptym, for oure lorde
Ihesu Criste hymselfe was baptized in the flode of Iordan by Seint
Iohn for to halowe the sacrament of baptym. For by the vertue of 955
Goddis wordis in baptym the devylle is drevyn awaye fro the yonge
childe, and his origynal synne is done awaye which he drewe of the
fader and moder, and by the grace of baptym it is helid in hym. And
if the yong childe borne be in perylle of dethe and no preest is þer
present, than a laye man shalle saye: 'I cristen the in þe name of the 960
fader and of the sone and of the holye goost. Amen.' And than the
laye man shalle put water on the childe and yeve name þerto, wheþer
it be man or woman childe, and this suffisith to the helthe of the
soule of the yonge chylde. And if anye childe is founden and is not
knowen wheþer it be cristenid or no, than the preest shal saye to þe 965
childe: 'If thou arte not cristenyd I cristen the in the name of the
fader and of the sone and of the hoolye goost. Amen.' And thaye that
holdyn the childe at the fonte shalle teche hym the *Pater noster*, the
Aue Maria and the Crede of the apostlis, for none maye be sauyd but
thurgh baptym and feith with gode werkis. And lete the preest be 970
ware þat he put not the childe in water if he was cristenyd before of a
laye man or of another preest, and the childe in lyke maner be ware if
that he comythe to age as þe decrees witnessith.

The .ij.de sacrament is **confirmacion** or confermyng, for that
confermyth and kepith the hooly goste in euery creature cristenyd. 975
And as sone as the fader and moder can, the childe after his baptym
he shulde be confermyd of a bisshops honde, and at the ferthist
within .v. yere. For if he passith that tyme by necligence and fallith
into dedlye synne than he shalle be welle shryven or that he be
confermyd. And also the fader and moder owith welle to be ware lest 980
thaye holde þer owne yonge childe before the bisshop to be
confermyd.

The .iij.de sacrament is **penaunce** that doith awaye alle synne
actual or of dede done, bothe venyalle and dedely synne. Goddis
sone ordeynid this sacrament, the which sone came fro hevyn into 985
erthe and did penaunce mekelye, not for hymselfe but for the
saluacion of his folke. And Iohn þe Baptist prechid penaunce into
remyssion of synnes. For whye penaunce, that is repentyng with

950 that] the A2

f. 172ᵛᵇ contricion of herte, | and with shryfte of mouthe and satisfacion of
990   werke, and with mekenes puttyng awaye alle envye that is þe devil
fro the herte of hym that doith penaunce, it distroyeth alle dedely
synne and drawith a man ayen to his creatour and it bryngith the
soule to grete ioye and clerenes.

The .iiij.th sacrament is the sacrament of the auter, þe which
995   confermyth and comfortith hym that doyth penance lest he turne
ayen and falle into synne. And þis sacrament reconsileth hym and
susteyneth hym that resceyvith it mekelye in clene lyfe. For whan
Ihesu Criste sopyd wyth his moost wel belouyd disciplis, than he
ordeyned this sacrament into the mynde of his passhion. And
1000   þerefore euery cristen man owith to receyue this sacrament with
moost grettist deuocion ones in the yere at the leste, þat is at Ester.

The .v.th sacrament is ordir that yevith power to hym that is welle
ordeynid, that is ordrid, to do his office and to halowe the sacrament.
For whye oure lorde Ihesu Cryste almyghty God yeafe power to
1005   preestis and to prelatis of the Churche that thaye shulde helpe other
men and to infourme them in the cristen feithe, and that þaye shulde
bynde and assoyle the people of þer synnes; and þat thaye shulde
mynister the sacramentis to oþer men, and moost soueranlye the
sacrament of the auter which is made by the vertue of Cristis wordis
1010   brought forthe of a very preest: for whye vertues ben in .iij. þyngis,
þat is in wordis, stonys and in herbis.

The .vj.th sacrament is matrymonye, which excludith dedely
synne in the werke of generacion betwene man and woman þat ben
weddid dewlye. God which is moost souereynlye wyse ordeynid the
1015   sacrament of matrimonye betwene Adam and Eve in paradise on
erthe. Matrimonye is a stronge ioynyng togeders betwixt man and
woman so that þaye maye not be departid in this lyfe but by dethe if
thaye be rightfullye weddid. And almyghty God ordeynid matrimonye for þe bryngyng forthe of children and for that chastyte shulde
1020   be kepte. Neuerthelese tho that ben weddid owith to kepe tyme and
houre with grete diligence, that is to leve contynentlye in hoolye
feestis by comyn assent for to be the more devoute than in there
prayers.

The .vij.th sacrament is the laste anoyntyng, that makith light
1025   syke men in perylle of dethe from bodelye peyne and gostelye. And
therefore after that man or woman hath take holye anoyntyng, he
owith to be þe more besye in the contemplacion of God, that is to
haue mynde the more in the seruyce of God.

991 penaunce] *add* for A2

The .iiij. cardynal vertues by which al mankynde ben rulid
and kepte in this worlde and þese ben tho: prudence,   1030
rightwysnes, temperance, and gostely strenght.

The holy goost techith the .iiij. vertues in the Boke of Wysedom,
that nothyng in this worlde is more profitable to man than these .iiij.
vertues and se the cause whye. For hosoeuer wolle do welle, furst it
behouith that he can do wel, that is to chese the gode from the evylle,   1035
and that of .ij. goodis he can chese the better; and prudence techith
vs this. And whan þou hast chose the gode fro the evylle or þe better
of the .ij. gode, than thou owist to forsake the evylle and do the gode
and to forsake the lesse gode and to do the more gode; and this
vertue is clepid rightwysnes. And for that .ij. thyngis lett and trouble   1040
a man to do gode and eschewe evylle, that is the prosperite of this
worlde that disceyvith a man by fals swetenes, and aduersite that
oppresseth hym by sharpenes, þerfore ayenst prosperitees thou owist
to haue mesure and discrecion, lest þou be ouer high; and this vertue
is clepid temperaunce. And ayenst aduersite thou owist to haue   1045
strenght and hardynesse of soule so that thou be not ouerthrowe and
caste downe; and this vertue is clepid gostely strenght.

These ben the .vij. werkis of mercy bodely, the which þou
owist to knowe.

The furst is to fede the hungry; the | secounde is to yeve drynke to   f. 173ra
þe þurstye; the .iij.de is to clothe the nakyd; the .iiij.th is to   1051
herborowe pylgrymes or þo that haue none herbore; the .v.th is to
visite prysoners; the .vj.th is to comforte the seke and the sorye; the
.vij.th is to bery þye even cristen whan thaye ben dede. And these
bene þe .vij. werkis of mercye that perteyn to the bodye.   1055
   'But howe shalle I do that am a religious man? For I cannot do non
of these dedis of mercye, for I am vnder the rule of anoþer man, and
þerfore it shulde moche more plese me to be a laye man so that I
myght performe these werkis of mercy.' But brother, thou shalte not
be disceyuid, as Seynt Edmonde sayeth. For whye it is more mede to   1060
the to haue petye and compassion in thyne herte on a wrecchid man
that suffrith pouertye than though thou haddist alle the possession of
this worlde and yeavist it to the pore for Goddis loue. For whye thye
selfe is more worthe than thye worldely goodis withoute comparison,

1065 and þerfore yeve thyeselfe and thou yovist more than þough þou
yeavist alle the worlde.

And oure lorde sayeth in the gospelle: 'Whate euer thyng ye haue
done to one of þese my leste in my name ye haue done it to me; for
whye, verye wylfulle pore men in spirite þat forsake al worldely þyngis
1070 and haue sewid me, whan þe sone of man shal come and sytte in the sete
of his magestye, than ye also shalle sytte on the .xij. tronys or iudicial
seetis and deme the .xij. kynraddis of Israel,' but no man shalle yeve þe
sentence but Criste alone. And also our lorde sayeth in the gospelle:
'Blessid ben pore men in spirite for þe reame of hevyn is þers.' He
1075 sayeth not: 'it shalle be þers,' but 'is þers' nowe. And þerfore if riche
men wolle haue hevyn þaye moste bye it of these pore men in spirite.

And oþer riche men þer be that haue grete gode in þer possession
and þaye spende it wysely to the plesyng of God in helpyng þer even
cristen in þer nede, and thaye loue not þer goodis but thaye loue
1080 God for þem. Suche ben the noble men of this worlde. And som þer
be þat haue grete richesse and loue þem inordynatlye and covetouslye, and oþer þer be that haue no rychesse but thaye desire
inordynately and covetouslye to haue tho richesse, and þese .ij.
maner of men ben ryche in evylle. And these ben the riche men that
1085 oure lorde spekith of in the gospelle: 'It is esyer that a camelle passe
thurgh a nedils eye þan suche riche men to entre into the reame of
hevyn.' And oþer ther be þat haue no richesse nor desire to haue
them nor love þem. And þese ben hooly men and religious, and these
ben the verry pore men, and the reame of hevyn is þers and this is
1090 the blessing of pore men.

And þerfore it behouyth þat riche men haue the contrary of this
blessyng. For if pore men in spirite ben blessid, for the glorye of
hevyn is þers, than thaye maye saye of suche inordynat and covetous
riche men in this maner: Cursid be proude rich men in spirite or in
1095 wylle, for the peyn of helle is þers. Thaye ben riche that haue riches
and loue them, or þey that haue no richesse but thaye loue them
inordinatlye and desire them covetouslye to haue them. And þey ben
pore that haue pouertye and loue it, either þey that haue richesse in
possession and loue pouerte and dispise richesse.

1100　　　The .vij. werkis of mercy goostlye.

The furst is to teche them that ben vncunnyng the lawes of almyghty
God. The .ij.de is to yeve gode councelle þer nede is and to counsel

them to do ryght to euery creature, and to counsel them to leve
rightfully in al þer doyngis. The .iij.de is to chastice þi servaunt[es]
whan þei offende ayenst God in þi seruyce, for þou shalte yelde a   1105
rekenyng to God for alle that be vnder þy rule, and þou shalte
vndernyme them and blame them whan thaye done amysse. The
.iiij.th is: thou shalte comforte them that ben hevy and sory with
comfortable wordis or with som oþer nedeful thyngis. The .v.th is to
foryeve them þat haue trespasid | and is sory and askith mercy and   f. 173rb
promyseth amendement. The .vj.th is to haue compassion of other   1111
mannys synne and infyrmyte and to counselle them for to forsake
there wickednes and to do penaunce and to drawe to vertue and to
contynewe þerin to his lyves ende. The .vij.th is to praye for þer
even cristen with compassion of herte.   1115
   Whan thou canst not helpe hym bodely nor gostelye with none of
these werkis of pety afore rehersid, than thou shalte praye God to
helpe hym. And þou shalte praye God to helpe bothe thye freendis
and enemyes, þat God of his mercy amende them and brynge them to
better levyng, for Seint Austyn sayeth: 'He that louyth his enemyes   1120
shalle be made here þe frende of God and his sones, and he that louyth
his enemyes his prayer shalle be raþer herde of God.' And by the loue
of oure enemyes the devylle is sonyst ouercome, and þerfore Seint
Austyn counseylyth vs in especial to love oure enemyes, for he sayeth
þat he knoweth no better medecyne to hele þe woundis of oure synnes   1125
than þat is. And oure lorde sayeth in the gospel: 'Love ye your
enemyes and than your rewarde shalle be grete.' For Seynt Austyn
sayeth: 'Oure very true lyfe here in this worlde is to loue oure freendis
and enemyes, and to hate them is euerlastyng dethe withoute ye
repent you and make amendis or ye dye.'   1130

   These ben þe .v. wittis: sight, heryng, smellyng, tastyng,
   and hondelyng.

In sight we offende almyghty God in desyring anye woman, or eny
woman desiryng man, fleshlye oute of matrimonye eiþer in dede or
in thought, or in desiring vnrightfully the goodis of þy neghbour, or   1135
in desiring to ete and to drinke so þat thou servist God the werse.
   In hyring we offende God whan we haue lykyng to here sclaunders
and bacbytingis of oure even cristen and oþer lecherous talkyngis
whereby þy mynde is take aweye fro God, and than alle thye delyte is
in suche foule talkyngis, wherefore þou shalte yelde a streyte   1140

1104 servauntes] servaunt A2

rekenyng before God but if þou repent þe or thou dye. And Seint
Austyn sayeth the devyl sittith on the tongis of the bacbyters and also
on the tonges of the wylfulle herers þerof.

1145 In **smellyng** we offende God by ouermoche takyng of metis and
drynkis for þe swete savour þerof, in ouermoche takyng that causith
vs to be seke and the werse disposid to serue God and to labour
trulye in þis worlde for oure levyng.

In **tastyng** we offende God also in etyng and drynkyng and in
takyng awaye oþer mennys thyngis, wherebye þou hast falle to these
1150 and stole þe goodis of thye neghboure.

In **foule handelyng** we offende God whan thou handelyst thye
wyfe or eny oþer woman lecherouslye, and by handelyng takyng
awaye þe goodis of thye neghboure, and also by herte in foule
thynkyng and by the feet in goyng to vnlefulle placis, whereby is
1155 causid ofte tymes bothe thefte and lecherye, manslaughter, envye and
wrathe, and slouth in Goddis seruyce, and bothe covetyse and
glotenye and al oþer synnes, for the which thou shalte yelde a
streyte rekenyng to God but if thou repent þe and make amendis
here or þou dye.

1160   These ben þe .vij. peticions of the *Pater noster* the which
          oure lorde Ihesu Cryste taught his disciplis howe thaye
          shulde praye to God the fader.

And he saide: 'Whan ye shalle praye saye ye this: "Oure fader þat
arte in hevyns, halowid by thye name. Thye kyngdom come to. Thye
1165 wylle be do, as in hevyn also in erthe. Yeve þou to vs this daye oure
eche dayes brede. And foryeve þou to vs oure dettis,"' that is, synnes
eyther peyne dew for synnes, '"as also we foryeve to oure
dettours,"' þat is, to them that haue trespasid ayenst vs, '"and
lede vs not into temptacion,"' that is, suffre vs not to be ouercome in
1170 temptacion, '"but delyuer vs from evylle, Amen,"' þat is, so be it.

This prayer passith alle oþer prayers in dignyte and profite. In
dignyte, for God hymselfe made þis prayer that knowith al the wylle
f. 173ᵛᵃ of God þe fader, and | which prayer plesith hym moost, and
conteyneth þo þyngis for which we wrecchis haue moost nede to
1175 beseche, for he allone knowith alle the wylle of God the fader, and al
oure wylle. And þerfore this prayer is moost prophitable to vs, for
therein is conteynid alle thyngis that we haue nede of in this lyfe and
also in the worlde to come. And þerfore oure lorde sayeth in the

gospelle: 'Whan ye praye nyl ye praye manye wordis, but ye shalle
praye in this maner and saye: "Oure fader þat arte in hevyns."' 1180

And this prayer as I saide afore passith alle oþer prayers, for þerin
is conteynid alle thyngis that we haue nede of in þis lyfe and in the
oþer lyfe to come; for þerin we praye God þe fader þat he delyuer vs
from alle evyls, and that he yeve alle goodis to vs, and that he make
vs suche that we do neuer evylle nor fayle of gode. And knowe thou 1185
welle that al evyles that greve vs, either it is evyl to comyng or passyd
or els evylle that we suffre nowe. And we praye oure swettist lorde
Ihesu Cryste that he delyuer vs fro evyl passid whan that we saye:
'And foryeve þou to vs oure dettis as also we foryeve to oure
dettours.' And we praye to be kepte from evylle to come whan we 1190
saye: 'and lede vs not into temptacion.' And we praye to be delyuerid
fro evylle present whan we saye: 'but delyuer vs from evil.' And eche
gode that is, eiþer it is temperal good or euerlastyng gode. We aske of
God temperalle gode whan we saye: 'Yeve thou to vs this daye oure
eche dayes brede,' and we aske of God goostlye good whan we saye: 1195
'Thye wylle be do as in hevyn also in erthe,' and we aske euerlastyng
good whan we saye: 'Thye kyngdom come to.' And we aske þe
confirmacion of al these goodis whan we saye: 'Thye name be
halowid.' These ben the .vij. askyngis or petycions of the gospelle
that oure lorde Ihesu Criste taught his discyplis. 1200

And also thou shalte wete that these .iiij. wordis before goyng, that
is 'Oure fader þat arte in hevyne,' techith vs howe we shulde praye
and whate maner men we shulde be in oure prayers. For in eche
prayer we owe to haue .iiij. thyngis, that is perfite loue to hym that we
pray to, and very hope to haue alle gode thyng that we aske, and 1205
stedefast beleve to hym in whom we beleve in, and we owe to haue
verry mekenes, for we haue no gode of vs selfe withoute the helpe of
God. And perfite loue is conteynyd in this worde 'fader,' for euery
creature kyndelye louyth his fader. And very hope is conteynid in this
worde 'oure,' for if he be oure fader, than we maye boldelye hope in 1210
hym and saye that he than shulde helpe vs in oure nede. And stedefast
hope and feithe is signefied in þis worde 'þat arte,' for whan we saye
'that arte' than we beleve and knowe that he is very God whom we see
neuer, and þis is rightfulle feithe. For whye feith is none oþer thyng
þan to beleve a thyng that maye not be seen. And very mekenes is 1215
sygnyfied in this worde 'in hevyns.' For whan we beleve and thynke
that he is in the hyest place and we in the lowist place, þan with this
remembrance we ben mekid to knowe oure freeltye.

And whan we haue al þese feyre vertues rotid in oure hertis, than
1220 we maye boldelye pray and saye with alle oure affecion and loue and
desire: 'Thye name be halowid,' that is to saye, thou arte oure fader,
conferme thye name in vs that we maye be so thye sones and
doughters that we do neuer no thyng ayenst thye gode plesyng, and
that we do euer alle thynge that ben acceptable to the, and this
1225 perteynith to þy heryng.

And for we maye neuer do that perfitlye while þat we be in this
caytyfe worlde, þerfore we aske: 'Thye kyngdome come to,' that is to
saye, þye kyngdom come to vs so þat thou regne in vs in þis lyfe by
thye grace, þat we may reigne in the in that oþer lyfe by glorye. And
1230 in this same askyng we praye for þem that ben in þe peynes of
purgatorye.

And for þat we maye neuer haue ioye withe the in hevyns if we do
not þy wille in erth, therefore we aske: 'Thye wylle be done as in
f. 173vb hevyn | also in erthe,' that is to saye, yeue þou grace to vs euer to do
1235 whate thynge that þou commaundist and to forsake alle thyngis that
þou forbedist, and this is as wel in hevyn as in erthe. And as
Mychael, Gabryel and Raphael, and alle hoolye angels and archaungels, patriarkis and prophetis, apostlis, evangelistis, disciplis,
martirs, confessours, virgyns, and as alle thye chosyn childryn do
1240 thye wylle in hevyn, so do the orders of people that ben in erthe; that
is to saye, þe pope, the cardinals, archiebisshops and bisshops,
abbatis and abbessis, pryours and prioressis, archedekyns and
denys, persons, vykers, preestis and alle other hooly orders; and
kyngis, princis, erlis, barons, pore men and riche men, clerkis and
1245 laye men, and alle þat ben before ordeynid by grace to euerlastyng
lyfe in eche reame, in eche generacion, in eche order, and in eche
age.

And for we maye not do thye wylle the while we leve in þis dedely
bodye if þat thou susteynist not vs, therefore we saye: 'Yeve þou to
1250 vs oure eche dayes brede,' that is to saye, moost blessid Lorde, yeve
thou to vs this daye strenght of body and of soule, and helthe of euer
eyþer. For ye shalle wete þat þer be .iij. maners of brede, that is
bodelye brede, as lyfelode and clothyng; gostelye brede, as techyng of
holye scripture; and brede of the sacrament of the auter, to comforte
1255 euer either kynde, that is to saye of bodye and of soule.

But for we be not worthye of vs silfe to haue eny gode the while
we dwelle in synnes tylle God do shewe his grace and godenesse to
vs, þerfore we aske of hym saying: 'Foryeve þou to vs oure dettis as

also we foryeve to dettours,' that is to saye, foryeve to vs whate euer
synne we haue do ayenst the in þought, speche and werke, and þis is   1260
as also we foryevyn to them þat done evyls to vs.

And for it is litle worthe to vs to haue foryevenes but if we after be
kepte from synnes, therefore we shulde praye this: 'and lede vs not
into temptacion,' that is to saye, suffre vs not, gode Lorde, to be
ouercome in temptacion of þe devylle, of the flesh and of the worlde.   1265
And not onlye to kepe vs from temptacion, 'but delyuer vs from
evylle,' bothe of bodye and soule, and from evylle of peyne and of
synne that is present and for to come, Amen, that is, so be it. And for
oure lorde Ihesu Crist sayeth in þe gospel: 'Whate euer thyng ye aske
the fader in my name he shal yeve it to you,' þerfore saye þou in the   1270
ende: 'by oure lorde Ihesu Criste that levith and regnyth with God
the fader and the vnyte of the hoolye goost and withoute ende.
Amen.'

This is the prayer that oure lorde Ihesu Criste taught his disciplis
in the gospelle. And vnderstonde that þou owist not to saye euerye   1275
worde by worde al that I haue writen here, but saye thou the nakid
letter by mouthe, and thinke in thye herte on þat I haue expownid of
eche worde by itselfe. And charge þou not to multeplye the *Pater
noster* or to saye manye *Pater noster*s withoute deuocion, for it is
better to þe for to saye onys the *Pater noster* with vnderstondyng and   1280
with a gode entente and meke deuocion than to saye it a .Ml. tymes
withoute vnderstonding, mekenes, and deuocion. For Seint Poule
sayeþ: 'I had leuer saye with meke herte and gode devocion .v.
wordis devoutelye than to brynge forthe .x.Ml. wordis by mouthe
withoute deuocion and vnderstondyng.' And in þe same wyse thou   1285
owist to do alle þye office in the churche, for this sayeth þe prophete:
'Saye ye the psalmes wyselye and synge thou the versis wyselye of
the psalmes.' To syng wyselye is to vnderstonde wyselye in þye herte
þat that thou sayest by mouthe, for if thye body be in þe quere, thye
lippis in the psauter and thyne herte in þe chepyng, than thou arte   1290
moost wrecchidlye departid in thyeselfe and thou arte not gracious-
lye herde of God. And for oure lorde Ihesu Criste sayeth in the
gospelle: 'Seke ye furste the reame of God and alle these thyngis
shalle be caste vnto you,' that is to saye, to howe many þyngis that
euer ye haue nede of temperalle godis, þo shal be yevyn to you   1295
withoute askyng, and þerefore ye shulde praye | to God onlye but for   f. 174ra
goostelye and hevynlye godis.

Orygynalle synne.

By the sacrament of baptym and by the vertue of Cristis passhion
1300 euery man and woman ben wasshen fro the bonde of originalle synne
that fylle to mankynde by the synne of Adam. For þe corrupcion of
that synne ayenst oure wylle contynuallye clevith to vs as longe as we
ben here in this lyfe for peyn of the furst synne, for þat we shulde
knowe oure owne silfe þerby and mekelye submytte vs to the mercy
1305 and godenes of God, knowyng verely that alle grace and godenes
comyth onlye of hym and nothyng of ouresilfe. But synne and
wrecchidnes and þis wasshyng by the sacrament of baptym and by þe
vertue of þe passhion of Criste suffisith to wassh vs from orygynalle
synne. And as for that synne, it suffisith to refourme vs ayen to
1310 euerlastyng blysse.

And for that a man after the sacrament of baptym wetynglye and
wylfullye doith ayenst the dome of reason that God hath put in hym,
and fallith folyly into synne that is dedely and horrible, and lightlye
for that horrible synne deservith euerlastyng dethe saue onlye the
1315 mercye of God, and þerfore oure lorde Ihesu Criste yett of his moost
plentevous grace and godenes hath ordeynid anoþer penaunce and
waisshyng to purge and clense mannys soule, the which waisshyng is
clepid by the ordynaunce of hoolye Church þe sacrament of
penaunce. Bi the which sacrament alle synfulle men and women
1320 haue a specialle remedye and a general fredom to be waish and
clensid fro the peryl of goostlye dethe for synne, if thaye wolle, and
than by the clennes of soule to come to the blysse of hevyn.

And in this wasshyng that is callid the sacrament of penaunce ben
.iij. wasshyngis to clense mannys soule by. The furst wasshyng is
1325 contricion, the seconde is confession, the .iij.de is satisfaccion. Of the
furst washing, þat is contricion, the prophete sayeth: *laboraui in
gemitu meo; lauabo per singulas noctes lectum meum lacrimis meis
stratum meum rigabo,* that is to saye, I haue traveilde in my sorowyng,
I shal waissh my bedde eche nyght and with my teeris I shal make
1330 moyste or wete the ouerhelyng of my bed. Of the .ij.de waisshyng,
that is confession, the prophete sayeth also: *Asperges me Domine ysopo
et mundabor; lavabis me et super niuem dealbabor,* that is to saye, Lorde
thou shalte sprynge me with ysope and I shalle be clensid, thowe
shalte wassh me and I shalle be made white aboue snowe. And of the
1335 thirde waisshyng, that is satisfacion, a fygere I fynde of the wordis
þat were saide to Nama Syrius: *Vade et lauare septies in Iordane et*

recipiet sanitatem caro tua atque mundaberis, go thou and be waissh .vij. sythes in þe water of Iordan and thye flessh shalle resceyue helthe and þou shalte be clensid.

And nowe I shalle shewe to you the nobley of the soule and his 1340 worthynes in his owne kynde if þat it had not be corrupte with the fylthe of synne. For oure maker, oure fourmer and oure creatoure almyghty God, by the myght and wysedom and alle the counseile of the hooly Trinite made mannys soule to his ymaige and to his lykenes, þat man so moche more feruentlye in brennyng loue shulde 1345 loue hym in as moche as he perseyuyth by gostelye knowyng that God hath made hym mervelouslye. þerfore þou soule take hede and considre þy worþynes and thye nobilite, for right as God is ouer alle hole oo God yevyng lyfe to alle thyngis and gouernyng alle thyngis in þere kynde, and right as God is and hath beyng, levith, and saverith 1350 gostelye by euerlastyng wysedom, right so in thye kynde after thye maner thou hast beyng, þou hast lyfe, and þou saverist gostely by knowyng of inwarde vnderstondyng. And right as in God be .iij. persones, the fader, þe sone and the hoolye goost, right so thou hast .iij. gostelye strenghtis: the furste is mynde, the secounde is reson, | 1355 and the .iij.de is wylle. And right as the sone comyth of the fader, f. 174rb and as the hooly goost comyth of the fader and of þe sone, right so of mynde comyth reason, and of mynde and reason comyth wylle. And right as God is the fader, God is the sone, and as God is the hoolye goost, not .iij. goddis but one God and .iij. persones, right so the 1360 soule is mynde, the soule is reason, and the soule is wylle, and yet not .iij. soulis but oo soule and .iij. gostelye strenghtis with þese strenghtis as for the moost excellent myght in þe soule.

And þerfore we haue in precepte of God to loue hym as he commaundith vs of al oure herte with al oure soules, that is to saye 1365 with al oure thoughtis and with alle oure inwarde vnderstondyng and alle oure wylle and alle oure mynde and with alle oure hole affeccion and discreccion withoute foryetyng, for thou arte richelye arayed with bewte of his lykenes, that is to saye made to his lyckenes as in clerenes and bewte of vertues. For right as God thye maker that 1370 fourmyd the to his lykenes is charite, gode, rightfulle, mylde, benygne, softe, pacient, mercyfulle, and of alle godenes and of noblenes as al hooly scripture makith mencion, right so thou arte made for þou shuldist haue in the charite and to be clene, hooly, fayre, honest, mylde, meke, benygne, debonayre, pacient and lowlye, 1375 and the more perfitlye thou hast these vertues in the, the more thou nyghist to Goddis presence and berist with þe þe symylitude and lykenesse of thye God that is þy fourmer and maker, for resonablye a creature sekyth hym to whom he is lyke. Than seke thou euer God, 1380 vsyng the myghtis of thye soule in his seruyce so shewyng and spendyng þye vertues to his wurship, for to that ende thaye were made and in this dignite and bewte richelye appareylde.

But ofte tymes these grete bewtees and vertues ben horryblye defacid with corrupcion of synne; but yette oure lorde Ihesu Criste 1385 hath ordeynid a gracious remedye to vs to aryse by ayen oute of synne as ofte as we falle. For as sone as we sorowe and morne for oure offencis done to God, and purpose to be mekelye confessid and to make satisfaccion to his power, than he shalle recouer ayen alle þo vertues by the godenes of God and contynewe forthe so, if he wolle 1390 not in the kepyng of þe commaundementis of God be necligent. And truste mekely in God and not in þysilfe, and praye God to be thye comforte and helpe by the merytis of his passhion, for that is þe sonyst remedye ayenst alle þe temptacions of the devylle, of the worlde and of the flesh, and by the meke remembraunce þerof thou 1395 maiste ouercome alle temptacions and perils of this lyfe.

But principallye, after doctours, synne þat defoulith the soule stondith in wylle whan it is not rightfulle, and than þer springith oute þerof evylle werkis as the wyckid frute springeth of the evylle tre, and this synne that is evylle makith vs fer fro God. For that þat 1400 is evyl is nought, as Seint Austyn sayeth vpon these wordis of Seint Iohn: *Omnia per ipsum facta sunt et sine ipso factum est nichil,* that is to saye, alle thyngis ben made by God and withoute hym is made nought. That is synne, as Seint Austyn sayeth, that nought is made withoute hym and þerfore men do nought whan þaye do synn. And 1405 also evyl that is synne is privacion or corrupting of alle gode, for it lackith alle godenes. And alle thyngis that ben done inordinatelye and ayenste the lawes of God haue no gode ende, and þerfore alle suche thyngis, wheþer it be in wylle or dede, it is synne, and so in as moche as it is synne it is nought.

1410 Oute of orygynalle synne and actualle synne comyth alle synnes. Orignalle synne is the gylte and corrupcion of the furst synne done by Adam that makith euery creature concupiscible to worldely and fleshlye vanytees. And that furste synne was also cause of hunger and f.174ᵛᵃ thurste, hete and colde, sorowe and drede, and also of manye | mo 1415 myschevi⟨s, and⟩ alle suche thyngis ben peynfulle to man for the synne of Adam. And actualle synne is the evylle desire in the herte

by malice or rancour saide by spech or perfourmyd in dede ayenste
the lawe of God, þat is to saye ayenst þe wylle of God. Whate man
þat doith suche actualle synne wylfullye and wetynglye, he puttith
wurship from God as moche as in hym is, and that shulde no man do   1420
wylfullye though he and alle erthely thyngis shulde perissh. And
synne of omyssion or commyssion is whan a man fallith from
godenes of thought, speche and dede and levith vndo that he
shulde haue do. This synne is omyssion. Synne of commyssion is
whan a man doith anye thynge inwarde or outewarde that he shulde   1425
not do.

   And Seint Austyn sayeth of the dowte betwene dedelye synne and
venyalle that þer is no synne so venyalle but it maye be made dedelye
while it plesith, and also in the contrary wyse there is no synne so
dedelye but it maye be made venialle by the displesyng of the synner.   1430
To the more declaracion of þese wordis Seint Austyn sayeth that
synne comyth of a vnresonable desire and wylle, and this vnresonable
desire is a wickid dilectacion, that is to saye whan a man is turnyd
awaye þereby fro the lykyng of godenes vnchaungeable, that is
almyghty God in whom euery man shulde reste with alle ioye and   1435
lykyng. But he that turnyth awaye fro God and settith al his loue to a
creature that is chaungeable, to haue his dilectacion in that creature
by thought speche and dede or by sensualite, and if that dilectacion
the which he hath than in þat creature be lasse than the lykyng that
he hath in God, þan is that delectacion venyalle synne. And if that   1440
delectacion wilfullye in that creature be as moche or more, or be putt
before and preferrid his lykyng þerto that he shulde haue in God,
than alle suche dilectacion is dedely synne while it lastith, that is to
saye tylle he repente hym. And þerfore euery daye examyne wiselye
thye conscyence and euer drede thou to offende God, and be thou   1445
ofte confessid and than þou goyst a syker waye to voyde alle þe
perylle of dedely synne.

   That prayers shulde be moost speciallye saide in þe masse
   tyme of alle people for .iiij. skyllis.

The furst is for the presence of oure lorde God onlye in his godhede   1450
as he is ouer alle, but also he is þer in manhede that he toke of the
virgyn Mary to saue mankynde for the loue that he had to mannys
soule. The .ij.de skylle is for the grete multitude of angels that ben
þer present euer more and ouer alle in wurship yeldyng to almyghty

1455 God. The .iij.de is for the grete profite and spede bothe to the bodye
and soule by the vertue of þat sacrament, bothe to them that ben
present and to þem in especial that resceyue it worthelye. The .iiij.th
is for the wonderful wurship yoven to man that at the worde and by
the vertue of wordis saide of an erthely man thurgh the presence of
1460 oure lorde and innumerable multitude of angels, so þat þer be so
manye commodytees and benefettis þat no tonge maye telle nor herte
þynke or comprehende. Therefore it is noo wonder though in the
tyme of masse prayer with deuocion shulde be vsid moost principallye if it be proferrid and yoven of oure lorde at þat tyme. And
1465 devocion shulde be vsid also in the tyme of seruyce that he is bounde
to saye, and also the prayers þat ben enioyned of þy gostely fader for
penaunce.

Howe a man shulde werke in þe .xij. articlis of the feith
with al mekenes.

1470 In the furst article thou shalte wurship God with alle þyne herte,
wylle and mynde, and serue hym onlye with bodye and soule, for he
is oure maker. And also we shulde wurship and blesse God at alle
tymes and to halowe and do reuerence to his holye name, for he
bought vs oute of the thraldom of þe feend, and euer to do wurship
1475 to oure lorde Ihesu Criste, for he is oure savyoure. 'For thou shalte
wurship thye lorde God and serue hym allone.' Mt.4°. And therefore
in þis commaundement is forbodyn alle wicchecrafte, enchantemen-
tis, charmes and coniuracions that men vse for þefte and other loste
f. 174ᵛᵇ thyngis, the which alle hoolye Churche forbedith | to be do, and also,
1480 ye shalle knowe for certein, alle astronomye and astrologye that
worche by þe tyme of mannys byrthe and vnder whate signe he
takith his iournaye and saye whate shalle falle to a man in tyme
comyng, and yet þeye knowe not whate shalle falle to themselfe and
thaye presume to telle whate shalle falle of oþer men. And þerfore al
1485 suche þyngis ben reproved by Seint Austyn and Seint Crisostome
and by other seintis, for thaye take vpon them the power that longyth
to God, and þerfore thaye that beleve to knowe suche thyngis
certeinlye þaye forsake the feith of cristen men and euerlastynglye
þaye deserue þe curse of God, withoute amendement be made or
1490 thaye dye by þe sacramentis of hooly Churche, for ye shulde beleve
tho thyngis that ben conteynid in the Crede and the Pater noster.
The worchyng of the secounde article is to conceyue Criste Ihesu

in penaunce and gode wylle, and bare Criste Ihesu by gode werkis
þat shulde come oute of gode wylle, and to be circumcysed with
Criste Ihesu by castyng awaye of alle synne.   1495

The worchyng of the .iij.de article is to teche them that be not
welle lernyd, and to hele them þat ben seke by compassion, and to be
crucified to the worlde by mortefying of þy flesh and to dye from
synnes, and to descende into helle by ofte remembraunce of the
paynes þerof, and to brynge oute soulis of the peynes of purgatorye 1500
by oure prayers and suffragies.

The worchyng of the .iiij.th article is to arise fro synne by gostelye
strenght into þe lyfe of vertues, and to shewe ensample into comforte
of oþer, and lightyn bothe þer inwarde wittis and outewarde by besy
techyng.   1505

The worchyng of the .v.th article is to ascende vp into hevynlye
thyngis by contemplacion into reprofe of the hardenes and vnbeleve
of hethen men, and also to comforte bothe the gode and þe bad in
this lyfe with prayers.

The worchyng of þe .vj.th article is that he which shal be baptized 1510
be repentaunt if he haue yeris of discrecion, and if he be a childe
than must the preest yeve credence to the fader and to the moder for,
as I sayde before, in this sacrament of baptym originalle synne is
waissh awaye and foryovyn; but yet here the preste muste beselye
aske whether that childe be caste oute and be foresake of þe fader or 1515
moder, or els wheder he be cristenyd of enye laye man. And also that
the preest knowe of baptizynge that a childe in perylle or in poynte
of deth it maye be cristenyd of a laye man or of a laye woman,
though it be þe fader or the moder of þe same childe. And also that
the godfader and the godmoder can þer *Pater noster*, þer *Aue Mary* 1520
and þer Crede, and þat thaye do there besynes that the same childe
can his beleve as sone as he hath yeris of discrecion, or els that thaye
charge the fader and the moder that þei teche hym as sone as theye
maye. Also in a childe that is founde, if men dowte of þe cristenyng
þan muste the prest saye in Latyn: 'If thou be not baptized, I baptise 1525
þe in the name of the fader, of the sone and of the hoolye goost.
Amen.'

The worching of þe .vij.th article is that he which shalle be
confermyd, that he be confermyd of a bysshop and that he be not in
dedely synne, and that the childe be confermyd within the age of .v. 1530
yere at the ferthist, and þat no man nor woman holde not þer owne
childe to confirmacion.

The worchyng of the .viij. article is that a man be sorye and contrite for his synnes in his herte with shame in openyng of his 1535 synnes and in fulle wylle to leue them, and þat he repente hym ofte after that he haþe synned and namely whan he hath synned dedlye, fulfyllyng his penaunce that is inioyned hym for satisfaccion, that he shewe his synnes to his person or parish preest or viker that hath power to assoyle hym, or els to aske leve to go to anoþer to whom he 1540 hath more devocion.

The worchyng of the .ix.th article is that a man resceyue the holye sacrament of the auter, that is God is bodye, onys in þe yere at the leest if he be a lay man [MS ends]

6 ST EDMUND OF ABINGDON

St Edmund Rich of Abingdon was born c. 1175. His father was probably a merchant. There is no certain chronology of Edmund's early education in Oxford and Paris. After Paris he returned to the Arts faculty in Oxford but then went back to Paris to study theology. When he returned to England he spent a year with the Augustinian canons at Merton before incepting in theology in Oxford. He may still have been teaching there when appointed to a prebend in Salisbury. In 1222 Edmund was made Treasurer of Salisbury with a prebend at Calne where he was obliged to live for three months of the year. So generous was his almsgiving that he was frequently obliged to live with the monks at Stanley Abbey, a Cistercian house near Calne, for want of funds. In 1227 he was ordered to preach the crusade by Pope Gregory IX, and in 1233 he became archbishop of Canterbury, nominated by the pope after three elections had been set aside.

Edmund subsequently had disagreements with his own monks at Canterbury, some of whom he excommunicated together with the king and the papal legate, Cardinal Otto. He went to live at the Cistercian abbey of Pontigny after the king and Cardinal Otto succeeded in having nullified a brief that Edmund had obtained from the pope. Pontigny, having been the abbey of exile of Thomas Becket, was seen as a refuge for prelates from England. Edmund died at Soissy, not far from Pontigny, on 16th November 1240. He had a reputation for great holiness and learning in his own lifetime, and four Lives were written of him soon after his death. He wrote the *Speculum Ecclesiae*, for which see the introduction to *What the Church betokeneth*, above p. 85.

Edmund of Abingdon's Life is in *SEL* 492–511, which this text follows, with much condensation after about l. 97. The source of the *SEL* text was the Life by Anonymous A, one of four known Latin Lives.[1]

The *ALL* text is printed by Blake (1962), pp. 163–173.

---

[1] Lawrence (1960), p. 60 and note 1; see note to l. 123 below.

Here endith the lyfe of Seint Appollynare, and bigynneth
the lyfe of Seynte Edmonde the Confessoure.

Seynt Edmounde the Confessoure that lyethe at Pounteney in
Fraunce was bore in Ynglond in the towne of Abyngdon. Mabely
the Ryche was his moders name. She was right holy, bothe wyfe and
wydowe, and vpon Seynt Edmoundis Daye the Kyng the sayde
Seynt Edmond was bore. And in his byrthe noo clothe was fowlyd by   5
hym, and he was bore in the furst spryngyng of the daye. And al that
daye tyl it was euyn he laye as he had ben dede. And than the
mydwyff wolde haue had hym buryed, but his moder sayde naye, and
anone thurgh the myght of God he revyved. And than he was bore to
the churche to be cristenyd, and bycause he was bore on Seynt   10
Edmondis Daye the Kyng he was namyd Edmond. And as this chelde
grewe in aige he encresyd gretely in vertu. And than the moder sent
the sayde Edmounde with his brother Robert to scole. And she had
.ij. doughters, Dame Mary and Dame Alys. Bothe theye were made
nonnys at Catesby in Northamptonshire by the laboure of Seynt   15
Edmond. And there moder gave theym yeftis to fast the Fryday, and
so she drewe theym to good levyng by yeftis and fayre beheestis, and
when thaye came to more aige it grevyd theym not. The moder
hirself weryd the hard heyre for oure lordis loue and lad hir lyff in
grete penaunce, but in a tyme as Mabely his moder put oute wolle to   20
spynne she toke hir spynners so moche for the *libra* that thaye myght
not leue thereon but complaynyd to Seynt Edmond hir sonne. And
he toke the yerne and rekyd it in the colys and the *libra* was sauyd
that she payd for and the ouerplewse was brente, wherefore she dyd
neuer so after to hir lyves ende.   25
    And than she sent hir .ij. sonnys Edmond and Robert to Paryce
too scole. And she toke theym mony for theyre costis wyth theym,
and she delyueryd to theym .ij. harde hayres made lyke shurtis, and
she prayd theym for here loue to were theym onys or tweys in the
weke and they shulde lake nothyng that nedid to theym. And then   30
thay fulfylled theire moders desire, and in shorte tyme after thaye
werid the heyre euery daye and euery nyght. This was a blessyd
moder that soo vertuosly brought fourth hir chyldren.

And then Seynt Edmond encresyd so gretely in vertu that euery
35 creature ioyed thereof and preysed God in his holy seruaunt
Edmond. And in a daye as his felowys and he wente to playe, he
left his felowship and went allone into a medowe vnder an hedge
saying his deuocions. And sodenly there appierid before hym a fayre
chelde in whyte clothyng and sayd: 'Hayle felowe that goyst allone.'
40 And than Edmounde [merveylid] from whens the chylde come. And
the chelde sayde: 'Edmond, knowyst [thu] me?' He sayde: 'Naye.'
And he sayde: 'I am thye felowe in scole, and in eche other place
where that thu goyst I am alweye on þy ryght syde, and yet thu
knowyst me not, but loke thu in my forehed and there thu shalte
45 fynde my name wryte.' And than Edmond lokyd in his forehed and
se wryte therein *Ihesus Nazarenus rex Iudeorum fili Dei miserere mei.*
And then the chelde saide: 'Drede the not Edmond, for I am thy
lorde Ihesu Cryste and shall be thye defendoure whyle thue leuest.'
And than Edmond fylle downe mekely and thankyd oure lorde of his
f. 73ʳᵇ grete mercy and godenes. And oure lorde | bade hym, when he shall
51 go to his bed and when he shall aryse, to blesse hym with the syngne
of the crosse, 'and saye the prayer affore wryten in mynde of [my]
passhyon, and the deuyll shall haue no power ouer the.' And anone
the chylde vanysshyd awaye, and Seynt Edmond vsyd euer after that
55 prayer and blessyng to his lyvys ende, and suffryd euer grete
penaunce for Goddis sake in weryng of the heyre.

And when he had contynued many yeris at Paryce at the scole,
than he came to Oxford. And he dyd neuer lechery nor consentyd
þerto, and that was a special grace of oure lorde. And on a daye he
60 came to an ymage of oure lady and put a ryng vpon hir fyngur, and
he promysed hyr verely neuer to haue other wyff but hir whyles he
levyd. And he greete oure lady withe these .iiij. wordis: *Aue Maria
gracia plena,* which was wryte in the ryng.

Hys oste had a doughter that labouryd gretely Seynt Edmond to
65 synne by hir, and she desyred long tyme to come to his chambir, and
at the last this holye man grauntyd hir. And she was ryght gladde
and spyed hir tyme and came to his chambir and made hir redy to go
to bed and stode nakyd before Seynt Edmond, and he toke a sherp
rodde and layde vpon the mayde tyll the rede blode ranne downe fro

35 sernaunt] *add* seynt LS   37 his] theyr LS   40 merveylid] merveyvid A2
41 thu] not A2   42 eche other] euery S   43 syde] hond S   44–5 there
. . . and] *om.* L   52 the(2) . . . affore] this forseyde prayer S   my] hys A2
58 came] come home and went S   61 whyles] as long as S

hir body in euery syde, and than he sayde to hyr: 'Thus thu shalt 70
lerne to caste awaye thye sowle for the fowle lustis of thye bodye.'
And ar he lefte of she had no lust to syn with hym, for all hir fowle
desyres were clene gonne. And after that she levyd a clene virgyn to
hir lyves ende.

Than sone after, Mabely his swete moder nyghed hir ende and 75
sente for Seynt Edmond hir sonne and yeaff hym hir blessyng and all
hir chyldren. And than she prayed hym for Goddis loue and oure
ladys also that he wolde se that hys susters were well guyded in the
nonry of Catysby afforesayde. And so she passid to oure lorde full of
vertues and is buryed in the churche of Seynt Nycholas at Abyngdon 80
in a tombe of marbyll before the rode. And this scripture is wryte on
hir tombe: Hir lyeth Maboly, flowre of wedows. And than Seynt
Edmonde made a chapell at Catysby, and after bothe his susters were
buryed therein, for the one of theym was pryoras of the same nonry
and dyd there many myraclys. And theye ben buryed before the high 85
auter in the same nonry.

And than this holy man Seynt Edmond dwellyd at Oxford and
contynued there in ful holy leuyng, for he weryd the hard heyre
knett with knottis lyke a nett. And the knottis stekyd faste to his
flessh, that oftyn tymes it causid his body to blede and to be full sore. 90
And in this maner was bothe hys shurte and hys breche imade. And
he bounde it faste with a corde to hys body, that the heyre myght
cleve fast to his body in euery place. Hyt sate so strayte vpon hym
that vnnethe he myght bowe his body, the which was a ful grete
penaunce to hym. And in a tyme whan his shurte of heyre was fowle 95
and tobroke, he toke it his man too brenne in a grete fyre. But he
cowde not brenne hem in no wyse, but euer thaye laye hole and
vnbrent in the fyre. Than his man toke an hevy stone and bownde
the shurte thereto and caste it in the water where was a depe ponde
and there he left theym, but he tolde hys maister that thaye were 100
brente.

Seynt | Edmond and his felowys on a daye came fro Lewkenowre f. 73ᵛᵃ
to Abyngdon, and as thaye came into a grete valey [there] thaye se
many black fowlys lyke crowys, among which there sate one that was
all totoryn with the other black crowys. And thaye cast hym from 105
one to another that it was grete pety to beholde it. Therefore his
felowys were nye madde for fere of that syght, and then Seynt
Edmond comfortyd hem and tolde theym whate it was. He saide that

'thaye beth feendis of helle that berith a mannys sowle that dyed at
110 the towne of Chalsegrove right nowe, and that sowle shall neuer
come in the blysse of heuyn for his cursyd leuyng.' And than Seynt
Edmond and his felowis wente to the towne of Chalsegrove and
fownde al thyng lyke as Seynt Edmond tolde theym. And fro thens
thaye wente too Abyngdon, and theire Seynt Edmond wente into the
115 churche and sayde his prayers lyke as he was wonte to doo, the which
prayer was *O intemerata*, the which he sayde euery daye in the
wurship of Ihesu Criste, oure blessyd lady and of Seynt Iohn the
Euaungelyst. And this prayer he vsyd to saye dayly or he dyd ony
wordely workys, but in a tyme he forgate to saye this holy oryson,
120 and than Seynt Iohn the Euaungelyst came to Seynt Edmond in a ful
gastfull maner and blamyd gretely Seynt Edmond. But after that to
his lyfys ende he neuer forgate to saye that holy prayer.

And after this holy man encresyd so gretely in Oxforde in all the
.vij. sciencis that all men had grete ioye of hym. And in a nyght as he
125 sate in his studye hys awne moder Maboly appierid vnto hym in a
vysyon, and she sayde to hir sonne: 'Loke fro henseforewarde that
thue laboure in devynyte and in no nother science, for that is the
wylle of God lyke as he hathe sente the worde by me.' This saide,
she vanyshed awaye fro hym, and after that this holy man labourid
130 alweye in devynyte to fulfylle the wylle of oure lorde Ihesu Cryst.
And he encresyd so merveylously in that scyence that al Oxford had
grete wondyr of hym for his grete connyng, for there was none lyke
hym in all Oxford. For he had that grace when he radde in the scole
of devynyte he profyted more to the herers in one weke than other
135 mennys techyng dyd in a moneth. For many one of his scolers
thurgh his gracious techyng forsoke the worlde and became relygious
men.

And in a daye as the holy man sate in the scole for to dispute of
the holy Trynyte, he came long ar his scolers came. And he felle in a
140 sclombryng as he sate on his chayre, and ther came a white dove and
brought hym the body of oure lorde, and he put hyt into his mouthe.
And than the dove flye vpwarde from hym, and heuyn openyd ayenst
hym as Seynt Edmonde behelde hit. And euer after he thought that
the savoure of oure lordis flessh was euer in hys mowthe, and thereby
145 he knewe full moche prevyte of the pure state of Ihesu Cryste and of
his magestye in hevyn. For he had mervelouse connyng aboue al
other doctors that were in Oxforde, for he expownyd so hye maters

---

121 gastfull] *add* syȝt and ferefull S   126 hir] hym S   129 she] *add* and S
130 oure . . . Cryst] god S   144 euer] *om.* L

to theym that they thought he was more lyke an angel than a man.
And in euery lesson that this holy man taught he thought in oure
lordis passhyon. 150

And in a nyght he studyed so long on his bokys that sodenly he
fylle aslepe and forgate to blesse hym and thynke on the passhyon of
oure lorde. And than the feende, that had gret envy to hym, laye so
hevye | on Seynt Edmond that he had no power to blesse hym with f. 73vb
the ryght honde ner with the lyft honde. And than Seynt Edmond 155
wyst not whate to doo, but at last thurgh the grace of oure lorde he
remembryd his blessyd passhyon. And then the feend had no power
ouer Seynt Edmond, but fylle downe anone fro hym. And than Seynt
Edmond commaundid hym by the vertue of oure lordis passhion that
he shulde telle hym howe he shulde best defende hym that he shulde 160
haue no power ouer hym. And the feende aunsweryd to Seynt
Edmond: 'þat that thue haste sayde and thought on the passhyon of
oure lorde Ihesu Cryst, for whate man or woman that hath hys
mende on oure lordis passhyon I haue no power ouer theym at no
tyme.' 165

And euer after Seynt Edmond the holy man had ful grete
deuocyon in the passhyon of our lorde and in holy orysons, for
therein was all hys delyte bothe nyght and daye. But when he ete,
slepte and rode, all that tyme he thought was but in ydelnes and hevy
onto hym. But all that he labourid in holy studye or bedis byddyng 170
or almesdede doyng, all suche thyngis was moost plesaunce to hym
and he was neuer wery of such werkys, for he was all hole yeuyn to
Goddys seruyce and to hys plesyng. And also he was a notable
prechoure, and gretely his techyng edefyed in the people that all
people had grete devosyon to hyre his prechyng. 175

In that tyme the pope sent his crosser to the bysshoppis of
Ynglonde þat thaye shulde chese a wyse clerke that shulde proclayme
the popys entent thurgh this realme of Ynglond for to haue helpe
and socoure ayenste the Turke, Goddis enmy. And so by one assent
theye chose Seynt Edmond to proclayme the popys wylle. And soo 180
he dyd that charge full welle and dyligently thurgh this londe, and
moche people he causyd to take the crosse and for to go into the
Holy Londe. And as a yonge man came with other to resseyue the
crosse, a woman that louyd hym lette hym of hys purpose and she

149 he] his S   thought] add was euer S   157 his] the S   passhyon] add of
oure lorde S   159 hym] the fynd S   168 ete] had S   169 he . . . was]
his thought was alle L   171 pleasaunce] plesaunte S   172 yeuyn] euer S
181 that] the popis S

185 drewe hym fast awaye fro thens with hir hondys. And anone bothe
hir hondis were styffe and harde as a borde and also hir hondis wax
all crokyd. And than she made grete sorowe and cryed God mercye,
and she prayed Seynt Edmond to praye for hir to oure lorde. And he
sayde to hir: 'Woman, wylt thue take the crosse?' And she sayde:
190 'Yee, Sir, full fayne.' And than she resseyuid it and was made hole.
And than she thankyd oure lorde Ihesu Cryste and his holy seruaunt
Seynt Edmond, and thurgh this grete myracle moche more people
toke the crosse.

In a tyme as this holy man prechyd at Oxforde in the churche-
195 yerthe of Al Halwyn and moche people was there to hyre his holy
prechyng, sodenly there waxed so derke weder that alle the people
were sore agast and moche people beganne to go awaye, the wynde
and the weder was so horryble. And than this holy man sayde to the
people: 'Abyde ye stylle here, for the power of God is strenger than
200 the feendis power, for thus he doyth for envye to distrouble Goddis
worde.' And than Seynte Edmond lyfte vppe his mynde to oure
lorde and besought [hym] of mercy and grace, and when he had
endid his oryson the weder beganne to withdrawe bye the other syde
of the churche. And all the people that abode there stylle to hyre the
205 prechyng had not one drope of rayne, but thaye that wente awaye fro
the sermon were thurgh wette with the rayne. And there fylle so
moche rayne in the Hye Strete that men myght neither go ner ride
therein. And than all the people preysid God in his seruaunt for this
grete myracle. And at Wynchester another tyme when he prechyd
f. 74ʳᵃ was shewid there | a lyke myracle, for there he chasyd awaye suche a
211 derke wether by hys holy prayer.

Than for his holy levyng he was chose hye chanon at Salysbury,
and there he was made rewler and tresourer. And there he levyd a
full gode lyve, for all the mony that he myght gete he yeaff hyt in
215 almes to pore folkys for the loue of God, that he had nothyng to leve
by hymself. And than he wente to thabbey of Stanley and soiournyd
there tylle hys rentys came in, for Maister Stephyn Lexton that there
was abbot, was somtyme his scoler in Oxford. He was so lytle an etyr
that men woundryd howe he levyd. And yett he wolde ete no
220 costelewe mete, for full selde he ete any flessh. And fro Shroftyde
tyll Ester he wolde ete no mete that suffryd the dethe, nor in Aduent
he ete neuer but Lente mete.

186–7 wax all] were S   189 the] this S   190 and] *add* anon S
191 than] *om.* S   196 derke] grete derkenes of S   199 strenger] byggur S
202 hym] *om.* A2   215 folkys] people S

And when the archiebisshopp of Canterbury was dede he was chose by all the covent to be there bysshopp. And anone thaye sent there messyngers to hym to Salysbury, but he was then at Calne, 225 which was then one of hys prebendis, there he was prevyly in hys chambir allone in his prayers. And one of his chapeleyns came into his chambyr and tolde hym þat he was chose archiebysshopp of Canterbury and that messyngers were come to hym for the same cause, but Seynt Edmond was nothyng gladde of the tydyngis. And 230 then the messyngers spake with Seynt Edmond and delyuerid to hym [ther] letters for to rede theym, and he sayde: 'I thanke you of youre laboure and gode wylle, but I am nothyng gladde of these tydyngis, but I wolle go to Salysbury and take councell of my felowys in this mater.' But when he came theder he was chose there in the 235 chapyter howse by all the feloushypp, but he denyed hytt in alle wyse to hys power. But the bysshop of Salysbury with his brethern chargyd hym by the vertue of obedyence that he shulde take it vpon hym, and then he mekely toke it vpon hym, fulle sore wepyng. And so thaye had hym to the hye auter, and there thaye beganne to syng 240 ful devoutly *Te Deum laudamus* ful merely, but euer this holy man wepte with full bytter tyres and sayde: 'Lorde, I beseche the to haue mercy on me thyne vnworthy servaunt, and yeffe me grace euer to guyde me to thy plesyng and wourshypp, and blessyd lady helpe me euer at my nede, and the holy virgyn Seynt Iohn þe Euaungelyst be 245 my socoure and helpe at my moost nede.'

And than he was brought fro Salysbury to Canterbury, and there he was stallyd archiebysshopp. And than he rewlyd holy Church full wysely and godely, that euery man spake gode of hym for he ledde his lyff in grete penaunce and almysdede, and euer he holpe the poor 250 in theyre grete nede.

In a tyme a pore tenaunt of hys dyed, and then his bayly fette the best beest that he had for his lordis heryott. And than the poor wydowe that had lost hyr hosbande and hir best beste came to this holy bysshopp and complayned to hym of hir grete pouertye. And 255 she prayd hym for the loue of God that he wolde yeff hir ayen hyr beest. Than seyde this gode bysshopp to the poor woman: 'Ye knowe welle that the cheff lorde must haue the best beest,' and sayde: 'Woman, yf y lene þe my beest, wylte thue kepe hym welle to my behofe tylle y aske it ayen of the another tyme?' And she sayde to the 260

232 ther] the A2   250 lyff] *add* in grete holines S   252 fette] fatt S
258 sayde] moreover he seide to the L, þen seyde the S   259 welle] *om.* S

bysshopp: 'Yee, sir, at all tymes to youre pleasyng or else God
defende, for I am fulle moche bownde vnto yowe that ye wolle to me
a poor wrecche shewe thys youre gode grace.' And so he lete sende
hir hyr best ayen, and she kept hytt stylle to hir lyfys ende.

265   And thys holy bysshopp was euer fulle mercyfulle to the poor.

f. 74rb And trewly he rewlyd and maynteyned | the right of holy Churche.
And therefore the devyll of helle had grete envy vnto hym for his
holy guydyng and sette debate betwene the kyng and hym, the which
kyng was Kyng Harry þat was Kyng Ihons sonne. And this kyng dyd

270   to Seynt Edmond leke as hys vnkylle Herry dyd to Seynt Thomas,
for alwey he was sturdy ayenst holy Churche. And yett Seynt
Edmond prayed hym oftymes to be mercyfulle to the Churche of
God and strenght [hem] in ther right, for the loue of God and of his
blessid modyr Mary. But for alle his godely entretyng the kyng toke

275   aweye the lybertyes and the fraunchyes thereof. And he thretenyd
gretely Seynt Edmonde, and whan he se it wolde no better be, than
he spake sherpely to the kyng and sayde: 'Though ye put me oute of
youre londe, yette I maye go to Paryce and dwelle there as I haue do
herebefore tylle ye be better dysposyd to holy Churche.' The kyng

280   hyryng this was euer moor and more ayenst hym and holy Churche.
Than Seynt Edmond cursyd all tho that troublyd holy Churche by
vnright and shame. And when the [kyng] herde of this cursyng he
was gretely meovyd ayenst Seynt Edmond, but alweye the holy man
kepte the right of the Churche to hys power and myght. And then

285   Seynt Thomas appierid to hym and bade hym holde vppe the right
of holy Churche with alle hys myght and rather for to suffre dethe
than lese the fredome of the Churche and to take þat [ensample] of
hym. Than Seynt Edmond fylle on hys kne and wolde haue kyssed
the fete of Seynt Thomas with weepyng teerys, but he denyed hytt.

290   And then he kyssed the mouth of Seynt Thomas and he vanysshyd
awaye. And then Seynt Edmond was more stedefast to holy Churche
than euer he was before and wolde rather dye than lese þe right
thereof. And he toke ensample by Seynt Thomas howe he wente
ouer the se into Fraunce. And þen Seynt Edmond went prevely ouer

295   the see intoo Fraunce, trustyng in God that the kyng wolde amende
his levyng and withdrawe his malyce fro holy Churche.
Than Seynt Edmond came to Pounteney and there he bode in

263 a poor] *om.* L   269 was . . . þat] Harry S   270 leke] *om.* S   hys . . .
Herry] kyng henre his vncle S   271 Thomas] *add* of Caunturbery S
273 hem] hym A2   283 vnright] vnryȝtfullnes S   kyng] *om.* A2
288 the(2)] holi S   ensample] in sample A2   290 hytt] in all wyse L, hym S
294 thereof] of holi churche S

fulle holy levyng, and euer he prayde for the gode state of the
Churche of Ynglond. And .vj. yere he dwellid stille at Pownteney in
fulle grete holynesse. And than this holy man waxyd seke and feble   300
and was counselyd to remove thens to a towne .xx. myle thens that is
callyd Solye. And than the monkys of the abbey of Pounteney made
grete sorowe for his departyng thense, but he comfortyd theym in
the beste wyse that he cowde and promysed theym to be there ayen
vpon Seynt Edmondis Daye the kyng. And as sone as he came to the   305
towne of Soly he waxe right sore seke, and he knewe welle he sholde
not long abyde in this worlde, and he desired to resseyue the
sacramentis of the Churche. And so he did with fulle grete reuerence
and passyd to oure lorde full of vertues in the yere of oure lorde
.Ml.ij.C.xlij. And fro the towne of Solye he was brought to   310
Pounteney vpon Seynt Edmondis Daye the kyng. He myght not
kepe his promyse to the monkis of Pounteney on lyve, and therefore
he kepte hys promys dede, for he was brought thedir and resseyuid
ryght devoutly and buryed with grete solempnyte and put into a fulle
worshipfulle shryne in the abbey of Pounteney before the high auter,   315
where oure lorde shewith many a grete myracle for his holy seruaunt
Seynt Edmond. |

Here endith the lyfe of Seynt Edmond the Confessoure,   f. 74va
and begynneth the lyf of Seynte Bryde.

320

7 ST BRIDE

Little is known for certain about St Bride, or Brigid, of Ireland, and her very existence has been doubted by some scholars. Stories told about her seem to agree that she was born in the fifth century somewhere near Kildare and died c. 525, having founded the monastery of Kildare.

The Life that follows depends on *SEL* 37–46, but is greatly condensed and has a slightly different sequence from the *SEL* version.

Here endith the lyfe of Seynt Edmond the Confessoure
and begynneth the lyf of Seynte Bryde.

Seynt Bryde the holy virgyn was bore in Yrelond. Duptak was hyr
faders name. He begate hyr on his mayde, that hyght Brosek, oute of
wedlok. And when his wyffe wyst yt she was gretely wrothe and
beganne to fare fowle with hir husbond Duptak, and she wolde not
suffre hyr [seruaunte] Brosek to dwelle noo lenger in hir howse. And 5
so hir husbond was fayne to put hir oute ferre into another countre,
and went with his servaunte to selle hir to straunge men. And than
for werynes þey rode in a carte and came by an howse where there
dwellyd an enchaunter, and he heryng the carte goyng by his howse
bade his man to loke howe many folke were in the carte, and he tolde 10
hys maister tweyn. And hys maister sayde that there bethe .iij., and
then he askyd the woman if she were with chylde, and she sayde:
'Yee Sir, forsothe, by this man that is in the carte with me.' And than
the enchaunter sayde to Duptak: 'Thue mayst be right gladde þat
euer thue begatyst this chelde, for she shalle be right a holy virgyn, 15
and alle thy wyfys chyldren shal be subgettis to hyr.' And than
another enchaunter tolde to Duptak that þis holy chylde shulde be
bore at the rysyng of the sonne and that hyr byrthe shulde be
wounderfulle, for she shulde neiþer be bore within howse ne
withoute.   20
    And so it happed that this Brosek was sette to seruyce by Duptak
in a worshipfulle mannys howse, and there she melkyd his kyne in
the feeld. And as she brought home the mylke in a vesselle and wolde
haue stepte ouer the threxholde in the halle, hir o fote within the hale
and the other fote withoute, she was delyueryd, the chylde lying 25
vpon the threxholde. And so she was bore neyther within the howse
ne withoute, after the sayng of the enchauntour. And the holy chylde
was wesshe in the same hote mylke that she brought in the vesselle.
    And after, this Duptak weddid this same Brosek, for his other
wyffe had forsake hym. And than this holy vyrgyn was crystenyd by 30
.ij. whyte angellis that cast oyle on hir hed and sayde the seruyce that
the preestis done and namyd hyr Bryde. And within shorte tyme
after she wexid so holy that oure lorde Ihesu Cryst shewyd many a
gloryouse myracle by hir, for in a day as she sate and hir hed coueryd

MSS A2L   5 seruaunte] seruauntis A2   16 subgettis] soget L

35 wyth a clothe, grete stremys of lyght shone on the clothe that laye on
hir hed, that alle folke wende hir hed had be sett afyre. And then hir
moder was right sore agast, and ranne theder to helpe hir chylde,
wenyng veryly that hir hed had brende. But when she came theder it
was the gloryous lyght of the holy goste shynyng on his spouse.

40   Another tyme, as this holy vyrgyn was in hir prayers, men herde a
man speke with hir, but thaye se hym not. And than the vyrgyn
sayde these wordis: 'This grownde is myne, this grounde is myne.'
But men wyst not what it menydde. But afterwarde there was bylde a
fayre churche in the worshipp of Seynt Bryde. And the people had
45 grete drede of hyr and bade hir fadir put hir oute of that londe, for
the people wolde not suffre hir there to abyde, but wente home into
there owne cuntre there hir modir dwellyd furst. And when she came
thedir the people had grete ioye to se the holy virgyn.

And than an holy wedowe desyred of Duptak hir fader to haue the
50 virgyn dwellyng with hir, and the wydowe and she wente thense |
f. 74vb towarde a grete company of people that stode and abode to see that
holy vyrgyn. And one of theym sayde: 'Loo þis is the holy virgyn
Mary is come here on erthe amonge yowe.' And one þat laye aslepe
awoke and cryed: 'I se oure lady Seynt Mary,' and tolde to the
55 people of whate stature she was and whate clothyng she weryd, and
anone Seynt Bryde appierid in the same clothyng and was gretely
honouryd of the people. Oure blessyd lady dyd hir a grete worshipp
that she made hir appiere lyke hirself in the syght of alle the people.
And after this the holy virgyn Seynt Bryde wente home ayen to hir
60 modir. And there she had the kepyng of .xij. mylche kyne and for to
yelde rekenyng of alle the mylke, botyr and chese that came of the
sayd .xij. kyne, and euer she solde faste awaye and yeaff the mony
thereof to poor folkys. The daye came that she shulde yelde
accomptis of hir deyry, but then she was full hevy, and to oure
65 lorde Ihesu fulle hertely she prayed, and when hir modir came to
resseyue hir accomptis she fownde grete plentye of euerythyng as
though she had solde right nought. And therefore who that trustyth
trewlye in our lorde shalle neuer be disseyuyd. And when hir fadir
knewe of this grete myracle he became crysten.

70   Another tyme this holy virgyn went into the felde to fecche home
hir shepe, and there fylle so grete rayne that hir clothis were thurgh
wette. And there she wolde haue hong vppe hir clothys to drye, but
she wyst not whereon, and she se the sonne shyne and heng hir

62 sayd] *om.* L   xij] *add* mylche L

clothis on the sonnebeem, and ther thaye hyng tylle thaye were drye. And than this holy virgyn Bryde dwellyd stylle in hir faders howse 75 and alle thyngis that she myght come by she yeaffe to poor folkys for Goddis sake. And hir fadir and modir were right [wery] of hir guydyng, and in especyalle hir stepmodir was alwey ayenst hir, that the fader was fayne to lede hir into fer cuntre for to selle. And there he came to the paleyse of the kyng and thought there to selle beste 80 hys doughter Seynt Bryde, for he was acqueyntyd with the kyng before, for the kyng had yevyn hym a fressh [scaberde]. And he went vnto the kyng allone and lefte his doughter withoute, and he toke his doughter his swerde to kepe tylle he came ayen. And in the meane tyme came a poor man to hir and axid hir gode for Goddis loue, and 85 she had no mony to yeue, but yeaff hym hir faders swerde that he lovyd fulle moche. Alle this tyme hir fader spake with the kyng to selle hym his doughter, and than the kyng sayde: 'Whye wylte thue selle thye doughter?' He sayde: 'For she is a strong theff and takyth aweye alle thyngis that she maye come by and yevith it aweye, I wote 90 not to whom.' And then he went ayen to his doughter to fecche hyr in to the kyng, but when he knewe þat she had yeve aweye his swerde he was nye madde for sorowe, for he louvyd nothyng so moche, and for grete wreythe wolde haue slayne his doughter had not men lettyd hym. And than the mayde was brought to the kyng 95 and [he] askyd hir whye she had yeue awey hir faders swerde 'that he louyd so moche, and I yeaff it vnto hym for grete loue,' and the kyng reprovyd hir gretely therefore. And then she sayde to the kyng ayen: 'Yf I had yowe in my power and my fadir also, yf a pore man aske me gode for Goddis loue and I had none other gode to yeve hym, I 100 wolde yeue to hym you bothe for my lordis loue, Ihesu Cryst, and alle your godis.' Than sayde the kyng to Duptak: 'Take thye doughter home ayen, for I wolle not hir haue.' And he yeaff the mayde a fulle gode swerde hir fader ayen to please. And so he had his doughter home ayen. And then he kepte his gode from hir as welle as 105 he cowde, but euer among this holy mayde caught somwhate and yeaffe hit to the pore folke.

And then | it felle that hir fader wolde haue maryed hir to a grete f. 75ʳᵃ duke, and she consent thereto before here fader, but she neuer consente thereto in hyr sowle, for she had leuer dye than lese hir 110 virgynyte. And euery nyght and daye she prayd to God that she

myght haue som dysfyguryng in hir vysage that this duke myght
lothe to haue hyr to hys wyfe. And so by the purvyaunce of oure
lorde she loste one of hir yene, and than this duke lothyd hir and
115 wolde not wedde hir in noo wyse. And than the fader cowde no
better doo but made hir a nune, whereof she was gladde and thankyd
oure lorde a thowsande tymes. And than forthwith she was professyd
of þe bysshopp, and anone she had hir eye ayen that she loste before.
And than oure lorde shewyd for his holy virgyn many a grete
120 myracle.

In a daye there came to hir a grete companye of lazar men and
askyd hir drynke for Goddis loue and she had none ale to yeve
theym, wherefore she was sory. There stode a grete tubbe with water
by hyr, and she blessyd it, and anone it turnyd into ale, and þan she
125 yeaffe it to the lazars to drynke, and theye were made clene of there
sykenes and thonkyd God and this holy virgyn of this grete myracle.
There came a woman and wolde haue borowid salte of hir and she
had more than the virgyn, and anone she blessyd the womans salte
and it turnyd to an harde stone, for she dyd it in scorne to preve
130 whate she cowde doo. Thre pore men came to hir and askyd almys,
and she had nothyng else to yeve, but yeafe theym togeder a cuppe of
syluer. And than thaye beganne to stryfe for the partyng thereof.
And þan this holy mayde toke the cuppe and brake it evyn on thre
withoute any instrument, and eche parte weyed lyke hevy, and thaye
135 thankyd oure lord and his holy virgyn Seynt Bryde.

And when she knewe that hyr endyng daye drewe nye than she
made hir redy, and she passyd to oure lorde fulle of vertues the furst
daye of Feueryere, *Anno Domini* .M.CC.xxij.

Here endith the lyffe of Seynt Bryde and begynneth the
140 lyffe of Seynt Edmond the Martyr.

---

112 myght(1)] *add* that she myght A2

8 ST EDMUND KING AND MARTYR

St Edmund became king of East Anglia as a young man c. 860. The Anglo-Saxon Chronicle records the arrival of a great Danish army in 866. It goes on to say that in 870 'it rode across Mercia into East Anglia and took up winter quarters at Thetford. And that winter King Edmund fought against them and the Danes had the victory and killed the king and conquered all the land.'[1] For all other details of Edmund's life we are dependent upon the earliest Life, by Abbo of Fleury, on which the *SEL* account (512–5), and in turn the Life below, depend.[2]

---

[1] Whitelock *et al.* (1961), pp. 45–6.   [2] Winterbottom (1972), pp. 67–87.

Here endith the lyffe of Seynt Bryde and begynneth the
lyffe of Seynt Edmond the Martyr

Seynt Edmond the Martyr was kyng of a partye of Ynglond that is
callid Northfolke and Suffolke, and he was a fulle gode man and a
softe and fulle of mekenes, and rewlyd his kyngdome fulle welle to
the pleasyng of God. But within shorte tyme ther came ayenst hym
.ij. fulle wyckyd and cruelle teraundis, the one of theym hight Hubba 5
and that other hight Hungar, that were callyd Danys, the which .ij.
enemyes came into this londe with a grete multytude of Danys, and
thaye arryved in the cuntre of Northumberlond. And there thaye
robbyd and slewe the people fulle faste and distroyed alle that cuntre.

And than that one that hight Hungar came into the contre there 10
Seynt Edmond was kyng, and he came vnware to the towne of
Burye. And there he and hys men slewe men, wemen and chyldren,
that grete pety it was to see. And thaye brende, rubbyd and distroyed
alle the towne, and thaye askyd after Seynt Edmond, but he was than
at a towne that is callyd Eglysdon. And than this wyckyd tyrand 15
Hungar went theder in grete haste, and he mette Seynt Edmond
withoute the towne walkyng allone, and there he toke Seynt Edmond
and bownde his hondis byhynde hym, and thaye ledde hym into a
thycke wode and there thaye woundyd hym fulle sore. And after
thaye bounde hym to a tree, and they shotte his body fulle of arowys 20
that noo place of his body was left vnwoundyd, that he appierid fulle
of arowys lyke as an vrchyn fulle of pryckis, that it was a pytious
sight to beholde. And this holy seynt toke alle these tormentis fulle
pacyently for oure lordis loue as though it had not grevyd hym. And
than þis wyckyd tyrand, seyng that he cowde not ouercome hym by 25
his tormentis, commaundid that his hedde shulde be smetyn of. And
than theye caste his hed into a thycke place of the wode of Eglysdon
for no cristyn people | shulde it fynde. But than there came a wolfe f. 75rb
and kepte þe hed with fulle grete diligence that no beste ne fowle
shuld devoure it, and it laye there in a thycke bussh. 30

And than long tyme after whan the grete persecucion was passyd,
the crysten people fownde the body, but thaye cowde not fynde the
hed, wherefore thaye made fulle grete sorowe. But at the last, bi the

MSS A2LS ·   10 that one] he S   23 sight] add to see and S

purvyaunce of oure lord, as thaye wente in the thycke wode the hed
35 spake and sayde: 'Here, here.' And than thaye with grete reuerence
toke this holy hedde oute of the thycke bussh and bere it to his
blessyd bodye and sette it thereto. And thaye bere than this holy
body to the towne of Burye, where his holy bodye nowe is
wurshipfully shryned. And fulle many a grete myracle oure lorde
40 shewith there for his holy kyng and martyr Seynt Edmond. And the
wolfe that kepte this hed made grete mornyng and crying when he
had forgo this holy hedde. And when the hedde was brought to the
body and sette thereto, sodenly the hedde ioyned to the body, and
than the body was fownde hole and sownde as though it had be neuer
45 woundyd, but a litle rede threde was sene shynyng as golde betwene
the bodye and the hedde there it was departyd in þe smytyng of. And
nowe in thabbey of Bury his holy body restyth, where oure lorde
shewith daylye for his holy kyng and martyr many a gloryous
myracle. And he suffrid dethe in the tyme of the wyckyd tyrande
50 Hungar aboute the yere of oure lorde Ml.CC.x.

Here endith the lyffe of Seynt Edmonde the Martyr and
begynneth the lyffe of Seynt Frydeswyde.

40 holy] seruant S   44 and sownde] *om.* S   48 holy] *add* seruant S

9 ST FRIDESWIDE

St Frideswide was born in the late seventh century. Her father Didan was probably a Mercian sub-king who founded a monastery in Oxford and made his daughter abbess. Blair says that although the central theme of the story below, the attempted abduction of Frideswide by Algar (whom *Vita A* calls *rex Leiecestrensium*), is a standard *topos* of medieval hagiography, abduction for dynastic ends was not an uncommon practice.[1] Frideswide died, perhaps on the traditional date of October 19th, in 727.

The Life below is a close adaptation of the *SEL* Life,[2] which is in turn dependent upon the Latin *Vita B* of Robert of Cricklade, printed by Blair.[3]

---

[1] Blair (1987), p. 90.
[2] Not in *Early SEL* or *SEL*, since it is not in the manuscripts on which they are based. It was edited by Lingley (1987) from MS A, and is currently being edited from MS P by Professor Sherry Reames. See Görlach (1974), pp. 196–7 and (1998), p. 92.
[3] See Blair (1987) and Thompson (1994).

Here endith the lyffe of Seynt Edmonde the martyr and
begynneth the lyffe of Seynt Frydeswyde.

Seynt Frydeswyde was bore at Oxford aboute the yere of oure lorde
.vij.C.xxvij. Hir faders name was Dydam and hyr modir hight
Safryde. þey were bothe crystyn and Frydyswyde was there heyre.
And when she was .v. yere olde she was sette to scool with other holy
wymen. Hir maistres hight Abyne and was a fulle gode woman, and   5
she taught this mayde Frydeswyde fulle welle and drewe hir to alle
godenes. And þan within shorte tyme aftir hir modir dyed, and she
prayed hir fader euer to leue chaste after. And than hir fader bylde
.ij. churchis in the towne of Oxforde, one of oure ladye and another
of Al Halwyn, there Seynt Frydeswyde lieth nowe in a shryne. In   10
that churche beth Blacke Chanons.

And than this gode man Dydam when he had bylde this churche
he fette his doughter there to be in the seruyce of God. And than she
forsoke hir heritaige and alle othir merchandyse only to be in the
seruyce of God in that same churche. And she leuyd there in grete   15
holynes in fastyng and in holy orysons, and hir levyng was so
vertewis that alle folke had grete ioye of hir. And thereof the devylle
had grete envye and came to hir on a tyme lyke a godely yong man,
and a grete meyne of devyls folowyng hym in mannys clothyng, and
sayde to hir that he was Ihesu Cryst, Goddys sonne, and tho that   20
folowyd hym were hys aungels come with hym fro hevyn. And he
sayde to hir: 'Com forth, my dere lemman and spowse, for it is tyme
that ye resseyue þe crowne of ioye and of blysse that euer shalle laste,
the which thue hast fulle welle deseruyd, and therefore knele downe
and honoure the steppis of my feete.'   25

And she beyng in grete drede prayd oure lorde Ihesu of helpe, and
she knewe veryly anone that it was the devylle was come theder to
dysseyue hir. And she sayde: 'Feend, howe mayste thue geve me þat
that thue mayste not haue thyself, for thue fellyst onys fro thens and
therefore thue mayst neuer come there ayen. Thye grete pryde was   30
cause of thye grete falle into the deppest pytte of helle, and so shalle
alle tho that folowe thy steppys, for alweye grete pryde wolle haue a
falle.' And than the devylle with grete crying and strong stynche
wente awaye fro hir and neuer durst more come to hyr. But anone he
wente to the kyng Algar and sette hym alle afyre in the love of   35

MSS A2L   33 crying] cry L

Frydeswyde, that he cowde haue no reste neyther nyght ne daye, his

thought was so moche on this | holy vyrgyn, and thought veryly to
haue adoo with hir flesshly. And anone he sente messyngers to fecch
thys holy nune vnto hym, for he was nye madde for hir loue, and
40 that thaye bryng hir in alle the haste in fayre maner, and yf she wolde
not: 'Constrayne hir to come to me.'

   And when thaye came to hyr, thaye dyd the kyngis messaige and
tolde hir that the kyng desired hir aboue alle wemen and wolde
wedde hir to his wyffe. And than she tolde theym that the kyng of
45 hevyn was hir spouse, and none other spouse wolde she haue. And
than thaye wolde haue brought hir to the kyng by strenght, but
anone thaye wexe sterke blynde. And than thaye repente theym that
euer thaye came there and anone thurgh the prayer of this holy nune
they resseyuid ayen þer sight bye the myght of oure lorde. And than
50 thaye wente ayen to the kyng and tolde hym alle by order whate was
byfalle theym. And than the kyng ferde as a wode man and swore she
shulde not so escape fro hym by hir wycchecrafte: 'For I wylle haue
my wylle of hyr, and than for spyte alle men that wolde shalle
defowle hyr body and make hir a comyn woman.' And anone he toke
55 his steed and rood to Oxford as a wode man, but he cowde not fynde
hir there, for she was gon thens in a bote by water with .ij. of hir
susters. And sodenly thaye came to the towne of Benton, and there
she abode long tyme in oure lordis seruyce previly with hir .ij.
susters, that were fulle holy nunnys also. And than the kyng dyd
60 grete hurte in the towne of Oxford because he myght not fynde hir
there and purposid to distroye the towne, but sodenly thurgh the
myght of God he was made blynde, and so contynewid to hys lyvys
ende in grete wrecchednes for his fowle luste, and therefor came ther
neuer [the] kyng there synnys.
65   And when the kyng was dede she came ayen to Oxford by the
towne of [Benesye], but there she abode .iij. yere and bylde there a
chapelle in the worship of God and Seynt Margaryte. And on a tyme
these holy nunnys compleynyd to hir that the water was fer fro
theym to fecche it, and than this holy virgyn Frydeswyde made hir
70 prayer to oure lorde, and sodenly there sprong vppe a fayre welle by
the churche wherein was fulle gode water and is yett, þat many a
fayre myracle hath be shewyd there.

   Vpon a Sonedaye a man wolde felle downe trees in a wode, and as

41 not] add come L   44 his] om. L   55 steed] palfrey L   64 the]
om. A2L   synnys] syn L   66 Benesye] Hengseye A2

he beganne to werke, sodenly his axe clevyd so fast to his handis that
noo man myght take it oute, for which thyng his frendis had grete 75
sorowe. And than he was conseylyd to go to this holy virgyn Seynt
Frydyswyde and prayed hir with grete mornyng to praye for this
man. And anone she prayd for hym to oure lorde, and he was
restoryd ayen to his furst helth. And anone aftir she wente fro
[Benesye] to Oxford, and grete people of the towne came ayenst hir 80
to resseyue hir with grete devosyon, where oure lorde shewid for hir
a grete myracle. A foule mesylle man came ayenste hyr among the
people and cryed faste on hyr and prayd hir for Goddis sake that she
wolde kysse hym with hir swete mouth if it were hir wylle. And than
this holy mayde was sore ashamyd and wente forth stylle, but euer 85
this mesylle cryed on hir withoute sessyng. And than this holy virgyn
fulle mekely kyssyd hym, and anone he was perfectly hole. And than
this man yeaffe thankyngis to God and to this holy nune Seynt
Frydeswyde, and so she wente to hir owne church and lad there a
fulle holye lyffe long tyme. 90
    And than at the laste she beganne to waxe right febylle for grete
sekenes that she had, and long or she dyed an aungelle warnyd hir
that she shulde passe hens. In the moneth of Octobre, the nyght after
Seynt Lucys Daye, that was on a Soneday nyght that she passyd hens
to the blysse of hevyn, and theder she was conveyed by Seynte | 95
Kateryne, Seynt Cecylye and with many other virgyns, and hir f. 75vb
bodye lyeth at Oxford in a fulle worshipfulle shryne in the pryery of
Blake Chanons that nowe is clepyd the churche of Seynt Frydeswyde. And there oure lorde shewith for hir many a gloryous myracle,
wherefore his name be preysyd worlde withoute ende. Amen. 100

Here endith the lyfe of Seynt Frydeswyde and begynneth
the lyfe of Seynt Edward the yong kyng.

80 Benesye] Hengseye A2   96 other] *add* holy L   102 *Rubric* kyng] *add*
and martir L

10 ST EDWARD KING AND MARTYR

St Edward was born c. 962 and was murdered at Corfe on 18 March 978. There are conflicting accounts of his burial and the removal of his body to a second (or third) site. His remains were translated to Shaftesbury in 980.

This Life is a much shortened version of *SEL* 110–118.[1] Christine Fell shows that the *SEL* version is a close translation of the *Passio Sancti Eadwardi Regis et Martyris*, which she edits and attributes to Goscelin, dating it 1070–80.[2]

---

[1] Görlach (1998), pp. 101–2.   [2] Fell (1971).

Here endith the lyfe of Seynt Frydeswyde and begynneth
the lyfe of Seynt Edward the yong kyng.

Seynt Edward the yong kyng and martyr was the sonne of Kyng
Edgar and was kyng but thre yere and .vij. monthis. And when his
owne moder was dede, his fader weddid another wyffe that was fulle
wyckyd, and by hir he had a sonne that hight Athelrede. This quene
labourid euer to dystroye this yong kyng Edward to make hir awne   5
sonne Ethelrede kyng, and fulle litle she lovyd this kyng Edward, for
stepmoders byn selde gode, for euer she labouryd with alle hir myght
to dystroye hym after that hir husbonde Edgar was dede. For when
he levyd he was a fulle gode kyng, for he chastysed rebyls and
cherysshid gode folkys, for he was alle rewlyd by Seynt Dunstone,   10
and that tyme was grete [ioy] and prosperite in alle this londe. For
when the hed is welle guydyd grete welthe folowith thurgh alle the
londe, and the contrarye is to the londe grete sorowe and payne. But
euer this wyckyd queen, thurgh the tysyng of the feend, labourid to
distroye this yong kyng Edward.   15
    Hit befelle on a daye that this kyng wolde ride an huntyng with his
knyghtis in the wode of Dorsett bysydis the towne of Warham, that
nowe is a fayre downe. And than the kyng departid awaye fro his
men and rode forthe allone to se his brother Athelred, that dwellyd
there besyde in a towne that is callid Corfe with his moder the   20
queen, where is nowe a strong castelle but þat tyme was none there.
But when this wyckyd quene se hym she was gladde, for she thought
then too haue hir desire that she had labourid abowte manye a daye.
And she welcomyd the kyng and made as though she had louyd hym
gretely, and commaundid hir men to fecche brede and wyne to the   25
kyng. And while he dranke, the boteler put a long knyffe thurgh the
kyngis bely and alle toslytte his guttis. And than this gode kyng
sporyd his horse, but or he passyd ferre from thens he felle fro his
horse and dyed. And than the wyckyd queenis seruauntis buryed the
bodye in a desolate place of the wode, that no man shulde knowe   30
where he were become.
    And when Seynt Dunstone knewe that this gode kyng was

MSS A2LS   4 hight] was callyd S   5 euer] euery day S   11 ioy]
om. A2   and prosperite] *om.* S   16 this] *add* yonge L   17 towne] *add then*
del. of Warham A2   22 gladde] *add* inowe LS   24 And] But L

mordryd he made grete sorowe, but halfe ayenste his wylle he crownyd hir sonne Athelrede kyng. And he sayde to hym: 'For as
35 moche as thue arte come to be kyng by wrong and manslaughter, therefore thue shalte haue grete sorowe and trouble to thye lyvys ende, and all shalle be for the dethe of thye brother Edward.' Who wolle knowe the sorowe that this londe had than, lete hym rede the lyffe of Seynt Alpheye, and there he shalle fynde sorowe inough that
40 felle to this Athelrede for the dethe of his brother. And alle the pore people sorowid gretely his dethe and cursyd theym that slewe this holy kyng Edward.

And manye a gode man wolde fulle fayne haue had this bodye buryed in a more worshipfulle place, but thay cowde not long tyme
45 knowe where he was buryed. But on a tyme as men of Warham and of the cuntree wente to seke this holye bodye with grete hevynes, one of theym se a grete lyght in the wode lyke a [pyller] of fyre strecchyng vp fro that place to hevyn. And the folkys drewe theder, and bye the purvyaunce of God [they] fownde there this
f. 76ra holy bodye and toke it vppe of the erthe with grete reuerence | and
51 bere it worschipfully with procession to the towne of Warham, and there thaye buryed this holy body in a churcheyerth of oure ladye at the este ende of the sayde churche, where nowe is a fayre chapelle of oure ladye. And in the wode where he was furste buryed is nowe a
55 fayre welle, and there oure lorde shewith many a myracle for hys holye martyr Seynte Edward, and is callyd Seynt Edwardis welle.

And this holye bodye laye in the sayde churcheyearth of Warham manye yeris, where oure lorde shewyd for hym many a grete myracle. At the laste therle Alpher, that lovyd moche this holye
60 kyng in hys lyffe, herde of the grete myraclis that God shewid for hym, counseylid the bysshoppis and clerkys, and also thurgh the conseylle of Seynt Wylfryde and Seynt Edithe that were nonnys at Wylton and were Seynt Edwardis susters, this holy bodye was take owte of the churcheyerthe of Warham and brought to the nunrye of
65 Shaftysbury. And bye the waye, as men bere the bodye by .ij. crepullys, anone thaye resseyvyd perficte hele and wente forthe with this holy bodye with grete myrth and ioye, and thankyd God and this holye seynte of there delyueraunce.

34 he] seynt dunstan S   34-5 as moche as] *om.* LS   37-40 who . . .
brother] *om.* S   43 had] *om* LS   47 pyller] perylle A2   49 they] thye
A2   55-6 there . . . Edward] *om.* S   61 clerkys] the clergye S
63 Seynt . . . susters] seyntis and susteris to seynt Edward S   65 by] *om.* S
66 crepullys] *add* mett with þe body of seynt Edward and S

And when this wyckyd queen herde telle of this grete myracles, she repentyd hir fulle sore and purposyd hir to ryde there this holy 70 body was to do hym worshipp and to aske foryevenes of the cursyd dedis that she had don to hym. But when she wolde haue ryden thether warde hir horse wolde not forthe in no wyse for no drawyng ne betyng, and than she lyght downe and went on hir feet, with grete repentaunce for the cursyd dedys that she had don to the holy seynte 75 Edwarde. And when she came to Shaftisburye, where this holy bodye was buryed, she dyd fulle grete reuerence therto and cryed God mercye and this holy seynt for hir grete offence. And aftirwarde she became a gode woman and ledde a holy lyfe to hir lyfys ende.

And when this holye seynte had layne in a walle manye yeris 80 besyde the high auter, at laste he appierid to a holye religious man and bade hym go to Dame Althrede, abbas of the place, and saye that she shulde purveye that his bodye were layde in a more worshipfulle place. And than she wente to Seynt Dunstone to praye hym of his helpe in this mater. And he came anone theder with grete multytude 85 of bysshoppis, abbottis, priours, and put this holy martyr in a fulle wurshipfulle shryne in the sayde abbeye of nunnys in Shaftisburye, where oure lorde shewith many a grete myracle for his holy martyr. And when this holye martyr was take oute of the yerthe to be putt in the shryne, there came oute of his graue a grete myste, and it smellyd 90 so swete to the people þat it was a verye hevynly comforde to them alle.

He was translatyd in the yere of oure lorde .Ml. and sumwhate more. And when Kyng Athelred was dede, Edward his sonne reyned after hym, that was a fulle gode kyng and graciouse, the which [lieth] 95 at Westmynster in a fulle worshipfulle shryne, and there oure lorde shewith for hym manye a gloryous myracle, wherefore oure lord be preysid, worlde withoute ende. Amen.

Here endith the lyffe of Seynt Edward the yong kyng and begynneth the lyfe of Seynt [Alpheye]. 100

73 on hir feet] on foote LS   77 fulle] *om.* S   82 and saye] *om.* S
95 lieth] light A2   97 lord] *add* god S   100 *Rubric* Alpheye] Alpheyne A2

11 ST ALPHEGE

St Alphege was born c. 953. As a young man he was a monk at Deerhurst but later became a solitary near Bath. After Dunstan re-founded Bath abbey he appointed Alphege abbot. In 984 Alphege succeeded Ethelwold as bishop of Winchester, and from 1005 until his death was archbishop of Canterbury. Alphege refused to flee Canterbury when it was besieged by the Danes in 1011, and was captured and imprisoned with a ransom set for his release. He said the country was too poor to pay the three thousand gold crowns demanded, and was taken to Greenwich. After a second refusal to pay the ransom, Alphege was murdered in 1012. This Life closely follows that in *SEL* 148–155.

Here endith the lyffe of Seynt Edward the yong kyng and
begynneth the lyfe of Seynt [Alpheye].

Seynt Alpheye the holye bysshopp and martyr was bore in Ynglonde,
and he came of noble kynred and was his faders heyre, but he forsoke
alle and became a monke at Derherst besidis Gloucester. But
afterwarde the gode kyng Edward yeafe that house of Derherst to
the house of Seynt Denys in Fraunce.   5
    And when Seynt Alpheye had be monke there long tyme he wente
fro thens to þe towne of Bathe to be there more in contemplacion
and reste of sowle. And within shorte tyme after he began to bylde
there a fayre abbey, and he endewid hytt with the order of blake
monkys, and hymselfe was | the furste abbott there and the founder   f. 76ʳᵇ
allso. And he lad there a fulle holy lyffe, and fulle welle he guydid his   11
monkys in vertuous levyng.
    And that tyme was Seynt Dunstone bisshop of Canterbury and
Seynt Ethelwolde bisshop of Wynchester, but within shorte tyme
after this Seynt Ethelwolde passyd to oure lorde fulle of vertues. And   15
than Seynt Andrewe appierid to Seynt Dunstone in a nyght, and
bade hym aryse anone and make Alphey thabbot of Bathe bisshop of
Wynchester. And so it was do with fulle grete solempnyte as oure
lorde by hys holy apostylle Seynt Andrewe had commaundid, and he
was bisshop there .xxxij. yere. And after that he was made archiebis-   20
shop of Canterburye bye the pope and also bye alle the clergye of
Ynglonde in the yere of oure lorde .Ml. and .vj. yere, and .vj. yere he
was archyebisshopp of Canterburye. And in the .vij.th yere came a
wyckyd tyrand oute of Denmarke into this londe, his name was
Erdriche, with a grete multytude of Danys, and brente and robbyd in   25
euery place where thaye came. And thaye toke manye lordis of this
londe and slowe meche people. That tyme was Ethelrede kyng of
Ynglonde and Seynt Edward the Martyr was hys brother. And Seynt
Edwarde the Confessoure was þe sonne of Athelrede, that lyeth nowe
at Westmynster in a fulle worshipfulle shryne, where oure lorde   30
shewith daylye for hym many a grete myracle.
    And after this þe Danys dyd fulle meche harme thurgh this londe.
The chefe princesse name of the Danys was Kyrkylle, and hys

MSS A2L   *Rubric* Alphey] Alpheyne A2   23 archyebisshopp] bisschop L
25 Erdriche] Eldryche L

brother Erdryche was maister of the hoste. Theye dyd grete sorowe
35 to the people, for no man was able to withstonde theym, for the kyng
Athelrede was a meke man and toke none hede to helpe his people.
And than Erdrych with the Danes wente towarde Canterburye, and
there he did fulle moche wyckydnes to the people, for he brente and
distroyed alle that he myght fynde, but at the laste he was slayne by
40 men of Canterbury. And when the prynce Kyrkylle wyste this he was
wode for angre and in grete haste wente to Canterburye, and there he
besegyd the towne of Canterbury and anone he gate it and brente
and distroyed alle that he cowde.

And than this holye bisshop Seynte Alphey came to this prynce of
45 Danys and prayd hym to take his bodye and spare the pore people
and the towne, but for alle that he slowe monkys, preestis and alle
that he myght fynde, and at laste toke this holy bysshop [Alphey]
and bownde his hondis and ladde hym with theym to the towne of
Grenewich besidis London, and there he put hym in pryson half a
50 yere and more. And the Frydaye in the Ester weke the devylle
appierid to this holy man in the pryson in lekenes of an aungelle, and
sayde to hym that it was oure lordis wylle that he shulde go owte of
prison and folowe hym. And this holy man levyd hym and wente
oute anone and folowyd this wyckyd aungelle by nyght, and he
55 brought this holye man into a derke valey, and there he wadid ouer
waters and dychis and myrys and heggis and euer this holy man
folowyd hym as welle as he myght for feblenesse, tylle at laste he
brought hym into a fowle myre þat was sette aboute with grete
waters, and there þe devylle lefte hym and vanyshyd awaye. And
60 than this holy man wyst that he was disseyuid by his wyckyd enmy
the fende, and cryed God mercy and prayed hym of helpe. And than
oure lorde sende his aungelle vnto hym and holpe hym owte and
bade hym: 'Go ayen into pryson to Grenewich, for tomorowe thue
shalte suffre martyrdome for oure lordis sake.'
65 And as he wente ayen to go into the pryson erely by the morowe,
his kepers that had sought after hym alle the nyght mette hym, and
anone thaye caste hym downe to grownde, and there thaye woundyd |
f. 76ᵛᵃ hym fulle pytuoslye, and than thaye brought hym ayen into pryson
and made there a grete smoldryng of smoke to dissese hym. And
70 than Seynt Dunstone appierid to hym and bade hym be of gode
comforte, for oure lorde had ordeigned for hym a gloryous crowne.

38 moche] add harme and L   47 Alphey] Alpley A2   54 this . . . aungelle]
hym L   57 welle as] om. L   69 there] therein L

And as thaye spake togeders, his bondis brake and alle his woundis were made hole anone thurgh the mercye of oure lorde, and when his kepers se this thaye drad fulle sore and anone this myracle was knowyn to the people, and thaye drewe fulle faste to se hym. And 75 than the iugis doubtid the grete people that came theder and toke hym oute of pryson and ladde hym to the place where he shulde be martryd, but the pore people made fulle grete sorowe for hym. And anone theye stonyd hym to the dethe in lyke wyse as thaye did Seynt Stephyn, and as he was allemoste dede, one that was his godsonne 80 smote hym with an axe on þe hed that he fylle to the grownde and yelde vp the spyryte to oure lorde Ihesu Cryste.

And than this wyckyd tyrandis caste the holye bodye into a depe water, þat goode men shulde neuer fynde hit, but bi the purvyaunce of oure lorde he was fownde anone bi the gode crysten people, and 85 than thaye reprovyd gretely these wyckyd tyrandis. And than thaye scornyd this holye bodye and toke an olde rotyn stycke and pyght it in the yerthe and sayde: 'If this stycke bere flowrys by tomorowe, we wolle repente vs and beleue þat he is a holye man, or else not.' And bi the morowe þey fownde this olde stycke grene and bare levys. And 90 when thaye se this grete myracle thaye belevyd in God and kyssyd the fete of this holye man, and thaye repentyd them fulle sore of there wyckyd dedis and cryed God mercy and this holye Seynte Alphey.

And than he was brought to London with grete wurship and 95 buryed in the churche of Seynt Pawlis with fulle grete reuerence, and there he laye buryed many a daye. And afterwarde he was brought to Canterburye, and there he was putte into a fulle worshipfulle shryne, where oure lorde shewith for this holye martyr manye a grete myracle. And alle tho that martyred this holy man þat repente 100 theym not dyed anone after cursidlye in dyuers maners for there cruelle dedys and wente to euerlastyng payne.

Here endith the lyfe of Seynt [Alpheye] and begynneth the
lyfe of Seynt Austyn.

72 brake] tobreke L   83 this] these L   103 *Rubric* Alpheye] Alpleye A2

12 ST AUGUSTINE OF CANTERBURY 1

St Augustine arrived in Kent from Rome in 596, bringing with him forty monks. Ethelbert the local king, a pagan married to a Frankish christian, gave the party permission to preach and provided a *mansionem* for them in *Durovernum* his capital. The mission was a success locally, and Ethelbert was baptised some time before 601. Although not a bishop when he arrived, Augustine travelled to Gaul for consecration in 597. At Augustine's request Pope Gregory sent fresh helpers in 601, and as a result Augustine ordained two bishops, Mellitus to London and Justus to Rochester. Shortly after Augustine's death in 604 these two bishops left for Gaul, leaving Lawrence, Augustine's successor in Canterbury, the only bishop of the Roman mission.

Despite Görlach's caution about the derivation of this Life from the *South English Legendary*,[1] we think the phrases recorded below in the notes are close enough to confirm that it is a shortened version of *SEL* 214–7.

---

[1] Görlach (1998) pp. 102–3 and Görlach (1974) pp. 172 and 278 note 183.

Here endith the lyfe of Seynt [Alpheye] and begynneth the
lyfe of Seynt Austyn.

Seynt Austyne the bysshop that brought cristyndom into Ynglonde
in the tyme of Seynt Gregorye pope of Room the yere of oure lorde
Ihesu Cryste .v.C.iiij.xx.ij. Seynte Austyne with fourtye felowys
aryved in the cuntre of Kente. And that tyme was kyng of that
cuntre one Albright, that was a fulle gode man in his lawe, and 5
suffryd theym to preche before hym, and oure lorde sende suche
grace to this kyng Albright that he and his people vnderstode right
welle his prechyng.

And than he tolde theym the feythe of Ihesu Cryste, and howe he
hathe bought man oute of þe devyllis boundis by his bytter passhyon, 10
and who that belevith in hym and kepith his byddyngis after this
presente lyfe shulle come to the blysse of hevyn. And than sayde the
kyng: 'I leke welle youre feyth and it be as ye saye, but I wolle that ye
preche your lawe to my people, and yf ye maye drawe theyme to
your beleve I wolle welle that ye so do.' And within shorte tyme he 15
had conuertyd to the feythe of Ihesu Cryst the moost parte of his
people and were crystyned by Seynt Austyn. And when the kyng
herde that he had conuertyd so many of his people than he resseyuyd
baptyme hymself. And | within shorte tyme after, alle this lond f. 76ᵛᵇ
became crystyn. 20

And than Seynt Austyn and his felowis were fulfylled with grete
ioye, and Seynte Austyne wente ayen to Roome to telle the pope
Gregorye of these gode tydyngis. And than he thankyd oure lorde for
this grete dede, and sente Seynt Austyn ayen into Ynglond. And
than he made anone .xij. bisshoppis in this londe to kepe the crysten 25
faythe, and he was the .xiij.th bisshopp, and was made archiebisshop
of Dovyr, that nowe is clepyd Canterburye. And anone after this
gode kyng Albright dyed in the .xx.th yere after he was cristyned and
the syx and fyfty yere of his kyngdom. And than Seynt Austyne lete
bylde the abbeye of Seynt Austyns in þe towne of Canterburye, 30
where he lieth nowe in a fulle worshipfulle shryne, and oure lorde
schewith there for his servaunte many a grete myracle, wherefore his
name be blessid worlde withoute ende. Amen.

MS A2   *Rubric* Alpheye] Alpleye   2 Gregorye] *add* was A2

Here endith the lyfe of Seynte Austyn and begynneth the
lyfe of Seynte Oswolde.

35

13 ST OSWALD

St Oswald, whose date of birth is unknown, was the nephew of Odo, archbishop of Canterbury 942–958. Odo, who had requested the monastic habit from Fleury for himself when appointed archbishop, sent Oswald to Fleury when he expressed a wish to become a monk. Oswald was ordained priest there and returned in 958, too late to see his uncle before he died. He then went north to another uncle, Oskytel, archbishop of York, and in 961 he was appointed bishop of Worcester. Nearby, in 962, Oswald founded a monastery at Westbury-on-Trym, and from there he later took the monks to found Ramsey, for which he had been given land in about 969. The introduction of monks to Worcester came later. Oswald became archbishop of York in 972, holding the two sees in plurality, and died in Worcester in 992.

This Life follows *SEL* closely and, as Görlach points out, comes from the PY MSS.[1] The source of the *SEL* Life is Eadmer's Life of Oswald.[2] There is no Life of Oswald in Caxton.

---

[1] See Görlach (1998), p. 106, Görlach (1974), pp. 146–7, and note to ll. 82–91 below.
[2] ed. Raine (1886), pp. 1–40.

Here endith the lyfe of Seynte Austyn and begynneth the
lyfe of Seynte Oswolde.

Seynt Oswolde the bisshop was bore in Ynglonde. Sir Odo, a fulle
worshipfulle man, was his vncle and he was cheffe of the kyngis
conseyle, the which kyng men callyd Athelston. He hadde grete
werre with the paynyms that tho were in this londe, and on a daye
there was a grete batell betwene the paynyms and the kyng, but bye 5
the help of oure lorde, the kyng had the better and slewe many one
of the paynyms and put theym to flyght, and in there fleyng the kyng
with his men slewe theym to the grownde. But at the laste the kyngis
swerde tobraste, and than his enemyes seyng that turnyd ayen, and
were therebye gretely comfortyd and made the kyng to flee bak. And 10
when this holye man Odo se the kyng flee, he sayde to hym: 'Sir
kyng, where is thye noble herte become? Drawe owte thye swerde.'
And than he lokyd and fownde anoþer swerde in his scabarde for the
swerde that he breke tofore. And when he se this he was fulle gladde
and drowe owte his swerde and turnyd ayen vpon his enmyes and 15
anone ouercame theym. And than the kyng thankyd God and this
holye man Odo.

And within a while after this the archiebisshop of Canterbury
dyed, and than this holye man Odo was made archiebisshop after
hym. And than this holy man Odo made Seynt Oswolde furste a 20
seculer chanon at Wylton and there he levyd a fulle chast lyve and
correctid his chanons that were vnder hym when thaye dyd amysse,
but thaye had hym in grete dyspyte and wold not be rewlyd after
hym because he was but yong and late come into the howse. And
when he se that he myght not rewle theym vertuoslye, he lefte that 25
howse and went to his vncle Odo that was archiebisshop of
Canterburye and tolde hym that he cowde not rewle his chanons
at Wylton, and therefore he wolde not take no more charge of
mennys sowlys, but he wolde be a religyous man in the howse of
Floryace in Fraunce where Seynt Benet lyeth, and forsake the worlde 30
and be a monke there. And when his vncle vnderstode this he
thankyd hertelye oure lorde and comfortyd Seynt Oswolde to
[fulfylle] hys holye purpose.

MSS A2LS   3 men] was S   callyd] *add* hym L   7 put theym] were put LS
13–14 the swerde] *om.* LS   14 he] the kyng S   31 vncle] *add* Odo S
32 oure lorde] allmy3ty god S   33 fulfylle] fylle A2

And when he came to the howse of Floryace the brethern
35 resseyuid hym with grete gladnesse for his holye levyng that thaye
had herde of hym. And there he contynued in fulle holye levyng,
that alle hys brethern had grete ioye of hym. But the wyckyd enmy
the feend had grete envye of his holye levyng, and oftentymes be
nyght he came to feer this holye man while he was in his orysons and
40 in holye meditacions, but anone he wolde blesse hym with the signe
of the crosse, and then he vanyshid fro hym crying and roryng. But
another tyme, when this holye man was in his prayers allone, the
f. 77ra feend came to hym in | the lykenes of an angelle and sayde that oure
lorde sende hym theder to bydde hym take sum reste and laboure not
45 his bodye so sore, for yf he take so grete laboure vpon hym he shulde
shorte his lyfe therebye, 'but oure lorde wolle that thue take lesse
laboure, that thue mayst contynewe the lenger in his seruyce.' And
he, merveylyng gretelye of this thyng, toke vppe his honde and
blessyd hym, and anone he vanyshyd awaye. And than he knewe that
50 it was his wyckyd enmye þe feend that came to dysseyve hym.

And anone after, this holye Seynt Oswolde came ayen into
Ynglonde to se his vncle Odo the archiebisshop of Canterburye,
but he was dede ar he came hider. And when he wyst it he made
grete sorowe and fylle down tofore his tumbe fulle sore wepyng, and
55 than he wente to his cousyn Oskatelle, that was the bisshop of
Dorchester, and dwellyd there long tyme with hym in grete hard-
nysse of levyng. And then yt fylle that the bisshop of Euerwyke
dyed, and Oskatelle was made bisshop there in his stede and wente to
Room to be sacryd of the pope, and he toke Seynt Oswolde with hym
60 theder. And when thaye had be there and had there entente of the
pope thaye returnyd homward ayen, but Seynt Oswolde abode stylle
in Fraunce where he was furst made monke, and there he con-
tynewed in holye levyng many yerys.

And that tyme was Seynt Dunstone abbot of Glastynburye, and
65 after Odo was dede he was chosyn archiebisshop of Canterburye.
And when he herde of þe holy levyng of Seynt Oswolde, he sente for
hym and desired to haue hym ayen into Ynglonde. And bye that
tyme he came hyder the bisshop of Worcester was dede, and then
Seynt Dunston and Oskatel made Seynt Oswolde bisshop there,
70 where he contynued in fulle holye levyng and rulydde his people so

35–7 thaye . . that] om. S   38 oftentymes] ofte LS   41 roryng] wryngyng
his hondis S   44 lorde] add god S   hym(2)] add that he LS   48 thyng] add
and A2L   48 he] the fynde S   49 than] add anon S   51 ayen] om. L
57 Euerwyke] add now ys callyd Yorke S   70 fulle] om. S

that alle men spake godenes of hym and thankyd oure lorde that euer
he came there. And than Seynt Dunstone, by helpe of Kyng Edgar,
that was a fulle gode kyng, and thurgh helpe of Pope Iohn, thaye
wente thurgh alle Ynglond and chargyd alle persons and vykers to
leve chaste from the synne of lechery or els to lese her churchis. And 75
for to se this werke fulfyllyd, Seynt Dunstone, Seynt Oswolde and
Seynt Athelwolde went thurgh alle this londe and putte oute suche
persons and vikers, and sett in holye men in there stedis that wolde
leve lyke a preste that shulde haue the cure of mannys sowle. And
theye toke awaye alle the godis of this wyckyd persons and vykers, 80
and with tho godis thaye byldyd here in Ynglond .xlviij. abbeys of
monkys and nunnys.

And þan Seynt Oswolde bylded the pryory of Worcester and sett
therein monkys where neuer was none affore. And thereof the
devylle had grete envye of the byldyng of that church, for in a 85
tyme as the werkemen wonde vp a grete stone for that werke of the
sayde churche, the devylle hylde downe so fast that stone that alle
the werkemen myght not remeove it, and thaye had grete mervayle
thereof what causid it to be so hevye. But anone after came this holye
man Oswolde and chasyd away the feende, and then a fewe men 90
myght wynde it vp anone.

And within a whyle dyed the bisshoppe of Euerwyke, and than the
kyng and Seynt Dunston made Seynt Oswolde bisshop of Euerwyke
and made hym to holde stylle the bisshopriche of Wurcester also.
But in a nyght, as this holye man and alle his monkys were at 95
Matyns, except one monke that wente to bath hym and lefte the
Matyns, and when he had do he wente and layde hym downe to slepe
in Seynt Oswoldis bedde. And anone the devylle came theder and
tormentyd hym fulle sore, that he cryed and made a grete noyse that
alle the monkis herd it and came theder anone and fownde hym in 100
Oswoldis bedde. And thaye askyd hym whye he made suche a noyse,
and he tolde theym that the devylle vexyd hym so sore because he
kepte not Matyns and because that he laye in Oswoldis bedde. And
then he repentyd hym, and the holye man forgaue hym that trespas
and chargid his monkys to be euer after at Matyns and other seruyce 105
in the churche.

77 oute] *add* alle S   79 preste] parson LS, *add* or vicare S   84 where] that
L, þat þere S   affore] *add* that tyme S   88 it] the seyde stoun S   90 man]
add seynt S   92 Euerwyke] *add* þat now ys callyd yorke   93 made] *om*. S
bisshop] archebischope S   of Euerwyke] there L   96 hym] hymselfe S
97 when] *om*. S   100, 103] in *add* seynt S   102 sore because] for LS
103 because] for LS   104 the . . . man] seynt oswald   105 chargid] *add* alle S
at] *add* hure S

f. 77rb   And another tyme as he came fro Euerwyk | to Wursester he
prechyd at the towne of Ramsey, and there came fro fer by water
monkys to hyre his sermon. And when thaye wente homward ayen in
110 a ship, sodenlye the shipp beganne to synke into the bottom of the
water. And then thaye callid for helpe to Seynt Benett and to Seynt
Oswolde, and anone Seynt Oswolde prayd to oure lorde for theym,
and anone the ship rose vp fulle of water, and the monkys were
sauyd by his prayer and beganne to lave oute the water that was in
115 the shypp, and soo came home to theyre howse in saftye and leuyd
[there]after more devoutly than euer thaye dyd before.

     And then Seynt Oswold came to Wurcester and levyd there a fulle
holye lyfe, and euery daye he refresshid .xij. poore men and wyssh
there fete and wypid theym fulle diligently. And anone after this
120 holye man beganne to wex feble for grete sekenes and anguyssh that
he suffryd daylye. And than he caste vppe his eyen to hevynwarde
and sate vp anone as though he had not be seke. And than his men
askyd hym whye he did so, and he sayde to theym: 'For nowe I se
my lorde Ihesu that wolle tomorowe sende after me,' and he prayd
125 theym alle to praye for hym to oure lorde. And at mydnyght he rose
vp to Matyns as other monkys dyd, and bye the morowe he
refresshyd and fedde his pore folkis lyke as he dyd when he was
hole and sayde the .xv. psalmys, and when he came to the laste
worde he cast vp his eyen to hevynward and se the fader, the sonne
130 and the holye goste. And so he passyd oute of þis worlde, and angels
of oure lorde were sene beryng his sowle to the blys of hevyn. And
than the monkys buryed his bodye there fulle worshipfully in the
church that he lete make, and afterward he was put in a fulle
wurshipfulle shryne there, where oure lorde shewith for his holy
135 bisshop many a grete myracle, wherefore his name be preysed worlde
withoute ende. Amen.

     Here endith the lyfe of Seynt Oswolde and begynneth the
     lyfe of Seynte Dunstone.

107 Euerwyk] Yorke S   108 fer] add contre S   110 the shypp] it L
111 And then] that L, And S   114 his] add holi S   116 thereafter] euer after A2
euer] om. S   124 after] for S   127 lyke . . . dyd] as he was wonte to do L
128 hole] in his heele S   132 fulle] om. S   133 church] add of Worcestre S

14 ST DUNSTAN

St Dunstan was born c. 909 near Glastonbury, where he was educated. Thanks to his uncle Athelm, archbishop of Canterbury, he was introduced to the court of King Athelstan, but was later expelled from the court and returned to Glastonbury. Dunstan was ordained priest with Ethelwold by the bishop of Winchester. He was made abbot of Glastonbury by King Edmund and served him and his brother Edred who succeeded him, but then fell out of favour with King Edwy, Edred's successor, and went into exile in the reformed monastery of St Peter's in Ghent. King Edgar seized the throne from his brother Edwy in 957, and Dunstan was recalled. He was made bishop of Worcester in 957, bishop of London in 959 and archbishop of Canterbury in 960. He died in 988.

The Life of St Dunstan follows the sequence of that in *SEL* 204–211, with two additional passages as noted below.[1]

---

[1] ll. 43, 121, and see also Görlach (1998) pp. 106–8.

Here endith the lyfe of Seynt Oswolde and begynneth the
lyfe of Seynte Dunstone.

Seynt Dunstone was of this realme of Ynglonde and oure lorde
shewyd myraclis for hym or euer he was bore, for vpon a
Candelmasse Daye, as alle folkys were in the churche with tapers
in there hondis, sodenlye alle there tapers wente oute at onys, and
thereof thaye had grete mervayle euerych one. And sodenlye as thaye 5
talkyd of this mervayle, Seynt Dunstonys moders taper was light
anone and brente fulle fayre bi the purvyaunce | of oure lorde. And A1 f. 53ʳᵃ
than al the peple tende þer tapyrs of hir tapre and thonkid God of
this gret myracle. And [than] was there an holy man that seid: 'This
childe that is in hir wombe shal light al Englonde with his holy 10
leuyng in tyme to come.'
Whan this holi childe Donston was bore in the yere of oure lorde
Ihesu .ix.C.xxv.ti, that tyme was kyng of this londe Athelston. And
Seint Donstons fader hight Herston and his moder Quendrede. Thei
sette ther son Donston to scole in the abbey of Glastynbury, where 15
he was aftir made abbot for his holy leuyng. And within a while aftir
he went to Ethelwolde his vncle, that [was] tho erchebishop of
Canturbury, and he was ful glad of his holi conuersacion, and he
brought hym anone to Kyng Athelston, and he made ful gret ioy of
hym also for his goode leuyng and made hym abbot of Glastynbury 20
by assent of Kyng Athelstone and of his brother Edmond. And there
he guydide ful wisely his monkes, that thei al drewe to holy leuyng
by his goode ensample. And that howse was made .iiij.C. and .iij. and
fifty yere or he of his moder was bore.
    And [Seint] Donstone and Seint Ethelwolde were bothe made 25
prestys in on day. And when he was made abbot of Glastynbury he
leuyd there a ful holy life. And when he was wery of preyng, he vsed
to werche goldesmyth werke with his hondes to sle therewith ydilnes.
And euer he yafe gret almes to pore folkes for Goddys sake. And in a
tyme as he sat atte his werke, his hert on Ihesu Crist, his mouthe 30
ocupyed with holy orisons and his hondes ocupied on goldesmythes

MSS A1A2LS   A1 begins at 7 of oure lorde   2 euer] om LS
3 folkys] peple S   4 hondis] add brennynge S   5 euerych one] om. S
6 light] tende LS   9 than] om. A1   12 whan] om. S   14 hight] was
callyd S   moder] add was callyd S   17 was] om. A1   tho] the A2L, ar S
19–20 of hym] om. A2S   20 also for] of S   23 howse] om. S
25 Seint] seind A1   26 he] seynt dunstan S   28 therewith] and put awey S
29 folkes] peple S

craft, the deuyl that had to hym grete enuye come to hym in the
euentyde as he was aboute to make a chalys, in the likenes of a fayre
woman with smylyng chere, and seid that she had gret thynges to
35 telle hym. And then he bade hir sey what she wolde, and anone she
bygan to telle hym many nyse tryffuls and no vertu was therin. And
than he supposid therby that she was a wikkid spirite, and anone he
toke hir bi the nose with a peyre of tonges brennyng hote, and the
deuyl bygan to rore and cry and fast drowe awey. But euer Seint
40 Donston hilde faste til it was fer within the nyght, and than he late
hir go. And therof she was ful glad that she was escaped oute of his
hondes and fled awey with gret cryyng and seid, that al peple myght
here: 'Alas, what shame hath þis carle to me do. Howe may I best
quytte hym ayene?' But neuer aftir she had no lust to tempte hym in
45 his smethy.

f. 53ʳᵇ   And than Kyng Ed|mond made Seint Donstone cheffe of his
conseil, and he yaffe hym ful goode conseil in al thinges to his lyves
ende. And than aftir Seint Edmond reyned his sonne Edwyne. And
anone aftir, Seint Donston and he fel atte striffe for his misgoydyng,
50 and Seint Donston rebuckid the kyng therfore, but none amendyng
was had but euer werse and wurse. [Wherefor] Seint Donston was
ful sory and dide the best he cowde to bring the kyng to
amendement, but it wolde not be in no wise, for within a while
aftir the kyng exiled Seint Donston oute of Englonde.
55   And than he seiled ouer the see and come to the abbey of Seint
Amande in Fraunce, and there he dwellyd long tyme in ful holy
lyvyng til Kyng Edwyne was dede. And then Kyng Edgar reyned
kyng aftir hym, a ful goode kyng. And than he sent aftir Seint
Donston to be of his conseil and receyued hym with gret reuerence
60 and delyuerd hym ayene his abbey of Glastynbury. And within a
while aftir dyed the bishop of Wursetter, and than Seint Donstone
was made byshop there aftir hym by the wil of King Edgar and Odo
erchebishop of Canturbury. And on that was there whiche was a holy
[man] seid that he shulde aftirwarde be byshop of Canturbury, and
65 so he was.
    And whan he had [long] be byshop of Wurcetter, then dyed the
bishop of London and also the bishop of Wynchester. And than
Kyng Edgar and Odo made Seint Donston byshop bothe of

44 neuer] euer A2   45 smethy] add werke S   49 misgoydyng] misdoyng S
51 was(1)] add made to be S   Wherefor] where A1   58 kyng(1)] om. LS   than]
om. S   64 man] om. A1   66 whan] om. S   long] om. A1   byshop] add
of A1   67 also] om. S   68 Odo] add archebischope of caunturbery S

London and of Wynchester. And within a while after died Odo
erchebishop of Canturbury, and than Kyng [Edgar] lete make 70
Donstone erchebishop there, and wel and wisely he goydide þis
londe to the plesyng of God, so that gret ioye and myrthe was that
tyme thorugh al Englonde. And euery man preysed gretly Seint
Donstone for his goode rule and goydyng. And than he bade euery
person to chese either to kepe goode life and chastite or else to lese 75
his personage. Thus Seint Donston, Seint Ethelwolde and Seint
Oswolde went thurgh al Englonde to se the rule of persons, and ⌜they
þat⌝ were not of goode leuyng thei put them oute of þer personages
and toke al ther goodes fro them and put in ther stede the moste holy
men þat wolde entende the wele of mannys soule and leuyd aftir the 80
plesure of God. And of the goodes that thei toke of the wickid
persons þei bylde here in Englonde .xlviij. abbeys of monkys and of
nonnys, as it is afore seid [in the lyfe of Seint Oswolde].

In a tyme as Seint Donston was atte Wynchester, there these
wickyd persons gate them frendship of serteyn lordis of this londe 85
and pledide gretly ayenst Seynt Donston, and they seid | to hym it f. 53ᵛᵃ
was her right to haue ther personages ayen that he had putte hem
oute of ayenst right and conscience. And than the rode spake, that al
men herde, and seid: 'Donston hath the right, and therfore trouble
hym no more for that mater.' But thei wolde not leue ther wickidnes 90
therby, but thei made anoþer gret day ayenst Seint Donstone in the
towne of Calne, and there thei thought verily to haue ther entent of
hym by lordiship, or else they wolde sle hym. And this gret day was
holde in a feyre chambre in the seid towne, and whan thei were in ful
purpose to do this cursid dede, sodenly euery pece of tymbre of the 95
house slode fro other, and there al his aduersaries were slayne or
hurte, that none escaped but Seint Donstone alone. And aftir that
[tyme] ther was no wickid person that wolde trouble hym no more.

Aftir that in a tyme as Seint [Donston] sat atte a prynces table he
see his fader and his moder aboue in the ioy of heuene. Than he 100
thonkid oure lorde of his gret goodenes that he wolde shewe to hym
that blessid sight. Anothir tyme as he lay abedde he se the brightnes

70 Edgar] Edgad *corr. in margin* A1   71 there] of Caunturbery S   and] *add* fulle
A2LS   73 Englonde] thys londe L   gretly] welle S   75 person] *add* and
vicarye A2, and vicare S   to . . . either] *om.* S   76 personage] beneficis S
77 persons] *add* and vikers A2S   77–8 they that] that they *corr. in margin* A1
78 leuyng] life and levyd not chaste S   personages] *add* and vicaraigis A2S
81 of(2)] with A2LS   82 persons] prestis S   83 in . . . Oswolde] *om.* A1L
85 wickyd] *om.* S   persons] *add* and vykers A2   88 than] *om.* S   89 the]
don S   94 feyre] grete S   seid] same L   96 house] chambre S
98 tyme] *om.* A1   99 Donston] Donstons A1

of heuene and angels syngyng that mery songe, *Kyrie rex splendens*
&c., the whiche was to hym a ful gret comforte that he myght see
105 suche gloriouse sightis here in this wrecchid worlde.

And he [loued] ful wel to harpe, and gret konnyng he had theryn,
but euer when he harpid his mynde was in heuene. In a tyme as he
harpid tofore diner he left of and went to mete, and he hynge vp his
harpe on the walle on an hoke. And when he was in myddys of his
110 dyner his mynde was al set in the ioyes of heuene and sodenly the
harpe sownyd a ful mery antyme that begynneth this: *Gaudent in celis*
anime sanctorum &c., in the whiche melody this holy man had ful
gret ioye, and al peple also þat herde it.

He was ful meche byholde to oure lorde that he wolde shewe to
115 hym suche heuenly comforte. And than within a while after he
waxyd feble and sike, and vpon Holy Thursday he sende for al his
men and askid them foryeuenes, and also he forgafe them ther
trespas that thei had offendide to hym, and assoylyd them of al ther
synnes. And the .iij.de day he passid to oure lorde ful of vertews
120 the yere of oure lorde .ix.C. .iiij. score and .viij. And his soule was
brought to heuene blisse with ful mery song of angels. And his
body lithe atte Canturbury in a ful worshipful shryne, where oure
lorde shewde for his holy seruant many a gret myracle, wherefore
f. 53ᵛᵇ his | name be preysed worlde withoute ende. Amen.

125   Here endith the life of Seint Dunstone and next bygynneth
the life of Seint Aldelme.

---

106 loued] loue A1   ful] *om* S   111 ful] *om.* L   114 ful] *om.* S
119 day] *add* aftyr LS

15 ST ALDHELM

St Aldhelm was born c. 639. He was related to the West Saxon king Ine. Educated first at Malmesbury and afterwards at Canterbury, he became abbot of Malmesbury in about 675 and bishop of Sherborne in 705. Aldhelm wrote letters, poems, a treatise on virginity and another on poetic metre. Only his (highly elaborate) Latin works survive. William of Malmesbury, writing in the twelfth century, claimed that an abbey copy of the Old and New Testaments was that bought by Aldhelm from sailors near Dover when he was visiting Canterbury to be consecrated bishop by Brightwold.[1] According to William, the altar and chasuble brought by Aldhelm from Rome were also still in Malmesbury.[2] Egwin of Worcester conducted Aldhelm's funeral at Malmesbury in 709.

This Life of Aldhelm closely follows that in *SEL* 211–214.

---

[1] William of Malmesbury, *De Gestis Pontificum Anglorum*, ed. Hamilton, *RS* 52 (1870), p. 365.
[2] *ibid.*, p. 376.

Here endith the life of Seint Donstone, and next begynneth the life of Seint Aldelme.

Seint Aldelme the confessor was bore in Englonde. His fader hyght
Kenton, he was the kynges brother of this londe that was clepid Ive,
and when the king was dede this Kenton was made kyng aftir hym.
And than this holy childe Aldelme was sette to scole in the howse of
Malmysbury where he was made aftirwarde abbot, and than he dide 5
there gret coste in bildyng and dide there make a ful rial abbey. And
when the pope herde of his gret holynes he sent for hym to come to
Rome. And than the pope made ful muche of hym atte his comyng,
and long tyme he dwellid there with the pope, and gette ful gret
priueleges to the howse of Malmysbury that no bishop of Englond 10
shulde haue ado there nor the kyng neyther to lette them of ther fre
eleccion, but for to chese ther abbot amongis themself. And when he
had gete al these preuelages of the pope he was ful glad and ioyful,
and he leued there many yere in ful holy leuyng.
    And than in a day as he seid messe in the churche of Seint Iohn 15
Latrans, when the masse was done ther wolde no man take his
vestyment fro hym. And than he se the sonnebeme shyne in at an
hole in the glas wyndowe, and he hyng his chesiple theron that al
men myght se this gret miracle. And the same chesiple is yet atte
Malmysbury, the couloure therof is purpul. 20
    And within a while aftir he come into Englonde ayen and brought
with hym ful gret pryueleges vnder the popis seal of ledde, and whan
he come to the kynge Yve and to Athelrede thei confermyd al that
the pope had grauntede to his howse of Malmysbury. This was the
yere of oure lorde .vij.C. and .vj. 25
    And than ther was a gret variaunce among the bishops of this
londe for the holdyng of Ester Day. But he made a boke that al men
shulde knowe for euer when Ester Day shal be, the whiche boke is
yet atte Malmysbury, and this abbey he foundyd in the worship of
oure lady. And Brightwolde, that was than erchebishop of Cantur- 30
bury, herde of Aldelmes holy lyvyng and sent for hym to be his
conseylour, and there thei leued togider many a day in ful holy life,
and ful ioyful were eyther of othir.

MSS A1A2L   1 Aldelme] Aldelyne L *throughout*   16 Latrans] *add* And
A1L   23 thei] þat L   24 was] *add* aboute A2L

And on a day as they were on the seesyde by Douer, ther seyled a
f. 54ʳᵃ ship with marchandise | not fer fro the londe, and than Seint
36 Aldelme clepid to them to wete if thei had ony ornament that
longith to holy Churche within the ship for to selle. But the
marchauntys had skorne of hym and thought he was not of power
to bye suche thynges as thei had, and so departide fro this holy man.
40 But anone ther fil on ⌐þem⌐ so gret tempest that thei were in poynte
to be lost. And than on of them seid: 'We suffre this gret trouble for
we toke in skorne the wordes of the holy man, and therfore late us al
desire hym to prey for us to oure lorde.' And than thei dide so, and
anone the tempest [sessid]. And than thei come to this holy man and
45 brought hym a feyre bible, the whiche is yet atte Malmysbury to thys
daye.

   And he was made bishop .iiij. yere byfore he dyed by Brightwolde
erchebishop of Canturbury and by Seint ⌐Egwyne⌐ byshop of
Wurcetter, and by them he was ful worshipfully brought on erthe.
50 And yet the bishop ⌐Egwyne⌐ come thyder fedyrd with cheynys of
iron fast lockid, and fro thens he went so to the pope of Rome,
whiche was to hym a ful gret peyne, God quytte his mede. And Seint
Aldelme or he dyed cursid al them that dide eny wrong to his seid
abbey of Malmysbery in brekyng of eny of ther pryueleges, and thei
55 that holpe that howse shulde haue Goddes blessyng and his. And
many days thereaftir he was translatide and put in a ful worshipful
schyryne, where oure lorde shewith dayly many a gret myracle for
his holy confessor Seint Aldelme, wherefore oure lorde be preysed
worlde withoute ende. Amen.

60   Here endith the life of Seint Aldelme the confessour and
next folowith the lyfe of Seynt Theophile.

40 þem] hym *del. and corr. in margin to* þem Al   44 sessid] *om* A1
48 Egwyne] Edwyne *corr. in margin* A1, Edwyne A2, Edwyne *corr.*L   50 Egwyne]
Edwyne *corr. in margin* A1, Edwine *SEL*

16 ST THEOPHILE

This 'Life' is part of a collection of Miracles of Our Lady which circulated widely in the Middle Ages and frequently included the miracles recounted here of St Theophile.[1]

The text follows that in *SEL* 221–238, but has omissions, curtailments and some differences of emphasis and additions. Görlach thinks it likely that it supplements *SEL* from an unknown source.[2]

---

[1] See Tryon (1923), Southern (1958) and Boyd (1965).
[2] Görlach (1998), pp. 109–110.

Here endith the life of Seint Aldelme the confessour and
next folowith the lyfe of Seint Theophile.

Seint Theophile was a gret clerke and was chosyn to be a bishop [by
al the peple], but he wolde not take it vpon him, for he seid he lackid
konnyng to haue the office of a bishop. And than the peple herde this
and chose anothir man to be ther byshop, whiche man hatid gretly
this clerk Theophile and putte hym awey oute of the mynster and   5
toke al his goodes fro hym. And he was brought into gret pouerte
and shame whiche byfore was a riche man and yafe muche goode in
almes to pore folkys for oure lordes loue. And when al his goode
were gon he was sore ashamed, that he durst not come among the
peple like as he was vsed to | do.   f. 54rb
    And as he went this mornyng by hymself alone, ther come a Iewe   11
to hym and askid hym whi he mornyd so. And than Theophile tolde
to the Iewe al his sorowe and pouerte. And than the Iewe seid: 'If
thou wilte be ruled aftir me I shal brynge the to a maystir that wole
make the richer than euer thou were.' And he seid he wolde do aftir 15
his conseil in al wise. And than he brought hym to the deuyl and
chargid hym that he shulde neuer make the signe of the crosse byfore
hym. And than the deuyl askid hym if he wolde be his seruaunt. And
he seid: 'Ye.' Than seid the deuyl: 'Thou must forsake thi beleue and
thy cristyndome, and thou must forsake God þat made the, and his   20
moder and al his seintis.' And than Theophile seid: 'I forsake al that
thou biddyst me and fully bytake me to þe.' And yet the deuyl seid:
'Thou muste make me a chartour of this couenandys with thyn owne
honde and seale hit with thi sele.' And than Theophile grauntid
therto. And than the deuel bare this charter with hym to helle and   25
lockid it ful fast in the depe pitte of helle, and than he thought that it
was siker ynowe to him and bade Theophile go home to his howse,
and there he shulde fynde golde and richesse withoute nombre.

MSS A1A2L   The A1 text breaks off at l. 119 **many othir Iewes** and the
missing passage, here reproduced from L ff. 226ra–227va, would have filled two folios of
A1. Görlach (1998), pp. 84–5, calculates that only one folio is missing from Al, with the
omission of one miracle, corresponding to *SEL* 45b. About 140 lines are missing from A1,
and the missing text would approximate more nearly to *SEL* 45c. The A1 text resumes
on f. 55ra at l. 270 **sorowe that ye.** The text of A2 contains only the Life, not the
Miracles, and ends at l. 93, **laste day of May,** after which follows the Life of Swithun.
Rubric Theophile] *add* the clerke L   1–2 by . . . peple] *om.* A1   5 the] þat
LA2   11 this] thus L, in the A2   28 richesse] *add* inow L

And whan he come theder he founde there riches in euery corner
30 of his howse, and than he bygan to pay his dettis and was a gretter
rewler than euer he was byfore. And hereof had al the peple gret
merueil, for he that was so pore a litel byfore howe he myght be so
sodenly riche. And than the bishop that had do Theophile so gret
wrong byfore sende for hym and cried hym mercy and delyuerid to
35 hym ayene al the goodes that he had take fro hym. And within a
while aftir the Iewe that brought Theophile to the fende was apechid
of hie treson, and the iugement geve that he shulde be hongid drawe
and quarterd and aftir brent, and so it was done, and so his mayster
that he serued quitte hym his mede. And so he doth atte ⌐laste to al⌐
40 that contynue in his seruyse, for euerlastyng peyne and deth is his
rewarde. And than Theophile vnderstode hymself that he was
brought in so gret myschefe, and þan he knewe by the Iewe howe
he shulde be serued aftir by his mayster the deuyl, and wiste wel
than that he shulde be dampned if he dyed in thys gret myschef.

45 And than he put hym al in the mercy of oure blessid lady and
f. 54ᵛᵃ wepte ful bittirly and made ful gret | mornyng for that cursid dede,
that he had so forsake oure lorde, oure lady and al his seintis. But
anone he went into a chapel of oure ladi, and there he fil downe
byfore an ymage of [hyr] and wepte and moornyd ful sore many a
50 day and many a nyght in ful gret abstynence, and cryed euer with
gret sobbyng to oure lady in that chapel .xl.ti days and .xl.ti nyghtis.

And atte laste oure lady had pety of him and she aperyd to hym
and seid: 'þu wrecchid man, howe durst thou desire me to prey for
the, that haste so forsake my sonne thy maker and bytake the fully to
55 the deuyl of helle.' And then he seid to oure lady with a ful peteous
cryyng: 'Nowe goode lady, helpe me atte my moste grettest nede,
and I shal be thy seruaunt in this chapel to my lyves ende and neuer
go oute til I dye.' And than oure blessid lady knelyd for hym to hir
sonne to haue foryeuenes for this wrechyd man Theophile. And than
60 oure lorde seid: 'Moder, I wole not denye hym that ye prey fore, do
with hym as it plesith you, for youre wil is my wil.' And than oure
lady come ayen to Theophile and bade hym be of goode chere, for
his synnes byn foryeuene hym, 'and therfore synne no more.' And
than Theophile with gret reuerence thonkid oure blessid ladi of hir
65 gret goodenes and blessid the tyme that euer she was bore, but he

37 hie] his L   39 laste to al] atte laste tha *with* atte *corr. to* the *and* tha *corr. to* al *in
margin* A1   al] *add* tho A2   47 had] *add* doo L   49 hyr] oure lady A1
56 moste . . . nede] nede and moste fere L

seid to hir al his sorowe was that he had not his chartour, for he
cowde neuer be mery til that he had it ayene, 'wherfore, blessid lady,
shewe thy goodnes so that I may haue it, for I beleue verily that what
thyng ye desire of oure lorde it is not denyed you. Therfore, blessid
lady, thynke on me.' And anone she vanyshed awey fro hym. And 70
than Theophile went ayen for to prey into the chapel of oure lady.
And the .iij.de day oure lady come and brought his charter and put it
in his honde while he slept, and than she vanyshed awey. And when
he woke he had his charter in his honde and was fulfilled with gret
ioy. And this graciouse dede was done to Theophile in a Satirday 75
nyght in Lent.

And the morowe aftir, that was the Sonday, aftir the gospel
Theophile come to the bishop and fil downe atte his feete and
tolde hym al howe the deuel had deceyued hym, and howe the deuel
had a charter of suche couenandys as he made with hym. And there 80
he shewde the same charter to the bishop, and he rad it byfore al the
peple, and than the peple wept for ioy and wolde haue kept the
charter for a [gret] myracle. But Theophile seid he myght | neuer be f. 54vb
sure til the charter were brent. And than the bishop lete brenne the
charter in a [gret] fire, and than was Theophile fulfilled with gret 85
ioye and his face semed to the peple as bright as the sonnebemme,
that thei had no power to byholde the brightenes therof. And than he
yaue al his goodes to the pore peple and swore a gret othe byfore al
the peple that he wolde neuer go oute of the chapel while he leuyd.
And anone aftir, God visited hym with so gret sikenes that he dyed 90
the .iij.de day aftir, and angels bere his soule to the blisse of heuene.
And his Day is halowed in [holy] Churche aboute þe·laste day of
May.

A Iews sonne sumtyme in Bretroyn vsed to pley [oft] tymes with
cristen yong men, and in an Ester Day they went to churche to 95
receyue the blessid sacrament. And when thei were howselyd, the
Iewe receyued the sacrament also like as thei ⌐dide⌐. And ther was an
ymage of oure lady that this Iewe had gret desire to biholde and
alwey his mynde was on hir while he was in the churche. And when
messe was done he went home to his faders howse, and than his fader 100
was glad that he was come home, for he had sought aftir hym. And
than he askid hym where he had be, and he seid: 'Atte churche with

71 for . . . prey] to his prayers A2, to prayer L   83 gret] gre A1   85 gret]
om. A1   92 holy] the A1   94 Bretroyn] Brytaigne L   oft] ought A1
95 yong] *add* children and L   Day] *add* as A1L   97 dide] seid *corr. in margin* A1

cristen men.' And when his fader wiste this he was madde for angre,
and hette his ovyn fire hote and cast his sonne theryn and stoppid
105 fast the ovyn mouthe, wenyng to brenne hym anone. But by the
purviaunce of oure blessid lady he was kepte vnhurte. And when the
Iewe is wife wiste that hir sonne was put into the ovyn, she went into
the towne and cryed and seid alas, hir husbonde had brent hir son in
his ovyn for that he was in the cristen mennys churche. And when
110 the cristen peple come to the ovyn, thei openyd it and founde the
yong man sittyng in the myddes of the ovyn and a fayre kerchyr
lyyng vpon the yong mannys hede that koueryd al his body. And so
by the purviaunce of oure blessid lady he was kepte harmeles. And
than the cristen peple toke þe Iewes fader and cast hym into the same
115 ovyn there [he] put his sonne, and anone he was al brent to pouder.
And than the cristen peple askyd the yong Iewe who had kepte [hym
so] harmeles in the ovyn, and he seid: 'That fayre woman that sat an
hye in the churche.' And than the Iewe and his moder, with many
L. f. 226ra othir Iewes, | were cristened thorough thys myracle and levyd aftyr a
120 fulle holy lyfe to þer lyves ende.

There was sumtyme a wyckid knyght that was a mansleer and a
robber by the hyewey and had many men with hym of the same
condicion, that robbid alle folkys that passyd by the castelle where
thys wyckid knyght dwellyd and toke there goodys fro them. In a
125 tyme it happyd that .ij. frioures come by þe castell where thys
wyckid knyght dwellyd, and anoon his men toke and wolde haue
robbyd them, but they cryed on them that they wolde brynge them
to ther lord. And so at the laste thorugh greet preyer they brought
them to hym, there hondys bownd byhynde hem, and when ther lord
130 sye them he bad serve them lyke as þey haue doon other. But they
spake so pitevously to hym that he yafe them lysens to passe fro them
f. 226rb harmeles. | And than the fryouris thankyd hym, and oon of them
desyred to preche byfore the knyght or he wente thens, and that alle
his men myght be þere to here his sermon. And then þe knyʒt
135 comaundyd that alle his men schulde be there. And then the fryour
stode in the myddys of them and bygonne hys sermon, but he seyde
to the knyght that there lakkyd oon of hys men. And then his felowes
wente and brouʒt hym thedyr, but he was fulle lothe þerto, for when
he come bifore þe fryoure he begon to tremble and quake. And than
140 the fryour coniurid hym in þe name of Ihesu Crist that he schulde
telle afore them alle what he was, and þan he confessyd byfore them

115 he] om. A1   116–17 hym so] trsp. A1

alle that he was a devylle of helle, 'and þis .xiiij. yeere I haue servyd
thys knyght and ever steryd hym to do these cursid dedys, and ever I
haue weytyd on hym bothe day and nyght for to strangle hym, but I
cowde not in no wyse, for he vsyd to sey every day .v. *Aue Maries* in 145
the worschip of the .v. ioies of our lady. And therfor I myght not
haue myn entente of hym, but and he had forgete it oone day I wolde
haue slayn hym anoon.' Tho seyd the fryour to them alle: 'Nowe ye
may se and knowe what a schrewed felowe ye haue had.' And than
the fryour chargid þe devil never aftyr to come there, and anoon he 150
vanysschid awey. And than þe knyȝt and alle his men toke greet
repentaunce and were schreven of the fryour, and aftyr that become
goode men and levid so to there lyves eende.

   Ther was sumtyme a riche knyȝt that honowrid greetly every feste
of owre lady þorugh the yeer in greet solempnyte, and fed | at every f. 226ᵛᵃ
feest moche pore peple in the worschip of owre lady. But it fylle in 156
schorte tyme that he come to greet pouerte, and than he was fulle
hevy that he myght not do as he dyd tofore. And in a feeste of oure
lady, when he hadde noo goode to fede the pore peple as he had do
byfore, than for schame he wente owte of hys place to a wodis syde 160
and walkyd there aloone in greet hevynes. Sodenly the devylle
apered to hym in the lickenes of a man and askid hym why he
wente so þere aloone. And than the knyght seid: 'Schame and
pouerte causith me thus to do, þat I dar not abyde at my place.'
And than þe devylle seide to hym: 'Yf thowe wylte promyse me to 165
brynge thy wijf hedir at a certeyn day, I schalle make the richer than
ever thow were.' And anoon the knyght grantyd thereto. And than
the devylle bade hym go home, for he schulde fynde goodis wiþowte
nombre at hys comynge home.

   He wente home and found every corner of his howse fulle of 170
goodys, and than he was fulfylled with greet gladnes, and so levyd in
greet prosperite alle that yeere that alle folkys had greet wonder that
he was so sodenly riche that was so pore a litle before. And than
when the tyme come that he must come to that place to mete wyth
the devylle and brynge his wyfe with hym, lyke as he had promysed 175
byfore, anoon he badde his wyfe make hyr redy for sche muste ride
with hym a litle wey thens. þan sche made hyr redy, but sche knewe
nothynge wheder sche schulde ride, but sche was a ful goode
womman and served fulle wele owre | blessyd lady euery day, therfor f. 226ᵛᵇ
who that servith hyr devoutely schalle not lese ther mede. 180
   Than sche was sette behynde her husbonde and reden forthe a

grete pace tylle they come to a chapel of oure lady. And than sche
praied her husbond that sche myght light downe and go into that
chapel to sey her prayers. Sche dyd so, and anoon sche fil aslepe, and
185 than owre blessyd ladye come owte of the chapel in lickenes of his
owne wyfe and sete vp behynd hym, he wenynge verely þat sche was
his owne wyfe, and so rede forthe to the place asigned. And anoon he
met with the devil and seide to hym: 'I thonke þe for the greet
goodnes that thow hast schewed me this yeere, wherefor I haue
190 brought the here my wyfe lyke as I haue promysid the.' And than the
devylle seide to hym: 'False knyght, þou lyest, for thow hast brought
with the Mary that is my most foo in stede of thy wyfe.' And when
the knyght herde this he was gretely aferde and wist not what to
answere. Than oure blessyd lady seide: 'Why woldyst thowe haue
195 this knyghtis wyfe?' And he seide: 'For I haue envy at hir goode
levynge, and nowe I had purposyd to distroye her that sche schuld
no more serve the, but thowe art ever my most foo.' And þan owre
lady comaundid the feende that he schulde go there as he schulde
never noye nor hurte more this knyght nor his wyfe. And then oure
200 lady bad the knyght that he schuld do penaunce for the greet offense
that he had doo to hir son and to hyr, and when he come home that
he schulde dele alle the goodys that he had of the deville to pore
f. 227ra men, and owre lorde schulde | sende hym sufficient goodis to lyve by
tyl his lyvis ende, and bad the knyght go to the chapel and take hys
205 wife with hym home and thanke her of there delyveraunce, and than
owre lady vanysschid awey fro hym. Then he rode to the chapel and
fonde his wyfe aslepe and toke her home with hym, and sche cowde
telle hir husbonde al that was befalle hym, and than they rode home
ayeen. And he cried God mercy of his greete offense and was
210 confessid of his greete trespas and dyd greet penauunce therefor,
and aftyr levyd a fulle holy lijf to his lyves ende. And owre lorde sent
them goodys inowh to lyve with, and [they] gave largely to the pore
for Goddis love, and passid owt of this wrecchyd lijf to the blysse of
heven. Amen.

215   There was sumtyme a worschipful knyght that forsoke the worlde
and went into a religious howse to be a brother there, but he had ful
lytle kunnyng. And than his bretheren dyd theyr laboure to teche
hym his *Pater Noster,* but for al that they cowde do they cowde teche
hym never more than these .ij. wordis *Aue Maria,* but they were ful
220 hevy that they myght teche hym no more, and when they se it wolde

212 they] *om.* L

noon otherwyse be, than they bad hym sey these .ij. wordys *Aue*
Maria euery day in the worschip of owre blessyd lady with þe best
devocyon. And so he dyd ever aftir to hys lyves ende. And when he
was dede, owt of his grave there spronge a feyre lyly ful of white
leves, and in every lefe was wreten with lettres of golde tho .ij.   225
wordis *Aue Maria*. And than al the peple had greet merveile of thys
sight and diggid in the grave and fownde the lely spryngynge owt of
his mowth. | And than alle the peple thankid oure blessyd lady of this   f. 227rb
greet myracle and ever aftyr had more devosion to serve hir to theyr
lyves ende.   230

   There was sumtyme in Inglond a knyght that had a childe by his
wyf, and sche toke hym with hir to chirche. And whan this childe
was there he lokid fast on the rode, and than he askid his modir:
'What man that is that so hangith on the crosse?' 'Sone,' seide his
modyr, 'this ys owre lord Ihesu Crist, that suffrid this bytter dethe   235
for alle mankynde, to brynge that were dampned world withowt ende
by theyr cursyd synne to the blysse of hevene by his peynfulle
passion.' Than seide the childe: 'What feyre womman is that that
stondith by him so sorowefully?' Sche seide: 'It is owre lady of
heven, hys blessyd modyr.' Than the child seide: 'Modyr, stode sche   240
thus by hym when he was slayn?' And his modyr seid: 'Ye, forsoth.'
Than seide the childe: 'This was greet sorowe and hevynesse to her
herte.' And than his modyr was right glad of hym and bad hym serve
wele oure lorde Ihesu and his blessyd modyr, and then he schulde
come to heven after this wrecchid lyfe. Then seide the childe to his   245
modyr: 'Else were I to vnkynde but I wolde love hym that hath
schewyd so moche love to me.' And euer after this child had his
mynde on owre lorde, and he servid hym fulle wele, for ever his
thought was on hym and the sorowe that his blessid modir Mary had
whan sche stode and se hir sone so slayne. This wolde never owt of   250
his mynde while he levid.

   Aftirwarde it fille that this childe dydde | a deedly synne, wherefor   f. 227va
he was in greet sorowe and wente to a fryour and was confessyd and
dydde greet penaunce for that cursyd dede, and euer when he met
the fryour he prayed hym to pray for hym. And also he prayed owre   255
lady to haue mercy on hym for the greet sorowe that sche hadde for
hir sone, to se hym suffre so bittir dethe on the crosse. And ever aftir
he was ful of greet sorowe to hys lyves ende for that synne.

   And than he wente to scole at Oxford, and there he dyed within
schort tyme after. And .ij. clerkys kepte hys body alle nyght, and oon   260

seyde to þe todyr: 'It is tyme to lyght hys tapyrs.' But the oon of hem
seyde: 'Lete vs abyde tylle the prestys come to fecche hym to
chyrche.' And than they bothe consentyd thereto, and anoon
sodeynly they fyl on slepe and se how angels bere the sowle of the
265 deed body to heuene. And owre blessyd lady wente byfore to guyde
hym the wey, and so sche brought hym before owre lorde. And than
sche knelyd downe byfore hym and seide: 'Here is my servaunt, that
hath wele servid the and me.' [Owre lorde seide:] 'Modyr, my wylle
is yowre wille, therfor doyth with hym as it plesith yowe, for he euer
A1 f. 55ra hath hadde grete pyte of yowre | sorowe that ye, moder, had when I
271 was hongyd on the crosse.' And then he was receyued and put among
the chosyn seruauntes of oure lorde. And oure blessid lady sent light
fro heuene to light the tapurs that stode aboute the dede bodi. And
the .ij. clerkys that slept by the dede body se this gloriouse sight in
275 ther slepe and the lightyng of the tapurs also, [that were light fro
heuene] by the purviaunce of oure lady. And than come the prestes
and beryed this body worshipfully, and the clerkys that wecchid with
the dede body al nyght tolde the prestis al that thei seyn in ther
slepe. And than al the peple glorified oure lady for this gret myracle
280 that she shewith for this yong man.

Upon Oure Ladi Dai in heruest, as an erchebyshop song his masse
in the towne of Tolewse, at the sacryng of the masse was herde a
voyce fro heuene that seid these wordes: 'Alas, the wickid Iewis,
howe thei put my sonne dayly on the crosse amongis them.' And as
285 sone as the masse was done the erchebishop with al the peple went
vnto a certeyn strete of þe towne where the Iewis dwellid and sought
al aboute, and atte laste there thei founde in a wickid Iewis howse an
ymage of oure lorde dispitously nayled and bete vpon the rode
hongyng with his .v. woundes bledyng. And than oure blessid lady
290 aperyd to the seid erchebishop and tolde hym that 'this the wickyd
Iewys dismembre my sonne ofte tyme, and therfore do thi power to
put them oute of this londe [and this londe] shal do wel and be in
gret prosperite, and thou shalt haue heuene blisse for thi labour.'

Here endith the life of Seint Theophile and next bygyn-
295   neth the life of Seint Swythen.

268 Owre . . . seide] om. L, oure Louerd aȝen sede SEL   270 ye] add my L
275–6 that were light/fro heuene] trsp. A1   292 and . . . londe] om A1

17 ST SWITHUN

St Swithun died in 862, and if, as this Life says, he was born during King Egbert's reign, he was born after 802. He became bishop of Winchester in 852 and was well known for his church-repairing and church-building. His remains were translated from his burial place outside the church to a shrine inside on 15 July 971, and into the new cathedral in 1093.

This Life of Swithun follows the wording and sequence of the *SEL* Life (274–9), with some omissions and two misreadings as recorded in the notes.

Here endith the life of Seint Theophile and next begynneth the life of Seint Swythen.

Seynt Swithen the holy confessour was bore bysides Wynchester in
the tyme of [Kyng] Egbert. He was the .viij. kynge aftir Kenulf, þat
Seint Beryne cristened, for Seint Austyn cristened not al Inglonde in
Kyng Athelbrightis days, but Seint Beryn dide cristen the west parte
of Inglonde in the foreseid Kyng Kenulf is days.   5
    And than this holy Seint Swythen seruyd oure lorde in ful gret
deuocion, so that al the peple had gret ioy of his holynes, and
Elmeston that was tho bishop of Wyncester made him preste. And
than he leued a ful streyte life and bycome a ful holy man, so that
Kyng Egbert made hym his chaunceler and chefe of his conseil. And   10
than the kyng Egbert put his sonne and his heyre, that hight |
Ethulfe, into his guydyng and preid hym to take goode heede to hym   f. 55rb
so that he were brought [vp] vertuously. And within a while aftir his
fader died, and than Ethulfe his sonne was made kyng aftir hym.
And he guydide this londe ful wel, that it encresed gretly in goode   15
leuyng by the counseil of Seint Swythen.
    And when Elmeston the bishop of Wynchester was dede, Seint
Swythen was made bishop there aftir hym, wherefore al the peple
were ful glad. And he by his holy levyng causid þe peple to do ther
tythyng trewly to God and to holy Churche. And where that eny   20
churche fil in decay Seint Swythen wolde amende it anone, and if
ther were eny churche to be halowid he wolde go thedyr on fote, for
he loued neuer pride nor rydyng on gay horse nor preysyng ne
flateryng of the peple. But nowe suche veyne thyngis beth gretly
byloued among hie estatis bothe spirituel and temporal.   25
    Seint Swythen goydyd ful wel his bishopriche, and ful wel he
amendide the towne of Wynchester in his days, for he made the gret
bridge of stone withoute the west yate of the towne. In a tyme ther
come a woman ouer the bridge with hir lap ful of eggis, and a
recheles felowe toke this woman and wrestelyd with hir and he breke   30
ther al hir egges, wherfore the pore woman bygan to wepe and cry
piteously for the losse of hir eggis. And than it happyd that this holy
bishop come by that same tyme and bade the woman lete hym se hir

eggis. And anone he lifte up his honde and blessid the egges and thei
35 were made holle and sownde euerychone. And than this woman was
fulfilled with gladnes, and she thonkid this holy man for this gret
goodenes and myracle that he had done for hir.

And then anone aftir dyed Kyng Ethulfe, and then his sonne
Egbert was kyng aftir him. And then was Athelbert made kyng aftir
40 hym. And in the .iij.de yere of this kyng dyed Seint Swythyn, and he
charged hys men to bery hym in the churcheyerde for cause the
peple shulde sette but litle prise by hym, for he loued no pride in his
lyfe. And he passid to oure lorde in the yere of oure lorde .viij.C. and
.vj., and he lay there in that churcheyerde or he was translatide [an]
45 hundred and nyne yere and odde days. But in the goode kyng Edgar
is days this holy seint Seint Swythyn was put in a ful worshipful
shiryne in the towne of Wyncester by Ethelwolde and Seint
f. 55ᵛᵃ Donstone, and in the same yere was Seint Edwarde the | martyr
shyryned atte Schaftysbury.

50 These holy bishops Ethelwolde and Donstone were warned by a
vision that thei shulde se these .ij. holy seintes Edward and Swithen
put in worshipful [schrynes], and so thei dide with ful gret deuocion.
And in like wise an holy man come to Ethelwolde and bade hym do
the same, and if he so do his sikenes that he hath had so long shal go
55 awey fro hym, and euer aftir he shal be holle to his lyues ende. And
also by the tokyn that he shal fynde on Seint Swythyn stone, þat
lithe on his berieles, ryngis of iron theron nayled fast, and anone as
thei sette honde on the ryng it come fro the stone anone and no
weme was seyn in the stone. And when þei had take up the stone fro
60 the grave thei sette the ryngis to the stone, and thei were fastenyd
anone therto. And than the bishop Ethelwolde and al the peple
thankid oure lorde for this gret myracle. And whan Kyng Edgar with
many bishops and gret multitude of peple were atte takyng up of the
holy body of Seint Swythen, suche a sauour come oute of his grave
65 that al the peple were fulfilled with that heuenely swetenes. And that
same tyme a blynde woman receyued hir sight by the merytes of
Seint Swithen, and many on was helyd there thurgh that heuenely
sauour that were byfore tormentide with ful gret sikenes. And yet
there oure lorde shewith by his holy seruant many a gret myracle,
70 wherefore his name be preysed, worlde withoute ende. Amen.

39–40 then . . . And] *om.* A2   44 an] and A1   46 seint] *om.* A2L
52 in] *add* a A1   schrynes] schryne A1   54 hath . . . long] *om.* hath A2, hadde
afore long tyme L

Here endith the life of Seint Swythen and next folowyth
the life of Seint Kenelme the holy martyr.

18 ST KENELM

The historical Kenelm was the son of Coenwulf, king of Mercia, who died in 821. We know that Kenelm witnessed some charters (see note to l. 21), but after that there is no record. The Kenelm legend developed after the revival of the monastery at Winchcombe in the tenth century.

The following Life of Kenelm depends upon *SEL* 279–291, and there are three points at which it is connected with the P version.[1] As Bennett and Smithers pointed out,[2] the source of the *SEL* Kenelm is the Latin *Vita* in Oxford MS Bodley 285, which has since been edited and translated by Rosalind C. Love.[3] Görlach demonstrates that a source additional to *SEL* must have been used by the writer, and this was, surely, the same Latin *Vita*, as the Life follows *SEL* closely, with few omissions, to l. 128, and thereafter depends on the *Vita*.[4] Details in the Life below which appear neither in *SEL* nor *Vita* are recorded in the Notes. We have not pursued sources further; the additions may be the embellishments of the story teller.

---

[1] Görlach (1998) 111–13; Görlach (1974) p. 283 note 227; and notes to ll. 19, 49, 129, below pp. 500–1.
[2] Bennett and Smithers (1968), p. 96.
[3] Love (1996).
[4] *ibid.* pp. 49–89.

Here endith the life of Seint Swythen and next folowyth
the life of Seint Kenelme the holy martyr.

Seint [Kenelme] the martir, that was kyng of a parte of Inglonde by
the contre of Walys, his fader that was kyng afore hym hight Kenulf.
He made the abbey of Wynchecombe and put thereyn monkes, and
when he dyed he was beryed in the seid abbey that he made, and that
tyme was Wynchecombe the gretest cite of that contre.   5
    In Englonde beth .iij. pryncipal waters, that is Temyse, Severne
and Humbyr. This kyng Kenelme was kyng of Wurcetterschyre,
Warwykeschire, Gloucetterschire, and the bishop of Wurcetter was
byshop of these .iij. [shyres] aforeseid, and also of Derbyschyre,
Chesterchire, Schropchyre, Staffordschyre, Herfordshire, Notyn-   10
ghamshire, Northamptonshyre, Bokynghamshyre, Oxfordschire,
Leycettershire, Lyncolneschyre. Al this was callyd the Marche of
Walys, and of al these contreys was Seint [Kenelme] kyng of, and
that tyme was Wynchecombe [cheffe] cite of al these contreys and
schires aforeseid. And | that tyme were in Englonde .vj. kynges, and   f. 55ᵛᵇ
byfore that was Oswolde kyng of al Englonde, and aftir this same   16
Oswolde is days was this departide in Seint Kenelmes days. Kenulfe,
that was Seint Kenelmes fader, was a holy man, and Dornemylde
and Queyndrede were Kenelme is susters. And this Kenulfe passid
to oure lorde in the yere .viij.C.xix., and then was Seint Kenelme   20
made kyng when he was but .vij. yere of age. And his suster
Dornemylde loued hym ful muche, and thei aftir leved a ful holy
lyfe to ther lyves ende. But Quyndrede his other suster turned al to
wickidnes and had gret envye that hir brothir Kenelme shulde haue
so gret riches aboue hir, and laboryd with al hir myght to distroy hir   25
yong brothir Kenelme, that she myght be quene and for to reyne
aftir hym.
    In a tyme she lete make a stronge poyson, and hir brother dranke
it onware, but by the myght of oure lorde he had none harme
thereof. And when she myght not haue hyr entent by that maner,   30
then she spake to Askaberd that was the ruler of this yong kyng and
byhight hym a gret sum of mony and also to haue his wil of hir if he

MSS A1A2L   1, 13 Kenelme] Knelme A1   4 seid] same L   abbey] add
of Wynchecombe A2   9 shyres] shyre A1   12 Al] And A2   14 cheffe]
ceffe A1   16–17 this . . . Oswolde] om. A2L   22 thei] add bothe A2L

wolde sle thys yong kyng Kenelme. And then anone the .ij. traytours
were sone accordide howe he shulde be slayne. And this same tyme
35 was this yong kyng aslepe and dremed a meruelous dreme, that it
semed to hym that he se a tre stonde by his beddeside that the
highnes therof touchid heuene, and it shynyd as bright as golde and
ful feyre branches were theron ful of blosomys and frute. And on
eche branche of this tre ther brend tapyrs of wex and lampys
40 brennyng also, that it was a ful glorious sight to beholde on. And
þan he thought that he clymbyd vpon the seid tre and se his ruler
Askaberd stonde benethe and felde downe this feyre tre that he stode
on. And whan this tre was so fel downe, thys yong king was ful heuy.
And then hym semyd that ther come a feire foule, he se neuer none
45 feyrer, and anone this brid fly vp to heuene with gret ioye. And aftir
his dremyng he awoke and had grete merueyle what this ment and
was ful heuy of this sight.

And atte laste he tolde his [dreme] to hir that was his norse, that
was clepyd Wolwelme. And when he had tolde hir al his dreme, then
50 she was ful heuy, and she tolde him what his dremyng was to
vndirstonde. She seid his suster 'and that false traytour Askabert
haue fully conspired thi deth, for he hath promysed Quendrede to sle
the, and that signifieth that he smete downe the feyre tre that stode
by thy bedside. And the bryd that fle up to heuene signifieth thi
f. 56ra soule, that angels shal bere to he|uene aftir thi martirdome.'
56 And anone aftir, this fals traytour Askabert desired this yong kyng
to go and sporte hym by the wodes side that was clepid Clent. And as
he walkyd þer he wax al heuy and leyde hym downe and slepte. And
anone this false traitoure Askabert purposed hym there to sle this
60 yong kyng Kenelme and bygan fast to make the pitte where he wolde
put hym in. But anone as God wolde this childe awoke and seid to
this Askabert that he laboryd in veyne, 'for God wil that I dye not
here, but haue this smale yerde, and there as thou shalt picche it fast
in the erthe, there I shal be martryd.' And then thei went fourth
65 togiders a goode wey thens til that thei come to an hawthorne, and
there he pight the yerde [into the erthe], and anone it began to bere
[greene] levys, and it waxyd to a feyre gret tre of asshe, that stondith
there til this day.

41 that] *om.* A2   44 none] *om.* A2   45 this] that A2L   48 dreme]
dre A1   49 clepyd] callid A2   51 suster] *add* Quyndrede L   66 into . . .
erthe] *om.* A1   67 greene] geene A1   gret tre] tree and a greet L   68 there]
add yit L

And there this fals traytoure smyte of this yong kyngis hed, and
anone his soule was bore to heuene with angels in the likenes of a 70
white dove. And than this wickid [man] drewe the body into a grete
valey bytwene .ij. hilles, and there he made a deppe pitte and beryed
hym theryn and cast the hed vpon the body. And when his hed was a
smytyng, he seid this canticle, *Te Deum laudamus,* til he come to this
verse, *Te martirum candidatus laudat excercitus,* and there he yelde up 75
the spirite to oure lorde in lykenes of a dove, as it is byfore seid.

Than this wickid man Askabert went anone to Quendrede and
tolde hir al the matyr howe he had done. And then she was ful glad,
and anone she toke on hir to be quene and chargid that no man
shulde speke of Kenelme in peyne of deth. And aftirwarde she 80
bycome an harlot of hir body and brought hir owne men to wrechid
lyvyng and into gret myscheffe. And long tyme this holy body lay
there in the wode of Clente, for no man durst fette hym fro thens to
bery hym in cristen beriels for this wickid quene Quendrede. But for
that she wolde suffre no cristen man to do hym plesure and conforte, 85
therfore oure lorde wolde that a simple beste shulde bere hym
felawship and do hym conforte. Ther was a wydowe there byside
that had a white cowe, the whiche went into the wode of Clent with
other bestis, but anone as this white cowe come ⌜to the⌝ wode she
wolde anone departe from the other bestis and go into the depe valey 90
where Seint Kenelme was beried. And there the cowe wolde sitte al
the day withoute eny mete and bere hym felawship, and euery nyght
she wolde come home with other bestis more fatter. And more mylke
she yafe that eny othir cowe | dide. And this she contynued many f. 56rb
yeres, whereof the peple had gret merueile that she myght be in 95
suche plite and ete no mete. But the peple seid that it tokenyd
sumthyng to commyng aftir. Men clepid that valey Cowbage there
Seint Kenelme was beryed.

In a tyme as the pope song his masse in Seint Petyr is churche of
Rome, sodenly ther come a white dove and lete falle a skrowe on the 100
auter where the pope seid his masse. And these wordes were writte
theryn [in] Englisshe with letters of golde. 'In Clent in Cowbage
Kenelme kyngis barne lithe vndir a thorne his hed of schorne.' And
when the pope had seid his masse then he schewid this skrowe to al

71 man] *om.* A1   drewe] threw L   74 smytyng] *add* of A2   82 tyme] *add*
after L   89 to the] hom *crossed through with* to the *in margin* A1   99 his] *om.*
A2L   100 skrowe] strowe A2L   102 in] *om.* A1L   104 skrowe]
strowe A2

105 the peple, but ther was no man that cowde telle whate it was, til atte
laste ther come an Englisshe man, and he tolde it byfore al the peple
what it was to mene. And than the pope thankid oure lorde and kept
this skrowe for a worthy relike amonge al tho that were in Rome.
And this fest of Seint Kenelme was halowid with gret solempnite
110 thurgh al the cite of Rome. And then anone the pope sent his
messengers into Englonde to the erchebishop of Canterbery, that
hight Wilfride, and bade hym with other bishops to go and seke the
place where this holy kyng Kenelme was beryed in Cowbage in the
wode of Clent. And then ⌈the⌉ place was sone knowe bycause of the
115 myracle that oure lorde [shewid] by the white cowe. And when the
erchebishop come to the place, he lete take the holy bodi oute of the
erthe with ful gret solempnite, and anone ther sprang oute of the
same graue a fayre welle, that is callid Seint Kenelme is welle, where
many a creature hath receyued helth that hath long tyme be sike.

120 And when this holy bodi was take oute of the graue, ther fel gret
striffe bytwene Wursetterschire men and Glowcetterschire men who
shulde haue this holy body. And then on that was a ful goode man
yafe conseil that al the peple shulde lye downe and slepe to reste
them, for the wedyr was tho right hote, and whiche of the .ij. schires
125 that God wolde that awakyd first shulde take the holy body and go
ther wey therwith. And so it happid that the abbot of Wynchecombe
⌈woke and al his meny and anone went fourth therwith towarde the⌉
seid abbey of Wynchecombe, and as thei come vpon an hie hille a
myle oute of the seid abbey thei were so sore athurste that thei wiste
130 not what to do. And anone thei made ther preyers to God and to this
holy kyng, and the abbot pight downe his croose in the erthe, and
f.56ᵛᵃ anone ther sprang up þer | a feyre welle. And there thei dranke and
refresshid them wel and toke up this holy body with gret solempnite
and with procession and brought him into the abbey, and anone the
135 bellys bygon to rynge withoute eny helpe of mannys honde.

And than this wickid quene dame Quendrede askid what al that
ryngyng ment, and thei tolde hir howe hir brother Kenelme was
brought theder with procession, and the bellys ronge ayenst hym
withoute mannys help. And than she seid in gret skorne: 'That is as

107 pope] *add* with alle the people A2L   114 the(1)] *ins. in margin* A1
115 shewid] shewith A1   116 take] *add* vppe A2L   119 tyme] *add* afore L
126 Wynchecombe] *add* and as thei come vpon an hie hille a myle oute of the seid abbey
crossed through with woke and al his meny and anone went fourth therwith towarde the
in margin A1   128 seid] *om.* A2L   131 croose] crosse A2
137 howe] that L   138 and] *add* how A2

trewe as bothe myn eyen fal oute vpon this boke.' And anone thei fil   140
oute of hir hede bothe at onys, and yet it is sene where thei fil on the
boke into this day. She rad in this psalme: *Deus laudem,* and anone
aftir she dyed ful wrechidly and was cast into the foulest myre that
was tho in al the contre.

And than the abbot with al the peple put this holy body of Seint   145
Kenelme into a worshipful schyryne in the abbey that his fader
Kenulf had made. And there oure blessid lorde schewith many a gret
myracle for his holy kyng and martir Seint Kenelme, wherefore his
name be preysed worlde withoute ende. Amen.

Here endith the life of Seint Kenelme the holy kyng and   150
martir and next bygynneth the life of Seint Chadde.

19 ST CHAD

Almost all we know of Chad is from Bede. In 664, when Wilfrid of York was overseas seeking consecration as archbishop, King Oswiu of Northumbria appointed Chad to York. Chad set off to Canterbury for consecration, but, as the archbishop had died, Chad then sought consecration from Wine, simoniac bishop of the West Saxons. In 666 Wilfrid returned to England and retired to Ripon, leaving Chad in York.

When Theodore arrived from Rome in 669 as the newly consecrated archbishop of Canterbury, he found only two active bishops in England, Chad and Wine, with Wilfrid possibly acting as bishop in Ripon. Theodore restored Wilfrid to York, telling Chad that his consecration had been irregular, but he reconsecrated him and allowed him to retire to his own monastery at Lastingham. His retirement was shortlived, as King Wulfhere of Mercia asked Theodore for a bishop and Theodore appointed Chad, who established his see in Lichfield. He died 2 March 672.

This Life is a condensed version of the Life in *SEL* 78–81.

Here endith the life of Seint Kenelme the holy kyng and
martir and next begynneth the life of Seint Chadde.

Seint Chadde was bishop of Licchefilde and borne in Englonde
aboute the yere of oure [lorde] .vj.C.xvj. in the contre of North-
umburlonde. And when the erchebishop of Euerwike, that nowe is
called Yorke, was dede, Kyng Oswy made Seint Chadde bishop of
Euerwyke and sent hym to the bishop of Canturbury to be sacred of 5
hym. But or he come theder the erchebishop was dede, and than he
was sacred of bishop Wyne, that was tho byshop of the Marche. And
fro thens he went to Euerwike and anone bygon to preche thurgh al
his diocise. And muche peple were brought to goode leuyng thurgh
his prechyng and with his goode ensample yeuyng, for he went on 10
his bare fete fro towne to towne, for on horsebak wolde he not ryde.
    And when he had long tyme be bishop of Euerwike and of
Licchefelde, then he bicome a monke of Seint Benettis ordre and
made a litle selle for hymself and .vij. other monkes to serue God
theryn. And ofte tyme he went oute of his selle on his bare fete and 15
prechid al aboute the contre and dide ful muche goode thurgh his
holy prechyng and for his goode ensample yeuyng. But he had euer
ful gret drede of lightenyng and thonderyng, that anone as he herde
suche | weder he wolde hast [hym] to churche and go euen to the hie f. 56vb
auter. And then atte last men askyd whi he was so sore agast of suche 20
weddyrs, and he tolde them that suche wedyrs were ful sore to be
dradde, for thei were the messengers of oure lorde, and suche oure
lorde shal sende to calle the worlde to the dredful day of dome. And
therfore eche creature aught to drede the messengers of oure lorde
ful sore, for no man knowith whom he wole smyte nor what time, 25
and therefore lete euery creature loue and drede oure lorde Ihesu
Crist with al ther hertis with al ther soules, for he is oure protector
and defender and none but he alone. Therfore we synful wrechis
aught to be ful sore agast of suche messengers of oure lorde, sith so
holy a man [had] so gret drede of them. 30
    And within a while aftir this holy man wexid ryght feble and

MSS A1A2L   2 lorde] om. A1   5 bishop] erchebisshop L   6 or] as
A2   7 tho] the A2   19 hym] om. A1   euen] add vppe A2L   20 askyd]
add of hym A2L   22 thei] these A2L   26 loue] leve A2   29 aught]
might A2   30 had] hath A1

drewe fast towarde his ende. Than in a day as he sate in his selle and a monke of his that hight Owyn sat with hym alone, for al the other monkes were in the churche, sodenly thei herd the swettest heuenely melody that euer thei herde, that come fro heuene. And anone thei
35 herde it on the toppe of ther selle, and there abode that heuenely melodi the space of an houre and more, and then thei herde it go vpwarde to heuene ayene. And hereby this holy man knewe that he shulde not long abide in this worlde, and anone he sent for al his
40 monkes and bade hem loue wel togiders and to be stidefast in [ther] ordre and kepe wisely the feith of holy Churche. And the .vij.th day aftir he passid to oure lorde ful of vertews into the kyngdome of heuene.

Here endith the life of Seint Chadde and folowith the life
45　　　 of Seint Cuthbert.

20 ST CUTHBERT

St Cuthbert was born c. 634. He became a monk at Melrose in 651 and went to Ripon (the 'celle' of l. 47) when land for its foundation was given to his abbot Eata at Melrose. Returning to Melrose, he became prior and c. 663 became prior at Lindisfarne. He was elected bishop of Lindisfarne in 685 and died in 687. Cuthbert was buried at Lindisfarne, but for seven years after 875 his body was taken with them by the Lindisfarne monks fleeing from the Danes. From 883 to 995 they remained at Chester-le-Street, going thence to Ripon and finally to Durham, where the community remained. In 995 Cuthbert was buried at Durham, his remains were translated in 999, and then again into the present cathedral in 1104.

This Life follows closely *SEL* 118–121, a greatly shortened version of Bede's prose Life of Cuthbert.[1] Our text shows minor agreements with the PY MSS of *SEL*.

---

[1] Colgrave (1940), pp. 141–307.

Here endith the life of Seint Chadde and next folowith the
life of Seint Cuthbert.

Seint Cuthbert was bore here in Englonde, and whan he was of the
age of .viij. yere oure lorde shewid for hym a faire myracle to drawe
hym to his loue. For in a tyme as he pleyed atte balle with othir
childern, sodenly there stode amongis them a feyre yong childe of
the age of thre yere, that was the feyrest creature that euer thei 5
byhilde. And anone he seid to Cuthbert: 'Goode brother, use no
suche veyne pleys nor set not thi hert on them.' But for al that
Cuthbert toke none heede to his wordes. And then the childe fille
downe to the grounde and made gret [heuynes] and wept ful sore and
wrange his hondes. And then Cuthbert and the other childern lefte 10
ther pley and confortide this yong childe and askid hym whi he made
so gret sorowe. And | then this childe seid to Cuthbert: 'Al my f. 57ra
heuynes is only for the, that thou vsist suche veyne pleys, for oure
lorde hath chosyn the to be an hed of holy Churche.' And then
sodenly he vanyshed awey, and thereby thei knewe that this childe 15
was an angel of oure lorde sent fro heuene to the confort of his
chosyn seruant Cuthbert.
   And anone he left al suche veyne pleyes and neuer more vsed them
aftir, but bygan to leue a ful holy lyfe, and desired of his fader that he
myght be sette to scole. And anone he drewe to goode levyng and was 20
euer in his preyers bothe nyght and day, and euer he preid to oure
lorde that he wolde yeue hym grace to do tho thingis that shulde plese
hym and to forsake al thyngis that shulde displese hym. And he leuyd
so holy a life that al peple had gret ioy of hym. And within a while aftir
Aydane the holy bishop dyed, and Seint Cuthbert, as he kepte shepe 25
in the felde, lokyd vpwarde and se angels bere the soule of Seint
Aydan the bishop into heuene with gret melody. And then Seint
Cuthbert aftir that wolde not kepe no more shepe, but went anone to
the abbey of Gervaus, and there he [was] made a grey monke,
wherfore al the couent was glad and thonkyd oure lorde, for he 30
leued there in gret fastyng and penaunce. And atte laste he had the
gowte in his kne by colde that he toke in knelyng vpon the colde stonys

MSS A1A2L   1 here] *om.* L   9 heuynes] heuenes A1   11 askid]
add of A2L   29 of] *add* Gervays or L   was] *om.* A1   30 was glad] were fulle
gladde A2L   32 colde . . . knelyng] knelynge and takyng colde L

when he seid his preyers, that his kne bygan to swelle that the senews
of his legge were shronke, that he myght not go nor strecche oute his
35 legge. And euer he toke it ful paciently and seid when hit plesid oure
lorde it shulde passe awey. And within a while aftir his brethern to do
hym conforte bare hym into the felde, and there thei met with a
knyght that bade them: 'Let me se and handle this Cuthbertis legge.'
And then when he had felyd hit with his hondes he bade them: 'Take
40 the mylke of a cowe of on coloure and iuse of smale planteyn and feyre
whete floure and sethe them al togyder, and ley hit therto hote like a
plauster, and it wol make hym holle.' And anone he was made perfite
holle, and then he thonkid oure lorde ful mekely, and knewe wel anone
aftir that it was an angel sent fro heuene to hele hym of his gret sikenes
45 and dissese by the purviance of God.

And than the abbot of that place was right glad of his recoueryng
and sent hym to a celle of thers to be hosteler, there to receyue in
gestis and do them comforte, and sone aftir oure lorde shewid ther a
f. 57rb fayre my|racle for his seruant Seint Cuthbert. For angels come to
50 hym thider ofte tymes in likenes of othir gestys, and he wolde serue
hem ful diligently with mete, drynke and al othir necessaryes, and
went oute to the bakhowse for to fecche them hote bred, but ar he
come ayene his gestis were al gon and no mete ete at al. And that
same tyme was a gret snowe, and then he lokyd to se by ther fete
55 what wey thei went, but he cowde se no steppe of them, wherfore he
had gret merueyle. And as he sought aboute he come by a chambre
where he smylled an heuenely sauour and went in and founde a table
spred with mete and drynke theron, and then he sat downe atte seid
table and ete and dranke and made ful mery, and thonkyd oure lorde
60 of his gret goodenes to sende hym suche gestis, whiche were his holy
angels sent fro heuene to his confort.

And euery nyght when his brethern were abed he wolde go into
the colde water al naked and stonde therin vp to the chyn til it were
mydnyght. And then he wolde go out, and when he come to londe he
65 myght not stonde, for he was so feble that ofte tyme he fil downe to
the grounde. And o tyme as he lay this come .ij. otyrs and liked euery
place of his body, and then went ayen to the see that thei come fro.
And then Seint Cuthbert rose vp al holle and went to his celle ayene,
and rose up to Matyns like as his brethern dide. But his brethern
70 knewe nothyng of his stondyng this euery nyght in the se vp to the

38 me] hym A2   44 his] add of his A1   66 this] there A2

chyn. But atte laste on of his brethern aspied and knewe of his doyngis and tolde therof, but he chargid hym to kepe his [counsel] while he leued.

And then within a while aftir died the bishop of Derham, and Seint Cuthbert was made bishop aftir hym. And then euer aftir he 75 leued a ful holy lyfe and brought muche peple to goode leuyng by his holy prechyng and goode ensample yeuyng. And aftir his deth he was translatid and put into a worshipful shyryne in the towne of Derham, where oure lorde shewith many a gret myracle for his holy seruant Seint Cuthbert, wherfore oure lorde be preysed worlde withoute 80 ende. Amen.

Here endith the life of Seint Cuthbert and next folowi[th] the life of Seint Feith.

72 tolde] *add* hym A2   counsel] cousel A1   74 bishop] *add* there L
82 *Rubric* folowith] folowid A1

21 ST FAITH

'St Faith's legend is untrustworthy and confused with that of St Caprasius.'[1] However, as she appears in the Martyrology of Jerome as having died at Agen she probably did exist, perhaps in the third century. Capras (l. 38) was, according to his legend, the first bishop of the city, and fled the persecution with his flock and saw the martyrdom of St Faith from his hiding place.[2] While her body was still lying there he confronted Dacian, and as a result was beheaded next day.

St Faith was a very popular saint in the middle ages and she appears in much vernacular literature. Her popularity arose in some measure because her relics were stolen from Agen in the late ninth century and taken to Conques, a large Benedictine monastery on the route to Compostela. Offerings made to her shrine there and to that of St Martin at Tours, also on the route to Compostela, largely paid for the building of a number of pilgrimage churches between Conques and Compostela.

In one work St Faith is named as co-patron of London, with SS Peter and Paul.[3] The cult was established in England in the twelfth century by Robert Fitzwalter and his wife Sybilla, who were captured by brigands near Conques when returning from a pilgrimage to Rome in 1100 and released after praying to St Faith. They took home two monks to found the monastery of St Faith at Horsham in Norfolk.[4] Bond records 23 dedications of churches to St Faith, and Dunbar 16 sole dedications.[5] Farmer notes that fifteen Benedictine monasteries in England celebrated her feast, which passed into the Sarum missal.[6] The parish church of St Faith under Old St Paul's Cathedral in London may have influenced her inclusion in this collection. The former parish church of Farringdon Ward was pulled down to make room for the extension of Old St Paul's, and the very beautiful crypt under the choir remained the parish church of St Faith, which Stow said was used by stationers.[7] The dedication survives in a crypt chapel in the present cathedral.

---

[1] Butler IV, p. 45.   [2] *ibid.*, p. 155   .[3] Dunbar (1904), I, 305.
[4] Eve (1994), pp. 12–24.   [5] Bond (1914), pp. 17, 117.
[6] Farmer (1992), p. 174   [7] Stow (1908), I 329.

Westminster Abbey also had a chapel dedicated to St Faith in the Revestry.[8]

Görlach shows in detail how close this Life is to that in the *South English Legendary*,[9] printed in *Early SEL* 83–86.

The Life that follows has been edited from S by Pahta.[10] It is slightly surprising that it does not appear in Caxton.

[8] Stanley (1890), p. 389; Bond (1909), p. 58.
[9] Görlach (1998), pp. 114–15.
[10] Pahta (1993).

Here endith the life of Seint Cuthbert and next [folowith]
the life of Seint Feith.

Seint Feith the holy vyrgyn bycome cristen in hir yong age and was
right holy of leuyng, that hir holynes sprang ful wyde. And then the
wickid tyrand and emperour Dyoclisian and his felowe Maxymyan
and the wyckid iustise Dacian, thei swor|ne the deth of al cristen f. 57va
peple, and al aboute into diuerse londes thei went and distroyd al þe 5
cristen men that thei myght finde, and then þei come to the towne
where this holy virgyn Seint Feith dwellid. And anone these wickid
tyrandys men brought this virgyn [before] Dyoclisian and Maximian
and Dacian the iuge, and when thei se hir thei grennyd vpon hir for
angre, and seid to hir: 'What art thou?' And then she made the signe 10
of the crosse and she preid oure lorde to make hir stidfast and strong
in his feith for to answere to his plesyng to Dacian the iuge. And
then she seid boldly to the iuge: 'I am a cristen woman and Feith is
my name, for I am nothyng aferd of thi tormentys.' And then bygan
Dacian to entrete hir with feyrenes, and seid: 'Feire mayde, I conseil 15
the to forsake thi beleue and thou shalt be a gret lady and haue al
thyngis to thy plesyng.' þen seid this mayde: 'Thou iuge, thou
spekist al in veyne, for I wol neuer forsake hym that hath me so dere
bought with his bitter passion, and I haue made a vowe neuer to
forsake hym while my lyfe lastith. Therfore do al thy tormentis that 20
thou canst to me, for I am able to suffre more tormentis than thou
canst devise, and therfore do what thou wilt, for I wole euer be a
cristen woman and worship almyghti Ihesu and not your goddis, for
they ben fendes and may neyther help themself nor you.'

And then the iuge ferde as he were mad, for the mayde seid so to 25
hym that his goddys were fendes. And then he commaundid to fecche
fourth a bed of bras and made the maide to do of hir clothis, and then
she stode there al nakid, and there she was lede in that brasyn bed, and
the tormentours strecchid hir oute alonge vpon the herde bed and
made a gret fire vndir hir and cast therin grese ful gret plente to make 30
the fire brenne the faster. And it semyd to al peple that the fire wolde
brenne up this virgyn anone. And then the tormentours turned this
virgyn in the brasyn bed that she shulde be anone al consumyd, but

MSS A1A2LS   *Rubric* folowith] folowid A1   5 al(1) . . . londes/thei went]
trsp. S   8 before] *om.* A1   12 to(3) . . . iuge] *om.* S   21 canst] *add* do L
25 for] because A2   so] *om.* A2   28 there] *om.* S   30 ful] *om.* LS
32 up] *om.* S   33 al] altogedre S

euer this holy maide made glad shere as though she had lay in a softe
35 feder bed. And when othir cristen peple herde that this holy virgyn
was so sore tormentide, thei fled awey oute of the towne and hid hem
for fere in dicchis and pittis in the contrey.

Than an holy man that hight Capras that was hid in a roche of stone
bysides the place that Seint Feith was torment in, and as he lokid oute
40 atte an hole towarde hir and se howe she was rostid in the fire, and
f. 57vb whan the fire bigan to brenne and was most feruent on hir, than | ther
come a white dove fro heuene and brought hir a crowne of golde that
schynyd brighter than the sonne and set it on the maydens hed, and
with hir wynges she blewe awey the fyre that none come nygh hir, but
45 she lay þerin ful ioyful. But none of al that were aboute hir se this but
only Capras, that was hid in the roche of stone, for al thei wende verily
that she had be brent in the fire. And whan this holy man Capras seigh
hir so preseruyd by the myght of oure lorde Ihesu, than he went oute
of the roche of stone and come into the place where Seint Feith the
50 holy virgyn lay in the bed of bras, and seid byfore al the tormentours
that he was a cristen man and wolde neuer forsake it for the drede of
Dacians peynes: 'For aftir tho tormentes I shal entre into the blisse of
heuene.' Then .ij. brethern that hight Prime and Felician com forth
boldly also byfore the wickid iuge Dacian and knoleched them cristen
55 men byfore al the tormentours.

And then Dacian was nygh mad for woo, and commaundide that
Seint Feithis hed shulde be smyten of, and Capras, Pryme and
Felicians hedys also. And then al these holy seyntis made ther
preyers to oure lorde knelyng on ther knees, and then anone aftir
60 ther heddys were smyte of eche aftir other. And then angels of oure
lorde bere ther soules to the blisse of heuene with gret ioye and
melody. And than this wickyd tyraunt Dacien commaundid to cast
ther bodyes in the moste foulest place that thei cowde fynde, but the
goode cristen peple fet awey the bodyes by nyght and beried them in
65 the most worshipful place that thei myght, wherefore God quytte
them ther mede in the blisse of heuene. Amen.

Here endith the life of the holy virgyn Seint Feith and
next bygynneth the life of the holy virgyn Seint Dorathe.

38 hight] was callyd S   45 of al] om. S   47 be] om. A2L   53 hight]
were callyd S   54 them] themselfe S   58 Felicians hedys] Felician hure
heedis smytyn of S   59 lorde] add ihesu crist S   anone aftir] aftyrward anon S
61 lorde] add god S   heuene] add everlastyng L

22 ST DOROTHY 1

There are no historical details of St Dorothy, believed to have been a virgin mártyred c. 300. Two versions of her life place her either in Caesarea under the governor Fabricius during the persecutions of Diocletian, or in Alexandria under Maximian. The manuscripts of Dorothy's Life in English known to us contain the Caesarea story, and they fall into three groups. We agree with Görlach (1998), p. 93, that the Additional Life is based on an earlier prose translation, and we present the text from the *ALL* as 'Dorothy 1' and the earlier version as 'Dorothy 2'. Kirsten Wolf's study[1] omits mention of only two of the MSS known to us which contain prose Lives of Dorothy: Oxford, Bodleian Library MS Eng. theol. e.17 (B), which is the same version as that in Dublin, Trinity College MS 319 (T1), our 'Dorothy 3';[2] and Cambridge, University Library MS Ll.v.18 (C), another copy of our 'Dorothy 2'.[3]

The source of the Caesarea story of St Dorothy in our MSS is summarised by Wolf (pp. 47–8).

---

[1] Wolf (1996), pp. 41–72.
[2] *ibid.* pp. 60–61 and notes 72–4.
[3] *ibid.* pp. 59–60 and notes 68–9.

Here endith the life of the holy virgyn Seint Feith and
next byginneth the life of the holy virgyn Seint Dorathe.

The right glorious virgyn and martir Seint Dorathe was borne of the
noble blode of the cenatours of Rome, hir fader hight [Dorathe]. In
that tyme the persecucion of cristen peple was wonder gret in the
londe of Romaynes, wherefore this blessid Dorathe, dispysyng the
ydols, forsoke Rome with al his possessions, as fildes, vynes, castels   5
and howsys and seyled with Theodora his wife and with his .ij.
doughters Cristyne and Calistyne to the reame of Capadoce into the
cite of Cesarem, wherein thei dwellyd and brought forth his holy
doughter Seint Dorathe.

   And whan this holy virgyn was cristened of the holy bishop   10
Appolynar, he named hir Dorathe, and anone she was fulfilled with
vertu and goodenes of the holy gost. | And she was of ful gret bewte   f. 58ʳᵃ
above al the maydyns of that kyngdome and she dispised this worlde
with al his vanytes, for she was a feruent louer of almyghti God and
loued pouerte. And she was ful of mekenes and chastite, wherfore   15
the fende had gret envie of hir goode leuyng and set the prouost
Fabricius afire in hir loue, that he wolde nedis haue hir to his wife.
And anone he sent for hir in al the hast and he byhight hir tresoure
and al maner goodes withoute nombre. This heryng, this holy virgyn
Dorathe denyed and dispised al erthly riches, and then withoute   20
drede she knowlechid hir byfore the prouost Fabricius a cristen
woman and that she was maryed to Ihesu Crist, and othir husbonde
wolde she neuer none.

   And when the prouost Fabricius herd this he was ny mad for
angre, and commaundide that she shulde be put into a tunne of hote   25
brennyng oyle, and she was so preserued by the myght of hir spouse
Ihesu that she felte none harme but ioyed theryn as though she had
be anoynted with a precious oynement of bawme. And when the
paynyms se this gret myracle, many of them were conuertid to the
feith of Ihesu Crist. But the tyraunt Fabricius seid that she dide al   30
this by wichecraft, and made hir to be shette in a depe prison .ix.
days withoute mete and drynke. But she was norished and fedde with
the glorious angels of oure lorde, so that when she come oute of

prison atte .ix. days ende and was brought byfore the iuge, then she
35 aperyd more feyrer than euer she dide bifore, wherfore al the peple
had gret merueile. And then the iuge seid to hir: 'But if thou wilte do
worship to oure goddys, thou shalt not escape the torment of iebet.'
Than she answerd hym sadly: 'I worship almyghti God, that made al
thynges, and not thy goddys, for they byn fendes.' And then she fil
40 downe flatte to the erthe, liftyng vp hir eyen to almyghti God and
preid hym that he wolde shewe hys myghte byfore al the peple, that
he is only almyghti God and none othir bysydys hym.

Than had Fabricius reysed vp an hye peler and set his ydol and his
god vpon it. And anone ther come a gret multitude of angels of
45 heuene with gret myght and cast downe this ydol, that no parte of
the peler myght neuer aftir be founde. And al the peple herde the
voyce of fendes in the eyre cryyng and seyng: 'O Dorathe, why doyst
thou distroy us and torment us this sore?' And for this [grete
myracle] many thousandys of paynyms were conuertide to the
f. 58rb feith | of Ihesu Crist and receyued the crowne of martirdome for
51 the knowlechyng of his holi name. And then he commaundid this
holy virgyn to be hongid on the iebet, hir fete vpwarde and hir hed
downewarde, and then al hir bodi was todrawe with hokys of iron
and she was betyn with roddys and scurgid with scurges, and aftir
55 this þei put fyrebrondes to hir tender brestes. And then whan she
was half dede, she was shet up ayene in prison til the next day.

The day folowyng she was brought forth ayene al holle withoute
eny hurte or dissese, wherfore the iuge had gret wonder and seid to
hir: 'O thou fayre maide, forsake thi god and beleue on oure goddys,
60 for thou mayste se howe merciful oure goddys be that this preserve
the, and therfore haue pety on thi tender body, for thou hast be
tormentide inough.' And then the prouost Fabricius sent fore hir .ij.
sustyrs Cristyne and Calistyne, and anone for drede of deth thei
turned awey fro the feith of Ihesu Crist and went to ther sustyr
65 Dorathe and conseiled hir to applie hir to the desire of the prouost
Fabricius and vtturly to forsake the feith of Ihesu Crist. But the holy
virgyn Dorathe conseiled hir susters with the gret swetenes of
heuenly confort, that she withdrewe them fro ther blynde errour
and made them fully the seruauntis of God, and thei knowlechid
70 themself cristen byfore the iuge.

And when Fabricius herd this he was ny mad for angre, and he
commaundid the tormentours to bynde þer bakkys togiders and cast

48–9 grete myracle] myrache A1

them bothe in a gret fire and so brent hem. And he seid to the holy
virgyn Dorathe: 'Howe long wilte thou trouble us with thi wichecraft? Eyther do sacrifice to oure goddys or else thi hed anone shal be   75
smyte of.' And than this holy virgyn seid with a glad semblant: 'Do
to me what torment thou wilte, for I am al redi to suffre it for the
loue of Ihesu Crist my spouse, in whos gardyn ful of al delites I haue
gadrid rosys and applys.' And whan the tyraunt herd this he
trembled for angre and commaundid that hir feyre visage shulde   80
be al tobetyn with stonys, so that ther shulde appere no beute in hir
visage but al disfiguryd, and so to be put in prison til the next day.
And then she come forth al holle and sounde as though she had
suffred no dissese, and was made more bewteuous than euer she was
byfore by hir spouse Ihesu Crist, for whos loue she toke vpon hir   85
these gret and sharp batayles.

And than Fabricius [commaundid] that hir hed shulde be smyte
of. And as | she was led towarde the place where the dede shulde be   f. 58va
done, on Theophilus, the scribe of al þe reame, seid vnto hir in
skorne: 'I prey the, sende me sum of the rosys and applys that thou   90
hast gadred in the gardyn of thy spouse þat thou preysist so muche.'
And than she grauntid hym his desire, notwithstondyng it was right
colde wynter that tyme and bothe frost and snowe. And when she
come to the place where she shulde be byhedide, she knelyd doune
on hir knees and made hir preyer to oure lorde Ihesu hir spouse for   95
al tho that worshipped hir passion, that thei myght be kept stidfast in
his feith in al ther tribulacion and to take it mekely, and specially to
be delyuerd fro al shame, gret pouerte and fals disclaundyr, and atte
ther last ende to haue verry contricion and remyssion of al ther
synnes. And also women with childe that calle to hir for help to haue   100
goode delyueraunce, and the childe to [be] cristenyd and the moder
purified. Also she preyd to God that whar hir life is wretyn or rad in
eny howse that it shulde be kepte fro al maner peryl of thondyr and
lightenyng and of alle fire and fro the peril of thefys and fro sodeyn
deth, and to receyue the sacramentis of the Churche atte ther last   105
ende for ther most soueryne defense ayenst ther gostely enemy the
fende. And as she had done hir preyer ther come a voyce fro heuene
and seid: 'Come to me, my dere spouse and trewe virgyn, for al thi
bone is grauntid to the that thou hast preyd fore, and whom thou
preyst fore shal be saued, and thou thiself shalt receyue the crowne   110

of martirdome, and then thou shalt receyue the blisse of heuene
withoute ende for thi labour.'

And than þis holy virgyn Dorathe bowyd downe hir hed to the
stroke of the swerd, and then anone there appered byfore hir a feyre
115 childe barefote and clothid in purpil with crispe heer whos clothes
were set ful of bright sterrys, beryng in his honde a litle maunde of
golde and .iij. rosys and .iij. applys therin, and profred the seid
maunde with rosys and applys to this holy virgyn Dorathe. To whom
the virgyn seid: 'I prey the bere them to Theophilus the scribe.' And
120 then the tormentoure smyte of hir hed and she passid to oure lorde
ful of vertues the .vj.th day of Feueryl, and she was done to deth by
Fabricius by the commaundement of Dyoclisian and Maximyan,
emperours of Rome, the yere of oure lorde .ij.C .iiij. score and .viij.
And as this seid Theophilus stode in the paleys of the emperour, this
f. 58ᵛᵇ childe aforeseid apperid | to hym and seid: 'These rosis and applys
126 my suster Dorathe hath sent them oute of the paradise of hir spouse.'
And anone the childe vanyshed awey. Then anone for that mer-
ueilous werke of oure lorde in this blessid virgyn that she sent by the
angel to Theophilus, anone he seid with a steryn voice of preysyng
130 he glorified the God of Dorathe for that gret myracle þat was
schewid there of rosys and applys in that tyme of the yere that
was so feruent colde, for al the grounde was then coueryd with frost
and snowe and no grene aperyng in no place. And then he seid
anone: 'He that sent thes thynges to me is of gret power, and therfore
135 his name be preised worlde withoute ende.' And then he was
conuertid to the feith of Ihesu Crist and al the peple of the cite.
Than this cursid tyrand Fabricius seyng this bygan to torment
Theophilus the scribe with many dyuerse tormentis, and atte laste
he was kut al to smale pecis and his flesshe cast to bestes and briddys
140 to be deuoured, but first he was baptised and then he receyued the
sacrament and folowyd the virgyn Dorathe to the blisse of heuene,
there to reyne in blisse and ioye worlde withoute ende. Amen.

Here endith the life of the blessid virgyn and martir Seint
Dorathe and next bygynneth the life of Seint Leger.

---

121 Feueryl] Feueryere A2   125 seid] *add* these wordys L   126 oute of] to
the from A2L   135 ende] *add* Amen A2   139 flesshe] *add* to be A1
142 blisse and] *om.* L   worlde] *om.* L

This Life closely follows the Latin Life printed in *LgAsupp.*, *De sancta Dorothea*, pp. 910–12.

All four manuscripts contain many individual errors and variant readings, and there is no particular reason for choosing any one of them as base. The only reading which might possibly suggest any affiliations between them is at l. 123, where the Latin text agrees with R alone, and therefore CMLb may share an ancestor containing the misreading.

The text of M was edited by Axon in *The Antiquary* 37 (1901), 53–55, and that of Lb by Horstmann in *Anglia*, 3 (1880), 325–8, in each case with minor mistranscriptions.

The right glorius virgine and martir Seint Dorothe was borne of the noble blode of the cenatours of Rome. The name of her fadyr was Dorotheo and her moder Theodora. In that tyme the persecucion of cristen people was wondyr gret in the lande of Romans, wherfore this blissed fader Dorotheo, dispisyng the idolls, forsoke Rome with alle 5 his possession, both feeldes, vynes, castelles and touwrs, and seiled with his wiffe Theodora and with his .ij. doughters Cristyin and Calistyin vnto they came into the | cite of Cesaream in the realme of f. 237ra Capadoce, wherin thay dwellyng brought fourth a doughter, of whos lyffe now we entende to speke. [When] this blissyd child was borne 10 she was previly baptizyd in the maner of cristen people of an holy bisshope Appolinari, and put to her a name takyn of her fadyrs name and moders and namyd her Dorothea. And she anon, fulfyllyd with the holy gost, taught with vertues of holy discipline. And she was wonderly fayre above all the maydons of that region, disspisynge the 15 world with all his vanitees, | a feruent lover of God with all pouerte f. 237rb and full of meknes and charite.

The fende, natt susteynyng her chastite, and for envy that he had to heer goodnes, he sett afyre in her loue Fabricion prouest of that [lond], the which the feend sterred so besely with prikkis of vnclene 20 love to this glorious virgine Dorothea that he send for her, behotyng her tresure and all maner goodes without numbre and for to take here for his weddyd wyffe withoute ony determinacion. This hyryng, holy Dorothea, dispysing as slym of the erth hym and all erthely

MSS RCMLb   1 right] *om.* C   and martir] *om.* CMLb   was borne] came downe CMLb   2 Rome] *add* the names of her fadyr and modyr R   The . . . was] Hyr fader hyght CMLb   3 moder] *add* hight Lb   4 wondyr] passing Lb   5 fader] *om.* CMLb   Dorotheo] Theodoro M, Doro *LgAsupp.*   idolls] *add* and R   6 possession] *pl.* C   both] *om.* M   both . . . vynes] that is to say wyffis Lb   both . . . touwrs] generally C   touwrs] howsis M*LbLgAsupp.*   7 doughters] *add* that hight Lb   Cristyin] Cristem CM   8 Calistyin] Calixtem C, Calistem M   vnto] tyll CMLb   8–9 cite . . . Cesaream/realme of Capadoce] *trsp. and add* and into *after* Capadoce CM, *trsp.* Lb   9 of] *om.* C   10 now] *om.* Lb   speke] *add* of C, *add* now by the grace of God Lb   When] Then R   blissyd] *om.* Lb   11 she] yt C   holy] *add* man Lb   12 and] *add* he CM   takyn] *om* Lb   13 and(1)] *add* her M   with] *add* vertues and discipline of almyghty god and of C   14 taught . . . discipline] *om.* C   of] and MLb   15 that] the M   16 his] *add* disceytes and C   a fervent lover] in a feruent love Lb   all] *om.* Lb   18 and] *om.* CM   19 he] *om.* CM   Fabricion] Fabrissiane C   20 lond] lord R   prikkis] vnforsing Lb   22 maner] *add* of CMLb   23 weddyd] *om.* CMLb   24 holy] *om.* C   dispysing] *add* all M   as] all Lb   of the erth] and mukke Lb   hym and] *om.* CM   hym . . . erthely] and worldly Lb

f. 237va riches and with|out ony drede, she knowliched herselff openly that
26 she was frely and truly maried to her lord Ihesu Crist, the which
Fabricius hyryng was all sett afire in wodnes, commaundyng anon
þat she were putt into a tonne of feruent brennyng oyle. And she,
with the help of her spouse Crist Ihesu, abode theryn withoute ony
30 disease, ioyng her therinne as thouh she had byn anoynted with a
[precious] anoyntement of bame, wher thourgh many of thes
paynems seyng this grete miracle weren conuerted to God. But
f. 237vb verely this tirant beleuyd that she did all | this by whichcraffte and
made here to be reclusyd into preson [.ix.] days withoute mete or ony
35 drinke. But yet was she norysshed and fedde with glorius angelis, so
that when she came out of preson and was brought before the iuge
she apperyd more fairer than euer she did before, wherof the people
wondrid gretly how she might be so fayre and so longe kepte in
preson withoute mete or drinke. Than sayd the iuge vnto here: 'But
40 yiff thu wurshep my goddis þu shalt not aschape the torment of this
iebett.' And she answerd sadly: 'I worshep only God and nott fendes,
for all thy goddys byn fyndes.' And then she fel downe prostrat to
the erthe, lyftyng vpp her yen to hevyn and praied oure lorde as he is
f. 238ra myghtfull that he wold | shew his grete myght how that he is only
45 God and non othyr besydes hym.

Than had Fabricius raised vp a grete pelour and sett his idoll
thervpon. And anon a gret multitude of angels commyng with grete
myght kast downe the idol, so that no part of that pylour myght be
found, and thos standyng abowte harde in the eyr cryng the voys of
50 fendis and said: 'O thu Dorothea, whi doyst thu distroie vs and

25 herselff] her lyff Lb   26 frely] verylye M   her] oure Lb   27 anon]
om. C   28 were . . . brennyng] shuld be sete in a boylyng vessell with C   feruent]
om. Lb   29 her] *om.* C   31 precious] preciuos R   anoyntement] *two words*
R, oyntment CMLb   of bame] *om.* C   thourgh] fore CMLb   34 made]
om. CMLb   comaunded Lb   into] in CM   .ix.] *number del.* R   ony] *om.* CMLb   35 yet]
om. CMLb   36–9 and was . . . preson] *inserted below column* R   36 brought]
add forthe Lb   37 did] was MLb   wherof] wherfore all CMLb   38 gretly]
om. CMLb   how] that Lb   38–9 kepte . . . preson] *om.* M   in preson] *om.* CLb
39 vnto here] *om.* C   40 torment] turnament Lb   this] the *corr.*
C, the M   41 sadly] and said M   42 for . . . fyndes] *om.* Lb   all] *om.* C   byn] ar C   then]
om. CM   prostrat] full strayte Lb   43 oure lorde] god Lb   43–4 as . . .
myghtfull] *om.* CMLb*LgAsupp.*   44 wold] *add* graunt and Lb   45 besydes
hym] but he oonly M   46 had] *om.* CMLb   raised . . . grete] arose up from his Lb
grete] hyghe CM   idoll] *pl.* C   47 anon] incontynent Lb   commyng] came C
with] *add* soo M   48 myght] *add* and RCM   kast] threwe CMLb   idol] *pl.* CLb
that] the CM   49 thos standyng abowte] they CMLb*LgAsupp.*   49–50 in . . .
cryng/the(2) . . . fendis] *trsp. with* voyces *pl.* CM, *trsp. with* erthe *for* eyre Lb
50 and said] *om.* CMLb   thu] *om.* CMLb

torment vs?' And for this glorius miracle many thousaundes of paynemes were openly converted to our lord Ihesu Crist | and entred into the crown of merterdome. And this holy virgine was hanged vpon the iebet her feet vpward, and all her holy tendyr body all todrawyn with hokys of iron. She was betyn with roddys, scorgyd 55 with scorgys, and after þat they sett hote firebrondis to her tender virgyn brestis, and she half dede was reclusyd in prison ayen intoo the moryn. The day folwyng she was brought fourth all hole withouten spotte or ony dissease, wherof the iuge wonderyd gretly and said to her: 'O thu fair maydon, yet thu shalt turne agayn for 60 now thu art chastised inowh.'

f. 238rb

And then he send | to her .ij. of her susters, Cristem and Calistem, the which for drede of deth were turnyd away fro Crist, and that thay [shuld] labour to þer suster Dorothea in the same wise for to withdraw her from cristen fayth. Then this blessyd Dorothe spake to 65 here susters so swetly and so graciously that she toke from them all the blyndnes of her hartys and conuertyd þem fully to God. Knoyng this, Fabricius toke her susters and bounde ther bakkys togedders and kast them both into a gret fyre and brent hem. And then he said to Dorothea: 'How longe lastyth | thi wychecrafte? Eyther do sacrifice and leve, other ellys resceiue the sentence of thy hedde to 71 be smetyn of.' And she answerde with gladde visage: 'Whateuer thu wult, I am redy to suffre for my lorde Ihesu Criste my spouse, in whos gardyn full of delyte I haue gaderyd roses and appollys.' Hyryng this, the tyrant tremelyng for anger within hymselfe 75 [commaundyd] that her fair visage [shulde] be all tobetyn with stones so that ther shuld appere no maner feture of fairnes in her

f. 238va

f. 238vb

---

51 many] om. C   53 merterdome] martyris Lb   54 iebet] add and C   all] om. CM   tendyr] om. MLb   55 iron] add and then M   roddys] add and M 55–6 scorgyd with] and Lb   56 þat they] this CM, om. Lb   firebrondis] fyry brondis M   her] the M   57 virgyn] virgyns M, om. Lb   57–8 ayen/intoo . . . moryn] trsp. C   58 moryn] morowe M   The] add morow Lb   61 now] om. CMLb   art] add nat C   62 Calistem] Calixtem C   63 the] om. CM   that] om. CMLb   64 shuld] shlud R   to] om. C   in . . . wise] om. Lb 65 cristen] the Lb   this] om. MLb   66 toke] by Lb   67 þem] add ayen M God] Ihesu Criste M   68 toke] add then M   toke . . . and] by her two susters and Lb   69 kast] threwe CMLb   and(2) . . . hem] om. Lb   hem] add to ashes C 70 lastyth] wolt thou drawe vs thus alonge with CMLb   71–2 to be] om. MLb 72 smetyn] smytyng M   answerde] add and saide M   gladde] add chere and M visage] chere Lb   whateuer] whanevir M   74 of delyte] delycious M 76 commaundyd] commaundyng R   shulde] shlulde R   all] om. Lb   77 stones] staves C, stavis and Lb, baculis et fustibus LgAsupp.   shuld] add nothing Lb   maner] add of C   of fairnes] om. CMLbLgAsupp.

f. 239ra face, and so kept into the mornynge. The day | folwyng she was
brought fourth fully curyd and made all hole and full of bewte by
80 oure sauyour her truwyst spouse, for whos worshep and love she toke
vpon her theis sharpe and trauaylous bat018ylles. And þen she receyved
the sentence of her hedde smytyng of.

And as she was ladde withoute the walles of the citee, Theophilus
the grete notary of the realme saw here and [behelde] her, and as in
85 scorne he prayed her that she wold sende hym rosys and appullys of
the gardyn of here spouse, and gretly he prayed her therof, the
f. 239rb whiche prayer | she graunted hym, natwithstandyng that it was that
tyme right grete coolde, both frost and snaw. And when she came to
þe place where she shulde be heddyd, she made her prayer vnto our
90 lorde for all them that in the worship of her name halowyn her
passyon, that thay may be kept and comforted in euery tribulacion,
and specyally be delyuered from the shame of pouerte and false
fame, and att ther ende that they may haue verray contricion and
remission of all ther synnes. Wemen with chylde that callene her
f. 239va name into ther helpe that þey may fynde comforte and | profite in
96 ther sorowis and tribulacions. Also she prayed that where her lyffe
were wretyn in ony house or place, that hit myght be kepte from all
maner of parellys of thounder or lyghtnyng or ony other fyre, and
also from the perell of thevys and all sodayne dethys, and to receyve
100 ther hevynly sacrament at ther last ende for ther souerayn defence
agaynst all goostly perellys. And as sone as she had made her prayer
then came a voyce from hevyn that said to here: 'Come my dere

78 face] visage CMLb*LgAsupp.*   mornynge] morow CMLb   79 fourth] *om.* Lb
and (1) *om.* M   all] *om.* CLb   and(2)] *add* made C   80 oure . . . spouse] her trusty
spouse and saviour Lb   81 sharpe] hard Lb   þen] whan C   81–2 she
receyved] he gaff Lb   82 of(1) . . . of(2)] that her hede shulde be smytten off Lb
83 as] *om.* Lb   withoute] thorowe C   walles of the] *om.* CM   walles] townewallis Lb
citee] *add* to þe place of execucion C, *add* Moreovir Lb   of] *add* all R   84 here . . .
her] and bihilde these thingis and Lb   behelde] he helde R   and] *om.* R
85 sende] shewe Lb   appullys] *add* out C   86 and . . . therof] *om.* C   therof] *add*
of M   87 that(1)] *om.* MLb   it was] *om.* Lb   88 tyme] tynee M, *add* was Lb
89 where . . . heddyd] of her martirdom Lb   where] *add* þat C   heddyd] beheded CM
made . . . prayer] prayed CMLb   91 may] *om.* Lb   and comforted] *om.* Lb
tribulacion] *add* and be delyuered therof M   92 specyally] *add* to CLb, *add* for to M
the . . . of] *om.* C   93 att] in CMLb   94 synnes] *add* and MLb
96 tribulacions] *add* and M   her lyffe] the lyf of hire C   97 house/place] *trsp.* Lb
98 of(1)] *om.* M   or(1)] and M, *om.* Lb   fyre] myschaunce Lb   99 also] *om.*
CMLb   to] þat þei may CM, thay that shall Lb   100 ther] the CMLb   hevenly]
holy Lb   last] *om.* Lb   souerayn] suffereynge C   101 perellys] enmyes C
made] don C   102 then] ther CMLb   102–3 dere . . . my] *om.* Lb

belouyd, cum my desyryd spouse, for all þat ye haue askyd and
prayed fore is grantyd | yow, and for whom ye praye shall be savyd.'   f. 239ᵛᵇ
Then the said virgine bowyde downe here blyssyd hedde to the   105
[stroke] of the swerde, and ther apperyd to here a fayre chylde
clothyd in purpur, barefote, with crispe heris, whos clothes were all
besprent with bryght steris, beryng in his hand a lytle panyer of
goold with .iij. reed rosys and .iij. appullys, and profered them to
thys blessyd virgine. To whom the virgine sayd: 'I pray yow, my   110
lord, that ye wyll bere them to Theophilus the scribe.' And annon
she receyved þe stroke of the swerde | and passyd to oure lorde the   f. 240ʳᵃ
.vj. day of February. She reseyvyd martirdome by Fabricion prefecte
vndyr Dyoclysian and Maximeon, emperowrs of Rome .CC.lxxxviij.
Theophilus standyng then in palise of the president, this childe   115
apperyd vnto hym shewyng to hym thes reed rosys and appulles,
seyng vnto hym: 'My suster sent thees vnto the from paradyse of
here spouse Ihesu Crist.' And anon the childe vanysshed away. Then
gretly wondryng, Theophilus brake owte in voyce of praysyng and
glorifiyng Crist the God of Dorothe, that in that tyme of soo grete   120
colde as ther was then in Februarij, that all the | lande was   f. 240ʳᵇ
ouercouered with frost and snowe and non grene apperyng in ony
place, thus saing: 'He that hath sende thees reed rosys and appullys
is of grete myght, of whom the name be blissyde withowtyn ende.'
And so by his prechyng and affermyng, all the citee was turned and   125

103 ye haue] thou haste M   haue] *om.* Lb   104 yow] the M   for . . . praye]
and for whom for whom þat þou prayest fore M, thay that ye pray for Lb   105 said]
blessyd CMLb   downe] *om.* Lb   blyssyd] *om.* CMLb   106 stroke] croke R, *ictum*
LgAsupp.   to here] *om.* CMLb   107 clothyd] *om.* C   all] *om.* C
108 besprent] spreynt CM, springelid Lb   lytle] *add* prety C   108–9 of goold] *om.* Lb
109 reed] *om.* CMLb   110 thys blessyd] the CMLb   110–11 yow,
ye] the, thou M   111 them] yt C   112–13 þe . . . reseyvyd] *om.* Lb
113 .vj.] .viij. CM, *om.* Lb, *Idus Februarius LgAsupp.*   prefecte] profeste M
114 .CC.lxxxviij.] *add* yere of oure lord god Lb   115 standyng then] *trsp.* CLb
in] *add* þe CMLb   president] emperour M   116 hym(1)] *add* and toke hym aparte M,
and toke hym this baskett Lb   shewyng] seyng CM   to hym] *om.* C   reed] *om.* CM
117 vnto hym] theis roses and apelles C, to hym these rosis and appils M   hym] *add* here
thus these rosis and appellis Lb   suster] *add* Dorothea CM   thees] *om.* CMLb
paradyse] þe gardyn C, the paradise M   118 Ihesu Crist] *om.* CMLbLgAsupp.
119 gretly wondryng] all forwondryng *corr. to* forwondrynd M, al forwondred CLb
voyce of] *om.* Lb   119–20 and glorifiyng] *om.* Lb   120 God] lorde M
that(2)] *om.* C   121 all] *om.* Lb   122 non] no CLb, no maner of M   ony]
no CM, noone Lb   123 thus saing] *om.* CMLb, *add* truly truly Lb   thees . . .
appullys RLgAsupp.] þis CMLb   124 myght] powere CMLb   ende] *add* Amen
MLb   125 and affermyng] *om.* C   turned and] *om.* CLb

conuerted to oure lorde Ihesu Criste. Seing this, Fabricion this
tiraunt he tormentyd Theophilus the scribe with many moo and
diuerse cruell maner of tormentis that Seint Dorothe receyvyd, and
att the last he was cutt all in smalle peces and comavnded to be caste
f. 240ᵛᵃ to bestis and to byrdes for to be devoured, butt | first he recevyd
131 baptym and after the holy sacrament of oure lordys body. And so,
folowyng this holy virgine Dorothea, he came to Crist that glorifieth
his seintes and he be glorifyed in them, the which beyng consubstanciall and eternall with the fader and the holy goost levith and
135 reigneth God by all the worlde of worldys. Amen.

126–7 Seing . . . tiraunt] The tyraunt seeyng this C, seyng this the tyrant M,
perseyuyng this the tyraunt Lb   127 he] *om.* C   127–8 and diuerse] *add*
maners of C, *om.* Lb   128 maner of] *om.* C   tormentis that] turmentours than Lb
that . . . receyvyd] then was sente Dorothea M, than Dorothea resayuyd Lb   receyvyd]
had C   129 cutt] *om.* M   130 to(1)] *add* wilde Lb   131 after] *add* þat
C, *om.* Lb   holy] blissid Lb   132 he] *om.* Lb   133 the] by C   which
beyng] *om.* Lb   134 eternall] coeternall CMLb*LgAsupp.*

This version is notably unstylish, with many clauses and phrases strung ineptly together, as in the first and fourth paragraphs. There are also apparent syntactical errors, such as omission of 'was' in l. 1 and use of the past 'forsoke' in l. 8 for the expected infinitive. In this edition no attempt has been made to 'correct' such lapses, but punctuation has been used to aid comprehension.

Here begynneth the lyfe of the gloryous virgyn and martir
Seynt Dorothe.

Thys gloriouse virgyne and martyr Dorothea, whos fadirs name
Dorotheus and her moder Theodora, whyche was comen of the noble
progeny of the most famouse and worthyest senatoures of Rome. In
whos dayes grewe full gretly the greuous persecucion of crystyn
peple euerywhere, but most specyally amonge the Romaynes,   5
whyche causyd thys blessyd Dorotheus fader of thys holy vyrgyne,
hatyng and despysyng the cursyd and abhominable mawmetry of the
Romaynes, forsoke the contre and felyshyp of the lothsome
Romaynes wyth all hys possessyons of castelles, houses, londes,
rentes and vynes wyth all other rychesses, and passyd ouer the see   10
wyth hys good wyfe Theodora and hys two doughtres, whos names
were Trystem and Calystem, and came into the region of Capadosy,
and entryng into a feyre cyte of that region called Cesarea and
dwelled theryn, wherein a gracious doughter was begoten, of whos
lyfe nowe wyth Goddys grace we purpose to speke of.   15
    Whan thys holy vyrgyne was brought forthe, anone after the holy
custome of crystyn relygion she was crystened full pryuyly of the
holy bysshop Seynt Appolynaris, whyche good man of her fadyrs and
modyrs names compownyd her name and namyd here Dorothea.
    Sone after, when nature had auaunsyd thys gracyous and holy   20
vyrgyne wyth more age and yet but tender of age to speke of, she was
so replenysshed wyth the diuersyte of vertues of the holy goste in all
partyes also well of body as of sowle, and so suffycyently taught in
gracious vertewesnes, all be hyt that nature had so excellently avaunsyd
her wyth singuler beawte, that the fame of her beawte wyth her other   25
singler vertues ouersprad all the maydones of that regyon. |
    To the whyche verteous bounteuosnes the enemy of all mankynde,   f. 3^r
the deuyll of hell, enuyed so sore, that may nat ne can nat susteyne
no creature to profyte that intendeth to grow in vertuos lyuyng, and
specially to that excellent vertew of aungelyke chastyte whyche that   30
he knew wele that thys yonge chosyn vyrgyne to aspyre to in suche
iuuent age, whos vertuos fame clerely dyd shyne thorought that
region, stered, meued and gretly excyted one of hys lecherouse

MSS T1B; B is defective and begins at l. 60 **gloryous**

dysciples, Fabricius by name, whyche kepte the offyce of prefecture
35 other elles by whom passyd all the jugementes of that region.

Thys wreched and blynde lecherous tyrant, so gretly meued and
stered wyth flesshly concupiscence, oppressyd hym so sore in
vnlefull desyre of thys gloryous vyrgyn that hys blynde nature
myght nat susteyne hit. Wherfore in all haste vnder the colour of
40 hys offyce he sent for hyr, and opened to thys chosyn vyrgyne the
synfull tresoure of hys abhominable desyres, behotyng her suche
plente of tresoure wyth plente of all other worldly goodes that he
supposyd shuld please her youthe wythouten any mesure for her
endowance, and also promysyng hyr to wedde lawfully after the
45 custome of that region.

Thys chaste, swete and gracyous vyrgyne, when she had herde hys
vnclene and blynde desyres, hys ryche promyses of hys erthely
tresores, sayinges and behestes, maydenly and holyly and in maner
wyth a lothyng indignacion she vtterly dyspysyd hem as she wolde
50 haue do cley or any other erthely corrupcion, opynly declaryng hyr and
boldly in hyr virginall langage saying and knowlechyng her by her
answere that she was dyspoused by her loue and feythe in spirituall
matrymony as trewe spousesse vnto owre sauyour Cryste Ihesu.

When thys blynde and lecherouse tyraunt had herde thys holy
55 vyrgynes answere, hauyng a maner of gladnes that vnder the colour
f. 3ᵛ of the offyce of hys | prefecture he myght execute the malycyous
vengeance conceued in hys vnclene hert, anone wexed so woode in
hys furyose tyranny that anone in all haste possyble, commavndyng
hys tormentoures, wythoute more langage or taryng, to caste that
60 gloryous vyrgyne into a ton of brasse full of hoote oyle feruently
boylyng.

But that blyssyd and louyng lord Cryste Ihesu, that comforteth all
hys louers in her moste necessyte and ys chyef refuge to all hys
louers in all maner of tribulacion, anone shewed hys myghty hande
65 of louyng and comfortable helpe to thys gracious vyrgyne Dorothe,
that wythouten any maner of peyne of that turment she felt none but
vnwemmyd. Wherfore she gretly reioyed, thankyng her spouse Ihesu
also louyngly as though she had be anoyntyd or bathed in the moste
precyouse and redolent bawme in erthe.

70 Anone after thys myracle seene, many of thos paynemes that were
present and beholdyng hyr paynefull torment and seyng thys grete

myracle of thys chosyn vyrgyne, pryuyly purposyd wythin hemselfe
in all the haste possible to be baptysed. And so were there many full
pryuyly conuertyd.

Thys blynde tyraunt Fabricius when he sawe thys grete myracle, 75
trowed and also veryly beleued that hit had be done by som magyke
otherwyse callyd nygromancy, commaundyng anone thys blessyd
virgyn to be put and closyd in a derke pryson .ix. dayes meteles and
drynkeles wythouten any maner of foode or sustenaunce. The
whyche blessyd vyrgyne in all thys tyme of her imprysonment was 80
so norysshed and fedde of blessed aungelles wyth heuynly food that
whan she was brought forthe before thys cursed iuge, and when he
sawe here beawte was manyfolde encresyd myche more fayrer then
euer she was before, whereopon all the pepyll that sawe her beawte,
meruelyng gretely howe so tender a virgyne | that was kepte so long f. 4ʳ
wythouten any foode myght apere so beauteuous, and therwyth 86
anone thys tyraunt blyndyd in malyce sayde vnto her: 'Trewly, but
thow worshyp my goddes anone thow shalt nat passe the punyssh-
ment of thys sharpe bed of iron,' whyche was full of prykkes of full
sharpe iron.   90

Thys holy Dorothe full mekely answered: 'I worshyp God and no
deuylles, for thy goddes that thow worshyppest be nought elles but
deuylles.' And than anone forthwyth thys blessyd vyrgyne fell downe
prostrate to the grounde, lyftyng vp hyr eyen into heuyn, praying to
almyghty God of hys eternall goodnesse to shewe there howe he ys 95
myghty and that ther ys noon other god but he alone.

And in thys meane tyme, whyles thys blessyd vyrgyn was in
deuoute prayeres to almyghty God, thys tyraunt Fabricius let areyse
a grete pylour, and theropon he let set the chyef idole of hys
mawmetry, whyche he worshyppyd most in his paynemes wyse for 100
hys god. And anone immediately God sent a grete multytude of
aungelles from heuyn sodenly, and wyth a grete hasty vengeaunce
threwe downe to grounde thys cursyd and lothsom mawment wyth
the pyllour that hyt stood on, in so moche that ther was no party of
the pyllour founde.   105

And sodenly therwyth was herde a voyce of deuylles crying in the

72 thys] hys B   73 the] *om.* B   76 trowed, beleued] trowyng, beleuyng B
magyke] *add* arte B   77 commaundyng] commaundid B   80 of] *om.* B
82 and when] *erasure* B   85 howe] *add* euer B   87 but] *add* yef B
89–90 whyche . . . iron] *om.* B   97 was] *add* thus B   103 to grounde] *om.* B
106 therewyth was] there were B   a voyce] voyces B

eyre: 'O Dorothea, why consumest thow vs and dryuest vs frome owre possessyons and dwellyng places? Thow lyuest to longe in thys erthe.' And anone forthewyth many a thowsand of paynems opynly
110 and feythfully were turnyd to crystyn feyth, whyche by the vyctoryous dethe of martyrdom entred into the kyngdom of heuen.

And then anone she was hangyd vp opon a gebet or gallous wyth her fete vpward and her hede douneward, and wyth hookes of iron
f. 4ᵛ her fayre and tender | body was all torente and torne, and wyth smale
115 yardes all tobetyn and wyth grete scorges all sore woundyd. And moreouer all these diuerse tormentes done, brennyng brondes were put to her maydynly brestes to consume hem awey wyth brennyng, and thus was she left halfe dede, and therwyth commaundyd to sharpe prysone tyll on the morow.

120 And on the morow when she was brought forthe, thys tyraunt her iuge sawe wele that there appered nether spot ne hurte of her former tormentes in no place of hyr beauteuous body, in so moche that he merueled gretly. And then anone he sayde to her: 'O swete and beauteuous vyrgyne, whether yet ye be remembred in any maner of
125 wyse toward [yowre] conuersyon, for ye haue bene somwhat chastysed for yowre inordinate rebellyon.' And anone he sente to her her two sustres Trystem and Calistem, the whyche for drede of temperall deth had forsake Cryste and were tornyd to paynemes lawe, and thus by hyr two sustres, yef they cowde haue brought hit
130 aboute, thys blessyd vyrgyn Dorothe shulde haue forsaken Cryste and be turnyd as they were to theyre hethen lawe.

But thys blessed Dorothe spake full mekely and seyde to her systres so feythfully, so blessydly, so heuenly, in so moche that she toke from hem the blyndnes of theyr hertes that they stood in at that
135 tyme and conuerted hem bothe aȝene to crystyn lawe. And anone as thys tyraunt Fabricius herde thys he commaunded anone bothe these sustres to be bounde togeder bak and bak, and bothe to be caste into a grete fyre to be brent. And so they were.

And than he sayde to Dorothe: 'How longe wylt thow wyth thyne
140 enchauntmentes and thy wychecraftes thus in thys wyse disceue vs in prolongyng thy lyfe in suche maner wyse? Other do sacryfice as thow

112 vp] om. B   114 torente and] om. B   torne, and] totorne B   115 sore woundyd] forwounded B   116 brondes] bondes B   122 beauteuous] bounteuous B   124 yet/ye be] trsp. B   125 yowre conuersyon] owre conuersyon Tı, youre comisyon B   128 and] that B   129–30 yef . . . aboute/thys . . . Dorothe] trsp. with and for yef B   131 be] add also B   132 and seyde] om. B   137 and(1)] to B   141 lyfe] selfe B

owest to do to owre goddys, that thow mayst lyue, or elles thyne
hede shal be smyte of anone.' Thys holy vyrgyne wyth a glad chere
answered and sayde: 'Whatsoeuer thow can thynke the | opon any   f. 15ʳ
maner of peyne, I am redy to suffer for the loue of my lord and   145
sauyour Cryste Ihesu, my chosen spowse, in whos precyouse
gardeyne so plenteuosly full of all maner delyces I haue gadered
rooses wyth appulles, where I shall ioye wyth hym worlde wythouten
ende.'

And when thys tyraunt, blynded in malyce, herde howe ioyfull she   150
answered, wexyng almost wood for wrethe, and malyce fretyng hym
by the hert full sore, and in hys cursed wyse grennyng, frownyng and
wyth an hygh wood voyce crying, commaundyd anone that her fayre
vysage synglerly replenysshyd so full of beawte shulde anone be all
tobetyn wyth staues and buffettes, that none impressyon of her fayre   155
vysage myght be knowen. And so hit was done tyll her tormentoures
wexed so wery that they myght no lengor susteyne. And so was she
sent to pryson ayene to be kept ther tyll on the morow.

And opon the morow, when thys gloryos vyrgyne Dorothe was
brought forth before thys tyraunt her iuge, forsoth ther was no   160
wemme ne no maner of hurt that apered in her maydynly body ne
vysage, for that same nyght before was she heled and cured by owre
sauyour Cryste Ihesu. And when thys tyraunt sawe thys myracle, the
whyche he cowde nat vnderstand for lak of feythe, anone he gaue
sentence of iugement that her hede shuld be smyte of.   165

And anone forthwyth was she lad wythoute the walles of the cyte
toward her iugement, where oone Theophilus, whyche was the
prothonary chyef of that region, and he was the most solempne
doctour of lawe of all that contre, sawe thys gloryous vyrgyne
Dorothe ladde toward her dethe, spake to her in thys wyse, in   170
maner scornyng her. Full desyrously he prayed her to sende hym
some rooses of her spowses gardeyn, for as he had herde her say
before her cursyd iuge in the tyme of her passyon, and thus in thys
wyse scornyngly he prayed her oftyn tymes. And anone thys blessyd
vyrgyn full of feythe promysyd hym to sende hym that he desyred,   175
natwythstandyng that tyme | he desyred thys hit was full colde, for   f. 15ᵛ
hit was in wynter season when all the erthe was bareyne.

---

142 owre] the B   144 thynke] bethynke B   147 delyces] delytes B
152 and(1)(2)] *om.* B   155 staues] stones B   156 vysage] face B   tyll her]
vnto the B   168 prothonary] prenotary B   and] for B   172 as] *om.* B   say]
add so B

And when thys gloryous vyrgyne came to the place where her
hede shuld be smyte of, she prayed to owre lord for all theym that in
180 the honowre and worshyp of almyghty god dyd any maner of thyng
in the remembraunce of her passion, that hyt myght be the cause of
theyr saluacion, and specyally fro worldly shame of greuouse
pouerte, also to be delyuered from shamefull sclaunderyng and
lesyng of theyr name. And also that they may haue grace, or they
185 departe from thys lyfe, to haue verrey contrycion and of all theyre
synnes plener remyssyon. Also for all women that wyth deuocion in
her name prayen or callen for helpe, and specyally in the tyme of
trauelyng of theyr chyldren, that they may sone haue releuyng and
helpe of theyr sorowes and dyseses, and also in what howse that a
190 booke of her passion were in or an image of hyr remembraunce, that
hyt may be preserued from all maner of perell of her fyre wythyn
hem, and that no maner of lyghtenyng hurte hyt.

And anone after thys prayer there was herde a voyce from heuen
aboue: 'Com on my wel belouyd, com on my spouse, thow haste
195 grauntyd in heuen all thy peticions and askynges, and also from
whom thow prayest fore shal be saued.' And then anone she bowed
downe her hede to the stroke of hym that shuld smyte her.

And anone sodenly therwyth there appered a passyng fayre chylde
yclothed in purpure, bare legges and feete, wyth a feyre crolled hede,
200 whos garment was powdred full of sterres, beryng a lytell basket in
hys hande wyth .iij. rooses and as many appulles and offeryng hem to
thys blessyd vyrgyn Dorothe, to whom thys gloryous vyrgyne sayde:
f. 16ʳ 'I beseche the, | my lorde, bere these rooses wyth the appulles to the
doctour Theophilus.'
205   And anone as thys was sayde, she bowed downe her hede and
suffred the stroke of a swerde, and so passyd she to God. The .viij.
Idus of February suffred she her martydome of the iuge Fabricius,
vnder the emperoures of Rome Dioclisian and Maximian, the yer of
Crystes incarnacion .CC.iiij.xx.viij.
210   And thys tyme stode myghty Theophilus doctor of her lawe in the
iuges palyce, and ther come to hym thys feyre chyld before sayde and
toke hym a parte besyde, and toke hym thys lytell basket wyth rooses
and appulles and seyde to hym in thys wyse: 'These rooses wyth
appulles my suster sent the from the delycyous gardyne of paradyse

180 of] om. B   184 may] myght B   191 her] add oune looks like onne B
191–2 wythyn . . . and] ne B   195 from] for B   201 as] also B
210 stode/myghty . . . lawe] trsp. B   212 parte] party B

of her spowse Ihesu.' And therwyth anone thys fayre chylde was 215
passyd away so sodenly that no creature cowde wete where thys
gracious chylde was become.

Then anone after thys, sodenly thys famous doctour Theophilus
brake owte anone into an hye and grete voyce of louyng and
praysyng, gloryfyng and gretly [magnyfying] Cryste Ihesu the 220
grete God of the vyrgyn Dorothe, that in the moneth of February
in so grete colde and froste whyche at that tyme had ouerfrozen the
erthe, when neyther felde ne orchard be wey of nature knoweth no
grenenes, ne bowgh can bere no leefe: 'Suche rooses and appulles
thys myghty lord Ihesu to whom he wyll he graciosly sendeth, whos 225
myghty graciouse and gloryos name must euer be blessyd world
wythouten ende. Amen.' Of whos testymony and affirmacion and by
whos prechyng all that cyte was conuerted anone to the feythe of
owre sauyour, and were baptysed and resceued crystyndom.

And anone when this cursyd tyraunt and iuge Fabricius sawe 230
thys, | that thys grete doctour Theophilus had thus conuertyd the f. 16ᵛ
pepyll and all the cyte hoole, anone many maner of tormentes, many
moo than euer Dorothe was tormentyd wyth, he let hym to be
tormentyd. And at the last he commaundyd hym to be all tohewen
into small gobettes, as who choppeth flesshe to the pot, and tho peces 235
of hys flesshe to be caste to bestes and to byrdes, and so malycyously
and tyrauntly to be deuoured.

But thys gracyous doctour Theophilus had furst receued the
sacrament of baptym, and also was comened wyth the preciouse
sacrament of Crystes gloryose flesshe and blood. And so by holy 240
martyrdom full of feythe he folowed that blyssyd and gloryouse
virgyn Dorothe, and changyd thys dedely lyfe and passyd to blysse to
owre sauyour Cryste Ihesu, that gloryfyeth hys loueres and seyntes.
And owre sauyour Ihesu ys gloryfyed in hem, that wyth the fader
and the holy gost consubstantly and coeternally lyueth and regneth, 245
God into the world of worldys. Amen.

---

215 was] *om.* B   216 wete] telle B   220 magnyfying] manyfying T1
232 many(2)] *om.* B   234 tormentyd] *add* with B   240 and] *add* hys precious B
242 thys] hys B   246 into] in B

25 ST LEGER

St Leger was born c. 616 and was ordained deacon at twenty. He was an abbot at thirty-five, and in 663 became bishop of Autun. Leger's political support for King Childeric II led to the exiling of Ebroin, mayor of the palace, who eventually returned and avenged himself upon Leger by having him blinded and mutilated. Two years later Ebroin succeeded in having Leger deposed as bishop and executed. Although Leger's murder was political, he was regarded by the Church as a martyr.

This Life follows closely that printed in *Early SEL*, 81–3.

Here endith the life of the blessid virgyn and martir Seint
Dorathe and next bygynneth the life of Seint Leger.

Seint Leger the holy bishop conuertid by his preching muche peple
to the feith of Ihesu Crist. And when the wickid tyraund Ebronyus
herd howe he had turned the peple fro his feith, than he in gret angre
sent for this holy byshop and [commaundid] his cruel tormentours to
put oute bothe his eyen, because he wolde not beleue on his false 5
goddys. But when his eyen were put oute yet he left not to preche
the feith of Ihesu Crist, but was more feruent then than he was whan
he myght se, wherefore these tyraundys were ny mad for angre and
constreyned hym blynde to go barefote vpon sharp rockys of stone.
And thei constreyned this holy man that was blynde to ⌐renne vpon 10
al þese⌐ scharpe rockis, and he euer prechyng to the peple the feith of
Ihesu Crist and sparyd neither for peyne ne for drede of the wickid
tyraundys.

   And than this Ebronyus commaundid that his tonge shulde be
kytte of oute of his hed, bycause he shulde not preche no more. But 15
then oure lorde Ihesu shewid there a ful gret my|racle for his holy   f. 59ʳᵃ
bishop Seint Leger, for he prechid aftir to al the peple as wel as he
dide bifore, wherefore these wickyd tyraundys were gretly abashed
and bygon to leue ther tormentyng. And as thei stode and merueyled
on this holy bishop, thei se a crowne of golde vpon his hed that 20
schynyd so bright that vnnethe thei myght se his face for the
brightnes therof. And then the iuge Ebronyus commaundide that
his hed shulde be smyte of. And ⌐then .iiij. wickyd tormentoures led
this holy⌐ bishop oute of the towne towarde the place where his hed
shulde be smyte of, and or thei come thider this holy bishop seid to 25
the tormentours: 'I conselle you to do youre office here or ye go eny
further.' And then anone .iij. of þese tormentours fille downe to his
feete and cryed hym mercy. And the .iiij.th lad this holy bishop to
the place assigned by the iuge, and there ful cruelly smyte of this
holy bishops hed.   30
   And then anone come a fire oute of helle and brent this cruel

MSS A₁A₂L   4 commaundid] conmaundid A₁   7 whan] whyle A₂L
10 man . . . blynde] bisshopp A₂L   10–11 renne . . . þese] go barefote vpon *del. and*
corr. in margin A₁   11 rockis] stonys A₂L   15 of(1)] *om.* A₂L   16 then
. . . holy] or thei come theder this holy bishop seid *del. and corr. in margin* A₁

tormentour, and fendys beryn his soule to the peyne of helle, and the angels of oure lorde bere the soule of this holy bishop into heuene with gret ioye and melody. And the goode peple beried his body aftir
35 with gret reuerence. And there oure lorde shewith dayly for his holy bishop many a gret myracle. And within .ij. yere aftir this cursid iuge Ebronyus come by the place where this holy man was beryed, and than the paynyms tolde hym what gret myracles his lorde Ihesus hath [schewid] there for this holy bishop. And then this Ebronyus
40 sent a knyght of his to the tombe of this holy bishop that seid: 'Cursid mote þei be that byleuen that a dede body may do eny myracle,' and with ful gret dispite with his swerd smyte depe into the tombe of this holy bishop, and seid: 'The deuel haue them al that beleue on this false bishop.' And forthwith come a gret [multitude]
45 of fendes and strangelyd this knyght and bere his soule with them into helle. And anone aftir died this wickid iuge Ebronyus, and fendes bere his soule to the pitte of helle for his cursid leuyng. And the angels of oure lorde Ihesu Crist [bere] the soule of his holy byshop Seint Leger to the blisse of heuene, there to reyne
50 euerlastyngly for his holy leuyng here, to the whiche blisse oure lorde bryng vs al. Amen.

f. 59rb

Here endith the life of the holy bishop and martir Seint Leger and next bygynneth the life of Seint Brandan. |

39 schewid] schewith A1   41 þei] thue A2   byleuen] belevyst A2
44 multitude] mutitude A1   48 bere] dere A1

26 ST BRENDAN

St Brendan lived at the end of the fifth century and became abbot of Clonfert, which he founded in 558. He was the hero of the *Navigatio Sancti Brendani* (*NSB*), a tenth-century text so popular in the Middle Ages that it was translated into several languages.[1]

As Görlach points out, the greater part of this Life follows that of *SEL* 180–204, with some lines and rhymes retained.[2] The *SEL* version is in turn derived from *NSB*, as has been demonstrated by Simon Lavery.[3]

---

[1] Selmer (1956), p. 145, O'Meara (1978).
[2] Görlach (1998), pp. 115–7.
[3] Lavery (1984).

Here endith the life of the holy bishop and martir Seint
Leger. And next bygynneth the life of Seint Brandan. |

Seint Brandan the holy man was a monk and borne in Irlond, and   f. 59rb
there he was abbot of an howse wherein were a thousand monkys.
And there he lad a ful streite and holy ⌐life¬ in gret penaunce and
abstynence and gouernyd his monkys ful vertuously. And than
within a while aftir come to hym an holy abbot that hight Beryn 5
to knowe of his wilfare and eche of hem to talke with othir, and so to
ioy in oure lorde Ihesu. And than Seint Brandan bigan to telle this
abbot Beryn of many wonders that he had seyn in dyuerse londes.
And when Beryn had herde al these wondyrs of Seint Brandan, than
he bygan to sigh and wepe ful sore. But euer Seint Brandan 10
confortide hym in the best wise he cowde and seid to hym: 'Ye
come hider to me for that we shulde be ioyful togiders, and therfore
for Goddys loue be mery and leue youre gret mornyng, and telle me
and vs [al] what merueyles ye haue sene in the Gret See of the occian
that compassith al the worlde aboute, and al othir waters come oute 15
of hym that gon into al the partyes of the worlde.'
    And then Beryn the olde man bygan to telle to Seint Brandan and
to his felawship al the merueyles that he had sene, ful sore wepyng,
and seid: 'I haue a sonne, his name is Mernok, and was a monk of
grete fame, the whiche had gret desire to seke aboute in dyuers 20
contreys by ship to fynde a solitary place wherein he myght dwelle
secretely oute of the worlde to serue God with more deuocion. And
then I consellid hym to seyle into an ilonde fer in the see bysides the
mounteyne of stouns, that is ful wel knowen. And when he come
theder with his monkes he liked that place right wel and serued oure 25
lorde there ful deuoutly.' And there Beryn see in a vision that this
monke Mernok was seiled fer estwarde in the see, more than .iij. days
seylyng. And sodenly to his semyng ther come a derke clowde and
ouerkeueryd them, that a gret parte of the day thei se no light. 'And
than as oure lordys wil was, the clowde passid awey and we se a ful 30
feyre ilond, and thederwarde we drewe where was ioye and myrthe

MSS A1A2L A1 breaks off at l. 416 in thys   *Rubric* Here . . . next] Here L
3 life] holy *del. and corr. in margin* A1   14 al] *om.* A1   19, 27 Mernok] *or*
Meruok A1, Mervok A2L, *see Note*   24 stouns] stonys or ellis callyd stouns L
30, 31 we] thei A2

inough, and the erthe of that ilonde schynyd as bright as the sonne, and there were the feyrest trees and erbys that eny man myght see and gret novmbre of precious stones that shynyd ful bright, and
35 euery erbe were ful of floures and euery tree ful of frute, that it was an heuenly ioy to dwel there.'

f. 59va And then | ther come to them a feyre yong man and ful curtesly welcomed them al and, clepid euery man by his name, and seid to them that thei were ful muche bounde to preyse the name of oure
40 lorde Ihesu, that wolde vouchesafe to schewe them that glorious place where is euer day and neuer nyght. And than this yong man seid: 'This place is called Paradise Terrestre, but by this ilonde is anothir ilonde where no man may come in. Also,' he seid, 'I haue byn here this half yere withoute mete, drynke or slepe.' But they thought
45 verily that thei had not be there the space of half an houre, so mery and [ioyful] þei were. And the yong man tolde them that 'this is the place that Adam and Eve shulde euer haue dwellyd in [and] al his osprynge if he had not broke the commaundement of God, for this is the place of ioy and myrth where is euer day and neuer nyght.'
50 And then this yong man brought them to ther schip ayen and seid thei myght no lenger there abyde. And whan thei were al schipped, sodenly þis yong man vanyshed awey oute of ther sight. And then thei within shorte tyme by the puruyaunce of oure lorde Ihesu come to the abbey ayen where Seint Brandan dwellyd, 'and than he and al
55 his monkes receyued us with ful gret ioye and askid vs where we had ben so long.' And than thei seyde: 'We haue ben in the Londe of Byheeste byfore the yates of paradise, where al mankynde shal dwelle aftir this life if thei kepe the commaundementis of God, wherein is euer day and neuer nyght and ioy and blysse withoute ende.' And
60 then thei seid al that it was a ful delectable place for al ther clothes smylled ful swete of that ioyful place.

And than Seint Brandan purposid verily to seke that place by Goddys helpe, and anone bygan to puruey for a goode ship and a strong, and vitayled it for .vij. yere and toke his leue of his brethern
65 and toke .xij. monkes with him to the shippe. But al thei fasted .xl.ti days, and leuyd ful deuoutly, and receyued oure lordis body, and went anone into the ship with his .xij. felowes. And than ther come

35 were] om. A2L   41–2 than . . . seid] om. A2L   43 ilonde] londe A2L
Also . . . I] And then this yong man sayde to theym ye A2L   46 ioyful] ioy A1
47 and(2)] om. A1   54 Brandan] Beryn L   55 us, vs, we] theym, theym,
thaye A2   65 with] add alle A2L

othir .ij. monkes and preyd Seint Brandan to seile with hym. And
then he seid: 'Ye may wel seile with me, but on of you shal to helle or
ye come home ayen.' 70

And then Seint Brandan made wynde up the seyle, and forth thei
seiled in Goddis name, and the ship seiled forth as faste as the arowe
fleeth fro the bowe. And when the sonne aros by the morowe thei
wiste not where thei were, for thei myght se no londe, but ther ship
was strong and goode, for | thei seiled .xl.ti days and .xl.ti nyghtis f. 59ᵛᵇ
euyn plat est. And than thei se an ilonde in the north [fer] fro them 76
and seiled thederwarde and se a gret rocke of stone appere aboue the
water, and .iij. days thei seiled aboute it or thei cowde gete in, but
atte laste thurgh the purvyaunce of oure lorde thei founde a litil
hauyn and went anone a londe euerychone. And then sodenly come 80
to them a feyre hounde and fil downe atte feet of Seint Brandan and
made hym goode chere in his maner. And then he bade his brethern
be of goode chere, 'for oure lorde Ihesu hath sent us his messenger to
lede us the wey into sum place ordeyned for us by oure lorde.' And
then the hounde went forth into a ful feyre halle, wherein thei 85
founde þe tablys spred and sette ful of goode mete and drynke. And
than Seint Brandan and al his felowes set them to the table and ete
and dranke and made them mery in the best wise. And than ther
were beddys ordeyned for them al, wherein thei aftir soper slepte ful
merely and toke ther rest aftir ther gret labour. 90

And then on the morowe thei went ayene to ther ship and seiled in
the see ful long aftir or thei cowde fynde eny londe, but atte laste by
the purviance of oure lorde thei see fer fro them a ful feyre ilelonde
ful of grene pasture, wherein were the whittest and feyrest shepe that
euer thei se and the grettist, for euery shepe was as gret as an ox. 95
And then ther come to them a ful goode man and welcomyd them al
and made them ful goode chere and seid: 'This is the ylelond of
schepe, and in this ilelonde is neuer colde weder but euer feire
somer, and that causith the schepe to be so gret and white. And thei
etyth the best gras and erbys that is in eny londe, wherefore thei ben 100
so feyre and grete.' And then þis goode man toke his leue of hem and
bade them seile furth right est, and within short tyme by Goddys
grace thei shulde come to a place like paradise where thei shulde
kepe ther Estertide.

And then thei went to schip ayen, and by the purviaunce of oure 105
lorde thei come within short tyme aftir to that ilonde. And when thei

68 to] that þey myght L   76 fer] om. A1   87 than] also A2L

come nye thider, thei myght not seyle therto for gret rockys of stone, but abode stil there byside. And then the monkes went oute of the ship vpon þe rocke and bygan to make a gret fire on the rocke and set
110 ouer a cawdron to dyght with ther mete, but Seint Brandan abode stil in the shippe, and whan the fire waxid right hote and ther mete was nye soden ynough, then this gret rocke lyke an ilelonde bygan |
f. 60ᵃ to meue, wherefore the monkes were ful sore agast and left ther mete there stille in the cawdron and highed them fast to ther schip, for
115 thei were ful sore adred and wist not what it was. But then Seint Brandan comfortide them and seid: 'Be not agast, for it is a gret fisshe of the se that is clepid Iasconye. He [laborith] nyght and day to putte his tayle in his mouth but for gretnes therof he may not.'

    And then anone [thei] wounde up the seyle [and seyled] evyn west
120 .iij. days and.iij. nyghtis or thei se eny londe, wherefore þei were right heuy, but in shorte tyme aftir, by þe puruyance of oure lorde, thei se a ful feire ilond ful of floures and erbys and trees, wherefore thei were ful ioyful and thonkyd oure lorde. And as sone as thei come theder thei went vp into the ilonde, and when thei had long gon in
125 this ilonde thei founde a right feyre welle, and therby stode a ful feyre tree ful of feyre bowys, and on euery bowe sate a feyre bryd. Thei sate so thicke theron that vnnethe a man myght se eny leffe of the tree, and euery brid sang so meryly that it was an [heuenly] noyse to here. Wherefore Seint Brandan knelyd downe on his knees and
130 wepte for ioy, and made his preyers to oure lorde to knowe what this birdes ment. And then anone oure lorde made on of the briddes fle fro the tree towarde Seint Brandan, and with the flykeryng of his wynges he made a noyse like a fidil that hym semyd he herde neuer a myryer melody.

135   And than Seint Brandan commaundide the brid [to telle] hym [what] causith them to sitte so thicke on that tree and syng so meryly. And than the brid seid to hym: 'Sometyme we were angels in heuene, but when oure maister Lucifer felle downe into helle for his hye pride, and eche of vs fil with hym aftir oure offence, sum lower
140 than sum, aftir ther trespas. And for oure trespas was litle, therfore oure lorde hath set us here oute of al peyne in ful gret ioy and

114 there] om. L   ther] om. A2, þe L   117 laborith] labored A1L
119 thei] the A1   and seyled] om. A1   122 and(1) . . . trees] trees and erbes L
128 heuenly] heuely A1   129 here] add theym A2   135 to telle] comaun-
dide A1   136 what] who A1   them] thym del. and corr. in margin in later hand A1
139 pride] add and A2

myrthe aftir his plesyng, and to serue hym this vpon this tree in oure
best maner that we can. And the Sonday is a day of rest fro al
worldly occupacion, and that day we ben al made as white as any
snowe to preyse oure lorde in that day in the best wise we can.' And   145
than the brid seid to Seint Brandan that 'it is .xij. monthis agon that
ye departide from youre abbey, and when ye haue seiled in the see
.vij. yere hereaftir, than ye shal see the place that ye desire to come
to. And al this .vij. yere ye shal kepe youre Ester here with us, and
atte .vij. yeres ende ye shal come to the Londe of Byheste.' And this   150
was vpon an Estyr Day that þis | bridde seid these wordes to Seint   f. 60ʳᵇ
Brandan. And than the brid fly ayen to his felowes that sat on the
tree. And then anone these fowlys bygan Euynsong so meryly that it
was gret ioye and comforte to here them syng. And then aftir soper
Seint Brandan and his felowes went to bedde and slepte right wel.   155
And by the morowe thei rose up bytymes, and then the briddes
bygon Matyns in the most mery wyse, and aftir that thei song Pryme
and houres and al the seruise that cristen men syngen here in this
londe.

    And Seint Brandan and his felowes dwellyd stil there .viij. wekys   160
til Witsontide and Trinyte Sonday was past. And then thei seiled
ayen to the ilelonde of schepe, and there thei vityllyd hem right wel
and made them mery and toke ther leve of the olde man and went
ayene to ther ship. And than this brid that spake byfore with Seint
Brandan and his felowes come ayene to them into the schip and seid: 165
'Ye haue byn [with vs] al this hie feste, and I am to you sende for to
let you wette that ye shal seyle fro hens into an ilonde wherein is an
abbey and .xxiiij. monkes therin, the whiche fro hens is many a myle.
And there ye shal holde youre Cristmas, and youre Ester with us like
as I seid byfore. And then anone Seint Brandan and his felowes   170
seiled forth in the Grete Occian, and anone ther fel a gret tempest
vpon them and were so troubled and tossid in the see that ⌐thei⌐ wist
not what to do, thei were so wery and feble, and ful long thei seyled
in the gret tempest and lokid fast aftir londe, but thei cowde nothing
se but the water and the firmament. But within a while aftir, by the   175
puruyaunce of oure lorde, thei se an ilelonde afer fro them, and then
thei preid to oure lorde on ther knees to sende them thider in safte.

144 we ben/al] *trsp.* A2L   145 to] *add* plese and L   146 that] *om.* A2
152 brid] fowle L   153 fowlys] byrdis A2   164 ther] *om.* A2L
166 with vs] ws A1   172 thei] that *del. and corr. to* they *in later hand in margin* A1
173 seyled] *add* forthe A2L

But it was .xl.ti days aftir or thei come therto, wherefore al the
monkes were so wery of that trouble that thei [rought] but litil of
180 ther lyves, and euer thei cried ful piteously to oure lorde to bryng
them there in safte, for thei were ful sore agast. But atte last thurgh
the help of oure lorde thei come into a litil hauyn, but it was so
streyte that vnnethis the shippe myght come in to cast his ankyr.
And than anone these monkes went to londe, and when thei had long
185 walkid aboute, atte last thei founde .ij. feyre welles, on of feyre clere
water and the todyr was sumwhat thicke. And then these monkes
thonked oure lorde that he had brought them thedyr in safte and
wolde right fayne haue dronke of this water. But Seint Brandan
f. 60va chargid them that thei | shulde take none withoute lisens, 'for if we
190 absteyne us a while, oure lorde wol puruey for us in the best wise.'

And anone ther come to them a feyre olde man with hoor heer and
welcomyd them right mekely, and he kyst Seint Brandan and led
them forth by many a feyre welle, til atte last thei come to a feyre
abbey, where Seint Brandan and his felowes were receyued yn with
195 gret honowre and procession, with .xxiiij. monkes al in rial copes of
cloth of golde and the crosse bore byfore them. And then the abbot
come to Seint Brandan and kyssed hym ful mekely, and toke hym by
the honde and led hym with al his monkys into a ful rial halle and set
them downe arewe on the benche. And the abbot of that place anone
200 wysshe al ther fete by rowe with the feyre water of the welle that thei
se byfore, and than he lad them to the fraytour and there he set them
amonge his couent. And anone ther come on by the puruyance of
oure lorde that serued them right wel bothe of mete and drynke and
set a feire whit loffe byfore eche monke, and white rotes of erbys he
205 set byfore them also, the whiche were right delycius, but thei wiste
not what rotys they were. And thei dronke of the water of that feyre
clere welle that thei wolde haue dronke of when thei come first
alonde, but Seint Brandan chargid them thei shulde not til that thei
had lycens of the abbot of that londe.

210 And than this abbot come and cheryd Seint Brandan and his
monkis and bade them: 'Ete and drynke for charite, for euery day
oure lorde Ihesu sendithe to us a goodly olde man that leyth this
tabyl and set oure mete and drynke byfore us, but we knowe not
howe it comyth, for we ordeyne neuer for no mete nor drynke for vs
215 this .iiij. score yere, but euer oure lorde wol puruey for his seruantis.
We ben in this abbey .xxiiij.ti monkys, and euery werke day oure

179 rought] brought A1   191 anone] add aftir L   olde] wolde A2

lorde sendith us to oure mete .xij. white loues, but euery Sonday and
holy day he sendith vs .xxiiij.ti white lovis. And the bred that we leue
atte dyner we ete it atte oure soper, and nowe ye byn here, oure lorde
hath sende .xlviij. lovys to us for to be mery togiders as brethern. 220
And alwey .xij. of us go to dyner while the othir .xij. kepe the quere,
and then we go to churche and thei come to dyner. And this hath
byn oure use this .iiij. score yere, for so long it is ago that we come
hider oute of the abbey of Seint Patrickis in Irlonde. And al this tyme
oure lorde Ihesu hath purueid for oure mete and drynke, but none of 225
us knowith howe it comyth to us but God alone, wherefore his name |
be preysed, worlde withoute ende. And here in this londe is euer f. 60vb
feyre wedyr, and none of us was neuer sike syns we come hider. And
when we goeth to Matyns, masse or eny oþer seruyse of oure lorde to
the churche, anone .vij. tapers of wex byn set in the quere by the 230
puruyance of oure lorde, and anone lightyd withoute mannys hande,
and thei brenne there bothe dai and nyght and neuer wastith as long
as we haue dwellid here, that is .iiij. score yere.'
    And then Seint Brandan went to the churche with the abbot of the
place, and there thei seid Evynsong ful deuoutly. And than Seint 235
Brandan byhilde up towarde the crucifix and se oure lorde hangyng
vpon the crosse, whiche was made of bright [cristal] and ful curiously
it was wrought. And in the quere were .iiij. and twenty setys, for in
that abbey were .xxiiij.ti monkys, and .vij. ful feyre tapyrs brennyng in
the quere that neuer were quenched, and the abbotis sete was made in 240
the myddes of the quere. And then Seint Brandan askid þe abbot howe
long thei had kept that silence that none of hem spake to othir. And
then he seid to hym: 'Forsothe this .iiij. score yere we spake none to
anothir.' And than Seint Brandan wepte for ioy to here of ther
conuersacion that was so holi. And then Seint Brandan desired of 245
the abbot that he and his monkis myght dwelle stil there with hym, but
þe abbot seid: 'Sir, that may ye not in no wise, for oure lorde hath
shewid you in what maner ye shal be goydyd til this .vij. yeres ende be
fulfilled. And thou with thi .xij. monkes aftir the .vij. yeres ende byn
fulfilled shal come ayen into Irlonde in safte. But on of the .ij. monkys 250
that come laste to the into the schip shal dwelle in the ielond of
ankres, and the tother monke shal go quycke to helle.'

    219 it] *om.* A2   oure(1)] *om.* L   229 or] *add* to A2L   to(2)] in A2L
237 cristal] cristral A1   242 none] neuer one A2L   245 conuersacion . . .
holi] holy conuersacion A2L   248 maner] *add* wyse A2   til] *add* þat A2L   ende]
om. A2L   249 ende] *om.* A2L   byn] *add* come and L

And as Seint Brandan knelyd in the churche, he se a bright
schynyng angel come in atte the wyndowe and lyght the tapers
255 euerychone and fly oute atte the same wyndowe ayen to the blysse of
heuene. And than Seint Brandan merueyled gretly that the tapurs
brent so fast and wastid not. And then the abbot seid: 'It is rad in the
olde lawe that Moyses seigh a busche of thorne al in light fire
⌐brennyng¬, but the more it brent the grener were the leuys, and
260 therfore merueile not of this thyng, for oure lordes power is as gret
nowe as it was than.'
  And whan Seint Brandan had dwellid in this abbey fro Cristmas
Euyn til .xij.th day was past, than he toke his leue of the abbot and of
al his couent and went ayen to his schip and seiled fro thens with [al]
f. 61ᵃ his monkys to|warde the abbey of Seint Hillariis. But thei had ful
266 gret tempest in the see, and were dreve hider and thyder in the see
and were in ful gret trouble, for thei were in that see from .xij.th tyde
til it was nye Palme Sonday. And þan by the puruyaunce of oure
lorde thei come ayene to the ylelonde of schepe, and there the olde
270 man receyued them with gret gladnes and kissid Seint Brandans fete
and al his monkes also. And then he brought them into a feire halle
and sette them to soper on Schere [Thursday], and aftir soper he
wisshe al ther feete and kyssed [them] lyke as oure lorde dide to his
disciples. And thei were there al nyght and Goode Friday al day, and
275 on Saturday that [was] Ester Euyn they toke ther leve and went ayen
to ther schip and seiled to the place where the gret fisshe lay. And
anone thei se the cawdron vpon the fisshis bak that thei left there .xij.
monyth byfore.
  And there thei went vp ayen and kept ther Resurreccion, and
280 euery monke seid his masse on the fishes bak. And aftir that thei
went to ship ayene and seiled the same day to the ielond of paradyse
where the tree was so ful of briddys meryly syngyng. And then the
same brid that cam to them [byfore came to them] ayen with ful
mery melodye, and welcomyd Seint Brandan and al his monkys like
285 as he dide the yere byfore. And ther Seint Brandan and his monkys
were fro Ester til Witsontide as ⌐thei¬ were the yere byfore, in gret
myrthe and ioy, and euery day thei herde that mery seruyse of the

259 brennyng] wenyng *del. and corr. in margin in later hand* A1   260 power is]
om. L   261 it] he L   264 al(2)] *om.* A1   267 were in(1)] had A2L
272 Thursday] Tursday A1   273 them] *om.* A1L   275 was] *om.* A1
276 ther] *om.* A2L   278 byfore] *om.* A2   283 byfore . . . them] *om.* A1   to
them/ayen] *trsp.* L   286 thei] as *del. and corr. to* they *in margin in later hand* A1
287 that] so A2

briddes that sat so thicke on the tre. And than the brid tolde to Seint
Brandan that aftir Witsontide he with al his monkys shulde go ayen
euery yere, til that the .vij. yere were fulfilled, to that abbey where   290
were .xxiiij.ti monkys and there to abide til the .vij. yere were
fulfilled from Cristmas to Candilmas. 'And thus ye shal labour euery
yere in the se in ful gret peril til .vij. yere be fulfilled. And than shal
ye come to that ioyful place of paradise and dwel there .xl.ti days in
ful gret ioy and myrthe, and then ye shal come home ayen yn safte to   295
youre owne abbey in Irlonde, and ther to ende your life and come to
the blisse of heuene that oure lorde hath bought you with his
precious passion.'

And then the angel of oure lorde ordeyned al thyngis that was
nedeful to Seint Brandan and his monkys in vytayle and al othir   300
necessaryes. And than þei thonkyd oure lorde of his ⌈gret⌉ goodenes
that he had shewde to them ful many tymes in ther gret nede. And
anone thei seiled in the Gret See there to abyde the mercy of God.
And as thei seyled in a ful gret tempest, anone thei | perceyued that a   f. 61ʳᵇ
ful gret fishe and a griselysche, castyng fire oute of his mouth,   305
folowid ful fast aftir ther ship, wherefore thei drad ful sore and cried
to God and Seint Brandan to be ther helpe. And anone by the
purviaunce of oure lorde ther come another grettir fishe than he oute
of the west and faught ful sore with hym, and atte last he had the
better and clove this gret fishe asondre in .iij. partis that had this long   310
tyme folowyd the schip of Seint Brandan. And whan that gret
[fisshe] had this slayne the tother gret fisshe than he returned ayen
into the same contre he come fro.

And then al the monkes thankyd God and Seint Brandan that thei
were so delyuerd from that gryselyche fisshe, but thei were in ful gret   315
heuynes, for ther viteyle was nye spent. But by the purviaunce of
oure lorde, there come a brid to them that brought them a gret
branche of a vyne ful of rede grapis, wherewith thei leuyd .xiiij. days.
And atte .xiiij. days ende thei come to a litle ielond where was many
a vyne ful of grapys. And than Seint Brandan thonkyd oure lorde   320
that he had so purueyd for hym and his monkes, and went on londe
and gadred there so many rede grapys þat thei leuyd þerby .xl.ti days
aftir in ther ship, seylyng in the see in many a gret storme and paryl.

290 were] be A2   291 were(2)] be A2L   abide] add euery yere A2L
294 ioyful place] place fulle of ioye L   297 you] add to A2L   301 gret] grtt
del. and corr. in margin A1   303 seiled] add forthe A2L   305 mouth] add and
A1L   312 fisshe(1)] fsshe A1   this] thus A2L

And as thei seiled this in the see in [ther] gret trouble, ther come a
325 gripe fleyng aftir the ship to distroye them al, wherefore they cryed
fast to God, for thei wend verily to be al distroyed. But anone by the
purviaunce of oure lorde, the brid of the feyre tre of paradise, that
had confortide them afore, come to them, and anone he fly to the
grype and smyte oute bothe his eyen and aftir anone he slowe hym.
330 Wherefore Seint Brandan thankid oure lorde of his gret goodenes
that he had so defendid them fro that gryselyche fowle. And then
thei seiled fourth in the see til it was Seint Petrus Day. And than
Seint Brandan with his monkys songe ther seruyse ful meryly, and
the see was there so clere that thei myght se al the fishes that were
335 aboute hem, wherfore thei were ful sore agast and conseyled Seint
[Brandan] to syng no more, for al the fishes lay as though thei slepte.
And than Seint Brandan seid: 'Drede you not, for ye haue .ij. Esters
kepte the Resurreccion vpon the grettest fishes bak of the see, and
therfore drede ye not of these lityl fishes.' And then Seint Brandan
340 went to masse and bade his monkys to syng in the best wise that thei
cowde. And anone al the fishes awoke and come aboute the ship so
f. 61ᵛᵃ thicke that | vnnethe a man myght see the water for the gret
multitude of fishes that come thereaboute. And anone as the masse
was don, eche fishe partide his wey, that none of them wiste where
345 thei bycome. And .vij. days aftir they seiled in suche clere water that
thei myght se al thingis in the water as [playnlye as] thei myght [se]
it in the londe, whereof thei had gret merueyle.

And then come a southe wynde and drofe them .viij. dais
northwarde, where thei se an ilonde ful derke, and foule stynkyng
350 smoke was theryn, and there thei herde gret blowyng and blastyng of
belowys, but thei cowde se nothyng, and there was gret ⌜thonder⌝
and lyghtenyng, wherfore they blessid them ful fast. And atte laste
come on startyng fourth al ful of brennyng of fire and stared vpon
them with his gret eyen, whereof the monkes were ful sore agaste,
355 and atte his departyng fro them he made the moste gastful noyse that
euer eny man herde. Wherefore þei were ful sore agast and blessid
them ful faste, but anone aftir thei come oute withoute nombre with
her tonges and hamers al brennyng hote and vpon the water thei
ranne ful fast aftir the ship. But thurgh the myght of oure lorde thei
360 hadde no power to hurte the schip nor the men, wherfore thei bygan

324 ther] the A1   326 to] *add* haue A2   336 Brandon] Bradon A1   thei] *add*
had A2   346 playnlye as] *om.* A1L   se(2)] *om.* A1   se it] *om.* L
351 thonder] powder *del. and corr. in margin* A1

to cry and rore and caste ther fire hamers aftir the schip, and than it semyd that al þe see was afire. And then the monkes were right sore agast and preid fast to oure lorde for to helpe them, for thei cast these fire hamers al aboute the ship in euery side, but ther come none into the ship. And it semyd to them that al the ielond was afire and 365 al the see also, for it smookyd and stank ful fowle, and ful long lastid ther roryng and cryyng aftir.

And then Seint Brandan tolde his monkes that it was a part of helle, and therfore he chargid them to be stidfast in the feith, for thei shulde se many a dredful place or thei come home ayene. And anone 370 come the south wynde and drove them ferther into the north where thei see an hille al afire and gret stynche and smoke come therfro, and the fire stode upon eche syde of the hille lyke a walle al brennyng. And then on of his monkes bygan to crye and wepe sore and seid his ende was come that he myght no lenger abide in the 375 ship, but anone he lepte into the see and cryed and roryd ful piteously and cursid the tyme that euer he was bore, and he cursid bothe his fader and moder that bygate hym, 'for nowe for my cursid leuyng I shal go into the euerlastyng peyne of helle.' And then | anone come the fendys and cast hym in the myddes of that gret fire, f. 61vb and tho was þe seyng of Seint Brandan founde trewe that he tolde 381 hym atte his first commyng into the schip. And therfore let euery man forsake his synne and cri God merci and do penaunce for his synnes here while he hath tyme and space, for atte the houre of his deth euery man shal have as he hath deseruyd, eyther ioy or peyne. 385

And then anone the wynde turned into the north and drove þe schip southwarde .vij. days, and atte last thei come to a gret bare rocke that stode in the see, and theron sate a nakid goste in ful gret sorowe and wrechidnes, for ofte the gret wawys of the see [bete hym] so that al his flesshe was gone and nothyng left but senewys and bare 390 bonys. And whan the wawys were gon, the canevas that hyng ouer hym bete his body with the blastes of the wynde, that it was a piteous sight to byholde. And than Seint Brandan chargid hym to telle what he was, and then he seid: 'My name is Iudas, that solde oure lorde Ihesu for .xxx.ti pens, that sitte this here, but I am worthi to be in 395 the grettest peyne that is. But oure lorde is so merciful that he hath rewardide me better than I hauye deseruyd, for my place of right is in that brennyng hille that ye come fro, for I am worthi to be in the grettest peyne that euer may be, that so falsly haue bytrayed my

389 bete hym] betym A1

400 lorde Ihesu that dide so meche for me. But I am here in this place
but certeyne tymes of the yere, that is fro Cristmas Eue til .xij.th
daye, and fro Ester til Withsonday be past, and euery hye fest of oure
lady, and from Evynsong on the Saturday til Sonday atte nyght. But
al othir tymes I lye stil in helle in gret brennyng fire with Pilate,
405 Heroude and Cayphas, wherefore cursyd be the tyme that euer I
knewe them.' And than Iudas preid Seint Brandan to abide there stil
with hym al that nyght, that he myght kepe hym there stil that the
fendes shulde not fecche him that nyght to helle.

And than seid Seint Brandan: 'By Goddys help thou shalt abyde al
410 this nyght.' And then Seint Brandan askid hym what clothe that was
that hyng ouer his hed. He seid it was a clothe that he yafe to a lepre,
'bought with oure lordys mony and not with myn whan I was his
purse berer, wherfore it doth me nowe ful gret peyne that it betyth
euer so fast on my face. And therfore let euery man alyve by ware
415 that he take awey no manys goode wrongfully, for he shal suffre
A2, f. 83va   peyne therfore here in thys | lyffe or in purgatory or in helle after his
deservyng. And these oxe tungis that hong here aboue me I yeave
them somtyme to .ij. prestis, and therefore the fysshis of the se
gnawe thereon and spare me. And the stone that I sytt on nowe laye
420 sumtyme in a place where hit esyd no man, and I toke it thens and
caste it into a fowle way where men were easid thereby, and therefore
it helpith me nowe, for euery gode dede shal be rewardid and euery
evylle dede punysshyd.'

And then þe Soneday ayenst evyn came a grete multytude of
425 feendis blastyng and roryng, and bade Seynt Brandon go thens that
thaye myght haue ther seruaunt Iudas, 'for we dare not oure maister
se but yf we bryng hym to helle with vs.' Then sayde Seynt
Brandon: 'I lett you not to do your maisters commaundement, but
doith the commaundement of oure lord Ihesu that is of more power,
430 by whos power I commaunde you leve hym here alle nyght tylle
tomorowe.' Then sayde the feendis: 'Howe darst thue helpe hym
that so betrayd and solde his lorde to the Iewes for .xxx.ti pens, and
causid hym afterwarde to dye the moost shamefulle dethe?' And then
Seynt Brandon chargid the feendis by the meritis of his passhion that
435 thaye shulde not noye hym that nyght. And anone the feendis wente
there waye roryng and crying toward there maister the grete devylle
of helle. And then Iudas thankyd Seynt Brandon fulle ruthefully,
that it was grete sorowe to here his grete mornyng.

426–7 oure maister/se] trsp. L

And then the next morowe betyme the feendis came ayen, roryng
and crying, and cursid the tyme that euer Saynt Brandon came there,   440
for he had causid theym alle that nyght to lye in oryble payne for
thaye brought not Iudas with theym. 'But we wolle revenge alle oure
iniuryes vpon | hym, for he shalle haue doble payne all this .vj. days   f. 83vb
for this one nyght.' Wherefore Iudas beganne to tremble and quake
that it was ruthe to beholde hym. And then the fendis toke Iudas   445
forthe with theym to helle.

And then Seynt Brandon and his monkys saylid forthe in the se
sowthwarde .iij. days and .iij. nyghtis, and on the Frydaye bi the
purviaunce of oure lorde thaye se an ylond. And than Seynt Brandon
began to sigh right sore when he se þat ilonde in the se, for he sayde   450
to his monkis: 'I se nowe Seynt Powle the hermyte that hath dwellyd
here .xl. yere withoute mete and drynke.' And when þaye came to
this ilond, anone thaye wente alonde euerychone, and then Seynt
Pawle the holy hermyte came ayenst theym and welcomyd theym
fulle mekelye. He was a fulle olde feble man, his here tyllyd downe to   455
hys fete bothe before and behynd, that no man myght se his bare
bodye in no place, and yett he had none other clothis on but onlye
hys hore here. And then Seynt Brandon stode in a full grete thought
and began to wepe fulle bitterlye and sayde to his monkis: 'Nowe I se
a man that levith more lyke an angelle than a man, and therfore,' he   460
sayde, 'we maye be ashamyd þat we wrecchis leue no better.' Than
sayde this holye man to Seynt Brandon: 'Thue arte better than I, for
oure lorde haþe shewid the moche more of his pryvite than euer he
shewid me, and therefore it is thue that shuldist be praysid and not
I.' And then Seynt Brandon sayd: 'We be monkis and maye laboure   465
for oure mete, but thue haste no mete by thyne owne laboure but
only by the purvyaunce of God, and holdist the euer pleasyd whate
so euer thue haste, and I cannot so do, wherefore thue, fader, arte
moche better than I.' And then Seynt Powle sayde to Seynt Brandon:
'Sumtyme I was a monke of Seynt Patryckis abbeye in Irelond, and I   470
was there wardeyn of þat place where men entyr into Seynt Patrikkis
purgatorye. And in a daye there came a man to me, and I askyd hym
whate he was, and he sayde: "I am your abbot Seynt Patryk." And
then he chargid me þat I shulde go the next morowe bytyme to the
see syde and there I shulde fynde a ship the which God had provydid   475
for me, and therefore I moste fulfylle his wylle. And then the next
daye I rose vp betymes and wente to the see syde, and anone I

447 in the se] so ferre L   474 me, I] the, thow L

fownde the shipp, lyke as Seynt Patryk had tolde me. And then
anone I wente into the ship and by the purviaunce of oure lorde
480 Ihesu I came into þis ilond the .vij.th daye after. And here I walkyd
vp and downe in this londe allone, tylle at the laste there came vnto
me an otyr goyng on hys hynder fete. And he brought me a flynte
stone and an yron to smyte with fyre in his .ij. fore clowis. And also
he brought with hym to me grete plentye of fyssh hangyng aboute
485 his necke, and then this otyr wente his waye. And than I smete fyre
and made me a gode fyre of styckis and sode my fyssh anone,
wherewith I levyd .iij. days, and at the .iij.de days ende the otyr came
ayen and brought me fyssh for other .iij. days, and this he hath done
this .lj. yere. And thurgh the myght of oure lorde Ihesu, there sprang
490 oute of this hard stone a fulle fayre clere water whereof I dranke
f. 84ʳᵃ inough euery daye. And I haue dwellid her þis .lj. yere, | and I was
.lx. yere olde or I came here, and so I am .j.C.xj. yere olde in alle.
And this I byde here in this ilond tylle God sende for me. For if it
pleasid hym I wolde right fayne be dischargid of this paynefulle lyfe.'
495   And then Seynt Powle bade Seynt Brandon: 'Take of the water of
this welle into thye ship what that pleasith the, for it is tyme that
thue go hens, for thue haste yett a fulle grete iorney to do. For thue
shalte sayle fro hens to an ilond that is .xl. days saylyng fro hens,
where þue shalte holde thyne Estertyde, lyke as thue hast don
500 before. And fro thens thue shalte sayle into the Londe of Beheest,
and there thue shalte abyde .xl. days, and after that thue shalte come
home ayen into thy cuntraye in safete.' And then these holy men
toke there leve eche of other and wepte fulle sore. And Seynt
Brandon wente anone to hys shipp and saylid .xl. days evyn southe
505 in fulle grete tempest. And vpon Ester Evyn thaye came to þere
good procuratour, and he made them fulle gode chere leke as he had
done to theym oftetymes before. And then he ladde theym to the
grete fyssh whereon thaye sayde Matyns and masse on Ester Daye.
And when the masse was done, þe fyssh beganne to meove and
510 swame forth fulle faste in the see. And alle the monkis stode on his
bak and euer he swam forthe fulle [faste in the se and surely and
fulle] sturnely, wherefore þe monkis were right sore agaste. And a
grete mervayle it was to se suche a fyssh as grete as alle a cuntre so
for to swymme so faste in the water, but by the wylle of oure lorde
515 the fyssh sett alle the monkis alonde in the paradyse of bryddis alle

489 sprang] *add* here L   490 whereof] of L   504 to hys] into the L
511–12 faste . . . fulle] *om.* A2   512 sturnely] *looks like* scuruely A2

hole and sownde, and wente his waye anon to the place where he came fro.

And then Seynt Brandon with his monkis thankyd oure lorde a thousand tymes of ther delyueraunce fro that grete fyssh, and thaye kepte there Estertyde þer tylle it was Trynyte Sonedaye, lyke as 520 thaye had done before other yeris. And alle this tyme þer procuratoure brought theym mete and drynke and alle thyngis that thaye neded. And then þay toke there leve there and wente to there shypp ayen and saylid forthe evyn este .xl. days, and at the .xl. days ende it beganne to hayle right faste, and therewith there came so derke a 525 myst that lastyd right long tyme, wherefore Seynt Brandon and hys monkis were fulle sore agaste. And then anone came there procuratoure and bade theym be of good chere, for thaye were come into the Londe of Beheest.

And anone as the myste was paste, thaye se þe fayrist londe 530 esteward that euer any man se, and it was so clere and so bright that it was grete ioye to beholde. And euery tre was fulle of frute, and the applis were ripe there than, lyke as thaye ben here in harvyst. And .xl.ti days thaye walkyd aboute in this plesant londe, [but thaye cowde fynde none ende of that londe,] and there was euer daye and 535 neuer nyght. And that was a fulle menable cuntre, neyther to hote ne to colde. And at the laste thaye came to a fayre reuer, but thay durste not go ouer. And anone there came to theym a fayre yong man and a fulle curteys, and welcomyd theym alle and kyssid them by rewe and callyd euery man by his name. And he honoryd gretely Seynt 540 Brandon and toke hym by the hande and sayde: 'Be mery, for this is the londe þat ye haue sought so long, but oure lorde wylle þat ye go hens within shorte tyme, and he wolle shewe | yowe moor of hys f. 84rb prevytees. When ye come ayen into the see, oure lorde wolle that ye charge youre ship with the frute of this londe and hye you hens, for 545 ye maye no lenger here abyde, but thue shalt sayle ayen toward thyne owne cuntre.' And sone after þue comyst home thue shalte dye, for this water that thu seyst here departith the world asondre. And in that other syde of this water maye no man come while he is here in this lyffe. And this frute that ye se here is euer this ripe euery tyme 550 of the yere, and alwaye this londe is as light as it is nowe. And he that kepith oure lordis bydis at alle tyme shalle se this londe or he passe oute of the worlde.'

And then Seynt Brandon and his monkis toke of this frute whate

555 thaye wolde, and also thaye toke with them grete plentye of precyous
stonys, and toke there leve of this yong man and wente to there ship
with alle þer stuffe with theym. But thaye wepte fulle sore that thaye
shulde so sone departe fro thens. And anone as thaye came to there
ship thaye made sayle and came [there wey] home in savetye within
560 shorte tyme after. And thaye were resseyvyd of there brethern with
fulle grete ioye and myrthe. And then anone this holye monke Seynt
Brandon waxid right feble and had but lytelle ioye of this worlde, but
alle his herte and mynde was onlye on the ioyes of hevyn. And within
shorte tyme after he passyd to oure lorde fulle of vertues, and he
565 lieth in a fulle fayre abbeye that he dyd do make hymselfe, where
oure lorde shewith daylye for his holye monke Seynt Brandon many
a grete myracle, wherefore oure lorde be praysyd world withoute
ende. Amen.

Here endith the lyfe of Seynt Brandon and begynneth the
570   lyfe of Seynt Crystyn.

27 ST MICHAEL

The traditional *Legenda Aurea* Life of St Michael, describing the appearances of the archangel and the hierarchies of angels, is alluded to in the rubric of MS A1.

The text presented here has only a slight connection with St Michael the Archangel. Sadlek asserts that 'the legend coheres because of the strong traditional association between Michael and the physical universe, an association that would have been part of the normal cultural background of its audience.'[1]

The text can be compared with St Michael Parts II and III, *SEL* 408–428. Some of the matter seems to come from another source (see notes), but most follows the *SEL* version very closely.[2]

---

[1] Sadlek (1988).
[2] Görlach (1998), pp. 117–9.

Here folowith an exposicion of the same mater here byfore
[reherssyd] made by another doctour of holy Chirche.

On Mychaelmas Day the churche makyth mencion of the gret
batelle that was made yn heuene by Seint Michael the archangel with
the dragon Lucifer þat for his hiegh pride felle fro the highest ordyr
yn heuene ynto the deppyst place yn helle. For of the feyrest angel
yn heuen for pride was made the fowlyst deuyl yn helle, for Seint   5
Michael put hym out of heuen and alle tho that consentid with hym.
But alle haue not like peyn, but aftir the quantite of [ther] offensis
sum byn vtturly bedampnyd and sum byn in on place and som yn
oþer places doyng ther penance. And some of them, as clerkys
supposyn, that offendyd not myche to be yn peyn til domes day, and 10
than to be restoryd ayen to the place wher thei felle fro.
    In the first begynnyng ther were .x. ordyrs of angellis wherof on
order fylle with Lucifer and so ther remayneth .ix. ordirs of angels.
And mankynde was made to fulle that nombyr ayen. But for the
trespas of Adam and Eue alle that come of them went to helle the   15
space of .v. thousand yere and more. And no remedy myght be
founde til our lorde toke flesshe and blode of the most pure virgyn
and modir Mary and become man and so dyed, and with his bittir
passion bought al mankynde to fulfille ayen the nombre that felle
with Lucifer. And the good angels sterith euer man to kepe them   20
from synne, and the bad angels that fillen with Lucifer euer sterith
men to synne and wrechednes both wakyng and slepyng, and lye ful
heuy vpon them. Sum clepe them the mare, for euer thei be redy to
greue and trouble mankynde for the gret enuy and malice that thei
haue to them, and so [these] wikid spirites greuyn bothe men and | 25
woman. For some tyme thei appere to men in the liknes of women in f. 178ra
wodes and in other desolat places and tempte them to lye by them.
And yn like wise thei appere in men is liknes to disseyue women.
And ful oft tymes of suche doyngis come ful gret sorowe to them
that haue don it, as some ther membrys [rotyth] away and sum   30
pynyth to the deth.
    Sum men haue seen gret companyes of them daunce in desolate

MSS A₁L   *Rubric* folowith . . . Chirche] begynneth the feste of Seynt
Michaelle L   reherssyd] reherssyth A₁   7 ther] other A₁   14 full]
fulfylle L   25 these] this A₁   29 gret] myche harme and L
30 rotyth] rotyd A₁

fildys and by wodys. Sum men clepe them eluys, and euer the labour
of these wikyd spirites is to bryng folkys to syn and myschefe. But
35 our lorde yaf to mankynde suche vertu and power that he may
withstonde his malice if he wole, for the wikyd spirites byn styed like
a tye dogge, for he may neuer bite ne hurte man but if he come
withyn his cheyne. So yn like wise the wikyd spirite may neuer hurte
mankynde but he come and consent to hym. But though he be tyed
40 he wole clepe folkys to hym by signes and sotil ymaginacions to
disseyue mankynde. But euer whan man fallyth to syn and wrechyd
leuyng the best remedy is to haue contricion, confession and to do
dew satisfaccion and to be ware that he come no more within the
fendys boundys. For and ye kepe you out of his bondys he may not
45 hurte yow no more than may the tye dogge that is tyed.

But the fende hath .v. fyngers by the whiche he clepith man to
him by dyuers tokyns and signes. With the first fynger he clepith
whan his mynde is steryd with foule lustys, and with the secound
whan þou hast gret delite yn the foule lustys. He clepith the with the
50 thride fynger when he consentith to do the syn. He clepyth hym with
the fourth fynger when he doith the dede. And he clepith hym with
the .v.th fynger whan he hath gret ioy and delite yn the same syn.
But God for his gret mercy and thourgh the merites of the holy
archangel Michael yeue us grace neuer to consent to the callyngis of
55 our wikid enemy the feend. Our lorde ordeyned heuene in the
highist place and helle in the lowist place, that is euyn in the myddys
of the erthe. And alle the erthe is not as gret as a balle in
[comparison] of heuen in largenes. For heuen compassith abought
alle the erthe as the white of þe egge doth the yolke, for heuen is ful
60 gret in compas, for the leste sterre therin is more than alle the erthe.
For onys in the dai and þe nyght the sonne goyth abought alle the
erthe, for at none tide it is here most hiest aboue thyn hede, and att
mydnyght vndir thi feet and vndir the grounde and comyth up ayen
by the mornyng and goith fourth yn his curse ayen. For the erthe is
f. 178rb rounde as an appil, so | that howe the sonne goyth in the day or in
66 the nyght he [schynyth] halfe the erthe. And whan the sonne is euyn
benethe us it is mydnyght here. Thus ye may the treuth knowe: take
a clere candyl and holde hit ayenst the on syde of an appyl, and it
wole yeue light to the on halfe of the appyl.
70   There ben .iij. firmamentis, as we may see. In the highest ben the

36 styed] tyed L   43 dew] *om.* L   51 doith] hathe greet ioy and delyte to do L
54 archangel] *add* seynt L   58 comparison] comparion A1   66 schynyth]
schynyd A1

sterres that is heuen. Ther aboue is the dwellyng place of almyghti
God the blissid Trinite, the whiche is euerlastyng, and we byn made
to be the enherytours of that glorious place. And bynethe this heuene
byn .vij. othir heuens that [byn clepid] planetes either sterres. The
first is clepid Saturnus, the secound Iupiter, the thride Mars, the 75
fourthe the sonne, the .v.th Venus, the sixte Marcurius, the .vij.th
the mone, that is lowist of the .vij. and next vnto this erthe. And by
these we haue oure disposicion, and the wedyr and the frutes on
erthe byn rewlyd by these .vij. planetes either sterres. For eche of
these .vij. hath dyuerse disposicion in mankynde that ben borne in 80
them, as sum to be lecherous and sum glotons, sum proude, sum
wrathful, sum envious, sum slouthful and sum ful of couetise, eche
aftir the planete that he is borne in. Theraftir schal ther geydyng be,
as some ben good and som byn euyl, and yeue hem qualite so to do.
But al men may eschewe the euyl and do good, and thei wole reule 85
them wisely aftir the commaundementes of God and to pray hym of
merci and grace. And also aftir these .vij. planetes beth named the
.vij. days yn the weke both yn Latyn an in Englisshe. And for the .ij.
planetes Mars and Saturne beth fulle wikid and litil good doth on
erthe, therfore sum men wole not gladly bygynne eny gret werke 90
vpon the Tewisday and on the Saturday neyther make no gret
bargeyns on tho days, for tho planetes byn ful wikid and ful litle
good doth to mankynde.

Among alle the planetes the sonne is most souereyn and chife of alle
other, for alle thei receyue ther light of hir. And without the sonne the 95
mone schulde haue no light, for she is alle blak of hir owne nature, but
the light that she hath she receyuyth hit of the sonne, for when the
mone is litle she receyvith litle light of the sonne, that is, when the
mone riseth yn the southwest. And litle and litle the sonne passith fro
hir, and than the mone receyueth more light til she come to the fulle 100
and than shynyth al nyght, and that is whan the mone riseth yn the est.
And whan he wanyth he [lesith] his light and [waxyth] ayen al derk
and blak att | the monþes ende. But the sonne schynyth euer yn on f. 178ᵛᵃ
place or in other of this worlde. And whan the sonne is gon vnder the
erth fro us and the mone aboue us in the nyght, than the sonne 105
sendyth hir light from hym by the on syde of this erthe. For the sonne
is more than erth an hundride sides and five and sixty sidys, as clerkys

---

74 byn clepid] beth clepith A1   either] or L   76 fourthe] add Sol whiche is L
.vij.th] add Luna þat is L   88 an] and also L   102 lesith] lesid A1   waxyth]
waxyd A1   107 sides, sidys] sithis L

seyn. And the erthe is .ix. tymes more than þe mone. The mone
semyth to us more than the sonne. The cause is for the sonne is so fer
110 and the mone is so nye. Ful meche space [it] is betwene erthe and
heuyn, for though a man myght go euery day .xl.ti myle he schulde
not come thedyr in .viij. thousand yere, as clerkys fynde by wretyng.
But a soule that is clene without ony spot of syn, when it passith out of
the body it hath the swiftenes of an angel, and it may be ther as sone as
115 a man can thynk as in the twynkelyng of an eye. But to helle is but a
litle way, and therfore it is to suppose that mo com to helle than to
heuen.

    Man was first made in paradise of the .iiij. elementes, that is to say
of the fire, of the watir, of the eyre and of the erth, of whiche man
120 and alle quicke bestys bethe made. Next the mone the fire is hiest but
the sonne drawith up the waters of the see and the moystyr of the
erth vnto him. And thourgh the gret hete of the sonne is drawe up
aboue the cloudys to the firy element, and ther it begynneth to
brenne anon. Therfore men bethe sore agast of suche thyng but it be
125 in hete. The lightenyng comyth therof whan hit turnyth to wete.
Therfore that drye vapur that [is] drawe up by hete of the sonne, it is
aboue made a cloude, and when it is sette afire aboue, anon it brekyth
thourgh the clowde. But ar it comyth thourgh it makyth yn the water
a gret blondyryng, as though a man toke a barre of iron brennyng
130 hote and put hit into the water it wolde make a gret noyse. In like
wise doyth the fire when it brekyth thourgh the clowde, and that fire
is clepyd lightenyng that schetith sodenly into alle this worlde. And
anon aftir comyth the thondyrclappe. Gret noyse ther is aboue or the
lightenyng come, but we may not here it for it is so fer fro us tyl the
135 lightenyng hath broke thourgh the clowde. For ther comyth ⌐neuer
lyghtnyng⌐ but aftir hete yn wete weder, for yn the pure somer is
selde eny thonder. For than is ful litle reyne to quenche the fire. And
in the pure wynter is selde herde eny thonder, for than is non heete
to drawe up the ⌐vapurs⌐ of the erthe for gret wete. But abought
140 Appril and May, whiche is betwene somer and wynter, and ayen aftir
f. 178ᵛᵇ heruest yn Septembre is the kynde | tyme of thondryng and
lyghtenyng. For in that tyme the wedyr is wete and hote also, and
ful oft tyme the thondyr sleythe men, castyth downe trees and
steplys and doth fulle meche harme.

    109, 110 so, so] *om.* L   110 it] is A1   116 com] go L   126 is(1)] *om.* A1
135–6 neuer lyghtnyng] lighti *del. and corr. in margin* A1   139 vapurs] water *del.*
and corr. in margin A1

I schal telle you the cause whi. For whan our lorde had bought 145
mankynde that was dampnyd with his bittir passion and had bounde
fast the fendes in helle, than he come thedyr and brast up the yatys
with ful gastful thondyr. And therfore sen that tyme the feendes beth
fulle sore agast when they here the thondyr, and fleyth aboute in
euery contre for fere. But yn suche wedyr thei do ful meche harme 150
bothe to men, bestys, trees and stepils. And for this cause it is that
ther comyth so myche myschefe of the thondyr and lightenyng. For
whan an howse is sette afire with the lightnyng, water wole not
quenche hit, for that fire comyth out of the water. The sonne that is
the norsher of al thynges yn this [worlde] sendith downe his hete ynto 155
the erthe, and that hete causith the water of the see and of the freshe
water to haue a gret brethyng upwarde, and hit goyth vp into the eyre
like a gret miste tyl hit come to right a colde place, whiche is amonge
the blak clowdys and other wedyrs a .ij. myle upwarde fro the erthe.
But when the sonne hath drawe up so that myst by gret heete, than it 160
may no ferther upwarde for the gret colde of the blak clowdys. And
than thes mystes turne alle to wetenes and waxith a watery clowde,
and heueryth a litil while til hit begynnyth to reyne, and so it fallith
ayen downe to the grounde. And oft for gret colde it fresith and
waxith snowe or it come to the erthe, and sumtyme for gret feruent 165
colde it turnyth to hayle stonys. For the gret hete of the sonne a
mornyng drawith vp to hym the dewe that fallith on the grounde on
the nyghtis. For when the sonne is gon downe, the hete of the sonne
fayleth, and so hit droppith to the erthe ayen. And than it confortith
bothe trees, gras and erbys and al maner of frutes and causith them to 170
encrese yn the nyght more than yn the day. For al reyne, al dewe and
al hore frostys and al mystys and clowdis, al these thynges comyth of
the water that the sonne drawith vp by his heete. For the water is
meche more than al the erthe, with the gret occian that ⌈goyth aboute⌉
al the worlde and [closyth] hit al aboute as the white of the egge goyth 175
aboute the yolke. And alle other waters byth but lymmys to the gret
occian, that come fro him by dyuerse veynes vndir the erthe and oft
comyth to the see ayen, that is the gret occian. | For alle the waters f. 179ra
that byn ebbyth and flowith, for the gret occian is alway in on. For the
mone is cause that the see ebbyth and flowith, and sodenly it waxith 180
and as sone it wanyth. For the mone is reuler of the see.

148 sen] sith L   155 worlde] wolde A1   163 heueryth] hoverith there L
168 nyghtis] add tyme L   174 goyth aboute] come fro hym del. and corr. in margin A1
175 closyth] closyd A1

This erthe is in the mydyl of the see occian, and she is ther in
liknes of a balle alle rounde. And helle is in the mydul of the seid
erthe, and it is the .vij.th parte of the erthe. For in the vttirmur party
185 of the northe may no man dwelle [for] gret colde. And in like wise in
the vttirmur party of the sowth [for] gret hete. For the north party is
fer fro the sonne and the sowth party is nye the sonne. And therfore
myche of this worlde is desolat for ouer meche hete and also for ouer
myche colde. Of these .iiij. elementes eche quycke thyng is made,
190 that is of erthe, of eyre, of water and of fire. Man hath of the erthe al
his body, and of the water he hath his blode and moyster, of the eyre
he hath his brethe, and of the fire he hath his hete. And eche quycke
thyng hath parte of these .iiij. elementes more or lesse. For he that
hath most of the erthe is sclowe as an asse, pale of colour, harde of
195 skyn, boystous, strong, pensiful, litle of speche, long wrethfulle, sone
olde, vnwildeful, stable and stydfast of chere. He that hath most of
the water schal be white and fatte, softe herre and crispe, and a gret
sleper, and sclow with a snevelyng nose, and of mouth of fewe
wordys, a litle drynker, schort brethid, meke, and of litle lust to
200 labour for his lifelode. He that hath most of the eyre schal be of
goode colour, fatte and neshe herryd, ful large, gret lechour, lawhyng
and of glad sembland and sumdele proude, and if [he] hath mete and
drinke ynogh he takyth litle thought. Litle while he berith wrath and
bith sone balled, glad, vnstable, and thynkith litle of that he hath to
205 do. He that hath most of the fire schal be smal and rede other blak,
with crispe herre, lene and angri, backebiter and boster, hardy and a
gret lyer, gret swerer and of many wordys, ful of lechery, proude and
of hie beryng, a gret drynker and wode in wrathe, hardy, light and
stronge and wel may wake.
210   And eche of these .iiij. elementes temperith other, that ther is no
man but he hath sum parte of alle. Than oure lorde ordeyned in
mankynde howe the frute schulde be gendryd betwene man and
woman togedyrs medled is like white foome yn colour, as clerkys
seyn. And withyn .xij. days aftir that it is begotyn, it is turned ynto
215 smale bollys eche hangyng aboue other. Of the hiest is made the
brayne, of the secounde is made the herte and of the thride that is
f. 179rb lowist | is made the lyuer. Thes byn the principal lymmes of
mankynde, and in them is al the life of the body, for if eny of
these .iij. were hurte thei might neuer be helyd, but it schulde dye
220 anone.

Aftir these .xij. days that this seede of man and woman hath byn so white, than it turnyth into thicke blode and changith his white color. And then .ix. days it thickith so and turnyth to blode. And the .xxj. dai it turnyth into fleshe, first a litle as the kynde may. And than it bygynyth to take the fourme of man, so that within the seide .xxj. days it hath euery lyme, and in lesse time [if] it be a man childe, for he is more hote than the woman childe. But euery lymme is ful litle and a smal wombe to beclippe alle from the first gendryng til it be boren. And he lithe al rounde and lithe in his modirs wombe as an hare lithe in hir fourme. His leggys [lithe] bowyd, his helys att his buttok, his kneys in either eye, his hede bowyd donwarde, the armys ayenst the bely, the elbowys towarde the schare, the hondys vndir the chynne. His bak is alle bowid that he lithe rounde.

Therfore man, whi art thou so proude and wilte not bowe to no man nor obey to the commaundementes of God thi maker, that can make the ful lowe when hit plesith hym? For thou schalt not escape fro hym, be thou neuer so hie in pride. In euery man byn .iij. soulis, but thei be not like good. Like as I tolde you byfore of the .iij. bollys that byn in manis body. In the lowist bolle whereof the lyuer is made bygynnyth the first life of the body and sendith norschyng to alle the lymmes of the body and causith them to wax and encrese in growyng more. And this soule of life is in euery tre and in euery erbe, and causith them to sprynge and to bryng fourth frute. Than of the secound bolle is made the herte of man, and therin is [the] secounde soule that bryngith life yn the herte. But for al these .ij. soulys, the body hath no power to ster ne meue til it be further brought. And than whan hit comyth to more age he hath [his] life and his wittys of the same soule, and so hath euery best, euery [fowle, euery] fishe and euery worme. And if thei be hurte yn eny of these .ij. soulys, thei dye anon. And thes .ij. soules dye when the body dieth, but ther is the .iij.de soule that is most worthy, for that soule come fro heuene and is felew to angel.

Our lorde put this soule first in Adam in paradise, and this soule is in mannys brayne, and þis our lorde hath medlyd oure wrechid flesshe to angels kynde. And this soule euery man berith with hym and geydith him here while the body leuyth. But this soule dieth not with | the body, for it schal euer leue in ioy or in peyne. And it

225
230
235
240
245
250
255
f. 179va

225 man] *add* or womman L   226 if] it A1   230 lithe] *om.* A1
244 the] this A1   247 his(1)] *om.* A1   248 fowle, euery] *om.* A1
250 dye] *om.* L   253 put/this soule] *trsp.* L

partith fro man att his dying. For al the reson and discression that man hath aboue a best, he hath hit of this soule. And by these .ij.
260 soulys that ben in the lyuer and the hert, att the departyng of the thride soule that neuer schal dye a man may knowe by the .ij. first soulys wheder the thride soule go to ioy or to peyne by certeyne tokens of them. For when the body dyed demewrely, the eyen closyd, the leggys [streight] fourthe and the body not disfiguryd but
265 of feyre colour, that is a tokyn that the soule shal be sauyd and come to heuen. And if the body be of foule colour, staryng eyen, and mowyng and grennyng with foule semblant, it is a tokyn of euerlastyng peyne. Fro the whiche God and Seint Michael us defende and aftir this wrechid life to brynge us to the life that
270 neuer shal haue ende. Amen.

Here endith the life of Seint Michael and next folowith the life of Seint Ierome.

262 soulys] *add* whether or L   264 streight] steight A1

28 ST THOMAS OF CANTERBURY

Thomas Becket, archbishop of Canterbury, was a figure of controversy throughout his adult life, as is apparent from the many Lives written shortly after his murder and since. Becket was born in 1118 to Norman parents in London, studied in London, Paris, Bologna and Auxerre, and became Chancellor to the young King Henry II in 1155. When Becket was appointed archbishop of Canterbury in 1162, he resigned the Chancellorship and became a supporter of the rights of the Church against those claimed by the Crown. After his rejection of the Constitutions of Clarendon, what had been a strong friendship with the king turned into a bitter struggle, with the king persecuting Becket, his friends and supporters. Becket exiled himself to France in 1164 and he appealed to the pope, as did the king. When he returned to England in 1170 his excommunication of those bishops who had crowned the king's son in his absence was the last straw to the king, who voiced his wish to be rid of Becket. The four knights who took him at his word murdered the archbishop in Canterbury Cathedral in 1170. Becket's violent death was followed by numerous miracles and he was canonised in 1173. The king's public penance at Canterbury was in 1174 and Becket's remains were translated in 1220.

This Life of Thomas Becket is, as Görlach points out,[1] dependent upon *SEL* 610–692, with additional material. The *SEL* Life itself depends 'on a version of Quadrilogus II made after Becket's Translation, but with the addition of "Becket's Tuesdays" at the end.'[2] Source materials for Becket study are numerous,[3] but we have been able to discover very little about the additions to *SEL* for this Life.

---

[1] Görlach (1998), p. 120.
[2] Duggan (1994), p. 106 note 7.
[3] Duggan (1980), ch. 6, 'Becket's Biographers,' pp. 176–226.

Here endith the life of Innocentes and next folowith the
life of Seint Thomas of Canturbury and of Gilbert Beket
his fader.

Gylbert Beket was Seint Thomas of Caunturbury is fader and borne
in the cite of London where Seint Thomas of Akers chirche is nowe,
and he was a ful goode man. And in his yong age he toke the crosse
and went into the Holy Londe, and toke with hym on Willyam that
was his man that he loued and trust right wel. And so when God 5
wolde thei come to the cite of Ierusalem, and there thei dide ther
pilgremage with ful gret devocioun.

And as thei were comyng homwarde ayene, thei were take
prisoners of the Sarasyns with many other cristen men with hem.
And thei al were brought as prisoners to the prynces howse that was 10
clepid Amyraud. And than he commaundide to putte hem into the
deppist dongeon of the castel, where thei suffred ful gret sorowe and
wo euery nyght, and al the day thei labored ful sore and had ful
seldyn any mete or drynke. But this prynce Amyraud had a gret
affeccion to talke with Gilbert Beket and wolde aske hym of the 15
cristen feith and of the rule of Englonde, and bycause he was
famylier with the prynce, al his felowes ferde the better for his
sake, and in especial for this prynces doughter louyd muche this
Gilbert. And in a tyme she seid to hym if he wolde wedde hir she
wolde forsake al hir heritage and bycome cristen for his loue. And 20
than she askid of hym of the rule of cristen feith and what shulde be
ther rewarde atte laste ende. And he answerd and seid: 'The blisse of
heuene is ther rewarde.' And than she askyd him where he dwellid.
He seid: 'In Englonde, in the cite of London.' And than she seid: 'To
London wol I come for thi sake if thou wilte promyse to wedde me to 25
thi wife.' And than he made hir promyse so to do.

But within a while aftir he and his felowe by the puruyaunce of
oure lorde escapid owte of prison and come into cristyndome in
safte. And than this prynce Amyraud was ny mad for angre and sent
his messengers aftir them, but thei cowde not ouertake them, as God 30
wolde, and than they | returned home ayene with sory chere. And f. 46ra
this mayde the princes doughtir [whan she] herd this she was ful
heuy and wepte ful sore. And in a nyght whan she se hir tyme she

MSS A1L   A1 breaks off at l. 1096 **hed like**. The text thereafter is from L,
f. 249rb.   *Rubric* of(2) . . . his] *crossed through by later hand.*   3 he(1)] *add* he A1
10 prynces] *add* of A1   32 whan she] *om.* A1

went away alone and come into many a wilde place, and so many
35 yeres wanderyng aboute hedir and thedyr and euer she askyd aftir
'London, London,' and 'Beket, Beket,' for more Englysshe coude she
not. And so atte last by the puruyaunce of oure lorde she come ouer
see into Englonde and so forth to London. And when she come
ayenst the place where Gilbert Beket dwellid, there Seint Thomas of
40 Akirs is nowe, she stode stil ther and many a sherewd boy wondryng
vpon hyr for she koude sey nothyng but 'London, London' and
'Beket, Beket.'

Hit happid that William, Gilbert Bekettis man that was with hym
while he was prisoner, knewe this mayde and went to his maister
45 Beket and tolde hym howe the prynces doughter Amyraud stode atte
his dore and muche peple wonderyng on hir. And then he anone
went to hir, and when she se hym she fel asownyng and lay as she
had be dede. And then Gilbert Beket toke hir up and confortide hir
in the best wise he cowde and led hir into his howse and bade his
50 men give hir mete and drynke. And in the mene tyme Gilbert went to
Seint Poulys churche where ther were .vj. bishops atte that tyme.
And then he tolde them of this wondyr, howe fer this hethyn maide
was come and forsake al hir heritage and to bycome cristen for his
sake if he wolde wedde hir. And then al these byshops merueiled
55 gretly of this thyng, and then the bishop of Chichester seid it was
best that he shulde wedde hir and make hir a cristen woman: 'For it
is thurgh the purvyance of God that she is so hyder come fro so fer
contre.'

And then Gilbert the next day brought hir to Seint Poulys
60 churche, and there the bishops met with hir and receyued hir
worshipfully and askid hir if she wolde become cristen if Gilbert
wolde wedde hir. And she seid: 'Ye forsoth, ful fayne, or else I wolde
not haue had so moche trouble for his loue. For this I am come hider
alone and forsake gret possessions, and al for hym only.' And when
65 the bishops vndirstode hir gret stedfastnes and goode wille to
receyue the feith off Criste, then anone she was baptized with the
ful assent of al the byshops and furthwith weddyde to the seid
Gilbert Beket in the churche of Poulys with ful gret solempnyte for
the gret myracle that oure lorde had shewid for that mariage. And
70 within shorte tyme aftir by the grace of oure lorde was bygotyn this
f. 46rb holy childe Seint Tho|mas.

57–8 fro . . . contre] *om.* L   60 met . . . and] *om.* L   68 Gilbert] *add* to the
seid Gilbert A1

And then anone aftir this seid Gilbert Beket had gret desire to go
ayene to the Holy Londe, but al his care was for his wife bycause she
was but late weddide and cowde not the langage of this londe, and
was more sadder than he was wonte to be afore. And than his wife   75
was ful heuy and thought in hir conceyt that hir husbonde was
displeysed with hir. And she seid to hym with mornyng chere: 'Sir,
whi be ye so heuy?' And he seid to hir: 'Forsoth, it is only for your
sake, for I am ful purposid to go ayene to the Holy Londe.' And then
she seid: 'If it be Goddis wille and yours, it shal plese me, for my   80
wille is youre wille, but I prey you, let Willyam your man abide
[here] with me to teche me the langage of this lande.' And then he
toke his leve of hir and went forth to the Holy Londe and was there
.iij. yere and an half or he come home. And when he come ayene into
Englonde he had a sonne of feyre stature and his name hight   85
Thomas. And then he was ful glad and thonkid oure lorde a
thousande tymes and made ful muche of his goode wife. And
within a while aftir he set this holy childe Thomas to scole, wherein
he encresid ful muche withyn fewe yeres and drewe al to vertues
lyvynge, that euery man spake goode of hym.   90

   And when he was of the age of .xxij.ti yere, his moder passid to
oure lorde ful of vertues, and aftir hir deth his frendes wolde fynde
hym no lenger atte scole. Than he bycome a worshipful mannys
seruaunt of this cite of London and kepte al his rekenyng, and his
maister loued hym and trust hym ful muche for his trewe seruyce.   95
And aftir that he dwellid with Tybaude, that was the erchebyshop of
Canturbury, and he loued hym so muche that he made hym his
erchedekyn and chefe of his counsel, and ful wel he hilde up the
right of holy Chirche. And he cherished them that were goode and
chastised them sharply that were euyl disposed. And ofte tymes he   100
went to Rome for the right of the Churche, for he wolde suffre no
wrong do therto if he myght let it. And then anone aftir, the Duke of
Normandye that hight Bloys dyed, and then was his sonne Herry the
secounde made kyng of Englonde, and he made Seint Thomas his
chaunceler and was al rulyd aftir hym.   105

   And then al this londe stode in ful gret prosperite, that al peple
preised gretly Seint Thomas. And he was right a gay man outewarde
to the sight of the peple, but inwarde secretly he leuyd ful streite
and in gret penaunce and cheryshid euer the pore peple and holpe

82 here] he A1   85 and . . . hight] whiche was named L   107 preised] *add*
ful L

f. 46ᵛᵃ them | if eny wolde do them wronge. And ful fayne he wolde be
111 quytte of his office with the kynge, for he thought that he cowde not
serue God and the kynge. And therefore in a tyme Seint Thomas
desyred of the kynge to be discharged of his chauncelership, but the
kynge wolde not forgo hym in no wise but [put] his eldist sonne
115 Harry into his goydyng, for he trust hym above al other and wolde
not forsake hym in no wise. And anone aftir he went ouer into
Normandy and left here Seint Thomas to rewle his sonne Herry and
al his rewme of Englonde in his absence. And within a while aftir
died Tybaude the erchebishop of Canturbury. And then the kyng
120 lete make Seint Thomas erchebishop aftir hym. That tyme he was
.xliiij.ti yere olde. And when he se that he shulde ⌐nedys⌐ be made
erchebishop, than he desired to knowe howe he shulde receyue it.
And than the kynge seid: 'Thou shalt be the hede of holy Churche
in this londe and al other folkes to be vnder thi rewle and none to
125 rewle the but only the pope of Rome.' And then Seint Thomas said:
'In this [condycion] I wole receyue the bishopriche of Canturbury
with a goode wille.'

And on Trynyte Sonday he was sacred erchebishop there with ful
gret solempnite, for ther was then the kyng Harry with .xvj. byshops
130 and many other gret estates of this londe. And anone aftir the abbot
of Evisham with other clerkes were sent to Rome to Pope Alysaunder
that was that tyme atte Mount Pelerys to fecche the palle of Seint
Thomas. And when thei come to the pope thei were anone sped of
ther message and returned home ayene with gret myrthe and ioy.
135 And Seint Thomas receyued the palle ful mekely and bygan to leue
ful streitly and were the sharp heire and so kept his bodi ful lene and
lowe so that his soule myght ⌐be⌐ mayster of the bodi, and then he
hopid to plese God. And next hym he wered the clothyng of ⌐a
monke⌐ and aboue that he wered the clothyng of a clerke, and so he
140 was monke within and clerk withoute and leued so bothe day and
nyght in gret penaunce and fastyng and in holy prayers to oure lorde
and to oure blessid ladi. And in his masse seyng ful deuoute with
plente of teris shedyng and hastely he vsid to sey his masse and vsid
to fare right wel atte his table, and ful litle he ete, for he was euer ful
145 streite to hymself and dide moche goode to other. Wherfor he was
gretly preised of al the peple.

114 put] *om.* A1   121 se . . . he] *om.* L   nedys] receyue *del. and corr. in margin*
A1   126 condycion] *om.* A1   127 goode] herte and L   128 Sonday]
add next after L   130 londe] *add* with hym L   137 be] not *del. and corr. in*
margin A1   138–9 a monke] among *with* g *del. and corr. in margin* A1

And then the kyng Harrys fader come oute of Nor|mandie into   f. 46vb
Englonde to se howe his sonne Harry rewlyd the reame. And as Seint
Thomas had knowlech of his londyng atte Sowthampton he toke
Harry the kynges sonne that was vndir his guydyng and met with the   150
kyng atte seid Sowthampton, and ther was ful gret ioye atte ther
metyng togiders, for eche clipped and kyssed oþer and thankid God
of eche other wilfaris. And then the kyng went thorugh his londe to
se the guydyng therof and was ful gladly receyued of al his peple,
and moche ioye thei made him. And the kyng was ful glad of the   155
goode rewle and goydyng and thankid God and his goode bishop
Seint Thomas. And then the kyng abode stil here in Englond many
yeres aftir, but when the kynge wolde do enythyng ayenst the
Chirche he wolde withstonde hit with al his power and myght.

And then it happid that the bishop of Worcetter and the bishop of   160
London that hight Gilbert Filiot dyed, and bothe these bishopriches
stode long tyme in the kynges honde, and he had al the profite of
them. And then Seint Thomas was ful heuy that holi Churche
shulde so be guydide ayenst the wil of God, and preid the kyng that
he wolde yeue tho .ij. byshopriches to sum vertues men. And then   165
anone the kyng grauntid his desire and made on Sir Roger bishop of
Wursetter, and on Sir Robert de Meke that was the erle of Glouceter
is sonne bishop of London. And then Seint Thomas thought that he
coude not plese God and the kyng, for the kyng bygan to do ful gret
wrong to holy Chirche, wherfore Seint Thomas was ful heuy and   170
thought to amende the state therof.

And the same yere he halowed the abbey of Redyng where is beried
William Basterd is sonne, and the same yere was Seint Edward
shyrynyd atte Westmynster by Seint Thomas. And within a while
aftir, the deuyl had gret enuye of the goode leuyng of Seint Thomas,   175
and sette gret debate and strife bytwene the kyng and hym. And then
the kyng sent for al the bishops of this londe and charged hem to apere
afore hym atte Westmynster ⌐atte a serteyne⌐ day, and so thei dide alle.
And than the kyng welcomed hem al and seid: 'Sirs, the cause that I
sent for you is this. Thomas the erchebishop of Canturburi wolde   180
distroy my lawe of this londe that hath ben vsed in the tyme of oure
forfaders, þat is this. Yf a clerk were a theffe and a | misdoer he wolde   f. 47ra
that my lawe shulde haue no correccion vpon hym, but that he shulde
be correctid by holy Churche. And me thynkith it were no reson, for

---

147 the] *add* the A1   Harrys] Herry the L   167 de Meke] Moreys L, Meluns
SEL   178 atte a serteyne] by seint Thomas *del. and corr. in margin in diff. hand* A1

185 then thei wolde not recke howe euyl dedes thei dide. And yet me
thinketh the hier that the ordre is, the better shulde ther leuyng be.'
	Then seid Seint Thomas to the kyng with ful demewre chere: 'Sir,
me thynkith that ye wolde make the clergy and holi Churche more
thral than the lay peple, for thei ben but onys ponyshed for on
190 trespas, but ye wolde that a clerke shulde be tweys corrected for on
trespas, that is, first by youre lawe and aftir by holy Churche lawe.
And that were ayenst the lawe of God that [thei that] euer ⌐prey⌐ day
and nyght for you and for your reme shulde stonde in werse case
than eny lay man. And therfore, Sir, haue pety on us and take not
195 awey the libertees and the franchis of holy Churche.' And then the
kyng seid: 'I wol manteyne the ryght of holi Churche in al wise
excepte the lawes that haue be vsid in the dais of oure forfaders,
them wol I mayntene.' And then seid Seint Thomas: 'Al your lawes
that we ben bounde to do and holde by right that is none hurt to holy
200 Chirche, them wol we kepe with goode wil and obbey to them in
euery poynte, and therfore we prey you to haue peti on holy Chirche
and brynge hir not to no thraldome for the loue of almyghti God.'
And the kyng seid to Seint Thomas: 'Nowe I knowe wel that thou
woldest fordo the lawes of my londe that were vsid in my forfaders
205 days, but I do the right wel to wete it shal neuer ley in thi power to
bring þat aboute.' And with this the kyng departed from Seint
Thomas in gret wreth and went to his chambir.
	And then al the bishops conseiled Seint Thomas that he shulde
obey to the kynges entent or else he shulde brynge this londe in ful
210 gret trowble, and lordes and knyghtis seid the same to him. And then
Seint Thomas seid: 'I take God to wittenes it was neuer myn entent
to displese the kynge or to take awey eny thing that longith to his
right or honoure.' And then al the bishops and lordes were right glad
and brought hym to þe kyng to Oxford where ther was with him atte
215 that tyme the moste parte of the gret lordes of this londe. And when
Seint Thomas come byfore the kynge vnnethes he wolde speke to
hym. And then he clepid al the bishops and the lordis byfore hym
and seid þat he wolde haue al the lawes to be holde ferme and stabil
that his forefaders had byfore hym, and there thei [were] newe
f. 47rb confermed | of al his lordes. And then the kyng charged al the lordes
221 bothe spirituel and temporel to apeire afore hym in his maner of
Claridon atte a certeyne day assignyd to come to his parlement or

else to falle into his indignacion. And then al the lordes departide
and went.

And this parlement was holde atte Claridon the .xj.th yere of the 225
kynges reyne and in the yere of oure lorde Ihesu Crist .xj.C.lx. and
.iiij. This was a ful noble parlement of lordis. First Kyng Herry
hymself, then Seint Thomas erchebishop of Canturbury, Sir Roger
the erchebishop of Yorke, Gylbert Filiot bishop of London, the
bishop Robert of Lyncolne, the bishop Nele of Ely, the bishop Roger 230
of Wurcetter, the bishop Hillary of Chichestir, the bishop of
Salsbury, the bishop of Herforde, the bishop of Chester. Of temporal
lordes, the erle of Cornewayl, the erle of Leiceter, the erle of
Gloucetter, the erle of Herford, the erle of Britaite, the erle of
Mygres, the erle of Mandevile, the erle of Chester, the erle of Ferees, 235
the erle of Arundel. Off barons, the lorde Lucy, the lorde Wareyne,
the lorde Walry, Sir Roger Pigot, Sir Richard Camvile, Sir William
de Browys, Sir Richard Dunstale, Sir Stele de Mombray, Sir
Humfrey de Bona, Sir Iosselyn, Sir William de Hastyng, Sir Hewe
Morele, Sir William Maloke, Sir Iohn Morestal, Sir Symond 240
Fitzpeerys, Sir William Mauduyt, Sir Geffrey le Here. Al these
lordes were there ayenst Seint Thomas, therefore God be his help
and goyder.

And then the kyng sittyng in his parlement with al his lordes askid
anone if thei wolde holde up al his lawes that had be usid in his 245
forefaders dais. And then Seint Thomas spake for holi Churches
parte and seid: 'Al olde lawes that byn rightful and not ayenst oure
moder holy Churche I graunt with goode wil to kepe them.' And
then the kyng seid to hym that he wolde not vndo o poynt of his lawe
and wexid ful angry towarde Seint Thomas. And then the bishop of 250
Salsbury and the bishop of Norwiche preid Seint Thomas to obey to
the kynges wil. And then Seint Thomas askyd respite of the kynge to
knowe al his lawes and then to yeue hym an aunswer therof. And to
sum of them he consentide, and many of them he denyed.

Thes ben the poyntes that Thomas consentide to. If eny bounde 255
man wolde be a preste he shulde not withoute licens of his lorde.
Also if eny persone holde eny lay fee, that he shulde do seruise to the
kyng therfore and the iugement therof in the kynges court. Also | if f. 47ᵛᵃ
any man were the kynges traitour, to be iuged by the kynges lawe.
Also if eny erand theffe stele the kynges iewelles and fle to the 260

224 went] *add* home L   250 towarde] ayens L   254 he(2)] *add* dyd not
consent but L

churche, then the kyng to iuge hym by his lawe. And in the same
wise euery man may fet his stolen goodes of the theffe in the churche
and kepe it as his owne. And also a churche youen by the kyng onys
to eny man he shulde neuer yeue it awey aftir withoute lycens of the
265 kynge to none house of religion. These thynges with many other
Seint Thomas grant with goode wille to the kyng.

But these that folowyn aftir he denyed in al wise to his power, that
is to sey: If a clerk and a lewde man pledide for the withholdyng of
the dewte of holi Churche, than that mater to be determined by the
270 kynges lawe as it hath be used to long ayenst right and consciens.
Also as for the yeft of eny churche by a lay man, if eny ple were
therfore it was pledid ayenst the right in the kynges lawes, for the lay
man was patron of the churche. And also that no bishop nor clerke
shulde go oute of Englonde withoute lycens of the kyng, and that he
275 shulde purchace no thyng atte Rome that shulde let the kynges
avayle, and hereto thei shulde be sworne or thei went oute of this
londe. The .iiij.th was that if eny man were acursid in holy Churche,
that he shulde fynde borowys and go quytte withoute penaunce if he
seid that he wolde amende. This was the kynges lawe. The .v.th if
280 that enye man hilde eny londe other seruise of the kyng and were
acursid in holy Chirche for his mysdedes, then the kynges baylys
shulde bryng hym afore the kynge and if he wolde amendes make by
[his] worde, he shulde go quytte fro holy Churche. The .vj.th was
that if eny bishopriche or abbey stode voyde it shulde fal into the
285 kynges honde and he wolde kepe it as long as it plesid hym and then
to geue it to on of his chapeleyns and then fourthwith to do the kyng
homage therfore or he were confermyd. The .vij.th was that if eny
man had a plee in holi Churche lawe, first he shulde go to the
erchedeken, to the bishop, and to the erchebishop, and if thei made
290 none ende therof than it shulde be brought into the kynges lawe and
no ferther go, and al the ple of holy Chirche atte laste muste ende in
the kynges lawe and take on hym the popis power. The .viij.th was if
a persone or a clerk pledide for the goodes that longith to holy
Chirche, anone the kynges baylys shulde take it oute of holy Churche
295 lawe and bring it into the kinges lawe. The .ix.th was that no citacion
f. 47vb oute of þe popis courte shulde be obeyed but were | al clene lefte
thorugh this londe. The .x.th was that al Petirs pens whiche were
wont to be sent to the pope of Rome, the kynge had them al and kept

them as his owne propre goodes. The .xj.th was if eny clerk were
take with thefte he shulde be iuged to the deth by the kynges lawe 300
and not by holy Chirche lawe.

And al these lawes and many mo the kynge hilde and kepte ayenst
the libertees of holy Churche, and seid he wolde not lese o statute
that his forefaders hilde, but he wolde maynteyne them to the vttirst.
This he seide .iiij. days afore Candilmasse atte Clarindon, and 305
chargid Seint Thomas and al the bishops of his londe to holde
these lawes [ferme] and stabyl. Then seid Seint Thomas to the kyng
with ful gret sorowe and mornyng: 'Nowe gracious ⌐kyng⌐, haue pety
on vs of holy Churche thi bedmen, and yeue us respite of this matir
til a certeyne tyme.' And then the kyng grauntid hym his axyng. And 310
eche man went home and Seint Thomas went to Wynchester with
gret sorowe, and whan other folk slepte he wept ful [bitturly] and
preid oure lorde to help holy Churche. And he hym thought verryly
to defende the right of holi Churche with al his myght and power,
but euer he was ful of sorowe that holy Churche shulde be brought 315
in thraldome in his tyme that was ful fre byfore his days. But then he
seid: 'Goode Lorde, I wote wel I have gretly offendid the, and
therfore this trouble cometh to holy Churche for my trespas.' And
therfore he purposed to go to Rome to be assoiled of his offense, and
went his wey towarde Canturbury. And then the kynges men seid 320
that Seint Thomas wolde not obey to his statutis. And when the
kyng herde this he commaundide his men to go to al his maners and
sese al his goodes into his hondes and gretly troubled his fermours
and tenauntys, and than eche man departide his way with ful gret
sorowe. 325

And when Seint Thomas come to the seeside he entred into a
shippe for to passe ouer the see, but anone as thei wolde haue seiled
fourthe the wynde fil contrary and then they come ayene to londe.
And the .ij.de tyme and the thirde tyme he dide the same, but he
cowde not passe ouer the se in no wise. And then he knewe wel that 330
it was the wil of oure lorde that he shulde turne ayene to Canturbury, and thedir he come ful pryuely in the euentide to his chambir.
And whan his men wiste it thei were fulfilled with gret gladnes and
receyued ful ioy|fully hym and sette hym to his soper. And then he f. 48ra
tolde them howe he had byn atte seeside to passe ouer the see to 335
Rome warde, and .iiij. tymes he seiled forwarde, but euer the wynde

drofe them to londe ayene, and then he knewe wel that it was not
oure lordes wil that he shulde passe oute of Englonde yet. 'And
therfore I am come nowe hider ayene. I trust to oure lorde for al oure
340 avayle.' And it was so in dede, for anone the next day come the
kynges messengers to Canturbury to sese al Seint Thomas goodes
into the kynges honde by the statute that was made atte Claridon,
like as thei had dispoyled al his other maneres as it is afore reherced.
And thei wende verryly that Seint Thomas had byn fled oute of this
345 londe. But as oure lorde wolde thei founde hym yet stil atte
Canturbury, wherefore thei were gretly abashed and turned ayene
to the kyng and tolde hym howe he was yet atte Canturbury.
      And then anone Seint Thomas went to the kyng to his maner of
Wodstok to besyke hym of better grace for holy Churche. And when
350 the kyng se hym he seid to Seint Thomas in skorne: 'May not we
bothe dwelle in this londe? Art thou of so gret and sturdy hert?'
Then seid Seint Thomas: 'Sir, that was neuer my thought, but I
wolde ful fayne plese you and do al youre desire so that ye hurte not
the libertees of holi Churche, for that I wol euer [maynteyne] to my
355 power while I leve.' And when the kyng herde this he was ful angry
with Seint Thomas. And then the erchebishop of Yorke labourid
with al his power to sette the kyng and Seint Thomas atte on, but the
kyng swore a gret othe that he wolde haue al the statutes of Claridon
holde of euery byshop in Englonde, and in special that statute if a
360 clerke were a strong theffe that he shulde be iuged by the kynges
lawes and not by the spiritual lawes. And then Seint Thomas seid
either he muste stonde myghtly with holi Churche or else [she]
shulde be brought vnder fote for euer, but he thought that it shulde
neuer be done by his consent, for leuer he had to dye for the right of
365 holy Churche.
      And so the kyng departide fro hym in gret wreth and seid he
wolde be awreke on this matyrs, and seid that a clerke shulde neuer
be his mayster in his owne londe. And then he chargid Seint Thomas
to apere afore hym and his lordes vpon the Tewisday aftir Seint
370 Lucies Day atte Northampton, and al the bishops of this londe to be
there also. And in the mene tyme al Seint Thomas londys anone were
f. 48ʳᵇ   sesid into the kynges hondis and thought veri|ly to distroy him atte
onys. And then Seint Thomas seid: 'God help me and holi Churche,
for ful fewe frendes we haue nowe,' and forthwith went to North-

ampton where the kyng hilde his gret counseil in the castel with al 375
his lordes. And when Seint Thomas come afore the kyng he seid: 'I
am come to obey youre commaundement, but byfore this was neuer
erchebishop of Canturbury this entretid, for I am hede of the
Chirche of this londe and am thi gostly fader, and it was neuer
Goddes lawe the sonne to distroy the fadyr that hath the charge of 380
his soule and must yelde rekenyng therof atte day of dome. And
thorugh thi steryng hast made al the bishops that shulde strenght me
and holy Churche to be oure most enemye, and thou knowist wel
that I may not fight, but I am redi to suffre deth rather then lese the
right of holy Churche.' 385
 Then seid the kyng: 'Thou spekist as a proude clerke, but I shal
abate thi pride or I leue the, for thou and I haue a rekenyng to make.
Thou vndirstondiste wel thou were my chaunceler many yeres, and
onys I lent the .v. houndred pounde, but thou madyst me neuer
rekenyng therof, and therfore withoute eny taryyng therof, pay me 390
that money,' or else he chargid his offisers to haue him to warde. And
then Seint Thomas seid to the king: 'Forsoth ye gave me that .v.C.
pounde, and atte that tyme I might haue had more and I wolde haue
desired it of you. And therfore it is vnsittyng to a kyng to yeue a
yefte and aftir when he is displesid to constreyne that man to pay it 395
to hym ayene.' And then the kyng seid in gret angir that he shulde
pay that summe euery peny or go to prison. And then .v. knyghtis
were bounde for these .v.C. li. to pay within short tyme eche of them
in an .C. pounde.
 And then Seint Thomas departide and went to his hoste. And the 400
next day he come ayene byfore the kyng if eny better grace myght
fal, but then it was werse than euer it was bifore, for the kyng callid
hym strong theffe and seid that he had stolen of his goodes more
than .xxx.ti thousand ponde in the tyme that he was his chaunceler,
'and therefore make the redy anone, for I wole haue a rekenyng of 405
euery peny.' And then al the lordes seid that Seint Thomas was vndo
for euer and like neuer to come oute of prison. And then he desired
to haue counsel in this mater and then to yeue the kynge an
aunswere. And the kyng grauntide hym, but he and his counseil
were fast lokkid vp in a chambre. And then the bishop of 410
Wynchester seid to hym: 'This shal be thyn aunswere. He made
the erche|bishop, and whan thou leftist thy office he askid then noo f. 48ᵛᵃ

dewte of the, and if ther had be suche dette owyng then he wolde
haue askid it, and also thou receyuest that bishopriche clere withoute
415 eny charge, and that tyme he made the quytte of al the charges done
byfore and no dette askid of [the] atte thy departyng. And therfore
me thynketh thou aughtist not to aunswere for nothing done byfore
while thou were chaunceler.'

But al the other bishops were clene ayenst Seynt Thomas saue
420 only the byshop of Winchester and the bishop of London, and [thei]
conseiled hym to obey to the kyng or else he wolde vndo al holy
Churche. Then seid the bishop of [Wurcetter]: 'God defende that
holy Churche shulde euer be vnder the kynges rewle, for then it were
clene distroyed.' And then Seint Thomas seid: 'God sende us better
425 counseil.' And then the bishops lete calle to them .ij. lordes and preid
them to haue respite of the kyng til the next day, and he grauntide
them. And euery bishop went home to his [loggyng] and the most
parte of Seint Thomas men [forsoke] hym. And then he toke pore
men by the wey and led them home with hym to his oste to sette
430 them to dyner and serued them hymself ful mekely and seid: 'These
ben goode knyghtis that wol not forsake me in no wise, but the
bishops that shulde helpe me and holy Churche ben nowe oure
moste foon, wherfore I prey almyghti God be oure helpe, for I wol
rather dye than suffir holi Churche to be brought in thraldome. And
435 I charge you al my brethren bishops bi the vertu of obedience that, if
eny seculer man set honde vpon me in violence, that ye fle anone fro
me and execute the gret sentence vpon ˹hym˺ or them that so done,
and rather for to dye than lese the right of holy Churche.'

And the Monday aftir [was] his day to apere afore the kyng and
440 his lordes, but he was so sike that he myght not. And then his
enemyes seid that he made hym for the nonys so sike, wherfore the
kyng sent for hym in gret angir. And then Seint Thomas preid the
kynge to pardon hym for that day, and the next day that was the
Twesday ˹he wolde come to hym though he shulde be caried vpon˺
445 an horsebere. And the Twesday erly in the morowe al the bishops
come to Seint Thomas and conseiled hym to obey to the kynges
entent in eny wyse, or else he shulde be distroyed and holy Churche
thurgh hym shulde be brought al vndir fote. And then seid Seint

414 thou receyuest] he resseyvid L   416 the] thi A1   420 thei] om. A1
422 Wurcetter] Vurcetter A1   427 loggyng] leggyng A1   428 forsoke]
forsokys A1   431 goode] goddis L   not] add for A1   437 hym] me del.
and corr. in margin A1   439 was] is A1   444 he . . . vpon] erly in the morowe
al the bishops come to seint del. and corr. in margin A1   445 the(3)] add alle the A1

Thomas: 'God defende that euer I do fulfille þe | kynges entent and   f. 48ᵛᵇ
bryng holy Churche into thraldome, yet had I leuer dye for the right   450
therof.' And he charged al the bishops to do the same and thynke
howe thei beth sworen to maynteyne the right therof. Nowe God
help Seint Thomas, for he had neuer more nede.

And anone he made hym redi to sey masse and [bygon] the office
of Seint Steuyn, *Etenim principes aduersum me steterunt &c.* And then   455
þe kynges messengers seid that the false bishop preid God to
distroye the kyng, wherfor ful many of these cursid tyrauntis
counseiled the kyng to distroye hym shortly, or else he wolde ouer
maister hym and then make king whome that plesid hym and make
suche lawes in this londe as he wolde, and rule bothe the spiritualte   460
and the temporalte atte his owne wille. And [thorugh] suche langage
the kyng was al sette in malice ayenst Seint Thomas and purposid
shortly to distroy hym. And when Seint [Thomas] had seid his
masse, he cast of his chisyple and dide on a cope and toke the pyx
that the sacrament was in and his crosse in his honde, for other   465
armure wolde he none haue to fight with for the right of holy
Churche, but anone went forth as Goddys knyght among al his foon.
Therfore God be his help, for other frendes hath he none.

And as Seint Thomas went towarde the kyng, the bishop Robert
of Herford wolde haue take his crosse and bore it as his chapeleyne   470
byfore hym, but he wolde not suffre hym so to do, and seid: 'While
that I bere it myself I drede no man.' And then the bishop of London
seid to the bishop of Herford: 'I rede the that thou do not so, for
then the kynge wol breke his angir on the.' And then Seint Thomas
come in this wise alone byfore the kynge and al his lordes. And when   475
he se hym he wexed ny mad for angir and seid to his lordes: 'Nowe
muste I nedys for shame be awreke on this false traitoure.' And then
seid al the lordes: 'Nowe may ye se that he is a false traytour to you
and euer hath byn, and yet he is proude and wole not knowe you for
his lorde that hath made hym so gret that had right nought but only   480
of youre yeftis, and therfore he may not haue to shameful a deth.'
And then the kyng lete proclame hym opyn traitour and al tho that
hilde with hym.

And then the bishop of Exceter knelyd downe to ⌜Seint Tho⌝mas
and preid hym to haue ruthe on hymself and them, or else he wolde   485

454 bygon] by A1   456 bishop] traytour Seynt Thomas L   461 atte] as L
thorugh] thorug A1   463 Thomas] *om.* A1   474 breke] wreke L (see note)
484 Seint Tho] his fete *del. and corr. in margin* A1

f. 49ra bringe al holy Churche to mischeffe. And then | Seint Thomas seid:
'Your counsel is nought and therfore I wol not obey therto.' When al
the bishops herde this, thei toke her counsel togiders and went to the
kyng and bysought hym of his grace, and seid al with o voyce that
490 thei wolde obey vnto hym in al wise and wolde forsake hym that
wolde distroy the kyng and þem thurgh his gret pride and folye.
'And therfore nowe we knowe for certeyne that he is a false
[forsworne] traitour bothe to God and you, and that we shal preue
vpon hym afore the pope of Rome, if ye wol yeue us licens therto and
495 deprive hym of his estate and dignite.' And then the kynge coude
them gret thonke for ther seyng, and preid them hertly so to do in al
the hast that thei myght and he wolde rewarde hem gretly for ther
costes.

   And then anone al the bishops come byfore Seint Thomas and
500 seid: 'Sumtyme thou were oure gostly fader and ruler, but nowe we
forsake the for euer, for thou art a false forsworne traitour to God
and to the kyng. And therfore we al excite the to apere atte Rome
byfore the pope to aunswere us ther that thou hast offended to the
kynge and us.' Then seid this holy Seint Thomas: 'I vndirstonde wel
505 alle youre desires, and by Goddys grace I hope sumtyme to come and
quytte me as a trewe man byfore oure holy fader the pope and you,
for God shal onys be the domes man bytwene you and me who of us
hath the right.' And anone as he had this seid the kynge sent for
Seint Thomas by the erle Robert of Leycetter and chargid hym to
510 apere anone byfore the kyng and his lordes withoute eny lenger
delay.

   And then Seint Thomas come yn byfore the kyng and his lordis,
and seid byfore them al that whan he was made erchebishop of
Canturbury by the kynges desire, 'he grantid me it so fre that no man
515 shuld haue eny correccion of holy Churche save only the pope. And
then ye seid that holy Churche shulde be quytte and fre of al
temporal seruise that longyth to the kynges courte. And for that ye
yafe [it] me so fre withoute eny condicion, me thynkyth ye ought by
reson to aske no ˹dette˺ of me, for if I had owyd yow so gret a summe
520 of mony ye wolde haue askid it me or this tyme. And therfore I let
you playnly wete, I wole neuer be iuged by the kynges lawes to pay o
peny that ye aske of me but if þe lawe of holy Churche wole it so
iuge byfore oure holy fader the pope of Rome. And there, al ye

---

493 forsworne] forsoworne A1   518 it] *om.* A1   519 dette] dewte *del. and*
corr. in margin A1

byshops, I charge you to apere | to knowe the right of this mater in f. 49ʳᵇ
the popis courte, wheder it be leeful for you to holde more with a 525
temporal kynges lawe or with almyghti Goddys lawe that is the lawe
of holy Churche.' And when he had seid these wordes he departide
fro the kyng and his lordes, and then al the lordes begonne to skorne
and mok Seint Thomas and made a gret cry vpon hym as though he
had byn a fole of the worlde, that al the towne of Northhampton 530
wondrid vpon hym alone and ferde so foule with hym that it was gret
pety to byholde.

And then he preid to God for [his] enemyes, and light vpon his
palfrey and rode towarde his loggyng with gret multitude of pore
peple aboute hym, and thonkyd oure lorde that he was skapid 535
hermeles oute of his enemyes hondes. And then he commaundide
that al the pore folke shulde dyne with hym in the howse of Seint
Andrews, and there he se hymself that thei were set al to mete, and
thonkid them of ther goode hertis and seid: 'I haue here no frendis
but God and you.' And as Seint Thomas sate atte mete and ful litil 540
he ete, but toke heede to him that radde the gospel byfore hym that
seid: 'If men pursue [the] in on towne, fle into another to helpe
thiself til ther ire be swaged.' Then the holy man thought that it was
the wil of God that he so dide, and so he purposed as sone as he
myght if the kyng in the mene tyme wolde be better avised. And 545
forthwith come .ij. lordys to warne Seint Thomas that the kynges
men had sworne to sle hym where euer thei myght fynde hym. And
then Seint Thomas lete make his bed in the churche by the hye auter
for surete of his body, but he slept not theryn but wakid and preid,
knelyng on his bare knees byfore the crucifix seyng the .vij. psalmes 550
and the .xv. psalmes and the letanyes, and aftir he opnyd euery auter
in the chirche and preid to al the holy seintes to prey for hym and
knelyd on his bare knees and wept ful sore. And euer he preid oure
lorde to be his help in this gret trouble, and aboute mydnyght while
al his men were aslepe he toke a frioure of Sypringham and .ij. or .iij. 555
of his men that he trust most and went pryueleche oute of the
chirche, and purposid to gete ouer the see in al the hast and go to
oure holy fader the pope of Rome.

And the same nyght that Seint Thomas went so awey fro
Northampton, on of his men dremyd that these verse of the Psauter 560
was rehercid to hym: *Anima nostra sicut passer erepta est de laqueo*

529 a] the most L   533 his(1)] *om.* A1   542 the] te A1   551 he
opnyd] vpon L   553 and] he L

f. 49va *uenancium. Laqueus contri|tus est et nos liberati sumus.* And al this was shewed by Seint Thomas, for he was atte Grantham fro North-ampton or it was day, and yet he went barefote that .xxv.ti myle. And

565 fro thens he went to Lyncolne, and there he was loggid atte a follers howse. This was on a Thursday, and the Friday he went .xl.ti myle by water to þe hermytage of Cypryngham, that stondith in the myddes of the water, and there he dwellid .iij. days. And fro thens he went to Seint Botulphis and to Hauelok and Offrey, that shulde be

570 his owne maner be right, and stode vpon the seeside, and there he dwellid .vij. days, and was there in a chambre nyghe the ⌐churche⌐ where he herd masse euery day thorugh an hole of þe walle, but no man knewe that he was there saue only the friour of Cypryngham and his owne men.

575 And vpon Al Sowlyn Day, that fil on a Twesdaye, he went by nyght into a ship and seiled ouer the see into Flanders and arived bysides the castel of Oye the same day, a mile out of Greuenyng. And when he was a londe he was clothid in a friours clothyng and was so wery what for sorowe and trouble of the see that he myght not

580 go for werynes. And then his [men] hired hym a mare for .iij. half pens to ride vpon, and then he cast his blak frioures cope on the mare and he himself sate aboue in his whit curtil of blanket and ride forth a goode pas towardes his logging.

And when thei were sette to soper he sette hymself lowist of al atte

585 tablys ende for he wolde not be knowe, and callyd hymself Friour Cristian. And there it was knowe in al the contre howe the kyng had mysdo Seint Thomas, and therfore his hoste supposid that this Friour was Seint Thomas the erchebishop of Canturbury that goythe towardes Rome this disgysid for he wolde not be knowen. But he

590 tolde his wife verily that it was he, and then thei dide hym better chere and brought applys, notis and other deyntees suche as thei had. But when Seint Thomas perceyued that his hoste knewe hym, then he was heuy and clepid his hoste to hym and preyed hym to kepe his counseile. And the next day he toke his hoste and went to the abbey

595 of [Charmaryes] that was .xij. long myle thens. He lay there the first nyght, the whiche abbey is besides the towne of Seint Omeryes, and fro thens he went to the abbey of Seint Bertyne, and there he dwellid a goode while to abyde the grace that God wolde sende.

571 churche] see *del. and corr. in margin* A1   575 Al Sowlyn] Alschalewen L
580 men] man *corr.* A1   587 his] *add* his A1   595 Charmaryes] Chamaryes A1

And in this mene tyme the kyng sent his bishops and his lordys
towarde Rome for to make ther compleynte vpon Seint Thomas. 600
And first | thei went to the kynge of Fraunce and brought him letters f. 49ᵛᵇ
fro the kyng of Englonde and tolde hym howe traitourly Seint
Thomas was gone oute of Inglonde, and therfor the king preid hym
that he wolde not suffre hym nor none of his to come into his londe.
And the kyng of Fraunce seid to hem: 'Sirs, me thynkith ye be to 605
heuy frendes to Seint Thomas, for if a man were a stronge theffe or a
bannyd man come into my londe, if he dothe none harme therein I
must nedes receyue hym for a tyme, and therfore may I not denye
Seint Thomas, for I knowe hym for right a goode man, and me
thynkyth ye bishops shulde holde moste with hym, for he is your 610
cheffe hede of holy Churche. For here in my londe I suffre the
bishops to haue ther fre libertees of al holy Churche, and so shulde
ye do also if ye dide wel.'
  And when thei myght haue none oþer comforte of Kyng Lowys of
Fraunce, thei toke ther leve of hym and went ther wey towarde 615
Rome to compleyne there to the pope vpon Seint Thomas. And
anone as the bishops and the lordes were departide fro Lowys kynge
of Fraunce, Seint Thomas sent to hym on maister Robert of Bosham
and [he tolde] to the kynge al the trouble that Seint Thomas hath
had in Englonde. And when he herde it he wepte ful sore for ruthe 620
and pety and seid: 'Loke what I may do for Seint Thomas, it shal be
redy atte al tymes.' And then the seid Robert Bosham departide fro
hym with gret ioye and come to Seint Thomas ayen to the abbey of
Seint Bertyne and tolde him what chere he had of Lowys the kyng,
and what chere he had made the bishops and the lordes of Englonde. 625
And then the seid maister of Bosham with other departide fro thens
and come to Rome, and there thei were not welcome, for the bishops
of Englonde and other lordes had greuosly compleyned vpon Seint
Thomas and fowle disclandride him byfore the pope. But then this
seid maister Robert of Bosham enformed the pope of the wronge 630
done to Seint Thomas atte parlement of Clarindon and what statutes
were made there ayenst Seint Thomas, and also howe he was
sompnyd to apere afore the kynge atte Northampton, and tolde
the pope in what trouble he was brought in there, and howe he went

606 man were a] *om.* L   614 Lowys] *add* kyng L   619 he tolde] *om.* A1
621 what] yf L   do] *add* eny thynge L   631–2 atte . . . Thomas] *om.* L
634 there] *add* and also he told the pope what statutis were made ayenst holy chirche at the
parlement in Claryndon L

635　thens barefote in a friours clothyng and had changid his name for he
wolde not be knowe, and so he come ouer the see into Flanders, and
tolde the pope of al his sorowe and wo, and al this was to holde up
the right of holy Churche. |

f. 50ra　And when the pope herde this he wepte for pety and thonkid God
640　that he had suche a prelate vndir hym to maynteyne the right of holy
Churche. And the next day aftir come ayene byfore the pope these
byshops and lordes of Englonde and tolde al the euyl that [thei]
cowde ayenst Seint Thomas. And first bygan the bishop of London
to telle his tale, and seid to the pope that Seint Thomas with folye
645　and pride wolde brynge al Englonde into gret trouble and distroy al
holy Churche and take awey the kynges franchise and his right fro
hym, 'but we wolde not in no wise consent to his euyl dede, and
therfor he hath caste his malice this ayenst us, for he myght not haue
his entent. And for no man wolde support his malice that is so cursid
650　this, he is stolen oute of Englonde to make his compleynte on the
kynge and us to youre highnes that we haue done hym vnright and
dreve hym oute of Englonde, but God knowith his owne folye
ᵣhathe do itᴸ and not the kynge nor we.' And then he sate downe. And
then the bishop of Chester seid to þe pope: 'Me thynkith ye ought to
655　correcte suche a proude man, that thrugh his malice settith al a londe
in trouble and [purposith] to distroy al holy Churche. And therfor
lete hym be sharply ponyshed to make al suche othir by ware by
hym.' Then stode up the erchebishop of Yorke and seid byfore the
pope and his cardynals that when Seint Thomas toke a silfe wille in
660　eny mater no man shulde brynge him therfro though it be neuer so
vntrewe. 'And therfore me thynkith it were a gret almesdede to
brynge hym fro suche folishe pride, for therwith he hath nye
distroyd al Englonde.' And then the bishop of Excetter seid: 'Ye
must nedes amende this thynges and many othir that byn amys, or
665　else holi Churche shal sone come to nought. This is treu that we telle
you, and therfore we beseche your highnes to take credence to oure
seynges, and if ye wole not beleue us, sende a legat with us into
Englonde and then ye schal knowe that we sey sothe.' And then
anone rose up the erle of Arundel and seid: 'For Goddis loue, holy
670　fader, here me, though I can speke no Latyn, in my moder tonge. We

635 thens] fro Northamton L　　642 thei] the A1　　643 cowde] add sey L
649 his] add cursyd L　that . . . cursid] om. L　　653 hathe . . . it] that he hath do
del. and corr. in margin A1, that he hathe doo L　　656 purposith] purposid A1
657 suche] om. L　　667–8 into Englonde] om. L

ben heder sent fro oure lorde the kynge of Englonde not to displese youre holy faderhede but to obey hym vnto you as lowly as any cristen prynce, and euer preyeth for your goode faderhode and euer entendith to do your plesure to his lyves ende. And no cristen prince maynteyneth better the lawe of holy | Churche than he doth, and therfore, and it plesid your highnes to make Seint Thomas oure erchebishop and primat of oure londe to leue his self wille, than I dar sey he shulde plese the kynge and sette al his londe in gret rest and oute of trouble. And if this be not done, oure londe is ⌐distroyed⌐ for euer, and þat were gret rewthe and pety.'

f. 50ʳᵇ

676

680

And then the pope seid to the bishops and al the lordes: 'Ye wete wel of right we may yeue no dome in this matyr til I haue herde Seint Thomas speke as I haue done you, for reson wole that I here bothe parties speke.' Then seid the erle of Arundel: 'Sir, ye must vndir-stonde that the kyng hath sette a day that we must nedes be then with hym in Englonde, and we dar not breke the kynges commaundement in no wise. And therfor we muste prey you of your holy faderhede to haue a better answere of you and a letter of credence that we may by youre power haue Seint Thomas ayene into Englonde, and then we trust by Goddys grace that al thynges shal be brought to a goode ende, or else it shal be vttirly distroyed.' And then seid the pope: 'I wote not howe sone the erchebishop wole come hedir, and therfore I counseil you to abide. And [when] I haue herde you bothe telle your entent, then I shal sette suche a direccion bytwene you that I trust to God ye bothe shal holde you ⌐plesid⌐.' And then the bishops and the lordes se that thei cowde not haue ther entent, sodenly thei departide and toke ther wey ayene towarde Englonde in gret wreth for thei cowde not spede aftir ther entent of the pope.

685

690

695

And al this tyme was Seint Thomas stil in the abbey of Seint Bertyn bysides Seint Omers in Picardi. And when that Seint Thomas knewe that the bishops and the lordes were gone ouer the see into Englonde, then Seint Thomas departide fro the abbey of Bertyn and toke his wey by nyght towarde Lowis the kynge of Fraunce. And when he knewe of his comyng he sent his men ayenst him to brynge hym to the kynge in safte, and when he come to hym he receyued hym with gret ioy and seid al that he had was atte his commaunde-ment, and yafe hym mony largely to [spend] and bade hym walke

700

705

672 as(2)] *add* lowly as A1   679 distroyed] vndone *corr. in margin* A1, lost and distroyed L   693 when] *om.* A1   695 plesid] pelsid *corr. in margin* A1
707 spend] spent A1

and sporte hym in what place he wolde of al his londe. And then he
thonkyd the kynge of his gret goodenes and seid he must nedes take
710 his iorney to Rome warde to speke with the pope. And then he toke
his lefe of the kyng and went towarde Rome. And then the kyng sent
his men with him to convey hym theder.

f. 50ᵛᵃ   And he | come to Rome vpon Seint Markes Day aftir none. And
then his cater went fourth to bye his dyner, for he and al his men
715 were fastyng, but he cowde not gete no fisshe, for al was solde or he
come, and so he went to his hoste ayene and tolde Seint Thomas that
he cowde no fisshe gete. Then he bade hym by suche mete as he
myght gete. And then he bought flesshe for him and al his men and
made it redy and set them to dyner and seruyd Seint Thomas with a
720 rostide capon. And when the pope had knowleche that he was come,
he sent a cardynal to welcome hym. And when the cardynal se that
he and al his men ete flesshe, he had gret merveil therof and toke his
leve and come in gret hast anone to the pope and seid: 'Holy fader,
this bishop of Englonde is no suche parfite man as ye holde hym, for
725 he this day etith flesshe mete and al his men, whiche is ayenst your
ordinaunce in al holy Churche thorugh al cristendome.' Then seid
the pope: 'I knowe right wel he is not so disposid.' And then the
cardynal confermed it with an othe that it was so in dede, wherefore
the pope sent theder another cardynal and bade hym to brynge to
730 him parte of suche mete as he ete, and toke a capons legge and put it
in his kerchir and brought it to the pope. And when he toke it oute of
his kerchir it was an hole fisshe that is callid a carpe. And then this
cardynal was gretly abashed and seid to the pope: 'Verely it was a
capons legge whan I put it into my kerchir.' And when the pope
735 herde this he had gret wondir of this thynge and sent for Seint
Thomas and welcomyd him and askyd of hym what mete he had to
his dyner. And he seid: 'Holy fader, I wolde haue ete fisshe, but I
come so late that al was gone, and then I bade my cater bye suche
mete as he cowde finde to selle. And so he bought a capon for my
740 dyner and other flesshe for my men.' And when the pope knewe this
gret myracle, he grantide .xl.ti days of pardon to al them that ete
flesshe on Seint Markes Day that dwel in his diocise.

And then Seint Thomas thonkid hym of his gret goodenes and
bygon to tel the pope of al the wronges that the kyng and the bishops
745 of Englonde had done to hym. And when the pope had herde his tale

716 tolde] *add* his maister L   720 knowleche] knowynge L

to the ende, he wepte for ruthe and pety that he was so wrongfulli
don to, and seid: 'Lorde, I yeue the thonkyngis that I haue suche a
bishop vndir me that wol not suffre holy Churche to lese hir
libertees, but rather to suffre deth than to brynge hir in suche
thraldome.' And then the pope chargid al the bishops | of cristyn- f. 50vb
dome bi his writtyng that thei shulde suffre no newe lawes to be 751
made vpon holy Churche by eny kynge or prince but rather to suffre
deth than grant therto, 'for al we may take an ensample atte Seint
Thomas howe we shulde rule holy Churche.' And whenne Seint
Thomas had tolde the pope al the newe lawes that the kynge hath 755
brought vpon the Churche of Englonde like as it is reherced afore,
euery article aftir other, then Seint Thomas besought the pope to
discharge hym of the erchebishopriche of Canturbury and wolde
haue delyuerd vp his rynge and preid hym lete some othir bishop
haue it that shulde sette the londe better in rest, but the pope and his 760
cardynals wolde not consent thereto in no wise but seid al with on
voyce that he shulde haue it stil, for ther was none so worthy to haue
it as he. 'For and we shulde putte anothir bishop there it shulde
cause the kyng then anothir tyme to be the bolder to bringe up mo
newe lawes on holy Chirche, and therfor ye must nedes haue it stil 765
yourself, for ther is none so able therto as ye.'

And then the pope comfortide Seint Thomas and seid: 'Loke what
thyng I may do for you, it shal be redy atte al tymes, and therfore be
strong and myghti to holde up the right of holy Churche.' And then
he seid masse byfore the pope in a whit chesiple, and aftir masse he 770
tolde the pope howe he shulde suffre deth for the right of holi
Churche, 'and bi this whit chesiple ye shal knowe the day, for when I
shal be slayne this chesiple that is nowe white shal be than red.' And
then the pope leide this chesiple in the place where he myght se hit
euery day. 775

And then Seint Thomas toke his leue ⌐of⌐ þe pope and went to the
abbey of Pontney in Fraunce, and there he dwellid long tyme in gret
abstynence and holy leuyng, for he wered alwey the herde heyre ful
of gret knottes that it made his fleshe ful of mater his shorte sat so
streite upon him. And there he had knowyng howe angry the kyng 780
was when the bishops and the lordes come fro Rome and tolde the
kynge howe thei cowde spede nothyng of ther purpose with the
pope. Then the kinge seid: 'Alas, this false traitour the bishop hath
do me gret a shame to putte me to suche a coste to sende my bishops

776 of] fro *del. and corr. in margin.* A1   784 me(1) . . . a(1)] to greet L

785 and lordes to Rome, and nothyng may spede for that fals traytour.'
And then he commaundide anone that al his kynne and frendes shulde
al be drevyn oute of Englonde, bothe sike and [hoole], yong and olde,
with al ther childern, wherefore al the common peple were right heuy,
f. 51ra and grucchid right sore ayenst the kyng for this doynge | as fer as thei
790 durst.

And then al these folkis went ouer the see with ful gret sorowe to
Pontney where Seint Thomas was dwellyng that tyme, and tolde him
howe thei were putte oute of Englonde by the commaundement of
the kynge 'for youre sake, and he hath chargid thorugh al Englonde
795 that no preste prey for you in peyne of deth.' And then Seint
Thomas was ful heuy for his kynnesmen, that thei were brought into
suche sorowe and trouble for his sake. And the moste sorowe of al
was that he had no goode to refresshe them in ther gret necessite.
But he comfortide them al in the best wise that he cowde and seid:
800 'God is the helper of al them that suffre wronges for his loue, and
therfore trust it verily he wole neuer suffre his seruauntis to perisshe
for defaute of mete and drynke.' For anone by the puruyaunce of
oure lorde the grettest men of the reme of Fraunce, when thei herde
of the euyl disposicion of the kinge of Englonde, howe wrongfully
805 [he] put oute of Englonde Seint Thomas for the right of holy
Churche, and al his kynnesmen also for the gret hate that he had
to Seint Thomas, then the seid men of Fraunce for pety and ruthe
sent to Seint Thomas ⌐goodes⌐ gret plente, wherewith he refresshid
hymself and al his kynnesmen.

810 And when the kynge of Englonde herde telle that Seint Thomas
and hys frendes were so wel refresshid in the house of grey monkes
at Ponteney, it happid the same tyme was a General Capitle of al
cristyndome of that order of Cisteans in Englonde that tyme.
Wherefore the kynge sent to them and chargid them to writte to
815 the abbey of Ponteney, that was an ordir of the seyd grey monkes,
and bidde them put oute that gret traytour and his enmye Seint
Thomas and al his kynnesmen, or else he wolde distroye al the
houses of that ordre within his londe of Englonde. Wherefore al the
hole Capitle was fayne to writte to the house of Ponteney and
820 charged them that they shulde no lenger kepe Seint Thomas nor his
kynnesmen, for and thei dide the kynge wolde distroye al the howsys

787 hoole] *om.* A1   795 preste] *add* schalle L   801 it] *add* welle L
805 he] *om.* A1   808 goodes] the *del. and corr. in margin* A1   812 Ponteney]
add and A1L

of that ordre within al his londe. And when thei herde these [thynges] thei were ful heuy, but thei durst no lenger kepe Seint Thomas, but put hym thens and al his kynnesmen, wherefore Seint Thomas was ful heuy and thonkid them of ther goode wil and gret 825 goodenes that thei had shewid to him and to his kynnesmen, and so departide fro thens, but he wiste not wheder to go, but anone he kneled downe and seid: 'Lorde that art the helper of al men and bestis and fedist them al, I prey the helpe me nowe in | this gret f. 51ʳᵇ nede.' And anone ther come a messenger fro Lowis the kyng and 830 bade hym chese his dwellyng in what place he wolde of al his londe, and he wolde pay for his costes and al his kynnesmen as long as it plesid hym to abide in his londe. Wherefore he thonkyd the kyng ful mekely of his gret goodenes and seid: 'Blessid be thou, Lorde Ihesu, that euer purveyst for thi seruantis that byn brought in sorowe and 835 wo, wherefore thi name be preised worlde withoute ende, Amen.'

And then the abbot of Ponteney brought hym forwarde on his wey, but Seint Thomas was ful heuy and wepte, and the abbot axyd hym whi he was so heuy syns the kynge had shewid to hym so gret kyndnes. And then Seint Thomas seid: 'I haue cause to be heuy, for 840 this nyght I dremyd that I striffe ayenst the kynge in the howse of Canturbury for the right of holy Churche. And me thought ther come .iiij. knyghtis and smytte with ther swerdis at onys vpon the crowne of myn hede. And then eche of them aftir other stered the breyne of myn hede that it fil on the stonys, but for myself I thonke 845 oure lorde Ihesu and am right glad to dye for the right of holy Churche. But for my [kynnesmen] I haue gret sorowe, for I knowe wel thei shal haue gret trouble for my sake.' And then he departide fro the abbot and preid him to vttir this thyng to no creature while he leuyd, and so he went forth .xij. myle thens to a place that is 850 clepid Seynys, and there the kynge of Fraunce founde hym and al his frendes atte his propre coste. And there Seint Thomas led a ful holy life longe tyme.

And then the kynge of Englonde come ouer the see into Fraunce, and Lowis the kynge was ful besy to brynge the kynge of Englonde 855 and Seint Thomas to be acordide, and thorugh his laboure were brought to speke eche [with] other. And when Seint Thomas come byfor the kynge, he fille downe atte his fete and seid to the kyng ful

823 thynges] thythynges A1, tydyngys L   825 goode . . . and] *om.* L
830 kyng] *add* of Fraunce L   834 be thou] *om.* L   839 had] *add* so A1
843 swerdis] *add* alle L   847 kynnesmen] knnesmen A1   857 with] to *del.* A1

sore wepyng: 'Sir, for Goddis loue haue pety and ruthe vpon holy
860 Churche that she be not this brought vndirfote.' Then answered þe
kynge bifore the kynge of Fraunce and al his lordes: 'It was neuer
myne entent to hurte holy Churche nor take awey o poynte of hir
libertees, but Seint Thomas wolde furdo the lawes of myn londe that
haue be vsid in my ancetters days byfore me oute of mynde. And ful
865 many a goode bishop haue byn in my londe byfore hym that seid
neuer ayenst my lawes as he dothe. Wherfor ye may vndirstonde that
the faute is in him and not in me.' And then al that there were seid
f. 51ᵛᵃ that | Seint Thomas was the cause of this trouble and not the kynge.
    Then seid Seint Thomas: 'Sirs, if the bishops of Canturbury that
870 haue byn byfore me had holde up al the libertees of holy Churche,
then this striffe shulde not haue byn nowe in my days, for al the
lawes that byn rightful and be not ayenst the libertees of holy
Churche them I holde with, and al oþer I wol deny to my power, for
else I shulde displese God, for the gospel seith: 'He that knowith
875 wrong done and wole not defende it to his power, he synneth dedly
and shal aunswere for his negligens therof byfore God atte day of
dome.' And then seid Lowys the kynge of Fraunce: 'Sir bishop, me
thynkith thou takist ouer muche vpon the to take awey the kynges
lawes that haue byn vsid in other kinges dayes byfore hym. And if
880 thou wilt be this presumptuously disposid to haue al thynges aftir
thyn owne wil and not aftir right and reson, I repent me that I haue
done so muche for the, for I knowe wel nowe thou doyste this of
malice and euyl wil and nothyng by right and conscience.' Wherfor
he chargid hym to avoide his londe, for he shulde no lenger abide
885 there in no wise.
    And then Seint Thomas was ful heuy that he was bothe put oute
of Englonde and of Fraunce, and he preid oure lorde Ihesu to be his
helpe, for al othir haue clene forsake him, but he thought euer rather
to suffre deth than to lese the right of holy Churche. And then he
890 come to his kynnesmen and told them howe the case stode with hym
and comfortide hem in the best wise that he cowde and seid: 'I am
the cause of your sorowe and not ye.' And then thei al comfortide
Seint Thomas and seid: 'Take no sorowe for us, for we wole laboure
with oure hondes and gete oure levynge right wel by the grace of
895 God, but al oure care is for you.' Then seid Seint Thomas to them:
'Be not heuy for me, for I trust to God. I shal begge and gete me
mete, for I am not to goode so to do. And God quytte them ther

875 he] *om.* L   880 this] *om.* L   882 doyste] *add* alle L   889 to] *om.* L

mede that me doyth helpe in this my gret nede.' And then thei al
seid: 'God defende that ye that bithe erchebishop of Canturbury
shulde stonde so herde bystade that he must begge his mete.' And 900
with this seynge al they departide eche man his wey.

And Seint Thomas purposid verily to go into a contre that is
bitwene Burgone and Provynce, for there it was tolde hym were ful
god peple and gladly they wole yeue goode for the loue of God. And
as he was goynge thederwarde, the kynge of Fraunce send for hym 905
by his messengers that he shulde co|me and speke with hym in al the f. 51ᵛᵇ
hast. And then he answerde them ful mekely and seid to them he
wolde come to hym with goode wil. And so he returned ayen with
hem and come to the kynges presence. And as sone as the kinge see
him he come ayenst hym and fille downe atte his fete and cried hym 910
merci and seid that he had gretly offendide God and him: 'For nowe
I knowe verili that ye haue the right and the kyng hath do you ful
gret wronge, wherefore I prey you take youre plesyng in eny parte of
my londe and I wole pay for your costes and for al them that be
longyng to you.' And then he laborid ful sore to make acorde 915
bytwene the kynge and hym. And the day was assigned to be
holde atte Mont Marteirs in Fraunce, where he hopid a goode
conclusion shulde be made bitwene hem.

And there thei come bothe, but al was in veyne, for the kynge seid
he wolde neuer be acordide with Seint Thomas but al the statutes 920
that were made at Clarindon shulde stonde ferme and stable. And
then seid Seint Thomas that wolde he neuer agre to, but rather he
wolde suffre deth than to obey to the lawes that byn contrary to
Goddis lawe and the distruccion of holy Churche. And then they
departide thens in gret wreth. And therfore Seint Thomas wepte ful 925
sore and preid God to help holy Churche, or else it was like to be
brought al vndirfote. And then on that was a clerke of Seint Thomas,
that hight Maister Robert of Bosham, seid to hym: 'This place is
clepid Mont Martire, wherefore I beleue that holy Churche shal
neuer be in pees in Englonde til ye be martird for the libertees of 930
holy Churche.' And then Seint Thomas seid: 'God sende grace that
it may be so, if holy Churche myght be brought in pees therby.'

And then ayenst mydsomer, the kynge beyng ful wroth towarde

898 helpe] *add* me A1   912 ye haue] thow hast L   912, 913 you] the L
913, 914 youre,your] thy L   915–16 ful sore/to . . . hym] *trsp.* L   916 was]
add sette and L   919 there] thedyr L   920 Thomas] *add* in noon other wyse L
925 therfore] then L   927 al] *om.* L   on] *add* seid A1   that] hys name L
928 seid to hym] that L   928–9 is clepid] hight L   930 be martird] suffre deth L

Seint Thomas, so departide oute of Fraunce and seyled into
935 Englonde to make Herry his sonne kynge by his life, and that
myght he not do withoute the assent of Seint Thomas, wherefore
ther fil gret sorowe within a while aftir, for these .iiij. bishops toke
vpon them to crowne his sonne Harry kynge withoute consent of
Seint Thomas, that is to sei the erchebishop of Yorke, the bishop of
940 London, the bishop of Salsbury and the bishop of Rochester. They
crownyd hym kynge atte Westmynster, and there the fader serued
the sonne atte feste of his coronacion with al the rialte that he cowde
in presence of al the peple.

f. 52ra   And when these tydynges come to Seint Tho|mas, he beyng then
945 in Fraunce, anone he sent to Rome and had the popis bullis to acurse
al them that consentide to that doynge, and suspendide al the
bishops that were doers therof and entredited al Englonde til thei
had made amendes of that trespas. But Seint Thomas kept the popis
bullys secret til he come into Englonde that he myght do the
950 sentence vpon them hymself. And sone aftir the olde kynge come
ayene into Fraunce. And than Kynge Lowis dide his best ayene to
sette them accorde. And so they were atte last, blessid be God, vpon
Mary Magdalenes Day in a place that is called Traytours Mede. And
so the pees was made like to the name of the place, for it was nothyng
955 holde in the kynges parte. But thei departide atte that tyme in loue
by her wordes, but I suppose it was not so in the kynges hert, for
sone after he breke his promyse. And then Seint Thomas sent
Maister Robert of Bosham to the kyng and bysought him that he
wolde yelde ayene to hym the goodes that his baylis had take awey of
960 his atte Canturbury and in other places. And then seid the kynge:
'For your gret hast ye shal abide, for parauenture he may so rule hym
to me that he shal not have o peny therof, but aftir his beryng so shal
I yelde hym his goodes ayene.' And than this Mayster Robert toke
hys leue of the king and tolde Seint Thomas the answere that he had
965 of the kyng.

And then Seint Thomas went ayen to the kyng to wete if he wolde
abyde by his promyse that he had made bifore. But when he spake to

935 by . . . life] of Inglond L   937 these] om. L   938–9 withoute . . . sei]
that was L   942 feste . . . coronacion] mete L   943 in . . . peple] that alle the
peple se that thynge L   944–5 he . . . Fraunce] om. L   948 of . . . trespas]
om. L   But] add when the popis bullys were brought to L   951 Lowis] add of
Fraunce L   954 made] om. L   957 sone] anoon L   And then] when L
958 and . . . him] om. L   960 places] add of hys L   961 For . . . ye] ye wole
ye be so hasty therfor he L   962 therof] om. L   963 Robert] add of Bosham L

the kyng of that mater he ferde as he sette not therby, and went forth
to here masse and bade his prest to sey a masse of Requiem, for he
wolde not kisse the pax with Seint Thomas. And aftir masse he 970
bygon to reherce to Seint Thomas the olde wreth bitwene hem and
howe he brought hym vp of nought, but the conclusion was thei
departide atte that tyme as though ther had be loue bitwene hem.
But it lastid not long.

And then Seint Thomas purposid verily to passe ouer the see into 975
Englonde, for he thought ful long that holy Churche was withoute
goode guydyng. And then he went to Lowis the kyng and thonkid
hym of his gret goodenes that he had do to him, and toke his leue of
the kyng and passid ouer the see into Englonde and londide atte
Sandewyche in Kent, and there the peple receyued hym with gret 980
ioy. And there he dide denounce the sentence of holy Churche vpon
them that had crownyd the yong kyng withoute his lic|ens. And then f. 52ʳᵇ
anone the seid bishops afore reherced maligned gretly ayenst Seint
Thomas. And than the peple come to him and warned him that .iiij.
knyghtis had sworne to sle hym and seid thei be atte Douer there to 985
wayte aftir hym that he shulde ⌐not ascape ther hondes⌐. And then
he preid al the peple to prey for hym that God wolde brynge hym in
safte to Canturbury that he myght see his churche onys or he dyed.
And then al the peple come ayenst hym with procession fro euery
towne bytwene Sandwiche and Canturbury, and so he was conveyd 990
to Canturbury in safte, blessid be God, and there he was then
worshipfully receyued to his owne churche with a solempne procession and ryngyng of bellis.

And when the .iiij. knyttis herde that Seint Thomas was come to
Canturbury, anone thei toke her wey to him warde in ful gret hast 995
and wodenes and seid that thei wolde sle hym anone but he wolde
assoile them that he had acursid. These were there names, Sir
Randolf de Wareyn, Sir Randolf de Broke, the bishop of Yorke,
the bishop of London, the bishop of Salsbury and the bishop of
Rochester, and Gerveys that was chereue, with meche peple, and 1000
come anone to this holy man and seid: 'Howe durste thou come into

970 aftir masse] when the masse was doon L   972 was] hadde be L
977 kyng] *add* of Fraunce L   978 that . . . him] *om.* L   978–9 of the kyng]
om. L   979 passid . . . see] wente fourthewith ouer L   londide] he aryvid vp L
980 receyued] welcomyd L   981 denounce] *om.* L   983 afore reherced] *om.* L
    gretly] *om.* L   985 seid] now L   986 that . . . hondes] *om.* L   not . . .
ther] ascape ther hondes *del. and corr. in margin* A1

this londe that hast this acursid the kyng, his bishops and us? Se
anone that we be al assoyled, or else we wul do to the like suche men
as thou hast made us.' Then seid Seint Thomas: 'Sirs, I may not
1005 vndo this cursyng, for it is done by the pope and not by me and the
consent of the kynge, that thei [that did so gret a deed] shulde knowe
ther gret trespas and make amendes of ther mysdedes.' And when
thei herd that the kinge had consentide therto, then slaked ther gret
malice and so departide thens in fayre maner and preid hym to vndo
1010 that cursyng. And the next day aftir these knyghtis come ayene to
Canturbury to Seint Thomas and preid hym to assoile them of that
cursyng. And then Seint Thomas seid: 'Sirs, I may not do it, for it
[is] done by the pope, but if ye wul finde surete to make amendis that
ye haue offendide to holy Churche, then ye may be assoyled, or else
1015 not.'

And then thei departide [thens] in gret wrathe and tolde the bishops
what he seid. And when thei herde this they manaced gretly Seint
Thomas, but anone aftir the bishop of London and the bishop of
Salsbury seid that thei wolde abide the lawe of holy Churche, but the
f. 52ᵛᵃ erchebishop of Yorke seid: 'I wol neuer abide the iugement of | hym
1021 that hath be euer our most foo. He hath don us meche shame and then
he wolde do us muche more. Though he hath of you power, of me
hath he none, for I am erchebishop as wel as he is. I haue a cheste
wherein is .viij. thousand pownde. Al that I wole spende to withstonde
1025 his malice and more to.' And then anone by his conseil al the bishops
went ouer the see to the kynge to compleyne on Seint Thomas, and
thei seid but if he toke better hede Seint Thomas wolde distroy his
londe, and tolde hym howe he had acursid 'al tho that were
consentyng to the crownyng of your sonne Harry.'

1030 And then the kynge was ny mad for anger, and went up and
downe and no man durst speke to hym til his angre were swagyd.
And then the kynge seid: 'This fals traytour hath acursid me also, for
I was cause that he was crownyd. Lo what shame this fals traytour
doyth to me and to my reme,' and seid: 'If I had men aboute me, this
1035 false prest shulde not this ouerled me in myn owne londe.' And
fourthwith these .iiij. knyghtis merkid the kynges wordes in ther
mynde and went anone into Englonde in al the hast. But when the
kyng wiste of þer goyng he was right sori and sent messengers aftir
them to bidde them come ayene, but they were fer seylyng in the see

1006 that (2) . . . deed] om. A1   1013 is] om. A1   finde] add me L
1016 thens] then A1   1037 into] toward L

that the messengers myght not brynge them ayen, wherfore the 1040
kynge was ful heuy, for it was not his wille that he shulde be slayne
in no wise. Thes ben the namys of these .iiij. knyghtis, Sir Reynolde
Beryson, Sir Hugh Morvile, Sir William Tracy, Sir Richard Brite.

On Cristemasse Day Seint [Thomas] made a sermon atte Canturbury ful sore wepyng, and preid al the peple to prey for hym, for his 1045
endyng day of this life was nygh come, 'for I must suffre deth for the
right of holy Churche.' And in that sermon he acursid with boke and
belle and candil al that were ayenst the right of holy Churche, 'and
special Sir Randolf Broke and Sir Robert Broke that had my
bishopriche to ferme in my absence, and thei spent the goodes of 1050
holy Churche vpon ther owne nedes.' And vpon Cristmas as this
kyng with his lordes sate atte diner, al the bred that thei hondlid that
were cursid, anone it waxid mowly that no man myght therof ete,
and that thei touchid not was fayre ynogh and good for to ete to hem
that were not acursid, but that the cursid men towchid, doggis wolde 1055
not ete it. And then these .iiij. knyghtis aforeseid that had sworne
Seint Thomas deth come to Canturbury vpon a Tuesday aboute
Euynsong | tyme, and went in to Seint Thomas chambre boldly and f. 52ᵛᵇ
seid that the kynge gret hym wel and chargid hym to make amendes
to the king for the wrong he had done hym, and se anone that he and 1060
al his bishops and lordes be assoyled anone, 'or else we wole sone
assoyle the that thi brayne shal lye in thi lappe.'

Then seid Seint Thomas: 'Al that is right for to do I wole do with
goode wille, but as for the cursyng I may not vndo that but ye
submytte you al to the correccion of holy Churche, for that was done 1065
by oure holy fader the pope and not by me.' Then seid Sir Reynolde
Bereson: 'Me thinkyth thou settist no prise by the kynges message. I
trowe thou woldist bynym the kynge his crowne and al his reme also,
but it shal neuer lye in thy power, for thi days byn [not] long but if
thou wilte be otherwise disposid to the kyng and his lordes. And 1070
therfore I charge the that thou assoile the kyng, his bishops and al his
lordes, or else I shal sle the anone with myn owne hondes.' Then seid
Seint Thomas: 'The cursyng I may not vndo hit for it is made by the
pope and not by me, but as for þe kynge, I wolde right fayne plese
hym, for I pray for hym and his londe bothe day and nyght, and 1075
vpon Mary Magdalene Day the kynge and I were acordide and that
this sentence shulde be done on them that had offendide ayenst the

right of holy Churche. And thou thyself knowist wel that it was so, for thou were there then, and many on mo than .v.C. men were there 1080 that tyme.'

Then on of the knyght bade hym: 'Be stil and disclandre not so oure kyng,' and if he dide so eny more he shulde repent it while he leuyd. And then Sir Reynolde Bereson with gret violence smyt Seint Thomas on the crowne as he knelid byfore the auter. And then 1085 Edward Gryme that was his croser putte his arme with the crosse ayenst the stroke that it was nye smyt of bothe his arme and the crosse. And the seid Edwarde went thens for fere, and so dide al the monkes that were atte Compleyn in the quere runne abowte as madmen hider and thider and wist not what to do. [Then] another of 1090 the knyghtis smete Seint Thomas on the same place and causid hym to bowe his hede ny to the grounde. Then the .iij.de knyght smete hym in the same place, that he fil downe on the grounde vpon a marbil stone. And then the .iiij.th knyght smete in the same place, that the poynte of his swerd breke ayenst the marbil stone, and then 1095 his brayne fil oute vpon the marbil stone medled with blode. And L, f. 249ʳᵇ then his brayne ran al aboute his hed like | a dyademe. And when thys holy man was deed they cryed ful lowde and faste and seyde: 'Go we hens nowe, for thys false traytoure is brought to eende.' Then þat cursid man Syr Robart Brok turned ayeen and pight his 1100 swerde thorugh his skulle depe into his braynepan and steryd owt alle the brayne owt of the skulle.

And then al these wikkyd men breke vp Seynt Thomas chambre f. 249ᵛᵃ and toke awey al the goodis that he had there. And then they | wente into hys stable and toke awey alle his horse, and they toke to Syr 1105 Robart de Brok alle the chartyrs and the other prevy wryttis, and bade hym bere them to the kynge into Fraunce to do hys wylle with hem at hys plesure, 'and yf there were eny man that wold sey the contrarye to yowr entent in oony poynt, anoon rere your baner ayenste hym.' And as these knyghtis robbyd Seynt Thomas, they 1110 founde in a chest .ij. schurtes of ful herde heyre made with greet knottys, and then they seide among þemselfe stylly that he was a good man. And as they wente owte of þe chirche after they had sleyn Seynt Thomas, they wexid so sore agast þat they were ny mad for fere, for þey thought verely that the erth failid vnder ther fete, that 1115 they wende verely to haue sonke into the erth al qvycke. William Tracy knyȝt tolde to the bisschop of Excetter in confession of the

1089 Then] The A1   1096 his brayne] *om.* L

holy lyfe of Seynt Thomas, and he repentid hym ful sore that ever he dyd that cursyd dede.

And anoon as the knyghtys were goon owt of Caunturbery, yt was knowen thorowe the towne anoon that Seynt Thomas was slayn. 1120 Wherfor alle the peple made ful greet sorowe and wente to the chyrche to se thys holy martir Seynt Thomas, and kyssyd his blessid body with many a bittyr tere. And hys face was fulle feyre and no blode sene thereon, saue a lytle streme of bloode that ran downe by hys nose fro the wounde. And then the monkys seyde his *Dyrige* and 1125 araied the body as they aught to | do and beryed the holy body with f. 249vb greet solempnyte byfore Seynt Austyns awter and bifore the awter of Seynt Iohn the Baptyst. And they that toke of his clothis seide he had bisschoppis clothynge above and monkys abyte vndyr, and next his flessche he werid the herde heyre ful of knottys. His schurte and 1130 his breche were bothe of the same heyre ful of knottis, that it stykyd fast to hys skynne. And al his body was stekyd ful of smale wormys that yt was a pitevouse syght to beholde, for the greet myght not come to theyre mete for the smale wormys. I trowe there was never no erthely man that suffryd the peyne that he dydde. He passyd to 1135 owr lord ful of vertues the yeer of owr lord .xj.C.lxxj. And he was .liij. yeer olde when he dyed.

And then at the last come tydyngis to the kynge as he lay in the castelle of Argentyne in Fraunce, that Seynt Thomas was thus slayn. Wherfor he swownyd for woo and come not owte of the castel .iiij. 1140 daies after þat, but ever wepte and made greete sorowe and seyde alas that ever he schulde knowe suche a cursyd dede doon by eny of hys men. The care and the sorowe þat he made was lyke to a coste hym hys lyfe, for ever he sorewyd bothe nyght and day. Then he sente anoon to Caunturbury and he preied the monkis for Goddys sake 1145 that they wolde preye for hym: 'For God knowith it was not my wylle nor my knowynge to do that cursyd dede, for the knyghtis wente fourthe vnknowynge to me, God I take to witnes, for as sone as I wyst yt I sende messengers to fecche | them ayeen, but they were f. 250ra fer seylyng in the see or my messengers come to the seesyde.' 1150

Then the pope euery day vsyd to loke vpon this whete chesyble that Seynt Thomas seyde schulde be rede when he were slayn. Yt happid the Tewesday in the Cristemas weke þat the pope lokyd thereon and then yt was rede. And he knewe then verely that Seynt Thomas was martryd for the right of holy Chirche. And then he 1155 commaundyd that a solempne masse of Requiem schuld be seide for

hym, and as the quere bygan the masse of Requiem, an angel of owre lorde began þis masse: *Letabitur iustus in Domino etc.* And then al the quere folowid after the angel. And then the pope and al his
1160 cardynalles thonkyd our lord that he wolde schewe them that greet myracle for his holy martyr Seynt Thomas. And then within a while after, Kyng Herry of Inglond, that was ful hevy for the dethe of Seynt Thomas, sent hys messengers to the pope of Rome and preyed hym for the love of God that he wolde haue pety and mercy vpon
1165 hym, for .iiij. of his knyghtys vnknowynge to hym 'haue slayn Seynt Thomas of Caunturbery, and God knowith it was never my wylle, wherefor I praye yow that I may be assoylid of that cursyd dede. And what penaunce ye enioyne me I schal do yt by the grace of God, for I submytte me to yowre grace to do with me what plesith yow, for I
1170 wole obey alle yowre correccion. Whatever ye byd me do, I schalle do yt by Goddis grace.'

When the pope herd the greet mekenes of the kynge, that he so lowly submyttid and obeied hym in alle thyngis and was so
f. 250rb repentant, | anoon for pete he sente .ij. cardynals to confesse hym
1175 and then to assoyle hym of the cursynge. And when they come to the kynge, he resseyvid hem ful mekely and preyed theym for the love of God that they wolde here his wrecchid confession and to haue pete vpon hym, for he wolde do 'with good wylle to make satisfaccion for the cursyd dede that is doon by my knyghtis ayenst my wil, I take
1180 God to witnes. For I was not so sory for myn owne faders dethe as I am for his dethe, nor for my moders dethe neyther.' When the cardynals sye that he toke so greet repentaunce, they assoylid hym and leied penaunce inowgh vpon hym. And then the kynge fulle sore wepynge, he seid he wolde do alle that they bade hym doo with good
1185 wylle, and seyde yt was to litle for his greet trespas. And he dyd of alle his clothys save oonly hys schurte and his breche, and wente owte of the chirche, and þere he was assoylid openly byfore alle the peple. And there he wepte ful byttirly for his offensis, and preied alle the peple to prey for hym. And then alle the peple wepte ful sore for
1190 pete of the kynge. And then the yonge kynge Herry his sone seid, ful sore wepynge, that if his fader myȝt not fulfille alle his penaunce, he seide to the cardynals, he wolde do ytt for hym.

Thus was this holy man Seynt Thomas doon to dethe, and within .xij. daies after yt was knowen at Ierusalem that he was do to dethe,
1195 for a holy monke of that contre dyed the same tyme, and hys abbot
f. 250va chargyd hym to apere to hym | ayeen, and [he] seide that he was

1196 he(1)] *om.* L

savyd and schulde dwelle in the blys of heven, and tolde hym of the greet ioy that he se there. And he seide the same tyme þat he come to blisse, the erchebisschop of Caunturbury Seynt Thomas was martirid in Inglonde, and his soule was to heven with greet multitude of 1200 angeles. And patriarkes, prophetis, apostelis, martyrs, confessoures and holy virgynes resseyved thys holy sowle with processyon and greet ioy into heven blys, and there they presentyd his sowle bifore the blyssyd Trynyte with fulle greet ioy and gladnes. Hys crowne was smeten of and his brayn alle sched owte and medled with dropys 1205 of bloode. Then seide owre lorde God to this holy bisschop Thomas: 'Thomas, come to my ioy and blysse, for thow hast bowght it with the schedynge of thy blode for the right of my Chirche in erthe. And for thy reward I yeve to the as meche ioy and blys as I yave to Seynt Petyr,' and set a crowne of schynynge gold vpon his hede, and the 1210 rede bloode was sene vndyr the crowne, the whiche was a gloryous sight to beholde. And anoon the foreseide abbot tolde the patriarche of Ierusalem alle that the monke had tolde hym, and then they thonkyd God for that gloryous martir Seynt Thomas. And within halfe a yeere after come pylgrymes to Ierusalem, and then the 1215 patriarche enquered of them what tyme Seynt Thomas dyed in Inglond, and they seid the Tewesday in the Cristemas weke, and than they knewe verely it was the same day and tyme that the monke tolde them.

And within .v. yeere aftyr | the martyrdom of Seynt Thomas there f. 250ᵛᵇ fylle greet stryfe betwene the fadyr and the yonge kynge hys sone, for 1221 he wexyd right prowde and sturdy ayenst hys fader, for alle the londe hylde hooly with the yonge kynge and set no prise by the fadyr. Wherefore the fadyr was ful hevy and ful of sorowe, and thought verely that he had that trouble for the dethe of Seynt Thomas. And 1225 then anoon he toke hys leve of Kyng Lowys of Fraunce and seyled over into Inglond and wente streight toward Caunturbury. And when he come a myle owt of the towne, he light downe of hys palfray and wente fourthe on his bare fete in his schurte tyl he come to the tombe of Seynt Thomas. And there he knelyd downe ful sore 1230 wepynge and hylde vp hys hondys toward heven and preied God and this holy martyr of foryevenes of his greet trespas. And there he knelyd a day and a nyght byfore the tombe of Seynt Thomas fulle sore wepynge, and preied to haue forgevenes of that greet trespas. And then the .iiij. knyghtis that slow Seynt Thomas suffryd aftyr ful 1235 meche peyne and sorowe to theyr lyves eende. And .iij. of these

knyghtis forsoke al that they had, and wente into the Holy Londe
and were ful repentaunte, and cryed God mercy and the holy martyr
Seynt Thomas for the greet offense that þey had doon to hym, and
1240 led theyr lyfe in greet herdenes to there lyves eende to make
amendys for theyr trespas. But Syr William Tracy abode stylle in
Inglond, and was aftyr right a fowle mesel, that hys flessche rootyd
f. 251ʳᵃ awey that men myght se hys nakyd | bonys, and he stonke so fowle
that noo man myght come nye hym. And then he plukked gobettys
1245 of his flessche and caste it fro hym, it stonke so fowle, and yet alle the
flessche was goon, that a man myght se of hym nothyng but senewes
and the bare bones. Alle thys he suffryd with goode wylle for hys
greet offense that he had doon to Seynt Thomas, and ever he cried
ful pitevously: 'Mercy Lorde, Seynt Thomas.' And within a while
1250 aftyr he dyed, and the .iij. knyghtis his felowes dyed alle in .iij. yeere
aftyr the dethe of Seynt Thomas. Now God for the love of Seynt
Thomas brynge vs alle to the blysse of heven. Amen.

The translacion of Seynt Thomas.

Seynt Thomas of Caunturbury lay in the erthe .xl. yeere and a halfe
1255 and more or he was translatyd and schryned, for Kynge Iohn wolde
not suffre hym to be translatyd in his dayes. But Kynge Herry his
sone dyd that worschipful dede thorough the sterynge of Stephyn
that was than erchebisschop of Caunturbury. And to se that this dede
were doo worschipfully, the pope Honoryus sente Randolfe hys
1260 legate with greet pardon to al folkis that come to visite this holy
martyr at the day of hys translacyon. For the whiche pardon come
thedyr many bysschoppis, abbottis, priouris, parsons, pristes and
clerkys, and also many a greet duke, erlys, barons, knyghtis,
serjeantis, sqyers and moche other peple withowt nombre, that þe
1265 contre abowte was not able to logge the peple that come thedyr. And
at Caunturbury was so greet prese that the bisschoppys and the
f. 251ʳᵇ lordys wyste not how for to do thys dede to haue the | bones owt of
the erthe. But Richard bisschop of Salisbury counseylid that it
schulde be do by nyght whyle the peple slepte, and so yt was
1270 doon. And so the prioure wiþ the covent toke owte of the erthe these
holy bones of Seynt Thomas the .vij. day of Iule vpon a Tewesday,
and the kynge with the legat and .ij. erchebisschoppis, with many
worschipful lordys holpe to bere on theyr schuldrys in a cheste these
worschipful bonys, and put them with greet reverence into the

schryne, when they had goon a processyon abowte the chyrche with 1275
greete multitude of peple folowynge to se this worschipful translacyon, for thys was doon on a Tewesday. And many a greet dede also
that Seynt Thomas dyd on the Tewesday, for he was bore on the
Tewesday, exilid owt of Inglond on a Tewesday, and vpon a
Tewesday owre lord appered to hym and tolde hym that he schuld 1280
resseyve hys martyrdom on the Tewesday for the right of holi
Chirche. And many other notable dedys he dydde on the Tewesday,
wherefor hys name be preysid worlde withowten eende. Amen.

29 ST JEROME

St Jerome was born of a wealthy family in Dalmatia in 331. He was sent to Rome to the secondary school run by Donatus, where he almost certainly learned Greek, and remained in Rome to study rhetoric. Jerome then travelled in Gaul, Dalmatia and Italy, and at the age of forty he set out for Jerusalem, although he was not to arrive there for many years. He stayed in Antioch for about two years, and there he had the dream recounted at the beginning of our text, as a result of which he changed his plans and went to the Syrian desert for two or three years. He then returned to Antioch, where he was ordained priest, and then went to Constantinople and studied scripture with the bishop, Gregory Nazianzen. Jerome returned to Rome in 382, beginning there his work of translating the bible, and meeting the women he greatly influenced, among whom were Marcella, Paula and Paula's daughter Eustochium. When Jerome left Rome in 385 it was for Palestine. He was joined en route by Paula and Eustochium, and they made a prolonged pilgrimage in the Holy Land before settling in Bethlehem, where Jerome remained until his death in 420.[1]

This Life is a translation made by Simon Wynter, of the Brigittine house at Syon, for Margaret Holland, duchess of Clarence.[2]

Lines 1–91 are from the Life in *LgA*, pp. 1002–9. MS Y includes some details from *LgA* omitted from the other MSS. Lines 55–58, 67–83, are authorial. The incident of the lion, ll. 1337–1455, *LgA* pp. 1005–7, is not in LJLb, but is added as chapter 20 to Y.

Lines 92–1299 are a translation, with omissions, from the letter of pseudo-Augustine to Cyril bishop of Jerusalem and Caps I–XII of the letter from pseudo-Cyril to Augustine, printed in Migne *PL* XXII 281–309.

Lines 1304–1332 are two chapters from the *Revelations of St Bridget*, IV.xxi and VI.lx.[3]

The text was printed from MS Lb by Horstmann in *Anglia* 3 (1880). MS Y gives the best text, and in using L as base we have edited conservatively.

---

[1] Kelly (1975).
[2] Keiser (1985) and (1987).
[3] Ellis (1982)

Here begynneth the lyfe of Seynt Ierome.

Seynt Ierome came of noble kynne and in his chyldhode he was sente
to Rome for to lerne, and he lerned Grewe, Latyne and Hebrewe.
And on a tyme, as he wryteth hymselfe vnto the holy mayde Eustace,
whan he studyed besyly nyght and daye in bokes of poetes and of
phylosophres bycause they saveryd hym bettyr than bokes of holy 5
scripture, yt hapned that abowte myd-Lent he was smytte wyth a
sodeyne and a fervent fevour in so moche that alle his body was dede
and colde vnto the herte. And when they were besy too dyspose for
his beriyng, sodeynly he was ravyssched tofore the dome of God.
And there he was asked what man he was, and he answeryd and 10
seyde that he was a cristen man. Then seyde the iuge: 'Thowe seyest
not sothe, for thowe art an hethen man and natt a cristen man, for
where thy tresour ys there ys thyne herte, and thy herte ys more
vppon worldly bokes then appon holy wrytte.' Then Ierome cowde
not answere. Then anoone the iuge bade bete hym anoone fulle 15
harde. And then he cryed and seyde: 'Haue mercy vppon me, Lorde,
have mercy vppon me.' And they that stode besyde prayed that he
myght have foryevenes, for he was but yonge. And then Seynt

MSS LYJLb
Preceding the text in Y is the following:
Here begynnyth the prologe ynto þe lyf of Seynt Ierom drawen ynto englysh as hit is
take of þe legende aurea vnto þe hygh pryncesse Margarete duchesse of Clarence by Syre
N. brothir and prest of þe monastery of Syon þe which is comynly callyd Shene.
There follows a letter of dedication, also in J and Lb, beginning:
Rigth noble and worthi lady and my ful reuerent and dere gostly doughtir in oure lorde
Ihesu.
At the end of the letter in Y is the following:
and þus endyth þe prologe and here begynneth his lyf as hit is drawe out of þe legende
aurea.
*After the letter of dedication J and Lb give a list of the 19 chapters that follow, with a
description of their contents. Y has 20 chapters and no contents list. The text of chapter 20, most
of which is translated from LgA, is here appended at the end of the Life.*
In almost all cases 'pope' has been deleted in L, and is silently restored in this text.

1 kynne] *add* and he was born yn a town callyd Strydon þat is betwyx .ij. contreyes of
þe which þat oon ys callyd Dalmatica þat oþer Panonia. His fadres name was Eusebius Y,
so LgA   2 for . . . lerne] to leve and þere he was crystenyd Y   Hebrewe]
add His master yn gramere was Donatus and yn rethoryk Victorinus Y, *so LgA*
5 phylosophres] *add* þat is to say of Tullius and of Plato Y, *so LgA*   6 scripture] *add*
which hym semyd were not eloquent Y, *so LgA*   8 they] his frendis Lb
15–16 the iuge . . . he] *om.* Lb   15 anoone fulle] *om.* LJ, *durissime LgA*
17 have . . . me] *om.* Lb

Ierome swore tofore the iuge God allemyghty and seyde: 'Lorde, yf
20 [euer] I haue eny seculer or worldly bookes or rede on hem hereafter,
f. 188vb then forsake me for a cristen man.' And | then by [thys] othe he was
let goo. And anoon he levyd ayeen and fownde hymselfe alle bewepte
and hys body sore and fulle of woundes of the betynges that he
suffred byfore the iuge. And fro that tyme forthe he studyed and
25 radde as besely on holy bokes as he hadde done tofore appon worldly
bokes.

Then he made hymselfe a monke and he levyd soo holyly in
chastysyng the lust of the flessch and withstandyng desyres of the
worlde that he causyd other that were relygyous to be bettyr for his
30 ensample. When he was .xxxix. yeere of age he was made a
cardenalle prest in the chyrche of Rome, and after that the pope
was dede alle folke cryed and seyde that Ierome was worthy to be
pope. But for as moche as he had vsed to blame flesschelynes of
mysgoverned clerkes and relygyovs peple, they with grete indig-
35 nacyon lay in wayte to do hym represse. And on a nyght when
Seynt Ierome schuld ryse to Matynnes as he was wonte, he dydde
appon hym a wommanes clothyng and so wente into the chyrche
wenyng that yt had be hys awne, whyche hys enemyes hadde [leyde]
by hys beddes syde to make folke wene that he had a womman in
40 hys chambyr and soo [to scorne hym.]

And when he sawe theyr malyce he fledde thens and came vnto
Constantynople, and there he communed with the bysschop of holye
scripture and syth wente into desert, and there he suffred grete
penaunce and desese .iiij. yeere togeder, whereof he seyde vnto the

20 euer] by errour L, *unquam LgA*   21 thys] hys L, *huius LgA*
28 chastysyng] *add* his body with Lb   of . . . flessch] þerof Lb   desyres] *add* therof and
Lb   29 were] *add* holy YJ   33 blame] *add* yn his wrytynges þe Y
34 mysgoverned] mysgouernance of J   35 represse] reprof Y, repreef J,
repreve Lb, *insidias LgA*   38 leyde] ledde L   39 had] *add* hadde YJ
40 to . . . hym] he scorned hem L   42 communed] comynd Y, comened J, comende
Lb   bysschop] *add* of þe cyte Y, *so LgA*   43 scripture] *add* whos name was
Gregorius Nazanzenus Y, *so LgA*   43–50 and syth . . . eny] But his fleynge out of
Rome was not only do be þe malyce of his pursuers but be þe mercyfull prouydence of god
þat þe Chirch of Rome þorough his laboure shulde haue holy wryt translatyd ynto latyn
out of þe trouth of Ebrew tonge where þorough þe iewes sholde no lengyr scorne crystyn
peple for lakke of knowynge of holy wryt. And þe grekys which mayntenyd hem þat we
had holy wrytt only of hem shulde knowe þat þorough Ieromes laboure we haue more
clerly out of þe welle of Ebrew þan þey hemsilf. But after seynt Ierom had studyed holy
scripture with þe seyd holy bysshop he went ynto Cyrye and þere he wrot þe lyf of þe
monke þat was take prisonere ynto hethennesse and afterwarde he went ynto wyldirnesse
to do penawnce as he had longe desyryd and so gladly he wente þereto þat he semyd rathir
to fle þan to go and þer Y   44 seyde] wryteth JLb, *narrat LgA*

holy Eustace: 'When I was in desert in that grete wyldernesse, where 45
ys a fulle horyble | dwellyng place alle tobrent with the sunne, me f. 189ʳᵃ
thought I was among the delytes of Rome. Alle my body was
deformyd and clothyd in a sakke and my skynne made blak lyke
vnto a Ethiop er a man of Ynde, every day wepyng and waylyng.
And when eny slepe come oppon me vnneth I wolde suffer my drye 50
bonys to rest vppon the bare erthe. Of mete and drynke I speke not
when they that be seke vse there but colde water and yt semyth
glotonye to ete enythyng soth. I was felawe of scorpyons and of
wylde bestes, and yet in thys colde body and in my dede flessche I
felte brennynges and sterynges of vnclennes. And therefor syth they 55
fele suche temptacyons that so dyspyce theyre bodyes and fightyth
oonly with theyr thoughtis, what suffre these men er wommen that
lyve in delytes? Sothely as the apostle seyth, they lyve in body but
they be dede in sovle. But owre lorde ys my wytnesse that after many
wepynges fulle often tyme me semed that I was amonge the 60
companyes of angeles.'
After that he hadde thus levyd in desert .iiij. yeer, he wente ayene
into Bethleem and there offred hymselfe as a wyse beste to abyde by
the crybbe of oure lorde. And there he gadred many disciples and
founded a monastery and levyd vnder the rule of the apostles, and 65
.lv. yeere and an halfe he travayled abowte the translacyon of holy
wrytte. And to hys ende he levyd a virgyne. Also he wrote the lyves
of holy fadres in a boke that ys callyd *Vitas Patrum.* He was also
wyse, | that what man had askyd hym eny questyon he schuld anoone f. 189ʳᵇ
withowt tariyng yeve hym a resonable and a sufficient answere. And 70
when ther had be set no certeyne service in holy Chyrche but
everybody sang and redde what they wold, the emperour prayed the
pope that he wolde ordeyne somme wyse man to sette dyvyne
service. And for the pope knewe welle that Seynt Ierome was perfyte
and most excellente in Latyn tonge, Grewe and Hebrewe and in alle 75
wysdom, he commytted vnto hym that offyce. And then Seynt
Ierome devyded the Sawter into Nocturnes and asigned to every
day in the weke a propyr Nocturne and ordeyned that *Gloria patri*
schuld be seyde at the ende of every psalme. He ordeyned also pistles

45 holy] *add* mayde JLb   46 fulle] foule Lb   48 clothyd] clad JLb
49 Ethiop er a] *om.* Lb   and] euery day JLb   51 erthe] grownde Y
70 answere] *add* He was so studyows yn his bokes þat he fastyd nygh ich day tyl euen Y, *so*
LgA   71 had] *add* ȝet neuere as vnto þat tyme YJ, *add* neuer Lb   be set] *om.* JLb
certeyne] maner J   72 emperour] *add* Theodosius Y   73 pope] *add* callyd
Damasus Y   dyvyne] diuerse Lb

80 and gospelles for alle the yeere and other thynges that longiþ to
devine service and sende them fro Bethleem vnto the pope, whyche
he and hys cardynalles resseyved and apreved and auctorised for
ever.

Then with abstynence and labour he wexe so wery and feble that
85 when he lay on hys bedde he myght not aryse but as he pullyd vppe
hymselfe with a rope teyed vntoo a blocke for to goo to do the
servyce þat longeth to be do in the monasterye. After thys he made
hymselfe a grave in the mowthe of the caue where owre lorde lay
when he was bore. And then after he hadde lyved .lxxxviij. [yeere]
90 and .vj. monthes he deyed and was buryed the yeere of owre lord
.CCCC. and .xviij. yeere.

f. 189ᵛᵃ   Of the lyfe and passyng of doctor Ierom and how Seynt
Austyn writyth in thys | wyse to Cyrylle bysschop of
Ierusalem.

95 O thowe worschipfulle preste Cyrylle, trowest thowe that scilence is
to be kepte from þe preysyng of the holy prest Ierome, that was
moste gloryous servaunt of crysten feyth and a corner stone of owre
moder holy Chyrche, in whom yt ys in maner groundede and made
sure, and nowe a schynyng sterre in hevenly blysse? Or ellys thow
100 dredist that I schuld speke of hym as a lypsyng chylde er as a man of
fowle lyppes, but for [hevynes] telle the glorye of God, and alle that
God made preyse hym in hys dedys, schulde a resonable creature be
stylle from preysyng whyle vnresonable creatures are not stylle?
[Therfor other I schalle speke er be stylle; yf I be stylle] I schalle be
105 bode crye with stones. Forsothe I schalle speke and nouȝt be stylle to
prayse the worthy Ierome, for thowgh I be vnworthy and insufficient,
while there ys noo preysyng feyre in the mowthe of a synner, yett I
schalle not cesse of hys preysyng. Therfor owre tunge and owre
honde be made serve and the tunge mote not cleue to owre palat, for
110 certeynlye thys man [is grete,] right holy and mervellous and to be
dredde above alle that be abowte vs.

86 blocke] balke YJ, wall Lb, *ad trabem LgA*   88 grave] cave Y
89 .lxxxviij.] .iiij.xx. and. xviij. YJLb   yeere] *om.* L   91 .CCCC. and .xviij.]
.CCC. and .xviij. YJLb, CCCXCVIII Graesse, CCCC *LgA*   92 and how] *om.* YJLb
98 groundede] gouernyd Lb   99 nowe] *add* he is Y   101 hevynes]
hevynesse L   104 Therfor . . . stylle(2)] *om.* L   105 crye] speke Lb
106 the] *add* hygh and YJLb   insufficient] *add* praysar YJLb   107 while . . .
synner] *om.* Lb   109 serve] sewre YJLb   110 is grete] as L

Grete he ys in holynesse of hys right excellent lyfe, grete in depnes of hys vnspekable wysdom, and grete in quantyte of hys right grete ioye. Merveylous he ys in vnwonte myracles and to be dredde for the grete power þat ys yeve hym of God. But howe grete thys gloryous 115 Ierome ys in holynesse of hys lyfe, howe schuld oo tunge make knowe when onethe | alle tonges of alle that be oo lyve in erth may not suffice f. 189ᵛᵇ to telle hys excellence? Be yt therefor lefulle to telle hym another Samuel, another Hely, anoþer Iohn Baptyste in holynesse of most excellent levyng. Iohn the Baptyst dwellyd in deserte and made lene 120 the body with scharpnes of mete and of clothyng. But moste gloryous Ierome was not of lesse levyng, the whiche as an hermyte dwellyng .iiij. yeere in desert had noo felawe but wylde bestes and scorpyons. And .xl. yeere togeder he never dranke wyne ne syder, but fled hem so moche that onethe he wolde here them named. He ete noo mete that 125 came nere fyre but oonly twyes in the vttrest nede of sykenesse. Next hys flessch he weryd a sacke of here and helyd hym above with a clothe most vyl. He knewe never other bedde but the erthe. Oones on the day oonly after Evensonge tyme he ete frute or levys or herbys or rotys, and after that yevyng hym to prayers he woke tyl two howres within 130 nyght, and then he slepte vppon the grownde tylle mydnyght. And anoone he arose and tylle day he entendid vnto redyng and to holy scripturys. He wept for right smale venyalle synnes so bytterly that he myght take noo more sorowe and he hadde slayne a man. Eche day thryes he bete hys flessch with so harde betynges that ryvers of blode 135 flowed from hys body. He eschewed as a tempest too speke eny idelle worde. Idelle was he never, but allewey occupyed in holy redynges or wrytynges er in techyng of other.

What schalle I sey | more? Yf I schuld seke the lyfe of alle seyntes I f. 190ʳᵃ wene I schuld fynde noone more holy then he. But for we named 140 Samuel byfore, we may schewe clerely that he Samuel was, for from hys moder tetys he was clepyd too dyverse studye of lecture and sette to service of holy scripture, soo that in the light of hys chyere alle flowed with wysdam. We se the light of bothe Testamentys and in the strenght off hys arme a grete parte of heretykes ys disperpelyd. 145 He ys the glory of owr vertue, translatyng both the old lawe and the

117 not] *om.* YJLb   118 telle] calle YJLb, *dici PL*   119–20 in . . . Baptyst] *om.* Lb   126 vttrest] vttirmust J, wittest Lb   127 with a clothe] *om.* J 133–4 he . . . and] a body myght haue wende Y, *thus with* men *for* a body JLb 135 hys flessch] hymsilf Y   136 flowed] ran Y   139 seke] speke Lb 140 we] he was J   142 lecture] lettrure J   144 with] *add* goostly Y, *add* godly JLb   145 disperpelyd] dyspersyd Y

newe from the langage of Hebrewe into Latyne and into Grewe,
disposyng bothe to abyde for ever vnto alle that come after,
declaryng many prevytees and dowtes. And araiyng the ordre of
150 dyvine service, he edefied ney alle the Chirche, soo that he appereth
grete in depnes of vnspekable wysdam. He cowde alle lyberalle
scyens soo perfytely that, as alle men seyth, noone appareth lyke
hym. And as I lerned myselfe by experience of many epistels of holy
wrytte that he sente vnto me, I fonde never noone lyke vnto hym, for
155 he cowde the langage and lettres of Hebrewe, Grewe, Calde, Pers,
Mede, Arabyke, and nye of alle nacyons as though he hadde be borne
and norissched amongyst theym.

What shal I sey more? Never man cowde nother knewe in kynde
that [that] Ierome cowde not. But, worschipfulle Fader, wene thow
160 not that I sey thys thynges wenyng that thowe knowe not the lyfe and
vertues of Ierome but by me, whyle thowe thyselfe were hys felawe a
longe tyme. But I calle God to wytnesse that for the holynesse of soo |
f. 190ʳᵇ [vnspekable] a man I may nat be stylle thowh I wolde, for merveyles
and myracles knowlyche ys holynesse, and also the selfe hevynnes in
165 whiche he ys grete and of more blysse then many of the seyntes that
be therein. Noo man dovte but that he hathe oon of the grettest and
hyest sett amonge the mansyons of the everlastynge fader, for whyle
every man ys rewardyd there after hys lyfe and merytes, and he was
of most perfyte lyfe, yt schewith that he ys oone of the grettest and
170 hyest cetezyns of hevenly Iherusalem, the whiche [that it] schulde
more sykerly and pleynly be belevyd of vs [tofore] alle men that owre
age hathe mynde [of], he appereth most mervellous in vnknowen
tokenes and vnnumerable myracles, of whiche the worschipfulle man
Eusebe declaryth summe vnto me by hys lettres.

175   But of other wondres that be doo there eche day merveylously as
[I here] by contynual relacyon, I pray the, right dere Fader, that when
ye may have leyser that ye wolde gader as many of theym as ye may
and sende them vnto me that am so desyrowse to here of so worthy
dedys and so profytable.

148 disposyng] *om.* Lb   152 scyens] service Lb   159 that(2)] *om.* L
163 vnspekable] vnspectable L, *ineffabilis* PL   170 that it] I L, that Lb
171 tofore] therfor L   172 of] that L   vnknowen] vnwont YJLb   175 be
doo] he doeth Y   176 I here] *om.* L   178 to here] an herar YJ, *peraudire*
PL

Howe Seynt Ierome the same hour that he dyed appered to   180
Seynt Austyn.

That the merytes of most holy Ierome be not hydde, I schalle telle
that byfelle me thorowe Goddis grace the same day of hys passyng.
For the same day and the same howre that the holy Ierome dyed of
the clotte off fylthe and of vnclennesse and was clothyd with   185
clothyng of ioye and | vndedelynesse, whyle I was in my selle   f. 190ᵛᵃ
thynkyng besely what glory and myrthe was in blessyd sawles that
ioye with Crist, desyryng to make thereof a schorte tretys as I was
prayed, I toke penne and ynke for to wryte a pystelle thereof vnto
most holy Ierome, that he schulde wryte ayeen what he felte in thys   190
matere, for I knewe welle that in so harde a questyon I myght not be
lernyd soo evydently of no man levyng as of hym. And when I began
too wryte the begynnyng of my letter, sodenly an vnspekable light
with a mervellous swetnesse of swete smelle entred into my selle at
Complyne tyme. And when I sawe yt I was so gretly astonyed that I   195
lost alle my strenght bothe of herte and of body. I wyste never that
the merveyllous hande of God hadde enhaunsed hys servant Ierome,
makyng hys merveylles knowen to moche peple. I wyst not that God
ˈof hisˈ wonte mercyes had dissolued his trewe servaunt Ierome from
corrupcyon of the body and araied hym so hye a sete in hevene.   200
    But for myne eyen hadde never sey suche a lyght, my smellyng
had never felyd suche a savour, I was gretly astonyed at soo vnharde
merveyles, and whyle I thought in myselfe what yt myght be, anoon
ther sowned a voyce owte of the light seiynge these wordes: 'Austyn,
Austyn, what sekyst thowe? Trowest thowe that alle the see schalle   205
be put into a lytelle vesselle, er wenyst thowe to close alle the erthe in
a lytylle fyste er to lett the fyrmament [from] contynuel mevyng, er
to lette the see from hys kynd course? | That never mannes ye   f. 190ᵛᵇ
[myght] se schalle then thyn eyen se, er thyn ere [here] that never
mannys herde? Wenyst thowe to mowe vnderstonde that never   210
mannys herte vnderstode ne myght thynk? What schalle be the
ende of an endeles thyng? What schalle be the mesure of thynge that

184 dyed] dyede YJ, did Lb   185 clotte] cote YJLb, *toga* PL   clothyd] clad
YJLb   190 ayeen] *add* to me YJLb   192 of . . . levyng/as . . . hym] *trsp. with*
alyve *for* levyng YJLb   196 never] not ȝeet þen YJLb   199 of his] *ins. in*
margin L   mercyes] meritis J   201 lyght] syght Y   203 be] *add* and L
207 from] *om.* L   208 kynd] wont JLb   209 myght] *om.* LY, *add* neuer Lb
here] herde L   210 mannys] *add* ere Y   212-3 What . . . mesured?] That
may not be mesure how shall hit be mesurid. Lb

may not be mesured? Rather schalle alle the see be speryd in a lytylle
pytte, rather schalle alle the erthe be holde in a lytille fyste, raþer
215 schalle the see cese ebbyng and flowyng, then thowe schuldyst
vnderstonde the leste partye or porcyon of the ioyes and blysse
that blessyd sawles in heven haue withowte ende but yf thowe were
taught by experience and tastyng of the same blysse that I am in.
Therfor travayle thow not to do thynges that been vnpossyble tylle
220 the ende of thy lyfe be come. Seche thow not tho thynges [here] that
may not be knowe but of hem that be in blysse, but rather travayle
thowe to do suche dedys that thow may be in possessyon [there] of
suche thynges as thowe [desyrest] to knowe here, for they that oones
enter thedyr go never owte ayene.'

225   Than I alle astonyd for drede and withowte strenght of herte toke
to me a lytylle boldenesse and seyde: 'Who arte thow that droppist so
swete wordes to me thus?' Then he seyde: 'I am Seynt Ierome prest,
vnto wham thowe hast bygonne to wryte a pystelle. I am hys sowle
that thys same howre in Bethleem levyng the burdon of the flessch
230 am ioyned vnto Crist and, felawed with alle the companyes of
hevene, clothyd in light and arayed with the stole of vndedly
f. 191ra blysse, goo vnto the everlastyng kyngdome | of hevynnes. And
from hensforthe I abyde no lassyng of ioye but [moryng] whan I
schalle be ioyned ayeen to the body that schalle be glorefyed, and the
235 glorye that I have nowe alle oone I schalle haue than with the body in
the day of the resurrexion, when alle mankynde schalle aryse and
owre bodyes schalle be changyd from corrupcyon, and we schalle be
resseyved vpp into the eyre to mete with Crist. And so we alle schalle
alweye be with owre lord.'

240   Than I, Austyn, not cessyng to wepe, answered and seyde: 'O
thowe worthyest of men, wolde God I myght be [worthy to be] thy
footeman. But haue mynde on thy servant, though I be most
vnworthy, whom thowe lovedyst in the world with so grete affeccyon
of charyte, þat by thy prayer I may be clensyd of synne, by thy
245 governaunce I may goo withowt stombelyng in the ryght wey of
vertu, by thy defence I may contynually be defended from my

213–14 see . . . pytte/erthe . . . fyste] *trsp.* Lb   218 in] *om.* YJLb
220 here] er L, *hic PL*   222 suche] *add* service and Lb   there] *om.* L
223 desyrest] desyres L   224 enter] euere J   227 to . . . thus] ynto my þrote
YJLb   Then he seyde] *om.* YJLb   Seynt] he sayde YJLb   231 clothyd] cladde
YJLb   233 moryng] mornyng LLb, *augmentum PL*   237 changyd] ioynyd
Lb   238 resseyved] rauysshid YJLb   241 worthy to be] *om.* L
246 thy] *add* bysy YJLb

enmys, and by thy holy ledyng I may come to the haven of helthe. And now lyke yt the to answere me to somme thyngys I schalle aske the?' Than seyde the sovle: 'Aske what thow wylte, knowyng that I schalle answere to alle thy wylle.' Than I seyde: 'I wolde wytte yf the 250 savles that be in heven may wylle enythyng that they may not gete.' The sovle answeryd: 'Austyn, knowe thow oo thyng, that the soules that are in the hevenly blysse are made so sure and so stabylle that there ys no wylle in them but Goddys wylle, for they may wylle nothyng but that God wylle. Therefor they may gete what they 255 wylle, and what they wylle God wylle and fulfyllyth yt. Noone of vs ys defrawded | of owre desyres ayenst owre wylle, for noone of vs f. 191rb desyrith enythyng but God. And for we have God alwey as we wylle, owre desyres ar alwey fully fulfylled, for we abyde perfitly in God and he in vs.' 260

O Fader Cirille, yt were to long to wryte in thys schorte pystelle alle thynges that gloryous soule answeryd and made know vnto me, but I hope with Goddis helpe after fewe yeeres to come to Bethleem to vysite hys holy reliques and than to declare more openly that I herde and haue wryte. Yf I schulde speke with the tunges of alle men 265 I myght in noo wyse worthely expresse howe sotylly, howe opynly and howe merveyllously that holy sovle, abydyng with me many howres, expressyd vnto me the vnyte of the holy Trenyte and the trenyte of vnyte, and the generacyon of the sonne of the fader, and the goyng forthe of the holy gost from the fader and the sonne, and 270 the ierarchyes of angelles and the ordres of angelles and of the blessyd sperites and theyr mynystracyons, and the blessyd ioyes of holy sovles, and other thynges profitabylle and harde to mannes vnderstondyng. And after thys the light vanyssched from myn eyen, but the swete smelle abode many dayes after. Howe merveyllous, 275 therfor, ys thys man doyng so many merveyles and schewyng to men so vnwoonte wondres. Therfore to hym crye wee and ioye wee and yeve we glorye vnto hys preysyng, for serteynly he ys worthy alle preysyng and we are not sufficient to prayse hym. For he ys entred into the howse of owre lorde bright and moste feyre where with|owte f. 191va dowte he hathe an everlastyng sete amonge the hyest mansyons of 281 blysse.

247 haven] heuene J, *porta PL*   253 that are] *om.* YJLb   254 them] heuin Lb   257 defrawded] descaudid *corr. in margin to* descayued J   267–8 holy . . . howres] *om.* Lb   269 sonne] same J   271 ierarchyes] *add* and ordres YJLb and(1) . . . angelles] *om.* YJLb   274 from . . . eyen] away Lb   275 smelle] sauoure Lb   abode] *add* with me Y   278–9 for . . . preysyng] *om.* Lb

Howe .iiij. other men had a vysyon of Seynt Ierom the houre of his deth.

285 But forthy that trowth schuld be declared by mo wytnesse than oone, I wylle conferme more playnly the trewthe of thys thyng. A worthy man called Seuere, excellent in wysdome and kunnyng, with .iij. other men beyng the same day and the howre of the passyng of Seynt Ierome in the cyte of Turone, sawe a vysion lyke vnto myn, of
290 whiche the same Seuere wytnessed vntoo me for that the heyh ioye of Ierome schuld not be hydde to the world, lest they that haue delyte to folowe the stappes of his holynesse, yf they know not that he hadde so grete rewarde, they myght wexe wery and cese fro the wey of holynesse. God wolde that they schuld se and knowe howe
295 many and worthy rewardes of holynes he hathe yeve vnto hym, that they schuld the more surely drawe after þe stappes of hys vertu, for the hope of reward lasseth the strenght of labour.

The day of Seynt Ierome passyng, at Complyn tyme the foreseide Seuere was in his owne howse and .iij. other goode men with hym, of
300 whiche .ij. were monkes of the monasterye of Seynt Martyne entendyng to holye redynges. Sodenly they herde in heven, in erthe and in the eyre innumerabylle voyces of moste swete songes vnherd and vnspekable, and the sovne of organs, symphans and of instrumentys of [alle] musyke with whiche as theym semed heven and
f. 191ᵛᵇ erthe and alle thynges sowned on every syde, so that wyth | swetnesse
306 of that melodye theyre sovles were nye in poynt to goo owte of theyre bodyes. And thus astonyed they loked vppe vnto heven and sawe alle the eyre and alle that was abowte the fyrmament schyne with brighter light then the sunne, owte of the whyche come the
310 swetnesse of alle swete odour. And then they prayed God that they myght wytte why alle thys was.

Than there came a voyce owt of heven and seyde: 'Let noo merveyle meve yowe nor thynketh yt not merveyllous thowh ye se and here suche thynges, for thys day kyng of kynges and lorde of
315 lordys Crist Ihesu comyth festfully ayenste the sovle of gloryous Ierome in Bethleem goyng owte of thys wykked worlde to lede hym vnto the kyngdome of hevene, so moche the more excellently [and hye] tofore other as he schyned tofore [other] in thys worlde by merytes of more hye and holy lyvyng. This day the ordres of alle

301 in erthe] myrth Y   303 sovne] same J   304 alle] om. L
308 the(1)] add erthe L   317-18 and hye] om. L   318 other] om. L

angelles, ioiyng and syngyng with suche voyces as ye here, come with 320
theyr lord. This daye alle the companyes of patryarkes and
prophetes, thys day alle holy martyres, thys day alle confessoures,
and thys day the gloryous and the moste blessyd virgine Marye
moder of God with alle the holy vyrgynes abowte her and the sovles
of alle that be in blysse come ioyfully and festefully ayenst theyr 325
contreman, theyre citezeyn, and other of heven with theym.' Thys
thynges seyde, the voyce was stylle, but the light, odour, and songe
abode an howre after and soo cesyd. By thes thynges, Fader, yt ys
schewed that he ys oone of the [hyghest] cytezens of hevenly Iher-
usalem. And no man dowte | but that, as hys wylle ys more nere to   f. 192ʳᵃ
Goddys wylle, so he may gete there what he wylle rathe `r´ then other. 331

How Seynt Iohn Baptyst and Seynt Ierome appered to
Seynt Austyn in a vysyon.

No man thynke that I am soo bolde to sey that Seynt Ierome ys in
the blysse better than Seynt Iohn Baptyst, for as owre savyour beryth 335
wytnesse noone ys more than he, nor that Ierome ys in the blysse of
heven tofore Peter and Pawle and other apostles that were specyally
chose and halowed of Crist hymselfe. Yet thouh reson forbede to sey
that Ierom schuld haue more glory in heven than theye, I se noo
resone why yt schuld not be lefulle to sey that Ierome ys even in 340
blysse with theym whyle he was not discordyng fro theym in
holynes. [And] syth God ys noone acceptor of persones but he
[dyssernith] the merytes of eche persone, he yevith to eche as he
deservith. If yt seme that Ierome schuld haue lasse ioye then Iohn
Baptiste and other apostles, yet the merytes of hys holynes, the 345
grevons of hys laboures, the bokes of hys wrytyng, the translacyon of
bothe lawes, the ordinaunce of the dyvine servyce, the frutes and
prophetes of goodenesse that he dydde not oonly to alle that be nowe
but also too theym that be to come, seme to prefe that Ierom ys even
to theym in blys. But lest I make a snare of skornyng to somme that 350
wolde deme that for carnalle affeccion where thorowe a man may
lightly erre from trewth, or for vnkonnyng of myselfe, I lykened
glorious Ierome to Seynt Iohn Baptyste or other apostles, I clepe

324 God] Ihesu Y   the(1)] *om.* YJ, her Lb   325 festefully] fastfully J
326 other] eyre YJLb   329 hyghest] *om.* L   331 rather] *final -r added in later*
hand L   334–5 in . . . blysse] *om.* YJLb   335 beryth] add of hym Y
342 And] *om.* L   343 dyssernith] dysservith LLb   346 grevons] grevys
YLb   348 that(2)] *add* we L   350 a snare of] *om.* Lb   353 clepe]
take Lb

f. 192ʳᵇ God to wytnesse that I schalle telle | a thynge that I lerned never of
355 man but by revelacyon of allemyghty God that heyneth and
magnyfyeth hys chosyn.

The .iiij.th nyght after his passyng, whan I thought desyrously
vpon the preysynges of moste blessid Ierome and bygan to wryte a
pistelle thereof vnto [the, aboute midnyght whane slepe come
360 apone] me, there byfylle me a merveylous vysion. There come
vnto me a grete multitude of angeles, and amonge theym were
twey men withowt comparyson, brighter then the sunne, so lyche
that ther semed noo dyfference save that oone bare .iij. crownes of
gold sette fulle of precyous stones on hys hede and that other but
365 tweyne, and they were clothyd with mantelles most whete and
feyre alle wove with golde and precyous stones. They were so
feyre that no man myght imagyne yt, and they bothe come nere
vnto me and stode stylle in sylence.

Than he that hadde .iij. crownes seyde vnto me thes wordes:
370 'Austyn, thow thynkest what of trowth thow schuldyst seye of
Ierome, and after longe thynkyng thow woste nere what to sey.
Therfor we be come bothe vnto the to telle the hys blysse. Sothely
this my felawe whom thowe seyst ys Ierome, whiche ys even to me in
alle wyse in glorye as he was even to me in his levyng. That I may he
375 may, that I wylle he wylle, and as I se God he seeth God, knoweth
God and vnderstondeth God, in whom ys alle blessydnesse of
seyntes. Nor noo seynt hath more or lesse blysse then other, but
[in] as moche as oone hathe more clere contemplacyon and sight than
f. 192ᵛᵃ another of the feyrenesse of God. That | crowne that I bere more
380 then he ys the aurealle of martyrdome by the whyche I ended my
bodely lyfe, for thowh Ierome for travayle and dyssecys, penaunce and
affliccions, wordes and repreves, and other grevous thynges whiche
he suffred ioyfully for Crist, and so beyng a very martyr hathe not
lost the rewarde off martyrdome, yet [for] he ended not hys lyfe by
385 the swerde he hathe not the aurealle that ys yoven in tokenyng of
martyrdome. The .ij. other crownes that bothe he and I haue are the
aureallys that are dewe oonely to virgyns and doctoures, by whiche
they are knowe from other.'

Then I answered and seyde: 'Who art thowe, my lord?' He seyde:

355 heyneth] heryeth Y, honourethe Lb, *exaltet PL*   359–60 the . . . apone] *om.* L
360 merveylous] wondirfull Lb   365 and(2)] Bothe YJLb   clothyd] clad YJLb
371 what . . . sey] *om.* YJLb   373 this] *add* ys L   375 God(1)] *add* so YJLb
376 blessydnesse] blesfulnesse Lb   378 in] *om.* L   381–2 penaunce . . .
repreves] *om.* Lb   384 for] *om.* L

'I am Iohn Baptyst, that am come downe to teche the of the glory of 390
Ierome, that thowe telle yt to other peple. For knawe thow that the
worschip that ys do to eny seynt ys do to alle seyntes, for there ys
noone envye there as in the world ys where eche man sekyth rather
to be above then vnder. Not so in heven, but there eche soule ys glad
and as mery of otherys ioye and blysse as yf he hadde yt hymselfe, 395
wherefor the ioye of eche ys the ioye of alle and the ioye of alle ys the
ioye of ech.'

Whan these thynges were seyde, the blessyd companye wente
theyr wey, and I woke of that swete slepe and felte in me so grete
fervour and brennyng of love and charyte that I felt never so moche 400
tofore, and from thensforth was there noone appetyte in me of envy
or of pryde as was tofore. God ys my wytnesse that there ys so
muche fervour [of] charyte [in] me that I ioye | more of anothers f. 192vb
goode than of myne. I desyre more to be vnder alle than to be above
eny. I sey not thys for too gete me veyne preysyng, but for noo man 405
schuld wene that thes were veyne dremes whereby we be ofte
scorned, but a trewe vysion by whiche we are other whyle taught
of God. Preyse we therefor God in hys seyntes, preyse we moste holy
Ierome that dydde grete thynges in hys lyfe and hathe resseyved
grete thynges in hys lyfe and also in his dethe. Man awght not to be 410
slowfulle to preyse hym wham God hath magnyfyed, ne wene noo
man to do wrong to Seynt Iohn Baptyste and to the apostels in
evenyng Ierome vnto theym, for they wolde gladly yf they myght
yeve [hym] of theyr glory. Therefor thowe that worschippest Seynt
Iohn and the apostles worschip also Seynt Ierome, for he ys even 415
vnto hem in alle thynges.

Sykerly therefor withowte drede, knowleche we with devocyon
that Ierome ys even vnto them in ioye, for yf we sey [that he] ys lesse
than Iohn we do derogacyon vnto Iohn. Thys tretys of the preysyng
of Ierome I sende vnto the, Fader Cyrylle, praiyng the that thow 420
scorne nat my lytylle wit but thowe wylte rede these preysynges that
I haue wryte of charyte. Yf alle tunges of alle men schuld preyse
hym, they were nat suffycyent. Worschipfulle Fader, haue mynde on
me synner whan thow standyst in that place where þe body of
Ierome lyeth, and commend me to hym with thy prayers, for no man 425

394 ys] *add* as YJLb   395 and as mery] *om.* YJLb   398 wente] yede Lb
403 of/in] *trsp.* L   404 to be(2)] *om.* YJLb   410 lyfe . . . his] *om.* YJLb
411 slowfulle] sloughfull Y, slawfull J, slewffull Lb   412 the . . . in] *om.* J
414 hym] theym L   418 them in ioye] Iohn YJLb   that he] who L
419 vnto] *add* him and Lb   420–1 thow . . . but] *om.* Y   425 to hym] *om.* J

dowte but whatever Ierome desyre in hevene he may gete yt, for he
may in noo wyse be defrawded of hys desyre. Fare wele, Fader, and
pray for me. |

430   Here endyth the pystelle of Seynt Austyn vnto Cyrylle and
       begynneth the pystelle of the same Cyrylle bisschop of
       Ierusalem vnto Seynt Austyn of the myracles of Seynt
       Ierom, and fyrst how .iij. dede men were areysed and her
       heresye destroyed by Seynt Ierome.

       To the worschipfulle man, worthyest of bysschoppes, Austyn
435   bysschop of Ypon, Cyrille bysschop of Ierusalem, lowest of alle
       prestes, sendyth gretyng and to yowe. Folowe hys steppys whos
       holynesse cesyth not to schyne in erthe, that ys to seye of gloryous
       Ierome whos mynde ys had in everlastyng blessyng. And howe
       worthy he ys thow woste welle thyselfe, for thowe vsedyst right
440   moche hys spekyng and doctryne. But I to speke of hym, syth I am
       in alle wyse wykked and vnworthy, I holde yt to moche boldenesse.
       But yet for thy cheryte compelleth me to wryte to the somme of the
       merveylous myracles that God lyst to do by hym in owre dayes to
       schewe hym glorious to the worlde and to [alle] folke, trustyng in thy
445   prayers I take yt on honde, and schortly I schalle telle a fewe of
       many, and fyrst I wolle bygyn at oone holy man Eusebi, disciple of
       the same Ierome.
       After the dethe of moste gloryous Ierome, there rose an heresy
       amonge the Grekes whiche come vnto vs that beth of Latyn tunge,
450   which heresye labowred to preve by wycked resons that alle saved
       sawles schuld not come to the sight and knowlech of God in whiche
       ys alle blysse tylle þe day of dome when they schulle be ioyned ayen
       to the body, and also that dampned sawles schulle haue no payne |
tylle that day. Theyr reson was thys, for lyke as the sawle with the
455   body hadde do wele or evylle, soo wyth the body yt schuld resseyve
       mede or payne. They seyde also that there was noo place of
       purgatorye where sawles þat hadde not do fulle penaunce for
       theyr synnes schuld be purged. And when thys wycked secte
       encresed we were so sory that vs yrked to lyve eny lenger. Than
460   I gadred togeder alle owr bisschoppes and other and enioyned hem

---

430–1 bisschop of Ierusalem] *om.* Lb   432–3 and(2) . . . Ierome] *om.* Lb
436 yowe] *om.* YJLb   438 blessyng] blys YLb   444 alle] the L
448 rose] was J   460 and other] *om.* Lb

to fastyng, that the power of God in noo wyse schuld suffer hys feyth so [to] be trowbled.

A merveylous thynge and in happes not sey tofore, .iij. dayes of fastyng and prayers fulfylled, gloryous Ierome apperyng [on] the nyght folowyng to his dere sonne [Eusebi] tofore seyde in his prayers and with vngreve speche conforted [hym] and seyde: 'Drede the not of thys wycked secte, for yt schalle soone haue an ende.' Than Euseby lokyd on hym, and he schone with so moche bryghtnesse that no mannes eye myght loke vpon hym, but wepyng for ioye Euseby myght vnnethe speke, but as he my3t he cryed and seyde: 'Thowe arte my fader Ierome, thowe arte my fader Ierome.' And ofte rehersyng the same wordes he seyde: 'Fader, why forsakist thowe me, why dyspisiste thowe my companye? Serteyn I schalle holde [the] and not leve the, ne thowe schalt not goo withowte thy sonne thowe louedest so moche.' Gloryous Ierome answered: 'My swete sonne, I schalle not leve the withowt confort, for the .xx. day after thow schalt folowe me and be with me in ioye withowt ende. But sey to Cyrille and vnto hys | bretheren that they and alle the clerkys that beth men of trewe cristen feyth, and also alle tho that be of that other secte, come tomorowe togeder to the chyrche of owre lorde where my body lyth. And make yowe the bodyes of the thre men that are thys nyght dede in the cyte to be brought vnto the place where my body ys buryed, and thow schalt ley vppon theym the sacke that I vsed to were, and [anoone they] schalle aryse and growndly distroye thys heresye.' Than gloryous Ierome bade hym farewele and apered no lenger.

On the morowe worschypfulle Eusebi come vnto me that was than at Bethleem and tolde me alle that he hadde seyne, and I, thankyng to God and to glorious Ierome, dydde do bryng the .iij. dede bodyes to vs alle gadered togeder in that place where owre savyour was borne of the clene virgyne, where also lyeth the body buryed of the gloryous Ierome. O merveylous mercy of God vnto man, in howe many wyse can he helpe theym that truste in hym, in howe many

465

470

475

f. 193va

480

485

490

461 to] *om.* YJLb   fastyng] *add* and prayours YJLb   in . . . wyse] *om.* YJLb schuld] *add* not YJLb   462 so] *add* to YJb   to] *om.* L   463 thynge] *om.* Lb 464 on] vnto L   465 Eusebi] *om.* L   466 vngreve] benigne YJLb   hym] *om.* L   471 thowe . . . Ierome] *om.* Lb   472 the same] þyse YJLb 474 the(1)] *om.* L   sonne] *add* whom YJLb   476 sonne] *add* he seyde YJLb   not] *add* forsake the nor Lb   withowt confort] be confortyd YJ, be vncomfortid Lb 478 they] *add* alle YJLb   479 cristen] *om.* Y   480 chyrche] cribbe JLb 484 anoone they] oone of them L   488 I] *add* doynge YJLb   489 do] *om.* YJLb   dede] *om.* YJ   493 wyse . . . many] *om.* Y

worschippes can he enhaunce hys seyntes? In thys mene tyme men of
495 the evylle secte scorned men of right beleve, but beth glad, alle men
of ryght feyth, and [preysyth] God in voyce of ioyng, for ye haue
resseyved mercy in the myddes of hys temple.

The worschipfulle man Euseby come vnto the bodyes of eche of
these dede men and knelyd on hys kneys, and holdyng vp hys
500 hondes to heven he prayed, alle men heryng, and seyde: 'God to
f. 193vb whom nothyng ys impos|sible, nothyng grevous, that doest grete
[merveyles] alone and dyspysist noon that hopyth in the, sende vnto
vs vertu [of thy] grace and strenght and here the prayers of thy
servantys. And that the feyth that thowe hast yeve mote abyde
505 vndefouled, and that the errour of that other may apere by merites
and prayers of the gloryous Ierome, brynge ayen into these bodyes
the sowles that thow hast made goo owte of them.' After thys prayer
he toke the sacke that Ierome vsed and towched the dede bodyes
therewith. And anoon they opened theyr eyen and schewyng alle
510 tokenesse of lyfe verely arose and begon with a clere voyce for to
telle openly of alle the ioyes of holy sowles and the paynes of
synners in purgatorye and in helle. For, as they tolde me afterward,
Seynt Ierome led theym into paradys, purgatorye and vnto helle,
that they schuld to alle folke knowleche what was do there, and after
515 bade theym go to theyre bodyes ayene and do penaunce for theyr
synnes that they hadde do, for the same daye and howre that
worschipfulle Eusebi schuld dye they schulde passe also, and yf they
dydde welle they schuld haue ioye with hym. And so yt fylle as I
schalle telle afterwarde. These thynges doo, the grete multitude of
520 peple both of trewe feyth and of her secte, seyng openly theyre
errour and the grete merytes of Ierome, yave to God grete preysynges that forsakith not theym that truste in hym. Thus, dere
Austyn, we be taught not to drede the pursuers of owre feyth, and
to knowe howe redy owre pytefulle lord ys to helpe alle that calle
f. 194ra vnto hym | in tyme of trybulacyon, and how myghti gloryous Ierome
526 ys to promote the prayers of them that in clene herte pray and truste
vnto hym.

494 seyntes] servantis Lb   mene] om. YLb   495 secte scorned] desyrith to
scorne Lb   496 preysyth] preysyng L   499 knelyd] knelynge YJLb
501 grevous] add ne harde Y   502 merveyles] merveylous L   503 of thy(1)]
om. L   thy(2)] add trew YJ   504 mote] me to Lb   506 gloryous] add loued
YJLb   513 helle] add and L   514 schuld] telle YJLb   knowleche] om.
YJLb   522 Thus] add by L   526 promote] ferthir Y   that] add be L

Of the foreseyde Eusebi and hys merveylous dethe and howe
Seynt Ierom appered vnto hym in the howre of hys passynge.

Whan tyme come that worschipfulle Euseby knewe that he 530
schulde passe, [as] he was enformed by the seyde vysion of Seynt
Ierome, the thyrde day tofore he was myghtly smete wyth a fevere.
And than he made his bretheren ley hym naked on the erthe and ley
vppon hym the sacke that gloryous Ierome vsed to were. Than he
kyssed alle his bretheren and benyngnelye comfortyng theym he 535
steryd them to abyde stabylle in theyre holy levyng. He ordeyned by
example of gloryous Ierome that he schuld be beryed naked withowte
the chirche in whyche the body of Seynt Ierome lyeth. After thys he
strenghyd hymselfe with the comunyon of the holy body of owre
lorde Ihesu Crist and commendyd hym to God and to Seynt Ierome. 540
And so he lay .iij. dayes withowte bodely syght or speche, hys
bretheren contynuelly seiyng and redyng theyre Sawter, the passyon
of owre lorde and other holy thynges. But forsothe yt ys harde and
ferefulle to alle that lyve in thys world thys that I schalle telle.
     The day that he schuld dey, .ij. howres before the passyng of that 545
blessyd sovle, worschipfulle Eusebi beganne to byhaue hym so
ferfully that the monkes that stode abowte hym fylle down to the
erthe for fere as men owt of theyre mynde, for other whyle hee |
turned vp hys eyen and wronge hys hondes togeder, and with a f. 194rb
ferfulle face and a harde voyce he sat vppe and cryed: 'I schalle not, I 550
schalle not, thow lyest, thowe lyest.' After thys he fylle downe ayen
to the erthe and festenyng his face to the grownde as muche as he
myght he cryed: 'Helpith me bretheren, that I peryssche not.' And
they heryng thys, wepyng and tremlynge for fere, asked hym: 'Fader
howe ys yt with yowe?' He seyde: 'Se ye not the multitude of fendes 555
þat wolde overcome me?' They asked hym: 'What wolde they that
thow schuldyst do whan thow seydest "I schalle not, I schalle not."?'
He answered: 'They labour and travayle me that I schuld blaspheme
the name of God, and therfor I cryed I schulde not do yt.' And they
asked hym: 'Why, Fader, haddyst thowe thy face to the erthe?' He 560
answered: 'That I schuld not se theyre lokyng, whiche be so foule
and horryble that alle the paynes in the world are right nat in regarde

---

531 as] and L   539 comunyon] comyng and percepcion Lb   542 bretheren]
add stondynge aboute hym YJLb   544 schalle] add now YJLb   560 haddyst]
hyddest YJ, *abscondebas* PL   face] add down YJ   erthe] ground Lb   561 theyre]
add grym Y   562 nat] *om.* J   regarde] comparisone Lb

therof.' Amonge thes wordes he began to do and crye ayeen as he
dydde tofore, and so come vnto the laste ende of his lyfe.

565   Hys bretheren that stode abovte hym, for fere and sorowe felle
downe as dede, not wyttyng what that they myght do, but God that
ys gloryous in hys seyntes, mervelous in hys mageste, [benygne] and
mercyfulle to theym that drede hym, he forsakyth not his servantes
in tyme of nede. For whan worschipfulle Eusebi came vnto the laste
570 ende, gloryous Ierome appered and benyngly comfortyd hym. And
whan he come, alle [that] innumerable company of feyndes for fere
f. 194ᵛᵃ of hym vanyssched awey as smoke, as many of the monkes | bere
wytnesse as by dispensacyon of God sey yt. But alle that stode aboute
herde howe that Eusebi seyde: 'From whens, Fader, comyst thowe?
575 Why hast thow taryed so long? I pray the forsake not thy sonne.'
And sodeynly alle they herde howe that Ierome answerd ayen:
'Abyde sonne, be not aferyd, for I schalle not forsake the whom I
love so moche.' Than after a lytylle whyle worschipfulle Eusebi
dyed. And the same houre dyed tho .iij. men that were areryd and as
580 I hope [went] with Eusebi vnto everlastyng ioye, for alle the twenty
dayes after that they wer areryd they yaue theym to soo moche
penaunce that withowte dowte they wer worthy to be rewarded with
endles blysse.

       Howe the forseyde thre men after they were areryd tolde
585   Cyrylle of the paynes of purgatory and helle.

I trowe yt be not to kepe sylence of tho thynges that I lerned of the
.iij. men in tho dayes that they levyd after they were areryd. For alle
that tyme I was contynuelly with somme of theym from mydmorowe
tylle Evensonge tyme, desyryng to knowe the prevytees of that lyfe
590 that we abyde after thys schort and passyng lyfe. But thouh that I
lerned many thynges of theym, yet nowe bycause of schortnes I may
telle but a fewe.
       On a tyme whan yt hapned me to go to oone of theym, I fownde
hym sore wepyng, and after I felte that he wolde take no comfort by
595 my wordes I asked hym [the cause of his wepyng. And whan I had
asked hym often and he answered not, at the last, compelled by my
long instaunce,] he answered and seyde: 'Yf thowe know tho thynges
that I had experience of the laste daye there schuld ever be in the

cause of wepyng.' Than I seyde: | 'I pray the telle me what thowe f. 194ᵛᵇ
sawyst.' He was stylle a lytylle and than he seyde: 'O what paynes 600
and tormentys are ordeyned nat oonly to the dampned soules but
also to theym that be in purgatory.' Than seyde I: 'Of thynge that I
knowe not I can yeve no serteyn sentence, but I trowe that they be
not lyke to the paynes and dysseses that we suffre here.' He
answered: 'Yf alle the peynes, tormentys and affliccions that myght 605
be thought in thys world were lykened to the leste payne that ys
there, alle that semyth here payne and torment schuld be but solace
and comfort. For yf eny man þat ys alyve knewe tho paynes by
experiens, he schuld rather chese to be tormentid vnto the ende of
the world withowt remedye with alle the peynes togeder that alle 610
men suffred fro Adam tylle nowe than to be oo day tormentyd in
helle or in purgatorye with the lest peyne that ys there. And therefor
yf that ye aske me the cause of my sorowe and grete wepyng, yt ys
the drede of the paynes that ar rightwysly yeve vnto synners. For I
knowe welle that I haue synned ayenst God and I dowte not but that 615
he ys rightwysse. And therfor merveyle not thowh I sorowe, but
rather thowe owest to be gretely amerveyled why men that wote
welle that they schulle dye at the laste by experiens of other leve here in
soo grete syke[r]nes and thynke not how to eskape so grete peynes.'
    [At] thys [wordys] I was towched with an inward sorowe so that I 620
myght not vnnethe speke, and I seyde: 'Alas, what ys thys that I
here? But I pray the telle me what dyfferens ys bytwene the paynes
of helle and purgatorye.' He seyde: 'There ys no | dyfference in f. 195ʳᵃ
gretnesse of payne, but in oo wyse there may be dyfference, for the
paynes of helle abydeth noon ende but [moryng] at the day of dome 625
whan the bodyes schalle be tormentid with the soules, and the
paynes of purgatorye haue an ende. For after that they haue doo her
penaunce ther they schalle be take vnto endles ioyes.'
    I asked: 'Be they that are in purgatory [tormentid] alle as lyche or
elles dyuersly?' He seyde: 'Dyversly, somme more grevously and 630
somme more esylye, after the quantite of theyre synnes. For in heven
alle blessyd sowles byholdeth the feyrenesse of God wherein ys alle
blysse. And thowe eche of theym haue as moche ioye as they can
wylle or thynke, yett they be not alle even in ioye, for somme haue

---

600 He . . . seyde] *om.* Lb   603 yeve] *om.* Y   608 þat ys] *om.* YJLb
613 sorowe and] so YJLb   617 rather *om.* Y   618 laste] leest YJ   other]
add that L   619 sikernes] sykenes LJLb, *securitate* PL   620 At] as L
wordys] worde ys L   625 moryng] mornyng LLb, morenynge J, *augmentum PL*
629 tormentid] *om.* L   630 He . . . Dyversly] *om.* Lb

635 more and somme haue lesse, after the dedys that they have do. And
yf thowe merveyle that there may be difference or dyversyte of ioyes
in seyntes [while] the oonly cause of her ioye ys God hymselfe, in
whom may be no dyversyte, the answere ys that the knowyng,
beholdyng and vnderstondyng of God ys alle the rewarde and ioye of
640 seyntes. And therfor thowh alle sowles in blysse se and knowe God
as he ys, yet somme se and vnderstand lesse then other and soo haue
lesse ioye, and somme se and vnderstonde hym more clerely and
haue soo more ioye. So may yt be seyde of the peynes of dampned
sowles, for thowh alle dampned sowles be in oo place of paynes, yet
645 they are tormentyd with dyverce peynes after the qualyte of theyr
synnes. For there ys so moche dyfference betwyxte paynes of cristen
f. 195ʳᵇ men and of hethen men, that the paynes of | hethen men in regard of
the paynes that false cristen men suffren been as yt were noo paynes,
and yet they be vnspekable and may nouȝt be thought of eny that
650 levith in erthe. And soo yt ys worthy, for crysten men resseyved the
grace of God in veyne and wolde not be amendyd of theyre synnes
whyle they levyd, holy scripture cryeng vpon theym contynuelly and
they sett nouȝt therby. I seyde: 'Yt ys right horryble that thowe
saiest, and wold God yt wer besely [festned] in the [myndes] of alle
655 that be alyve, that they myght sese from synne for drede of payne yf
they wole not for love of yoye.'

Of the deiyng of these .iij. men areryd and howe Seynt
Ierom comforted them in ther passyng.

'Now I pray the telle me howe yt was with the the last day whan
660 thy sowle passed from the body.' He seyde: 'Whan the howre of my
dethe come, þer come so grete multitude of evylle sperytes and
fendes in the place there I lay that for multitude they myght not be
numbred. The lyknes of them was suche that there may be thought
noo thyng more peynfulle ne more horryble, for any man alyve wold
665 rather put hymselfe to bren in the hattest flambes of fyre than he
wold se the formes of theym in twynklyng of an eye. Thes fendes
come vnto me and brought vntoo my mynde alle the synnes that ever
I dydde, steryng me to trust no lenger vnder mercy of God, for I

636 difference . . . of] dyuers YJLb   637 while] whiche wylle L
643–4 of(1) . . . peynes/of(2) . . . sowles(1)] trsp. and add þat longen vnto þem J
650 crysten] add fals Y   654 festned] festred L   myndes] myddes L
657 the] add first Y   668 vnder] on þe YJLb

myght not eskape ne withstonde theym. And whan alle the strenght
of my speryt fayled soo that I was nye in poynt | to assent vnto f. 195va
theym, gloryous Ierome come with a grete companye of angelles 671
aboute hym seven tymes brighter then the sunne and comfortyd me.
And whan he se the wycked sperytes howe harde they trobled me, he
was gretely steryd ayenst theym and seyde with a ferfulle voyce:
"Yee sperytes of wykkednesse and of alle cursydnesse, why come yee 675
heder? Wote yee not welle that he thys schulde be stedfaste by myn
helpys? Levyth hym anoone and withdraweth yowr wykkednesse
from hym as fer as the Eest ys from the West."

And anoon with these wordes alle that companye of cursyd
sperytes were aferde, and with grete cryenges and weylynges they 680
wente owt of the place there I lay. And then gloryous Ierome bade
somme of the angelles that they schuld not go fro me but abyde tylle
he come ayeen. And with the tother angelles [in hast he went his
way. And whan he was gone, the angelles] that wer lefte to kepe me
they comfortyd me and gan to byhote me feyre yf I wolde suffre and 685
abyde with stronge herte. And amonge these wordes of comfort an
houre passed, and than come Seynt Ierome ayeen, and stondyng in
the dore he seyde: "Comyth in hast." Than sodeynly my sowle lefte
the bodye so grevously and bytterlye that no mannys mynde myght
vnderstond what angwyssche and dysseses they were but yf he lerned 690
theym by experience as I haue. For yf the vnderstondyng of alle men
schulde esteme alle angywysshe of sorowes they cowde, yet they
schuld counte theym as nou3t in regard of [departyng] of the sowle
from the bodye.'

But whyle he tolde [me] thys and many moo thynges fulle harde 695
and dredefulle to alle men, the | whyche I wryte not here for lenght f. 195vb
of tyme, the daye began to ende, and therfor he must nedes leve to
telle thoo thynges that byfylle hym after hys deth whyche I desyred
most to here.

Howe the sowles of thes .iij. men stode byfore the dome of 700
God and howe Seynt Ierom led them to se the ioyes of
heven and the paynes of purgatorye and of helle and syth
bad them goo ayeen to theyr bodyes.

676 stedfaste] socowryd YJLb   678 from hym] *om.* Y   as(1)] *add* fast and as Lb
683–4 in . . . angelles] *om.* L   686 stronge] *add* peyne of Lb   692 esteme]
ymagyn Y   693 departyng] despartyng L   695 me] *om.* L   697 of
tyme] *om.* YJLb

The nexte day after, I cleped the tother tweyne with hym to wete
705 howe they acordyd that by wytnesse of theym alle thre I myght be
taught more surely. And whan they began to telle me that þe tother
hadde tolde me tofore I seyde: 'Though these thynges been profitable
and yt ys not veyne to speke of hem often, yet levyng thes that I haue
iherde, I pray yowe tellyth forth what byfalle yowe after ye were
710 departyd from the body.' Than seyde he that spake on the day
tofore: 'What askist thow, Cyrylle? Yt ys not possyble to telle yt
fully, for sperytuelle thynges may not be comprehendyd of owre
wyttes. Thowe knowest that thowe haste a sowle and yet what a
sowle ys thowe knowest not. Also thowe knowest that God ys, but
715 what he ys thowe mayst not knowe in thys lyfe but be exsample. So
ys yt of angelles and of alle vnbodely thynges, for whyle there ys
many thynges knowe in kynde that for febylnesse of owre lytylle
vnderstonding we may not vnderstonde, howe schuld we vnderstonde heven and sperytualle thynges that be in alle wyse strange
720 from the knowyng of kynde?' Than I seyde: 'Yt ys as thowe seyest,
but I pray the telle as thowe may.'

f. 196ʳᵃ   Than he seyde: | 'These men that be here with me schalle bere
wytnesse that had experience of þe same thynges as welle as I, so
schalle I telle as I may. Whan my sowle was dyssolued from the body
725 with so many angwyssches and sorowes as I seyde tofore, sodeynly
and vnspekably in þe twynkelyng of an eye yt was ibore tofore the
presens of God demyng. But howe er of whom yt was bore I knowe
not, and yt was no merveyle, for nowe I am in the hevy bodye and
then was the sowle withowte body or flessche. There tofore the iuge
730 was the sowles of many rightwysse men with tremelyng and with
vnthynkable feerys to wyte what the iuge schulde doo. Alas, why
knowe not they that be dedly to whom schalle befalle as then befelle
vs? Certeyne were not the vnknowyng thereof they schuld not synne
so ofte as they doo, for we dydde no synne in alle the tyme of owre
735 lyfe that myght be hydde from the iuge, but alle that ever we dydde
was als clerely knowe to alle that stode there as yf they had be
present, in so moche that the leste of the thoughtys that ever we
thought apperid as yt was.

704 hym] me Y   710 day] morowe Lb   715 be] add experience of Lb
717 knowe] om. Y   719 heven] heuynly YJLb   721-2 as . . . seyde] thou me
than so as Lb   722 seyde] add As YJ   723 I] thou. He sayd Lb
728 was no] is YJLb   731 vnthynkable] vnspekable Lb   to wyte] om. YJLb
737 of] add alle YJLb   737-8 that . . . thought] om. Lb   apperid] add there YJLb

'Bythynke the with howe many and howe grete feerys we were
smytte; at that tyme there stode many fendes beryng witnesse of alle   740
the evels that we hadde doon, declaryng in the tyme and the place
and the maner. And we owreselfe myght not sey nay to þat that was
putte vnto vs both, for eche of vs knewe welle that yt was trewe, and
also that the iuge knewe alle thynges and was most rightfulle. Alas,
alas, what schalle I sey? What sentence abode we than? For mynde   745
thereof I quake yett and I am aferde. Owre wyckednesse | cryed after   f. 196rb
vengeance vnto the iuge, and oneth appered there eny goode wherby
we myght haue hoope [of] mercye, and alle that were there cryed that
we were worthy to be in torment and in payne. And whan there
fayled nothyng but oonely to yeve the sentence ayenst vs that ys yove   750
ayenst synners, gloryous Ierome, bryghter than sterres, with Seynt
Iohn Baptyst and with Peter prynce of apostels and with grete
multitude of angels come into the trone of the iuge and prayed that
owre sentence myght be taryed a whyle and that [we] myght be yeve
vnto hym for the reverence and devocion that we had to hym, and   755
[for nede] to destroy the foreseyde heresye. And as he wolde, so yt
was graunted hym.
    'After thys, he with the blessyd companye ledde vs with hym and
declared [vnto] vs where alle trewe cristen sowles haue everlastyng
ioye that may not be spoke, that we schuld bere wytnesse thereof.   760
And than he ledde vs to the paynes of purgatorye and to helle, and
not oonly he schewed vs what was there but he wolde also that we
schulde asaye the peynes by experience. And whan alle thys was
doone, that tyme that worschipfulle Euseby towched owre bodyes
wyth Ierome sakke, the same gloryous Ierome bad vs turne ayene to   765
owre bodyes and that we schulde bere witnesse of alle that we hadde
se, and byhotyng vs that yf we dydde dewe penaunce for owre synnes
we schulde at the .xx. day after haue endeles blysse with worschipfulle Euseby that schuld passe from thys worlde the same tyme. And
so were owr sovles | ioyned ayeen to owre bodyes.'   f. 196va
    O dere Austyne, many ferfulle thynges lerned I of thoo .iij. men,   771
whyche yf they wer impressyd or expressyd to mannes mynde they
schulde vtterlye reende awey from theym the love of alle erthely
thynges and the grete besynes that ys hadde thereabowte that nowe

739 Bythynke] But þenke Y   740 beryng] om. Y   741 in] om. YJLb
748 of] and L   751 than] add alle YJLb   754 we] yt L   756 for nede]
folowed L   foreseyde] om. YJ, said Lb   759 vnto] om. L   trewe] om. Lb
761 the . . . of] om. YJLb   769 tyme] day and the same oure Lb   770 sovles
. . bodyes] bodies ioynyd to oure soulis ayeyne Lb   772 or expressyd] om. YJLb

775 make many a man to erre. But for I abyde [thy] comyng to vysyte the
relyques of gloryous Ierome as [thy] lettres makyth mynde, I leve of
now, and I wylle towche of the sepulture of worschypfulle Euseby
and sith speke forthe of the myracles of gloryous Seynt Ierome.

Of .ij. myracles that Eusebi dyd or he were beryed.

780 Whan thys holy man was dede abowte mydmorowe, anoon there
schewed many myracles to bere wytnesse of the holynesse [of his lyff,
of whiche I wille telle twayne.] There was a monke of the same abbey
that for wakyng and wepyng hadde loste hys syght. And anoone as he
towched the worschypfulle body of Euseby he hadde hys sight ayeen
785 as he hadde tofore. Another man ther was that hadde a fende within
hym and was owte of hys wytt and come and met with vs as we were
beryng the body of holy Euseby, and anoone he was delyvered and
made hoole. Thenke we here inwardly howe holy thys man was in
lyfe that my3t do so grete merveyles so hastely after hys dethe.
790 Thenke we of hys holynesse with grete drede, for syth he that was so
holy hadde so perylous a trowble and temptacyon at hys ende, howe
schalle we synfulle wrecches askape that howre and we noote howe
f. 196vb sone we schalle come therto? Than we buryed the body | of the holy
Euseby with dewe worschip but naked as hys mayster was, by the
795 chyrche in whyche the holy body of gloryous Ierome ys buryed. And
in the chyrcheyerde of the same chirche the bodyes were beryed of
the forseyde .iij. men that dyed the same howre.

Howe an heretyke called Sabynyan was behedyd and
overcome be the merytes of gloryous Ierome.

800 Ther was an heretyke called Sabynyam that seyde ther were .ij.
wylles in Crist somtyme dyscordyng, in so moche that he seyde Crist
wolde many thynges that he myght not doo. And with thys heresye
he dydde vs so moche sorowe that I may not telle yt with wordes, for
he peruertyd the folke that ys commytted vnto vs as a ravysschynge
805 wolfe. And for he schuld meynten hys heresye the more effectually,

775, 776 thy, thy] the L   777 I wylle] awhile Lb   779 dyd . . . he] wrougth
ere his body YJLb   780 abowte] add mydnyght or Lb   781-2 of(2) . . .
twayne] om. L   782 was] add a man Lb   784 he hadde] om. JLb
786-7 were beryng] bare YJLb   789 merveyles] myraclys YLb   dethe]
ende YJLb   795 the . . . of] om. Lb   798 was] add meruaylously YJLb
802 wolde] add make L   803 with] add any YJLb   804 folke] flock J

he made a tretyse therof and seyde that gloryous Ierome hadde made
yt to make vs to yeve feythe therto. But I knowe welle that gloryous
Ierome made a pystylle ayenst the same errour a lytylle tofore he
dyed, and therfor I clepyd the same heretyke on a Sonday with alle
hys dyscyples vntoo the chyrche in Iherusalem for to dispute and 810
repreve hys errour. There was gadred also the same tyme alle owre
bysschoppys and many other trewe cristen men, and so the houre of
disputacyon enduryd from noone tylle even.

When the foreseyde heretyke leyged ayenst vs the seyde tretis that
he fadred vppon gloryous Ierom, Syluan archebysschop of Nazareth 815
myght not suffre so moche wronge to be put on Ierome, for he lovyd
and | worschypped Seynt Ierome with soo moche affeccyon and f. 197ra
devocyon of herte that [at the] begynnyng of enythyng that [he dyd]
he asked helpe first of Seynt Ierome, and therefor he was callyd
Ierom ny of alle folke. He arose ayenst thys heretyke and blamyd 820
hym scharply for the wykkednesse that he dyd. And when that they
had longe stryve and eche of theym seyde ayenst other what they
myght, at the laste they acorded togeder thus, that yf Seynt Ierome
by the Sonday at noone openly amonge alle peple seyde that
Sabynyam lyed falsly in that he seyde Seynt Ierom made that 825
tretys, the heretykes hede schulde be smeten of, and elles schuld
the archebissoppis hede Syluan be smyt of. And thus eche man
wente home.

And alle that nyght we yaue vs to prayers, askyng helpe of God
that fayleth noone that trustyth in hym, but he ys grete and right 830
preysable and there ys noo numbre of hys wysdom. Whan the houre
came on the next day, the heretyke with hys disciples come into the
chyrche and wente abowte as a rampyng lyon sekynge to devowre the
servaunt of God. And alle the peple of trewe feythe stode in the
chirche clepyng the name of gloryous Ierome. But gloryous Ierome 835
feerde as thouh he had slepte and nought take kepe of theyre prayers,
and alle the trewe crysten peple stode astonyed and alle bewepte and
amerveyled why that gloryous Ierome abode so longe. And when
there appered nothyng of myrakylle, the heretyke cruelly called on
Syluan to doo that he hadde behight. Than holy Syluan wente intoo 840

811 repreve] preue YJLb   also . . . tyme] togeddir also Lb   812 the houre of]
oure YJLb   814 foreseyde, seyde] same Lb   leyged] laid Lb   818 at the] ys
L   he dyd] om. L   819 of] add God and of YJLb   seynt] gloryous YJLb
823 Ierome] add shewyd YJLb   824 Sonday] secunde day YJLb
824-5 openly . . . Ierom] þat he had falsly YJLb   827 the . . . of] Siluanes
þe archebysshoppes YJLb   837 alle(1) . . . peple] I, alle bewepte YJLb   and(2) . . .
bewepte] om. YJLb

the place where he schuld be hedyd, ioiyng as though he hadde goo

vnto a feste, | and alle bysschoppys and crysten men that stode there wepyng he comfortyd and seyde: 'Ioieth with me, my dere frendes, ioieth and be not hevy, for God levyth not ham that hopyth in hym.'

845 Than he knelyd downe and seyde: 'Moste holy Ierome, helpe me yf yt plese the. And thowh I be worthy moche more torment than thys, yet leste falsenesse haue place, doo thowe socour to trewthe. And yf yit be not lefulle that I be holpe, be vnto me mercyfulle in the howre of my dethe, that I be not departyd from the endeles blysse.' And

850 than he helde forthe hys nek and bad the turmentour smyte. And he lyfte hys swerde on hye, desyryng to smyte of the worschipfulle bysschoppys hede at oo stroke. Than sodenly, alle men seyng, come gloryous Ierome and put vp hys honde and hylde stylle the swerde and bade Syluan aryse. And then he blamed the heretyke, schewynge

855 howe he hadde vntrewly made that tretys and myssevnderstonde the scripture, and therefor he thretyd hym. And then vanyssched Ierom fro the syght of alle the peple, and anoon as the gloryous Ierome was gon, the heretykes hede fylle vppon the ground smyt of from the body as thouh yt had be smyt of with a swerde att oo stroke. And

860 when they se thys grete merveyle so sodeynly they wer astonyed and thanked God, and then þe dyscyples of the heretyke turned vnto the way of trewthe.

Loo how the truste that thys worschipfulle bysschop hadde vnto God and to gloryous Ierome was effectualle, for he dred not to dye

for trewthe, yevyng ensam|ple to every crysten man that sparyth to

866 dye for trewthe. Syth Cryste yaue hys lyfe for vs to by vs from thraldom, we owe not to be aferde to yeve owre lyfe for hym whan tyme ys, for noo man may gete the crowne of blysse but yef he fyght therfor lawefullye.

870 Howe the fende appered in lyknes of the forseyde bysschop Syluan and sclawndred hym mervelously, and howe he was delyuered by Seynt Ierom.

For I haue seyde somwhat of Syluan, I wylle sey another thyng of hym as merveyllous as the fyrst, [whereof be] als many wytnesse as

875 there been folke dwellyng in the cytees of Nazareth and of Bedleem

842 and(2)] add oþir YJLb   855 myssevnderstonde] vndirstond Lb   860 so] om. YJLb   865–6 yevyng . . . trewthe] om. Y   865 every] alle J, all cristene men for he is no trew Lb   868 crowne] ground Lb   874 whereof be] wherefor by L

that se yt wyth her eyen. The olde serpent the fende that for hys pryde was caste downe into the depnesse of helle, havyng envy at thys goode man Syluan, grevously he was steryd ayenst hym and gylefully he trauayled too sclaunder hym, that as many as he hadde encresed by ensample of hys holynesse and goode conversacyon vnto 880 goode levyng, soo by hys falle they myght be steryd vnto evylle.

On a nyght folowyng, the fende in the lykenesse of thys holy man Syluan appered vnto a worschypfulle woman lyeng in her bedde and besyed hym to come vnto her vnlefully, askyng the consent of her body. Than the womman, not knowyng the man, was aferde, and 885 seyng herselfe aloone in her chamber wyth a man wyst not what to doo, [but] cryed lowde and often, so that wyth her besy cryenge they awoke that were aslepe, not oonly in the same howse but also her ney|boures f. 197vb abowte. And alle they came rennyng to the wommans chamber and asked her what her eyled, and sche beyng sore aferde tolde theym. But 890 in the mene tyme that gylefulle serpent hydde hym vnder her bedde, and they sought abowte longe to wete whatt man yt was, and at the last they founde hym. And whan they behelde hym with many candylles lyght, they wende verely yt had be Syluan the archebysschop. And than alle they stode astonyed in maner owte of theyre wyttes, not 895 wetyng what to sey ne doo, seyng bothe hys holynesse and that foule and abhomynable dede. At the last they asked hym why he hadde doo suche wykkednesse, and he answered: 'What dyd I amys thouh thys womman clepyd me for too do thys dede?' The womman heryng with wepyng answered that he seyde vntrewly. Than he, wyllyng to stere 900 men more ayenst the servaunt of God for to make theym sclaunder hym the raþer, he began to speke [so] fowle horryble wordes of vnclennes that no man myȝt suffre theym for fowlenesse, but with dyspyte and grete repreves they compellyd hym and made hym goo owte of the howse. And on the morowe they tolde abowte what was 905 doone and cryed that Syluan the archebysschop was an ipocryte and worthy to be brente, in soo moche that alle Nazareth was so steryd ayenst the archebysschop that in noo wyse they myght not here hys name but yf they cursed hym. A, merveylous pacyence of thys man and a token of grete holynesse. Whan he herde alle thys sclaunder and 910 reprefe he meved nott oones hys mowthe to speke eny evylle worde, ne

878 goode man] worshipfull bysshop YJLb   879–81 he . . . levyng] be ensample of his holynesse had encrecyd yn the weyes of holy conversacyon YJLb   882 folowyng . . . in] he took YJLb   883 worschypfulle] add and a gret YJLb   884 besyed] visittid Lb   887 but] om. L   898–9 amys . . . clepyd] agaynys this womman thoughe she callid Lb   900 vntrewly] vntrewe YJ   902 so] to L   908 in . . . wyse] om. YJLb

f. 198ʳᵃ hys herte was noothynge | steryd to vnpacyence, but alleweye he
thanked God and seyde hys synne hadde deservyd yt.

Alas, Austyn, what schalle I sey? Not oonely I flee as moche as I
915 may wronges and repreves, but ofte I am greved with a fewe wordes.
I desyre the rewarde of hevene, but I take not kepe to traveyle
therfor. And yet I wote wele there may noo man come there but be
the wey of traveyle and of affliccyon and dyssese. And what schalle I
elles deme whyle I fynde myselfe descordyng from holy men in my
920 lyfe and maners but that I muste be founde descordyng from theym
at the howre of dethe in my rewarde? Yt ys fulle grevous and hevy to
me to thynk on holy mennys lyfes and on myn. Yt ys merveylous to
here howe men rede and speke of holy men as I doo as I haue herde
howe they dydde. Thus I sey to schewe myne owen foly I knowe
925 welle that I haue often herde of the same Syluans mowthe, that he
thought hymselfe never so wele at ese as whan he se hymselfe
dyspysed and of alle folke trowbled and throwe down. But thys
sclaunder of hym grewe soo ferre that yt wente into Alysawnder and
Cypre and other londes and cytees so moche that for dyshoneste noo
930 man come within hys dore. Merveylous God syttyng above and
seyng alle folke, he suffreth hys servauntys to falle into trybulacyons
and dysseses for the better, but he fayleth not theym whan that
nede ys.

After a yeere was past that the fende had vsed suche malyce ayenst
935 the servaunt of God, the holy bysschop Syluan lefte alle other
thynges and wente prevely vnto the chyrche where the body of
f. 198ʳᵇ gloryous Ierome ys | beryed as to a haven of refute and of socour, and
there at hys tombe he sett hym downe to pray. And after that he
hadde abyde there .ij. howres in hys prayers there come a man into
940 the chyrche fulle of the speryte of malyce, and fyndyng the holy man
there in hys prayers he ran to hym as a dragon and repreved hym,
seiyng þat he labowred contynuelly for to stere wommens hertys to
vnlefulle lustys. But the innocent lambe Syluan, ioyeng of hys owen
despyte, answeryd not. Than he with hys ryght honde drowe owte
945 hys swerde that he bare by hys syde and lyfte yt vp to haue put yt in

915 greved] begylid Lb   916–17 but . . . And] vnto traveyle þerfore I take no
kepe but Lb   919–20 myselfe . . . maners] my lyffe and maners of holy men Lb
921 at . . . of] in my JLb   in my] and in JLb, and my Y   923 men(2)] mennys
dedys YJLb   923–4 as(2) . . . howe] and wylle nothynge doo as YJLb   927 of
. . . down] trode down of alle synnars Y, as Y with folk for synnars JLb   929 for
dyshoneste] þer durst JLb, þer thurste (corr. in margin in later hand) Y   935 Syluan]
om. and punctuate here. Add The same bysshop YJLb   937 and of socour] om. YJLb

Syluans throte. And when the worschypfulle bysschop put ayenst
hym thys worde: 'Helpe, gloryous Ierome,' he turned the swerde into
hys owen throte and so he slewe hymselfe.

   After yt hapned that another wycked man come into the chyrche
and, wenyng that the holy bysschop Syluan had slayne hym, he toke 950
hys swerde to haue islayne the bysschop and, to telle schortly, he
slewe hymselfe as the tother hadde doo byfore. Onethe was he falle
vnto the grownde or other .ij. men come into the chyrche and seyng
these men dede they wende the holy man had doo yt. And therfor
oone of them that was more cruelle bygan to crye and called hym 955
thefe and seyde: 'Howe long schalle thy malyce endure? Thow
steryst wommen vnto the fowle wylles of thee flessch and therto
sleest men thus pryvely. Certeyne thys day schall be an ende of thy
wyckednesse.' And anoone he ran with hys naked swerde to haue
slayne hym. And when Syluan hadde seyde | thys worde: 'Helpe, f. 198ᵛᵃ
gloryous Ierome,' þis man slewe hymselfe as the other .ij. men hadde 961
do byfore with hys owen honde. The tother man that came with
hym, seyng thys, was aferde and ranne owte at the dore and cryed
owte and seyde: 'Cometh heder alle folke and se thys wykked Syluan
that not oonly defouleth wommen but alle with hys wycchecrafte he 965
sleeth men.'

   Than alle the peple, men and wymmen, come rennyng and cryeng
that Syluan the bysschoppe was worthy to be brente. And whan thys
come to my eerys I wente theder wepyng and fulle hevy, and there I
sawe howe amongyst the cruel wolfes stode that meke lombe ioyfulle 970
and mery as yf he hadde be in grete prosperyte. Noothyng he seyde
elles but: 'I suffre thys rightwysely, for I haue synned ayenst my
God.' They bet hym, they pulled hym and led hym vnto torment,
and he was so moche the more glad as the torment was more
grevous. But anoone [as] he was led owte at the chyrche dore, 975
sodeynly was seene gloryous Ierom ryse vp owte of the place wher he
laye so [bright] that no mannes eyen myght endure to loke vpon
hym. And thys he apered that alle myght se hym, and with hys right
honde he toke Syluan by the right honde and with a ferefulle voyse
he bad theym that helde hym leve of, which voyse and vysyon was of 980

952 hadde doo] dyd YJLb   957 the] þi YJLb   of . . . flessh] om. YLb
967 peple] add of JLb   men . . . wymmen] om. Y   971 prosperyte] profyte
corr. in margin in different hand J   972 wysely] corr. to worthyly in margin J
974 and . . . torment] om. Lb   975 as] om. L   976 was seene] om. YJLb
ryse vp] was see YJ, was rysyne Lb   977 bright] buryed L   978 And . . .
hym] om. Lb

so grete power that thoo that were there wer aferde and fylle downe streight to the erthe as dede men.

In the mene tyme, a womman bownde honde and feete that was vexyd with a | fende was brought to the chyrche for helpe by the hondes of many men. And anoon as the wommans fete toched the chyrche dore the fende began to crye [ferefully] by her mowthe and seyde: 'Mercy, gloryous Ierome, for by the I am tormentyd tofore my tyme.' Then gloryous Ierome seyde vnto hym: 'Thow wykked speryte, goo owte of thys servant of God and telle the wykkednes that thowe hast doo ayenst Syluan, schewyng thyselfe in the lyknes of Syluan to alle folke.' Than anoone, as gloryous Ierome badde, the fende apered in lyknes of Syluan so that alle men myght haue wende that yt hadde be Syluan the erchebysschoppe. And there he tolde alle that he hadde doo for to sclaundyr the servaunt of God, and after that with grete gronyng the fende vanyssched awey. And then gloryous Ierome not levyng the riȝt honde of the blessyd bysschop seyde vnto hym with a softe voyce: 'What desyrest thowe, my moste dere Syluan, that I shalle doo more for thy love?' He answered: 'My lorde,' he seyde, 'that thowe leve me here no lenger.' Than he seyde ayeen: 'That thow askyst, yt schalle be doo. Come therefor anoone after me.' And thys seyde, he appered noo lenger. But after the space of a schort howre Syluan the archebysschop passed vnto God, and then alle the peple was astonyed and merveyled. After the body of worschipfulle Syluan was borne vnto the chyrche of Nazareth wyth dewe worschyp with the multitude of peple of Nazareth and of Bethleem. And in the chyrche of Nazareth we buryed that body as was semyng, but many wordes myght not expresse | fully the [wonders] of thys worschipfulle bysschop. But for I haue more to sey of Seynt Ierome I leve of.

1010   Howe twey hethen men that · come to vysite gloryous Ierome were mervelously delyvered from theves and from grete perylle of dethe.

Twey worthy hethen men, ryche and goode men on þer maner, herynge of the grete myracles of gloryous Ierome come fro the cyte

981 and] *add* alle þe strength of þeyr bodyes faylynge þey YJLb   982 streight to] vpon YJLb   983 bownde] *add* bothe Lb   983–4 that . . . a] and full of þe YJLb 986 ferefully] ferefulle L   991–2 to . . . Syluan] *om.* Lb   995 gronyng] cryengys YJLb awey] *om.* YJ   998 thy love] the YJLb 999–1000 he(2) . . . ayeen] seyde gloryows Ierom YJLb   1002 God] cryst YJLb 1003 peple] *om.* Y   1005 peple] *add* bothe YJLb   1008 wonders] wondes L, wordis Lb   1012 grete . . . of] *om.* YJLb

of Alysaunder with moche ryches and fervent devocyon to vysite the 1015
relyques of gloryous Ierome. And goyng in theyre wey hit hapned
hem to here the steppes of men in a grete woode, and they wente
ferther and they founde neyther steppes of men nor of horse. And
therfor they clepyd vpon the name of gloryous Ierome and holy
commytted theym vnto hys kepyng. In the same wode ther dwelled a 1020
prynce of thefes havyng vnder hym more than .v. hundred theves,
sendyng somme oo wey and somme another wey to slee men and to
bryng theyre goodes vnto hym. Thys prynce seyng these .ij. men, he
clepyd .iij. theves and bad theym go and slee theym. And when they
had take ther armour and were nye at theym, wher they se tofore but 1025
.ij. than they se innumerable multitude of angellis, and oone goyng
tofore theym so bright þat noone myght loke vpon hym. Than tho
theves were aferde and wyste nott what to do, but turned ayeen, and
when they were fer fro theym they loked ayeen and they se but .ij.
And then they began to pursewe theym ayeen, but as soone as they 1030
come nere they se as they dydde byfore. Than were | they more f. 199rb
astonyed, and then in alle the haste they wente to ther prynce and
tolde hym. And he called theym folys and cleped other .xij. theves,
goyng hymselfe with hem, and they alle goyng togeder a whyle they
dyd se but .ij., and when they come nerre they sawe as many as the 1035
tother dyd byfore. Than they were aferde and theyre hertys trembled
and alle the strenght of theyre bodys fayled.

And when they come ayeen to theymself they thought that they
were wyllyng and wolde pursewe after theym prevely to se what
schulde falle. Whan even come vpon these pylgremes they wyst not 1040
what to doo ne where to be logged, and therfore they turned to the
.xij. theves to aske covnseyle of theym, wenyng that they hadde be
weyefaryng men as they were. And when they turned toward the
theves they see but .ij. and then were they bolde to mete with theym.
And after that they met, the theves asked whens they were and 1045
whether they wolde. They answered and seyde: 'Wee be men of
Alysaunder goyng to Bethleem for to vesyte the relyques of blessyd
Ierome.' The theves asked what men they wer that come wyth
theym. The tother merveyled and seyde that they se noon syth they
come into the wode butt theym and other .iij. Then the prince of 1050

1017 here . . . in] erre of þe wey ynto YJLb   1017–18 and . . . neyther] where þey
see no YJLb   1021 theves] om. YJLb   1022 wey(2)] om. YJ   1026 of
angellis] om. YJLb   1033 cleped] tooke Y   1034 goyng togeder] om. YJLb
1035 dyd] were aferre þey YJLb   1037 fayled] add for fere Lb   1039 were . . .
and] om. YJLb   1041 logged] leyghyd Y   1050 butt] saaf YJLb

theves tolde theym alle as yt was, praiyng theym to telle hym what
was the cause. And they seyde that they knewe noo cause, but yf yt
were for they commytted theym vnto the kepyng of gloryous Ierome.

Then the theves, sodeynly enspyred wyth the holy goste, fylle
f. 199ᵛᵃ downe at theyre feete | askyng theym foryevenesse, and syth lad
1056 theym to theyre felawes. At the begynnyng of the nyght they come to
the tother theves abydyng after theym and tolde hem as yt hadde
befalle, praiyng theym to leve alle þer synnes and goo with hem to
visite the bodye of gloryous Ierome. The tother thevys scorned them
1060 and seyde that they wolde slee theym yf they spake any more thereof,
but they cesyd not therefor. And then many of the theves arose and
drewe owte theyre swerdes, but then they callyd helpe of Seynt
Ierome and then þey myght not lyfte vp theyr swerdes ne put theym
vp tylle they that þey wolde haue slayne prayed to gloryous Ierome
1065 for theym.

O, the vnspekable mercy of owre sovereyne savyour, þat in so
many wyse bryngeth whom he wolle to the knowleche of trowthe.
[Anone] alle the companye of theves seyng thys thanked and praysed
God and gloryous Ierome and made a vowe to vysite hys relyques,
1070 and when morowe come, moo then .CCC. theves that were there that
tyme lefte the wode and wente with the forseid men of Alysaunder
vnto the tombe of gloryous Ierome, tellyng thes wordes. Then the
hethen men [were] baptysed and, levyng alle the vanyte of the
worlde, wente into a monastery, and the theves also yave theym vnto
1075 holy levyng by the grace of God and by the merytes of gloryous
Ierome.

How Seynt Ierome saued .ij. yong men [from dethe] that
come fro Rome to vysyte hym.

When twey yonge men goyng fro Rome toward Bethleem to vysyte
f. 199ᵛᵇ the relyques of | gloryous Ierome yt hapned theym too come by a
1081 vylage .xij. myle fro Constantynople. And .ij. myle from that vylage
or they come thereto .ij. men were sleyne, wherefor men of that
towne gadred theym togeder and began to seke abowte whoo yt
schuld be that dydde that dede. And when they hadde alle sought

1056 the nyght] *om.* J   1062 callyd] callyng after YJLb   1066 sovereyne]
om. YJLb   1068 Anone] when L   1070 and] Therfor YJLb   1072 of
... Ierome] *om.* J   wordes] wondres YJLb   Then] There YJLb   1073 were] *om.* L
baptysed] *add* theym L   1077 from dethe] *om.* L

they founde noone but oonly tho .ij. yonge men [that come fast by, 1085
whom they toke, wenyng they hadde slayne the tother men. Whereof
the yonge men] were amerveyled and swore as moche as they myght
that they knewe not thereof. But they set nought be þer wordes, but
led forthe tho yong men in alle the haste to theyre vilage and sith
sent theym to Constantynople with grete acusyng. And there with 1090
rygour of grete tormentys they were compellyd to knowleche them
gylty where they were not gylty, and so they were dampned and
demed to be behedyd.

Alas, what herte myght consente ar kepe theym fro wepyng to here
so many waylynges of innocentys whyche were arayed both with 1095
[yougth] and with gretnesse of noble byrthe, for wepyng and weylynge
and syeyeng contynuelly they seyde: 'Gloryous Ierome, ys thys the
reward that thowe yevest to them that serve the? Ys yt thys that we
haue deservid with traveyle of owre wey? Alas, thowe cytee of Rome,
thowe knowest of owre byrthe. We wende [not] that thowe schuldyst 1100
haue be so vnknowynge of owre ende.' Thus were they ledde into a
place where they schulde be behedyd, moche peple stondyng there
and abydyng. And there they kneled downe and hylde vp theyr
hondes, and wyth a lowde voyce they seyde: 'Gloryous Ierome,
anker of owre helth and [hauyn | of] owre hope, bowe thy eeres f. 200ra
vnto owre prayers at thys tyme, so that yf we dydde not thys synne for 1106
which we be punyssched that we may fele of thy wonte pyte the helpe
of thy delyveraunce. And yf we be gylty let vs be dede as nede asketh.'
And when þey hadde seyde thys they put owte theyr nekkes to the
smyters, seiyng nothyng but: 'Helpe, gloryous Ierome.' 1110

What merveyle though the mercyfulle helper Ierome myght not
absteyne hym fro schewyng mercy to so many teerys of hem that
come vnto hym, while the hertys of alle that stode abowte of the
selfe tormentowres wer mevyd vnto compassyon. Than they lyfte
vp theyre swerdys and smote on theyr nekkes, but ther nekkys toke 1115
the strookes as though they hadde been of stone, and they smote
ayeen and ayeen, but they felte theym but as they hadde be smytte
with a stree. Whereof arose amonge the peple grete merveylle to
alle that stoode abowte, and a grete multitude come rennyng to se.

1085–7 that . . . men] whyche L   1090 with(2)] add grete L
1092 dampned and] om. YJLb   1094 consente . . . theym] conteyne hit YJLb
1096 yougth] thought L, add and wyth gret feyrnesse YJLb, juventutis et pulchritudinis
maxima venustas PL   1097 syeyeng] fyghtynge J   1100 not] om. L
1105 hauyn of] ever | haste been L, auxilii portus PL   1110 Helpe] add help YJLb
1112 so] see J   1118 amonge . . . peple] om. YJLb

1120 At the last the iuge that demyd theym come hymselfe and bade
hem smyte ayeen that he myght se. And they smote, but her
nekkes wolde not be hurte. And than the iuge merveyled gretely
and wyst not what yt myght be, but thought that they hadde vsed
some wychecrafte, and therefor he commaundyd that in alle the
1125 haste they schulde be made naked and brente. Then they made a
grete fyre abowte theym and put in oyle and pycche the rather to
distroy her lyfe, but he that delyveryd theym fro swerdes cowde
also helpe theym crieng contynuelly vpon hym in the fyre. The
f. 200rb fyre brente faste and the flames | assendyd vp right hye, but the
1131 yonge men by the helpe of gloryous Ierom restyd theym as in a
mery herber.

At the last the iuge wolde wete wheþer yt was by meracle or by
wycchecraft, and he bad that they schuld be hanged .viij. dayes, and
yf they levyd so then they schuld goo whether they wolde. But the
1135 presence of gloryous Ierom fayled theym nott, for mervelously he
kepte theym alle thoo .viij. dayes, holdyng vp theyre fete wyth hys
hondes. On the .viij. day alle the pepulle of the cytee and of townes
there abowte and the iuge hymselfe wente to the galowes, and ther
openly they sawe thys gloryous myracle, the kepers tellyng theym
1140 what they hadde sey. Then alle merveyled and preysed gloryous God
and worschipful Ierome and dydde grete worschip to the yonge men.
And then moche pepille wente from Constantynople vnto Bethleem
to vysite the relyques of gloryous Ierome. And anoon the yonge men,
castyng fro theym alle worldly besynesse, entred into the monastery
1145 where gloryous Ierome levyd, nyght and day entendyng to prayeng
and to penaunce and to holy levyng.

Howe a monastery of nonnes was destroyed for covetyse
and for symonye.

The myracle of thys yonge men tofore ys to vs cause of grete
1150 merveyle, ioye and devocyon, but thys that folowyth yeveth cause
of grete drede, namely to relygyous pepulle. In a contre called
Thebayde there was a monasterye of nonnes abowte .ij. yeere agoo
ryght feyre and worthy, and ther was abowte an .CC. ladyes honest
f. 200va in maners | and relygyon and contynuelle reclusyon. Nowe eche

1123 thought] þough JLb   1136 .viij.] *om.* YLb, the J   1138 there] *om.* YJ,
come Lb   1140 gloryous] *om.* YJLb   1141 worschipful] gloryows YJLb
1144 besynesse] vanyte Lb, *add* and L   1153 and(2) . . . was] wheryn were YJLb

oone blesse bothe theyr eeres that the toon lett not go owte alle that the 1155
tother takyth in, for he that schalle sayle into the depe see, haue he
never so goode a schyp and hoole, yt avayleth hym not yf oone hole be
lefte in the bottom where water may come in and drowne hym.

Why sey I thys? The mater of thys storye schalle be schewed
forth. For the foreseyde monastery had many vertues and holynesse 1160
of levyng, but yt kepte oo synne of symonye that causyd yt to be
dystroyed. For by the instruccyon of the fende the nonnes hadde
thys ambycyon, that when eny schullde be resseyved a nonne
amonge theym, they toke her [not] so moche for charyte and
mercye as they dyd for loue of money, for þer schulde noone 1165
entre to abyde in that monastery but yf sche brought a serteyne
sum of money with her. In thys monasterye was a nonne fer in age
that had caste from her the loue of alle erthely thynges and fro her
chyldhode entendyd oonly to God in prayers and fastyng, and gretly
sche horryd and hated thys vyse that was amonge theym. To her in a 1170
nyght beyng in her prayer as sche was wonte, gloryous Ierome
appered in grete lyght and bad her goo on the morowe and telle the
abbes and the tother nonnes that but they cesyd of that synne they
schuld fele the sodeyne vengeaunce of God. And when he was agoo
sche merveyled gretely what he was that yaue her thys grete charge, 1175
and alle that nyght sche abode wakyng.

On the morowe sche range the chapyter belle. And when they wer |
alle gadred merveylyng why they wer called so hastely, thys holy lady f. 200vb
arose vp amongyst theym and tolde what sche had see and herde.
Anoon alle the tother scorned her and seyde that sche was a foole and 1180
sche my3t in happes be dronke over nyght and dreme suche thynges,
but sche takyng thys reprefe defendyd her with the schelde of
pacyence and, [sorowyng] of theyr obstynacy but ioiyng of her
owne despyte, wente to her wonte prayers, besekyng contynuelly
God þat yt befelle not her sustres as sche had herde.   1185

And .x. dayes after that, sche abydyng in her prayers in a nyght,
abowte mydnyght gloryous Ierome appered vnto her and badde her
goo withowte drede and telle her sustres as sche had warned theym
tofore. Then sche asked: 'Who arte thowe that byddest me doo these
thynges?' He seyde: 'I am Ierome,' and anoon hee was goo owte of 1190

1155 blesse] lesseþ Lb   1156 for] notwithstondynge Y   into . . . see] om. Y
1159 sey/I] trsp. YJLb   be schewed] shewe YJLb   1160 forth] om. YJLb
1164 not] om. L   1165 schulde] myght YJLb   1166 monastery] abbay
Lb   1173 but]   add yef YJ   1180 and(2)] add how JYLb
1182 takyng] thanking Lb   1183 sorowyng] sorowed L   1185 God] om. YJLb

her syght. But sche, knowyng theyre hardenesse, wyst not what too
doo nor sey, yet at the laste sche thought that sche hadde lever be
holde of theym woode and dronke þen to doo ayenst the wylle of
God. Therfor sche dydde gader her sustres as sche dydde byfore to
1195 haue tolde theym what sche se and herde. But as soone as they se her
aryse, or sche began to speke they wente owte of the chapter howse
with mowes and scornes. The .iij.e nyght after abowte mydnyght
gloryous Ierome with an vnspekable multitude of angelles appered
vnto thys lady beyng aslepe and bad her aryse and goo owte of the
1200 monasterye, that sche were not smyt with the sodeyne sentence that
f. 201ʳᵃ schuld come | vpon theym. But when sche prayed with grete wepyng
that they myght be spared, gloryous Ierome bad her goo in haste to
the abbes and vnto her sustres and telle theym that but yf they dydde
penaunce for there synne that same nyght there schulle falle the
1205 vengeaunce of God, and [yf] they abode obstynate then sche schuld
goo and no lenger abyde in that monastery.

Then thys nonne fulle of angwyssch and of hevynesse wente to the
chapyter and ronge the belle hastely. The abbes awoke, and when
sche wyst who yt was sche was wrothe and came to the chapter and
1210 blamed her gretely and wolde in noo wyse here noo worde of her,
seiyng that but sche wolde leve that tydyngis sche wolde noo lenger
abyde in the place with her. That lady answered: 'Tary not to doo
that thowe seyst, for I wylle no lenger abyde in thys place, for
gloryous Ierome hath appered vnto me and seyth that thys mon-
1215 asterye schalle anoone be smyt with the wreth of God.' Then the
abbesse, wenyng that sche hadde seyde thys of madnesse, bad the
keper of the place dryve her owte of the gate, and when sche hadde
be owte a whyle sche bade take her in ayeen, hopyng that thereby
sche wold cese of suche dedys. But thys nonne was glad to goo and
1220 fulle of sorowe and wepyng for the myschef comyng to the place.

O ferfulle God, stronge and myghty, and hoo schalle withstonde
hym? Alas, why drede men hým nott þat prouoke so moche hys
wrethe and may not flee yt nor flee from hys hondes, but hys grete
dome muste nedys take theym? At the leest wrecchys be aferd by thys

---

1192 at . . . laste] *om.* Lb   1196 howse] *om.* YJLb   1204 there(2) . . . falle]
þey shulde fele YJLb   1205 yf] *om.* L   abode] *add* stylle YJLb   obstynate] *add*
and L   1208 hastely] *add* wherwith YJLb   1210 in . . . wyse] *om.* YJLb
1211 but] *add* yef YJ   wolde . . . tydyngis] lefte such þynges YJLb   wolde(2)] shulde
YJLb   1215 wreth] wreche YJ   1217 place] gate YJLb   of(2) . . . gate] *om.*
YJLb   1218 sche bade] *om.* YJLb   1223 yt . . . from] *om.* YJLb
1224 leest] *add* ye Y, laste JLb (*JLb punctuate at* laste.)

ensample. Here they that trust | in theyre rychesse, that God sterith f. 201rb
vnto wrethe with drynesse of theyr couetyse, what dome God sente 1226
from heven vpon thys monasterye, turnyng awey theyre face from
hym for the loue of money. Onethe was thys nonne goone owt at the
doore but sodeynly anoon alle the monasterye felle downe to grownde,
sleyng alle the nonnes so there abode not but oon alyve. But thys lady 1230
wente into a monasterye in a contre faste bye, and there sche levyd in
grete holynes. To thys myracle I wolle ioyne other, schewyng the
ferefulle domes of God that the harde hertys of synne my3t be turned
into softenes of penaunce.

How .iij. heretykes were mervelously punyssched for 1235
offence ayenst Seynt Ierome.

An heretyke of þe Grekes dysputed openly on a Sonday with a preste
in þe cytee of Ierusalem. And when the prest for defense on hys
party alegyd an auctoryte of Seynt Ierome to dystroy the resons of
thys Greke, then the Greke with a bolde voyse was not aschamed to 1240
sey that Seynt Ierome lyed of alle trewthe. And for he dydde suche a
wikkednes with hys speche he spake never worde after.

Another that was an Aryen heretyke, when oon had brought oone
auctoryte of Seynt Ierome ayenst hym in dysputacyon and the
heretyke had boldelye seyde þat he lyed, anoon he was smytte 1245
with the vengeance of God. For he hadde not fully endyd the
worde but that he cryed alle the day after wythowte cesyng: 'Mercy,
mercy, gloryous Ierome, for I am tormentyd of the with harde
peynes.' And he cryed thus alle the day | as moche as he myght. At f. 201va
Compleyn tyme, alle men seyng that were there, wrecchydly he 1250
deyed.

Another heretyke se in the chyrche of Syon an ymage of gloryous
Ierome, and he seyde: 'Wolde God that I hadde had the in honde
whyle thowe levedist, that I myght haue sleyne the wyth my swerde.'
And then he pulled owt hys knyfe and smote yt in the throte of the 1255
ymage. A, howe grete ys thys Ierome doyng these many myracles.
Thys heretyke myght smyte hys knyfe in the throte of the ymage,
but he myght not get owte hys knyf from the ymage ne hys honde

1225–6 that(2) . . . couetyse] *om.* Lb   1225 God sterith] styre God YJ
1226 dome] *add* that L   1230 not but oon] not oon YJ, noon Lb
1233 synne] synnarys YJLb   1238 of Ierusalem] *om* Lb   1240 then the
Greke] *om.* Y   voyse] spyryt Y   1241 lyed] lyght YJLb   trewthe] *add* lyed
YJLb   1256 these] thus YJLb   myracles] meruieylys YJLb

from the knyfe tylle yt was knowe openly. But anoone there come
1260 blode [flowyng] owte at the wounde as of a levyng man, whyche
cesyth not yett in schewyng of the myracle.

In the same tyme thys was doone the iuge of the contre was in the
chyrcheyerde, to whom gloryous Ierome appered with a knyf in hys
throte askyng of hym to doo vengeaunce for that offense, tellyng hym
1265 how yt was. The iuge was astonyed and alle that were there, and
goyng vnto the chyrche they se the heretyke stonde with hys knyfe in
the throte of the ymage. And as soone as they se yt he my3t take
awey hys honde. Then they toke hym, and for he abode obstynatly in
hys evelle, seiyng that he sorowed for nothyng safe for that he slewe
1270 not Ierome in hys lyfe, then the multytude of peple with stones and
staves and swerdys and sperys slew hym.

Howe Seynt Ierome [delyveryd] a man owte of preson
from oo londe into another within a ny3t space. |

f. 201ᵛᵇ Iohn my nevew whom thowe knowest arayed with alle feyrenesse,
1275 whom I telle too me in stede of a sonne, tolde the as I wene what
byfylle hym, but yet that [yt] may the better be hadde in mynde I
wylle wryte yt. The same Iohn was take .ij. yeere agoo of men of the
londe of Perse and they sold hym to the offycers of the kynge of
Perse. And for hys excellent feyrenes he was ordeyned to serve the
1280 kynge. And when he hadde be a yeere there wyth grete sorowe and
werynesse in the kynges courte, the same daye a twelmonthe servyng
the kynge att mete he myght not for hevynes kepe hym from
wepyng. And when the kynge see yt and had askyd besely and
knewe the cause, he badde serteyne knyghtys take hym and put hym
1285 in a castelle. In the nyght that folowed, he beyng in the castelle alle
bewepte in hys slepe, gloryous Ierome come vnto hym and as hym
thought he toke hym by the honde and led hym with hym vnto the
cyte of Ierusalem. On the morowe Iohn awooke and, wenyng that he
had be amonge the knyghtys, he founde hymselfe in the howse there
1290 I dwelle. And then he was nye madde for merveyle and cowde not
wele wytte whether he was in the castelle or in my house. And at the
laste he come to hymselfe and cryed, and so he awoke them that were

1260 flowyng] folowyng L   1268 abode] did Lb   1272 delyveryd] delyveyd L
1275 telle] chese YJLb   a sonne] sum Lb   1276 yt] ye L, hit YJ, I Lb
1280 there] om. YJLb   1281–2 the(2)... mete] om. Y   1284 put] kepe YJLb
1285 that folowed] folowynge YJLb   1290 I dwelle] he dwellid Lb   he] y Lb

aslepe. Then come they alle rennyng to me with grete ioye and seyde
Iohn was come. Yet [I was] dowtefulle tylle I went myself and se
hym present whiche I wende hadde be in bondes among the Persees. | 1295
Than he tolde vs howe he was holpe, and we thonked and preysed   f.202ra
God and gloryous Ierome, by whos merytes and prayers owre lorde
delyver vs from alle evylle and brynge vs to the cyte of alle wele, to
dwelle wyth hym in endeles ioye and blysse. Amen.

Here endyth the pystelle of Cyrylle to Seynt Austyn of   1300
Seynt Ierome. And here begynneth howe owre lady
commendith Seynt Ierom in the Revelacyons of Seynt
Brigytte.

Whan Seynt Brygitte was on a tyme in her prayers, sche seyde [vnto]
owre lorde: 'Blessyd be thowe, my Lorde God, that arte .iij. persones   1305
and oo nature. Thowe arte very goodenesse and very feyrenesse and
power. Thowe arte very rightwysnesse and trewth, by whom alle
thynges lyve and haue theyr beyng. Thowe arte lyke a flowre
growyng syngulerly alone in the feld, of whyche floure alle that
neyhed therto resseyved swetnesse in theyr tastyng, relevyng in   1310
theyre brayne, delectacion in theyre syght and strenght in alle theyre
membres, so alle that neyhe vnto the are made the feyrer by levyng
of synne, wyser folowyng the wylle of the and not of the flessche,
more rightwysse folowyng the prophete of the soule and the
worschyp of the. Therfor, moste pytefulle God, graunte me to   1315
loue that that plesyth the myghtly, to withstonde temptacyons and
to despyce alle worldly thynges and to holde the besely in mynde.
   The moder of God answeryd the salutacion: 'Gat the that goode
Ierome by hys merytes that wente from false wysdome and founde
trewe wysdom, that despysed erthly worschyp and [wan] God   1320
hymselfe. Blessyd ys that | Ierome, and blessyd are they that follow   f. 202rb
hys techyng and levyng, for he was a lover of wydowes and myrrowr
of alle that profyted in vertu, and a doctour and techer of alle

1294 I was] they were L			1295 in bondes] om. Lb			1301 And . . .
begynneth] om. YJLb			1304 vnto] into L			1305 .iij.] add and oon, thre yn
YJLb			1306 oo] add in YJLb			very . . . and(2)] om. Lb			goodenesse] add
and verrey wisdom YJ			and(2)] Thou art YJ			1310 neyhed] drawith Lb
1312 neyhe] drawith Lb			1317 holde . . . besely] be holden busye Lb			in] add my
YJLb			1318 God] add oure lady YJLb			1320 erthly] add
wisdome Lb			1320-1 and . . . hymselfe] om. Y			1320 wan] when L
1321 hymselfe] add			seyde		L			1322 wydowes] wisdommys			Lb
1323 profyted] were parfett were Lb

trowthe and of clennes.' Another tyme owre lady seyde to Seynt
1325 Brygytte: 'Doughter, haue mynde howe I tolde the that Ierome was a
lover of wydowes, a folower of perfyte monkes and an auctour and
defender of trowthe, that gate the be hys merytes that prayer that
thowe seydist. And nowe I [adde] to and seye to Ierome was a
trompe, be whyche the holy gost spake. He was also a flowme
1330 inflamed of that fyre that come vpon me and vpon the apostles on
Pentecoste Day. And therefor blessyd ar they thatt thys trompe
heryth and folowe therafter.' Amen.

   Y omits the final 'Amen' and adds a further chapter (f. 20r):

   How be þe byddynge of Seynt Ierom a lyon was kepere of
1335   an asse and of þe wysdom and pacyence of Seynt Ierom,
   Capitulum 20

Seynt Ierom, prest and relygiows man, whan he dwellyd yn
Beethlem, which is .vj. myle fro Ierusalem on þe south syde, on
an even as he sat with his bretheryn and herde þe holy lesson of here
1340 collacyon þere come sodeynly a lyon haltynge ynto þe monastery,
and whan þe bretheryn see hym þey ran awey for drede. But Seynt
Ierom went ayenst hym as ayenst a gest to receyve hym. Than þe
lyon shewde his foot þat was hurte to Seynt Ierom, wherfore he
callyd his brederyn ayen and badde hem waysshe þe lyons foot and
1345 seke bysily where þe sore was, and so þey dyd, and þey fonde þat þe
sole of his foot was as hit had be woundyd and kut with knyves. And
after þey had do cure and leyde medycynes þerto hit wex hoole, and
þe lyon, levynge alle his wyldnesse and fersnesse, dwellyd amonge
theym as a tame best.
1350   Than Seynt Ierom, seenge þat God had not sent þat lyon to þeym
oonly for helynge of his foot but also for þeire profyȝte, be cownseyle
of his bretheryn he enioyned þe lyon þis offyce, þat he sholde dryve
Y, f. 20ᵛ to pasture and kepe an asse which | thei had to fecche home wode fro
þe parke. And þe lyon obeyed, for euery day yn maner of a shipherde
1355 he had out þe asse to his pasture and abode with hym contynually as
his felow and defensour. And such tyme as þe asse was wont to be
brougth home for to laboure þe lyon brougth hym home bothe for to
fette his owen mete and for to brynge home þe asse. But on a day hit
happyd þat while þe asse was yn his pasture þe lyon felle sore aslepe,

and marchawntys þat come be þe wey and see noþynge but þe asse 1360
stale þe asse and had here forth with þeym. And whan þe lyon
awooke and fonde not his felow he roryd and went abowte rorynge,
and whan he fonde hym not he turnyd home soryly to þe yatys of þe
monasterye, but he þurst not entyre as he was wont for shame.

Whan the bretheryn of þe hows see þat he come latter þan he was 1365
wont to doo and þat he brought not þe asse with hym, þey wende þat
for hungir he had ete þe asse, and þerfor þey wolde not yeue hym his
mete þat he was wont to haue, but þey seyde vnto hym: 'Goo and ete
þat oþer dele of the asse as þou hast begonne and fulfylle þi
glotenye.'   1370

Neuerþeles, for þey were yn doute whedire þe lyon had do such
trespas, þey went ynto þe pasture and sought alle aboute yef þey
myght haue fownde eny token of þe asse þat he had be slayn, and
whan þey cowde ryth nouȝt fynde þey turnyd home and tolde Seynt
Ierom alle þat was doo. Than Seynt Ierom bad þeym put þe lyon to 1375
þe same offyce þat þe asse was wonte to vse, and so þey dyd. They
hew wode and leyde hit vpon þe lyon as þey were wont to do vpon
þe asse and he suffred and bare hit pacyently.

On a day whan þe lyon had do his laboure, he went out ynto þe
felde and ran abowte fro place to place as yef he wold haue wyst what 1380
had befalle of his felaw þe asse. And þus sone he see aferre how þe
marchawntys come with þeire camelys lade and þe asse goynge
before hem, for the maner of þat contre ys þat whan þey goo ferre
with þeire camelys þey make an asse go before hem with a rope
abowte his nekke to lede hem þe ryght wey. But whan þe lyon knewe 1385
þe asse he ran vpon þeym with a gret rorynge, and alle þe men fledde
and ran awey for drede. Than þe lyon ferfully cryenge and rorynge
smot þe grownde strongly with his tayle, and made alle þe camelys as
þey were lade with marchawndyse goo before hym home to þe
abbeye.   1390

Whan þe bretheryn see þis þey tolde Seynt Ierom, and he bad þat
þey shulde waysshe þeire gestys feet, þat is to say þe camelys feet,
and yeve hem mete and abyde þe wyll of oure lorde þervpon. Than
þe lyon ran abowte þe monasterye and with glad and favnynge chere
he felle down prostrate at eche brotherys feet and waggynge his tayle 1395
he semyd to aske foryefnes of þe trespas, þat he had not do as he
sholde haue do, or ellys more veryly he made ioye for þe fyndynge of
his felowe.

But Seynt Ierom, knowynge yn spiryt what was to come, bad his

1400 bretheryn make redy þat was necessarye for gestys þat were
comynge. And while he was spekynge þer come a messengere to
hym and seyde þat men were come to þe yate þat wolde speke with

f. 21ʳ þe abbot. Seynt Ierom went | vnto hem and þey felle down prostrate
at his feet and askyd hym foryefnesse for stelynge of þe asse. But he

1405 benyngly lyfte hem vp and bad hem ryse and took hem ynto þe
abbey and shewyd hem gret charyte and humanyte. And afterwarde
he delyuered þeym þeire camelys with alle þeire marchawndyse and
bad þem take þeire owen and stele noon oþer mannys. Than þey
prayed Seynt Ierom þat he wolde take half þe oyle þat þey had yn

1410 here caryage yn þe wey of charyte, but he wolde not assente.
Neuerþeles þey compellyd hym so ferforth þat vnnethe he bad his
bretheryn take hit. And þey behyghte þat þey wolde yeve so moche
oyle eche yere to his bretheryn and to charge theire eyrys with þe
same for euyre after.

1415 In this is shewde gret charyte of Seynt Ierom þat he had yn
kepynge of hospytalyte, for not only he receyvyd men but also bestys
to his charyte, and þerfor he wrytith hymsilf and sayeth þus: 'In my
monasterye,' he sayeth, 'we entendyd of herte to hospytalyte, for we
receyve alle with glad chere and waysshe þeyre feet, saf only

1420 heretykys.'

And as þe holy man Severe wrytyth of hym, he was so excellent yn
connynge of Latyn, Grew and Hebrew þat yn all connynge noon was
lyke vnto hym, for whatsoeuer was askyd of hym he had redy a
competent answer withoute eny delay. And yef þer were take hym a

1425 book of Grew, he wolde rede hit forthwith yn Latyn, and a Latyn
book ayenward as redily yn Grew withoute stomblynge, as yef þe
same langwage had be wryte before hym þat he redde.

He translatyd þe book of Danyel out of þe tonge of Calde and þe
bok of Iob out of þe tonge of Arabyke ynto Latyn. And þerfor sayeth

1430 Seynt Austyn þat hys wysdom and eloquence shone as þe sonne out
of þe east ynto þe weste. And oo þynge he laboryd euer yn alle his
studye, þat þe enemyes of Crystys Chirche shulde alwey be his
enemyes, and þerfor he had contynualle werre agenst wykkyd lyvarys
and mysbelevarys. And þerfor heretykes and lollardys hated hym,

1435 because he impugnyd þeire heresyes so myghtyly and wysly that
noon myght withstonde hym.

Clerkys also hatyd hym, for he sparyd not to blame þeire ynsolent
lyvynge and þeyre synnes, but alle good folke lovyd hym and had
hym yn worship. And how pacyently he took alle detraccyon and

persecucyon þat was doo ayenst hym he shewyth hymsilf yn a pystyll 1440
þat he wrot *ad Gallam*, where he wrytyth þus: 'I þonke God,' he
sayeth, 'þat I am fownde worthi to be hatyd of þe worlde, for þey
calle me a wykkyd doare. But I kan goo to þe kyngdom of heuyn be
ynfamye and be good fame, be sklawndire and be good loos. And
wolde God þat for þe name of my lord and for his ryghtwysnesse alle 1445
þe myslyvarys of þe worlde shulde pursewe me. Wolde God þat alle
þe worlde shulde ryse agenst me to my repref so þat I mote deserue
to be preysid of Cryst and þat I mote hope to haue þe mede of his
behest. For hit is an acceptable and a desiderable temptacyon,
whereof mede and rewarde is hopyd to be had of Cryst yn heuyn, 1450
and cursynge and sklawndire is not grevows whan hit is chawngyd
for þe praysynge of God. And þat trybulacyon is ioyfulle and
pacyently to be suffred | which getyth grace here and endles blys f. 21ᵛ
hereafter. To þe which grace and blys oure lord Ihesu brynge vs
þorough prayers and desertys of this gloryows Seynt Ierom. 1455
Amen.

Here endith þe lyf of þe holy doctoure Seynt Ierom.

1455 this] *add* and Y
There follow in Y, J and Lb two Latin prayers.

For details of Augustine's life, see 12 Augustine 1 (from MS A2), above, pp. 169–172.

We have no direct source for the Life printed here from MS L. Part of the story of Augustine's visit to Les Ponts de Cé (ll. 20–48, 63–71) is based on Goscelin.[1] The incident at Compton (ll. 151–202) closely follows the account in Brompton's *Chronicle*.[2] The adventure in Dorset is in Goscelin and in William of Malmesbury.[3] In both these accounts the fish tails were attached to the clothing of Augustine and his band, and likewise in the same story told by Wace and Laȝamon.[4] It is, however, to the Wace/Laȝamon versions that we owe the addition that the men of Dorset had tails thereafter.

[1] Goscelin, *Vita S. Augustini episcopi Cantuariensis primi* in Mabillon, ed., *Acta sanctorum ordinis S.Benedicti* (Paris, 1668), pp. 498–534.

[2] Robert Twysden, ed., *Chronicle of John Brompton* in *Historiae Anglicanae Scriptores* 10 (London, 1652), cols. 736–7.

[3] Mabillon p. 526, and William of Malmesbury, *De Gestis Pontificum Anglorum*, ed. N. E. S. A. Hamilton, *RS* 52 (1870), p. 184.

[4] Laȝamon, *Brut*, ed. G. L. Brook and R. F. Leslie, *EETS* OS 277, 1978, vol. 2, p. 772, ll. 1470 ff., and Arnold, Ivor, ed., *Le Roman de Brut de Wace*, (Paris, 1940), vol. 2, pp. 717–8. See also G. Neilson, *Caudatus Anglicus: a mediæval slander* (Edinburgh, 1896).

Here begynneth the life of Seynt Austyn bisschop.

Seynt Austyn was sent into Inglonde to preche the feyth of Cristys
lawe by Seynt Gregory the pope of Rome, the whiche had a greet
zeele and lovynge to Ynglonde, bycause on a tyme he walkid in the
citee of Rome, that tyme beyng a cardynalle, he sawe .ij. childryn led
by the strete of a merchaunte to be sold and he enquerid of whatt 5
londe they were. And the merchaunt seid: 'Holy fadir, of Inglonde,'
affermynge that alle the children of that londe were of suche beawte.
And then Seynt Gregorie askyd if the peple of that londe were
cristen. And they seyde: 'Nay, forsothe.' And then he was greetly
meevid with pety and compassion and seid: 'It is greet pite that the 10
prince of derkenes schal haue power and lordschip of so feyre a
peple.' And then Seynt Gregory did seye these wordis: 'O Inglissche
peple ben in beawte like angillis, wherfor it is sittynge that theyr
dwellyng schuld be in hevyn amonge angelis.' And than he hymselfe
purposid to take þe labour vpon hym to come into Inglond to preche 15
there the cristen feithe, as it is schewed more pleynly in his owne
lyfe. But | he was let for dyuers causys, for soone aftir he was chosyn   f. 208va
[pope] by þe eleccion of alle þe cardynalles.
    And then he sente Seynt Austyn to fulfil his entent wiþ a goodly
felischip of monkis and clerkys to þe nombre of .xl. persones. And 20
when þey come to þe prouince of Andegauensy callid Pont Say a
myle fro þe ryuer of Lygerym, purposyng to haue restid þem ther
and for to tary al nyȝt, but what for multitude of pilgrimys and for þe
greet scornynge of wemen they myght not reste there in noo wise, for
there were a greet felischyp of evyl disposid wommen that scorned 25
them and drofe them out of the town. And withoute þe towne þer
was a feir brode elme vndyr þe whiche they purposid to reste them
alle that nyght. But oon of these yonge women that was moore ferser
and bolder than eny other of þem pursued them so nye that they
myght not reste them there þat nyght neyther. And when Seynt 30
Austyn lifte vp his staffe to remeue fro thens, sodenly his staffe flye
out of his honde with a greet violence the space of .iij. forlongis and
styckyd stylle in the erthe. And when Seynt Austyn come to his
staffe and pullyd it out of the erthe, by þe grace of almyghty God
there spronge a feyre welle of clere watyr, the whiche refresschid ful 35

swetely theym alle. And then abowte þat welle they restid alle that
nyght. And they that dwellid there nye aboute sawe a greet light alle
þat nyght strecchyng fro heven vpon them and couered the place
wher these holy men lay. And in þe morowe Seynt Austyn wrete in
40   the erthe wiþ his staffe besides this welle thees wordis folowynge:
f. 208ᵛᵇ   'Here had Austyn | the servaunt of the servauntis of God hospitalite,
whom þat Seynt Gregorie [pope] hath sente to converte Inglonde.'
And vpon þe morowe, when the holy men were goon, þe dwellers of
the cuntrey þat sawe this light thoruȝ alle the nyght come to the
45   same place, and þer they fonde a feyre welle of the whiche they
merveylid greetly. And when they sawe þe scripture wreten in the
erthe, they were greetly aschamyd bycause of theyr vnkyndenes
schewid vnto these holy men, and then they repentyd þem ful sore.
      And aftir they dydde do bylde a chirche in þe same place in the
50   worschip of God and Seynt Austyn, the whiche aftyr þe bisschop of
Andegauensy halowid, to þe whiche halowynge ther resortid so
moche peple that they trad vndyr foote alle the cornys aboute þe
seide place in so moche that it myȝt raþer be callid a pleyn floore
clene swepte raþer than errable londe for to bere corne, for ther nas
55   oo man that wolde spare more his owne corne than other mennys.
But they hopid and trustid in the mercy of God that by the meritis of
Seynt Austyn that they schulde not be disseyved, for when the tyme
come of repynge that londe bare more corne and bettir þan other
dydde that was not trodyn beside that place. And the hyȝe auter of
60   that chirche stondith ouer þat writing that Seynt Austyn wrote with
hys staffe in the erthe beside the welle. And yet into this day ther
may no womman entyr into that chirche nor draw water at the welle.
And yet there come þedir a noble womman that seyde that sche was
not gylty aȝens Seynt Austyne and purposid mekely with a tapur in
f. 209ʳᵃ   hir honde to tempte the seynt and to | offir hir tapur in the seide
66   chirche, but the sentence and graunte of almyghty God may not be
revokyd, for as soone as sche biganne to entre the chirche hir
bowellys and her synewes bygan to breke, and so sche fylle downe
to the erthe deed to the ensaumple of alle oþer wommen, wherfor we
70   may vndirstonde that iniurye don ayenst a seynt dysplesith greetly
almyghty God.
      And fro thens soone aftyr they come into the coostys of Inglond.
And they arivid vp at the ile of Tenet in eest Kente where in that
tyme reyned Kynge Athelbert, the whiche was riȝt a good man and a

42 pope] *erased*   58 þan] *add* than

meke to the peple in þe lawe of paynymes that he was tho of. To 75
whom Seynt Austyn sente a messanger schewynge to hym the cause
of hys comynge fro the courte of Rome too brynge hym right ioyful
and confortable tydyngis, yf that he wolde obey hym and his
prechynge he wolde promyse hym the ioy of heven that ys everlastynge, and there to reigne eternally lyke a kynge with allemyghty 80
God wiþowte dowte. And then Kyng Athelbert herynge this
commaundid that they schulde abyde and tary in that same ile,
and he comaundid that they schuld haue alle thyngis that were
necessarye to theym tylle the tyme that he myȝt aske consent of his
lordys of this mater what were best to do. And wiþin fewe dayes 85
aftyr the kynge come to the same ile and kepte residens without in
the feld in the opyn eyre. And then he commaundid Seynt Austyn
and his felowschip for to come and speke with hym.

And then they, armyd ful of vertu, come into the felde like
Goddys knyȝtis, folowynge a crosse in the stede of a baner, | seiyng f.209rb
the Letany for þer owen helpe and of the herers also. And in þat 91
place Seynt Austyn made a glorious sermon before þe kynge, in the
whyche he declarid ful notably the cristen feith opynly to a greet
nombre of paynyms then there gadryd to the greet availe of the
kynge and of alle hys peple. And when this sermon was doon þe 95
kynge seyde to them: 'Youre promys ben ful feyre that ye brynge,
but bycause they be newe and we haue not herde of them heretofore,
þerfor we may not anoon geve consent therto. Neþeles bycause ye
ben come as pilgrimes fro ferre contreies, we wylle not be grevous
nor hevy vnto yow, but we wole resseyve yowe mekely and we schal 100
mynyster to yow syche thyngis as ben necessarie. Noþer we wylle
forbede yow, but as many as ye can converte to your religion by
youre prechyng ye schalle haue licence to baptise þem and to be fully
of your lawe.' And then the kynge yave theym a dwellinge place in
the citee of Dorroburnence that now is clepid Canturbury. And 105
when they drowe nye the citee they come in with procession
besechynge almyghty God and al his seyntis of socoure and of
helpe for to take awey hys wrathe fro that citee and for to enflawme
the hertis of the peple to resseyve ther doctryne.

And then Seynt Austyn and his felawschip began to preche there 110
ful devoutly þe word of God abovte in þe provynce, and alle the
peple that were wele disposid were soone conuertid to the feith, so
that within a while myche peple were baptised. And then they
folewyd the steppis of thyse holy men and by ther holy lyvyng | and f. 209va

115 by grete myraclis schewyng, and anoon there grete fame roos in þe
contre.

And when this came to the kyngis eere, anoon he came to þe
presence of Seynt Austyn and he desired to here hym preche. And
then þe worde of God enflawmed hym so wiþin his soule þat as
120 soone as þe sermon was doon he felle don to the fete of Seynt
Austyn, and he brake out mornyngly into þese wordis: 'Alas,' seyde
he, 'woo is me that I haue errid so longe and knewe not this that
thow tellist, for þy promyssis ben so dilectable þat I þynke it alle to
longe tylle I be cristened. Wherefor, holy fadyr, I requyre the for to
125 mynystre to me þe sacrament of baptym.' And then Seynt Austyn,
seynge the greet obedience and desire þat þe kyng had to be baptisid,
with wepynge teeris he toke vp the kynge and cristyned hym wiþ al
his meyne, and then he enformyd hem diligently in þe feiþ wiþ greet
ioy and gladnes. And when alle þis was doon, Seynt Austyn
130 desirynge þe helpe of the peple of Inglond wente on his fete
toward the citee of York.

And when he come nyʒe to þe citee there met hym a blynde man
that seide: 'O thou holy Austyn, helpe me that am ful nedy.' And
then Seynt Austyn seid: 'I haue no siluer, but suche as I haue I yeve
135 the,' and seide: 'In the name of Ihesu Crist arise vp al hoole.' And
wiþ that word he resseyved his siʒt, and then he beleuid in oure lord
and he was baptysed. And vpon Cristemas Day he baptised in the
ryver callid Swale .x.Ml. men withowte wommen and children. And
f. 209ᵛᵇ there was so greet multitude of peple | resortynge to the seide ryuer,
140 the whiche was right depe, that no man myʒte passe over on foote,
and yet by þe myracle of God there was neyþer man, womman nor
child in eny perille, but they that were sike were made hool boþe in
body and in soule. And in the same place is bylde a chirche in the
worschip of God and of Seynt Austyn.

145   And when he had prechid the feiþ of Crist to þe peple and hadde
confermyd them stedfastly in þe same, then he turnyd ayen fro York,
and by þe wey he mette with a lepour askyng helpe of hym. And
when Seynt Austyn hadde seyd these wordis: 'In þe name of Ihesu
Crist be thowe clensid from al thy lepour,' and then anoon al his
150 filthe fil awey and a feir newe skynne overcouerid his body, so that he
semyd a feir new yong man. And also as Seynt Austyn come into
Oxfordschire to a towne that is callid Coniton to preche the worde of
God, to whom the curat seid: 'Holy fadir, þe lord of þis lordschippe
hathe ben often tymes warned of me to pay his tiþis, and ʒit he

wiþholdith þem, and I haue acursyd hym and ȝit I fynde hym the   155
more obstynate.' To whom Seynt Austyn seyd: 'Sone, why payest
not thy tythis to God and to holy Chirche? Knowyst thow, knyȝt,
that thy tythis byn not thyne but ben Goddys?' And then the knyȝt
answeryd to Seynt Austyn: 'I know weel þat I tylle the grownde,
wherfor I owght as wele to haue þe .x.th parte as þe .ix.th parte.'   160
And when that Seynt Austyn cowde not turne his entent, þen he
wente to messe, but fyrst he commaundyd by þe vertu of almyghty
God that alle tho that were acursyd schulde | anoon go out of the   f. 210ʳᵃ
chirche. And then ther rose vp sodynly the body of a dede man and
wente oute of þe chirche into the chyrcheyarde with a white clothe   165
vpon hys hede and stode stylle there tylle masse was doon. And then
Seynt Austyn wente into the chirche to þis wyckyd goost. And then
he requirid hym for to telle hym what he was. And then he seyd that
some tyme he was lord of that same towne, and bycause that he
wolde not pay his tithis to his curat he acursid hym, and so he dyed   170
not assoyllyd of that curse and wente to helle. And then Seynt
Austyn commaundid hym that he schulde brynge hym to the place
where hys curat was buryed, and so þis caryon of this dede knyȝt
wente byfore and brought him to the graue. And then Seint Austyn
seyd that al men myght knowe þat boþe lyf and dethe is in þc power   175
of God. And then he seyd: 'I commaunde the in the name of God to
aryse, for we haue nede of the.' And then he aroos anoon and stode
byfore hym and al the peple. To whom Seynt Austyn seide:
'Knowyst thow thys man, brother?' 'Yee,' he seyde, 'but wold
God I had never knowen hym, for he was a withholder of hys   180
tithys and in alle hys lijf an evylle doer.' To whom Seynt Austyn
seyd: 'þu knowyst weel that oure lord is merciful, wherfor we
wrecchys his creaturis most be mercyful, and as longe as þe peynis
of helle dothe endure lete vs be mercifulle.' And then Seynt Austyn
toke þis preste a rodde, and there thys knyȝt knelynge on hys knees   185
was assoyled. And then he commaundid hym to go to his graue aȝeen
and there to abyde tylle the day of dome, þe whiche | entryd into his   f.210 ʳᵇ
graue and anoon he fal to asschis.

    Than Seynt Austyn seide to the prest: 'How longe haste thow
leyne here in thy graue?' And he answeryd and seyd: '.j.C.lj.ti yeere.'   190
And then he seyde: 'How is it with the?' 'Wele, holy fadyr,' he seyde,
'for I am in everlastynge blysse.' 'Wylte thow that I pray to almyghty
God that thow abyde here stylle with vs for to make stydefaste þe
hertis of men in trew byleeue?' And he seyde: 'Nay, holy fadyr, I

195 pray yow trowble me not, for I am in a place of reste.' And then
Seynt Austyn sayde to hym: 'Goo in pees and pray for me and for
alle holy chyrche.' And then he entrid into his graue, and anoon he
was turned into erthe. Of thys syght the knyght was fulle sore aferde
and with ful sore quakynge come to Seynt Austyn and to his curat,
200 and there he askyd them forȝeuenes of al hys trespas, purposynge
ever aftyr to pay his tithys to God and to holy Chirche and to folowe
the doctryne of Seynt Austyn.

And aftyrward Seynt Austyn entryd into the contre callyd
Dorsettschyre, and there he was resseyved of alle the peple lyke an
205 aungylle. And he come into a towne where myche peple were, the
whiche refusyd hys prechynge, and they trowblyd hym so that he
myght not reste in that towne, but anoon they drofe hym owte aferre.
To whom Seynt Austyn seyde: 'þe rightful iugement of almyghty
God falle vpon yow bycause ye wole not resseyve the doctryne of
210 hym.' For it is seyde that they kast vpon hym the taylis of ray
f. 210ᵛᵃ fysschis, | for the whiche they had a greet sykenes after in there
nether ende lyke acordynge to the same whiche was to them a greet
repreef many ȝeeris aftyr.

And in another place where were peple of false feyth, for they
215 scorned the promyses of Seynt Austyn and he made hys prayer
besechynge almyghty God that the pot of worldly fylthe þat þe
profete sawe in the face of the northe alle brennynge myght be
broken with the rodde of iron, or ellys that þe seyd pott myght sethe
in hys furneys more bytter to that eende þat they the whiche repreve
220 the worde of God myght be the more scharpely punysschid. And
anoon alle þe mysbylevers were brent with a fyre invisible so that
ther skyn apperyd rede as bloode. And whan þe peyn was so greet
that they myght not suffre it, then they were constreyned to axe God
foryevenes. And so they felle downe to the feet of Seynt Austyn,
225 besechynge hym that he wolde pray for them that they myght be able
to resseyve the sacrament of baptym and to be relesyd of there greet
grevous brennyng peyne. And whan Seynt Austyn had prayed for
them, anoon that merveylous fyre was qwenchyd over alle that contre
so þat it was never more seyn in that contre.

230 On a tyme as Seynt Austyn was in his prayers, oure lord apperid
to hym and confortyd hym with a gentylle and a famulyer speche,
seiynge: 'O thow my good servaunt and trewe, be thow confortyd
f. 210ᵛᵇ and doo manly, for I þy lord | God am with the in alle thyn affeccion
and myn eerys ben open to thy prayers, and for whomsoever thow

axe eny peticion thow schalt haue thy desire, and the yate of 235
everlastynge lyf is open to the, wherein thow schalte ioy with me
withouten ende.' And in this same place where the fete of oure lord
stode he fixid his staff into the grounde and made an ende of hys
iourney. And there a welle of clere watyr spronge vp in þe same
place, the whiche welle is callyd Cerne and it is in the contre of 240
Dorsett. And also there is bylde a chirche in the same place in the
worschip of our savyour bycause he apperede there to the blessyd
Seynt Austyn.

Also besyde the costys of the same contre there was a yonge man
that was bothe lame, defe and dombe, and by þe prayers of Seynt 245
Austyn he was made alle hoole, and after that he wax ful desolate and
wantone of his speche and he infect the peple with iangelynge in the
chirche and talkynge, so that his olde sykenesse hauntyd hym ayen
bycause of his mysgydynge. And ȝit at the laste he fel to repentaunce
and axid forȝeuenesse of God and of Seynt Austyn. And then Seynt 250
Austyn praied for hym, and then he resseyvide perfite helthe as he
had byfore.

The .iiij.de day bifore the Nativite of Oure Lady is halowid the
Translacion of Seynt Austyn, in the whiche nyght a cytezyn of
Caunturburye beynge that tyme at Wynchester sawe heven open 255
ouer the chirche of Seynt Austyn and a brennynge laddyr schynynge
ful bryght and aungils | comynge downe to the same chirche, and alle f. 211ra
the monastery semyd as yt hadde be afyre of greet light that come fro
the laddyr, so that he merveyled what yt schulde mene, for he
vndyrstode nothynge of that translacyon of Seynt Austyn. And when 260
he knewe the trowthe and what it signyfied, þen he yaf laude and
preysynge to almyghty God and to his holy confessour for that
glorious sight etc.

There was also in the day of þe translacion .ij. enemyes vnable to
be reconsylid, for eche of them hadde slayn others fadyr. And when 265
they mette in the chyrche of Seynt Austyn, the oon wolde haue falle
vpon the tother, and they hadde no power too drawe there swerdys
within the chirche. And then they thought to goo owt at the chirche
dore, but when they come thedyr they hadde no power to goo out,
but there stodyn stylle as men amasyd. And then they ascryvid this 270
dede to the prayers of Seynt Austyn, and then everiche of them askid
mercy of oþere, and so they were made goode frendis and loved ever
aftir ful wele togedyrs as they had ben bretheren or as the fader and
the sone.

275 On the auter of Seynt Austyn ther felle a brennynge candylle, þe
which brente the space of .iij. foote vpon the myddis of the auter that
was ful richely dight, and that tyme the kepers were alle awey, and
by the myracle of Seynt Austyn it brent no ferther but cesid by
hymsylfe. And when the kepers come and sawe this they thonkid
280 God almyghty that by the merytis of Seynt Austyn hadde preservyd
f. 211rb them fro that merveillous and sodeyn aven|ture.

Also in a tyme a greete multitude of Danys assayled þe hous of
Seynt Austyn at Caunturburye, and for fere the [monkys] fledde
awey. And then oon of the felischip of Danys stale a palle fro the
285 auter of Seynt Austyn, and as he bare it awey to haue hidde it vndyr
a selle, then the clothe clevid so fast to hym as yt were hys owen
skyn, so that ther myght no man take it fro hym without they
schulde haue slayne hym. And when they sawe thys, then they were
sore aferde and wente to the tombe of Seynt Austyn and axyd
290 foryevenesse, promysynge þat þey wold resseyve cristendome. And
then anoon the clothe felle fro hym and then al they resseyvid the
feythe of Criste and were baptysed.

There was a merchaunt in Ingland that hyght by name Hagano
and his wife hight Emme, the whiche was greet wyth chylde and
295 many tymes in þe poynt of dethe that there cowde no man nor
womman promytte hyr lyf. And then aftyr in hyr slepe a feyre
archebisschop apperide to hyr and bad hyr do make a candylle of þe
mesure of hyr stature and of the mesure of the gretnesse of hyr bely
in the worschip of God and Seynt Austyn, and to sende it to the next
300 chirche that is halowyd in the worschip of hym and lete this candylle
brenne there, and sche schalle be made hoole of hyr sykenes and be
delyuered of hyr chylde wiþout eny perylle. And when sche was
awakyd sche commaundyd that thys visyon were fulfillid, and anoon
sche was delyuered of hyr chylde withowte eny perylle. |

f. 211va A wedowe there was that hadde but oon doughter of the age of
306 .viij. yere, the whyche mayde felle sodeynly dombe, the whiche was a
greet hevynesse to hyr modyr and sche ceesyd not to seke remedies
in visytynge holye placis. And at the last hyr gostly fadyr counseylid
hyr to vysyte the tombe of Seynt Austyn with fasting and wacchynge
310 and to be there in hir prayers alle the day and the nyght. And as the
monkys were at Matyns in the nyght, sche knelynge in hyr prayers
prayed ful hertly for hyr doughter, and sche prayed not in veyn, for
the mowthe of the seyde mayde was opened by myracle of the

283 monkys] monkyd

blessyd Seynt Austyn, and then sche spake clerly, praysyng God and
Seynt Austyn.   315

Also another mayde was dombe fro hyr byrthe. Aftyr that sche
had sought many holy placis, at þe last sche come to the tombe of
Seynt Austyn, and as hir frendys wacchydde alle the nyght in ful
devoute prayers abowte the tombe, and whan the monkis were at
Matyns and red the gospelle of the prophecie of Zachary, wherin is   320
made mencion how the mowthe of Zacharye was opened þe whiche
hadde be closyd a certeyn tyme by the power of God, and whan þat
clause was red thys maydes mowthe opened, and than sche spake
with a lowde voyce and seyde .iij. tymes: 'Lord, spare vs.' And when
they askyd hyr why sche seyde thoo wordys .iij. tymes, sche seyde   325
that sche se 'a man araied lyke an archebisschop, the which wold
haue put the ende of his crosse into my mowthe, and for fere it
causid me to sey tho wordys aforeseid.' And | aftyr that sche spake f. 211vb
right wele and perfytely, wherfor they ȝafe laude and preysynge to
God and to hys holy servaunte Seynt Austyn.   330

Three cytezyns of Caunturbury bought of tryars of syluer aschis
and swepynge awey of syluer, hopynge by þe wassching of the seyd
asschys they myght haue sum avayle by gaderynge thereof and
wynnyngis. This was doon in a towne where the iewyllers owyd
but lytille favour to the seyde merchauntys, and they put matyrs of 335
suspesyon vpon theym. And then they were atachyd by officers, and
they were cruelly ponysschid in prison with iron and with streyte
feters abowte theyr fete and manaclid faste by the hondys and
cheyned faste by the neckys and teyd to the walle of stoon. But .ij.
of them gate suretees, and for .xx.d they wer delyuered out of prison. 340
And the .iij.de was a semely yonge man but he had neyther money ne
cowde gete no borowes to helpe hym with, wherfor he was the more
cruelly ponysschid by grevous turmentys. And when he was in the
myddys of his sorewis he remembryd Seynt Austyn, and then he
cryed mekely to hym for helpe, and anoon by the stroke of a   345
thondyrclappe the house bygan to tremble so mervelously that the
fetyrs of his feet al tobrake and felle of, and his manaclis also. And
the walle that his necke was tyed to was alle toschake and in poynt to
falle downe, thys doon in the nyght. And on the morowe the kepers
come to the prison with myche peple of the towne, the whiche   350
merveylid gretely of this myracle. And they enquered of the prisoner
by whos | merytis this myracle schulde be schewyd. And the   f. 212ra
prysoner seide: 'Yt was doon by the meritis of Seynt Austyn.' And

then the kepers toke of hym for theyr fees the asschis that he hadde
355 bought of the argentoures and suffrid hym to passe freely whether
þat he wolde, wherfor he yaf lawde and preysynge to God and to this
holy Seynt Austyn for his delyueraunce oute of that greete duras etc.

Adelstanus the noble kyng of Ingland gadrid togedyr a navey of
schippys in the havyn of Sandwiche to diffende hym fro his enemyes,
360 the whiche purposyd to distroy his londe. And this noble kyng had
ful greet deuocion to Seynt Austyn and he lovyd ful wele the
Chirche of God. And as he rode to Sandewiche warde, he light
downe at Caunturbury purposynge to visite the holy place of Seynt
Austyn, and to aske counseyl of the abbot Alfenothus, the whiche
365 [prayed] the kynge to tary and dyne with hym. And then the kynge
grauntyd hym, for he was ful glad to talke with hym and that causyd
hym to tary and to dyne with hym. And bycause of his longe tarieng
oon of his princis waxe rebelle and stoburne ayenst the kynge and
prowdely and vngoodely callyd the kynge cowarde, and seyd that he
370 durst not mete with his enemyes or else he wold not tary so longe
there. And then the kynge, þat was ful meke in speryte, seyde to
hym: 'I am no coward, but I tary to here better counseil than thow
canst telle me, for it ys my wylle to overcome myn enemyes withowte
f. 212ʳᵇ blode schedynge.' And then the prowde prince | wolde take no hede
375 to the kyngis counseile, but seyde with an high sperite that he wolde
go forthe with suche peple as he hadde and sle alle his enemyes with
stronge honde. And so in greet wrath he departid fro the kynge and
toke his peple wiþ hym and rydde forthe owt of the towne. And
whan he came to an hille that is callid Chele Hille not ferre fro the
380 monastery of Seynt Austyns estwardes, there the wrath of God fille
vpon this prince. For as he stode amonge his men and lokid abowte
hym and he sawe the erthe open and a ful depe pyt within, and out of
the pytte ascendid an horrible fowle derkenesse that made hym and
al his men so agast that they wolde haue fledde, but they wyst not
385 whether. And as the prynce smote his horse with his sporis he fel
downe of his horse and brake his necke. And as the peple fled they se
the seide derkenes take vp the body of the prince and bare it into the
seide hole. And then the peple turned ayen to the kynge and told
hym al this by ordre. And when þe kynge herde it he seide with
390 mornyng chere: '*Dominus iustus concidet cervices peccatorum confun-*
dantur et conuertantur retrorsum omnes qui oderunt Syon,' that is to sey,
the rightwise lord schalle cutte downe the pride of synners, and alle
they that hate the Chirche schalle be confoundid and overturned

365 prayed] pray L

bakward. 'Loo,' seide the kynge, 'the rightwisnes of oure lord hathe
ponysschid this man bycause he hatyd and dispisid the holsome 395
counseile of the Chirche, and the counseile | also of Seynt Austyn f. 212ᵛᵃ
and of hys monkis, wherfor of riȝt he fallyth into curse that dispisith
to be blessid.'

In the towne of Norwiche þer was a preest whos name was callid
Wilfagus, the whiche byldyd a chirche in the worschip of Seynt 400
Austyn. And there was a riche man dwellyng þerbesyde þat more by
strenght than by right made a clayme to the grownd whereon this
chirche was byldyd, so that the preest myght not be in pees for þe
þretenynge and cryeng of þis riche man. And our lord seyng this his
grete coveytise toke awey hys mynde and made hym lyke an 405
vnresonable beest, so that he knewe neþere his owne goodes
neyþer oþere mennys. And then his frendys sought for remedye in
manye holy placis, but noon helpe myght be fownde. And at the laste
it fylle in theyr myndys to bring hym to the same chirche of Seynt
Austyn where he trowblyd so the preest, and there they wecchid in 410
prayers alle a nyght. And on the morowe whan he wakyd of his sleep,
he knewe hys frendys as wele as evere he dydde bifore, and he seyde
that he se an archebischop enter into the oratorye where he lay, and
with his touchynge he was made hoole.

In Leicetter in a chyrche of Seynt Austyn ther was an ankres, the 415
whiche had be closyd ther þe space of .xv. yeere, blynde and myght
se noothynge. And sche kepte alleweies þe bookis and the veste-
mentys of the chirche euery nyght, and euery mornynge sche
deliuered them ayen to the prestys. And at the last it plesyd
almyghty God to restore hyr sight ayen by the meritis of Seynt 420
Austyne, for she sawe hym in a | nyght appere to hyr in the lykenes f. 212ᵛᵇ
of an archebisschop with .ij. oþere bisschoppys ryally arayed for to
doo there devyne service. And on the morowe when a preste come to
haue his book and vestementis, he spake to hyr by signes lyke as he
vsyd to doo bifore, and then he se hyr byholde hym with an angelly 425
loke. And then sche tolde hym that sche myght se right wele. And
then sche and hyr curat thankyd almyghty God and holy Seynt
Austyn for þis greet myracle.

The wyfe of an artificer of the chirche of Seynt Albons kepte a
blynde womman for almis the space of .xvj. yeere, and yit this goode 430
artificers wyfe had ful lytil to take too, and yet sche kepte this blynde
womman of almis so long tyme that Seynt Austyn had pyte of this
goode wommans pouerte consyderynge hir goode wille to hyr in a

nyght in a vision, and bad hir take hir blynde womman with hir and
435 go to Caunturbery and visite hys tombe and sche schulde resseyve
hir sight. 'And as for your costis by the wey, God schal purvey for
yow sufficiently.' And whan sche awoke sche tolde this to the blynde
womman and then they were bothe right glad of thys tydynges. And
the next day they toke theyr iorney, and within schort tyme aftyr
440 they come to Cavnturbery to the tombe of Seynt Austyn, and ther
they made theyr prayers ful devoutly, and thys was in the day of his
translacion, and betwixe noone and Evensonge tyme sche was
restorid to hyr syght. And then alle the peple yaf laude and
preysynge to God and to Seynt Austyn for this greet meracle,
445 whos name be praysed world withoute eende. Amen.

31 ST BARBARA

This Life of St Barbara is based on the Latin Life by Jean de Wackerzeele, a Flemish Augustinian fl. 1370–1400.[1] The English text follows the Latin, but is a highly elaborated version rather than a translation, so that the Latin seldom throws light on instances where the two English MSS differ.[2] The heightened writing is especially apparent in the letters between Barbara and Origen, ll. 355–421, and 486–597 where the number of rhyming words suggests that these passages could be derived from a verse Life; but the only such Life known to us, *IMEV* 3994, in Bodleian Library, MS Rawl. poet. 225, is not their source. The Latin prose source of these passages, however, is in heightened language, with much repetition and word-play, the elaboration of which the English translator may have been trying to reflect by using rhymes. (See notes to ll. 355 and 486.)

---

[1] de Gaiffier (1959), Derolez (1991).
[2] We have consulted a microfilm of Brussels, Bibliothèque Royale MS 21003, cited as Br in the notes.

Here begynneth the lyfe of Seynt Barbara virgyn and
martyr of Crist and also of her kynrede in .xvj. chapiters.
And this is the fyrst folowynge.|

Dyvyne scripture and very trewe gospel of God makith pleyn   f. 251va
mencyon howe that owre swete savyoure Crist Ihesu, lord of alle
the worlde and hede of alle holy Chirch bothe above in heven and
here in erthe benethe, warned hys trew and feytheful servantys of
the manyfold persecucyons, trybulacions and diseases that they   5
schulde suffre for hys sake in tyme to come long and many a
daye before, to that entente that they schuld suffre theym the more
easely whan they came; and so for to comforte theym and make
theym the more strenger in suffrynge of suche persecucyons seyde
these wordys vnto theym: *Trademini a parentibus et amicis in mortem,*   10
the tyme schal come that ye for me be your owen fadris and frendes
to dethe [schal be putt].

     Thys was fulfyllid in the blessyd and glorious virgyne Seynt
Barbara ful surely while sche aftyr diverse turmentis and peynes was
behedid by her owen fadyr, and so graciously by martirdome passyd   15
owt of thys moste wrecchid lyf worldly, nowe reignyng with Criste in
everlastyng lyf, ioye and blysse of heven amongis alle aungilles and
seyntis, as schalle be declaryd nowe more dyffuselye. What tyme that
Alisaunder the emperoure of Rome callyd Alisaunder Aurelius, by
the meanes and praiours of Mammea his modyr, sesyd from   20
schedynge of cristen mennys bloode and was convertyd and turned
to cristen feithe in Pope Vrbans tyme the fyrst, whiche brought
many ful grete estate to the cristen | feith and martirdome and at the   f. 251vb
laste suffryd martirdome hymselfe, in whos daies also aboute the
contrey of Alisaunder that right famous and worschipful doctor   25

MSS LCo
     The Latin text referred to below as Br is Brussels, Bibliothèque Royale MS 21003.
     Co begins on f. 1: In the worshyp of oure lorde Ihesu Cryst and of his moste blessed and
glorius modere oure lady Seynt Mary, Saint Birgit, Seint Austeyn and of all the seintis of
heven, here begynneth the lyf and passion of the blessed virgyn and martyr Seint Barbare.
First of hir fadere and modere and of here holy name and conuersacion. And this in the
first chapter of this boke nowe folowynge vndire this forme *and continues as L.*
     In margin of L above the beginning of this Life, in a later hand, Sente Berbara virgyn and
martir of Christe.

     12 schal be/putt] *trsp.* L   22 tyme] dayes Co   23–4 and(2) . . . martir-
dome] *om.* Co

Orygene prechyd and taught the feith of Criste, as who sey over alle
the world moste specially aboute Alisaunder.

Than aftyr this seide moste cristen emperoure came oone
Maxymyan, Dyoclysian son, and succedid though yt were by
30 wronge enherytaunce. And he by his stronge honde and myghty
power, ayens decre and wylle of alle the senatours and lordes of
Rome, made hymselfe emperour and dyd moche sorowe and grete
hurte to the cristen peple for the hate that he hadde to Origen, and
alle for the convertyng of the seyde emperour Alisaunder his
35 predecessour vnto cristen feithe, and therefor he was the more
wooder and cruel ayenst men of holi Chirche. And so amonges other
he pursued Mammea, Alysaunder moder, and alle her householde
with moste cruelte and feersnesse, so that in hys dayes was passynge
grete persecucion and mordrement amonge cristen peple thorowe-
40 owte alle the worlde to the vtter destruccion of the feythe and
vndoyng of alle holy Chirche. And he myght haue had hys wylle, for
he comaundyd openly by his lawes þat wheresoevyr ony cristen man
or woman myght be fownde, anoon they schuld be put to dyverse
turmentis and peynes and at the laste withowte any grace or mercy
45 lese theyr [heedes].

And his cruel wodnes was so ferslye disposed and sette ayens the
f. 252ʳᵃ cristen peple that within a moneth of hys | reigne .xvij. thousand of
cristen peple were mordred and slayn. Wherefor by the rightwisse
iugement of God suche a manqueller myght not lyve halfe his dayes,
50 but within the .iij.de yeere of hys reigne he deyed a myschevous
dethe lyke as a wrecche of ylle disposision schuld do. Netheles
whyles he thus cruelly reigned in hys empyre, in the parte of the
worlde aboute Egipte was a greete duke, a noble and a riche, sauf he
was a paynyme and a worschipper of idolles, oone clepyd Dyoscorus.
55 And thys duke dwellyd in a cite of Egipt clepyd Solys, to the whiche
cite, as some [storyns] say, Ioseph with our lord Ihesu and our
blessyd lady Marye hys modyr fledde for fere of Herode whan he
pursued Crist in tyme of hys byrthe. Of the whiche cite Isaie the
prophete spekith fulle clerely in his boke of prophecie the [.xix.]
60 chapitre. And as some storye seythe also, this cite was somtyme
clepid Nichomedia, bicause that oone Nichomede kynge of Bytomy

29 succedid . . . yt] succesyd yf Co   40–1 of the feythe/and vndoyng] trsp. Co
45 heedes] goodes L, et ad vltimum capitali sententia Br   51 of . . . disposision] om.
Co   52 in the] add Est Co   56 storyns] storyes L, historiographorum Br
57 fere] drede Co   59 .xix.] om. with space for insertion of numeral L
60 storye] storyns Co

belded it and made it vp of his owne coste and so calde it aftyr his
owne name, as the vse and maner of greet lordys is.

This seide duke was a passyng grete pursuer of cristen peple. And
he was not callyd Dyscorus for nought, for this name Discorus is as 65
moche to saye as favoure or worschip of goddys. And so he was a
favowrer and worschiper of false goddys, wherein he sett alle hys
delyte and ioye. This name also Discorus cometh of this worde Dya,
whiche is as moche to sey as twoo or tweyne, and of thys worde
Scorus, | whiche is as moche to sey as abhomynacion or hate, for so f. 252rb
he was abhomynable and hateful in two dyverse waies, that is to saye 71
bothe to God and to man: to God for hys ydolatrie and infidelite in
cruelle pursuynge of cristen peple; to man for ayenst al manhode,
nature and kynde he behedyd [his] owne doughter, as it aftyr schal
be declaryd. þis duke hadde a noble lady and a quene to his wife 75
clepid Pya, whiche pryvely in her sowle, though sche were no cristen
womman, yet after her name Pya sche was pitevous and hadde pite
vpon cristen peple and folowed cristen feythe. And aftyr the seynge
of sum storyes, sche came of þe same stokke and progenye that oure
lady came of, howebeyt that sche was weddyd to an hethen man. And 80
by her thys duke opteyned the crowne and was made kynge, but aftyr
her decesse for his cruelte he hadde noon advayle of his kyngdome
safe oonly a name withowte a prophite, as many haue in these dayes.

Netheless these two grete astates, by the specyalle grace and
worchyng of God, had a doughter betwene them so feyre, so 85
semely, so sadde and so lovely a creature to loke vpon that al that
sawe her merveyled of her beaute, for they sawe never noon so feyre
a lady in tho dayes byfore. And this feyrenes God endewed her with
al, it is to suppose that the owteward fayrenes of the body schuld be
an evident signe and token of the inward feyrenes of the sowle. 90

This yonge lady by the wyse providence of God was clepyd | Barbara, f. 252va
whiche is as moche to sey after interpretacion as straunge, for sche
keped her self straunge and clene from the worschypynge of idols
and veyn goddys worscheped amonge the hethen people, and gave
her oonly to the worschippe of oo God and to the loue of oure moste 95
blessyd lorde and saviour Crist Ihesu, verray God and man, whom
sche loved specially aboue alle thynge and toke hym for her maker.

63 owne] *om.* Co   65 Dyscorus] *add* not L   74 his] *om.* L   *In
margin of L, level with* l. 81 And by her thys duke *is a four line verse, the first line of which
appears to be in the hand of the marginal insertion above the beginning of the life.* hope well and
have well / so it maye fall / But hope not to myche / and at last lose all.   86 so
lovely] lowly Co

And so thys name Barbara is as moche to sey also as the doughter of
whete or the doughter of corne, for so by trewe feythe and beleve
100 and love of God was the doughter of oure lord Ihesu Crist, [whiche]
in holy scripture lykneth hymselfe to corne and seith: 'But yf the
corne be caste in the erthe yt growith not nor multiplyeth not.' For
whan he was caste down in the erthe by the Iewes in tyme of his
passyon, than gan hys name and his doctryne to growe and multiplie
105 amonge cristen peple be trewe feythe and bileve, and nowe ys
knowen for the moste parte thoroweowt alle the worlde. So that
like as it is the propurte of every goode chylde naturally to folowe the
condicions of the fadyr, right so thys holy virgyne was the veray
folower of our lord Ihesu Criste in suffryng of martirdome, bitter
110 payne and passyon for his sake, takynge hym for her cheef fader
before alle creaturys in the worlde. And thowgh sche came of the
hethen by the fadyr syde, yet after the decesse of the quene Pya her
f. 252ᵛᵇ moder, most cristianly as a lylye among thornes | and breres grewe
and encresed from vertu [to vertu and kept the clennesse of
115 virgynyte] and chastyte bothe of sawle and body right vertewesly
alle the dayes of her lyf, with alle other vertuous condicions and
maners.

Here begynneth the secunde chapiter howe this glorious
virgyne Seynt Barbara was set to scole and within a lityle
120 while came to grete cunnyng and by manyfolde resons and
dyvers argumentis sche came to the knowlech of almyghti
God Ihesu Criste.

Whan this yonge lady was set to the scole be her fader too lerne, and
there was riȝt besy for to come vnto vndirstondynge of letture and
125 within a litil while sche came to right grete cunnynge, at the laste the
eeyen of her sowle opened and lightned by the specialle grace of
God. As sche oftentymes after the custume of the gentyls came to
the idols temples and there sawe dyvers ymages of men purtreyed
and made by mannes hande and worschipped of the peple as goddys,
130 anoon sche bygan wisely and warely to aspye what this wikkid
erroure and supersticion mente, nor never wolde leve nor sese tylle
sche came to the knowleche of the truthe.

99 by] she be Co   100 whiche] *om.* L   101 seith] faith Co
112 hethen] *add* peple Co   the(1)] her Co   the(3)] *add* good Co   114-15 to . . .
virgynyte] *om.* L   123 this] *add* fayre Co

Vpon a day when sche came into oone of these sayd templis and
there sawe þe peple do so grete worschip to idols and mawmetes,
anoon sche bigan to aske many questions and seide to them that there   135
were present: 'Howe say ye, syrs? What be alle these fayre
symylitudes of men, and what meneth this that ye thus worschyppe
theym?' 'Pease,' seyde they, 'and calle theym not to symylitudes of
men but sy|mylitudes of goddes, [for they be goddes and wylle be   f. 253ra
worschiped as goddes,] and as a thynge seyen and not knowen, for   140
though they seme men to our sight yit they ben verray goddys in
dede.' 'Why,' quod sche, 'were not these men sumtyme whom ye
nowe worschip as goddes?' 'Yis,' seyde they, 'men they were as we
be. But they were a grete dele bettyr than we and hadde power to do
here in erthe what they wolde as goddes.' 'Wele,' seide sche, 'yit   145
haue I not myn entente and desyre. Yef these be goddes as ye say
they be, I wolde fayne know how many there be of theym in nombre
in þe world and what theyr names be, for no man worschipeth a
thynge vnknowen and nothynge is knowen but by his name.' 'O fayre
lady,' seyde they, 'this is a straunge question of yow and nede not be   150
asked, for ther be so many of theym in the worlde that neyther there
names ne nombre may wele be knowen for the grete multitude of
theym, while oone is worschipid in this place, annother in that place,
yche of theym after þat men haue devosion and desire vnto theym.
Netheles for as moche as ye desyre to knowe the nombre and names   155
of the greet multitude, we schal reken vp a fewe vnto yow of theym,
that when ye knowe theym it schal suffice yow in worschippynge of
theym to worschip alle withowt any knawlege of moo.'

'First among the Egipcians in Egipt oone clepid Vsis was
worschiped for theyr god. After hym amonge the Cretes Iubiter,   160
amonge the Romaynes Quyrynus, amonge the Mawrynce Iuba,
amonge the Latynes Faunus, amonge the Attenys Mynerva,
amonge the Sames Iuno, | amonge the Paphyns Clitera, amonge   f. 253rb
the Nemyns Volcanus, among the Iraxyns Liber, amonge the
Epiromis Ceres, amonge the Lyddyns Appollo, amonge the Eristans   165
in Troy Neptunus, so that whosoever knowe thees, by theym schal
he come to the knowleche of moo after whos proporcions these be
ordeyned and made.' 'Ye,' seide sche, ' "Be these ordeyned and made
after theyr proporcions." I vndirstonde not halfe aright what thys
meneth that ye sey "thees be ordeyned and made after theyr   170

138 not to] no Co   139–40 for . . . goddes] om. L   142 quod] seid Co
157 that . . . theym] om. Co   162 amonge(2) . . . Mynerva] om. Co

proporcions." If they be ordeyned and made, then schuld yt seme well that they be no veray goddys of theymselfe but rather after mannes opynyon. I wolde fayne knowe therefor,' sche sayde, 'what thys meneth that ye say "thees be ordeyned and made after the

175 proporcion of other goddes."' 'O madame,' seyde they, 'we see welle ye muse greetely vpon our goddes that we say thees be ordeyned and made after the proporcions of oother goddes. But forsothe ye nede not to muse so moche as ye doo, for thys ordynaunce and makyng is so grete and so merveilous in hymsilfe that and it myght be

180 expressed it schulde be vnleful for anybody to denye or sey they be no goddes.'

Of these wordes therefor this holy virgyne Seynt Barbara hadde grete wondre, and day and nyght had grete musynge in her mynde howe this myght be that thees idols were goddys thus ordeyned and

185 made by mannes hande. And the more sche musyd therevpon the
f. 253ᵛᵃ more was sche combered within herselfe, notwith|stondynge sche asked counseyle of grete philosophers and lerned men in the lawe.

And thof sche were a paynym and an hethen womman, yit sche by the special light of grace geven to her of God sche founde by her

190 owen wytte and natural reason howe yt was oone to be veray God in hymselfe not made by mannes honde, and that made and vnmade myght never stande togeder vnyversally in alle parties, but nedys that oon muste be trewe and that oother vntrewe, so that by this reason sche vnderstode and perseyved welle that moche peple of the worlde

195 were in grete erroure for lakke of knowlege of hym that ys veray God.

Herto also forthermore sche began for to lay forthe oother reasons and to argue with herselfe and seide thus: 'If men be oure goddys as I am enformed they be, than schulde it folowe me semeth thereby that

200 goddes muste nedes be borne into the worlde as men be and passe owte of this worlde ageyn be dethe as men doo, for no man is there in the worlde but that first he is borne and than at the laste he passeth owte of the worlde by dethe. But for to say God is borne or deide, me semeth it is ayenst alle reason, for the godhede is a thynge as me

205 semeth that neyther hathe begynnynge nor endynge, but man hathe a begynnyng and an endynge and therfor he may not be God. Also man hathe his begynnyng of the erthe, whiche was made or he. Yif man therfor made of erthe schuld be God, it schuld folowe that God

175 proporcion] porcions Co   176 muse] muste Co   goddes] wordes Co
183 had grete] lay Co   191 honde] *om.* Co   202 worlde] *add* ayeyn Co

schuld have a begynnynge, that is to sey the erthe, | and by this   f. 253vb
reason schuld I calle the erthe God rather than man, for the erthe   210
was made or man. Also the erthe is neyther of hymselfe, neyþer the
water nor the fyre nor the eyre nor noon of alle the .iiij. elementis be
of theymselfe, neyther the fyrmament above is of hymself, but rather
after the sentence of philosophres that trete of nature al these be
creaturis and made. And so ys man also, and hath a parte of al .iiij.   215
elementis. Wherefor it muste nedis be concludyd by alle these resons
þat oon there is the maker of alle these whiche was in hymself
essencially before eny creature [was made, he beynge hymselfe no
creature nor] made, but rather the maker of alle creaturis, and therfor
yf any schulde be God propurly it schulde be he. Hym therefor   220
certeynly, withowt that I knowe more than I know yit, schal I seke
with al my herte and that right besyly. And my devoure schal I doo
yf I may haue grace to come to hys knowlege by any meane and that
ful diligently, for I trust and byleve verely that he ys verey God
aloone and no mo but he as it ys.   225

'Also yt may be schewed by many other dyuers resons, for and he
were not oone alone there schulde never be so goode accorde
betwene creaturis as there ys. Howe schuld the sunne, the moone,
the sterres and oother planetes kepe theyre contynuel course but yf
there were oone to rule them never chaungeable in hymself, ever of   230
oo wylle? If there were twoo or thre goddes, than me semeth that
oone schulde seye: "Go forthe," that oother schulde seye: "Stonde
stylle." And so they | schulde ever be at variaunce and chaungeable   f. 254ra
in wille, but chaungeablenesse is not in his creaturis. Wherefor it
appereth welle that he is allewey oone and ever of oo wylle,   235
disposyng alle thynge as it plesith and likyth his mageste, the
planetes to kepe her mevable course aboue, þe erthe to be stabylle
with his propurtees benethe, the eyre to be dyuers, the water to be
moiste, the fyre to be hote, and every thynge after hys kynde to do
what it is ordeyned too, alle be oone assent and accorde after his   240
propurte. Howe schuld þe worlde endure so longe and kepe so goode
acorde and certeynty in his variauncis or variacions betwene the day
and the nyght for to haue the sunne schynynge in the day tale, the
mone in the nyght tale, hote in somer, colde in wynter, a mene

211–12 the . . . alle] neyther the erthe neyther the fyr nor non of Co   213 rather] om.
Co   218–19 was . . . nor] not L   220 propurly] add me semeth Co   Hym]
om. Co   225 Co punctuates after he   232 schulde seye] om. Co
233 ever] om. Co   234 but] add this Co   242 varauncis or] om. Co

245 betwene bothe in hervest and in veer, the lond to kepe his boundys,
the see to kepe hys boundys, but if there were oo lorde and oo God
to rule theym alle after his owen entente and wille? If there were so
many goddes in the worlde as men make by theyr errour and vanyte,
than so goode accorde betwene creaturis myght ther never be.

250 'Oo God therfor withowte any moo qvestyons I beleve verely that
there ys, whiche bereth not the worlde vpon his schuldres as a man
overladen with a byrthen, or rulyth it by astronomye or be rennyng
of sterres, nowe forward now bakwarde, as semed the grete astronomyar Athlaus to do, whiche for his greete cunnynge was supposid
f. 254ʳᵇ to rule the sterres and bere alle the worlde | vpon his backe. But by
256 his owne vertu, power and strength he holdiþ vp and conteyneth all
thynge wiþin hymselfe and rulith yt more easely withowt comparison
than a man wolde rule the leste peyre of balaunce or any other
thynge with the leste fynger of his hande, to whom alle thynge oweth
260 to obey, to drede and to worschip both aboue and benethe, in
hevene, in helle and in erthe.'

Aboute suche maner of thoughtis thys right wytty and glorious
virgyne Seynt Barbara in her childehode whiles sche was yonge and
wente to scole sette her herte and mynde. And by suche resons of
265 natural philosophie whiche sche lerned and hadde right excellently,
and by the grace of the holi goste moste specially, at the laste sche
came vnto hevenly philosophie whiche stondith in knowlege of hym
that is verray God and in consideracion of hys werkis. When sche
therefor here with alle hadde redde the feire fables and feyned
270 lesyngis of dyvers poetes and hadde overswomen the depe see of
Aristotille and Plato is bokis, than sche sighed and within herself
saide: 'Alas for sorowe, why lakked these grete philosophres the
knowlege of veray God and hadde so grete wyttes gyven to theym?'
And whan sche sawe the lyves of theym that were holden for goddis
275 amonge the peple wreten here and there in bokis and paynted alle
abowte the walles in the temple, sche prevely in her mynde behilde
theym, discussid them, repreved theym and as a moste rightwyse
f. 254ᵛᵃ iuge condempned theym as | for nought, havyng this consideracion
allewey within herselfe and seiyng thus: 'If the lawe condempne
280 theym to be hanged and put to the dethe þat slee theyre [owne]
faders, than was Iubiter worthy to be hanged for he kylled the fader
of Saturne. Howe therefor may he be called god that dyd suche a
wyckid dede and bi the lawe was worthy to be dede hymselfe? Eyther

254 do] *om.* Co   256 strength] myght Co   280 owne] *om.* L

the lawe muste erre or ellis Iubiter errid, or ellis it is leful for goddes
oonely to slee theyre [owne] fadres and haue this prerogatyfe to 285
theymselfe for to do as cursidly as they liste and be not punyssched,
and so to kepe within theymselfe bothe eqvyte and iniquyte. Howe
[was yt] leful to Iovis for to defoile his owen sustyr and to haue so
manye concubynes when men suffre not suche a wyckid dede to go
vnpunyssched? Therfor either the lawe [is] nought or elles these 290
goddys be not. But the lawe wele I wote is goode, and therfor these
goddys be nought that were not aschamed to do so cursyd and
wycked dedys. Wherefor it is passand grete merveyle to me howe
men can thynke that these be goddis whiles they lefte no wycked
deede vndo behynde theym.' 295

Suche and many other argumentis like this sadde and welle
advised holy and blessid virgyne made by herselfe in the courte
[and] counseil howse of her sawle, and allewey kepte her counseile
pryve to herselfe, and herewith also as often tyme as sche was stered
by her fader to go too the temples of the seyde idolles sche wente 300
with body but not with | herte. And whan sche sawe the pepille, as f. 254vb
welle the lordes as the comynalte, knele and bowe theyr hedys to
stokkes and trees, metal and stones, sche thought it was a fulle
wycked vsage and supersticion and right a blynde devosyon. Than
forthermore sche bethought herselfe howe sche myght behaue her to 305
wynde awey from theym if it come to her lotte to do the same as they
dyd. Thought sche: 'Schalle I knele or schal I wrestelle there ayenste
and not knele? Schal I, that am sensible and haue witte and reson and
may fele and vnderstonde, knele and worschip theym that be
insensible, or schal I, that may bothe here, speke and se, smelle, 310
handel and goo, worschip theym that may do noon of alle these? But
thofe they seme men, yit they be noon. What schal I do? And if I
knele not before theym, what schalle I answere to theym þat aske of
me why I knele not? Yif I knele with my body and not with my herte,
what schal it advayle me or what schalle it hurte me? Nowe verely I 315
wote never what is beste to do. But and yf I hadde oones the
knowlege of hym that is veray God wolde I leve alle this crafte and
for hys sake dispise alle straunge goddys and oonely holde me to hym
and worschip hym.'

And so amonge al suyche agonyes and many dyvers conflictis thys 320

285 owne] owre L   288 was/yt] trsp. L   290 is] om. L   291 goddys]
om. Co   298 and(1)] of L   299 also] om. Co   306 wynde] wende
Co   308 haue] om. Co   320 suyche] add grete Co

holy and discrete virgyne wiste never what was beste to do. But yit
thof sche were yonge and lusty of age, allewey sche made the body
subiecte to the speryte and kepte her virgynyte for the grete desyre
f. 255ra that sche had after the knowlege of God, whiche | alwey reigned in
325 her sawle, overcame and quenchid clene alle maner of batayle and
inordynate lustes and steryngis of the flessche.

The .iij.e chapitre tellith of the lettre þat Seynt Barbara wrote
vnto Origen for to haue the more open knowlege of God.

After thys came preysable [tythynges] to the sayde cyte of
330 Nychomede, how there was right a wyse and a famous doctor, oone
clepid Origen, in Alysaunder, and he was so excellent a clerke in
schewynge and declarynge of hym that is veray God that no
philosophyer myght withstonde hym nor seye ayenste hym, Stoykis
nor [perypatetykis], that he commandyd and preved by open ensam-
335 ples oo God to be verely and no moo, confoundyng the false and veyn
worschip of idols and mawmettys. And whan these [tythynges] ran
abrode and came to Seynt Barbara is eere, sche was ful glad and mery
in her sawle, and alle her sorowe began to passe and drawe faste to an
eende. Than sche bethought herselfe with wise deliberacion howe and
340 by what meane sche myght come by the informacion of thys seyde
doctor, alwey beyng aferde in her mynde to schewe or telle Dioscorus
the kynge her fadyr the prevy counseilis of her herte. For sche sawe
hym so fervently abowte the worschipynge of his goddes that sche
durste nat yit displese hym, specially for he had no mo chyldren but
345 her aloone, but more specially for he hadde made a vowe to kepe her
chaste and gyf her to oone of the goddes of Veste, that sche schuld do
f. 255rb worschip and service | to her alle her lyf dayes and lyve in chastite, and
so it semeth welle that sche dredde to displese her fader more for
brekyng of chastite than for anythynge els. Whan therefor sche wyste
350 never howe to doo, for sche cowde fynde no trusty man to open her
counseile to, at the laste sche made a lettre to this saide worschipful
doctor Origene dwellyng in the seyde contrey of Alisaundre, and by
this lettre sche opened vnto hym alle the previtees of her hert vnder
this fourme that folowith.
355   'Dyscrete and right noble Fadyr, bothe in name and fame, dew

327 tellith] om. Co   329 tythynges] thynges L, rumore laudis Br
334 perypatetykis] ypatetykis L, peripateticorum Br   336 tythynges] thynger L
346 goddes of] add one cleped the godde of the Co   353 this] om. Co

reverence and worschip be vnto yow of suche a symple mayden as I am. For as moche as I here and vndirstond that ye be the worschiper and schewer of hym that ys veray God whom my desyre is to knowe, I beseche your holy fadirhode to accepte me at this tyme and to helpe me nowe in my desyre. This hath ben my desyre alwey from the 360 tyme that I came to the yeres of discrecion, to knowe God and to worschip hym oonly and to serve hym with devocion. Goddis haue I seen many oone, so for too speke after mannes opynyon, but fayned and false haue I founde them everichone by prefe and trew argument and right reason. Figures of men also have I beholde, made bothe of 365 sylver and of golde, and som of stone and tree, but these wele I vnderstonde that neyther they may go nor stonde nor haue the leste sensible lyf that a creature hath in any degre, and made never so welle thof they be of golde or of syluer or of any | other mater be it f. 255va never so vile or precious, yet wele I wote other than they be made of 370 schalle they never be nor bettyr, and so the selfe trowþe techith vs. Wherefor my commyng to theym hath not be to worschip or do them reverence, but rather to come to knowlege of theym by more pleyn and open evidence, and thus experience hath enformed and taught me that al suche figures insensible be and neyther may fele, speke, 375 here nor se nor helpe theymselfe nor theyr worschipers, whatsoever they be.

'Questions also haue I asked dyvers and many if these were men so worschipped for goddes, and it was answered to me right strangely that men they were and lyved theyre lyves ful greetly amysse. Than 380 me thought it openly expressed that these were false goddes of men so worschipped, and gessyd that man with begynnynge and endynge myght never be veray God and so wykked in levynge, for I can perceyve noone other wyse in my mynde but God is he that ever hathe be [and ever schalle be], worlde withowten eende. And tyme be 385 made, as me semeth it is, than is he God certeynly that hathe made tyme and before alle tyme ys. But man wele I wote was made in tyme, and of right schorte tyme he is. Therfor to say þat man is God me semeth it gretely amysse. Never therefore wille I beleve whyles I haue right wytte and mynde that dedely man ys God and hathe so 390 schorte an eende. Nevertheles in many thynges I stande in right grete dovte, and in my sawle often tymes I have right grete merveyle and

356 mayden] handmayden Co
368 made] make Co   373 to(2)] be Co
om. L   387 tyme ys] tymes Co

367 they may go] goo may they Co
378 if] of Co   385 and . . . be]

f. 255vb wonder | howe God hathe made the worlde and rulith it alle aboute and yit from mannes knowlege is so ferre asondre. For man ys so

395 blyndid by ydolatrye, wylful maners and wikkid supersticion that God his maker he lettyth goo by and loveth hym in maner of season. But hym verely ever haue I loved, for he hathe made me, or ellis I am deseyved, and my lyf to me hath grauntyd and hiderto thus graciously me hathe guyded. To hym therefor haue I made myn

400 advowe that thus my lyf to me wolde leen never to cese to I hym knowe and it may be by aany meane. Wherefor to yowe now, worschipful fader of so grete name and [fame], me thynkith beste to open my herte in the begynnynge of thys frame and let yow knowe howe lothesom I am of these vayn goddes be lettre, where as I may

405 not speke to yowr faderhode by mowthe nor expresse myn entent no bettyr, that so by your fadirly informacion alle feeres and dowtes putte clene awey from me I myght come to his knowlege and cognycion and so [do] service to his high maieste, for ye haue knowlege of hym and it be as it is tolde me. Wherefor nowe I beseche

410 your faderhode as lovly as I can that ye take awey thys derke and blak clowde of ignoraunce from me and brynge me to that bright light schynyng of knowlege that ye haue. For hym that ys veray God I wolde knowe ful fayne, whiche alle thynge bothe seen and vnseen hathe made after his entent, whether he be verely oone or ellys

415 tweyne, lyke as I before haue preved by manyfolde and dyverse
f. 256ra resons and argumentis. | Who also he is, howe goode and howe excellent, I pray yow hertely to open vnto me. And let worde be sente to me by messenger if ye can thynk me ever worthy in your famyliarite. And that lorde whom thus I love and sette my truste and

420 bileve in, preserue yow in helthe of sawle and body to his pleasure and worschip everlastynge. Amen.'

This lettre Seynt Barbara, whan sche hadde founde a man sche cowde sadly truste to ful wisely and warely, sente it forthe to the seyde doctour Origen dwellyng in the seide cite of Alisaunder. And,

425 for thees two citees Alisaunder and Nichomede were right ferre in sondre, sche stode ever in grete fere and hevynesse for her messenger lest, eyther by any infortune, eyther by eny sikenesse or adversyte, eyther by any oother sodeyn case þat myght falle vpon hym by the

393 alle] om. Co   396 lettyth] add hym Co   in] add no Co   400 leen] leue Co   402 fame] name L   406 bettyr] letter Co   408 so] om. Co do] to L   416 resons and] om. Co

weye, her purpose and desyre schulde be lette and come to noon
effecte and perfit eende. Wherfor sche wepte many tymes and ofte   430
and contynuelly prayed for her messenger and sayde thus: 'Lorde
God, whose love and desire of knowlege hathe been with me so
longe, Lord, whom I beleve to be God oonely withowt felawe and
peer, Lorde, in comparison of whose maieste and power alle goddes
that mannes blyndenes worschippeth be nought and wronge, Lorde,   435
whiche lightnes mannes herte or thow come therto þat it schuld se
and feele the whan thowe comest, Lorde, whiche haste made me to
desire the or ever I herde of the, and be natural reason hast brought
me from the vnwisdom of idols to thy wisdom in parte and knowlege
of thyselfe, Lorde, and these thoughtis and fervente desires | whiche f. 256rb
I haue and feele be of the, or and yf it plese thy goodenesse thus   441
thyselfe to schewe to me, now guyde and kepe the messenger whom I
haue sente to thy servaunte. I beseche the that neyther he nor I never
dye tylle I haue worde of my desyre whiche I haue and labour aftyr
so besylye.'   445

The .iiij. chapitre of the lettre þat Origen wrote vnto Seynt
Barbara for to enforme her the more openly in knowlege of
the Godhede and blessyd Trynyte.

Longe continuaunce and perseueraunce hadde in praier and vertuous
lyvynge, this holy virgyn Seynt Barbara beganne to fayn herselfe   450
syke as to the estimacion of her fadyr Dioscorus, because he schuld
not knowe her counseile nor whereaboute sche was besy and labored
by herselfe. The whilste schortly to saye, the messenger came into
Alisaundre and fonde this fulle wise clerke before rehersed, Origen,
within the [palace] of that worschipful matrone and lady Mammea   455
the modyr of Alisaunder the emperour, as in the begynnynge more
openly it is expressid, where he founde hym ful besily occupied in
techynge of this lady and her howseholde cristen faythe and religion.
And whan he hadde doon his message and delyvered Seynt Barbara
lettre to Origen and he hadde redde it over and vnderstode it, anoon 460
he was so merye and so gladde within hymselfe that forthewith he
felle downe and kissed the grounde for ioye and gaf thankyngis and
praysyngis to God, whiche of his infinite goodenesse hadde [raysid]
suyche a | womman from the harde stony errour and mysbileve of f. 256va

44 haue and] *om.* Co   452 labored] a lorde Co   455 palace] place L,
palatium Br   463 raysid] resseyvid L, *suscitauerat de saxo* Br

465 hethen peple and brought her so mercifully vnto the moste stedfast
feith and bileve of cristen peple, herewith endewyng her so largely
with his grace and mercy.

Then he wolde nott hyde this lettyr from the saide lady Mammea
but anoon he schewyd it openly vnto her and to her meyne, and then
470 he commendid the merveilous feythe of this virgyne vnto theym.
Than they magnyfied God more specially that to his chosen and
feythefulle lovers dothe so gracyouslye. Than he exortyd theym to
make theyr hertys more stedfast and stable in cristen feithe and
beleve by the ensample of suych an hethen womman. And than he
475 steryd theym to have more fervente love and charyte in theyre sawlys
to God and to theyr even cristen, and confermed theym and made
theym so fervente in the love of God that aftyr that tyme wolde they
never seke other nor worschip other god but whom þis hethen
womman sought and worschipid so wilfully and with so grete
480 besynesse and stody. Than also forthermore this noble doctor and
right sadde fader in grete haste began to write ayeyn to thys seyde
holy virgyne, and in his lettre fulle wittely and clerely like a man of
holy Chirche and Cristes lawe and loore answered to euery poynte
that sche desired to knowe in her lettre before, as now it folowith
485 vndir þis fourme.

'Ryght devoute doughter in owre lorde Ihesu Crist, veray God and
f. 256vb man, whom I am servaunt to bothe day | and nyght and contynuelly
worschip and preche after my power thof I be vnworthy, that lorde I
besech most high of power and myght as hertly as ever I can to kepe
490 and preserve yow bothe sawle and body in goode helþ and prosperite. The werkys of God ever merveyllous and newe to hys trewe
servauntis be alwey cause of new ioy and gladnes, and make many
oone þat never before hym knewe to haue in hym right wondirful ioy
and swetnesse. Who ever harde or cowthe thynke yt trewe any
495 hethen man or womman so enspired with God and his grace for to
turne from hethen peples errour by hymself, and after cristen feithe
so wilfully to sue, and myght nott wele mervayle of so wondirful a
case? Varely devoute sawle, right fewe or noon hadde ever this grace
geven to hem of God so soveraynly withowte a mayster in knowlege
500 of God to folowe thys trace in esspecialle and he were oones
encombred in the snare of ydolatrye. But ye lakke nothynge els
nowe, as be your wrytyng is expressid, sauf oonely more openly to

482 clerely] clerkly Co   492 make] *om.* Co   494 cowthe] knoweth Co
497 sue] sowe Co, *declinare* Br   wondirful] worder full Co   498 ever] neuer Co

knowe who and howe goode and excellent he is. Who he is ye knowe
ful welle, for þat lesson in partye have ye lerned afore by his
auctorite, but that and other schalle I nowe teche yow more 505
openly after that I fele, and this in as fewe wordes as I can, be
suych lefe as [he] thereto wille graunte me.

'This name God, therefor, is a name by hymselfe betokenyng a
synguler substaunce, and suych a synguler substaunce, doughter.
And so I wille ye vndirstonde me that no man therto hymselfe schuld 510
presume to avaunce, for no man | may be callyd God propurly but f. 257ʳᵃ
oonly he. Be the whiche lesson, though it be schorte, yit may ye
vndirstonde and se that this name God is godly and makith alle
thynge in every degree, and knoweth it in hymselfe or ever it be, and
loveth alle thynge that he hathe made ful syngulerly and welle. This 515
name God also, for to speke after the Grekes and more openly, ys as
moche to sey as "I beholde or se", for so God alle thynge beholdeth
and seeth in hymselfe ful certeynly, and nothynge may be hydde
from his sight and godly mageste.

'Forthermore I wille that ye knowe for more certeynte and open 520
evidence that this name God is sumtyme as moche to sey as "I
renne" or "I swyftely goo", for so God as who say alwey renneth,
and so swifte is he that in every place over alle and ever lyke soone he
is present, and so but he may be no moo, not that in his rennynge he
meveth fro place to place as we doo, but by this rennynge is 525
vnderstode that by presencial power he rewlith alle thynge mevable
and vnmevable, and herewith merveylously disposiþ alle thynge in
his fourme in suych wyse and so that in hymself he is alwey oone and
in hys werkys vnchaungeably stedfast and stabille. Other names there
be many oone þat longe to his excellence and highnes, as for to calle 530
hym myghty, greete, goode, large, everlastynge, and suych other
lyke, whiche betokeneth noþyng ellys in hym the trowthe to expresse
but that he is the selfe myght, the self goodenesse, the self ever-
lastyngnes, and so forthe of alle other longe to declare or speke.

'Besyde hym | therfor propurly noon may be callyd goode, greete, f. 257ʳᵇ
high or myghty, for alle such terms withowt accedentalle qualite or 536
quantyte to hym been impropred moste specially, and never may he
be other than he is in noo degree, for he passith all qualitees and
quantitees moste excellently. And what schal I say more of thys

507 he] ye L *ipse* Br   512 ye] *add* bothe Co   513 se] shee Co
and(2)] euery dele and that god Co   515 thynge that] that euere Co
532 ellys] *om.* Co   539 schal] *om.* Co   thys] his Co

540 godhede and mageste while it passeþ mannes wytte to speke of so
high dyvynyte? And I calle hym goode, the selfe goodenesse and
moste beste he ys. And I calle hym myghty, the self myght and
moste myghty he is. And I calle hym wyse, the selfe wisdome and
moste wyse he ys. And I calle hym vertuous, the selfe vertu moste
545 vertuous he is. And schortly to sey, no name may he be callyd by that
goode is, but that he hathe alle the propurtees therof moste
soveraynly and withowte any mysse. As ensamples therfor alle
suche names and callyngis of God be put vnto vs that we be
thaym sumwhat schuld vndirstonde howe goode he ys, howe
550 excellent and howe vertuous, and that he in his werkis is ever
oone withowt felowe and peere alwey poste alone.

'Moreover now I pray yowe take goode hede to me and oo lesson
schal I brynge to mynde, and this is the knowlege of the blessyd
Trenyte whom in yowre lettre I can notte fynde. The Trenyte
555 certeynly is he that oo God is in persones .iij., alle of oo nature and
oo kynde, fader, son and holi goste thus named they be. Be wisely
ware of my wordes and se them welle to the ende. These .iij. lyke as
f. 257ᵛᵃ they be oo God in substaunce, | right so in persones they be verely
.iij., and yet as oo God they be to be hadde in worship and
560 reverence, for as oo God alle .iij. be knyt togeder in power
vnyversally and never may be departyd in godhede thof they be
depertyd in persone, nor never owght to be called of vs .iij. goddes or
.ij., for than it were likly that they schuld be of dyvers condicions,
and than for vs it were grete foly to worschip theym as we doo. But
565 thys surely in God in noo wyse may be so, for all .iij. persones be oo
God and no moo, noon withowt another, noon before another by any
processe of tyme, but alwey hole togedyr the son in the fader, the
fader in the son, the holy goste in bothe two, whose charite and
communyon knytteth alle .iij. in oon and togedyr dothe theym
570 combyne.

'Oo God therfor in Trenyte, .iij. persones in vnyte, thus holi
Chirche techith vs to beleve and dothe determyne, the fadyr never
withowt the son, the son never withowte the fadyr, the holi goost
never withowte the fadyr and the son. And yit is not the son the
575 fadyr and oo God by hymselfe, [neyther the fadyr the son and oo
God by hymselfe, neyther the holi goost fadyr or son and oo God by
hymselfe], but alle .iij. togider oo God in vnyte, not made but

vnmade, withowt begynnyng and withowt endyng, of whos habitudis
or relacion, natures, processe and generacion it passyth mannes wytte
clerely to speke or ever so high to clymbe. Here, therefor, to 580
worschip hym lat vs now mekely oureselfe enclyne and withowt
any lenger processe alwey to hym warde let vs entende, for whoso wil
not beleve thus he schal never be saved nor never come to the
presence of God, where ioy and gladnes ys worlde | withowten ende. f. 257vb

'Thus vnderstand ye nowe, doughter, and kepe thys faithfulle lesson 585
ever in mynde, and whan ye have seen this lettre and redde it, if ye
stande yowe in dowte of anythynge, aske ye covnseile of the messenger
whom I sende to yow and he schal satisfie alle yowre desyre by such
bokes as with hym he schalle brynge to yow. Forthermore right
specyally I warne yow before of oo thyng, that and ye for Cristes 590
sake suffyr never so many turmentis and paynes or dethe and it be, be it
never soo sore, yit never dowte nor be aferde of any suche turmentyng,
for Cryste seyth hymself: "Whosoever in this worlde lesith hys lyfe for
me, in heven schal he fynde it ageyn and lyve with me for evermore,"
which he graunte both yow and me with goode helthe, welfare and 595
prosperite both gostely and bodyly dayly to encrese fro vertu to vertu,
alwey better and bettyr to hys endles worschip. Amen.'

The .v. chapitre of the grete comforte that Seynt Barbara
resseyved by Origens lettre sente vnto her by oone of hys
clerkys. 600

Thys lettre the worschipful fader and doctor Origen betoke to oone of
his clerkis, and in alle goodely haste sente it forth to Seynt Barbara
with her owen messenger and his clerke togeder, that so her messenger
schuld be guyde too his clerke and brynge hym into the contray that
this holy virgyne dwellid in. And as they wente togedyr in theyr 605
iorney, grete desyre they hadde to come into the costys of Nichomede,
revolvynge often tymes in þer myndes by many dyvers wysdoms howe
they | myght behave theym whan they came into the cite and into the f. 258ra
kynge Dyoscorus paleys Seynt Barbara fadyr, and howe they myght
convey thys lettre for to kepe it from the kyngis knowlege and satisfye 610
hys doughter of her entente, that hadde so greete desyre to become a
cristen womman and to resseyve the grace of cristyanyte.

Whan therfor they come nye to þe seyde cite they herde telle þat

---

584 worlde] *om.* Co   587 yowe] then Co   597 endles worschip] worshippe
endelesly Co   Amen] *in margin* L   611 to become] for to come Co

Seynt Barbara lay syke in her bedde of long tyme. And whan they
615 herde thys they thought yt a goode meane and convenyent for to
brynge theyr purpose aboute, for than they acordyd togedyr that
Seynt Barbara messenger schuld goo before and sey that he had
brought a phisician with hym owte of Alysaunder whyche schuld
make the kyngis doughter hoole of al her sekenesse, whiche sekenesse
620 ye schalle vndyrstonde was no bodely sekenesse, as before in partye
is declared in the begynnynge of the .iij. chapitre, but it was the
fervent love that sche had to God whiche maketh many devoute
sowles to seme as they were seke owtwarde whan they be fulle well at
ese in theyr sowles inward and brenne fulle hote in love and charyte
625 to God, and so dyd sche. Her messenger therfor came before and
tolde hys ladye alletogedyr prevely howe he hadde spedde in hys
iourney, and howe thys holy fadyr Origen had sente oone of hys
clerkys vnto her which schulde satisfye her of alle her desire, and
because no man schuld vnderstand what was doon openly he seyde
630 that he hadde brought a phisicyan with hym owte of Alysaunder
f. 258rb which stode | at the yate and desyred for to come in for to schewe hys
phesyk, for he wolde make the kynges doughter hole of alle her
sekenes.

Whan sche herde thys it wente to her herte more swetter than any
635 hony, and than sche avoyded alle her meyne from her, sauf suche as
sche trusted, and than sche thankyd God with alle mekenesse of
herte and seyde thus: 'Oo moste desyrous God, I thanke the verely,
for now I trust vnto thy grace and mercy after my trowbles to come
too thy knowlege so longe desyred of me moore saufly and sowndly
640 than a schip aftyr manyfolde wyndes and stormes cometh to the
haven owt of the trowbles see.' And with thys sche commawndyd the
clerke to be callyd in. He come in therfor and sayde: 'Madame, owre
lorde Ihesu Crist veray God and man save yow.' Sche rose anoon and
resseyvid hym ful reverently, havynge the name of God in grete
645 worschip and this clerke in reverence. Also within a lytille while after
thys, tydynges came to her eere that her fader cam to visite her, and
whan sche herde thys anoon sche wente and leide her downe ageyn
to bedde and feyned herselfe syke to her fader as sche was wonte to
doo ofte tymes before for the saide causes. Whan her fader þerfor
650 came in and sawe thys straunger ther standynge and knewe not hys
comyng, anoone he beganne to bowe the browes vpon hym and

615 convenyent] convayaunce Co   622 many] *om.* Co   645 reverence] *add*
and worshipp Co *and punctuate after also.*   lytille] *om.* Co

seyde: 'What felawe is thys, and why is he here?' Then his doughter answeryd and seyde: 'Fadyr, it is a phisician comen owte of Alisaunder, and he hathe | made covenaunte with me to make me hole of alle my sekenesse. And he tellith me that he hathe so connyng a man to his mayster that ayenst the vse of alle other phesicians not oonely he makith the peple hole in theyr bodyes but also in theyr sowles.' And when her fader herde thys he was ioyfulle and glad and right wele plesyd and gafe her lycence and leve to speke with hym as ofte as sche wolde. And so he departyd from hys doughter and wente abowte other besynesse and occupacions that he hadde to doo.

Whan therefor her fader was goone and they hadde leysor to speke togeder, eche of them beganne to open theyr hertys to other. And Orygenes lettre was brought forth and redde by goode avisement and welle vndyrstande, so that aftyr the tenour of the same lettre, whatsoever lakked therein in fulfyllyng of her desyre sche askyd yt of thys worschipful clerke and brynger of thys lettre. And he answeryd therto and declaryd yt ful clerely, and whan sche knewe howe the fadyr and son and holi gost was oo God in Trenyte fully and perfitly, and that the son the seconde persone in Trenyte was sente from the fadyr and had take mankynde vpon hym, and called man from his errour and redemed man owte of his thraldome be his moste blessyd passyon, and wassched man from hys synnes by the sacrament of bapteme' and ordeyned that sacrament and other for a perpetualle remedye for man, than sche desired with alle her herte to resceyve thys | sacrament and made alle the haste sche cowthe therto for to brynge yt to an ende, save yt myght not be do so sodeynly because of her fader.

Netheles grete comforte sche resceyved of these wordes. And never was the qvene of Saba more comfortyd by Salamons wordes than sche was by these, wherefor sche gave preysyngys and thankyngis to God, and fro that day forwarde was bettir cheryd and more gladder than ever sche was before. And so sche wente forthe and tolde her fadyr that sche was right wele amendyd, wherof he was right gladde, mery and iocunde. After thys, therefor, thys noble lady and virgyne Seynt Barbara beganne to lyve a newe lyfe and to haue al her mynde vpon God, kepyng his lawes bothe day and nyght. And from that day forwarde sche beganne to rede bokes of holy scripture, the holy Gospels, Paules Epistles, the Psalter and

f. 258va

655

660

665

670

675

f. 258vb

680

685

---

652 Then his] The Co   659 right] myght *with* m *blurred as if attempted deletion* Co   677 to an ende] abowte Co   687 vpon] vpwarde to Co

690 other dyvers bokes sent vnto her by Origen, wherby sche myght
come the more verely vnto the knowlege of God and cristen feythe
and vertuous lyvyng. Wherfor by suych vertuous excersise and
stody, wythin a lytylle while sche came to grete knawlege and
vndirstandyng of scripture, havynge no mayster for to teche her
695 save oonely the holy goste which inspireth the hertys of hys chosyn
and techith whom he wole.

Here than nowe [because] longe dylatyng of wordes makith colde
hertys sone dulle and wery, lat vs nowe passe over with these maters
tyl another tyme and speke we of her martyrdom and causes therof as
f. 259ra God wil dispose | vs and gyve vs grace, levyng behynde the
701 manyfolde [frutes of] goode werkis and vertuous dedys that sche
brought forthe to God many oone ful secretly by contynuelle labour
and besynesse and be dayly devocions and prayers.

705 The .vj. chapitre howe Seynt Barbara was put vp into a
towr by her fader that the peple scholde not se her bewte.
And how sche refused weddyng and alle the riches of the
worlde for the vertu of chastyte.

Evermore contynuelly thys gloryous virgyne thus occupied in vertu
710 and thus lightned by grace, and plesaunte to Criste moste soverayn
kyng of blysse more than ever was the quene Hester of the Olde
Testement, whyle sche vpon a day toke her walkyng vp and down
within the palyce and the kynge Dyoscorus her fader mette with her
and fixid hys ey3en vpon her and behelde her beavte, hym thought
715 sche was passynge fayre to beholde and lovely to loke vpon. And
whan he herde telle and perseyved oones that her feyrenes and
beaute was openly knowen abrode bothe ferre and nere, howebeyt he
knewe nott yit the feyrenesse inwarde of her sawle, whiche was more
excellent a grete dele in the sight of God than was the owteward
720 fayrenesse, he bethought hymselfe howe he myght hyde thys
feyrenesse fro the syght of the peple, that they schulde not beholde
her nor loke vpon her ymage and feyrenesse so custumably as they
were wonte to doo.
And thus lyke a cursyd and a wyckyd man he mysvsed the

697 because] the cause L   701 frutes of] seintes and L, *fructibus* Br
705 by . . . bewte] *om.* Co   706–7 and . . . worlde] *om.* Co   713 the(1)] *add*
place and L   714 fixid] festned Co

goodnes of nature that | God sente and gave vnto hym not to be f. 259ʳᵇ
hydde but to be schewed to hys honour and worschip, for he is the 726
maker and gever of alle feyrenesse and beaute. Atte laste, notwithstondyng alle thys, he sought a convenyente tyme and toke counseyle
of hys lordes howe he myght do in thys case. And so be theyre
counseyle he sente forthe hys messengers, of the moste discreteste 730
and wyseste men he hadde, into dyvers contreyes and regyons to seke
abovte and brynge with theym of the kunnyngeste werkemen they
cowde fynde, bothe masons, ioyners and carpenters that bothe cowde
hewe, grave and kerve in stone and in tymbre. And whan thes
werkemen were brought byfore the kynge, anoon he made cove- 735
naunte with theym to gyve every man after hys deservynge and
werkemanschip, and tolde theym what a towre that he wolde have
made of .iiij. sqvare, so feyre, so royalle, so costelewe, so strong and
so high that no man for to distroy it or hurte yt myght come þereby.

Than every man in alle the haste they myght beganne to make 740
redy alle that ever was nedeful and necessarye to thys werke, to make
scharp theyr instrumentis, to poolyssch and make redy the stonewerke, to frame the tymber werke, too plane the bordes, to dresse the
fundament for to sette the byldynge vpon. And within a fewe dayes
the towre was made and sette vp after the kynges commaundement 745
ful hye and ful ryalle to beholde vpon. And for thys towre was
square, if wyndowes had be made in every parte | thereof the hete of f. 259ᵛᵃ
the sunne wolde haue distempered the howse by vnkyndely hetes.
Therfor the kynge commaundyd that there schuld be made but two
wyndowes, oone of the northe and another in the sowthe, for hym 750
thought it vnworthy to make any wyndowes into the eest or into the
weste, leste whan the sunne rose the brightnesse thereof schold be
grevous to his doughter and let her of her reste in the mornyng, or
when the sunne wente [adowne] att nyght the howse schuld be
distemperate to her be any inordynate heetes before in the day tyme 755
or sodeyn colde comyng in the nyght tale.

And so whan thys towre was made and alle thynges ordeyned
therein nedeful and necessarie and resonable as belongeth to a kyngis
doughtres ryalte, the kynge toke hys doughter and put her therein in
þe moste royalle wyse as for the moste noble and richeste tresour that 760

725 goodnes] goodis Co   731 wyseste] wylyest Co   738 so(1)] *add* grete so
Co   739 to] *add* noye hit or Co   746 beholde] *add* and to loke Co
748 distempered] distroubled Co   754 adowne] adowte L   758–9 a . . .
ryalte] the roialte of a kyngis dowghter Co

he hadde. Aftyr thys, whan sche came to yeeres of age for to be weddyd, many a noble [lorde] and many a myghty prince desyred for to have her to hys wyfe, and to that entente bothe wrote and sente theyr messengers in the moste solempne wyse to her fader and
765 besought hym by many dyvers meanes and prayers for to haue hys goode wylle in thys case. But he in no wyse wolde graunte therto, but refusyd everichone and answerid every man by and by and sweryng by his god Hercules that 'Verely no man schuld haue my doughter from me, for sche ys myn hope and my trust, my huswyfe and my
f. 259vb keper vp of | my lyfe, and alle the comfort that I haue and ioye to
771 loke vpon with myn eyhen in this worlde.' Netheles, at the laste, what be covetise and desyre of worldly worschip, what by counsayle and enformacion of hys lordes and barons abovte hym, which counseilid hym that he scholde consente to oone of theym that
775 desyred to haue her to hys wyfe, and seyde that he wolde stande in the more favour and love of lordes, and bothe he and sche shulde have than theyr delytes and ryches and domynacions of thys world the more, at the last he went vp into the tour to his doughter and began to exhorte her and tempte her lyke as the devyl temptyd owre
780 lord Ihesu Cryst vpon the hylle, declarynge to her what kyngdomes, what riches, what power, what dominacions and delectacions of the worlde sche schuld haue if sche wolde be weddyd, and seyde: 'Doughter, not a fewe meanes be made to me for the whiche before I supposed schuld never haue be, but forsothe, doughter, if
785 that fortune befall to þe whiche is lykly to falle, I schal consent and not be there ayenst. Telle me, þerefor, doughter, wylte thow be wedded and it be desyred of the and asked?' þis he seyde not fynaly that he wolde haue her weddyd, but for to atempte and preve whether sche wolde consent thereto or noo.
790   Then this beautevous virgyne Barbara moste prudently answeryd to her fader, openly refusynge and forsakyng alle the dominacions and powers and delytes of the worlde, and sayde: 'God forbede, Fader, that ever I schuld be wedded thus. God forbede that I ever
f. 260ra and my herte | goo from yowres or yowres fro myn. I schalle telle
795 yowe, Fader, lyke as it is in myn herte. No man is there in the worlde so noble nor so fayre, noon so stronge nor noon so riche, for whoose love the entente I am set in may be withdrawen. Not and it were the emperours sone that I myght haue the crown and dominacion of alle

the empyre by hym, for I am set another wey, Fader, and haue another
purpose right fer from thys.' 'In what purpose, doughter, trowest 800
thowe?' seyde he. 'Forsothe, Fader,' seyde sche, 'I schalle telle yow.
Let these feyre wordys and manyfolde behestes of lordes goo from
me. It ys fowle to myn yehen to se and beholde alle these golden
araymentys so fayre and so dyvers. I sette not by alle these precious
broches, and owches of golde I despise and trede alle vnderfoote. I 805
forsake alle thys service done to me of so many servauntys and
mayne abowte me, and it is inowh to me, Fadyr, if I haue and stande
in your goode grace. I have avowed chastyte, whiche vertu and it be
welle ponderid there is nothynge in the worlde accordynge thereto,
and thys ys the cause why I haue no deynte of noothynge so moche 810
as thereof, but despise alle the richesse and vanyte of thys world
oonely for the vertu of chastite.'
   Whan her fader herde thys, anoone he beclypped her and kyssed
her and was gladde that he fownde her so welle accordyd to his
entente, wille and desyre. And than anoon he made promyse to her 815
and answered her verely that sche schuld have alle thynge that was
profitable and delectable vnto her, and that þe | towre schuld be f. 260ʳᵇ
[made more] feyrer and commodious that ever yt was before with
bathes and with stewes, condytes and lavours paynted alle abovtes in
the moste royalle wyse. And so he came down fro hys doughter and 820
gave the messengers an answere and sent them hoome ageyne to
theyre lordys voyde as they came, hymselfe abydyng allewey vpon
the werke to se yt were done like as he made ensuraunce to his
doughter, thys to be a signe and token betwene hym and her and as a
perpetualle bonde that sche schulde never be wedded to man erthely 825
but oonely lyve chaste.
   In the meane whyle it hapned that this kyng Dyoscorus was sente
for to the emperour and was commaundid by hym for to go forthe
abowte his nedys into ferre contrey. And because he myght not byde
at home, for he was compellyd to go forthe by a grete lorde whiche 830
was there at that tyme and hadde the rule of that londe vnder the
auctorite of the emperour and was above þis seyde kynge Dioscorus,
therfor he callyd the werkemen togedyr and made couenaunte with
theym alle in grete and tolde the maysters of hys werke hys advise
howe this werke schuld be perfourmed. And than he commyttid alle 835

807 if I] to Co   812 the . . . chastite] that vertue Co   814 accordyd]
acordynge Co   816 answered] ensured Co   818 made more] *trsp.* L
823 he] *add* hadde Co   826 oonely] alwey Co   828 forthe] *om.* Co

his goodes to the truste and kepyng of his doughter and callyd alle
his cheef knyghtis togeder and toke counseyle of them what wey they
schulde take, and so by theyre counseyle went forthe and toke his
iourney and was owte fro home a grete whyle. |

f. 260va

841   The .vij. chapitre how Criste and his aungellis appered to
      Seynt Barbara and of her .iij. wyndowes. And how sche
      was baptyzed by Seynt Iohn Baptiste.

Resonable tyme and conveniente seson hadde, whiles her fader was
absent and made so long tariynge from home, this glorious virgyne
845 and servaunt of God wente vp into the sayde towre for to see the
werke thereof alle abowte. And when sche come by a certeyn lavatory
or bathynge place made in the same tour to her comforte and solace,
ther sche sawe the sunne, the mone and the sterris with other dyuers
planetes above graven and paynted so curiously that al that ever
850 behelde yt my3t wele merveyle and wonder of so royalle and precious
a werke. And as sche stode besyde thys bathe and bethought her of
the mevynge of the sunne, the mone and the sterres whose figures
sche sawe paynted ther and of theyr begynnynge and influence,
anoon the aungelle of God came to her from heven and brought and
855 gave to her hevenly wisdom as moche as sche was able to resceyve,
whereby sche myght vnderstonde sufficiantly alle thys and alle that
ever was nedeful for her to vnderstonde and knowe to her helthe.
And so, for the holy gost restyth vpon theym that [be] veray meke
and quyete in sawle, therfor sche deserued to haue that grace gyven
860 to her of the holi goste for to haue an aungelle to declare vnto her alle
the poyntes consernyng þe feith and beleve of holi Chyrche, whyche
sche lerned before in partie resonable by Origens lettres, as it is

f. 260vb

declared | before.
      Netheles now this aungelle more openly declared vnto her and
865 tolde her of Criste and of hys holy incarnacion, howe he became man
for her sake and for the love of alle mankynde, and howe he of his
owen fre wylle and goodenesse and by specialle pryvelege hadde
imprynted and sett hys marke vpon her and marked her in the herte
with the vayle off chastyte, that sche schuld never resseyve other to

---

836 and kepyng] om. Co   841 Seynt Barbara] her Co   841–842 and . . .
wyndowes/And   .   .   . Baptiste] trsp. Co   842 baptyzed] baptithed Co
843 was] add owte and Co   850 and precious] om. Co   853 sawe] shawe Co
858 be] by the L   862 resonable] add playnly Co   867 wylle and] om. Co

her paramour and love but oone. And herewith anoon owre lord 870
Ihesu Criste also appered vntoo her hymself in a lyckenesse of a feyre
yonge chylde, in whom sche had more delyte than may be expressyd.

Than the aungelle tolde to her what dyuers turmentis and peynes
and dethe owre lord Ihesu had suffred for her and for the
redempcion of mankynde frely of his owen free wylle withowt 875
compellyng of any other. And with this also he told her before
howe many dyvers turmentis and peynes sche schuld suffre for þe
name of Criste, and that sche schuld not oonely be crowned in heven
with the crowne of virginis but also with the crowne of doctoures,
prechoures and martyrs. And while the aungille spake thus vnto her 880
and exhortid her and steryd her that sche schuld dispose and make
her redy to suffre martyrdome for love of Ihesu Crist her spowse, the
seide chylde owre lord Ihesu Criste anoone turned as thof he had
bene alle blody and as thof he hadde suffred passyon the same tyme.
Wherefor sche was passand sorye and compuncte in her herte, and 885
stode as thof sche hadde | ben alle in another worlde and owte of f. 261ʳᵃ
herselfe for sorowe. And of very compassion and with alle bitternesse
and deuocion sche wepte and wayled for the byttyr payne and
passion that owre lorde Ihesu Crist had suffred for her, so that the
aungelle whiche sayde before that sche schuld be crowned with .iij. 890
crownes myght wele sey to her commendacion with the prophete
that is wreten in the Psalter boke: *Specie tua et pulcritudine tua intende
prospere procede et regna*, for thowe haste the now, so fayre and
beautevous in sowle, be sadde remembraunce of Cristys passyon and
by veray pyte and compassyon of the same haste made yt to the so 895
paynfulle and bitter. Therfor nowe go forthe and procede and reigne
by contynuaunce every day better and better, and thowe schalt be
crowned in heven with the threfold crowne of virgine, prechoure and
martyr.'

And so from thys day forwarde this holy virgyne to the ensample 900
of alle virgines had her mynde so moche in the remembraunce of
Crist and hys passyon, and set her mynde so moche vpwardes to God
and hevenly thynges aboven in heven, and was so stedfaste and stable
in the feith of holy Chirche, what now be the aungelles wordes, what
before by Origen lettres, and what moste specially by grace of the 905
blessyd Trenyte ful clerely knowen in her beleve, that sche myȝt sey
wele with Seynt Poule and with alle cristen peple, howbeyt sche had

870 oone] hym Co   875 free] *om.* Co   887 sorowe] sowe Co
896 procede . . . reigne] proce aygne Co   897 and better] *om.* Co

not yit resseyved the sacrament of baptem of water: *Nostra autem*
conversacio in celis est, our conversacion and our levyng verely is and
910 schulde be alletogeder in heven with God almyghty. |

f. 261rb   After thys therfor that thys holy virgyne had seen oure lord Ihesu
and resseyved thys comforte of the aungelle, sche revolued and
considered and vnderstode welle in her mynde that it was behouefulle for every man and woman to be lightned with the light of trewe
915 feythe and beleve of the blessyd Trynyte. And whan sche wente
forthe in the tour and sawe .ij. wyndowes and no moo, sche asked
alle the werkmen why they hadde made it so. They answeryd and
seyde: 'Madame, youre fader wolde haue it so.' 'What,' quod sche,
'hathe not my fader made thys tour for me?' 'Yis, madame,' seide
920 þey. 'Wele than,' quod sche, 'sith thys ys thus that my fader made
this tour for me and comawndid yow to make but .ij. wyndowes
therein, it belongeth to yowe for to obeie to me in my faders absence.
And so I wille that ye in my name make vp the thirde wyndowe in
the eeste parte, for it plesith me to have yt soo.'

925   Thus seyde this holy virgyne, for sche wolde haue .iij. wyndowes
in worschip of the blessyd Trynyte whom sche worschiped and loved
with alle her herte. Than the werkmen, thof they were somwhat
adredde of Dioscorus the kyng her fader, yit they obeyed to her
commaundement and made vp the .iij. wyndowe lyke as sche
930 commavndid theym. And this was doone by the gracious disposicion
of God for a perpetualle remembraunce of the holynesse of thys
blessyd and glorious virgyne Seynte Barbara, for sche was so holy in
f. 261va her levynge þat sche desyred | to have a specyal knowleche of the
blessyd Trynyte before her baptem. And otherwyse it myght not be
935 þan God provided and ordeyned from the begynnynge by his
eternalle wisdom, for from thys daye forwarde thys holy virgyne
by thys meane made her redy to suffre martirdome, as it schalle be
schewed afterwarde by processe of narracion.

Aftyr thys therfor, thys holy virgyne thus alle besette with vertues
940 roundeabowte, wente ayen to the sayde lavatorye or bathe and there in
þe eest parte thereof with her right thomb made dyvers tokens of the
crosse in the harde pylers of marble, the whiche crosses be there yit into
þis day to the sterynge of the hertes of the peple beholdynge a grete

908 of water] *om.* Co   918, 920 quod] seide Co   920 fader] *add* hath Co
927 thof] therof Co   931 God] *om.* Co   of thys] and Co   932 was] *om.* Co
936 for] *om.* Co   939 therefor, thys] *om.* Co   943 a grete] so grete a Co

myracle doone of God by the meritis of Seynt Barbara. And whan sche
wente downe into the seide bath and fownde no water therein, anoon 945
sche felle downe prostrate and wepte and made her prayers to God and
seyde thus: 'Lord Ihesu Crist, whiche by Moyses thy servaunt
broughtest owte water of the harde stone in deserte, open now to me
here in this same place the welle of fressche rennyng watyr, and blisse
and halowe þe same water. Lorde, I beseche the that I may be baptized 950
therein in the name of the holy Trenyte, fader, son and holy goste, and
be clensyd and have forgevenes of alle my synnes as thow arte of
myghtis moste.' With this sche sette downe her right foote into the
sayde bathe, whiche step is seen there yit, and anoon sprange vp a welle
with so grete plente of watyr that | it came nerehande to her naville, f. 261vb
which water was anoon devided into .iiij. parties in maner of cross- 956
ewyes, and so there ran owte .iiij. stremes as it hadde be the .iiij. floodes
of paradise. But oo þing was doon more merveillous and more worthyer
than alle thys, and more to be commendyd and preysed in thys glorious
virgyne. For in maner lyke as Criste whan he was baptizid in flum 960
Iurdan the water was halowyd by touchynge of [his] holy body, right so
nowe it liked the Trenyte to halowe þis water by touchyng of the body
of þis holy virgyne, that whatsoever devotely entre into this bathe or
welle is made hoole of alle maner sekenesse and thereby resseyveth
grete grace bothe bodily and gostely. 965

This bathe or welle therfor may wele be lykned to the ponde where
as our lord made the man hole of the palsey, and to the fressche
sprynge welle that the woman of Samarie desired of our lord to drynk
of, and to the water and wasschyng place of Syloe where as our lorde
made the man that was blynde borne to se, for whosoever can visite 970
this place devoutely there may he be made hole from the tremlyng
palsy of lecherye and from the thrustelewe synne of covetyse and from
the blynde custume and longe continuaunce in the synne of pryde and
other synnes. So that nowe thys may welle be called the welle of lyfe
for the manyfolde lyvely vertues and graces that it hathe and for the 975
manyfolde myracles that hath ben schewed there by the merytes of
thys seyde gloryous virgyne. In this same welle or bathe, therefor, by
the disposicion of God which knoweth | his chosen from other, to f. 262ra
whom noþing is impossible, this holy virgyne and lambe of Criste was
wasschen and resseyved the holy sacrament of bapteme by the glorious 980
precursor and messenger of Criste Seynt Iohn Baptiste, whiche
depped her hede .iij. tymes in the same water in the name of the

959 and more] *om.* Co 961 his] thys L 963 whatsoeuer] whosouere Co

blessid Trinyte and in tokenyng that sche was deed and buried with
Criste, as who sey from alle worldly lyfe, and rose vp ageyn with hym
985 from dethe to lyfe and began to leve a newe lyfe alle spiritualle and
gostely. And lat not this gendre any scripulnes or dowtefulnesse in
mennes hertys nor let not men be the more lother to heere this storye
and tretice because it is sayde that this special bechosen virgyne of
God Seynt Barbara was baptized by Seynt Iohn Baptiste, for we rede
990 and fynde in dyuers places that holy sawles and seyntes beyng in
heven haue comen and doone service to man here benethe in erthe ful
besely.

Thus we rede of Seynte Petyr prynce of þe apostles howe he came
to the holy virgyne and martyr Seynte Agas whiles sche was in
995 preson, and restored her brest ageyn whiche was kutte of, and made
hole her woundes that sche had resseyvid by many dyuers tormentis
and peynes before. Thus we rede also of Seynt Mertyn, Seynt
Nicholas, Seynt Austyn and of many other seynte now glorified in
blisse howe they haue mynystred and holpen theyr servauntis and
1000 lovers ful tendyrly be manyfold myracles and benefetis. And what
merveyle ys it thowh this blessid virgyne Seynt Barbara was baptized
of Seynt Iohn Baptist while sche folowed hym in the scole of vertu so
f. 262rb perfitly? Seynt Iohn of al goode | lyvynge bare the maistry, for he was
forme of holynes, ruel of riȝtwisnesse, myrrour of virginite, title of
1005 clennesse, ensample of chastyte, and he schewed vnto vs the veray
wey of penaunce and taught how synnes schulde be forgeven and
preched of trewe feith and beleve.

And this holy virgine not oonly folowed Seynte Iohn in [these
vertues but also in many moo, folowynge the same Seynt Iohn in]
1010 straytenesse of penaunce, and lyved by herbes and rotes and
honysukklis moste perfitly after tyme sche was oones baptized, so
that we may not saye but it was worthy that such a vertuous and
blessyd virgyne schulde be baptized of Seynt Iohn Baptyste whils
sche thus perfitly folowed hym in vertuous levyng and gave herselfe
1015 so fulle and hole to the love of Criste. Wherefor if Criste gave oones
a grete commendacion to Seynt Iohn Baptiste of his byrthe when he
seide there was never man borne of woman gretter of byrthe than he,
moche more in maner myght he nowe say to the commendacion of
the vertu of this blessyd virgyne there was never woman borne vpon

984–5 and . . . lyfe] om. Co   986 scripulnes] scrupilosnes Co   1000 lovers]
lyvers Co, viatoribus Br   1002 scole] shole Co   1008–9 these . . . in] om. L
1012 was] add wele Co

erthe moche more vertuous than sche. And if the holy woman Iudith   1020
deservid the blessyng of God for her vertuous levynge, and the
goode womman Ruth also to be commendid amonge the peple for
her vertu so openly, moche more this holy virgyne was worthy to
have þe blessynge of God and to be commendid and magnyfied and
preysed of alle thoo that knewe her lyfe, and so nowe to be   1025
commendid of vs whiche nowe in parte have herde howe goode
sche was and howe vertuous.

Forthermore aftir this, this gracious | virgyne wente vp into the   f. 262va
tour ageyn alle merie and glad. And whan sche sawe her faders
mawmettis and ydols alle becovered abowte with golde and precious   1030
stones, anoone sche tooke goode herte vnto her in the holi gost, and
the blessyd Trinite made her so stedfaste and stronge in trewe feith
and beleve and gave her the victorie of alle her enemyes so myghtely
þat sche nether dredde fader nor noone other man, but boldely
spytte vpon the faces of the ydolles and seide: 'I pray God alle they   1035
that haue made yowe and set theyr truste in yowe may be doone to
like I schalle doo to yowe.' And herewith sche toke theym and brake
theym alle to gobettys and peces. And whan sche remembrid these
verses in the Psalter: *Beatus qui intelligit super egenum et pauperem*,
[and] *Dispersit dedit pauperibus iusticia eius manet in seculum seculi*, and   1040
vnderstode welle that whosooever wolde helpe and releve theym that
were pore and nedy schuld have grete rewarde of God and resseyve
hys blessynge everlastyngly, anoone sche gadered togedyr these
seyde peces and gave theym in almes to pore folke.

And than sche abode stylle in þis tour and gave her to prayer and   1045
to preyse God contynuelly bothe day and nyght with spiritual laudes
and preysyngis in thought, worde and dede, also after the saynge of
the prophete in the Psalter booke: *Benedicam Dominum in omni
tempore, semper laus eius in ore meo.* Than sche desired also therewith
to haue the blessyngis conteyned in the gospelle wherewith God   1050
blessith his chosen, and so to be blessid | with poverte in sperite that   f. 262vb
sche myght be made riche in the kyngdom of heven; to haue the
vertu of veray mekenesse that sche myght be exalted and brought vp
into large possession of the lande of blisse; to wepe and wayle and
suffre the hevynesse of this worlde that sche myght resseyve ever-   1055
lastyng comfort above; to hungre and thruste and allewey to haue an

1038–9 these verses] this verse Co   1040 and] *Et* L, *Et iterum* Br
1042 rewarde] thanke Co   1044 folke] peple Co   1048 booke] *om.* Co

appetite after rightwisnesse and rightfulle levynge; and to be bettyr
and bettyr that sche myght be replete hereaftyr with hevenly metys
and drynkes where as never schalle be hongre nor thrust nor lak of
1060 perfeccion; to be the doughter of mercy and of pite that sche myght
come to the fader of mercy, God almyghty; to be clene and pure of
herte that sche myght se God in the face clerely; to be peasible with
God, with herselfe and with her neyburgh, that sche myght be called
the doughter of pease of God; to suffre persecucion for God and his
1065 rightwissenesse that sche myght reigne with hym as a quene in blisse;
and to suffre paciently the cursyngis and wickid wordes and evel
langage and lesyngis of malicious peple whereby sche myght opteyne
graciously the crowne of heven be everlastynge ioye and glorye, so
that be these meanes and hevenly desyres sche alletogedyr com-
1070 mytted her wylle to Goddys wylle, euery day encresyng from vertu
to vertu, tylle at laste after the aungels wordes sche sawe God of alle
vertues redy to crowne her in heven with the crowne of blisse among
alle his holy martyrs and seyntes.

f. 263ra   The .viij. chapitre of the mysterye of the .iij. wyndowes
               made be Seynt Barbara to the worschip of the blessid |
1076   Trinite. And howe a marbille stone closed her vp and
               caried her forthe into an hylle. And of the schepard turned
               into marbille and his schepe into grassehoppis.

Upon a certeyne day long tyme aftir this, whan thys kynge
1080 Dioscorus the fader of that moste blessid virgine Seynt Barbara
was come home, and whan he wente to se thys tour if it were
perfitely made vp like as he had commaundid before he wente owte,
and when he sawe .iij. wyndowes made and remembred how he had
ordeyned before there schulde be but .ij., than he asked of the
1085 werkemen who durste presume to take vpon hym to make the .iij.de
wyndowe ayenst hys commaundement. Oone of theym answerid
and seide: 'Sir, if it please your hyenesse, my lady your doughter
commaunded vs so.' Than he called his doughter and kyssed her
and seide: 'Doughter, why be there .iij. wyndowes made here? Was
1090 yt youre wille to have it so?' 'Ye forsoothe, Fader,' seide sche, 'and
for thys skille I haue ordeyned the .iij.de wyndowe, for .iij.
wyndowes gefe light to every man that cometh in, where as .ij.

1057 rightwisnesse . . . levynge] rightwis lyvynge Co   1058 bettyr] holere Co
1076 her] hit Co

wyndowes let men to se.' 'How so?' seide the fader, 'how may .iij.
wyndowes geve more light than .ij.? Than sche ful of the holi goste
answered and saide: 'Three open and evidente lightes Fader, there   1095
be, fader, son and holi goost, not .iij. goddys but oone veray God in
persones .iij., the maker of heven and of erthe and of alle that is
conteyned therein, in whom every man oweth to beleve and do
dewe reverence and worschippe to.' And herewith sche was so
enflawmed with the hote brennynge fyre of charite within for the   1100
whiche puttith a|wey alle feeres and dredes worldly that sche spake f. 263ʳᵇ
to her fader and saide: 'Forthermore, Fader, in .ij. wyndowes is
grete mysterie, but I fynde gretter mysterye in .iij. wyndowes a
grete dele. By .ij. wyndowes I vndirstande the condicions of
mankynde whiche standith in man and woman, withowte the   1105
whiche .ij. kyndes noo man may be naturally, for no man may be
borne into this worlde but by man and woman. By the sowthe
wyndowe þerfor, whiche is hote, I vnderstand man, for man is of
hote complexion. By the northe wyndowe, whiche is colde, I
vnderstande woman, for woman is of colde complexion, so that for   1110
to take example and speke of the nature and condicions of mankynde
I holde it right convenient and accordynge for to have but .ij.
wyndowes. But for to take exsample and speke of the nature of the
Godhede and blessyd Trinite, and if it please your faderhode for to
here me paciently ye schalle here and knowe by me that ye never   1115
knewe afore.

'Fader, I wille that ye vndirstande me. The Godhede is that
thynge whiche hathe made alle that ever ys of nought, bothe visible
and vnvisible. And he is .iij. in persones, fader, son and holi gooste,
and oone in godhede, vndevided, vnseparable and vndepartable in   1120
his godhede thof he be departable in persones. And thof the fader be
fader by hymselfe in that he is fader, yit he may never be withowt
the son nor withowte the holi goost in that he is God. And the same
is to be vnderstonde and beleved bothe of the son and of the holy
gooste. | Thus Fadyr, and it lyke yowe, schalle I schewe more openly f. 263ᵛᵃ
by ensample of this towre and be the .iij. wyndowes nowe made   1126
therein. This, thof it haue .iij. wyndowes, yit it is but oo tour in
substaunce, and yit every wyndowe hath hys ful light be hymselfe,
and every wyndowe hathe a difference from other, for the eest
wyndowe ys not the northe wyndowe, nor the northe wyndowe the   1130

1110 that for] *om.* Co   1120–1 vndevided . . . godhede] *om.* Co
1127 therein] *add* be me Co   This] *add* towre Co

sowthe wyndowe, nor the sowthe wyndowe the eeste or the northe
wyndowe, but these .iij. wyndowes togeder in oone tour makeþ the
tour to have his dewe forme and schappe. Thus, Fader, for to speke
by ensample, it is of the blessyd Trinite. Every persone is fulle God
1135 in hymselfe, the fader fulle God in hymselfe, the son fulle God in
hymselfe, the holi goost ful God in hymselfe. And yit neyther the
fader is the son, neyther the son the fadyr or þe holi gooste, neyther
the holy gooste the fadyr or the son, but alle .iij. togedyr oo veray
God aloone, fader, son and holi goste, distincte in persones and not
1140 in godhede. Of the which persons, oon of theym is veray God and
man and that is the son, seconde persone in Trenite, owre lord Ihesu
Crist, whiche, because he is man, hathe take me to his spouse by
commaundement of his fader [and of his owen free wille and
goodenes or ever the, Fader,] beganne to take your iorney owteward
1145 from home. And therfor to hym haue I promysed to kepe my
virginite and to kepe me clene and feitheful for evermore, from
whos love no tribulacion nor angwissche, no persecucion nor hungre
f.263ᵛᵇ nor schame nor swerde | nor blame nor nothyng in the worlde may
departe fro me. But and if it falle to my lotte for to dye for hys love,
1150 ȝit schalle I putte my body in ieberdye and stayne it with the rede
bloode of martirdome, trustyng to his grace and goodenes for to be
clothed hereaftyr with the rede precious purpour of holy martyrs in
everlastynge ioie and blisse.'
      Whan sche hadde seide this, anoone her fader forgate hymselfe and
1155 felle downe to the grownde for woodnes and lay like a dede stokke
alletogedyr owte of hymselfe. Within a while after he came ageyn to
hymselfe and remembred the wordys of his douȝter, and when he
vnderstode that sche was become a cristen woman and had take Criste
for her spouse, anoone in a grete wodenes he drewe owte hys swerde
1160 and wolde haue renne thorugh her notwithstondynge alle the love he
had to her before. Then this holy virgine was nothynge lothe to dye for
Cristes sake, but havyng pite and compassion vpon her fader praied
for hym that God wolde haue mercy on hym. And even sodeynly the
merveilous mercy of God was redy, for anoone forthewith a grete
1165 marbille stone by the werke of God closed her in and toke her vp and
caried her forthe vp into an hille fulle of stones and caves, and so sche
was preserved of God at that tyme and delyvered from the cruelte of
her fader by open myracle as ye may see.

1143–4 and(1) . . . fader] *om.* L   1148 nor swerde] *om.* Co   1149 fro] *om.* Co

In this hille were .ij. schepardys the same tyme kepynge theyr
schepe and sawe whan alle thys was doone. And whan the fadyr 1170
sought his doughter al aboute | and cowde nowher fynde her, at þe f. 264ra
last he wente owte of the cite vp into this hille and asked of the
schepardis if they sawe his doughter. Than oone of theym, havynge
pite and compassion vpon thys lady, dredynge what schuld falle of
her whan he sawe her fader stonde there in suych a woodenes with 1175
his swerde drawen, wolde not discover her but seyde: 'I sawe her not
nor I wote not where sche is.' That oþer scheparde was cruelle and
cursed and thought it was not wele doone to suffre the fader so longe
to be trobled aboute the sekynge of his doughter, [and] boldely with
his fynger schewedde where sche was. And therfor God of his 1180
rightful iugement wolde not suffre suych a wycked dede goo
vnpunyssched, but anoon forthewith the same schepard was turned
into an ymage of marble and his schepe into grashoppis, which
ymage of marble and grashoppis yit into this day be at the schryne or
sepulcre of this glorious virgine for alle men to beholde and too 1185
wondyr vpon.

Whan this blessyd virgine therfor herde the voyce of her fader,
anoone obediently [she] came to hym withowte any tariynge and
wilfully offred herselfe vnto hym. And whan the fader sawe his
doughter so freely come to hym, anoone he hadde ruthe and pite on 1190
her and put vp hys swerde into the schethe and wolde not sle her in
noo wise but thought to correcte her by another meane. Whan
therfor he had thus fownde his doughter, he bette her grevously
and plukked her be the heere of her heede and drewe her downe
from the hille and brought her home ayeen | into his howse and f. 264rb
there chayned her faste with chaynes and lokked her vp in a narowe 1196
derke dongeon and wold no more speke with her tylle on the
morowe. And yit this was nought inowh but he muste doo oo
wycked dede vpon another and commaunded kepars to wacche
vpon her al nyght that sche myght no wey eskape but that sche 1200
schulde be take and brought ayeen. Sche therfor abode there alle
nyght and resseyved grete comforte be the felisschip of aungells.
And so sche commendid and commyttid her martirdome and cause
oonely to God, and seyde with the prophete: *Adhesit anima mea post*
te, 'Lord, I besech the that I never be departid from the, but that 1205

1179 to be] *om.* Co   and] *om.* LCo   1181 goo] *om.* Co   1187 blessyd]
glorious Co   1188 she] *om.* LCo   1199 dede] torn Co   1200 no . . .
eskape] not escape no way Co   1205 *te*] *add* me L

my soule and mynde be so knytte to the as I thy trewe folower
everlastyngly may be.'

The .ix. chapitour howe Seynt Barbara was comen and her
fader hadde labored alle that he myght and sche was
1210   brought before the iuge and after many grete turmentis
and peynes was put into preson, and how our lorde Ihesu
came and appered to her in the same preson and comforted
her and made her hoole of al her woundes.

Sodeynly whan the morne was comen and her fader hadde labored
1215   alle that ever he cowthe for to make her revoke and go from her holy
entent and purpose and in no wise cowde brynge it aboute, in a
greete wodnes he wente to the chief iustice of the cite beyng that
tyme oone callid Marcian, and tolde hym alle togedyr what an hevy
case was behapned of his doughter whiles he was owte aboute the
f. 264va   emperours | nedes, that is to sey, howe sche was turned from the
1221   worschipyng of theyr goddes to the worschip of Crist, having suych
maner of wordes to the sayde iuge. 'An vngracious fortune is befalle
to me, and in an vnhappy tyme was I made [goo] owte abowte the
emperoures nedes, and therefor haue I loste my doughter. A
1225   sekenesse longe enduring it is, an happe and ever it be hoole. This
madnes and fonde opinyon, if it were newe and fressche in my
doughter, paraventure it schulde be taken awey from her. But now
let her be fette hedyr and entretid scharpely to se of .ij. thynges what
sche wylle doo, whethyr sche wylle contynue forthe in this opinyon
1230   or ellis paraventure for fere and smartnes of peynes wille leve it and
go therefro, or ellis, and sche holde it stille and wille not leve it, by
the goddys whom I worschip and beleve in, after dyvers turmentis
and peynes I schalle smyte awey this madnes myselfe with myn owen
swerde her nek of by the harde schuldres.'
1235   And whan he had seide thus to the iustice, he made hym to swere
also be the power of his goddys that he schulde sende for his
doughter and put her to moste grevous turmentis and peynes. The
iuge sware therfor and anoone forthewith alle he sente his officers for
this glorious virgine. And whan sche sawe theym stonde aboute her
1240   and knewe welle inow whether and wherfor they came, anoone sche
beganne to make her prayers to God and seide: 'Lord God, to whom

1208–13 *Co has space here for insertion of chapter heading*   1223 goo] *om*. L
1231 it stille] forthe therwith Co   1240 whether and] *om*. Co

alle maner strenght is subiecte to do what thow wilte, for the am I
drawen, for the | am I haled and ledde forthe to the barre like a theef. f. 264ᵛᵇ
Never was I wonte to be in suych places, Lord, thow knoweste.
Come with me, I beseche the, stande with me and make me stronge 1245
in sowle and arme me with the armure of thy myght and power, for
nowe I go to bateylle, not my batelle, Lorde, but thyne. And nowe I
go with my enemyes to batelle, and that is moche more perilous than
if I wente with my frendes. I haue right grete nede to be armed with
thyne armour, and that ful surely that I graciously myght withstonde 1250
and overcome theym and bryng to the open signes and tokenes of
victorie. Woman, Lorde, thow knowest welle is more weyker than
man, but thow maiste make a man of a woman. Make me nowe
therefor, goode Lorde, that I never be aferde of these berded and
brasen faces, but be thowe with me oonelye and I schalle overthrowe 1255
theym everychone. I trust in thy mercy, and a grete wonder and
confusion schalle it be to theym and if that they be overcome by me,
and a grete worschip schalle it be to the and paraventure not a fewe
sawles wonne thereby, wherefor nowe helpe me, Lorde, right hertely
I beseche the.'   1260
  Anoone as sche had made this prayer to God sche was brought
before the iuge sittynge in iugement, and fyrst and formeste sche lifte
vp [her] eyhen and herte to God and beganne to speke to the iuge
and seide: 'Syr iuge, why hast thow sente for me, and wherto am I
brought before the? Wilte thowe knowe my feithe? I am a cristen 1265
woman, and veray God I worschip as I can, dispising alle ydolles and
mawmetrie.' Than seide the iuge to this glorious virgine: 'Thow arte
poysened,' he seyde, 'with the | poyson of desseyte, and therefor f. 265ʳᵃ
thow spekist lyke a dronken woman and arte so poysened and
overdronken þat thow arte so bolde to answere or any question be 1270
asked of the. And who hathe thus poysened [the]? Thowe arte
desseyvid, doughter, verely, and the trowthe is otherwyse than thowe
wenyste for.' Than answered the holy spouse of Criste and seide
ageyne to the iuge: 'Nay,' sche seide, 'I am not poysened nor
desseyved, but I knowe the trowth. And I wene not it is trowthe 1275
that I beleve, but I knowe verely it is soo and may be noone
otherwise than trowthe verely.'
  Than the iuge Mercian seide ageyn to this virgine: 'Turne the

1242 maner] *om.* Co   1249 frendes] *add* Wherfore Co   1262 and formeste]
om. Co   1263 her] *om.* L   speke] *add* fyrste Co   iuge] *add* hyrself Co
1269–70 so . . . arte] *om.* Co   1271 the(2)] *om.* L   1277 verely] *om.* Co

from this errour, [doughter,' he seide, 'turne the fro this errour]	and

1280 leve it. It is no merveyle thof this errour and supersticion haue desseyved the, for many oone haue be desseyved [therby,] also they that haue be riȝt aged and witty.' Seynt Barbara answered: 'I am turned,' sche seide, 'alle redy, for byfore I erred and worschiped mawmettis as thowe doyste, but nowe am I turned to the worschip of

1285 my maker, and therefor nowe I erre not but kepe the right wey. Nor this is eny errour or supersticion that wee cristen peple folowe and kepe, but that is errour and supersticion that ye vse amonge yowe in worschipyng and enclynyng youre hedys to ydols and mawmettis and take no hede þat they be made by mannes hondes of insensible stones

1290 and metalles.' þe iuge answered and seide ageyn to þis virgine: 'I am meved,' he seyde, 'with a maner of mercy and pite vpon the for thowe arte so yonge and so fayre and so bevtevous, wherefor, first for

f. 265ʳᵇ love of thy fader to whom | we desire to restore the ageyn clene purged from alle thys fonnednes, we schalle assay if we can brynge

1295 this abowte. But and if thow contynue forthe in this fonnednes and wilte not leve it, [at] the laste we schalle preve be experyence how stronge thow arte.'

Seynte Barbara answered: 'Arte thowe,' sche seide, 'meved with mercy vpon me? Be meved with mercy to thyselfe. Thretenyste

1300 thowe me with peynes? Drede thow the peynes comyng to the. Temporalle paynes schalle brynge me to everlastynge reste, and temporalle dignytees, worldly ioies and delites schalle brynge [the] to everlastyng peynes.' Than the iuge Marcian with these wordes was passynge wrothe and angry, and anoone be the suggestion of

1305 Dioscorus her fadir commaunded this virgine to be beten [naked with scorges] and roddis, saiynge thus: 'When betynges come, wordys schalle sease.' But this glorious virgine was right ioyfulle of this betynge and glad that sche was ever worthy to suffre suych peynes for the love of Criste. Wherefor sche thanked God and seide:

1310 '*Benedictus Deus qui non amouit deprecacionem meam et misericordiam suam a me.* Blessid be God in his high maieste for he haþ not dispisid my praier nor withdrawen his mercy fro me. This day have I abiden, this day haue I sought after longe, and now right graciusly [haue I yt fownde.'

1315 And while sche was thus grevously] beten and for no payne wolde

---

1279 doughter . . . errour] *om.* L   1281 therby] *om.* L   1296 at] al L

1298 sche seide] *om.* Co   1302 worldly] *om.* Co   the] *om.* L

1305–6 naked/with scorges] *trsp.* L   1313–15 haue . . . grevously] *om.* L

leve her opynyon, the iuge commaunded her to be brought ayene
tofore hym. And than he beganne to speke such maner wordys | to   f. 265ᵛᵃ
[her] and saide: 'Whereof is thy skynne [made], of horne? Whereof is
thy breste made, of stone? Why wilte thow not leene to holsom
counseille? Why arte thow not aferde of scharpe betyngis? Why takes 1320
thowe no hede of the grete bloode that thowe arte come of? Eyther be
wedded to some grete lord after thy degre, or ellis doo service to the
goddas Veste to whom thy fader hathe avowed thy chastyte, or els,
and thowe wylte do noone of these but dispise the emperours
commaundementis and make no sacrefice to our goddis after the 1325
vse and custome of the citee, thowe schalte fele in thy body at the
laste what payne schal come thereof to the.'

    Seynte Barbara answered: 'Doo thowe,' she sayde, 'alle thy rygour
that thow canst, for I am so stronge that I wylle never goo from the
wey of rightwysnes. But I hadde lever suffre alle peynes in my body 1330
then oones I wolde declyne from the pathe of rightwisnes. To
worschip hym that ys oo God and veray God, there is nothynge so
riȝtwis, for he seythe: "*Ego sum Deus et non est alius preter me*, I am
veray God and noone other God there ys but I." But to obey to the
emperours commaundementis and lawes and worschip ydolles and 1335
mavmettis whom devils inhabyte, there ys nothynge so vnrightwysse,
for they haue mowthes and speke not, iyen and se not, eeres and
heere not, nooses and smelle nott, handes and [feel not], feete and
goo not, lyke as seithe the prophete in the Sawter of theym and theyr
worschyppers: "*Os habent et non loquntur, oculos habent et non* 1340
videbunt &c.'"

    Then | the iuge spake ageyn to this virgyne and seide: 'Many f. 265ᵛᵇ
wordes,' he seyth, 'thow haste, and moo then be nedefulle. Leve alle
thys iangelynge and bowe to oure counseyle. Yit maiste thowe be
saved and thowe wylte, for oo falle and trespase axeth oo rysyng and 1345
correccion.' Herto this holy virgyne, strengthed in the holy gooste
and stablissched in the feyth of holy Chirche, answeryd and seyde:
'There is noone other saluacion,' sche seyde, 'but my lorde Ihesu
Crist, savioure of alle the worlde, whiche hathe brought me in the
veray wey of saluacion.' Anoone, therefor, as the iuge herde this, he 1350
was confusyd and overcomen. And when he perceyved that the peple

1318 her] *om.* L   made] *om.* L   1320 of] *add* so Co   1323 goddas] goddis
of Co   1328 she sayde] *om.* Co   1329 canst] *add* to me Co
1336 inhabyte] *add* and dwell in Co   1338 feel not] *om.* L   1339–40 of . . .
worschyppers] *om.* Co   1342 iuge] *om.* Co   1343 he seyth] *om.* Co

vndirstode he was thus confusid and overcomen be thys holy virginis wordes, anoone he roryd like a woode lyon and commaunded her clothys to be doone of and her body to be alle tobete and rente with
1355 scorgis fulle of hookes made of bulle synewes withowte eny mercy or pyte, and aftir thys to be rubbid moste grevously alle her body with rough clothes of heyre moste scharp and paynfulle.

O the wycked and cruelle tiranny commaundyng such tormentis vnto a tendre body. But the herte of so clene a virgine myght never
1360 be withdrawen from the love of Crist for any of these peynes, but rather was more stedfaste and stronge to suffre them for the love that sche hadde to her veray spowse Ihesu Criste. And thoff these peynes were longe so that alle her precious body ranne on bloode and her woundes were rubbid with salt, and this wickid tyraunte hadde
1365 commaunded her to be putte in a moste derke preson and rollid vpon
f. 266ra schellis | and scherdis and scharpe harde stoones, and thought he wolde prolonge her dethe with moste cruelle peynes and put her to moste grevous tormentis or ever sche dyed but yf sche wolde be entretid and goo from her feythe, yit sche toke alle this fulle
1370 paciently and was right ioyfulle and gladde to suffre suche tormentis and paynes for the name of Ihesu. Wherfor the same nyght abowte mydnyght came grete light from heven aboute her into the same preson, and in the same light owre saviour Ihesus, in whom sche putt alle her hoope and truste, came and appered vnto her and comfortid
1375 her and seyde: 'Barbara, my wele belovid doughter and [spowse], be stronge in the feythe and of goode comforte, for there is right grete ioye made bothe in heven and in erthe of thy passion. Drede never the thretenyngis nor paynes there of thys wickid tiraunte, for I am with the and schalle delyuer the from alle the sore woundes thowe
1380 haste resceyved for me and make the hoole.' And anoone herewith sche was hoole from alle the woundes that sche hadde, so that ther was not the leste signe or tokyn of any wounde seen vpon her, and then our lorde blessyd her and made a sygne of the crosse vpon her and vnto her sight assendid ayene vp into heven. Of this vision and
1385 comfort therfor this blessid virgyne hadde more ioy and gladnes then enybody can speke or thynke, wherfor sche thanked God with alle her herte and seide: 'Lorde, gramarcy, for now am I save in beholdynge of thy maieste and glorye.' |

1361 stronge] strenger Co   1368 moste] more Co   1375 spowse] spowses L
1378 there] om. Co   1381 that(2)] add she had that Co

The .x. chapter how Seynt Barbara was putte to moo
tormentis and peynes after the [firste] makyng hoole. And
how sche was led aboute the cite naked and beten with
scorgis. And how the aungelle of God brought her a
garment from heven and kevered her body and made her
hoole ayeen of alle her woundes.

Forthewith the nexte day folowynge this [bestialle] man and wickid
iuge and scheder of mannes blode sette in iugement ayeen and
commaunded this holy virgine to be brought byfore hym. And when
he sawe her body alle hoole and more feyre then ever it was before
and no signe of any stroke appere vpon her, he brake owte with a
lowde voice and seide with a grete sperit: 'O the pite, O the mercy, O
the benyvolens of our goddis. ȝit haue they not lefte the destitute nor
forsaken the, ȝit be they so merciful and kynde to the and so besy
aboute thyne helthe and to saue thy lyfe þat they have rewthe vpon
the and have made the hoole this same nyght of alle the woundes
thow haddest of vs yisterday. Now maiste thowe see þat thow haste
doone theym wronge, nowe maiste thowe se that they be not so cruel
as thow holdeste them. If they schulde haue schewed theyr cruelte
and a doone as they hadde cause, they schulde not a made the hoole
but a turmentid the with more gretter peynes. But nowe yt schewith
welle that they haue schewid this mercy to the because thowe
schuldiste remembre how gracious they be and turne and do
sacrefice | vnto theym.'

[Then Seynt Barbara the holy spouse of Criste answered and seide
to the iuge:] 'Stoppe thy mouthe and leve thy wickid langage, thowe
blasphemer of God allemyghty. Thy false goddes that thow worschi-
pesste here in vayne, in the depe derke pitte of helle they lye in
everlastyng payne and like vnto the they be and other that
worschippe theym, withowte mercy and pite and vndirstondyng of
the trouthe and may helpe no man nor make hym hole, for and if
they myght they wolde rather helpe and socour theymselfe. And
therfor alle ye that are owte of the trew beleve and set your beleve in
theym and make your oblacions and sacrefice vnto theym, ye rather
encrese your paynes thereby in helle than ye dispose yowe for to
haue forgevenes of synne. But [y] in stede of encens offre devoute

1395

1400

1405

1410

f. 266va

1415

1420

1390 firste] fiste L   1395 bestialle] testialle L   1403 saue] haue Co
1408 a(1)(2)] haue Co   a] haue Co   1413–14 Then . . . iuge] om. L
1424 y] om. L

1425 prayer to my lord Ihesu Crist whiche hath made me hoole of alle my
woundes, and in stede of sacrefice I offre myselfe vnto hym, and for
his love I am redy to putte my body to alle maner of turmentis and
peynes. And thowe, wickid iuge, and there were eny grace in the,
thow myght consydre and see what my lorde ys be the grete
1430 benefeetes that he hathe schewed to me. But thowe arte [blynde]
and wylte not knowe thy maker, for þe deville thurgh thyne owen
malice hath blynded the and made the so harde hertid that thow
maiste not see.'

Than the iuge [perseyvyng] that sche was more strenger in the feithe
1435 of Criste after her helthe [recouered] than ever sche was before,
commaunded his tormentoures to hange her vp in a gibette alle
nakyd, her fete vpward and her hede downeward and her holy body
f. 266ᵛᵇ to be | rakked thorough moste cruelly with flessch hookis and other
dyvers instrumentis, and than hote brennyng lampes or cressettes to
1440 be putte to her sydes to brenne the woundes to her more peyne. And
whan this was done so that alle her blessyd body ranne a blode lyke
stremes owt of a welle, this holy virgyne thanked God and was more
meryer than ever sche was before. This wicked tyraunte commaunded also hoote glowynge plates of iron to be holde to her
1445 sydes so that what by the woundes, what by the lampes or cressettis
and brennyng plates, sche schulde feele and suffre moste horrible
paynes that myght be thought.

O moste cruelle tyraunte, þat myght fynde in thyne herte to
assigne such peynes to anybody. But this most holy virgine stode
1450 alletogeder armed in the love of God and was nothynge aferde of so
grevous passions, but suffred moste paciently and thanked God in
hope and truste of remedye, synging and seiynge thus: 'Nowe am I
glad in allemyghty God, nowe am I ioiful in my herte, now haue I
grete delite in my saviour Criste Ihesu, now haue I a cause to thanke
1455 God and praise God, for now wote I wele the peynes and sorowes of
this worlde be nothynge like to the ioies that every true cristen man
and womman schalle resseyve and haue for ever herafter.'

Whan the iuge herde this he fared lyke a wood man owte of his
witte and commaunded her to be take downe and set in a peyre of
1460 stokkes before hym, and her hede to be troden vnder foote, and alle
f. 267ʳᵃ to be bette with iron hamers tille alle the pament ranne | a bloode.
Whilste therfor this holy virgyne laboured in this maner of paynes,

1430 blynde] blynded L   1434 perseyvyng] perseyved L   1435 recouered]
om. L   ever] om. Co   1445 by(1)(2)] for Co   1448 O] add thou Co

sche made her praiers to God and seide: 'Lorde God whiche arte in
heven, bowe thyn eeres of grace and here me. Thowe arte my kynge,
thow arte my God. For the am I brought to reprefe, for the am I   1465
mokked and scorned. Thow arte my cause and occasion þat I suffre
this. Helpe me, Lorde, and defende me and arme me ayenste my
enemyes, for I knowe verely that alle my helthe and welfare is of the.'
When the iuge herde this he was more woder and bethought hym
what he myght doo or what peynes he myght devise for to make her   1470
leve this lay, and anoon like a woode beste and like a serpent fulle of
venom commaunded his turmentoures to take theyre swerdis and
cutte of her brestes be longe layser, þat sche schulde feele the
stronger peyne in þe longe cuttyng of theym.

O how grete and plentevous is the swetnes of God that made this   1475
holy virgyne to suffre so manyfolde paynes with soo grete swetnes as
thow alle had bene as a play and a sporte. The grete love þat sche
hadde to Criste made the daies of turmentis and peynes seme to her
but schorte, soo that whilest her brestys were a cuttynge owte sche
suffred moste paciently and turned her face to the iuge and seide: 'O 1480
thow cruelle beste, O thow [man] cruelle owte of kynde that gnawest
and renteste of my pappis as it were with wolfes tethe, knowest
thowe not that the more thow [turmentist me in my body in erthe
the more thow encresist my victory and crowne in heven?] This
drawynge owte of my brestes is a comforte and a | refresschynge to f. 267rb
me. Why arte thow not aschamed to take and cutte awey womans   1486
beaute? Why arte thowe not aschamed to kutte awey in me þat thow
somtyme dydest sowke in thy moder? Wolte thow make me a man?
Spare not hardely, I am glad thereof. It plesith me welle for to be a
man that I may overcome the the more manfully. It is convenyent   1490
that the brestis whom child never dydde sowke be drawen awey from
the body that the armes may be at more large to fight.'

And when this holy virgyne hadde seide thus sche loked vp to
heven warde and made her prayers to God and saide: 'Lorde God,
whiche syttis in the high trone of thy maieste and demeste alle the   1495
world be rightwisnes and equyte, be to me as a lord and defende me.
Be to me as a place of comforte and refresschynge and [kepe] me in
savegarde from alle enmyes noiyng me. Varely, Lorde, myn enmyes

1474 cuttyng] *add* off Co   1479 a] in Co   1481 man] *om.* L, *add* vnkyndly
Co   1482 it were] *om.* Co   1483-4 turmentist..erthe/encresist heven] *trsp.* L
1483 in erthe] *om.* Co   1486 and cutte] *om.* Co   1490 the(1)] *om.* Co
1497 kepe] helpe L

be risen vpon me [and gnawe vpon me] as doggis that gnawe vpon
1500 karyon, and to my breestys they be not aschamed nor aferde to putte
theyre cruelle handis. Lord, thow maist se and howe they haue goode
sporte to beholde my bloode renne down fro me. Thow arte alle my
love and alle my truste and fidelite. For the I am now like a man, my
brestes taken awey and goone, but I beleve verely that thow schalt
1505 restore them ayen to me in everlastyng felicite, where nothynge that
is grevous or vnhoneste schalle be, nor nothynge that sowneth to any
imperfeccion.'

When therefor this holy virgynes brestes were cutte of as now
f. 267va before is saide, and this moste wickid tyraunt sawe | that he myght
1510 not prevaile nor have his entente, than yit he ful of vervent malise
and wickednesse wolde not anoone determyne her dethe as he was
purposed tofore, but he added malice vpon malice and commaunded
this chaste virgyne thus pitevously araied, thus wounded and thus
turmentyd, to be ledde naked rownde abowte alle the cite and to be
1515 betyne with scorges and roddes, that alle the peple myght se and
wonder vpon herre. Where was there ever such another [turmentour?
Where was there ever such another] woo or payne? Where was there
evere so ferefulle and horrible a dede don be man? But this our
saviour, merciful Ihesu, suffred to be doone to his chosyn spowse
1520 here in the erthe þat sche schulde haue the more victorie and be
crowned with the more gracious and brighter crowne in heven. For
this virgyne was not overcome be this turmentry, thof the vertu of
honeste in her were aschamed vertuously, for when [alle thes] cruelle
commaundementis were doone the moste care that sche hadde was
1525 for her nakednes of body, wherfor sche lifte vp her eien to heven and
made her praiers to God and saide: 'Lord God, whiche coveriste the
fyrmamente with clowdes and yeviste coloure manyfolde and dyvers
to flowres and lilyes growynge in the feeldes, so that Salamon the
roialleste kynge that ever was, was never so coverde with vesture nor
1530 clothes as be they, be my defender and helper, my goode Lorde, now
at þis tyme I beseche the, and cover my body with the clothis of thy
f. 267vb mercy that noone of these wicked paynes | nor these paynemes nor
no man els may now beholde nor loke vpon me vnreverently.'

1499 and . . . me] om. L   1500 nor aferde] om. Co   1510–1 vervent malise
and] maliciouse Co   1513 this] add moost Co   1514 the] add province and
the Co   1516–17 turmentour . . . another] om. L   1517 there] om. Co
1519 saviour/merciful] trsp. Co   Ihesu] om. Co   1521 gracious, brighter] gloriouse, hyere Co   1522 thof] thorowe Co   1523 alle thes] this L
1530 be(2)] add thou Co   my(2)] om. Co   1532 paynes nor these] om. Co

And whyle sche prayed thus, anoone almyghty God, which hathe
cure and charge and rule of alle [his] creatures, sente his aungelle to   1535
her with a feyre white garment from heven and coverde her body
therewith so honestely that there was never woman nor mayden
more goodely araied when sche schuld be weddyd to her newe
husbond. And herewith the aungelle comfortid her and crossid her
and blessid her and made her soo hoole of alle her woundes that   1540
there was not the leste signe or token of any hurte seen vpon her
body. The turmentoures also that drofe her forthe and bette her with
roddes and scorges sodeynly were made blynde euerichone by the
grete brightnes of this hevenly garment sente to her from heven, so
that then every man beganne to commende and praise this gracious   1545
and glorious virgyne and had her in grete reverence and worschippe.
And than sche herselfe was more gladder of this victorie than ever
was Iudith that noble lady whan sche had smyten of Olyfernes hede
by the harde body.

The .xj. chapiter of other grete tormentis done to Seynte   1550
Barbara. And of the peticions grauntid vnto her of God.
And howe sche was behedid by her owne fader vpon whom
God toke vengeance sodenlye.

Anoone within a litille while after, when this holy virgine come into a
certeyne strete of the seide cite called Thaslasser, the pepul of the   1555
same strete toke her and brought her ayeen before | the seide iuge   f. 268ra
Marcian. And when the iuge sawe that sche was alle hoole and more
feyrer and ruddier and bettyr cherid in the face and merier and more
bettir araied than ever sche was before, he was gretely astonyed
within hymselfe and cowde not speke a word, but satte stylle lyke a   1560
mased man and like a man alletogedre madde and owt of his witte.
Whan this holy virgine perseyved this, sche cryed vpon hym and
seide: 'A thow wycked iuge and confused and confounded lyke vnto
thy fader the deville, why arte thow trowblid of this grace schewed to
me by my spowse and lorde Ihesu Criste in alle his yiftes so free? I   1565
pray God that alle they that worschip ydolles and mawmettis and
sette theyre ioye in theym be brought to confusion and schame as
thow arte.'

1535 his] these L   1545–6 gracious and] om. Co   1555 strete] add were
wikked and Co   1560 a] oon Co   1563 and(1)] all Co   and confounded]
om. Co   1564 thow] add so Co

Than the iuge come ageyne to hymselfe, and stered by his [meyne]
1570 for to revenge hym on these wordes, like a rorynge lyon commaunded this holy virgine to be caste vpon naked swerdes sette
vpright by and by and her body to be made fulle of woundes moste
cruelly. And at the laste whan he se that he cowde not haue the
better of her he beganne to wex woode with hymselfe and grenned
1575 vpon her like a dogge and seide: 'A thow wicche, thow by thy
wicchecrafte takest awey mennys wittes from theym and makest
theym witles.' And than he spake to his meyne and seide: 'Have awey
this wicche from me and slee her, for and sche lyve eny lenger I am
so enfebled I schalle not lyve.' Than alle his meyne, officers and
f. 268rb peple that stode aboute hym, consentid to | her dethe and seide: 'Let
1581 this wicche be dede that thus by her new maner of charmes and
wichcraftes takeþ mennes wittes from theym withowte potacions and
drynkis, oonly by her wordes.'

Anoone therefor forthewith alle the iuge gave sentence of dethe
1585 vpon her and seide thus: 'The mageste of emperoures hath made
decree that whoevir wylle nat do make sacrefice with ensence to owr
goddis he schalle falle in the sentence of his hede stryken of,
whatsoever he be.' Whan this sentence was gyven this holy virgyne
thanked God with alle her herte, and like Sampson myghtely and
1590 strongely withstode the emperoures commaundementis and was redy
to suffre alle maner of turmentis and peynes rather than sche wolde
oones applie to his entente. And herewith also sche dispisid the iuge
and alle his meyne and kepte herselfe stedfaste and stable ever in the
feith of Criste and wolde never go therfrom to deye therfor. Than yit
1595 notwithstondyng alle this, the foreseide kynge Dyoscorus this holy
virgine is fader was not satisfyed hereby. But whan he sawe that the
iuge was overcome and cowde do noo more, anoone [he] was redy to
schewe his cruelte, faryng like them that be gladde whan they haue
doone schrewedly, and so he reioysed hymselfe in his owne
1600 lewdenes, malice and wykkednes to the encrese of his peynes in
the pitte of helle, and lyke a woode beste sette honde vpon this holy
f. 268va virgine as though he hadde | forgoten clene that ever sche was his
doughter, and like a woode man drewe her forthe with hym to the
hille where sche schulde be hedyd. Sche therefor to be the veray
1605 folower of Criste, which whan he wolde deye for mankynde vpon the
crosse came before to the place of his passyon to schewe that he

1569 meyne] maner L　　　　1582 potacions] eny pocionz Co　　　1586 do] om. Co
1597 he] om. L　　　1601 woode] wylde Co　　　1605 mankynde] mannes kynde Co

suffred passyon wilfully, right so nowe this holy virgyne with grete
ioye and gladnes for to haue the more glorious victorie and crowne in
heven wente before her fader to þis hille and songe and seyde with
herte and mowthe: 'How may it be but þat I in my soule schalle be 1610
obediente and subiecte to my lorde God almyghty? Of hym haue I
alle my helthe, he is my lorde, he is my God and brynger vp to
blysse, he wylle never forsake me as I truste and beleve verely, hym I
worschippe and love as I can, for he is my saviour and helper in tyme
of nede, to whom alle my desyre is to come. He be preysed, thanked 1615
and magnyfied everlastyngely for the grete grace and mercy that he
hath schewed to me. For nowe I consider wel and se that by his grace
and goodenes it is that I am so stedfaste in trewe feith and beleve and
may never be departyd from hym, nother by tormentis nor paynes of
any wicked men, nor never enclyne from the right wey of trowthe 1620
vnto false doctryne.'

And whan this holy virgyne hadde seide thus and considered that
her lyfe was but schorte here in this worlde and how nye everlasting
ioie and felicite was comyng to her, anoone sche gave her to prayer
devotely and beganne to make her | bone and peticion to God and f. 268ᵛᵇ
seide in this wyse: 'Lorde Ihesu Crist, whiche hath made bothe 1626
heven and erthe and alle þat therein ys, Lorde, whiche haste made
the see, the londe, the fisschis, the fowles, the schowres, the dewes,
the clowdes and the raynes, Lorde, whiche haste walked vpon the see
and staunched the flodes of theyr [roughnes] and the wyndis of 1630
theyre blowynge and boystous blastis, Lord, whiche hast spred abrod
thy precious armes vpon the crosse and schewed thy grete mercy to
mankynde, bothe to goode and to yvelle, with innumerable myracles,
benefetis and graces many moo than may be rekened or rehersid,
here me now thy servaunt, moste merciful God, in this my laste 1635
necessite and nede. And for thow hast be my lord God from my
yonge age and graciously defended me and kepte me hyder to nowe,
merciful saviour, to whose commaundement alle thynges be obedient, make me to make a goode ende of my lif and agony, and graunte
me this grace of thy mercy, that whosoever be in any necessite or 1640
nede and remembre me and calle vpon me may haue comforte of thy
large pite. And for them, Lorde, I pray moste specially, that be
yerely devocion worschip and kepe the day of my passion to thy
lawde and praysyng, that they never deye sodeynly but that they may
be verely contrite and confessid of theyr synnes and resceyve thy 1645

1630 roughnes] rightwisnes L   1640 thy] *add* grett Co   1641 me(2)] the Co

blessid body or they go hens, that the deville haue never power in
theym to kepe them from thy face of glorie. Remembre not theyre
synnes, Lorde, at the day of dome to theyre confusion and schame,
f. 269ʳᵃ but haue mercy vpon theym and | forgeve theym. Thow knoweste
1650 welle, moste benynge lord and oure alther maker, that man is fraile
and redy to falle.'

And whan this holy virgyne had made this praier to oure lorde
God and seide 'Amen', anoon sodeynly came a voice fro heven and
seyde: '*Veni electa mea, veni sponsa mea formosa, veni coronaberis*
1655 *aureola quam tibi ab eterno preparaui in regno meo;*' this is to sey in
Englissch: 'Come to me my [chosyn sowle, come to me my] wele
belovid spouse, alle feyre and beutevous. Come and thow schalt be
crowned with the crowne fulle glorious whiche I haue ordeyned for
the from withowt begynnyng and reigne with me in my kyngdome in
1660 ioie and blisse everlastyng. And nowe it is graunted and given to the
alle that ever thowe haste desyred and asked of me.'

Then thys holy virgine heryng this voice was right ioyfulle and mery
in sowle and thanked God right gladly, and than sche leyde forthe her
feyre white and holy necke that her precious hede schulde be smyten of
1665 by the wickid handes of her owen fader. And so it was done vereli in
dede as the ende preveth, for the kyng her fader Dioscorus toke owte
his swerde and, like as he made promyse to her before, right so nowe in
a grete woodenesse smote of her hede and sente her soule to heven by
his synne and wickidnes, whose body before he brought into this world
1670 by grete laboure and besynesse. And thus the yere of oure lorde
.CC.lxvij. Maxymyan emperoure of Rome, Marcian iuge and ruler in
the cite of Nichomede, as it is before rehersid, this glorious virgine
f. 269ʳᵇ Seynt Barbara the .iiij. day of Decem|bir suffred glorious martirdome
for Criste, sche beyng aboute .xv. yere of age, whose sowle was borne
1675 vp to heven gloriously of aungelles with grete ioye and gladnes and
there now reigneth with Criste for ever in blys.

Aftir this, whan this glorious virgine thus victoriously was
deceased in owre lorde Ihesu and her agonye and payne were
alletogeder overpassed and doone, and whan this seide kyng
1680 Dioscorus her fader was come downe of the hille where as he
hadde behedid his owne doughter, he settyng fulle littille by this
that he hadde doone suych a wicked dede, allemyghty God, whiche
reserveth to hym due punysschement for synne, wolde not [suffre]

1648 and schame] *om.* Co   1654 *formosa*] *add mea* Co   1656 chosyn . . .
my] *om.* L   1683 suffre] *om.* L

such an horrible dede go vnpunyssched, but sente wildefyre from
above whiche brente hym and consumyd hym soo vtterly to assches   1685
and powder that there lefte not the leste crome of hym vnconsumed.
And therewith there came a grete wynde and bare vp these assches
abrode into the [eyre] as thycke as it hadde be motes in the
sunnebeame and caste theym downe alletogeder in an hepe into
the fyre of helle, where as now it is to suppose he is buried bothe   1690
soule and body world withowte ende, and there lieth in dovble
paynes after his deservyng, from the whiche God kepe vs all. Amen.

The .xij. chapter how Seynt Barbara was buried firste by a
cristen man and a preste. And how afterward sche was
translated and schryned amonge the paynemes for the   1695
manyfolde myracles schewed among them thorugh her
merytes.|

[L]este therefor this precious iowelle and holy body of this glorious   f. 269ᵛᵃ
and vndefiled virgine and martir Seynt Barbara schuld be devowred
of doggis or of hoggis or eten of any other beestes or fowles of the   1700
eyre, oone Valentinus, a cristen man and a preste, vnknowen to
Seynt Barbara while sche lyved, whan he knewe that sche was dede
and suffred martirdome for the feyth of Crist, anoon he made redy a
bere whiche longe tyme before he had ordeyned for hymselfe, it is to
suppose. And the same nyght folowyng he toke his carte and wente   1705
and fette and brou3t this holy corse with hym, and after tyme he
hadde sette the heede and the body togedyr and wrapped yt in
clothis with many precious oynementys and spices, with grete
reverence and worschip he beryed it in the same cite. And in this
same place of her berielle he didde make vp a lytylle praty chapelle,   1710
in the whiche to the worschip of God, be the merites and
intercession of this glorious virgin and martir [be] many grete and
wonderful myracles done many tymes and ofte, for [ther] the blynde
be restored to sight, the halte [to] goo vpright, the deefe to heeryng,
the dome to spekyng, the lame to helthe, the sory to welthe, the   1715
vexed with wicked sperites to right wytte and lay, and many other
grete myracles be schewed there yit into this day.

1684 wildefyre] fire Co   1688 eyre] cite L   1692 from . . . whiche] wherfrom
Co   1695 translated and] om. Co   1698 Leste] Beste L   1699 vndefiled]
vndefouled Co   1706 and fette] forth Co   corse] body Co   1712 be] by L, ar
Co   1713 ther] om. L   1714 to(2)] om. L   1716–17 other . . . myracles]
another mirakle Co

The peple therefor of the cite, thof they were paynemes, whan
they sawe these grete and innumerable myracles wrou3t among them |
f. 269vb euery day encresyng more and more, they ordeyned a feyre schryne
1721 and a corious bothe noble, riche and precious, alle coverid with golde
and precious stones. And this schryne they ordeyned that this
glorious virgyne schulde be translate and hadde in more reverence
and worschip than ever sche was before. And so when this schryne
1725 was redy they leyde her body þerin, and with grete ioy and gladnesse
lifte [it] vp on high into the chefe temple of the seide cite hangynge
[it] by .iiij. chaynes of golde fulle reverently with many feyre lampes
and lightis thereaboute brennyng ful clerely. This was done by the
grete providence and wisdom of God for to schewe the high
1730 excellence of hys holy spouse Seynt Barbara, for these .iiij. cheynes
betoken the preceptis and counseylis conteyned in þe .iiij. gospellis
writen by the .iiij. evangelistis Mathew, Marke, Luke and Iohn,
whiche sche fulfilled ful surely, and the .iiij. cardynal vertues where
after sche disposed her living fulle vertuously. And these chaynes
1735 were not made of golde for nou3t, for golde is a noble and a precyous
metalle amonge alle metalles, and so was sche right noble and
precious in the sight of God be the vertu of chastite, moste precious
of alle precious. This schryne also was lyfte vp and hanged on high
by the seyde cheynes of golde with her precious body, in tokenyng
1740 that sche was a clene virgine and in her mortalle body leved an
angelles lyfe alletogedyr set vp to hevenwarde ferre fro erthely and
f. 270ra worldly lyfe, so that | sche myght sey contynuelly like as seide the
holy man Iob, which in maner lyved suche a lyfe: 'Suspendium elegit
anima mea', that is to sey, my life is as a thynge hanged vp on high,
1745 alletogeder sette vp to God warde and hevenlynes, ferre from the
concupiscens, delectaciones and vanitees of the worlde and world-
lynes. And thus was doone her first translacion.

The .xiij. chapiter of the meanes of her seconde translacion
from the paynemes to Rome.

1750 Criste, Goddis sone in Trynyte, his charite is so grete and free with
large habundaunce of grace, mercy and pite that no resonable
creature there is whatever he be but that he may be partyner of

1726 it] om. L   on] and Co   seide] om. Co   1727 it] om. L   1737 chastite]
charytee Co   1738 hanged] changed vpp Co   1742 contynuelly] conueniently
Co   1746-7 and worldlynes] om. Co

his passyon, and he wole be even equalite, for he is veray God and man and makeþ excepcion to no persone. Blessyd mote he be that wille calle vpon hym for grace and mercy, but he be special previlege 1755 hathe visite the peple of cristiante and sette vpon hym his marke of knowlege before alle other syngulerly. And he is not so merciful and gracious to vs or to vertuous peple but that he is as scharpe and rightwys to synfulle pepulle. He therfor, considerynge the synne and vice that sumtyme reigned in the worlde, specially aboute the partes 1760 of Egipte amonge the peple of that londe, whiche folowid theyre lustys and didde as they wolde and not as they schulde, euery day encresynge in theyre synnes more and more, nor never wolde leve theyr wickidnes and amende theym but contynue forthe in theyre infidelite and mysbeleve, thought for to destroye theym, wherefor he 1765 sterid and reysed | vp the hertes of cristen peple that lyved in trewe f. 270rb feith and bileve of holy Chirche and desired his [worshippe and] encrese of cristen feith, but they schulde gedyr togedyr and goo forthe toward the lande of Egipte for to make these rebelles and peple owte of bileve subiecte to the dominacion of owre modyr holi 1770 Chirche and to his lawes.

Whan this noble oste therfor and feithfulle congregacion of cristen peple were gedrid togedyr and wente forthe and scowred the contreyes abowte, alle the parties suche as helde and folowed the secte of the paynemes and many an heretyke besyde, and alle suych 1775 as they cowde fynde owte of bileve and wolde not be convertid to cristen feith, they punyssched them and entretid fulle scharpely, but alle suche as wolde be convertid to cristen feith and doo penaunce they resseyved to grace and to mercy and made them cristen peple. So that thof the cristen peple were gretely hurte and often tymes 1780 stode in grete perille bothe of themself and of theyre goodis, yit allewey they wente forthe and hadde the victorie, for allemyghty God faught with theym and for theym. And therefor in scripture he is callid God of batelles, for he hathe power both in heven and in erthe to gefe the batelle and the victorie to whom it plesith hym. And 1785 nothynge there is that may resiste or lette his power but that he may doo what he wylle, for he is lorde of alle and comunly withstondeth alle prowde peple and giveth alle victorie and his grace to theym that be verey meke. For as moche | therefor as our lorde Ihesu Criste is f. 270va

1758 vs or to] om. Co   1767 worshippe and] om. L   1768-9 but . . .
forthe] om. Co   1774 the parties] om. Co   1775 many an heretyke] heritikis
Co   1778 to . . . feith] om. Co

1790 lorde of alle his creatures, he wylle not that the holy and precious
bodies of his chosen seyntes here in erthe schalle be entreted
vnreverently or hadde in disworschip whose devote sowles reigne
with hym perpetuelly in heven, but rather that they schalle be hadde
in grete reverence and worschip, theyre bodies translate and exalted
1795 in the chirche after theyr excellence and meritis of levynge. Wherefor
it is wreten in the Olde Testement that Enoch that holy patryarke
pleased God so moche in his livynge that allemyghty God translated
hym into paradise terrestrial. And if he for his holy levyng deserved
to be translate into thys place of ioy here in erthe, yit beyng in bodely
1800 lyfe in tyme of the Olde Testament, moche more the holy bodies of
Cristes seyntes whos sowles be in heven owght to be exalte and
translate and hadde in grete reuerence and worschip in the chirche
among cristen peple in tyme of the Newe Testament. And so nowe
also it was worthy that the holy body of the glorious virgyne and
1805 martir Seynt Barbara the spowse of Crist schold be translate from the
paynemes and hadde in more reverence and worschip, as ye schalle
here afterwarde.

Whylest sche was so excellente in vertues lyvynge, so stronge in
the feith, so stedfaste in hope, so fervent in charite, so paciente in
1810 adversite, so straite in penaunce doynge, so meke, so pure, so
innocent and so perfite in alle her levynge, for worschip is dewe to
f. 270ᵛᵇ vertu, and worship [to] every goode | dede is the rewarde and mede,
saiying our lorde God allemyghty 'danti michi honorem dabo gloriam,
whosoever to my worschip liveth vertuously I schal rewarde hym
1815 with the worschipfulle mede of endeles glorie.' In processe of tyme,
therfor, the forseide oste of cristen peple came to the seide cite of
Solis or Nichomede, where as the peple, thof they were paynemes,
hadde firste translate the glorious body of this glorious virgine Seynt
Barbara, as it is seide.

1820 And whan they hadde leyde seege to this cite and with grete
difficulte had wonne and goten yt, such as were owte of the beleve
and hateful to God they murthered and distroyed, but alle such that
wolde be converted and do penaunce they resseyved to grace and
mercy to the encrese of the feith of holy Chirche, as it is saide before.
1825 Also and alle this was doon, it is to suppose verely and withowte

1795 Wherefor] om. Co   1801 owght] owe Co   1805 the(1)] add holy Co
1808 vertues] vertuous and punctuate after lyvynge Co   1809 the] om. Co
1812 to] of L   1814 to my] do me Co   1821 yt] add all Co
1822 distroyed] distrewde Co   1825 Co punctuates after Also

dowte be the hande of God, that this noble tresoure the body of this
glorious virgine schulde be take from the paynemes vnworthy to
haue suych a iewelle amonge theym, and after the ordynaunce of
God be translate and brought to our moder holy Chirche and exalte
amonge cristen peple and had in dewe reverence and worschip. For 1830
there is no convenience nor accorde betwene God and the deville,
nor it was not convenient nor accordynge that the holy body of so
holy a virgine schulde be in so fowle a place where as ydolles were
worschipped. For sche while sche lyved dispised alle ydolles and
ydolatrie, in so moche that sche toke the kynge Dioscorus her fadyrs 1835
idolles of golde and alle | tobreke them and gave theym awey be f. 271ra
pecemele and almes vnto poore folke, knawynge verely that our ioie
schulde be in God and that be almes [is] gate to vs the kyngdome of
blisse, as it is also more expresly seide before in the .vij. chapiter.

The .xiiij.e chapter of the grete myracle þat was schewed 1840
amonge cristen peple be the merites of Seynt Barbara in
her seconde translacion.

And praysyng be to our lord God almyghty, which for vs in his
manhode hath suffred vpon the crosse and goten the victorie, for be
his helpe it was verely that this seyde cite was taken of the cristen 1845
peple so graciously. Wherefor whan they thorowe Goddis helpe had
taken this cite, and after the comons of warryoures bothe wounded
and hoole wente aboute the stretes in the cite laanes and howses for
to gete goode and for to dispoyle the cite, at last they came into the
temple, not for to pray but because they supposyd to fynde moche 1850
tresour therein. And a merveylous thynge, they came not theder to
seke the mercy of God in that temple, and yit they fownde this
blessyd virgine and martir Seynt Barbara there helper. And thof they
never knewe her nor herd of her before, yit they founde her a
gracious helper vnto them, for as many cristen peple as came into the 1855
temple wounded and hurte, sodenly and anoone they were hoole
everichone. And what may we say, thof this were merveillous to
theym and so nowe to vs, but that thys was doone be our lord
God and | swete saviour Ihesus. Than the peple, greetly awondred, f. 271rb
were ioyful and gladde and thanked God and sought more wysely 1860

1832 holy] om. Co   1837 that] add all Co   1838 almes] almesdede Co
is] it L   1843 And] Laude and Co   1847 the comons] comon gyes Co
1852 the . . . God] god and his mercy Co

aboute if they myȝt fynde and knowe the cause more redely of so
grete a benefice and sodeyn helthe schewed vnto them, for man
naturally desirith to know the cause of every thynge. And no
merveyle though allemyghty God schewed this grete myracle nowe
1865　amonge cristen peple by the merytes of this holy virgine Seynt
Barbara, for he sumtyme in the olde lawe tolde his peple afore by
Moyses what myscheff, what hevynes, what sorowe, what warre and
what destruccion schuld falle vnto theym for there synne be theyr
enemyes bothe withowte and within. But when allemyȝti God
1870　perseyved that there enemyes entendid for to destroye his peple
vtterly, and thought also that suche victories as they hadde was of
themselfe and not of God, than he withdrewe his hande and wolde
not punyssche his peple no lenger, but gave hem power over theyr
enemyes for to overthrowe ther pride and destroye them, that they
1875　schuld knowe verely his peple hadde a lorde to punyssche theym
whan he wolde and delyuer hem whan it likid hym.

　Right so it was now for allemyghty God, considerynge the grete
pryde and infidelite and mysbelevynge that rayned amonge the
paynemes, and also that they dispised cristen peple and sette
1880　Criste at nought, and most of alle for he wolde haue the body of
f. 271va　this glorious | virgine Seynt Barbara translate and borne awey from
theym to be hadde more glorious in reverence and worschip, therefor
now he smote the paynemes downe and distroyed them and made
cristen peple hoole of theyr hurtes and woundes that they victor-
1885　iously schuld make the seconde translacion of this sayde glorious
virgine.

　The peple therefor, ioyful and gladde and gretely awondred of the
vertu and grace [shewde] amonge them, not yit knowynge pleynly
the vertu of God, wente forther into the temple for to serche better
1890　aboute and wolde not cease til that they had theyr desire. And lo
anoone by grace of God they founde that they wold haue, for they
founde the glorious body of this blessid virgine hanging be foure
cheynes of golde in a feyre schryne of golde alle besett with precious
stones, with lampes and lightis brennyng rownd aboute in the moste
1895　ryalle wyse as it besemed right weel for suche an holy virgyne to
haue for the blessyd virginite and martirdome þat schone ful
syngulerly in her, as it is seide before. For sche was not sloutheful
and sluggisch or ydille with the fonnde virgines that lay and slepte

1862 benefice] benefete Co
1878 mysbelevynge] myslyvyng Co
1888 shewde] om. L

1867 what(4)] add sorow L
1881 Seynt Barbara] om. Co

and were put owt of heven gates for they wolde not make redy to
mete with theyr lord whan he came to calle theym to his weddynge 1900
of blisse, but schynynge in vertu more brighter than the sunne, redy
to mete with our lorde and to entre with hym as a kyngis doughter to
the kyngdom | of heven, alle besette with pacience, loue and charite f. 271vb
and with alle maner of vertues and feith of holy Chirche on every
syde. And sche forsoken and forgate her fadyr and alle temperalle 1905
worschipis and riches and dominacions and power and alle worldly
vanyte, and at laste, as it is seyde before, for the love of her spowse
Ihesu Criste suffred martirdom and dethe by her owen wycked fader
handes, wherefor sche deservid thus to be worschipid in erthe.

When the peple therefor sawe many grete myracles doone and so 1910
grete solempnyte and worschip aboute thys schryne in the temple,
and amonge alle other they founde an aged man and a preest of the
gentils sittyng besyde the same [schryne], they askid of hym what
alle this mente. But the preste was so aferde whan he sawe them
come in, and stode in grete drede of his lyfe, supposyng þat they 1915
wolde sodenly haue kylled hym and made an ende of hym, that he
cowde not speke a worde. Whan they behelde the preest and
perceyved that he was so gretely aferde, anoon þey spake feyre
and easely to hym and asked of hym ageyn what was in this schryne
and what it mente þat there was so grete solempnyte, worschip and 1920
preciosite doone thereaboute. Than the preeste answerid and seyde
that in the same schryne was the glorious body of the excellente
virgine and martir Seynt Barbara, sumtyme a kyngis doughter, and
moreover rehersed alle her lyfe vnto theym and tolde theym howe
sche was behedid by the kynge Dioscorus | her owen fader and gave f. 272ra
her sawle to Criste her spowse, to whom sche made a specialle preyer 1926
for her servauntes and worschippers before her dethe, affermynge
also that after her bitter passyon and dethe, by her meanes were
doone innumerable myracles in the same cite, and this was the cause
that so grete solempnyte reverence and worschip was made and 1930
doone to her body aboute the schryne.

When the cristen peple herde þis and sawe theyr felisschip that
were wounded and hurte in batelle hoole by the merytes of this
glorious virgyne, anoon with grete ioye and gladnes gave preysyngis
and thanking to God for his merveylous werkis in his seyntes, and 1935
forthewith ranne and fette alle the bodies of cristen peple that were

1908 wycked . . . handes] fader Co   they] that Co   1910 sawe] add so Co
1912 they . . . aged] an aged fonde Co   1913 schryne] scryne L

slayne in the same batelle and brought theym into the temple everichone. And anoone allemyghty God, whiche is merveilous in power, more merveillous in grace and mercy, but moste merveilous
1940 of alle in his seyntes, for to geve a worschipful name for evermore to this glorious virgyne Seynt Barbara [forthewith] by her merites and by the prayers of cristen peple alle these dede bodies were raysed from dethe to lyfe.

Than was ioye and than was gladnes. And than alle everichone alle
1945 hoole togeder for þe grete deuocion and love they hadde to God felle downe flatlyng vpon the pament and wepte for ioye and thanked God and preysed God and blessid God in his moste holy spowse Seynt
f. 272ʳᵇ Barbara. And verely welle myght they blesse God and thanke | hym that so blessidly hathe chosen cristen peple to be theyre lorde and
1950 theyre God and to make theym eyres of heven in schewyng of so manyfolde benefetis and graces amonge theym to the worschip therefor of our lorde Ihesu Criste, whiche ys the werker of every goode dede that is doone. And to the laude and memorie of his noble spowse Seynt Barbara, the cristen peple with alle myrthe and gladnes
1955 and with alle deuocion and swetnesse mekely and reverently toke this precious body, and for to translate it into a more worschipful place didde alle theyr labour and besynes, so that they hadde so grete ioye and gladnes of the fynding of this glorious body and sperytualle tresour that they forgate alletogeder the strokes that they hadde in
1960 victorie and batelle before, and wente forth to Rome with the same body where it was leyde fulle reverently with alle ioye and worschip in a place called Seynte Kalixte churcheyerde, in the whiche chircheyerde restith the bodies of many an holy seynt fulle gloriously. And thus was doone the seconde translacion.

1965   The .xv. chapitre of the thirde translacion of the glorious
       virgine and martir Seynt Barbara.

Eternal God aftyr thys, whiche is conditour and maker of alle the worlde and disposeth tyme from tyme to schewe the habundaunce of his goodnes more plentevously after the highnes of his mageste and
1970 to oure informacion and recommendacion of his chosen seyntes, like
f. 272ᵛᵃ as this | holy virgyne had a synguler and a specialle knowlege before many oþer of the blessid and glorious Trenyte, right so he wolde also

that sche to her more worschip schulde be translate from place to
place .iij. tymes, that is to sey oones in her owne cuntrey, whan sche
was taken from the place that sche was first beryed in by the 1975
paynemes and translate into the temple, as it is seyde before in the
.xij. chapiter, another tyme whan sche was taken of this place by
cristen men and brought into the seyde cite of Rome, as it is seyde
before also in the next chapiter, and the thirde tyme whan sche was
translated from Rome into the cuntrey of Italye into a cite thereof 1980
clepid Placencia by the grete kynge and emperour of Rome called
Karolus Magnus. And this translacion was doone thus.

Charles, emperoure of Rome and kynge of Fraunce, hadde right a
devoute woman to his sustir, oone clepid Angilburgh, whiche in the
same seyde cite Placencia founded a noble monasterye of monkes of 1985
Seynt Benettis ordre, whiche monasterye amonge the comon peple
was clepid Seynt Sixte monasterye or the monasterie of Seynt Sixte.
Whan this noble emperoure therefor vpon a tyme came to Rome to
visite the holy apostles Petir and Poule, he mekely and devoutely
made supplycacion to the pope, than by name called Honorius the 1990
first, that he wolde vouchesafe to graunte hym and give hym the
worschipful body of the holy virgyne Seynt Barbara | martir of f. 272vb
Criste. The pope be the meke prayers and holy devocion of this
noble emperour enclyned to hys entente, and with his cardynallys
and clergie of alle the hole cyte of Rome with the peple folowyng 1995
wente in processyon wyse to the seide chirchyerde of Seynt Kalixte,
and with grete solempnyte, deuocion and prayer mekely by his owen
persone lifte vp the precious body of this glorious virgine and
betoke it vnto the emperour, save the hede he kepte to hymselfe for
the moste precious tresour and for a perpetualle memorie and 2000
witnesse in tyme to come that the body of þis virgine lay there
sumtyme before. And this was doone not oonely that so noble an
hede schulde be kepte of the hedes of the Chirche and Cristys vicars
here in erthe, holy fadirs and popes of Rome, but also for thys hede
schulde be hadde in more reverence and worschip because it was in 2005
the holy cite of Rome, whiche is hede of alle Cristes Chirche here in
erthe.

Then the noble emperour Karolus Magnus, whan he was enriched
with so riche and precious iewelle, was not a litille glad thereof but
gave thankyngis and preysyng to God, and in alle goodely wyse and 2010

1977 taken] add oute Co   1978 men] peple Co   1981 Rome] add Charlys
Co   1990 by . . . called] beynge Co   1995 hole] holy Co

with alle dewe reverence and worschip made redy alle thyngis
necessarie to the thridde translacion of so precyous a body and
hadde it forthe with hym into the seyde cite of Placence, and there
schryned yt the thyrde tyme with alle diligence in the seyde
2015 monasterye of Seynt Sixte, whiche his suster beforeseyde fownded
f. 273ra and made vp alle newe, the yeere of our lorde .viij.C. | .iiij. score .xv.
the .xij. day of Februarye, the same day noted and marked for þe
holy translacion of this gloryous virgyn and martyr of Criste Seynt
Barbara for evermore.

2020   Than beganne a newe light of grace too sprynge amonge the
Placentynes, lyke in maner as it didde sumtyme amonge the Iewes in
Quene Hesters dayes, for than was daunsynge and skyppynge,
worschippe, ioye and gladnesse amonge the peple, namely amonge
the monkes of Seynt Syxte whiche than myght wele sey of thys
2025 gloryous virgyn that ys wreten in scripture by the wyse man to her
lavde and preysynge: *Venerunt michi omnia bona pariter cum illa*: alle
encrese of grace and goodenes is come to vs by this gloryous virgyne
Seynt Barbara.

    This gloryous translacion is conteyned alletogeder in a certeyne
2030 cronycle of the seyde emperour Karolus Magnus, whiche for his
holynesse by specyalle priuylege ys clepyd Sanctus Karolus, and this
was doone for the thyrde translacion.

    The .xvj. chapiter of the feeste of the Invencion of Seynt
    Barbara.

2035 In processe and longe tyme after thys solempne translacion rose grete
contrauersy and rumour amonge the peple of the seyde cite of
Placence, sum saiyng of suspecion that the body of thys gloryous
virgyne Seynt Barbara, what by yiftis, what also by prayers, was
borne awey owte of the seyde cite of Placence. And many oone
f. 273rb affermed the same in many other dyvers places, saiyng that | they
2041 hadde the holy body with them when they hadde but a parte therof,
takynge paraventure after Aristotles saiyng a parte for the hoole.

    The same rumour also and contraversy was made for the hede off
thys glorious virgine, and no merveil thof suche rumour began to
2045 ryse amonge the peple for the relykis as wele of the hede as of the
body of thys holy virgyne, thof they be but smale and litille in
quantite, yit wheresoever they be hadde they be of grete dignyte,

2026 *pariter*] *om.* Co   2032 for] *om.* Co

reverence and worschip and preciosite. And therefor the peple,
wheresooever they myght knowe eny relykes of thys virgyne or
any chyrche or chapelle made to her worschippe they wente thedyr 2050
thykke and threfolde to worschip theym with alle deuocion and
mekenes. Neuertheles alle thys was doone be the ordynauns and
suffrauns of God, sercher and knower of alle hertes, to whom yt
pleased at the laste to remeue and take awey alle thys dubitacions and
dowtes and let men haue open knowleche where this precyous body 2055
lay in certeynty, as nowe yt schalle be schewed more clerely.

The Placentynes, therefor, thus stryvyng togeder, som holdyng oo
wey, som holdynge another, the abbot and covent of the seide
monastery, with alle the devocion and reuerence that they cowde,
went vnto the place where as the body of thys gloryous virgyne was 2060
schryned, and moche pepulle feythfulle and trusty beynge there
present the abbot opened the schryne and | fownde the body liynge f. 273va
therin like as it was leyde in the same day of her translacion the yeere
of oure lorde a thousand .iij. hundred .iij. score and .x.. And this
serchynge of [this] gloryous body was not done in the day of her 2065
translacion for nought but that, by invencyon and fyndynge of this
noble body, her translacyon schulde be hadde in the more reuerence
and worschip and spoken of bothe ferre and nere thorow owte alle
the worlde, and also that thys day not oonely schuld be kepte in the
worschip of her translacion but also in worschip of her invencion.   2070

Thus than alle questyons and maters of altercacion was ceased
amonge the Placentynes, and be the meritis of this excellent virgine
and glorious martir Seynt Barbara alle were made acorded and were
of oo herte and oo wylle in sawle and loved and dwelled togeder
cherytably as bretheren. So that verely and withowten dowte thys is 2075
the body of the venerable virgine and martir Seynt Barbara, whiche
after many cruelle kyndes of turmentis and paynes, abidynge the
smytynge of of her hede by that moste feerse kynge her fader
Dyoscorus, praied our lorde Ihesu Crist her spowse for her devoute
worschippers, as it is more clerely schewed in her moste holsom lyfe 2080
and passion in the .xj. chapitre before, that he wolde not suffre
theym goo owte of this laborious preson of thys presente lyfe tylle
they, contryte and confessyd, were confermyd and armed by the
reseyvyng of his holy body | veray flessche and bloode.   f. 273vb

Wherfor now this holy virgyne, glorified in blysse, may wele sey to 2085

2048 and worschip] *om.* Co   2063 yeere] *add* then Co   2065 this] *om.* L
2066 translacion] *add* not L

alle her cuntreymen, seruauntis, oratours and children of Cristis
Chirche here benethe in erthe, and þat fulle comfortably: *Imitatores
mei estote sicut et ego Christi*, that ys to say: lyke as I haue folowed
Cryste, right so folowe ye me, and than in heven your everlastynge
2090 mede and reward schalle be. And this ys the cause it is to suppose
that sche bereth the palme and signe of a chirche, in tokenyng that
sche of alle her enemyes hadde the victorie and was the veray trewe
folower of Criste and his Chirche, and so schulde wee.

Thus than ys declared how þis gloryous virgine and martir Seynt
2095 Barbara, by manyfolde tribulacions and persecucions, turmentis,
peynes and martirdome, as a meke lambe folowed Criste the veray
lambe that taketh awey oure synnes and waisscheth vs dayly in the
bloode of his blessyd and gloryous passyon. Wherefor now sche
foloweth hym in the mery paradise of blysse, berynge the crowne of
2100 glorye vpon her hede, besette with the fressche florisschyng rooses
and lilies on every syde of ioye and gladnesse, davnsynge amonge the
virgynalle felisschip of hevenly virgynes withowte ceasynge and
werynesse, saiyng and syngynge with aungels and seyntis the new
songe and praysyng to the holy Trinite *Laus tibi Domine rex eterne
2105 glorie*. To this blessid virgine, therefor, and martir lat vs pray þat
sche wille pray for vs to oure lorde Ihesu Criste kynge of blysse, that
f. 274ra we may be his folowers graciouslye | clensed from alle maner of
synne and never to be subiecte to other but too hym and for hym,
whom he so dere hath bought with his precyous bloode for to make
2110 vs partyners of hys glorie amonge alle aungels and seyntes, *Qui cum
patre et spiritu sancto viuit et regnat Deus in secula seculorum. Amen.*

Here endith the life of Seynt Barbara. And begynneth
meraclis.

There was sumtyme a knyght whiche hadde Seynt Barbara in grete
2115 reverense and worschip, in so moche that he vsed and had in
custome for to faste in the Vigil of her passyon and martirdome,
keping and halowynge her Day moste holyly. Wherfor he was not
deseyved of grete reward, for there is noo goode dede vnrewarded
that is done to worschip of God and his seyntes.
2120 This knyght had many enemyes that were grete and myghty of

2112–13 of . . . meraclis] and martirdome with the translacions and inuencion of the
glorious spouse of Criste Seynt Barbara. And after here foloweth the miracles of the same
glorious virgyne Co   2117 holyly] holely Co

power, and so on a tyme it hapned he felle into their handes and forthewith they stroke of hys hede. His horse alle bloody ranne home to the knyghtis place, his servauntis and they that were in the seide place se thys, they were gretely astonyed. They wente to a preste for to haue his counselle, and so thorowe his advice they toke the wey 2125 towarde the place where theyr mayster was slayne, the preste goyng with them with the sacrament. Whan they were come to the place, they founde the hede departed from the body. The preste neighed nye. The sperite of this knyght whiche was in the hede seyde vnto hym: 'O,' he seide, 'thow servaunt of God and brynger of my 2130 savyour, | be not slowe ne dowtefulle for to come to me, for by the I f. 274rb may resseyve helthe bothe of sowle and body.' The preste was than aferde, wenyng and supposyng it hadde be sum fantasie or sum wickid sperit, wherefor he durst not come nye. Than eftesones, thorow the sufferaunce of God and helply meanes of blessid Seynt 2135 Barbara, the hede seide ageyne to the preste: 'Come nye and ioyne my hede to my body, and thorow hym that is helthe of alle creatures and by the merytes of my blessyd lady Seynt Barbara I schalle be save and made hoole.'

After than the prayers were made and done for hym to allemyghty 2140 God, the kny3t arose hole and sownde in so moche that there appered no maner of marke or token of his wounde. The knyght than affermyd by his trowthe vnto theym that were there present, in confirmacion of this myracle, that for fastyng of the Vigile and halowynge solemply the Day in the whiche Seynt Barbara suffred 2145 martirdome, sche therefor defendid hym and kepte hym that he schuld not dye to the tyme he had resseyved the sacrament of the Chirche, and moreover sche promyttid hym ioy everlastyng after his deth. Þan aftir this he was confessyd vnto the preste and resseyved the blessid sacrament, and after the debate and warre was ceased 2150 betwix hym and his aduersaries thorow the merites and helpely meanes of blessid Seynt Barbara. And he rested in oure lorde Ihesu Criste and his sowle wente to heven blysse.

Miraculum. | There was on a tyme a cursed and a moste wycked f. 274va man in levynge, ledynge his daies in gladnes and ioye of wickyd and 2155 malicious dedis. Wherfor he schuld haue be distroyed and lost at hys ende hadde not bene the grete meritis of Seynt Barbara and the mercy of God whiche vouched safe to dye for synners, and of his

goodenesse and grete mercy gave hym that grace þat he become the
2160 servaunt of thys virgyn Seynt Barbara. And so in maner of a custume
he vsed dayly for to do sum maner of service vnto her, but yit he
seased not of hys wycked dedys.

It hapned that his wickidnesse was not vnknowen to the iuge of
the cite of Colayn, whiche toke hym and put hym in presun. And
2165 after he was compellyd too telle his wickid dedis, he was dampned
and demed to be done vpon the racke as the maner of that contray ys.
Then his armes, his leggis and the chyne of his backe were broken
vpon the whele and he was putte qwycke vpon the whele, and soo he
schuld pyne to dethe. This done, he was also wacched and kept a day
2170 and a nyght of men ordeyned to kepe hym that no man schuld take
hym awey.

But almyghty God, to whom it is appropred to be mercifulle and
at alle tymes redy to spare synners that wylle amende theym thorowe
the meritis of his spouse Seynt Barbara, he sente to the synful man
2175 neyther aungelle nor archangelle ne yit his spouse Seynt Barbara, but
he sente vnto hym his owne dere moder to his comfort, which
f. 274ᵛᵇ moder | and lady of alle comfort and of mercy abhorred not this
synner, but easely and cherefully sche seide vnto hym: 'Truste thow
verely,' sche seide, 'that for the service that thowe haste done to our
2180 dere doughter Barbara thowe mayst not dye to the tyme thowe be
confessid and hast resseyved thy gostly foode, the blessid body of my
son, but yit notwithstondyng thow schalt suffre moche more turment
or thow þat resseyve. Therefor dowte not, loke þow be of goode
comfort in thy sawle and haue feith and trust in me and in Barbara,
2185 the spouse of my son, whiche is my wele belovid doughter.'

þus than after he was thus comfortyd and thus swetely spoken to
of our lady and also of hir gracious presence, he toke strenght vnto
hym, saiynge to hymsylfe as the prophete saith: 'In Domino sperans,
non infirmabor. I truste in God, I schalle not be syke, for withowte
2190 fayle this is the promyse that my lady Barbara fulfilleth, not oonely in
me but also in alle theym that wylle pray vnto her.' Than a fewe
daies after this, he that putte hym to his iewes, seyng that he was on
lyve and wexed more strenger and better of chere than he was byfore,
he was gretely angwissched in hymselfe, and so for malice and envie
2195 that he myȝt not overcome hym and haue his wylle fulfilled puttyng
hym to deth schamefully, eftsones he put hym to paynes and

2168 (1)vpon . . . whele] om. Co　　　　2180 dere] om. Co　　　　2183 not] add
but Co

turmentis. And so he toke hys spere and didde bete hym therewith to he had geven hym .xix. woundes. And whan this man was thus gretely wounded, he gave vp a crie. Men rode to hym on horsebacke and other ranne | vnto hym for to defende hym, for þey supposed f. 275ʳᵃ that sum wolde haue spoyled hym or ellis haue schortyd his lyfe, and 2201 as they were comynge the light of the day beganne to apere. Þan they seide: 'Yf there be enybody here, speke in the name of God.' This turmentour that had wounded hym, whan he herde men speke, he fledde. Than he that was on the whele seyde: 'I was putte here on 2205 this whele .iiij. daies paste, but thorowe the merites of þe blessyd virgine Seynt Barbara, I may not deye to the tyme I be confessyd and haue resseyved the blessyd sacrament to my comfort. And this is seyde to me of oure ladies owne mowthe, that glorious virgyn and moder of God, and also of the meke virgyne Seynt Barbara, for our 2210 lady tolde me of the cruelnesse of thys tormentour and of the woundes he schuld geve me.'

When the peple herde this they went streyte vnto Colayn, and there they tolde openlye what they had seen and herde. The peple of the cite were gretely astonyed of this and merveiled. Þe clergie were 2215 fulle of ioye and gaf thankyng to God for his rightwisse iugementis, and so in procession they came to the place where the man was rakked, and by the comaundement of the iuge they brought bothe the man and the whele that he was put on into the cite and toke hym downe. And than they herde hym telle howe and on what wyse he 2220 was comfortid of our lady and of Seynt Barbara, and howe that for the litille service that he did vnto Seynt Barbara he myght not dye withowte schryfte and howsylle. | Than after he was confessid and f. 275ʳᵇ had resseyved moste devootelye the blessid sacrament of the awter, he gave vp his sperite vnto the handes of allemyghty God and so 2225 passed. And his graue is yit vnto thys day in Colayn vnto the worschip of allemyghty God, whos mercies haue never ende, whiche our lorde graunt vs thorowe the merites and prayers of the blessid spovse of Criste Seynt Barbara. Amen.

Miraculum. In the contray of Braban in a certeyne monasterye of 2230 the ordre of Premonstries callid Lordis Parke, there was a monke that gave hym gretelye vnto the service of the blessyd virgyn of God Seynt Barbara. This monke on a tyme rode into a certeyn water that he knew not, and so vnwarly bothe he and his horse were drowned, paraventure thorowe the providence of God that the merites of his 2235

blessyd virgyn Seynt Barbara schulde be the more notefied and knowen. And as he and his horse schulde haue sonken downe to the bottom of the water, there was a virgyne redy at hym and helpid hym and brought bothe hym and his horse save vnto the londe and to the
2240 banke where he was fyrste or he entred into the water.

　　And whan he was suyr and syker of the lande, with drede and reverence he seide: 'Feyre virgyn, what be ye?' Sche than smylyngly and manerly with a lawghyng chere seide: 'I am Barbara the servaunt of my lord Ihesu Crist that thow hast done fulle thankful service to,
f. 275ᵛᵃ and þerfor | God hathe geven to the that grace þat thow schalt never
2246 dey sodeynly withowte howsylle and schryfte as longe as thow hast devocion to me.' And for this he was afterwarde the more devoter vnto the blessid virgyne Seynt Barbara, so that after he was made abbot of the same place and monasterie. And than in alle that he
2250 my3t he stered other to haue her in worschip, bryngynge often to mynde this myracle that God had schewed thorow her meritis vpon hym.

Miraculum. There was on a tyme a wrecched man that neyther knewe the lawe of God ne þe feith of holy Chirche ne yit the rewarde
2255 of goode peple in the blisse that is to come, for he was a paynym and of the kynrede of gyauntes. But yit notwithstondyng he hadde a grete devocion vnto Seynt Barbara, and in his maner he purposed in hymselfe for to do her service, so that in the Day of her martirdome as the yeere cometh abowte, for hir sake and to her worschip he vsed
2260 to doo grete almesse, whiche Day also he kepte worschipfully, for that day he wolde haue the more pite and be in more ioy and gladnesse than in any other day.

　　This gyaunt, not that giaunt that the prophet spekith of: *Exultauit v[t] gigas ad currendam viam a summo celo egressio eius* and toke
2265 flessch and bloode of the virgyn Marie, but thorowe the merites of Seynt Barbara he entendid vnto heven. This giaunt, when his deth was comen that no man may escape, in bataille he was taken presoner
f. 275ᵛᵇ of his enemyes. | Sentence was given vpon hym that his hede schuld be stryken of. Aftyr this he was beried and forgeten as dede as ofte
2270 tyme men are. But the sothefastnes of the promyse of God and the vertu and perfeccion of loue that he had to his spouse Seynt Barbara is gretely to be merveyled be that þat folowith.

For .lx. yeere after he was beried there were dichers þat delvid and
dichid in the same place where he was beried, and there they founde
a grete hede and a fayre, havynge goodely heere therevpon, alle 2275
fressch and bloody as if it hadde bene kitte of the same day. They
were amerveiled thereof and astonyed, wherfor they wente to the
bisschop of the diocise and tolde hym alle the mater as it was doone
in dede. The bisschop than considered in hymselfe and thought that
this myght not be withowte grete mysterie and the prevey domes of 2280
God. What dyd he than, not oonly the bisschop but also alle the
peple wente to praier and yafe them to fastynge that they myght have
verey knowleche what this bemente. And after they had gone aboute
with procession with alle devocion for the same, within a maner of
feere and drede they wente vnto the hede there as it was. And whan 2285
they had founde it, the bisschop chargid yt in the name of the holy
Trenyte that he schulde answere hym and telle whose hede he was
and how longe it hadde layne there and why it was so fressche and
apered so newly stryken of.

Than forthewith the hede answered and seide: 'I am the hede of a 2290
paynym and of a giaunt, and I | haue leyne here beried the space of f. 276ra
.lx. yeere, abidynge the wille of my lorde God. Knowe ye for
certeyne þat I schuld haue bene dampned, but thorowe the praiers
of the blessid virgyn and martir of Criste Seynt Barbara I schalle not
dey to the tyme that I haue resseivid the sacramentis, [that is the 2295
sacrament] of baptem and of penaunce. Than alle the peple blessyd
God and glorefied hym and hys spouse Seynt Barbara. The bysschop
than baptised the hede, and after that it confessid and repentid, and
no dowte of but that it had speritually the sacrament of the awter,
whose sowle as they alle stode aboute they se it assende vp to heven. 2300
And forthewith the hede waxe drye like vnto other hedis þat lye
buried.

Herefor lovyng and praysyng, glorie and service be done of alle
creatures vnto God for his goodenesse and to his blessid spowse
Seynt Barbara, worlde withowten ende. Amen. 2305

Miraculum. In the Vigile of the Nativite and of the Birthe of Our
Lord Ihesu Crist there was certeyn merchauntis and wollemen that
were gretely blynded with [avarice], having no reverence vnto the
holy day whiche our lorde commaunded to be kepte and seith:
Sabatum sanctifices. Thes merchauntis toke theyre iorney owte of 2310

2295–6 that(2) . . . sacrament] *om.* L   2308 avarice] a variaunce L

Inglonde from Seynt Botulphus wharfe vnto theyr owen contrey, notwithstondyng the solempne feest of Cristemasse. They entred into the schip and forthe they wente, but almyghty God, to whom bothe the see and the wynde be obedient, raysed vp the sperite of
2315 tempeste and drowned these wicked men except tweyn of them
f. 276rb whiche had devocion vnto the blessid spouse | of Criste Seynt Barbara, and they were of the cuntrey of Braban. And for the devocion that they had vnto this glorious virgine, though the schip went to wracke and they were caste in the water, yit they myght not
2320 be drowned, but flotered vpon the water .iij. daies on .ij. boordes. At the laste thorow the prayer of Seynt Barbara, notwithstondyng dyverse partes of theyr bodyes were as it were dede for colde, yit at last they came to londe.

　　Than were there fisschers to whom these .ij. men tolde of theyr
2325 grete perilles and laboures that they were in, mekely besechynge them that they wold for the love of Seynt Barbara helpe them and releve them, for they seyde that it was the wille of God for the merites of his meke spowse Seynt Barbara virgyn and martir that they schuld not passe owt of thys wrecchid lyfe withowte schrifte
2330 and howsylle. Whan these fisschers herde this they wente for a preste, whiche brought the sacrament with hym and came to theym, to whom these .ij. sike penytentis and syke men were schreven and confessid, and afterwarde with alle devocion they resseyved the blessyd body of oure lorde Ihesu Criste, the sacrament of the
2335 auter. And than forthewith they thanked God and betoke theyr sowles vnto hym and to his blessid spowse Seynt Barbara, and thus they passed and gave vp theyr speritis and their sowlys wente to heven. And therfor seith Seynt Iohn the Evaungelist: *Beati quem in Domino moriuntur*, blessyd be they that dye in oure lorde.

f. 276va **Miraculum.** It hapned on a tyme in the cite | of Colayn in the
2341 chirche of Frere Menowres in the Solempnyte and Feste of the glorious martirdome and passion of the blessyd spowse of Criste Seynt Barbara, which is there had in grete reverence and worschip, in so moche that to this chirche cometh grete concourse of peple
2345 with ther oblacions and to her devyne service and to here the worde of God preched, as the maner is there yeerely.

　　Whan these devote peple were thus gadered, Sathan was amonge

theym, for loo there was a ribalde, an vnthrifte, that stode in the wey
as the peple came with theyr offrynges toward this chirche, that was
abowtewarde for to haue lette these peple of þer devocion, whiche 2350
blasphemed Seynt Barbara and seide vnto the peple: 'It schuld
advaile yow more for too geve me these offryngis than to her that
ye calle your Seynt Barbara, for sothely,' he seide, 'the myracles that
are rehersed and seide of her are as trewe as and ye se me lye nowe
dede bifore yowe.' This lesynge wolde he not suffre vnponyssched of 2355
whom it is seide: *Perdes omnes qui loquentur mendacium*, for forthewith
withowte eny more tariynge this wickid man toke owte his wepen
that he bare by his side and stroke hymselfe to the herte, and in the
presens and sight of theym that were abowte hym, sodenly he felle
downe dede. And thus God is redy to punyssche theym that 2360
blaspheme his spowse Seynt Barbara, and he is redy to schewe
mercy and grace to alle them that haue her in | worschip and f. 276vb
reuerence.

Miraculum. On a tyme vnder a noble and a worschipfulle prynce
callid Raynolde Selrye, in a walled towne clepid Nouomagion, there 2365
was an honest man, prudente and wise, and he was a burgeys of the
same towne, whiche spowsed and wedded a wyfe that was welle
disposed and fulle honest in her behavynge. These two persones, this
man and his wife, the forseide prynce and lord of the town loved
enterly for theyr goodenesse and goode [disposision]. This burgeis in 2370
his yonge age had that excellent spouse of Criste Seynt Barbara
gretely in reverence and worschip, in so moche that he vsed dayly for
to doo vntoo her sum maner of service, supposing there thorowe sche
schuld be a meane for hym vnto God, paraventure thynkynge in his
sowle that many disseses and sekenesse schulde come vnto hym 2375
afterwarde. And therefor he purveyed betymes to make her a meane
for hym, remembryng the saiyng of the apostle: *Dum tempus habemus
operemur bonum ad omnes.*

This man on a tyme loste his witte and felle into a madnes, and for
because he cowde not rule hymselfe his frendes ordeyned oone for to 2380
governe and rule hym. On a day in a mornyng he came from the
chirche home to his howse. He wente vp into his chamber prevely
that his keper wiste not of, and there he fonde his wife devotely
kneling and praiyng. And whan he se sche toke no hede of hym, he
loked abowte and there he founde a scharpe knyfe whiche he was 2385

2354 and(2)] *om.* Co   2357 more] *om.* Co   2370 disposision] disposion LCo

f. 277ʳᵃ wonte to bere abowte hym. | He bare this knyfe prevely vnder his
gowne and wente into his stable and in a hoole of a poste not fully
bored thorowe he put the hafte of the knyfe and the poynte toward
hym and with alle his myght he ranne ageyne the poynte of the
2390 knyfe. And so he steked hymselfe to the herte and thoroweowte the
body to the poynte come owte at his bak.

Loo, notwithstonding this wicked dede, yit here was schewed the
grete myght of God thorowe the merites of his blessid spouse Seynt
Barbara. He covered the wounde with his gowne and came ageyn
2395 into the chambre to his wife and schewed her what he had done. His
wife se his wounde, for sorowe and woo sche cried and felle downe as
dede. The meyne that were in the howse herd her crye and they
came vnto her for to helpe hir. At the last whan sche came vnto
herselfe ayeen sche seide: 'Take hede,' seide sche, 'to your mayster,
2400 anaunter he haue not slayn hymselfe.' Than oone of the wemen
servantis toke vp her mayster gowne, and whan sche perceyved what
he had done sche was astonyed, and forthewith sche went owte and
called in his frendes and neyboures and also his curate for to here his
confession and for to gif hym his rightis.

2405 This man than was schreven and made his confession with grete
contricion and moste devotely and afterward with grete instaunce
and mekenes he desired the sacrament, but the preste for drede of
the temporalle lawe durst not comyn hym. The prince þat loved
hym so entierly was the same tyme in the same towne, and whan he
f. 277ʳᵇ herd | what he had doone, he dispised not in his owen persone after
2411 the ensample of Criste for to come to his servaunt, for veray love
that he had to hym compellid hym so to do. This man that was
hurte se that the lorde was comen fulle devoutely, and with wepyng
teeres he besought hym of mercy and that he wolde vowchesafe to
2415 forgyf hym that trespace and offence that he had done to hymselfe
and that he schuld not dey temporally therefor, and that for as
moche as he didde abide the mercy of God, whiche he trusted for to
haue thorowe the praiers and meritis of that moste blessyd virgyn
Seynt Barbara.

2420 This worschipful prynce than heryng hym sey thus, in maner like
vnto Ioseph Iacob son, that was mevid with pite vnto his bretheren
whan he toke theym to grace, so had he pite of this man, for gladly
he wolde haue obeied vnto the Chirche, and also hym thouȝt he
muste kepe iustice and rightwisnes. Then he toke the preste on syde

2408 comyn] comen Co

and wysely he enquered of hym wheþer the lawe of rightwisnesse 2425
and of iustice myght be relesed for that manslaughter or nought, and
wheþer he myght be beried in cristen berielle or not. The prest
answered and seide: 'Ye, he myght welle.' And thereto he was
compellid by dyuers causes, and specially for the promyse that
God made to his spouse Seynt Barbara in the hour of her deth 2430
and martirdome, 'whose mercy,' seide he, 'this syke man hathe
goten, for he hathe made his confessyon and schryfte moche more
discretely and | with more compunccion and contricion than ever I f. 277va
herde eny man make. And moreover as he schewed vnto me and
tolde me owte of confession þat he myght not passe owte of thys lyfe 2435
withowte the sacramentis no more than they do that do service vnto
Seynt Barbara as her lyfe maketh mension. And this was for the
service that he had done vnto her by his dayes.'
   Whan the prynce herde this he thanked God right devotely and
his spouse Seynt Barbara, and vtterly forgave this man alle that he 2440
hadde deserved by rightwisnes for to haue be done by the lawe to
hym for his owen hurte. Than after this man was assoyled of the
preste and had resseyved the sacrament, he made a token to them
that were abowte hym that oone of them schulde drawe owte the
knyfe. And whan it was drawen owt he gaf vp the sperite vnto 2445
almyghty God. This was right mervellous to alle them that were
present. Then, for the myracle myght be the more magnyfied and
praysed, the prince commaunded the dede mannes body to be
opened. Whan this was done the knyfe was founden go thorow the
herte even the myddes thereof. Phisiciens and surgeons and other 2450
wyse men that were there present they seide it passed nature that the
man so hurte schuld lyve so longe withowte it were by myracle. And
so from that tyme forthe the seide prynce and other grete estatis that
were there with hym, with other also of lower degre, after that tyme
were the more devotelyer sette to serve | Seynt Barbara, praysyng our f. 277vb
lord Ihesu Criste in her.   2456

Miraculum. There were .iij. abbottes of þe ordre of Cistews that
were goyng toward theyr Generalle Chaptour as the maner is. Then
oone of them, whiche was abbot of a monasterie clepid Alberdenser,
a ful religious man in his behavynge and a dreder of God, whose 2460

2427 or not] *om.* Co   2441 be . . . lawe] bene Co   2444 of them] *om.* Co
2447 the(1)] *add* more L   2448 prince] duke Co   2450 even] *add* thoroghe
Co   2459 Alberdenser] Alverdenser Co

name was Iohn, bothe he and these two other abbottes must nedes in
theyr wey passe thorowe a woode that was right perilous and ful of
theves. And as they passed thorowe this woode they herde a mannes
voyse crie vnto theym owt of the woode ferefully and horible to here.
2465 And this voice semed to theym as if it had be in the moste perilous
place of the woode, whiche seide to this abbot that was clepid Iohn in
this wise: 'Syr abbot Iohn, in the reverence and worschip of the name
of Criste, come and helpe me.' They were all aferde of the voice and
they stroke theyr horses with spurres for to haste theym owt of the
2470 woode and owte of that ferefulle place.

Than the voice began to crye ageyn to theym more besely and
seyde: 'Syr abbot Iohn, in the name of Criste, helpe me.' This abbot
herde the name of Crist twyes named. He was strenghthed with that
name, and with the grace that God gave vnto hym he turned hym
2475 toward the place where as he supposed that he herde firste the voise.
And whan he came there abowte and hovyd stylle to herken where
the voise was and cowde nothynge here, he seide: 'O goode Ihesu,
what voise may this be that in thy name prayed me for to come helpe
f. 278ra hym?' He lokid abowte hym and he did | se a mannes hede stryken of
2480 liyng vnder a stokke, havyng his eyen open, which seyde: 'Fader
abbot, be not aferde but calle hedyr thy two brether and I schalle
telle yow the wonderful merveyles þat allemyghty God hathe
wrought in me, wrecchid synner, thorowe the meritis of that glorious
virgyn and martir Seynt Barbara.'

2485 Than this abbot callid to hym the two other abbottis and alle
theyre meyne, and whan they were comyn and sawe the hede they
were gretely amerveiled. The hede than seide: 'I sey and telle it
openly for a trouth. I was sumtyme a marchaunt and had riches
inowh and bare my merchaundise here and there abowte. And more
2490 than thre dayes sythen, I come amonge these bussches and theves
toke from me my goode and stroke of my hede like as ye that be
present may se now. And for that my sawle was fallen into so many
synnes, devels therefor as it had bene hailestones felle abowte me
downe owt of the clowdes for to take my sawle with them to
2495 everlastynge turmentis and paynes. But loo, the blessid virgyn and
martir of Crist Seynt Barbara, for a litylle service that I didde to her
dayly, and namely in the Day of her passion and martirdome whiche
alwey I kepte solemply, sche therfor was with me and now sche

covereth me with clothyng of her brightnes. And that ye may haue
ful evidence and knowlege hereof, take me from this place and bere 2500
me to my body whiche is on your right honde hidde and covered in
the thyknes of the woode, and diligently in the name of Crist set my
hede to my body as it was before. And than | I schalle arise and go f. 278rb
with yow and that I may, be the sacramentis of the Chirche, resseyve
forgifnes of alle my synnes and trespace.' 2505
Vnto these wordes than these abbottis were agreed, and in the
name of Crist alle thyng that the hede desired they fulfilled in dede.
Than whan they sett the hede to the body, anoone he rose vp as if he
had not bene hurte at alle and wente forthe with them to a litille
towne besyde. And there he wente into a chirch and made his 2510
confession to this abbot clepid Iohn with teeris of contricion and
lamentacion for his synnes. And after fulle devotely he resseyved of
the curate of the same chirche in presence of them alle the blessid
sacrament of the auter, and also in the presence of moche other
seculer peple that knewe hym welle before, and so than graciously he 2515
passed to our lorde Ihesu Criste.

Miraculum. It was so on a tyme in the contray of Braban in a
certeyne place where as lieth buried the body of a holy bisschop and
martir clepid Sanctus Rumoldus, there were dyvers men that in the
Vigile of the martirdome and passion of þe excellente virgine Seynt 2520
Barbara whiche were loggid in an ostre. And whan they herde whose
Even and Vigile it was, they rehersed and tolde among them how
many greete thynges our lorde wrought and schewed for this blessid
virgyne. And they were so gretely edefied in her werkis in so moch
that some seide they wolde for her sake and love ete no flessche in 2525
her Vigile. Som there were also that were sterid with more devocion,
for | they seide they wolde not oonly absteyne from flessche but also f. 278va
they seide they wolde faste in her Vigile, for they knewe wele and
vndirstode by enformacion of an holy woman that was the keper of
the holy virgynes relikes that who that wolde yeerely remembre and 2530
thynke devotely with sum maner of devocion done vnto this blessid
virgine Seynt Barbara, that they myght not dye ne passe owte of this
lyfe withowte veray trewe confession and resseyving of the blessid
sacrament of the auter.
The man that kept the ostrye herde alle this. Presumptuously he 2535

2525 sake and] *om.* Co

seide: 'And I haue made to roste a goode fatte capon and I schalle ete thereof. And than schalle be seen whether I schalle not be schreven and make my confession and resseyve the sacrament before I dey or not as welle as ye.' This man theyre oste, whan he had seide thus,

2540 then the same nyght he wente to his reste hoole and sownde, but on the morne after he was founde sodenly dede in his bedde.

Miraculum. There was on a tyme a man that was comen of goode kynred whiche hadde devocion vnto the nobille and worschipfulle virgyn and martir of Criste Seynt Barbara, in so moche that he wolde

2545 yeerely worschip her with fastynges and praiers in the Vigil of her passion and martirdome, and the Day folowynge he wolde kepe holy and worschipful, and this he vsed of longe tyme. It hapned on a day afterwarde as he sat with moche other feleschip in a taverne |

f. 278ᵛᵇ drynkyng wyne of syluer peces, and at even whan the peces schulde

2550 be gadered togeder, the taverner in þe tellyng of his peces he lakked oone of them. Than anoone the taverne dore was schitte faste that noon of them schuld passe to that they were serched by and bye. Grete noyce was made in the taverne and grete clamour for stelynge of this pece and that he schulde be punyssched that had stolen it.

2555 The thefe than whiche had stolen it wente and put it prevely in a litille bagge of thys trewe mannes whiche had devocion to Seynt Barbara, and than he went boldely and made hem to serche hym. And whan they had do so, he lepe owt of the dore and wente his wey.

At the laste this goode man as though he had be gylty of the dede

2560 was takyn and brought before the iuge and for a thefe he was iuged too be honged, and so he was, wherfor grete sorowe and lamentacion was made for hym, not oonly of his frendes but also of many other. Than whan nyght was comen and the swyne of the towne that alle daye had bene in the feeldes schuld come home, as they came by the

2565 galowes and theyr kepers folowyng them, this man that was hanged seyde vnto hem: 'Come,' he seide, 'and take me downe, for I lyve yit.' When they herd this they wolde not take hym down forthewith, but they wente to the cite and tolde the peple bothe grete and smale, and specially vnto his frendes and to suych as loved hym that he was

2570 on lyve.

f. 279ʳᵃ Than the peple whan they herde this, boothe | moste and leste, wente vnto the galowes and there they founde hym on lyve, and they asked hym than howe it myght be that he didde lyve. He answered

2552 of them] *om.* Co

and seide: 'I may not dye, for the blessid virgyn and martir of Criste
Seynt Barbara holdeth me vp with her blessid handes.' Than, by the 2575
advyce and consente of the iuge, he was taken downe of the galowes
and there than he tolde two thynges. First was how he hadde ever in
reverence and worschip the solempne Feeste of the blessid virgyn
Seynt Barbara in the which sche suffred her martirdome, for that day
specially he dydde synguler worschip vnto her. He tolde them also 2580
how he was hanged giltlees and withowte cause, and howe that he
that caused hym to be hanged schulde that same yeere deye a
schamefulle dethe. After than he had taken sum mete and was
welle comfortid and refressched, he wente home to his owen howse
and lyved longe tyme after and contyneved eftesones more devotely 2585
in the service of Seynt Barbara. Than, within schorte while after, this
wycked man, this thefe aforeseide, was take for sleynge of a man.
And by the meanes of iustice and rightwisnesse he was put vnto a
schamefulle dethe, and than he knowlechid openly how that he
hadde stolen the foreseide pece and prevely had put it in the litille 2590
bag of this goode man whiche was servaunt to Seynt Barbara.

Miraculum. On a tyme the peple of the contrey of Normandye
whiche are clepid Normandes came saylyng by the see toward the
contrey of Flaundres with a grete | puyssaunce of armed men. And f. 279rb
what tyme they came to a certeyn place clepid Tarby nye vnto 2595
Kalgant, theyr adverseries met with theym and did fight with them
and overcome them and had the victorie and distroyed nye alle theyr
schippes and slewe them that were therein, in so moche that there
was so grete bloodeschedde and distruccion of the Normandes that
theyr blood colored and made rede the water of the see. 2600

Amonges these Normandes there was a certeyn knyght that of
longe tyme did specialle service to Seynt Barbara, whiche was
drowned and caste in the see with other. But yit this notwithstondynge he had his herte and mynde to Seynt Barbara, and therfor sche
helped hym so that he was cast nye vnto the banke of the see and 2605
myght not be drowned ne dey withowt the sacramentis of the
Chirche. This man thus stode in the water whan it flowed and in
the sande and gravelle of the see vp to the hede more than .xv. daies,
clepynge devotely vpon þe chosen spowse of God Seynt Barbara that
sche wolde vowchesafe to be his helpe, that he schuld not dey 2610

withowte confession and resseyvynge of the blessid sacrament of the
awter.

There were fisschers that came to fissche abowte the same place,
and whan the water was clere and at the ebbe they herde the voyce of
2615 this knyght swetely and devoutely cryenge and praiynge on this wise
for his help: 'O thow moste blessid virgyn and martir of Crist Seynt
Barbara, whom I haue so longe servid, forgete me not but for that
f. 279ᵛᵃ grace that ys | [grawnted] vnto the of allemyghty God helpe me,
synner, that I may resseive or I dey the sacramentis of the Chirch,
2620 that is to sey, veray trew confession and the sacrament of the awter.'
The fisschers than herde hym pray thus mekely and devotely. They
came to a preste that dwelled nye vnto the same place and tolde hym
what a voyce they had herde, supposyng it had be but a fantasye. But
notwithstondyng that, the preest lyke a discrete man toke a stole
2625 aboute his necke and also the blessid sacrament and alle that longed
to the reverence and worschip thereof whan yt ys borne abowte, and
he came with the fisschers in theyr bote vnto the same place. And
whan he was comyn thedyr he herde the voyce of this knyght lyke as
the fisschers didde afore. And than the preste wente vnto the knyght
2630 there as he was and than with grete devocion and diligence he lifte
hym vp owte of the sandes, and after he had herde his confession he
mynystred vnto hym the blessid body of oure lorde the sacrament of
the awter. And whan this was honestely and reverently doone the
sowle of hym passed vnto our lord and his body is worschipfully
2635 beryed in Flawndres at Skluse.

Miraculum. There was a man in the contray of Almayne dwellid
in a walled towne called by name Wolflaghen that had the blessyd
spowse of Criste Seynt Barbara in grete love, in so moche that he
vsed daily for to sey certeyne prayers vnto her. He vsed also yeerely
f. 279ᵛᵇ for to faste her Even as the yeere come | abowte and keped the Day
2641 of her martirdome solempne and holy as reson is. This man thorow
instigacion and suggestion of the deville by violence oppressid [a]
womman and dydde lye by her.

It hapned that he was taken therewith and by comaundement of
2645 the iuge he was betaken to preson. And whan he was compellyd to
knowleche his wicked dede he was iuged to be deede. The sentence
was given in þis wise, whiche was that he schulde be taken to a
turmentour whiche schuld fasten hym myghtely abowte the myddel

2611 withowte] *add* veray trewe Co   2618 grawnted] grawted L   2642 a]
and L   2646 sentence] *add* of iugement Co

and bynde hym faste vnto a stake sett faste in the erthe as the maner
is of that contray. And so there were certeyn persones that were 2650
charged of the iuge for to kepe hym þat he schuld not be taken thens,
but he schulde be so diligently kepte in the same place in that peyne
to the tyme he were dede moste schamefully. Then this wrecchid
man thus tormentid and payned thre daies togider he cried moste
dolefully vnto theym that passed forthe by hym, and namely to his 2655
kepers: 'What profiteth yowe to kepe me thus? Sothely,' he seide,
'thorow the merites and praiers of my most holy lady Seynt Barbara,
for the service that I haue doone to her, I may not dey to the tyme I
be schreven truly and haue resseyvid the blessid sacrament of the
awter, whiche schalle be my defence ayenst my gostelye enemyes.' 2660
    When his kepers herde this they wente vnto the iuge and tolde
hym what they herde and seen. Then by the commaundement of the
iuge he was remeved fro the grownd where he was sette, and than
the | preste was brought to hym with the sacrament, our lordis f. 280ra
blessid body, too whom he was schreven and confessid. And after he 2665
had resseyvid with alle ioy and gladnesse the blessid sacrament, he
gave vp the sperite, which ascendid vp to heven everlastyngly to
rayne with that glorious virgyn and martir of Criste Seynt Barbara.

Miraculum. There was on a tyme a payntour that was a cunnyng
man of his crafte, whiche on a tyme paynted the story and the lyfe of 2670
this glorious and blessid virgyn of Criste Seynt Barbara. And when
he came to that place of her storye where as the schepard detecte her
and bewreyed her to her fader was turned by the myght of God into
an image of marble and his schepe into smale bestes called
greshoppis, he hadde forgeten to make them in theyr fourme 2675
and schappe as they schulde be made, and the season and tyme was
not that any myght be fownden. Wherfor this payntour knelid downe
devotely and besought this worschipfulle spowse of Crist Seynt
Barbara that sche wolde vowchesafe to schewe hym the likenesse
and the fourme of them. And as he praied thus there came sodenlye 2680
oone of these greshoppys lepynge byfore hym. He loked welle vpon
hym and marked his likenesse and schappe and closed hym faste in a
boxe and so paynted forth her story and made this greshoppe so
kyndely in his likenesse in so moche it semed to alle that loked
therevpon as though it had bene a greshoppe on lyve beyng. Than 2685

2668 and . . . Criste] *om.* Co   2672 schepard] *add* þat Co   2675 forgeten]
add them L   2685 beyng] *om.* Co

f. 280rb after this the payntour came to his boxe and founde nothyng | within, and yit the boxe was close as he lefte yt.

Miraculum. In the same fraunchyse not fer from the towne there this payntour dwelled, there was an howge towre of a castelle that 2690 felle down to the grownde because that the grownde and foundement was olde and feble. And in the fallyng of this tour ther was a damyselle fylle therewith that was a servaunt in the same castelle, whiche hadde devocion to the spowse of Criste Seynt Barbara.

This damyselle was oppressid and couered with as many stones 2695 and erthe that an hundred waynes of oxen myght not lede awey. There were there sum peple nye that did se this damyselle thus oppressid. They were meved with mercy and pite, and anoon they did gete laborers there that with cartes and karres myght haue awey the stones and erthe from her. And so, yf they myght save her lyfe, 2700 alle a day longe than they didde spende abowte the sauacion of this damyselle. At the laste they came almost at her, and than they fownde that alle the membres and partes of her body were dede and alle tocrussched for the grete oppression of stones and of erthe. Than sche began to crye with a lowde voice and seide: 'Beth not aferde, for 2705 I lyve yit,' sche saide, 'and I may not dye to I haue resseyved the sacramentis, that ys the sacrament of penaunce and the sacrament of the awter. And this is for the service, thowh it be litille, þat I haue doo to the blessid virgyn and martir of Crist Seynt Barbara.' Whan f. 280va they vnderstode this, anoon there was | brought vnto her a preeste 2710 for too mynyster vnto her the sacramentis. Aftir this was doone dewly as it oweth to be, this damyselle yafe vp the sperite whiche passed and wente vp to allemyghty God.

Miraculum. There was on a tyme a riche yonge man whiche neyther hadde fader nor moder on lyve, that gave hym gretely 2715 vnto the service of the blessid martir and spowse of Crist Seynt Barbara, in so moche that he was brought in custume devotely to sey or to do sumthynge dayly vnto her worschip, and namely in the Day of her passion and martirdome.

Hereatt the deville had envie that this yong man had suche a love 2720 to hyr and did so many goode dedis vnto her worschip, wherefor he thought that he wolde sowe sum schrewed thynge amonge his goode dedis for to withdrawe hym fro her service. Than he wente to and excited and stered his frendes that they schulde stere hym to take a wife, so that by the love of his wife his love schuld be the more abated from thys blessyd virgyn Seynt Barbara. This doone, his 2725 frendes and kynnesfolke than þey steryd and in maner compellid hym to be wedded. And so they were sette vpon a damyselle whiche they thought lykly for hym, and so at the laste he agreed vnto theym.

In the meanewhile, on a nyght this yonge man hadde a dreme. Hym thought he was in a gardyn whiche was a feyre gardyne, a mery 2730 and a iocunde to beholde, where hym thought he sawe many feyre maydyns whiche | were feyre to beholde, amonge whiche hym f. 280ᵛᵇ thought he sawe oone of them passand feyrer than other which turned her bakke and hidde her face fro hym. Than was there another of thes feyre maydons that sawe this other mayde her felowe 2735 turne awey her face from this yonge man. Sche asked her why sche did soo and why that sche was soo hurte in hym that sche turned awey and did hide her face. Then sche seyde: 'This yonge man gave hymselfe gretely to my service and to be my servaunt, and now he begynneth to love another with whom he schalle be so gretely 2740 tangled and tyed that he is lyke to serve me no more, for thus hathe he done, he hathe trouthe plited another of fervent love and sett me on syde.' [This other virgyn harde this. Sche seyde:] 'I schalle be messenger on this behalfe.'

Than come sche to this yonge man and seide: 'Why is this 2745 dameselle displesid thus with yowe, and why haue ye deservid her indignacion ayenst yowe?' He answered and seide he knewe her not ne noon of theym. Than sche seide ageyne to hym: 'Knowe thow for certeyn that alle we be hevenly creatures, and sche this that schewith her to haue indignacion at the ys Barbara the holy spowse of Criste, 2750 to whom thow haste thus gretely offendid, and that for as moche as thowe haste put her service on side and purposist to love another.' And forthewith sche declared vnto hym how that the devylle had disseyved hym, bryngynge his matrymonye abowte. 'And yf thow wilte know [what I am, I wille thow know] for certeyn that I am 2755 Kateryn, famylier felowe with Barbara. And if it plese the, I am ful redy to reconsile the vnto her, and | that be my prayers.' f. 281ʳᵃ

And after that he was thus entised by the swete wordis to her love

2731–2 where . . . beholde] *om.* Co   2743 This . . . seyde] *om.* L
2749 sche] here Co   2755 what . . . know] *om.* L   2758 the] thies Co

ageyn, he answered mekely and seide how he was redy at alle tyme to
2760 put her displesaunce on syde so that sche wolde resceyve hym ageyn
to grace. Than Seynt Kateryn promysed hym that sche wolde gete
hym grace and forgifnes. And so she toke hym by the hande and
brought hym to Seynt Barbara. What than, than she shewed her
feyre clere and beautevous face vnto hym and resceived hym to grace
2765 and to her service ageyn. And than she seide vnto hym moreouer:
'Dispose for thy housholde,' quod she, 'for within schorte while
thow schalt passe owte of this lyfe, and thow and I schalle haue
everlastyng ioy and blysse togeder.'

This yonge man than whan he waked he wolde not take this for a
2770 dreme, but he knew verely it was a vision. Than at the morne he
called togeder his housholde and such that were his frendes and tolde
them that he wolde not procede no ferther in that processe of
matrimonye for other thyngis that were to hym behapned in the
meane tyme. Within a while after sekenes toke hym, and anoon the
2775 prest was sent for, to whom he tolde thys visyon. The preste than
mynystred the sacramentis vnto hym, and after this was deuotely
doone he yelded vp his soule to almyghty God and gate that
everlastyng reste and qvyetnes in ioye and blisse with Seynt Barbara.

Miraculum. There was on a tyme a merchaunt which toke his ship
f. 281ʳᵇ with other feliship for to sayle over the see. And after he | had sayled
2781 a certeyn tyme he rose hym vp vnwarly and be a sodeyne chaunce he
slipped owt of the ship and felle into the see in the sight of his
felisschip and they myght not helpe hym. And whan they had done
alle theyr power to helpe hym and myght not, they passed forth
2785 theyr wey, supposynge they schuld never haue seen hym more.

A merveilous thynge and the grete power of Criste gretely to be
wondred, and also the grete power and auctorite of this blessid
martir and spowse of Crist Seynt Barbara, to whom this man was
besy to do servyce, and therefor in perelle of deth she was redy to
2790 helpe hym and bare hym vp above the water to the tyme that another
ship came forthe by, where the peple that were therein herde hym
calle vpon Seynt Barbara and se hym in perille. They came to hym to
helpe hym and so they toke hym saufe into theyr schip and kepte
hym, and thorowe the guydynge of Seynt Barbara they came more
2795 rather to the porte save and sownde than the ship that he felle owte

2771 housholde] kynnesfolke Co   2774 hym] this yonge man Co
2781 sodeyne] certayne Co   2791 where] wherfore Co   2795 L punctuates
after sownde

of bifore. Than this man gave thankyngis to God and to this blessid
virgyne, and also to them that had thus delyvered hym from perille,
and so he wente out of the ship and stode vpon the see banke. Than
he loked aboute and se dyvers shippes, but he fownde nou3t his owen
ship. At the laste as ferre as he myght loke and perseyve he se 2800
comyng his ship that he felle owt of drawyng to the see banke there
as he stode.

Oone of them than þat were in the ship seide to his felowes: | 'Lo, f. 281ᵛᵃ
I se yonder owre felowe whom we trowed had be drowned in the
see.' And other sayde nay it was nat he, but he was lyke hym. Than 2805
he seide: 'Verely it is he.' When they were come to the londe,
havynge no dowte but that it was he, they asked hym howe he
escapid that horrible and perylous deth of drownyng, for they se
welle whan the water of the see swolowed hym vp. Than he
answered them and seide: 'I was wonte,' he seide, 'and I haue 2810
bene vsed therto many yeeres devotely, for to faste the Vigile and
Even of the martirdome and passion of the gloryous virgyn and
martyr of Crist Seynt Barbara, and also for to kepe her Day folowyng
to my power. And therfor I trust that thorowe hir worschipfulle
prayers that I schalle not passe owte of this lyfe withowte the 2815
sacramentis of the Chirche, and than schalle I commende my
sawle to my lorde God.' And after this than he tolde them that
thorowe the helplye meanes of Seynt Barbara there were other
shipmen that toke hym owte of the water into theyr schip and so
delyverid hym from the floodes of the see [withowt any harme and 2820
sette hym vpon the see] bank. Than aftir this that marchaunt,
notwithstondynge that he was devote to Seynt Barbara before, yit
after he gave hym more devotely vnto her service.

Miraculum. It hapned on a tyme in the Day of the worschipful
passion and martirdome of the blessyd virgyn and martir of Crist 2825
Seynt Barbara, there was an hermyte of the religion and ordre of
Seynt Avstyn that stode vp and | preched to the peple the story of f. 281ᵛᵇ
Seynt Barbara and the lyfe as maner and custume is in the cuntrey of
Braban in a chirche of Seynt Iohn the Evangeliste, whiche prechour
in the ende of his sermon brought forthe in wrytynge a myracle of 2830
her and seyde: 'There was a man *in ducatu Iuliacensi* that was
synfulle, vile and foule and vnprofitable to his owen sowle. In his

2806 Verely] *add* quod he Co   2807 havynge no] and hade not Co
2809 swolowed] sloppt Co   2820–1 withowt . . . see] *om.* L

levyng he was in condicion like a sowe and a swyne, frende and felowe vnto noon but to his owen wombe and to his owen glotonye,
2835 for he enforsid hym dayly to etynge and drynkyng and to glotony, dredyng that he schulde never haue had inowe ne haue bene fulfilled.

On a tyme as this drynker and gloton lay aloone dronken in his howse as he was wonte to do ofte tymes and custumably, it hapned hym by vnchaunce that both his howse and his neybowres howses
2840 were sette afyre, and this man that for dronkenesse myght not helpe hymselfe was alle tobrente in the same fyre. Than his frendes ranne vnto his howse for to helpe hym, and whan they se they myght not helpe hym, the howse beynge allemoste brente, they were right sory.

Aftir this than more than a yeere came the heyres of this man
2845 willynge to bylde vpon the same grounde, bryngyng with theym a laborer for to haue awey the rubussh that was in the same place. Than as the laborer labored in dyggyng and in delvynge he herde a voice seiyng to hym in this wise: 'Delve no depper.' The laborer toke no hede to this voice but labored forthe on. Eftesoones he herd the
f. 282ra voice say: 'Delve no depper.' And at | the laste he seide: 'Thow
2851 comyste to nye me with thy delvyng.' The laborer than was astonyed and aferde leste it had bene an evelle sperite that had seide thus, wherefor he seyde: '*Benedicite,*' seide he, 'who is there?' '*Dominus,*' seide the voice, 'I am that man that was wonte to dwelle here.' Than
2855 seide the [laborer]: 'How may that be, for that man thow saist thow arte was brente vnto asshes.' The voice seide: 'Thow saist trew. I was brente alle to asshes except my tunge oonly, in the whiche life is yit. And I may not dey withowte veray confession and resseyvyng of the sacrament of the blessid body of my lord Ihesu Crist. For allethowgh
2860 I levid the daies of my life vndiscretely, yit I lefte not of but that I did sum maner of service though it were litil to my lady Seynt Barbara, the blessid virgyne and martir of Ihesu Crist, and þat I didde dayli. And therefor thorow her worschipful prayers that she hath made for me to our lord Ihesu Crist she therefor hathe gete me
2865 that grace and mercy of God that he wille spare me.'

Whan the laborer herd þis he wente anoon in alle haste vnto the curate of the same place and tolde hym what he hadde herde. Than the curate withowt tariyng with grete devocion and not with litille mervaile anoon put vpon hym prestes arayment and toke the blessid
2870 sacrament, the blessid body of Crist, and but oone man byfore hym

2837 dronken] drynkynge   2842 hym] *add* for they were dredfulle lest he shulde periche Co   2855 laborer] labored L   2870 but] put Co

for to bere the li3t, but there folowed moche peple after the preste
to the same place. Than the preste called after the voyce, and
forthewith the voice answerid in audience of moche peple and seide
as | he didde bifore. The forseid laborer than toke his instrument f. 282rb
that he had in his hande and remeved awey the rubissch and the 2875
erthe [where]abowte he herde the voice speke twyes or thryes
before. And there they founde the tunge qvycke and on life
withowte any hurte, whiche tunge made confession to the same
preste more perfitly and more clerely than ever the preste herde eny
make confession before. Than the prest leyde the sacrament vpon 2880
the tunge, with the whiche the sowle of that man whiche was
secretely hid in the tunge was gostely refresshid and so, havyng
remyssion of alle his synnes, the tunge turned into asshes, but the
sowle was ioyned to owre lorde and wente vp to everlastyng ioies.
And this myracle this forseid prechour bare recorde of and affermed 2885
for trew *per verba sacerdocii* by his prestehode, for he hymselfe, he
seide, was in his owen persone presente with moche other peple
where and whan this myracle was doone.

Miraculum. Aftyr this, in the same day and in the same chirche, the
forseide prechour rehersed and tolde this myracle that folowith of 2890
the same blessid virgyn. 'There were,' he seide, 'in a feliship .vj. or
.vij. scolars whiche were sente of theyr frendes to a certeyn cite, and
also it was an vnyversite, for to lerne and to gete kunnynge and
science. And whan they were comyn to this vnyversite they were
wele witted and applyed theym fervently to gete kunnynge and 2895
science. Nevertheles it hapned that oone of them, thorowe instiga-
cion of | the feende of whom comyth alle evylle, for a certeyn iniurye f. 282va
that was done vnto hym of a certeyn citezen of the cite, the scolar
didde sle hym, wherfor anoon forthewith he was take and brought
byfore the iuge þat was that same tyme in the cite. 2900
    'The lawe of this cite was that for such offense the armes and the
thyes schulde be broken of such a trespassour and bownden qvycke
vpon the racke, and by longe peynes he schuld ende his lyfe. Whan
this was done to this man his felowes aforeseid with grete sorowe and
hevynes they folowyd after hym vnto the place where he schulde 2905
suffre his tormentis and paynes, and there they abode the iustice and
the peple goyng home ther wayes. And whan alle wer gone save they

2871 moche] *add* other Co   after . . . preste] *om.* Co   2876 where] *om.* L
2895–6 and science] *om.* Co   2897 feende] devell Co

alloone there they [wepte] and wayled for theyr felowe to the tyme
they cowde no more here hym sorowe nor wayle. And than they
2910 knewe noon other but that he was dede and passed. With grete
sorowe þan they departyd from hym and began to go home theyr
weies. And they thought they wolde pray for hys sowle to our lorde
Ihesu Crist.

'On the morowe folowyng the seide scolars for hevynes and sorowe
2915 wyst not what to do. Than they wente agayn to the same place where
the daye before they lefte theyr felowe dede. And whan they were
comyn thedyr they beganne to sorowe and wayle for theyr felowe, and
thus they cried and seide: "O most dere felowe, wayleawey, wayleawey, moste dere and feithfulle frende, where schalle we leve the and
f. 282ᵛᵇ what shalle we sey to thy frendes | when we come home into our
2921 cuntrey? Wayleawey, goode felowe, what may we do for to helpe the?
And if we wold help the, we may not. God be merciful to the and
brynge thy sawle vnto everlastyng blisse." Thus and in like wise they
seyde often, makynge theyr mone with grete waylynge and sorowyng
2925 for ther felowe. And as they were thus sorowing, they herde theyr
felowe that was on the racke calle theym with a lowe and a stylle voice.
They gave hede vnto the voice and they thought theyr felowe shuld be
on lyve. Than he spake to them and seide: "O my felowes," he seide,
"what haue ye done that ye haue awaked me of so convenyent and so
2930 goode a slepe?" His felowes answered and seide: "Alas for sorowe, alas
for sorowe, O beste belovid felowe, how bitter, how harde, how
paynfulle was thy slepe." Than he seide: "Ye wote not what ye say. I
haue rested and slepte bettir than ever I didde in my lyfe, for I haue
rested me on the lappe of that blessid virgyn and martir of Crist, Seynt
2935 Barbara, whiche is a moste feytheful besecher vnto God for hem that
love her, whom I haue evermore served of my yowthe, but yit not with
suche diligence as I schuld haue done. She hathe purchased for me,
thorowe her merites and prayers whiche she hathe offred vnto God for
me in my vtter nede, that I am helid and curid of alle my woundes,
2940 hurtes and peynes in my body and in alle the partes thereof. Cometh
nere," he seyde, "and loseth me and I schalle go hens with yow."
Thorowe whos wordes than and myracle these forseid scolars were
f. 283ʳᵃ [so] ioyfulle and glad that theyr ioye and gladnes myght not be | tolde.
'Than they losyd hym downe of þe racke as he bad theym and

2908 wepte] wente L   2910 noon other] no more Co   2914 morowe]
morne Co   2923 blisse] ioyes Co   2926 lowe] softe Co   2942 scolars]
add his felowes Co   2943 so] om. L

wente his weyes with theym hole and sauf withowte any wekenesse 2945
or febilnesse. But for as moche as they dredde the lawe of the cite
and also the frendes of hym that was slayn, they durst not entre with
theyr felowe into the cite, wherfor they toke theyr counseil eche with
other what was for to be done. And so they were agreed that sum of
theym schulde lede hym into a woode besyde, and sum of them 2950
wente to the iuge of the cite and tolde hym alle that was done, and
also of the myracle whiche such a myracle hathe not bene herde,
besechyng hym that he wolde vouchesauf, for the loue of God and at
the reverence of the blessid and meke virgyn and martir of Criste
Seynt Barbara, that he wolde go with hym to theyre felowe that 2955
bifore he hadde putte on the racke, which was verely cured and
helid, as they seide by myracle, of alle his hurtes and paynes. For
withowte his diffence and proteccion, they seyde, they durste not
brynge hym forthe for drede of his frendes whom he hadde so slayn.

'To whos [supplicacions] and praiers than the iuge agreed. But yit 2960
for as moche as he dowtyd and merveiled of that was tolde hym of
these scolars, therfor forthewith he hymself wente forthe with
theym for to se this merveilous sight, and moche oþer peple
folowid hym after. And whan the iuge was comyn there as he
was and founde alle trew that was seyde and had resceyved this 2965
man hoole and safe, he lovyd God and praysed hym and also his
wele belovid spowse and | virgyn Seynt Barbara. Than he toke this f. 283ʳᵇ
man and ledde hym with hym into the cite, and whan he was seen
of his aduersaries they ranne ageyn to the iuge and they desired of
hym that he wolde do iustice ageyne on hym and put hym to the 2970
deth. The iuge than answered and seide: "This scolare," he seyde,
"at youre requeste after the lawe he was iuged and put vnto the
dethe vpon the racke. And so he owght no more be iuged
therevpon, ne I dare not do yt, for allemyghty God," he seyde,
"thorowe the meritis of his meke spowse Seynt Barbara hathe 2975
saved hym and hath perfitely helyd hym of alle his woundes and
sores."

'Thus than this scolar was delyvered. But yit for drede of his
aduersaries he durst not abyde there no lenger, but wente home
into his owen contrey and servid Seynt Barbara more devotely than 2980
he did byfore and contynued in her servyce to his dethe.' And this
forseid prechour seide feithfully that he sawe the same scolar and

2947 was] he hade Co   2960 supplicacions] supplicions LCo

herde hym telle þis myracle with his owen mowthe, and that yit
within the same yere that he prechid this myracle to the peple.

2985 **Miraculum.** In a ducherie clepid Gilrens there was a knyght whiche
in suche thynges that longed to dedes of armes he was wele taught
and had experience in. And right besy he was and a famovse man in
suche thynges that longed to batayle and to warre. This knyght, on a
tyme in the Vigile of the passion and martirdome of the blessid
f. 283va virgyn Seynt Barbara, came with his men with | hym sodenly and
2991 vnwares vnto a place where as he se a servaunt of his somtyme whom
this kny3t hated dedely. He se hym thresshyng in a barne. He light
downe of his horse and with a greet feersenesse he went towardis
hym purposyng to haue slayne hym. He drowe owt a sharp swerde
2995 and sette the pomelle thereof to his owen breste and didde renne
with the poynte of his swerde ayenst his servaunt. There cowde noon
lett hym, but with a grete myght he threwe hym downe to the
growned and shoved hym thorowe with his swerde, but yit he cowde
not slee hym, wherfor he was meved with more woodenesse.

3000 Than he toke the swerde with bothe hondes and he bete hym
dyvers tymes therewith and shoved hym eftesones thorowe in dyvers
places of his body. And besy he was for to haue streken of his hede,
but yt wolde not be for hym. Then he bete hym so longe with the
swerde that the swerde bowed lyke a sythe or a sykylle, but in alle þis
3005 he didde hym noon harme as thowh his body had bene of yron and
the knyghtis swerde but a strawe. This knyght at the last was wery
for labour and [marveled] moche that he cowde not sle hym. And
than he toke goode hede to his criynge whyche besought hym right
ofte and withowte ceasynge that he wolde haue mercy vpon hym,
3010 saiynge in thys wise: 'Right dredefulle and ferefulle lorde, haue
mercy vpon me and spare me, for ye laboure,' he seide, 'in vayn, and
ye may not performe your wylle in me, for I trust stedfastly that I |
f. 283vb schalle not dey withowt confession and reseyvynge of the blessid
sacrament, the blessid body of my lorde God. And that for as moche
3015 that I haue fasted lyke as I haue vsed of longe tyme for to do the
Vigile and Even of the blessid virgyne Seynt Barbara, which Vigile is
as thys same daye.'

Then the knyght se that this was a myracle and above nature. He

2989 Vigile] *add* and L　　2991 vnwares] at vnwarnes Co　　2992 hym] *add*
stande Co　　　　3003 for . . . Then] *om.* Co　　　　3005 noon] no more Co
3007 marveled] labored L　　4　3009 withowt] *add* shrifte and Co

toke hede vnto his praiers and forgave hym al his trespace and become afterwarde his veray feithfulle mayster and frende and in the 3020 honour and worschip of the meke spowse of Crist, Seynt Barbara. This knyght than righted his swerde that was bifore bowed and put it vp in his shethe, and bothe he and hys men wente theyre weies. And there he lefte his servaunt in pease withowt any more harme or hurte. 3025

Aftir thys than this forseide knyght had a certeyn presoner in his daunger, whiche for dyverse trespace that he knowlechid hymselfe he was demed to be deede and to haue his hede streken of. Than the knyght commaundid that his hede shulde be streken of with the same swerde whiche myght not fasten nor do no harme before in 3030 the servaunt of Seynt Barbara. And this the knyght didde for to preve his swerde for the more evidence and token of the thyngis aforeseide. Than the tormentour that shuld put this gilty man to dethe toke the knyghtis swerde and at oone stroke he stroke of this wicked mannes hede. Than the knyght and hys men tolde openly 3035 for veray trowthe this myracle and alle these thynges as they were done to the peple. And they loved and thanked God and his blessid | spowse Seynt Barbara, and they made theyr avowes forthewith that f. 284ra they wolde from thens forthe gyve them to her service the more devotely. 3040

Miraculum. There was on a tyme a symple poore womman that was of symple reputacion and lytelle set by of the peple, which had in goode custume to be often confessid and shryven. And bifore or she wolde go to shryfte she vsed for to sey sum certeyn praier to the blessid spowse and martir of Crist Seynt Barbara as to her lady and 3045 maystres that she wolde teche hyr howe she schulde be confessid, whiche symple poore womman on a tyme come to be confessid of her gostely fader, whiche was person and curate of a chirche of Seynt Dionyse.

She dressid her downe behynde hym for to be shreven, but she 3050 had forgeten for to sey her praier to Seynt Barbara that she was wonte to sey byfore her confession. She remembrid her of her praier but she cowde not brynge it to mynde, ne also no synne that she shulde haue be confessid and shreven of. She sat stylle as yf she cowde not haue spoken. At the laste she prayed the prest for to 3055 abide her to she came to hym ageyn. Than she wente forthe and at

the laste seide devotely her praier. And whan she had doone she
come ageyn to the preste, and than she made her confession with
suche an hertely contricion so clerely and playnly that the preste
3060 was gretely amerveyled, for hym thought he had herde never suche
another confession before. And after this womman had made thus
f. 284rb her confession she was the more devetelyer sette and | gave herselfe
afterwarde more fervently vnto the service of Seynt Barbara.

Miraculum. There was a knyght whiche on a tyme came casuellye
3065 amonge his enemyes. They were more myghtyer and stronker than
he was, and so they felle vpon hym and toke hym and hanged hym
vpon a tre and wente theyr weyes. Than .iij. daies afterwarde there
was another knyght and a special frende vnto this knyght that was
hanged, and whan he herde hereof he seide vnto his famulyar
3070 meyne: 'I wille ride,' he seyde, 'for to see my wele belovid felowe
and frende that is thus hanged of hys wicked and cruelle enemyes.'
His servauntys and his meyne counseyled hym the contrarye and
they seyde: 'Goode syr,' quod they, 'lett not suche thoughtis
vnqvyet your herte. What shalle ye do ther where ye shulle fynde
3075 nothynge els but grete cause of hevynesse and of sorowe? For whan
ye se hym hange whom ye so gretely loved by his lyfe, it is no
dowte of but that your herte shalle be newly wounded with sorowe
and hevynesse ageyn.' But for alle this seiyng they myght not lette
hym from his purpose. But after that he had made hys compleynt
3080 to God for his wele belovid frendes deth, he cowde not for the
tyme refrayne hymselfe from wepynge. Netheles forthe he wold
algates, wherefor he seide to hys men: 'Cease,' quod he, 'of your
wordes and go we ride forthe, for sothely I wille goo se my wele
belovid frende.'
f. 284va Whan this knyght and his men were | comen to the tree where the
3086 knyght hynge, he cowde not refrayne hymselfe but brake owte into
grete lamentacion and wepynge, and with often rehersynge he seide:
'Weileawey, my dere frende and my felowe, weileawey, ye were he
that I loved as my lyfe, for I loved yow before alle other. Wayleawey
3090 that I hadde not bene nygh yow for to haue defende yow what tyme
this violence was done to yow, or ellis if yt hadde so hapned that I
myght haue deied and haue bene hanged with yow, for I wolde not
haue bene aferde for to haue deied with yow. It is sorowe vpon
sorowe to me now for to lyve in this worlde. It were better for me to

3085 men] mene Co   3089 lyfe] selfe Co

be dede than hereafter for to ioye vpon erthe.' Than whan this 3095
knyght had thus mornyd and made this lamentacion, he that was
hanged spake vnto hym and seyde: 'Cessith, my dere frende, and
sorewith no more for me.' Than seide this knyght: 'O my lorde and
my wele belovid, is there yit lyfe in yowe that haue hongen on this
tree .iij. dayes?' He answered: 'I lyve,' he seide. 3100

Than this knyght and his men light down of theyr horses and toke
hym down of the tree, and than they asked by what myght and vertu
he myght so lyve and was so longe hanged. To whom he answerid:
'My frendis,' he seyde, 'þis schalle I telle yow. There was no day of
my life sithen I vnderstode goode from eville, were I never so gretely 3105
in besynesse but that I wolde saye before my besynesse sum specialle
prayer to oure lordis .v. woundes and sumwhat to that blessid virgyn
and modir | of God our lady, and also sumwhat vnto the lovynge and f. 284vb
praysynge of the meke spowse and martir of Crist Seynt Barbara.
And specially that was for that I herde of oone that prechid of her 3110
that she had purchased and geten graunte of hir spowse Criste Ihesu
to alle them that serve her, that they shalle not deye withowten
verray confession and resseyvyng of the blessid sacrament, the body
of Crist. And therefor,' he seide, 'the blessid virgyn and moder of
God oure lady and the spowse of Crist Seynt Barbara, þey haue 3115
stonde alle this tyme vndir me and haue susteyned and borne me vp
and haue made praiers for me in the sight and presence of owre lord
and they haue gete me grace that I shalle not perisshe, whiche grace
is graunted to alle theym that do [them] trew service. Therefor I
beseche yow hertely that ye wylle fecche to me the curate of the 3120
nexte chirche and that he wille brynge with hym the blessid
sacrament the body of my lorde.'

This doone like as he desired, he made a perfyte confession and
right devotely he resseyved the sacrament. Than thys other knyght
after he hadde seen this feyre myracle, with grete ioye and gladnes he 3125
gave lovynge and praysynge to allemyghty God and to his moste
purest and clennest virgyn our lady and to the blessyd spowse and
martir of Criste Seynt Barbara. And than he seide to the knyght þat
was takyn downe of the tree: 'My dere frende and my beste belovid,
now is my sorowe turned into ioye and my hevynes into gladnes. 3130
Therefor | lete vs now ride togeder and I shalle brynge yow savely f. 285ra
and surely to your owen maner and dwellynge place.' Then he

3105–6 so gretely in] evell occupied or hade I neuer so grete Co   3119 them]
penaunce then *with* penaunce *crossed out and subpuncted* L

answerid in presence of the preste and of other that stode aboute:
'Feithfulle [frende],' he seide, 'I thanke yowe for alle thynges, but
3135 this that ye desire I may nat do in no wise, for sothely the blessyd
moder of my lord Ihesu Crist and his spowse Seynt Barbara haue
shewed me a more delectable contray than any mannes mynde may
thynke or tunge may expresse, vnto the whiche I haste and entende
withowte eny tariyng.' And whan he had seyde thus, forthewith he
3140 gave vp the sperite to allemyghty God.

Miraculum. There was a preste on a tyme that bare the blessid
sacrament, the body of our lorde, to oone that was syke in his
parisshe. And as he wente by the see banke he herde besyde hym a
moste febillest voice as if it had bene the voice of oon that had leyn in
3145 diyng, which voice waylyngly called vnto the preste. The preste lokid
abowte hym and he se not ellis but the boones of a dede man neyther
havyng skynne nor flesshe but brought to suche a consumpcion that
vnneth the bones abode in theyre iunctures, owte of the whiche
bones there sovnded a voice, as it semed to the preste.
3150 Than with grete fere and drede and also with grete merveile he
came nye to the bones and spake to them, and he asked whether the
voice was there that he herde or nott, or whether the voyce came of
God or not of God. Than a voice out of the bones answered to the
f. 285ʳᵇ preste and seide: 'Syr,' quod the | voice, 'I am the voice of a man that
3155 by infortune was drowned in the see, and after the naturalle
disposicion of þe see it hath caste me here. And here I haue bene
a longe tyme lyke as ye may considre be that ye se. But for as moche
as I vsed in my daies to serve that holy virgyn martir and spowse of
Crist Seynt Barbara, I may not deye withowte veray confession and
3160 resseyvyng of that blessid sacrament of the awter, and that hath she
purchased of God for me and for alle that doo her service.'
 The preste than, whan he herd this, he brought to his mynde that
it is so seide in her legende, and her myracles declare the same. Than
the preste sat downe by the man that was thus drowned and herde
3165 his confession, whiche was perfetely made, and afterward like as he
desired bifore, he resseyved the sacrament. And than he thanked
God and his spowse Seynt Barbara, for than he knewe wele that for
the promyse that was made vnto hir of God he was thus graciously
saved. And whan he had seide thus, fulle graciously he passed to
3170 oure lorde and gave vp the sperite.
 3134 frende] frendes L

Miraculum. There was on a tyme a bisshop that came devotely by a certeyn place where as bothe men and wemmen were put to deth for her demeritis, which place was as it were a myle from the cite. This bisshop listened and hym thought he herde the voyce of a womman vnder the grounde wrecchidly sorewyng and criyng, prayng the bisshop with a ferefulle voyce | of helpe and soker, whiche voice seyde in this wyse: 'O worshipfulle and holy fader, wille ye vouchsafe to come to me and haue mercy vpon me?' The bisshop whan he herde thys, he merveyled moche. He came nye to the place where hym semed he herde the voyce and asked who was there, and whether the voyce were of God or nott. The voice vndir the grounde answerid and seide: 'Ye, sothely, holy fader, it is of God. Fader,' seide she, 'I am a synfulle womman whiche many yeeres goone for my demerites and trespace by the meanes of iustice and right-wisnesse I was iuged to be dede. And here I am dolven vnder the grounde, but thorowe the goodenesse of our saviour Ihesu Crist, at the instaunce and prayer of his meke spowse and martyr Seynt Barbara because that I fasted her Even, and also by my lifetyme halowid her Day, wayleawey that I didde no moore, but yit for this litille service she hath kepte me to thys tyme on lyve, so that withowte verey confession and resseyvynge of the blessid sacrament of the awtere whiche is grauntyd of God to alle her worshippers I may not deye. Therefor I beseche yow, benyngne fader, that ye wille helpe me therto.'

Whan the bisschop herde this, anoon forthewith he sent oone of his men for a curate, and also he sente to the iuge of the cyte, and he desired they shulde come thedyr to hym and that the curate shuld brynge with hym the sacrament, and the iuge shulde come to geve licence to take her owt of the | grounde. Whan the prest and the iuge were comyn, and shortly for to sey, the erthe was abated and taken awey, the womman was founden standynge vpright in the place and pitte, beyng on lyve as she was whan she was putte therein many yeeres byfore. The custume and maner was there at that tyme in that contrey that wommen for theyr trespasse shuld be putte qvykke in the grounde so for to dye.

Thus this womman than, after that she had tolde in the presence of grete multitude of peple what she had seide to the bisshop beynge in the grounde as it is seide bifore, and after she hadde made her confession moste clerely to the seyde bisshop, the bisshop toke the

3175
f. 285va

3180

3185

3190

3195

f. 285vb
3200

3205

3201 place and] *om.* Co

3210 stoole of the preste and mynystred to her the sacrament, and so this
womman devotely resseyvynge our lordes blessid body she gave vp
the sperite vnto the hande of [allemyghty] God, whose body, in the
presence of the bisshop and many moo that were there presente,
vanysshed awey as if it had leyne dede from the tyme that she was
3215 put first in the grounde.

3213 allemyghty] allemyght | ty L   3215 grounde] Co adds: *Explicunt miracula
beate Barbara ad presens et non terminentur in hoc seculo.*

Now Barbara the spouse of criste that moche art of myght
For the loue of thi spouse that loved the of right
Saue vs from all soden chaunces be day and be nyght
So that after this wreched lyfe we may come to endles li[ght].
Amen
On the next folio of Co in a later hand is written:
Think not the time I pray you ouer long
To reade the verse of Barbara bright of hue
A worthy saint and daughter to a king
Whose actes of fame here partly do ensewe
This lilly sweete this flower of fragrant smell
Vnto the rose full well I may compare.

NOTES

1. ST EDWARD THE CONFESSOR

15–16 **Seinte . . . fonte** This story is not in Aelred nor in his sources, but it is in William of Malmesbury's life of St Dunstan (*Memorials*, pp. 309–10).

42–43 **slewe . . . Alphey** See *Alphege*, 11, pp. 163–67.

66 **Brightwolde** Beorhtweald, monk and abbot of Glastonbury, from 995 or 1005 bishop of Ramsbury. His vision is in *Vita Edwardi regis qui apud Westmonasterium requiescit*, see Barlow (1962), pp. 8–9.

109–13 **Now hath . . . emperoure** We have been unable to find a source for this claim.

112 **importable** impossible or very difficult to pay, *MED importable* adj. (b).

153 **did consecrate** 'unxerunt et consecraverunt in regem.' Aelred 744 D.

174–5 **Salomon . . . wysedom** 3 Kgs. 4:34.

200–229 This story is found only here.

204 **neyde** compulsory tax. *MED* does not record this sense, but see *OED need* sb. 10.

258–9 **.iij. childrenne . . . Chaldeis** Dan. 3.

260–1 **Ioseph . . . fro hym** Gen. 39. 'Pharao' should be 'Potiphar'.

262–3 **Susan . . . preestis** Dan. 13:12–26.

263–6 **Iudith . . . myschefe** Judith 13.

285–6 **He was . . . touchid** 'Diligit ille sed non corrumpitur, diligitur illa nec tangitur.' Aelred 748 B. For **broken** see *MED breken* v. 23a, fail to maintain chastity; for **touchid** see *MED touchen* v. 6, have sexual contact with.

289 **fals stok** 'compulsus generi se miscuerit proditorum,' Aelred 748 B. See *MED stok* n. 2(a), line of descent, lineage, ancestry.

290 **generacion** *MED generacioun* n. 1a (a), sexual intercourse. 'operi supersederet conjugali,' Aelred 748 B.

295 **estate** *MED estat* n. IV 16a, the formal pomp appropriate to occasions of state.

297 **soufte** *MED sofi(e* adj. 4(b), mild, restrained; 'in risum modicum', Aelred 749 A.

301–10 **Danys . . . drowned** Svein Estrithson, king of Denmark, outlived Edward. He died in 1074.

352 **orphalyns** *MED orphelin* n. does not record this spelling.

374 **falle in** failed in the performance of; *MED failen* 1 does not record this spelling.

409 **bounde . . . vnbounde** Matt. 16:19 and 18:18.

451 **recchid oute** *MED rechen* v.(1) (d), to stretch out, straighten, 'extenduntur', Aelred 755 A.

452   **kernels** *MED kirnel* n. 4(b), any pathological lump, tumour.
  bouchis not in *MED* with this spelling. See *MED bocche* n. 1, boil, tumour, running sore, ulcer.

454 **lete . . . go** allow him to walk.

458 **discryve** ascribe, *MED descriven* v. 2(b), to interpret or explain something, does not give this sense.

602–4 **Seint . . . curyng** 1 Cor. 12:8–9.

611 **chambirleyne** 'cubiculariis', Aelred 762 C.

617–18 **voyce . . . Egipte** Matt. 2:13.

618–19 **dreme of Danyelle** Dan. 2.

619–20 **dreme(2) . . . true** Gen. 41.

628–9 *Non . . . gloriam* Ps. 113 (B):1.

640 **Bruham** 'Bruheham', Aelred 764 A; 'Bruhellam', Osbert XVI, l. 8, p. 96; Brill, Bucks.

734 **hylle of Selyon** Mt Celius. The story of the Seven Sleepers of Ephesus is in *LgA* pp. 670–5. There the sleepers are walled up for 372 years, although the chronology is questioned at the end of the tale. Barlow (1965) deals with the occurrence and content of this story.

739–40 *Surget . . . gentem* Matt. 24:7.

763–805 **Essex . . . hym** This story is not in Osbert and the location of the church is not mentioned by Aelred, to whom, according to Barlow (1962), p. xxxvi fn. 1, it is unique. A much simpler version is told about St Edmund King and Martyr in the Life of St John the Evangelist in *LgA* p. 96.

776–80 **And as thaye . . . wylde beestis.** This is an unsatisfactory attempt to translate the gist of two of Aelred's sentences: 'qui die quadam a publica strata declinantes devia quaeque secuti sunt. Et ecce sole ruente dies clauditur, aer suffunditur tenebris: viri quid agerent, quo diverterent, non occurrit. Illis itaque subsistentibus et de his quae acciderant conferentibus.' Aelred 769 D–770 A.

843 **with . . . breest** wholeheartedly, see *MED hole* adj. (2) 7(b); *brest* n.(1) 5(a).

882–3 **had defoulid his faders bed** 'ascendit cubile patris sui et maculavit stratum ejus, vivente adhuc archiepiscopo Roberto cathedram Cantuariensem invadens; ob quod a summo pontifice suspensus.' Aelred 773 B. Stigand was appointed archbishop of Canterbury in 1052 after archbishop Robert of

Jumièges fled to Normandy. The current pope, Leo IX, did not accept Stigand, who eventually received the pallium in 1058 from Benedict X, a 'non-canonical' pope. For the whole situation, see Barlow (1963), pp. 77–81, 302–8. Lanfranc accused Stigand of expelling the lawful archbishop, invading his see, and using his pallium to celebrate mass, the latter being cited as evidence that he was usurping and not merely taking over the administration of a vacant diocese. Barlow points out that this may not be true, as Stigand exercised no metropolitan rights before receiving his pallium from Benedict X (p. 304).

979 **clonkyn** shrivelled, wasted, *MED clingen* v. 2(a).

stronkyn tightly drawn, not recorded in *MED*, but see *strengen* v. (2).

1020 **opteynid** 'excepissent', Aelred 777 D, 'captured' or 'intercepted'. Here 'captured' seems required, but *MED obteinen* gives no instance with this sense.

1052 **laste houre** Compline.

1092 **newe** 'nova lex, novus pontifex, nova jura condunt, novas promulgant sententias.' Aelred 780 A.

1096 **fyel man** 'falli potuisti ut homo', Aelred 780 A. *MED* yields no possibility for **fyel**, which presumably means 'fallible'.

1130 **alowid** praised (?), 'propalaret,' Aelred 781 A, 'manifested'.

1254 **norysshid forthe** The Aelred text 'depascor et non consumor' (785 D) requires the sense 'consumed with pain,' which *MED* does not record.

1300 **meyne** religious community, not in *MED* in this sense, but see *meine* n. 1(a), (c), (d).

1311, 1340 **.vij. psalmys** The seven penitential psalms, nos. 6, 31, 37, 50, 101, 129, 142 (AV 6, 32, 38, 51, 102, 130, 143).

2. ST WINIFRED

4 **Teuythe** In A2 u/n are indistinguishable. Caxton prints Tenythe, the Latin Lives read *Teuyth*.

3. ST ERKENWALD

This life follows Tynmouth up to l. 43, **vncorupte**, and again for ll. 55–95, 791–802. Lines 44–55 and 96–231 are from *Vita Sancti Erkenwaldi*, Whatley (1989); the miracles follow the sequence of *Miraculi, ibid.*, with nos 7, 8 transposed.

101 **softe . . . worde** 'sermone modestus', *Vita* ll. 31–2

102–3 **plantid . . . charyte** This is an exact translation from *Vita* ll. 32–3 'caritatis radice plantatus', an allusion to Eph. 3:17 'in caritate radicati'.

108 **hym, hym** The Latin makes clear that these refer to the 'chare'.

123 **wode thyngis** 'insensata', *Vita* l. 50

125 **pertable** able to share in, *MED partable* adj. 2 (a)

132 **and . . . hym** is an addition to the Latin, which reads 'filios suos'.

202–3 **water . . . Moyses** Exod. 14:21.

204 **Ely . . . rest** 4 Kgs. 2:11.

mounte of rest 'requiem intronizandus', *Vita* ll. 151–2

233 **doctours house** 'in doctoris gentium familia', *Miraculi* I.1. 'Doctor gentium' was a common mediaeval epithet for St Paul. (See, for example, *Pardon of Rome*, 4.210, p. 80.) The story is about St Paul's School.

242 **a nonne** This nun is not in *Miraculi*.

265–7 **For . . . God** This is an awkward condensation of the Latin which is here an apostrophe to the reader, pointing out that as the boy could, by the merits of St Erkenwald, turn aside the anger of his teacher, so we, by those same merits, ought to be able to turn aside the wrath of almighty God, *Miraculi* I, 61–5.

275–6 **And . . . hym** This awkwardness is a result of a slight change in the story from *Miraculi*. The man throws down his burden just as one of the ministers comes out of the church, and he is truculent towards the minister, not caring what anyone will say to him. 'cepit resistere uacuus, quid quisque loqueretur de irreligiositate ipsius nequaquam sollicitus', *Miraculi* II, 32–3.

288 **he kepte . . . to** If not a scribal error, this is a relatively rare example of adverbial 'to'.

341 **that** is redundant.

403 **Morys** Maurice, bishop of London 1086–1107.

420 **there here** their hair was uncovered, 'sparsis crinibus', *Miraculi* IV, 40.
heddis head coverings, *MED hed* n. (1) (e).

431 **glasse wyndowis** There is no mention of windows in *Miraculi*.

461 **Richarde** Richard of Belmeis I, bishop of London 1107–1127.

471 **collyke** The infirmities mentioned in the Latin are a dryness ('ariditas') and a contraction ('contractio') of the hand, *Miraculi* V, 23–4. The only lexicographical reference to colic not being of the colon is at *OED colic* sb. 1, A. Flint, *Princ. Med.* 1880 'often applied to paroxysmal, spasmodic pain in other parts.'

472 **yere daye** The scribe presumably had in mind the anniversary of the death of Erkenwald (see *OED Year-day*, 2), but the Latin ('post mortem illius quarto anno' *Miraculi* V, 20) makes it clear that it was during the fourth year after Erkenwald's death that Benedicta came daily to his tomb to pray for healing.

508–9 **an . . woman** 1 Cor. 7. 14

536–7 **Amelyne, Breed** 'Hamelinus', 'Albereda', *Miraculi* VII, 29–30.

540 **afraye** attack (of illness), *MED affrai* n. 1(a), attack (but attack of illness not recorded).

562 **syke** the sick man, 'egrotus', *Miraculi* VII, 66.

642 **symple wrecche** Arcoid, canon of St Paul's. See Whatley (1986) pp. 342–3 and (1989) pp. 25–56.

682–9 **Then he . . . creature.** Lacking in *Miraculi*.

759 **Bede** *HE* IV, 11.

763 Whatley points out that this is the only complete piece of chronology in *Miraculi*, which underlines the basically liturgical motive of the collection, *Miraculi* p. 228, XIV note 10.

791–803 **After . . . of them** These lines are a close translation from Tynmouth, p. 398.

806 **alene** a foreigner, *MED alien* n., *alien* adj. The Latin reads: 'quidam de transmarinis partibus aduena', Miraculi XV, 5.

819–20 *in pontificalibus* 'uestibus niue candidioribus ac sacerdotalibus indutum, quemadmodum archiepiscopi missam celebraturi uestiuntur', *Miraculi* XV, 18–19. On this hint as to Erkenwald's primacy, see Whatley (1989), p. 229, XV note 3.

841 **axys** MED acces(se n. [OF *acces*, Lat *accessus*] 1 (a) any attack of illlness characterised by fever, but esp. of malarial fever or ague; (b) an attack of fever, esp. one of the periodic attacks of an intermittent fever.

847 **temptacion** 'in fornace huius temptationis', *Miraculi* XVI, 7–8, in the furnace of this trial.

849 **but for . . . nowe** 'sed ut in futuro iuuenilem petulantiam uirga correctionis studeas edomare', Miraculi XVI, 8–9, 'but so that in future you will study to overcome the waywardness of youth with the rod of self-discipline.' The translator has changed the sense of the passage and added a redundant clause.

854 **than he tolde** In *Miraculi* XVI, 14–16, the old man says 'Erkenuualdus nuncupor, habens sepulchrum in dextro latere altaris sancte fidis uirginis et martyris.' This was in the crypt, see Whatley (1989), p. 229, XVI, note 3.

866 **cheste** 'testudo crypte', *Miraculi* XVII, 6, the vault of the crypt.

884 **Goslamis** see Whatley (1989), p. 230, XVIII, note 1.

891 **Alwyne** 'Aeluiue', *Miraculi* XVIII, 16 *(OE Ælfgyfa)*, abbess of Barking c. 1060–c.1122, Whatley (1989), p. 230, XVIII, note 3.

907–8 **like . . . hole** Acts 3:2–8

909 **brake . . . voyce** 'conclamauit dicens', *Miraculi* XVIII, 38. See *MED* breken v 28 (c), break out. *MED* does not record the verb **b- up**.

923 **London** 'Linconiensis', *Miraculi* XIX, 3. The Latin places the miracle in Luton.

928-32 **And also . . . Erkenwolde** This passage is in neither *Miraculi* nor Tynmouth.

4. PARDON OF ALL THE CHURCHES OF ROME

The MSS of the *Liber Indulgentiarum* edited by Huelsen and referred to in these notes have the following sigils: **M**, Munich, Bayerische Staatsbibliothek, Clm 14630; **R**, Rome, cod. Vat. Reg. 520; **V**, Rome, cod. Vat. lat. 4265; **Ri**, Florence, Biblioteca Riccardiana cod. 688; **St**, Stuttgart, Staatsbibliothek 459.

9 **when . . . is(1)** the day of the patronal festival.

10 **.vij.** only five follow, which are listed in **Ri** in the same sequence. Capgrave, p. 63, adds two more, the altars of Simon & Jude and of the Holy Cross.

19-23 **And Pope . . . lentis** This passage translates the Latin of MS **R** with one exception. The Latin mentions pardon for 'offensis parentum sine manuum iniectione', but the text here has pardon for laying hands on parents. Early penitentials listed penances graduating in severity for degrees of dishonour done to parents, from cursing to striking them. Here pardon was granted for this sin except in its most extreme form, but the translator has misunderstood the original and omitted 'sine', stating that pardon for striking one's parents was included.

25 **Holy Thursdaye** Maundy Thursday, the day before Good Friday.

41 **Conuercion . . . Poule** Feast of the Conversion of St Paul, 25 January.

42 **Daye . . . Innocentis** Feast of the Holy Innocents, 28 December.

47 **Seint . . . Spayne** The cathedral of St James at Santiago de Compostela in Galicia.

52-4 **Pope . . . God** 'papa Bonifacius dixit: Indulgentia Lateranensis numerari non potest nisi a solo deo', Huelsen **R** item 3, p. 140.

57 **daye . . . halowyng** the anniversary of the consecration.

59-60 **Seint . . . Daye** 10 November.

67-8 **brede . . . proposicion** shewbread of the Temple, Exod. 25:30.

80-1 **cote . . . dede** See *Jerome*, 29.481-5, p. 337.

88-95 **And . . . Amen** 'Constantinus imperator dixit ·post baptismum suum Silvestro papae: ecce d. m. ecclesiam domino consecravi, infunde benedictionem. Et ait papa Silvester: Dominus noster Ihesus Cristus qui te mundavit a lepra per

suam misericordiam et purificavit fonte perhemni, ita mundet omnes huc venientes
et sit éis remissio omnium peccatorum.' Huelsen V item 4, p. 141.

106 **ben . . . to** A thousand years of pardon are added, on the feast days just
mentioned, to the forty-eight years and as many lents of pardon already granted
every day.

108–9 **Assumpcion . . . Natyuyte** 15 August to 8 September.

120–1 **stonys . . . dyed in** pilgrims to the Holy Land were led to sites where
tradition asserted that St John the Evangelist said mass for the Virgin and where
she had died. They frequently took from those sites stones as souvenirs which
then came to be regarded as holy relics.

127 **feest of them** Stephen 10 August and Lawrence 26 December. 'In eadem
ecclesia in festis sancti Laurentii et sancti Stefani centum anni. In festo
dedicationis ipsius ecclesie centum anni et totidem quatuor tempora et totidem
quadragene et remissio tertie partis omnium peccatorum. Et durat ista
indulgentia per omnes octavas festivitatum beate Marie. Et quicunque visitaverit
dictam ecclesiam quolibet die Mercurii per unum annum, potest liberare unam
animam de penis purgatorii.' Huelsen **Ri** item 13, p. 142.
127 **dedicacion** anniversary of the consecration of the church.

140 **oyselle** vinegar, MED *aisel* n.

142 〈**bawme**〉 **of Ynnocent** Error for 'Vincent'. The scribe left a space here.
Capgrave records in this church: 'There is a cloth þat seynt ion baptist wered.
There is a laumpe ful of bawm whech bawm ran fro þe heid of seint uincent.'
(p. 77). By Brewyn's time this has become 'a lamp filled with "balsamo" in
which floats the head of blessed Vincent, the martyr.' (p. 55).

155–6 **Sebastian . . . eyre** In his Life in *LgA* p. 167, Sebastian was martyred
and his body thrown into the sewer lest his remains should be honoured by
christians. The following night he appeared to Lucina and revealed the whereabouts of his body, asking that it be buried near the remains of the apostles.

157–60 **There . . . deseruyd** translates part of the Latin of Huelsen **R** item 6,
p. 142.

164 **alle . . . Maye** the only MS showing all Sundays as opposed to one Sunday
is Huelsen **V** item 8, p. 143.

166–8 **Pope Gregory . . . pardon** translates part of the Latin of Huelsen **R**
item 6, p. 142.

169–70 **þer . . . þerto** Huelsen **R** item 6, p. 142 with 27 popes.

175–9 **there . . . wryten** 'est omnium peccatorum remissio ad preces filie
Theodosii imperatoris, que aportavit cathenam de Ierusalem qua cathenatus fuit
sanctus Petrus apostolus. Papa Pelagius predictam ecclesiam consecravit et
antedictam indulgentiam concessit.' Huelsen item 83, **St** 8.

179–80 **Vite . . . Macello** should read *Viti et Modesti et Crescentie in macello*, the latter being a reference to the local meat market. Lines 207–11 translate Huelsen item 103, St 9, with **iiij.th.** for 'tertie'.

187–9 **And . . . lentis** translates Huelsen item 76, St 11.

192 **in Pyncis** St is the only one of Huelsen's MSS to add these words to the name of the church. Huelsen item 39, St 14.

193 **Vrcy** *Ursi*, only in St. Various accounts of this name are given by the authorities, but it seems to have been applied to the church of *S. Andrea de Urso*, or *de Ursis*, named after a local family named *de' Boccacci di Orso*.

    Marcellyne This church of *S. Marcelli* is incorrectly called *Marcellini* in St. Huelsen item 56, St 16.

194–5 **Saturnyne, Marcellyne and Peter** two churches found only in St, 17,18.

196 **Ceryce and Iulycte** is incorrectly named. It should be *Cyri et Iohannis*. Huelsen item 34, St 19, reads *Cire et Io*, Ri reads *Curcii et Io*.

199 **Eustace** should be *Eustachio*, but St reads *Eustasio*. The description of this church translates Huelsen item 38, St 21.

201–2 **And . . . pardon** translates Huelsen item 23, St 22.

203 **Alle . . . Angels** Huelsen item 16a, St 23, reads *Sancto Angelo*.

203–4 **And . . . pardon** Huelsen items 42,19, St items 24, 25.

205 **end of folio in MS A2** At this point A2 omits the Church of St Ambrose, Huelsen item 13, St 26, a copyist's error.

206 **Ierome** Huelsen item 46, St 27, (only in St and Ri).

207 **Alexij** translates Huelsen item 12, St 28.

208 **de Thoure** only St, Ri read de. The church is *S. Salvatoris in thermis*, Huelsen item 93, St 29.

209–10 **chapelle . . . smete of** The chapel of the three (not four) wells is in the church of *S. Anastasii ad aquam Salviam*. A difficulty is that Huelsen has omitted item 30 of St from his lists, probably because this church is one of the nine principal churches of Rome in the Vatican MSS which he deals with at the beginning of his study. **Ri** provides a clue: 'In ecclesia Triumphantis (scr. trium fontium), ubi beatus Paulus fuit decollatus et in ecclesia sci. Anastasii et S. Marie in scala celi cuique mille anni et totidem quadragene.' Huelsen item 8.

211–12 **in the waye** 'in via' St, other MSS read 'extra portam', 'de portu', Huelsen item 92, St 31.

215 **Syngnano** *Sitignano*, Huelsen item 48, St 33.

217 *de Carceribus* *de curtibus*, Huelsen item 79, St 34.

223 **Seint Michael** Only in St item 38, other MSS *Sant Angelo*.

224 Seint Mathye *S. Mathei* **St** item 39. The church of St Matthew in via Merulana.

229 Anastace see note to ll. 209–10.

236 Horose The scribe has had difficulty with his exemplar. The church is *S. Tome* (Huelsen item 101, *Thomaxo* **St** 43,) and the rest of the line translates the Latin of **St**.

238 Seyint . . . Latyn *S. Iohannis ante portam Latinam.* The text translates Huelsen item 49, **St** 44.

249 Iohn and Poule should read Iohn and Iames (see text ll. 198). *SS. Iohannis et Iacobi* are unique to the Stuttgart MS, Huelsen item 50, **St** 52.

251 Liace should read *Luce.* This church appears only in **Ri**, **St**, Huelsen item 55, **St** 54.

255–83 And in . . . of pardon. These lines translate Huelsen items 71, 59, **St** 58, 59.

260 Neptymus *Neptune.*

286 Mynorcya *de Minerva.* We can find no explanation for this reading. Huelsen item 61, **St** 61.

287–8 and . . . pardon(2) This phrase occurs only in **St**, Huelsen item 64, **St** 62.

289 Transpadiun *in Transpadina.* The text translates Huelsen item 73, **St** 63.

291 in þe Feelde *de Campo.* This church appears only in **Ri,St**; only **St** reads in. Huelsen item 60, **St** 64.

292 in Portica *de Porticu.* Only **St** reads in portico, Huelsen item 69, **St** 67.

294 þe Pytte *de puteo.* See Glossary pytte.

296 Oure . . . Water This is probably a mistranslation of *S. Maria de Aqua Salvia.* According to the entry in *Huelsen* for V item 12, p. 144, a chapel of this name was in the church of *S. Anastasii* (see note ll. 209–10.) Huelsen's own catalogue says that the ancient name of this church was *SS. Vincenzo ed Anastasio alle Tre Fontane*, and it is now known as *S. Anastasii ad Aquam Salviam.*

300 Scala Greca 'scola greca' **St**, all other MSS read 'scola grecorum', Huelsen item 72, **St** 69.

301 Libera . . . inferni The only mention of this chapel in the MSS edited by Huelsen is item 108 from **M**. It was a small church built in the fourteenth century above that of *S. Maria Antiqua*, and was sometimes known as *S. Maria liberatrice*, or *S. Maria de Inferno.*

305 Seint Susanne This church is only in **St**, Huelsen item 100, **St** 72.

306 wyfe . . . Alexij Only **St** mentions this fact, Huelsen item 90, **St** 73.

307 Potencyan *S. Potentiana*, Huelsen item 85, **St** 74.

308 **Praxiede** *S. Praxedis*, Huelsen item 86, **St** 75.

309–10 **and . . . at** This phrase has been added in **St**.

310–11 **and . . . reliques** This seems to be the only phrase in this text unique to the writer.

313 **Felicitas** only in **St**, Huelsen item 40, **St** 77.

315 **Radegunde** This apocryphal church is the one certain link between MS A2 and **Ri**. See the introduction to this text.

316 **Pernelle** *Petronillae*, Huelsen item 84, **St** 80.

319 **Iulyan** In this position (83) **St** has *S. Clare* (Huelsen item 32). The listed indulgences do not match, and this may be a case of a simple omission. The very generous indulgences do match the following entry in **St**, *S. Viviana*, (Huelsen item 25, **St** 84.)

321 **Agathe** only in **St**, Huelsen item 10, **St** 85.

322 **Margrete** illegible in **St**, Huelsen item 106, **St** 86.

323 **Crystyne** *Christiane*, this church only in **Ri, St**, Huelsen item 30, **St** 87.

324 **Peter . . . prison** This is almost certainly 'ecclesia que dicitur Custodia, in qua incarcerati fuerunt b. Petrus et Paulus', listed in only three of Huelsen's MSS (item 82).

332 ff. The heading is in the manuscript margin, and the text is from the *Revelations of St Bridget*, Book VI, chapter 102.

5. WHAT THE CHURCH BETOKENETH

1–109 **The churche . . . þe churche** cf. Durandus I.1.

20 *Ego . . . hostium* John 10:9.

25–6 *sapiencia . . . septem* Prov. 9:1. *et* is not in Vulgate text.

34–5 **Blessid . . . theris** Matt. 5:3.

50 *Domus . . . vocabitur* Matt. 21:13.

56 *quia . . . peccatorum* 1 Pet. 4:8.

62 **book** nave, *MED bouk* n. 2(a).

68–9 *Ego . . . mundi* John 8:12.

74 *Vos . . . mundi* Matt. 5:14. 'et bonorum . . . exempla' is not in Matt. 5:14.

78 **crucyfyxe** 'crux triumphalis' Durandus.

111–18 **The white . . . people** cf. Durandus I.2.

120–54 **It is . . . Eve** cf. Durandus I.3.

147 **Ioseph** *add* 'fame afflictum' Durandus.

155–64 **For by . . . God** cf. Durandus I.4.

166–9 **For þer . . . lyfe** cf. Durandus I.5.

171–80 **Whan . . . masse** cf. Durandus III.2.

181–95 **The awbe . . . with** cf. Durandus III.3,4.

182 **desolate** *MED* records spellings 'dis(s)olat' under *desolat(e*. Since the word here must mean religiously or morally lax, it must be an error for *dissolut(e* adj. 1(a).

194–5 **scorge . . . with** Mark 15:15.

196–204 **The stole . . . peler** cf. Durandus III.5.

205–12 **The fanon . . . passhion** cf. Durandus III.6.

211 **right arme** an error for left arm and an addition to the Durandus text which reads: 'Manipulus etiam representat funem quo Iesus comprehendus a iudeis ligatus fuit'.

213–28 **The chesiple . . . scorne** cf. Durandus III.7.

216–17 *quia . . . peccatorum* 1 Peter 4:8; 'et omnia . . . continent' is not in 1 Pet. 4, but reflects Matt. 7:12 or Matt. 22:40.

220–1 *Amice . . . nupcialem* Matt. 22:12.

229–40 **Furst . . . charite** cf. Durandus IV.4.

236 *Asperges . . . me* Ps. 50:9.

243–65 **Oure . . . erthe** cf. Durandus IV.6.

266–81 **The meke . . . vs** cf. Durandus IV.7.

270–1 *Dixi . . . remisisti* 'Dixi: Confitebor adversum me iustitiam meam Domino; et tu remisisti impietatem peccati mei', Ps. 31:5.

277 **Lorde . . . synner** Luke 18:13.

282–91 **The encense . . . God** cf. Durandus IV.8.

294–309 **The kyssyng . . . beganne** cf. Durandus IV.9, 11.

304–5 **Anticriste . . . Iewis** The two men from heaven who will confront the Antichrist were identified from early patristic times as Enoch and Elijah, see Charlesworth (1985), I, 769, note 14a.

311–20 **Thaye . . . them** cf. Durandus IV.12.

321–33 **Furst . . . ouresilfe** cf. Durandus IV.13

334–51 **It . . . glorefye** cf. Durandus IV.14.

336 **Boaz . . . felde** Ruth 2:4 The error (Ruth for Boaz) may be because the writer was thinking of his source.

336–7 **angel . . . Gedion** Judg. 6:12.

353–63 While . . . *regnat &c.* cf. Durandus IV.15.

364–76 The epistle . . . Churche &c. cf. Durandus IV.16.

377–85 The grayle . . . life cf. Durandus IV.19.

378–9 Doith . . . comyng Matt. 3:2.

386–95 *Alleluya(2)* . . . lyfe cf. Durandus IV.20.

396–402 The tracte . . . hevyn cf. Durandus IV.21.

403–10 The sequence . . . *te* cf. Durandus IV.22.

404 togeders not in Durandus IV.22, confuses the sense. Each has a double stole.

409–10 *Beati* . . . *te* Ps. 83:5.

411–26 Furst . . . the cf. Durandus IV.24.

427–30 Whye . . . kyngdom 'Et nota quod quattuor sunt euangelia de beata maria vt dicetur in septimo parte sub festo assumptionis.' Durandus IV.24.

431–43 The Crede . . . Amen cf. Durandus IV.25.

432–4 feith . . . helthe Rom. 10:8–9.

437 kunne know by heart, *MED connen* v. 5(b).

442–3 *et quem* . . . *Ihesum* John 17:3.

444–53 *Sanctus(2)* . . . hym cf. Durandus IV.34.

454–60 In the margin is written: 'pro prima sancti dei omnes quam estis consortes communi oracio omni sancto, pro secunda de profu[n]dis, pro tercia deus quam caritatis cum deus caritas est.'

454–65 The grettist . . . *fideles* cf. Durandus IV.51.

466–87 The yevyng . . . evylle cf. Durandus IV.53.

488–96 *Ite(2)* . . . godenes cf. Durandus IV.57.

497–519 The blessyng . . . þerof cf. Durandus IV.59.

503–4 *Benedicat* . . . *terre* Ps. 66:7.

506–7 *Venite* . . . *regnum* Matt. 25:34.

512–13 brake . . . knyfe cf. Luke 24:30 The sentence is not in Durandus.

521–31 The Evensonge . . . benefettis cf. Durandus V.9.

533 *Conuerte nos* 'Converte nos, Deus, salutaris noster' is the Versicle recited at Compline.

533–48 Complyn . . . this cf. Durandus V.10, but 621–28 does not represent the Latin text: 'Et attende quoniam ad primam et ad completorium Apostolorum symbolum non dimittimus, quia cuncta opera nostra in eius nomine incipimus et concludimus, in que credimus. Similiter ad vtrumque officium confessionem, et Miserere mei Deus adiicimus: vt quicquid in nocte peccavimus, aut in die deliquimus, per confessionem et penitenciam diluamus, adimplentes illud: Confitemini alterutrum peccata vestra.'

537 *Deus in adiutorium* The verse quoted, Ps. 69:2, is the opening verse of every Divine Office.

541–8 **And also . . . welle this** It is not the Creed that is said at Compline, but the Confiteor. These sentences only approximate to Durandus.

550–64 **The Matyns . . . ende** cf. Durandus V.4.

558–9 **devylle . . . flesh** the phrase, repeated at l. 1393, is from the Litany.

561–4 **Seinte . . . ende** The belief that this hymn was jointly composed by Ambrose and Augustine at Augustine's baptism dates back to the ninth century and is repeated in his Life in *LgA* p. 847. Voragine attributes the story to Honorius (of Autun)'s *Speculum Ecclesiae*.

565 **Laudes . . . Matyns** 'De Laudibus matutinis', Durandus.

565–75 **The Laudis . . . ship** cf. Durandus V.4.

572–3 **.viij. . . . ship** Gen. 7:13.

578–9 **.viij. . . . bestis** Gen. 8:18–19.

584–5 **roost . . . honyecombe** Luke 24:42.

595 **taught and lightid** instructed and enlightened.

597–610 **Whan . . . crosse &c** cf. Durandus VI.80.

605 *Mandatum . . . invicem* John 13:34.

611–24 **By the . . . temptacion** cf. Durandus VI.81.

632–5 **Seint . . . sore** This story from the *Dialogues* is in Exaltation of the Cross, *LgA* p. 938.

642 *Deus . . . peccatori* Luke 18:13.

644 *qui plasmasti . . . Deus* cf. Life of Thais in *LgA* p. 1039.

654 **feythfullye** *Sp.E.* adds 'uni soli Deo, et ipsum fideliter adorare.'

655–6 **and alle . . . þerin** om. *Sp.E.*

657 **goost** *Sp.E.* adds 'sunt tres persone.'

661–2 **whether thou . . . takyng** 'whether you have maintained faithfully towards him that which you promised in assuming Christianity.'

662 **cristendom takyng** 'baptismo' *Sp.E.*

662–5 **And euery . . . thyselfe** 'Per illud preceptum ordinatur homo erga Deum Patrem omnipotentem.' *Sp.E.*

667 **of(1)** *Sp.E.* adds 'tui'.

668 **oure . . . Cryste** all Latin MSS read 'Paulus', but this should read 'Iacobus', as the quotation is from James 5:12. The translator may have been thinking of Matt. 5:37. (Forshaw (1973), p. 57, note 12).

670 **in as moche as in you is.** not *Sp.E.*

675 **and lyfe** Only 4 of Forshaw's MSS have this reading (p. 57, note 17).

682 **halowid** *Sp.E.* adds 'Modo indulge pro Deo, nec habeas pro malo, et dicam tibi quomodo debes sabbata custodire.'

682–3 **And if . . . daye** 'Si sis sanus corpore' *Sp.E.*

687–94 **and beseche . . . of God** These sentences replace three sentences of *Sp.E.* about attendance at the Divine Office and at mass, hearing and memorising a sermon, sharing the food provided with the poor, and giving thanks.

691 **of power** See *Aldhelm* 15. 38, p. 188.

695 **loke . . . tauernes** 'non ibis ad tabernam' *Sp.E.*

695–6 **veyne . . . placis** 'ad luctaciones vel ad coreas, nec ad alios ludos vanos' *Sp.E.*

697 **pore . . . bedrede** 'miseros et languidos' *Sp.E.*

698–700 **bothe . . . bothe** 'et ita dies festivales in servicio Dei finire. Et illud preceptum ordinat hominem ad recipiendum Spiritum sanctum.' *Sp.E.*

713 **neither . . . bodelye** not *Sp.E.*

715 **his** *Sp.E.* adds 'propriis'.

715–17 **whan . . . soule** 'et quando ipsum ponit in loco mortis, sicut in carcere, vel in alio loco qui posset esse occasio mortis.' *Sp.E.*

718 **tysyng, eggyng** 'incitamentum' *Sp.E.* These must be taken together to account for the '.ij.'.

726–7 **both . . . synne** not *Sp.E.*

731 **and (1) . . . gydyng** not *Sp.E.*

734–6 **that he . . . do to** 'nam qui non vult suo proximo dampnum facere per se, nec debet alteri, qui sibi dampnum facit, consentire, nec consulere, nec auxiliari.' *Sp.E.*

738 **lowe dameselle** not *Sp.E.*

739 **but kepe . . . enye** not *Sp.E.*

741–2 **that is . . . matrimonye** not *Sp.E.*

744–5 **that is . . . godis** not *Sp.E.*

754–5 **God . . . Synaye** Exod. 31:18

760–1 **or highnes . . . cristen** not *Sp.E.*

763 **souerayne** 'superiorem' *Sp.E.* The Latin clearly refers to a religious superior, so there is a change of emphasis here.

764 **spice** 'species' *Sp.E. MED spice* n. (2) 1(e), a sub-class or branch of sin.

769–71 **whan . . . richer** 'quando homo alterius bonum minuit ut ipse melior apparere possit' *Sp.E.*

770 **discresith** belittles, *MED decresen* v., diminish.

773–4 **vnshamefastenesse** 'impudencia sive inverecundia' *Sp.E.*

775 **eiþer hie beryng** om. *Sp.E.*

777 **noble** nobility, high rank; perhaps an error for 'noblei'.

778 **grace** 'fortune' *Sp.E.*

778–9 **gode . . . love** 'gracia, bona fama' *Sp.E.*

781 **possessions** *Sp.E.* adds 'familia'.

791 **necligent** 'negligencia' *Sp.E.* This use of the adjectival form for the noun, not recorded in *MED*, is probably an error.

792 **rennyng . . . thought** 'vagacio mentis' *Sp.E.*

794–5 **and . . . God** 'contra misericordiam' *Sp.E.*

796 **vnsittyng** 'inepta' *Sp.E.*
   gladness *Sp.E.* adds 'luxuria, immundicia'.

797 **and . . . evils** *om. Sp.E.*

798 **of synne** 'cordis' *Sp.E.*

807 **hymselfe** *Sp.E.* adds 'accidia ipsum tormentat.'

813 **the which . . . maner** 'et ait isto modo' *Sp.E.*

816 **that . . . cristen** 'id est erga proximum suum' *Sp.E.*

817 **reioyse** 'possidebunt' *Sp.E.*
   þat . . . hevyn 'scilicet perpetuam' *Sp.E.*

819 **for . . . trespasse** not *Sp.E.*

825 **with . . . God** not *Sp.E.*

826 **in . . . seruyce** not *Sp.E.*

836 **and . . . made** not *Sp.E.*

837 **myldenesse or sobyrnesse** 'mansuetudinem' *Sp.E.*

842–5 **and . . . disceyuid** not *Sp.E.* At this point *Sp.E.* has a sentence about lechery which our text lists after gluttony.

850 **sykenes** *Sp.E.* adds 'plures quam scio nominare.'

852–3 **and(1) . . . soule** not *Sp.E.*

855–6 **that . . . &c.** not *Sp.E.*

858 **Nowe** 'Iam habes infirmitates et earum medicinas. Postea' *Sp.E.*

861–3 **spirite** . . . **lorde** Is. 11:2–3.

862 **cunnyng** 'sciencie' *Sp.E.*

865–7 **And** . . . **helpe** 'Et vide qualiter. Primo debet homo dimittere malum' *Sp.E.*

868 **And for** 'Postea' *Sp.E.*
    to(2) . . . **cristen** not *Sp.E.*

871 **flateryng** . . . **softenes** 'blandiciam' *Sp.E.*

874 **alle, of this worlde** not *Sp.E.*

894–5 **for** . . . **cristen** not *Sp.E.*

903–4 **can, maye** 'sciat', 'possit' *Sp.E.*

904 **wolle** 'velit' *Sp.E.*

905 **none** . . . **vertues** 'scienciam, potenciam, nec voluntatem' *Sp.E.*

913–14 **wonderfulle liberalle,** 'mirabiliter liberalis' *Sp.E.*

914 **and** . . . **yeftis** not *Sp.E.*

915 **euery(1)** . . . **houre** not *Sp.E.*

932–3 **and(2)** . . . **synne** not *Sp.E.*

939 **man** *Sp.E.* adds 'tercia die.'

941 **of(1)** . . . **honyecombe** Luke 24:42, not *Sp.E.*

960 **man** *Sp.E.* adds 'vel mulier'

962–3 **wheþer** . . . **childe** not *Sp.E.*

968 **holdyn** 'tenent' *Sp.E.* cf. l. 981 holde, *Sp.E.* 'teneant', present or sponsor for baptism or confirmation.

970 **with gode werkis** not *Sp.E.*

972–3 **and** . . . **witnessith** 'ne fiat irregularis, et puer similiter, secundum decretum.' *Sp.E.*

976 **And** . . . **can** not *Sp.E.*

980–2 **fader** . . . **confermyd** The early Councils of the Church laid down that the spiritual relationship between sponsors and godchildren was exactly equal to the relationship between parents and their children. Parents could not, therefore, sponsor their children for confirmation, as this would technically become an incestuous relationship. All pastoral manuals of the time contain this warning.

984 **or** . . . **done** not *Sp.E.*

990 **envye** . . . **devil** 'inimicum' *Sp.E.*

997 **that** . . . **lyfe** not *Sp.E.*

1003 **that . . . ordrid** not *Sp.E.*

1010–11 **vertues . . . herbis** This refers to an earlier passage in *Sp.E.* (Forshaw, chapter 6 §20) which explains that knowledge of God's wisdom can be attained by meditating on the qualities of his creatures within the order of things; stones have existence only, plants existence and life, beasts existence, life and sentience, and mankind all three with the addition of intelligence.

1013–14 **þat . . . dewlye** not *Sp.E.*

1014 **is** *Sp.E.* adds 'summe bonus et'.

1017 **departid** 'separari' *Sp.E.*

1017 **but** *Sp.E.* adds 'per iudicium sancte ecclesie aut'.

1017–18 **if . . . weddid** not *Sp.E.*

1021–3 **that . . . prayers** not *Sp.E.*

1024 **makith light** 'alleviat' *Sp.E.*

1025 **peyne** 'a pena' *Sp.E.* For **gostelye peyne** see *MED pein(e* n. 3(a), suffering endured by soul in purgatory or hell, and cf. l. 1167.

1027–8 **that . . . God** not *Sp.E.*

1032 **Boke of Wysedom** Wis. 8:7.

1055 **bodye** *Sp.E.* adds 'Sed iam posses ita michi dicere.'

1056–7 **I(2) . . . mercye** 'non habeo potestatem dandi cibum, necque potum, vestimentum, nec hospicium, quia non habeo ex quo possum illud facere; nec ego possum visitare incarceratos, nec confortare egrotos, necque sepellire mortuos, quia sum in alterius voluntate constitutus.' *Sp.E.*

1060 **as . . . sayeth** not *Sp.E.*

1067–90 These lines involve omissions from the source, with some re-writing. The two paragraphs in *Sp.E.* (73, 74, Forshaw pp. 71, 73) continue the question and answer form of the preceding paragraph, but the questions are here omitted. The questioner, a religious in both source and this passage (l. 1056), wants to know if it is not better (at **worlde** 1066) to have goods and give them away than to sacrifice one's self; to judge or to be judged (at **to me** 1068); to possess, or to be promised, the joys of heaven (at **alone** 1073). 1072–3 **but . . . alone** is an addition to the source which elucidates the judgement process. The final question (at **spirite** 1076) is who are the truly poor and the truly rich, and the answer ll. 1077–80, a re-writing of the source, is clearly aimed at wealthy laity.

1072 **kynraddis** tribes, *MED kinrede* n. 4(a).

1089 **þers** *Sp.E.* adds 'Ita enim dicit Christus in evangelio: 'Beati pauperes spiritu, quoniam ipsorum est regnum caelorum.'' This omission from our text must surely be an eyeskip by the translator 'caelorum . . . caelorum'.

1091 **þerfore it behouyth** 'oportet ergo' *Sp.E.* The sense requires 'It follows, then,' *MED bihoven* v.2a(a).

1120–2 **Seint . . . God** a free paraphrase of *Enchiridion ad Laurentium* XIX, 70.

1123–6 **Seint . . . is** We are unable to trace a source for this.

1127–30 **Seynt . . . dye** a free paraphrase of *Tractatus CXXIV in Joannis Evangelium* I, 13.

1138 **lecherous** dissolute, *MED lecherous* adj. 2(b).

1141–3 **Seint . . . herers** a free paraphrase of *Tractatus CXXIV in Joannis Evangelium* I, 13.

1149 **falle** become desirous? *MED falle(n* sense 47, examples are of the heart.

1160 The heading in *Sp.E.* begins: 'Posterius debes cognoscere que sunt septem peticiones oracionis dominice, que auferunt omnia mala et procurant omnia bona.'

1166–7 **that . . . synnes** not *Sp.E.*

1167 **peyne dew** that is, ecclesiastical penalty incurred, *MED pein(e* n. 1a(b).

1168 **þat . . . vs** not *Sp.E.*

1169–70 **that . . . temptacion** not *Sp.E.*

1171 **passith** *Sp.E.* adds 'et excellit'.

1172 **prayer** *Sp.E.* adds 'et ideo facit ille magnum dedecus et magnam irreverenciam Iesu Dei Filio, qui sibi accipit verba ritmica et curiosa, dimittitque et relinquit oracionem ipsemet composuit.'

1175–6 **wylle, wylle** 'voluntatem', 'necessitatem' *Sp.E.*

1176–8 **And . . . come** This replaces a passage in *Sp.E.* condemning those who multiply their prayers.

1186 **euyl to comyng** 'malum futurum', cf. **to commyng**, *Kenelm*, 18.97, p. 209.

1193 **good** *Sp.E.* adds 'bonum spirituale'.

1199 **askyngis or** not *Sp.E.*

1200 **discyplis** *Sp.E.* adds 'et amicos'.

1205 **gode** not *Sp.E.*

1207–8 **withoute . . . God** not *Sp.E.*

1211 **that . . . nede** 'quod nobis tenentur' *Sp.E.*

1212 **hope and** not *Sp.E.*

1213 **knowe** 'confitemur' *Sp.E.*

1216 **beleve . . . thynke** 'cogitamus' *Sp.E.*

1217–18 **with . . . remembrance, to . . . freeltye** not *Sp.E.*

1219 **feyre** 'quatuor' *Sp.E.*

1220–1 **and(2) . . . desire** not *Sp.E.*

1225 **heryng** 'laudem' *Sp.E. MED heriing(e* vbl. n. praise.

1239 **thye chosyn childryn** 'electi tui' *Sp.E.*

1242 **prioressis** *Sp.E.* adds 'et omnes sui subditi.'

1243 **persons, vykers** 'rectores' *Sp.E.*

1245 **by grace** not *Sp.E.*

1250 **moost . . . Lorde** not *Sp.E.*

1251–2 **euer eyþer** 'utriusque' *Sp.E.*

1255 **euer either** 'utramque' *Sp.E.*

1257–8 **tylle . . . vs** not *Sp.E.*

1267–8 **of(2) . . . synne** 'pene et culpe' *Sp.E.*

1271–3 **that . . . Amen** not *Sp.E.*

1274 **his disciplis** 'nos' *Sp.E.*

1278 **charge þou** 'cures' *Sp.E.*
   multeplye 'multiplicare sepius' *Sp.E.*

1279 **withoute deuocion** not *Sp.E.*

1281 **and . . . deuocion** not *Sp.E.*

1282 **mekenes** not *Sp.E.*

1283 **with . . . devocion** 'in corde meo devote' *Sp.E.* 1 Cor. 14:19.

1285 **withoute deuocion** not *Sp.E.*

1287 **Saye . . . psalmes** Ps. 46:7–8

1291 **departid** 'divisus' *Sp.E.*

1293–4 **Seke . . . you** Matt. 6:33

1296 **askyng** 'interrogacione' *Sp.E.*

1296–7 **þerefore . . . godis** 'ideo debes scire quid habebis in gaudio celesti' *Sp.E.*

1326–8 *laboraui . . . rigabo* Ps. 6:7.

1330 **ouerhelyng** covering. *MED* does not record this vbl.n., but *OED* cites an Old English example under *overhele* v.

1331–2 *Asperges . . . dealbabor* Ps. 50:9. 'Domine' is not in the Vulgate text.

1336–7 *Vade . . . mundaberis* 4 Kgs. 5:10. This chapter contains the story of Naaman, a leper who was captain of the host of Syria.

1399–1400 **For that . . . nought** cf. Augustine, *Tractatus CXXIV in Joannis Evangelium* I, 13.

1401 *Omnia . . . nichil* John 1:3.

1410–26 **Oute of . . . not do** These lines summarise the elderly Augustine's views of the Pelagian controversy.

1415 **myschevi⟨s and⟩** Worm holes and marks on the text make these letters illegible.

1427–44 **And Seint . . . repente hym** cf. *De Civitate Dei* 21.27 and 11.17.

1434 **the lykyng** *MED liking(e* vbl.n. (1), 1(d), beauty, attraction.

1436 **lykyng** *ibid.*, 1(a) feeling of pleasure.

6. ST EDMUND OF ABINGDON

20–25 **but . . . ende** This story is not in *SEL* nor in any of the published lives of Edmund.

21, 27, 96 **toke** *MED taken* 31 (b), gave. *SEL* uses the same verb in all these instances. See Glossary for other examples.

24 **ouerplewse** surplus. *MED overplus* does not cite this spelling.

71 **caste . . . sowle** a misreading of *SEL* ll. 116–8: 'Maide þu schalt lurny þus . awei forto caste / þi fole wil of þi flesch . wiþ suche discipline. / Heo þoȝte lute of fol þoȝt . er þis gode man wolde fyne.'

77 **she . . . hym** *SEL* l. 132 makes it clear that his mother told Edmund 'þat þu somwhar þi sostren do . in a nonnerie.' She did not specify Catesby and Edmund had some difficulty in finding a suitable house. 'Ac wel vneþe he miȝte hit do . wiþoute symonye.' *SEL* l. 148. According to the hagiographers, Catesby was the only religious house prepared to accept his sisters without a dowry, and he regarded payment of such a dowry as simoniacal, but see Lawrence (1960), pp. 107, 109, showing that the house at Catesby was endowed with property by both Edmund and his brother William.

96–101 **But . . . brente** The inconsistencies between singular and plural pronouns for the hair shirt reflect those in *SEL* ll. 179–184.

104 **there sate one** Görlach (1998), p. 98, points out that this is a misreading of *SEL* l. 189: 'A lute blac sac as þeȝ hit were . among hem þis foweles bere.'

110 **Chalsegrove** Of all the contemporary Lives of Edmund, only that by Anonymous A, which Lawrence considers to be the source of the *SEL* Life, has this reading. Other *SEL* MSS have 'Stafgrene'.

149–50 **And in . . . passhyon** 'Ne þoȝte noȝt þis holi man . so moche in his lessoun / þat euere among his þoȝt nas mest in Godes passioun.' *SEL* ll. 277–8.

176 **the pope sent his crosser** 'þo þat of þe croserie . þe pope sende fram Rome' *SEL* l. 319. croserie, see *MED croiserie* n. (a), crusade against pagans.

'Crosser' is an unrecorded noun from *MED croisen* v.2(b), to invest somebody with the insignia of a crusader.

178–9 for to . . . Turke 'þat me wende to Ierusalem' *SEL* l. 322.

182 take . . . crosse take a vow to go on crusade. Those who took such a vow undertook to wear a cross on their clothing, and thus were known as *crucesignati*. See *Thomas of Canterbury*, 28.3, p. 285.

216 Stanley a Cistercian abbey, dependency of Quarr, now King's Stanley, near Stroud, Glos.

217 Stephyn Lexton Stephen of Lexington, formerly of Quarr, and earlier a student of Edmund at Oxford.

222 Lente mete food prescribed for any period of fasting. Compare *What the Church betokeneth*, 5.576–85, 625–39, pp. 103, 104. *SEL* l. 404 reads: 'noþing þat þolede deþ.'

227 chapeleyns 'chamberlayn' *SEL* l. 415. As Treasurer of Salisbury Edmund would not have had chaplains.

235 he was chose Edmund had already been appointed. (See l. 228.) The sense requires 'he was advised to accept.' 'þer come fur & ner / To consailli him of þisse þinge . þe red was sone ido / For gladliche at one worde . hi radde him alle þerto.' *SEL* ll. 440–2.

240 thaye had hym 'him bere' *SEL* l. 456.

242–6 Lorde . . . nede this prayer is not in *SEL*.

259 lene (*or possibly* **leue**) 'Gode wyf he seide if ich take þe . aȝe þi best to lone' *SEL* l. 483. The sense requires 'lene'.

261–4 at all tymes . . . ende These lines have no equivalent in *SEL*.

270 vnkylle 'grandsire' *SEL* l. 496.

282 cursyd excommunicated, 'amansed' *SEL* ll. 516, 518.

300 .vj. yere a misreading of *SEL* ll. 541–2. Edmund stayed in Pontigny for about six months, having chosen to go there because Stephen Langton had been there for six years.

303 Solye 'Soycie' *SEL* l. 560, Soissy, a convent of Augustinian Canons.

7. ST BRIDE

17 another enchaunter The second enchanter does not make an appearance until later in *SEL*, when Brosek is sold to him.

22 **worshipfulle mannys** In *SEL* this is the second enchanter and it is he, not Duptak, who marries Brosek.

29–32 **And than . . . Bryde** In *SEL* this is a vision of the enchanter.

32–9 **And within . . . spouse** This story of Bride's childhood in *SEL* precedes our l. 33.

47 **there owne cuntre** The ambiguity here is a result of great condensation by the writer of the *SEL* account. Bride returned to her own country with her stepfather.

68 **fadir** 'steffader' *SEL* l. 163.

82 **scaberde** 'swerd' *SEL*. The sequence of this passage is different in *SEL*.

125 **made clene** *SEL* makes no mention of a cure.

127–30 **There . . . doo** The story in *SEL* ll. 257–8 differs. Bride had no salt but 'Mid a blessinge he[o] turnde to salt . a gret hard ston.'

130 **pore** 'sike' *SEL* l. 259.

138 **.M.CC.xxij.** The year of Bride's death is not in *SEL*.

8. ST EDMUND KING AND MARTYR

5 **Hubba** Ubba is the name given by Abbo 5.5 to Halfdan, Hingvar's brother.

6 **Hungar** 'Hinguar,' Abbo 5.4.

15 **Eglysdon** *Haeglesdun*, Abbo 11.16. The whereabouts of this place has been much debated. In the early twelfth century, c.1100, Herbert Losinga granted to his new cathedral priory at Norwich the church at Hoxne 'with the chapel of St Edmund where the martyr was killed,' and by the late fourteenth century popular belief was that Eglysdon was Hoxne. However, in the mid-tenth century the patron of the church at Hoxne had been St Ethelbert, beheaded in 794 on the orders of Offa of Mercia. Gransden (1992), p. 89, believes the identification of the Hoxne church with Edmund may be a case of substitution of one king for another. Ridyard (1988), pp. 218–9 and notes 31, 34, favours the discoveries of West (1981–4), who points out that there are, within five miles of Bury St Edmunds, a field-name Hellesden, and a short distance away Sutton Hall, Kingshall Farm, Kingshall Street and Kingshall Green. Ridyard cites Hermann's identification of the site of the initial burial of Edmund at *Suthtune* as additional evidence to support West's view. The case for Hoxne was made by Whitelock (1970).

9. ST FRIDESWIDE

This Life is not included in the EETS edition of *SEL*. It was edited from Bodleian Library MS Ashmole 43 (A) for her thesis by Lingley (1987), and is currently being edited from MS P by Dr Sherry Reames. Citations of *SEL* for this Life are from A unless otherwise stated.

2 **Dydam** 'Dydam' *SEL* P, 'Didan' *SEL* A, 'Didanus' *Vita B*, 2, l. 5

5 **Abyne** 'Abyne' *SEL* P, 'Ailȝiue' *SEL* A, 'Algiva' *Vita B*, 2, l. 11

9 **.ij. churchis** This is a misunderstanding of the *SEL* text, in which Didan builds one church in honour of the Holy Trinity, the Virgin Mary 'And eke of Alle Halwen,' *SEL* l. 18, but see Blair (1987) p. 89 and notes 42, 43.

10 **in a shryne** not *SEL*.

11 **Blake Chanons** Augustinian Canons.

30–33 **Thye . . . falle** not *SEL*.

35–6 **sette . . . Frydeswyde** 'et virginis Frideswide iam amore tactum impudico inflammat' *Vita B*, 8, l. 3, not *SEL*.

57 **sodenly** 'sodeynliche' *SEL*, 'Sub unius hore spatio decem miliaria transferuntur' *Vita B*, 12, l. 6.

59–60 **dyd grete hurte** Görlach (1998), p. 101, could find no source for this addition to *SEL*. However, *Vita B* 13, ll. 4–5: 'Hinc iratus rex et amentium more intolerabili permotus furore, civitatem terribiliter intuens, in eius subversionem coniuravit', may have given rise to this version.

66, 80 **Benesye** Frideswide's intention in moving to Binsey is, according to *Vita B*, to seek solitude while within reach of the sisters in Oxford. 'Hengseye', Hinksey, also a village near Oxford, but unconnected with Frideswide, is substituted in A2.

66 **.iij. yere** In *Vita B* Frideswide remains in Bampton for three years, returning to her own monastery in Oxford only when nearing her death.

77–8 **this man** The sense requires 'hym'. *SEL* and Latin source are of no help as the text here is a condensation of *SEL*.

84–5 **wylle/stylle** remnant of rhyme in *SEL* ll. 91–2.

94 **Seynt Lucys Daye** 'Seint Lukes Day' *SEL* l. 168. This is a misreading. St Lucy's Day is 13 December, St Luke's Day is 18 October. *Vita B* gives the time of Frideswide's death as the early hours of 19 October. Cf. *Thomas of Canterbury*, 28.369–70, p. 294, where these feast days are similarly confused.

98 **Blake Chanons** not *SEL*, which reads 'a wel fayr chanounrye.'

10. ST EDWARD KING AND MARTYR

4 **quene** Alfthryth.

18 **a fayre downe** *i.e.* the former wood of Wareham is now a bare hillside. 'adoune' in *SEL* has been taken otherwise and incorrectly by both Horstmann and d'Evelyn & Mill, as adverbial 'down', which is accepted and cited by *MED*, sense 3(d). *SEL* reads: 'In a uair wode in Dorsete . þat bi side Waram was / þat fair wode was þulke tyme . ac nou he is al adoune / Bote þornes & þunne boskes . þat stondeþ biside þe toune,' (ll. 42–44) translating 'in siluam . . . quae iuxta uillam quae dicitur Werham admodum grandis tunc habebatur, sed nunc rara tantum spineta nucumque arbores neglecto situ campis late patentibus ibi cernuntur', Passio p. 4, ll. 11–13.

20–21 **towne . . . none there** *SEL* translates this directly from *Passio*.

39 **lyffe . . . Alpheye** see *Alphege*, 11.32ff., p. 165. The *SEL* St Alphege, ll. 148–155, makes rather more of the ravages of the Danes.

59 **therle Alpher** ealdorman Alfhere.

59–60 **that . . . lyffe** which of these two loved the other is no clearer in *SEL* ll. 153–4: 'An hei eorl þer was alonde þo . þat ihote was Alfer / þat seint Edward louede muche . þo he was aliue her.'

62 **Seynt Wylfryde** 'þe abbesse of Wiltone' *SEL* l. 166.

62–3 **nonnys . . . susters** 'And to seint Edith þe holy womman . þat nonne was þo þar / þat was seint Edwardes soster . & þe kynges doȝter Eggar,' *SEL* ll. 167–8. These two were mother and daughter as the Latin makes clear: 'quaedam uenerabilis uirgo, soror ipsius sancti, magna uitae et morum honestate pollens, Edgit nuncupata, quae supradicti regis gloriosissimi Edgari et eiusdem Wilfridae, nondum Dei consecratae, filia fuerat. (*Passio* p. 8, l. 27 to p. 9, l. 2.) Görlach (1974), pp. 151–2, records no variants in *SEL* MSS that would account for this suppression of Edith's relationship to her abbess.

82 **place** 'Go he seide to Sseftesburi . to þe abbesse of þe house' *SEL* l. 221.

93–4 **.Ml. . . . more** 'A þousand ȝer it was & on' *SEL* l. 253, translating: 'qui erat annus ab incarnatione Domini millesimus primus', *Passio* p. 13, ll. 10–11.

94 **Edward** Edward the Confessor, for whom see pp. 1–38.

11. ST ALPHEGE

15 **after this** *SEL* makes it clear that St Ethelwold died soon after Alphege became abbot of Bath.

20 **.xxxij. yere** 'twenti ȝer & two' *SEL* l. 37.

33–4 Kyrkylle, Erdryche 'Kyrkel was þe prince ihote . . . His broþer was maister of is ost . Edrik was is name' *SEL* ll. 67–70. In fact the Danish army was divided into two parts, one led by Thorkell the Tall, the other 'by Hemming, Thorkell's brother, and by a chief named Eilaf.' 'Erdryche' (*SEL* Edrik) is probably suggested by Eadric Streona, a Mercian on the English side, who later acquired a reputation for treachery (Stenton (1947), pp. 376–7).

49–50 half a yere and more 'half a ȝer and somdel more' *SEL* l. 94. Alphege was imprisoned for about seven months.

12. ST AUGUSTINE OF CANTERBURY 1

1–2 Seynt . . . Room The grammatical difficulty presented by the unamended text is paralleled by: 'Seint Austin þat Cristendom . broȝte into Engelonde / Riȝt is among oþer iwis . þat he beo vnderstonde / Sein Grigori þe holyman . pope was of Rome.' *SEL* ll. 1–3.

6–8 oure lorde . . . prechyng 'þat oure Louerd hom sende grace . hore prechinge vnderstonde.' *SEL* l.48. This statement is necessitated by the preceding in *SEL* l.15: 'Hi dradde hom sore for hi ne couþe . þe speche of Engelonde.'

13 I leke . . . saye 'Swuþe fair þing it is he sede . þat ȝe bihoteþ me / Were ich siker þat it were soþ' *SEL* ll. 57–8.

22–3 Seynte . . . tydyngis 'Seint Austin wende aȝen þo . þe pope he tolde at Rome.' *SEL* l. 83.

24–7 And than . . . Canterburye 'Twelf bissops he made in þe lond . to wardi Cristendom / þe þritteþe he was him sulf . as oure Louerd ȝaf þe cas / Erche bissop at Douere . þe ferste þat euere was.' *SEL* ll. 88–90.

27 Dovyr, that nowe is clepyd Canterburye Perhaps an attempt by the scribe to rectify *SEL* l. 90: 'Erche bissop at Douere.' The Roman name for Canterbury, *Durovernum*, may be the source of the confusion in *SEL*, which also reads 'Douere' at l. 70, in a passage not in our text about a house at Canterbury given to St Augustine by the king.

13. ST OSWALD

21 seculer . . . Wylton Wylton should read Wynton, for Winchester. This inaccurate story comes from Eadmer. It is dealt with in detail by Robinson (1919), p. 13.

30 **Floryace** *Floriacum*, Fleury, also known as Saint-Benoît-sur-Loire, one of several reputed sites of the relics of St Benedict.

51–3 **And anone . . . hider** The 'PY' MSS of *SEL* omit lines explaining that Odo, when 'old & feble,' sent for Oswald (Görlach (1974), p. 268 note 58, and also notes to ll. 120, 129 below).

73–82 **thaye . . . nunnys.** This passage parallels *Dunstan* 14.74–83, p. 183, which reflects the identical passages in *SEL* Oswald ll. 119–20, 126–30 and Dunstan ll. 139–40, 146–50.

95–6 **this holye . . . Matyns** In *SEL* Oswald is in the habit of praying (presumably in the church) while his monks are asleep. There is no mention of Matins. The story in Eadmer is about the monk Ægilricus who goes to sleep in a seat frequently used by Oswald.

120 **anguyssh** *SEL* MSS PY 'much anguisse and tribulaciouns he hadde,' a line not present in the other MSS.

129 **worde** 'word,' *SEL* MSS PY, 'vers' *SEL*.

14. ST DUNSTAN

17 **Ethelwolde** 'Aldhelm' *SEL*. Dunstan's uncle was Athelm, archbishop of Canterbury 914–923.

43 **carle** 'calwe' *SEL* (bald) reflects Osbern's Latin, where the devil, who has an attractive head of hair, taunts Dunstan for his tonsure and exclaims: 'O quid fecit calvus iste!' (*Memorials* p. 85). In none of the Lives of Dunstan does the devil appear as a woman, but it is a common motif in medieval saints' lives and our writer may have got the idea from this devil's 'formosa caesarie'. See Townsend (1991).

48 **Seint Edmond . . . Edwyne** Edmund, mistakenly here referred to as Seint, was murdered in 939 and succeeded by his brother Edred, at whose death in 955 Edmund's son Edwy came to the throne.

63–4 **a holy man** 'Odo' *SEL*. The *SEL* text elaborates on Odo foretelling that Dunstan will succeed him as archbishop.

71, 74 **goydide, goydyng** guiding, guidance, *MED giden* v., *giding(e* ger.

83 **afore seid . . . Oswolde** See *Oswald*, 13.73–82, p. 177 and note. Caxton in his Life of Dunstan in *GoL* repeats this reference to the Life of Oswald, but fails to include the Life itself.

84–98 **In a tyme . . . no more** not *SEL*. Accounts of this meeting at Winchester and the subsequent one at Calne occur in the lives of Dunstan by Osbern, Eadmer and William of Malmesbury. (*Memorials* pp. 113, 213, 308.)

85 **persons** These were the secular clerks of Winchester, who were given the choice of becoming monks or leaving the Minster.

91-2 **gret day . . . Calne** A revival of the claims made at Winchester.

93 **lordiship** This refers to the authority of the 'serteyn lordis' of l. 95 above.

99 **atte . . . table** 'in a priue place' *SEL* l. 156.

103 *Kyrie . . . splendens* 'a murie song þer inne / þat me singeþ зute in Holy Churche . wanne me deþ masse bigynne / Kyrieleison Cristeleyson' *SEL* ll. 163–5.

111–12 *Gaudent . . . sanctorum SEL* gives 4 lines of this hymn in English.

121–4 **And . . . Amen** not *SEL*.

15. ST ALDHELM

2–3 **Kenton** Aldhelm's father may have been Centwyne, king of the West Saxons, d. 685, a predecessor and relative of Ine, but not his brother.
   Ive All MSS read 'Ive', *SEL* 'Yne'. Ine was king of Wessex c. 688–726.

23 **Athelrede . . . confermyd** 'And Aildred þe king of þe March . þat þo was god & hende / þe priueleges forþ wiþ þe pope . confermede boþe to' *SEL* ll. 44–5. Athelred, king of Mercia, was overlord to Ine, king of Wessex. His grants of lands to Malmesbury Abbey were recorded among its earliest charters.

27 **he . . . boke** Aldhelm wrote a letter, at the request of a synod convened by Ine, to Geraint, king of Dumnonia, in whose lands some clerics were continuing to observe Celtic use in dating Easter.

29 **this . . . founded** Aldhelm succeeded Maildubh, the founder, as abbot of Malmesbury c. 675.

38 **he . . . power** 'for he þoзte pouere & milde' *SEL*, l. 70. *MED pouer(e* n. 2 *ben of þ-*, to afford (something); 6(f) *ben of þ-*, to have authority. Aldhelm seemed to the sailors either to be too poor to afford the price of any of their wares, or to have had no authority to negotiate on behalf of the Church. William of Malmesbury says that Aldhelm tried to negotiate a lower price for the bible, at which the sailors objected.

49 **brought on erthe** 'an eorþe broзte' *SEL*, l. 89, buried. See *OED earth* sb 1, I 3, and *MED erthe* n.(1) 6 (c).

50–51 **fedyrd . . . lockid** According to Faricius' *Life of Aldhelm*, Giles (1967), pp. 138–9, Egwin was on his way to Rome wearing penitential fetters when he learned of Aldhelm's death and so went to conduct the funeral before proceeding to Rome.

16. ST THEOPHILE

11 **this mornyng** scribal spelling makes the meaning ambiguous. The text almost certainly means 'thus mourning'.

30–31 **was a gretter rewler** is a condensation of *SEL*. Theophile, who had lost his **poer** when he refused the bishopric, now, according to *SEL* l. 81, 'richere neuere he nas' and with this money, 'As louerd & sire he was iholde . wel muche is poer was.' (l. 82).

92–3 **aboute** . . . **May** 'is day falþ in þe ȝere / A litel biuore Aueril' *SEL* ll. 197–8. Görlach (1974), p. 279 note 184, states that Theophilus does not appear in any English calendars.

94 **Bretroyn** 'Buturie' *SEL* l. 201. 'in civitate Bituricensi,' (cited by Southern (1958), p. 192, from two Latin MSS), i.e. in the city of Bourges. The legend of the Jewish boy appears in Latin collections in four versions described by Wilson, *Stella Maris* (1946), pp. 6–7.

98 **gret desire** seems to mean intense pleasure, and is an unrecorded sense of **desire**. See *MED desir* n. 'To oure Leuedi is ymage mest . him þoȝte is herte drou / His herte him ȝaf þat þulke ymage . mest louie he miȝte / Out of is þoȝt ne com he[o] noȝt . after þe uerste siȝte.' *SEL* ll. 210–212.

128–9 **at the laste** . . . **hym** *SEL* makes it clear that the friars prayed their captors not to rob them but to deliver them unharmed to the 'wyckid knyght'.

146 **.v. ioies** these five joys are the Annunciation, the Visitation, the Nativity, the Presentation of Christ in the Temple, and the Finding of the child Jesus in the Temple.

158–9 **a feeste** . . . **lady** 'oure Leuedi day' *SEL* ll. 307, 309. Feast of the Annunciation, 25 March.

159 **goode** provisions. *MED god* n. (2) does not record this sense of foodstuffs, but it occurs here and in *Thomas of Canterbury*, 28.798, p. 306.

170–73 **He wente** . . . **a litle before** not *SEL*.

179–80 **euery** . . . **mede** not *SEL*.

236 **brynge that were dampned** Perhaps **tho** has been omitted before **that**, which begins a new line.

281 **Oure Ladi Dai in heruest** Feast of the Nativity of the Virgin Mary, 8 September.

282 **Tolewse** 'Tolete' *SEL* l. 488, 'In Toleto', i.e. in Toledo, *Stella Maris* 9,1. All other versions of this story, which Tryon (1923) calls 'one of the more popular legends of the virgin' situate it in Toledo. See Wilson (1946), p. 166.

17. ST SWITHUN

2 Kenulf An error; it was Cynegils, king of Wessex, who was baptised by Birinus in 635.

10 chaunceler not *SEL*. Swithun was chaplain to Egbert.

12 Ethulfe Ethelwulf, son of Egbert.

19–20 And he . . . tythyng There is a change of emphasis here from *SEL*. 'þe king also to alle gode . to Holy Churche he broȝte / So þat þoru heste of þe kyng . and þoru is wissinge also / Echman wolde þoru al þe lond . is teþinge wel do.' *SEL* ll. 38–40.

24–5 But nowe . . . temporal. This is an authorial comment.

28 west 'est' *SEL* l. 53.

29 lap 'bagge' *SEL* l. 57.

30 wrestelyd 'biclupte hure in ribaudie' *SEL* l. 59.

31 al . . . egges Another change of emphasis. Not all her eggs were broken: 'hure eiren nei echone.' *SEL* l. 60 This is confirmed in l. 66 'and he blessede þe eiren tobroke'.

38–40 And then . . . Swythyn Ethelwulf died in 858 and was succeeded by his eldest son Ethelbald, with Ethelbert his younger son as sub-king. Ethelbald died in 860, and Ethelbert succeeded. The confusion here is naming Ethelbald as Egbert. Swithun died in the third year of Ethelbert's kingship.

43–4 .viij.C and .vj. 'He deide eiȝte hondred ȝer . and in to & sixtiþe ȝere' *SEL* l. 81. Swithun died in 862.

45 odde days 'And almost þerto fortene niȝt . ar he were þanne ido' *SEL* l. 86

48–9 in the same . . . Schaftysbury not *SEL*. This may be a misunderstanding of *SEL* or use of an *SEL* text different from the edited version. Swithun appeared to Edgar, Edward's father, and said that he should be translated 'in herre stude' (l. 90). Edgar then consulted SS Athelwold and Dunstan. Perceiving that it would be a propitious time for his own translation because there was a good king as well as a good bishop, Swithun then appeared to the holy man of l. 99 with his message for Athelwold.

53–90 All MSS agree in this passage, but there is an omission from the source. In the corresponding passage in *SEL* Swithun appears in a vision to the holy man who is to act as his messenger to Athelwold, and tells him that as soon as he sets off to deliver the message the illness from which he has long suffered will be cured. A further sign will be given to Athelwold, that the rings of iron in the stone will be removable as a sign of the message being genuine. The holy man and Athelwold go together to the stone, where the rings are easily removed and replaced.

63 **takyng up** It is odd that there is no mention of the re-interment in the new shrine which in *SEL* is a 'vair ssrine' (l. 157) in 'seinte Petres churche' (l. 156), and no mention of the second translation into the new cathedral in 1093.

18. ST KENELM

7–13 **This . . . Walys** These lines truncate *SEL* ll. 21–39 and thereby make it read as if all the counties listed ll. 11–14 were part of the bishopric. But *SEL* l. 11 'and also' refers to the king, and while all the following counties belong to the March, the last five are in the diocese of Lincoln, and Nottinghamshire is in the diocese of York.

15 **.vj.** 'Vif' *SEL* ll. 9,19. *SEL* lists the kingdoms.

16 **Oswolde** This may be a reference to King Oswy, 642–670.

18 **Dornemylde** 'Borunuld/Borwenuld' *SEL*, Borewenild *Early SEL*, Burgenhylda *Vita Kenelmi*. Love (1996), p. 54, note 1, suggests that this sister, who appears in no other source, is fictitious, a foil to her 'wicked' sister.

19 **Queyndrede** Cwoenthryth, Kenelm's sister, was abbess of Southminster, Kent in 824 (Love (1996), p. 54, note 1).

susters 'sustren' MS P *SEL*, 'douȝtren' other *SEL* MSS, l. 78; see Görlach (1974), p. 283 note 227.

20 **.viij.C.xix.** Coenwulf died in 821. The date here agrees with that in the Anglo-Saxon Chronicle.

21 **made kyng . . . age** Kenelm almost certainly predeceased his father, who was immediately succeeded by Ceolwulf. Winchcombe charters datable to between 803–811 were attested by a Cynhelm 'princeps' or 'dux' (Love (1996), p. lxxxix and note 3.)

31, 41 **ruler** 'maister . . . þat is wardein was' *SEL* l. 105, 'procuratorem intimum' *Vita Kenelmi*. The sense is 'tutor', which *MED* does not record.

32 **to haue . . . of hir** 'and of hure al is wille' *SEL* l. 112. This is taken up in ll. 80–82.

44 **hym semyd . . . foule** 'To a litel foul he bicom' *SEL* l. 129.

49 **Wolwelme** thus MS P *SEL*, 'Vuluuenne' *Vita Kenelmi*; see Görlach (1974), p. 283 note 227.

51–5 The interpretation of Kenelm's dream comes from the *Vita Kenelmi*, pp. 56–59.

80–82 **aftirwarde . . . myscheffe** not *SEL*, not *Vita Kenelmi*, but this may be our writer's inference from l. 32.

102 **Cowbage** On this place-name see Humphreys (1938) and Love (1996), p. 63 note 7.

102–3 **In Clent . . . of schorne** 'In Clent Coubach Kenelm kinges bern / Liþ vnder a þorn heued bireued' *SEL* ll. 267–8. Our version attempts a rhyme, or perhaps modernises 'bireued'. *MED* records *bireven* v.1, *b- of hevede*, behead, no later than 1250. The lines from *SEL* appear in three MSS of *Vita Kenelmi*, see p. 66 apparatus.

111–12 **erchebishop . . . Wilfride** 'Wolfred' *SEL* l. 279, Wulfred, archbishop of Canterbury 805–832.

116–17 **erchebishop . . . erthe** The archbishop merely authorises the translation in *Vita Kenelmi*, but it could be inferred from the Latin that he took part in the proceedings.

118 **Seint . . . welle** This spring became a centre of Kenelm's cult, see Love (1996), p. 68, note 2.

124 **for . . . hote** not *SEL*, not *Vita Kenelmi*.

126 **abbot . . . Wynchecombe** not *SEL*, not *Vita Kenelmi*.

128–9 **hie . . . abbey** This is an accurate description of Salter's Hill, east of Winchcombe abbey (Bennett and Smithers (1968), p. 315, note to ll. 247–56.) *SEL* gives the distance as half a mile.

129 **oute of** 'wiþoute' *SEL* MS P, 'bi este' other *SEL* MSS; see Görlach (1974), p. 283 note 227.

131 **abbot . . . erthe** not *SEL*, not *Vita Kenelmi*.

135 **bellys . . . honde** not *SEL*, not *Vita Kenelmi*.

139–40 **That is . . . boke** not *SEL*, not *Vita Kenelmi*, but see Love (1996), p. 72 note 3, for Giraldus Cambrensis' version of the tale, with this exclamation by Quendrede.

142 *Deus laudem* Ps. 108 (AV 109), one of the imprecatory psalms (see *ODCC* p. 824 and Love (1996), p. 71 note 5.) The *Vita Kenelmi* makes it clear that Quendrede was singing the psalm backwards 'contra illum' and that it was when she reached the verse 'Hoc opus eorum qui detrahunt mihi' (v. 20) that her eyes fell out.

19. ST CHAD

2 .vj.C.xvj. This date may be correct. *SEL* reads: 'He was sone after þulke tyme . þat seint Austin com / And prechede verst in Engelonde . & broȝte Cristendom / Aboute sixe hondred ȝer . and sixty and tene / After þat oure Louerd Crist . an eorþe aliȝte ich wene' (ll. 3–6).

4 **dede** 'þe erche bissop of Euerwik . deide þo by cas' (*SEL* l. 8). Wilfrid was not dead, see introduction to this Life.

13 **a monke** . . . **ordre** Görlach (1974), p. 147, points out that only MSS PY of *SEL* read 'monkes . þe order of seint Benet he nom'. Chad was already abbot of Lastingham.

20. ST CUTHBERT

7, 13 **veyne pleys** 'idel game/s' *SEL* ll. 8, 21, 26.

9 **heuynes** 'deol' *SEL* l. 12.

29 **Gervaus** 'Gireuaus' *SEL* l. 35, 'Mailros' *Bede* (Melrose). Gervaus, a Cistercian house founded in 1150 at Fors, moved to Jervaulx in 1156 (Knowles (1950), p. 251). Görlach (1974) p. 270, note 83, suggests *SEL* Gireuaus may be a misreading of 'Gyruensi' (Jarrow) which occurs some lines later.

40 **planteyn** 'plauntayne' *SEL* MSS PY, 'sage' *SEL* l. 52.

41 **whete** 'wete' *SEL* l. 52, 'triticeam . . . farinam', *Cuthbert* p. 160, wheat flour.

71 **aspied** 'aspyed' *SEL* MS Y, 'vnderȝet' *SEL* l. 97.

78 **Derham** 'Duram' *SEL* l. 100, but actually Lindisfarne. 'That Lindisfarne is replaced by Durham in [*SEL*] 100 is not surprising with a 13th century southern author.' Görlach (1974) p. 270, note 83.

21. ST FAITH

56 **madde for woo** 'wod-wrothþ' *Early SEL* I. 99. The sense seems to require *woo* to mean 'anger', but neither *MED* nor *OED* records it in this sense.

22. ST DOROTHY 1

2 In other Lives, Dorothy's father is named Dorotheo and her mother Theodora.

132 **feruent** severe. *MED* does not record its use with reference to cold.

23. ST DOROTHY 2

13–14 **And . . . discipline** The Latin ends this unsatisfactory sentence at l. 15 **region** and omits the rest of the paragraph. It reads: 'Dorothea . . . repleta est', whereas the translator has supplied 'was' only in ll. 14–15 'was wonderly fayre.' A second 'was' is required after 'anon' in l. 13.

70 **How . . . wychecrafte?** 'quousque, malefica, nos protrahis?' *LgAsupp.*

24. ST DOROTHY 3

32 iuuent young, adj., this form recorded as noun but not adj., which is *juven* in *MED*.

44 endowance dowry, not in *MED* or *OED*.

52 dispoused espoused, not recorded in *MED*, but cf. *epousen* and *spousen*.

125 yowre conuersyon 'owre conuersyon' T1, 'youre comisyon' B. Conversion (meaning to the judge's gods) seems the most likely sense, though in that case 'yowre' might have been expected. B 'comisyon' might result from the loss of abbreviated *er* and confusion of minims, but if correct would refer to the judge's command, in which case 'owre' would seem more appropriate. The former, with the emendation to 'yowre', seems on balance the more probable.

25. ST LEGER

32–5 and(2) . . . reuerence These lines seem to reflect the style of the prose writer, cf. 'Seint leger was wel faire i-bured : is soule to heouene wende' *Early SEL* l. 37.

37–9 come . . . Ebronyus Perhaps the exemplar had two more lines at this point. This visit is not in *Early SEL* nor *LgA*.

47–51 And . . . Amen. These lines again seem to reflect the style of the prose writer, cf. 'And he himsulf to þe Ioie of heouene : after is deþe gan gon. / Nou god for þe loue of seint leger : is swete grace us siende, / þat we aftur þusse liue : moten to þe Ioye of heouene wiende.' *Early SEL* ll. 52–4.

26. ST BRENDAN

19, 27 Mernok is confirmed by *NSB* and *SEL*. However *n* and *u* are often indistinguishable in A1, so this may be *u* for [v]. Caxton shares the A2L spelling 'Mervok'.

26–9 Beryn see in a vision It was Mernok who had the vision that his godfather was coming and then sailed for three days to meet him. They then sailed through the darkness together for a whole day, *NSB*.

44 this half yere The young man tells them that they have been on the island for a year *NSB*, *SEL* l. 60.

47 There is no mention of Adam and Eve in *NSB*, *SEL*.

64 vitayled it There is no mention of provisions in *NSB*, *SEL*.

65, 67 .xij. 'fourteen' *NSB*.

68 .ij. 'three' *NSB*.

102 est 'west' *NSB, SEL*.

117 Iasconye *iasc* is Irish for fish.

157–8 Pryme . . . seruise *SEL* ll. 219–222 is specific about all the canonical hours.

162 to the . . . schepe possibly a misunderstanding of *SEL* and in turn of *NSB*. 'þo com atte Trinite . þis godemon to hom þer / þat spak wiþ hom in þe lond of ssep' *SEL* ll. 225–6.

167–8 ilonde . . . monkes After 8 months they will find the island of the community of Ailbe, *NSB*. 'ȝe ssolleþ after seue monþes . yse[o] a uair ile / þat Abbey is ycluped' *SEL* ll. 233–4 ('yle of Aylbey,' *Early SEL*, l. 394.) St Ailbe was a contemporary of St Patrick and was the subject of a voyage legend of his own. The monks are not mentioned in *SEL* until l. 291. See Görlach (1998), p. 116 note 184.

178 .xl.ti days This telescopes the time scales of *NSB, SEL*; 3 months and 40 days *NSB*, 'Four monþes hi wende in þe se' *SEL* l. 243, 'ȝute after þat sein Brandan . ferst þis ile ysey / In þe se hy wende forty dawes . ar hy miȝte come þer ney' *SEL* ll. 247–8.

195 .xxiiij. 'Voure and twenti freres' *SEL* l. 291, 12 monks *NSB*.

195–6 rial copes . . . crosse the monks came in procession bearing crosses and reliquaries *NSB*, 'a crois touore hom bere / Wiþ tapres in eiþer side . monekes it were echon / Reuested in vaire copes' *SEL* ll. 268–70. There seems to be a misinterpretation of 'cope' here. This word in *SEL* probably indicated a *cappa*, the hooded cloak worn by monks for processions and ceremonies in choir. This garment developed in time into an elaborate vestment worn by priests, which seems to be described here. See *MED cope* n. 2(b) and 3.

253–4 bright . . . angel a flaming arrow *NSB*, 'a vury arwe' *SEL* l. 333.

258 light fire a bright fire, *MED light* adj. (1) (a).

265 towarde the abbey of Seint Hillariis There is confusion here between time and place. *NSB* says that the journey shall continue until the beginning of Lent, and *SEL* l. 345 'to seint Hillare day' (14 January).

267 .xij.th tyde Feast of the Epiphany; not recorded in *MED*, but see *OED Twelfthtide*, first example 1530.

290 to that abbey 'in þe ile of Albay' *SEL* l. 390, see Note to 167–8.

325 gripe 'gryphon' *NSB*.

337–9 you . . . ye . . . ye inconsistent syntax. 'Wat beoþ ȝe quaþ sein Brandan . war of be[o] ȝe ofdrad / Vpe þe maistres rug of alle visses . ȝe habbeþ imad ȝou glad.' *SEL* ll. 449–450.

351 **thonder** the noise was like thunder *NSB, SEL.*

358 **vpon the water** 'To þe brymme hy orne of þe se,' i.e. to the shore, *SEL* l. 478, as in *NSB*, but *Early SEL* l. 481 reads: 'Op-on þe watere heo ornen faste.'

361, 364 **fire hamers** lumps of burning slag *NSB*, 'oules' *SEL* (*MED oul* n., flesh hook, instrument of torture).

404–5 **Pilate . . . Cayphas** *add* 'Annas' *NSB, SEL.*

417 **oxe tungis** *SEL* gives 'tongen' (wrongly glossed by the editors as 'thongs'), and mentions neither the ox nor the fish. In a legend of Judas he gave iron forks for holding cooking pots, or in some versions tongs, to two priests. Our author, not seeing how tongs could support the cloth, has turned them into 'ox tongues' and invented the feeding fish to give them a function.

448 **Frydaye** 'þe ueorþe day' *SEL* l. 607.

471–2 **Seynt Patrikkis purgatorye** There is no reference to St Patrick's Purgatory in *NSB*, in which Paul the hermit is a former monk of St Patrick's abbey in Ireland and guardian of the brothers' cemetery, where he meets St Patrick and is commanded by him to travel to the island he now inhabits. St Patrick's Purgatory, a cave on Station Island, Lough Derg, Co. Donegal, is traditionally the place where Patrick had a vision that all who made a pilgrimage there would receive a plenary indulgence and be granted a sight of the punishments of the damned and the joys of the redeemed.

491 **.lj. yere** 'þo ich hadde þer þritti ȝer . in þis liue ibe[o]' *SEL* l. 649.

492 **.lx. yere olde** 'And fifti ȝer ich was old . þo ich gan hider gon' *SEL* l. 652.
.j.C.xj. yere olde 'an hondred ȝer . & twenti' *SEL* l. 653.

548 **world** 'lond' *SEL* l. 713.

552 **bydis** commands. This seems to be from *MED bidden* v. 4b, to require, command, order, but no noun with this spelling is recorded, cf. *MED bed(e* n. 1(c), order, commandment.

27. ST MICHAEL

4–11 **For of . . . felle fro** The first of the three passages mentioned by Görlach (1998), pp. 117–8 as being possibly from a different source. There is no parallel in *SEL.*

14–20 **But for . . . with Lucifer** The second of the passages without a parallel in *SEL.*

22–23 **and lye . . . the mare** 'And ofte hi of liggeþ men . þat me clupeþ þe mare' *SEL* l. 228, Often those that men call incubi lie upon people. The prose changes the sense by treating the relative clause as the start of a new sentence.

33 eluys *Catholicon Anglicum* of 1483 gives 'lamia, eumenis' (fury) as Latin for elf, see Lewis (1964), p. 124.

36 styed restrained. Not in *MED*, first recorded in *OED* for 1610.

46–52 The third passage not found in *SEL*. The devil's five fingers are enumerated in *SEL* but the two passages seem otherwise to be unrelated.

70 .iij. 'atte' *SEL* l. 413, but the apparatus records the reading 'ei3te' in MS J, which must be correct as the text then treats of eight.

77–83 And . . . in For the influence of the planets upon mankind, see Lewis (1964), pp. 105–9, but he does not mention the traits listed here.

83 geydyng behaviour. *MED giding(e* ger. (e) does not record this spelling.

106–12 For the sonne . . . wretyng For the dimensions of the medieval universe and distances in the cosmos, see Lewis (1964), pp. 97–8.

120 Next . . . hiest The four elements are earth, water (lighter than earth), air (lighter again) and fire, lightest of all, so that fire is at the circumference of nature and forms a sphere just below the moon (Lewis (1964), p. 95).

129 blondyryng disturbance, not in *MED* in this sense, see *blondering*.

140–1 aftir . . . Septembre 'efsone fram heruost . forte seint Clementes day / þanne is þonder kunde inou . and li3tynge also' *SEL* ll. 562–3. St Clement's Day is 23 November.

145 I schal . . . whi 'þare uore ich mot 3ou telle more . of kunde of þe þonder' *SEL* l. 568

155 norsher provider of nourishment, *MED norisher(e* does not record this sense.

157 brethyng upwarde *MED brethen* v.(1) 3 (a), *brethen up*, to rise as vapor.

183–4 And helle . . . erthe This truncates and changes the meaning of *SEL* ll. 649–652: 'Eorþe is amidde þe grete se . as a lite bal al round / And pur helle amidde eorþe . wo so so3te þe ground / And 3ute as gret as eorþe þinch . & as lite as he is / þare nis bote þe seueþe deol . þat men wonieþ on iwis.'

196 vnwildeful 'no3t wiluol' *SEL* l. 670. No forms with *d* are recorded in *MED* or *OED*. This sense is first recorded for 1570.

211–15 Than oure . . . aboue other is a very free rendering of *SEL* 691–8: 'þo oure Louerd made uerst mon . he made him iwis / Of al þis foure elemens . as man 3ute is / þo made he cunde in echman . as 3e mowe alle iwite / Bitwene men & womman . of wam we beoþ bi3ute / Vil a þing him is þe sed . of wan man is isprengd / Boþe of man & of womman . togadere it is imengd /

Of wyȝt colour it bileueþ . as it is iwrite / Forte aboute twelfþe day . þat it is biȝite.'

215 bollys 'bollen' *SEL.* See *MED bolle* n. 4(e), 'shell' or layer [of an embryo]. These two instances are the only recorded cases of the word in this sense.

228 wombe renders 'web' *SEL* l. 715, meaning 'membrane', see *OED web*, sb. II 6.

28. ST THOMAS OF CANTERBURY

The text of each column is lightly crossed through, probably as a result of the following: 'Archbishops, bishops, deacons etc. to preach the word of God, showing the difference between things commanded by Him and ceremonies used in the church. Thomas Becket, sometime archbishop of Canterbury, shall no longer be named a saint, as he was really a rebel who fled the realm to France and to the bishop of Rome to procure the abrogation of wholesome laws, and was slain upon a rescue made with resistance to those who counselled him to leave his stubbornness. His pictures throughout the realm are to be plucked down and his festival shall no longer be kept, and the services in his name shall be razed out of all books. Westminster, 16th November 30 Henry VIII (1538).' Brewer & Gairdner (1862–1910), XIII pt. II, p. 354, item 848.

2 St Thomas . . . chirche 'þat is nou an ospital . irered of sein Thomas' *SEL* l. 84. The hospital of St Thomas of Acon in Cheapside, between Ironmonger Lane and Old Jewry, was founded in the late 1220's by Thomas fitz Theobald of Helles, who stated in his charter that the property had belonged to Gilbert Becket and that the archbishop had been born there.

3–84 toke the crosse . . . come home. The so-called Saracen legend of Becket's parentage links him with the crusades. It appears in *Quadrilogus I* and also in the Chronicle of John Brompton, (Brown (1930), pp. 28 ff.). For the crusades see also *Edmund of Abingdon*, 6.182, p. 136, and note.

40–1 and . . . hyr attached clause containing a present participle, typical of MS A1.

92–3 fynde hym no lenger 'is fader him nolde finde' *SEL* l. 161. His father would no longer provide for him at school, *MED finden* 17(a).

102–4 Duke . . . Englonde This is a mis-reading of *SEL* ll. 175–6: 'So þat þe duc of Normandie . ymad was al in pes / Henri king of Engelond . after Steuene þe Bleis.' Henry II's father was Geoffrey of Anjou, and Henry was made Duke of Normandy in 1151, before succeeding to Anjou at his father's death that same year. He became king of England on the death of Stephen of Blois in 1154, in accordance with the Treaty of Wallingford (1153).

128 Trynyte Sonday Thomas appointed the Octave of Pentecost to be the principal feast of the Holy Trinity. The feast was universally enjoined by Pope John XXII in 1334.

131 **Alysaunder** Alexander III.

160–1 **bishop(1)** . . . **dyed** a misreading of *SEL* ll. 295–8: 'Suþþe it biuel þat þe bissop [.] of Wircestre ded was / And sire Gilberd Foliot . as God ȝaf þat cas / þat was bissop of Herford . ibroȝt was ȝute to more / And ymad bissop of Londone.'

166–8 **Roger . . . London.** A misreading of *SEL* ll. 311–4:

'Sire Rogger he made a godman . bissop of Wircestre / Sire Roberdes sone þat was . eorl of Gloucestre / Bissop he made of Herford . an holyman inou / Sire Roberd de Melons.' Roger, son of Earl Robert of Gloucester, became bishop of Worcester, and Robert of Melun became bishop of Hereford as a result of Gilbert Foliot's move to London.

172 **he halowed** 19 April 1164.

174 **shyrynyd** 13 October 1163.

176 **hym** There is an omission here of *SEL* ll. 327–96, which are also omitted from *SEL* MSS PY, a pointer to the source of this text.

222 **Claridon** Clarendon, a favourite hunting-lodge of Henry II about three miles south-east of Old Sarum, in the centre of the forest of Clarendon.

232–41 **temporal lordes . . . Here.** The list here follows that of *SEL* ll. 503–519 with scribal slips and omissions. Errors are: **Britaite** for 'Brutaine', **Mygres** for 'Aungeo', **erle of Ferees** for 'sire William de Forers', **Pigot** for 'Bigod', **Camvile** for 'Caunvile', **Stele de Mombray** for 'Nel de Moubray', **Morele** for 'Morvile', **Maloke** for 'Malet', **Morestal** for 'þe marchal' and **le Here** for 'de Uer'. Barlow (1986) does not list those present at Clarendon, and not all are in his index.

271–3 **Also . . . churche.** omitted from *SEL,* an indicator of the use of a supplementary source.

316–18 **But . . . trespas.** These lines replace *SEL* ll. 631–654.

329 **.ii.de . . . thirde** The boat made two attempts to leave the shore in *SEL* and *Quadrilogus.*

351–6 **Art . . . Thomas.** not in *SEL.*

369–70 **Tewisday . . . Day** 'þe nexte Tiwesday þat were / Biuore sein Lukes day' *SEL* ll. 735–6. The writs summoned the Council for Tuesday 6 October 1164, and the court sat on Tuesday 13 October. St Luke's Day is 18 October and St Lucy's Day 13 December.

392 **.v.C.** 'an hondred' *SEL* l. 773

419–22 **But . . . Churche** This sentence is intended to summarise the bishops' discussion, *SEL* 839–74 (part of which is missing from MSS PY), but should refer to the bishop of Worcester rather than London, since the latter was in fact Thomas's main opponent.

455 *Etenim . . . steterunt* Ps. 118:23 'Etenim sederunt principes et adversum me loquebantur,' the Introit for the mass of St Stephen.

467–8 **foon, none** rhyme surviving from *SEL* ll. 961–2 'fon', 'non'.

473–4 **I . . . the.** The advice was given to Thomas, not to the bishop of Hereford. *SEL* ll. 839–46.

474 **breke** (wreke L). We can find no other example of this expression, but see *MED breken* v. 16(a), to disclose or reveal, and cf. *OED wreak* II 3, to give vent or expression to.

550–1 **.vij. psalmes** See note 1.1310, p. 473.
.xv. psalmes The Gradual psalms, nos. 119–33 (AV 120–34).

551 **opnyd euery auter** It is not clear what this means. There is no reference to it in *MED*. Altars were customarily covered with expensive palls and perhaps these in turn had protective covers. High altars frequently had surrounding curtains which were drawn back for services, but this would not have applied to smaller altars within a church. There is no equivalent phrase in *SEL*.

561–2 **Anima . . . sumus.** Ps. 123.7

567–8 **hermytage . . . water** perhaps Catley, Lincolnshire, see Barlow (1986), p. 115.

569 **Seint Botulphis** Boston, Lincs. **Hauelok** 'Auerholt' *SEL* l. 1149, Haverholme in the fenland west of Boston.

Offrey 'Estreie' *SEL* l. 1151, Eastry, near Sandwich, Kent, a manor belonging to the archbishopric. The scribe has confused it with Offekerque (*Offrigi Capella*) near his point of arrival in France.

577 **Oye** Oye, between Marck and Gravelines, Flanders, about four miles from Gravelines.
Greuenyng *Greveninga*, Gravelines, Flanders.

595 **Charmaryes** Clair-Marais, Cistercian abbey near St Omer, Flanders.
long myle a mile or more, *MED long* adj. 1 (f).

600 **Rome** The pope was at that time in exile at Sens, France.

654 **Chester** 'Chichestre' *SEL* l. 1306, which is correct.

713–42 **And he come . . . diocise.** This story is in none of the lives of Thomas. The diocese of Canterbury did, however, enjoy an exemption from the obligation to fast on St Mark's Day into the sixteenth century. James Pilkington, in *The burnynge of Paules church in London in 1561*, criticises the 'monstrous fast on St Marke's Daye' from which Londoners living in the Canterbury diocese are exempt. In 1100 eight churches in London belonged to Christ Church, Canterbury, and a further church was half owned by Canterbury. These are listed in Douglas & Greenaway (1953), item 280, pp. 954–6, and it may be that their parishioners enjoyed Canterbury privileges, since Pilkington mentions Cheapside as being half in the London diocese and half in Canterbury. Of the eight

Canterbury churches in London in 1100, the parish of St Mary le Bow straddled Cheapside, while that of St Pancras was wholly to the south.

767–75 **And then . . . day.** This story is not in any of the lives of Thomas.

777 **Pontney** Pontigny, Cistercian monastery nine miles from Auxerre, France.

798 **goode** provisions. See note to *Theophile*, 16.159, p. 498.

811 **grey monkes** 'Greie monkes of Cisteus', *SEL* l. 1539. Cistercians are usually referred to as white monks.

813 **Cisteans** for Cîteaux, appears to be the spelling in both manuscripts, though *u* and *n* are often indistinguishable, especially in A1.

813 **in Englonde** The General Council met at Cîteaux on 14 September 1166.

851 **Seynys** Sens, 21 miles from Pontigny. Thomas went to St Columba's abbey, a Benedictine house.

917 **Mont Marteirs** Montmartre, supposed site of the martyrdom of St Denis.

953 **Mary Magdalenes Day . . . Traytours Mede.** The meeting was on 22 July 1170 in a meadow on the east bank of the Loire between Fréteval and Viévy-le-Rayé, locally known as Traitors' Mead.

969 **Requiem** The ceremonial kissing of the pax is omitted from masses for the dead. See *What the Church betokeneth*, 5.534–477–87, p. 100.

980 **Sandewyche** 'Wiʒtsonde' *SEL*

1002–4 **Se anone . . . made us.** Those excommunicated by the pope are threatening to behave towards Thomas in such a way as to deserve excommunication.

1006 **consent of the kynge** The king had agreed at the Peace of Fréteval that his son should be crowned anew by Thomas because the previous coronation had not been carried out by him, and that Thomas should indeed punish those bishops who had acted without authority.

1132 **And al . . . wormys** 'Fol of wormes was is fleiss ek . to al oþer wo / In no creature ich vnderstonde . neuere nere iseie mo / For in eche stude of is fleiss . þo þicke hi were isete / þat þe grete ne miʒte come . for þe smale to hare mete / Faste hi crope and ssoue ek . as eneten al aboute / Ac þe smale cleueþ faste to . þe grete leuede wiþoute.' *SEL* ll. 2253–8.

1143 **a coste** have cost, see *OED a* v. and *MED haven* v. 12c (a), infinitive as auxiliary or quasi-auxiliary.

1151–61 **Then . . . Thomas** This is not in *SEL* nor other sources. The point being made is that Requiem masses are not said for martyrs (because they are already saints in heaven by virtue of their martyrdom), and by singing the text quoted, '*Letabitur . . . Domino*' (Ps. 63:11), the Introit of the mass for a martyr, the angel is revealing Thomas's sainthood.

1257 **Stephyn** Stephen Langton.

29. ST JEROME

12 **an hethen man** 'Ciceronianus' *LgA*.

13–14 **and . . . wrytte** not *LgA*.

19 **God allemyghty** not *LgA*.

21 **then forsake me** 'te negabo' *LgA*.

27–30 **Then . . . ensample** not *LgA*.

33 **flesschelynes** 'lasciuiam' *LgA*.

42 **communed** 'didicit' *LgA*.
   bysschop 'Gregorium Nazianzienum' *LgA*.

43–4 **and(2) . . . togeder** not *LgA*.

53 **enythyng** *add* 'coctum' *LgA*.

55 **brennynges . . . vnclennes** In *LgA* these were caused by visions of 'choris puellarum'.

55–8 **And . . . delytes** not *LgA*.

58–9 **they . . . sovle** Rom. 8:13.

62 **ayene** not *LgA*.

67–83 **Also . . . ever** not *LgA*.

91 **.CCCC. and .xviij.** '.CCC. and .xviij.' in the other MSS, and variously 'CCCXCVIII' and 'CCCC' in versions of *LgA*; a typical scribal confusion of numerals.

92 **doctor** doctor of the Church, theologian of outstanding repute and sanctity, *MED doctour* n. 1(a).

120–21 **Iohn . . . clothyng** 'Elias et Ioannes Eremitae, magnis ciborum et vestium asperitatibus carnem maceraverunt' *PL*.

123 **and scorpyons** not *PL*.

124 **.xl.** 'quinquaginta' *PL*.

136 **tempest** 'pestem' *PL*.

141–3 **Samuel(2) . . . scripture** 1 Kgs. 1:24.

142 **clepyd . . . lecture** 'de vanis litterarum studiis verberibus evocatus' *PL*.

144 **wysdam** 'divina gratia' *PL*.

149 **prevytees and dowtes** 'aenigmata et obscura dubia et nodosa' *PL*.

167 **sett** 'sedibus' *PL*, *MED set(e* n. 2, 4(a), dwelling-place.

184–5 **dyed of the clotte** 'put off the mortal body.' *PL* reads 'exutus putredinis et immunditiae carnis toga.' *MED* records no instance of the spelling 'dyed' for 'did', which seems to be required here, and it seems likely that an early copyist substituted it, thus obscuring the idiom 'do off', which Lb recognised and restored. L 'clotte' for 'cote' may be an extension of this error, but in view of the uncertainties it seems best to let it stand.

189 **prayed** *add* 'nostri Severi, quondam venerabilis Martini Turonensis Episcopi discipuli' *PL*.

192 **lernyd** 'doceri' *PL*, taught.

207–8 **er(2) . . . course** not *PL*.

213 **speryd** 'clauderetur' *PL*, *MED speren* v. (1), 4(b), to confine.

215 **see . . . flowyng** 'caelum a motu continuo desisteret' *PL*.

236–9 **when . . . lord** not *PL*.

259–60 **for . . . vs** not *PL*.

272 **mynystracyons** 'mysteria' *PL*.

303 **symphans** 'tympanorum et psalteriorum' *PL*.

336 **noone ys more than he** Matt. 11:11.

346 **grevons** 'gravia' *PL*, *MED grevaunce*, which records this spelling. A noun is required, which rules out the reading 'greuous', though as so often *u* and *n* are indistinguishable. Y and Lb subsituted *grevys* for this unusual spelling.

368 **stylle** 'paulisper' *PL*, for a little while.

407 **scorned** 'deluditur' *PL*.

436 **sendyth . . . yowe** not *PL*. Another noun must have been lost after 'and', and MSS YJLb try to put it right by also removing 'yowe' in order to join this to the next sentence.

484 **growndly** 'radicitus' *PL*, *MED groundli* adv. (b), thoroughly, completely.

518 **dydde welle** 'bene agerent poenitentiam' *PL*.

523-78 **we . . . hym** a paraphrase of the Latin.

526 **promote** *MED promoten* v.(e), to advance (someone's cause). There is no example in *MED* of prayers being promoted.

536 **holy levyng** 'sancto proposito' *PL*.

554 **heryng** 'videntes' *PL*.

567 **benygne** *MED* records no sense which would fit this context for L's reading **huge**.

568 **to theym that drede** 'amantibus' *PL*.

575 **I pray . . . sonne** not *PL*.

649 **eny** The Latin requires **by eny**, 'a viventibus' *PL*. All the English MSS omit **by**.

650 **cristen men** 'illi' *PL*, that is, the false christians. MS Y is correct.

693 **departyng** separating, 'dissolutionis' *PL*.

710 **departyd from the body** 'dissolutionem corporis' *PL*.

715 **be exsample** 'per speculum et in aenigmate' *PL*.

717 **in kynde** 'in natura' *PL*.

720 **knowyng of kynde** 'a naturae cognitione' *PL*.

790–3 **Thenke we . . . therto** not *PL*.

815 **fadred vppon** 'intitulabatur' *PL*.

824 **seyde** 'ostenderet' *PL*.

833 **rampyng** 'rugiens' (roaring) *PL. MED raumpen* v. does not record this sense, but it appears under *raumpant* adj. (c).

898 **thouh** 'si' *PL*.

915 **I am greved** 'frangor' *PL*.

981–2 **fylle . . . men** 'omni vigore corporis destituti, in terram velut mortui cecidere' *PL*.

1163 **ambycyon** 'abusio' *PL*

1197 **mowes and scornes** 'magnis cachinnationibus' *PL*.

1211 **leve that tydyngis** 'cessaret hoc agere' *PL*.

1217 **keper** 'ostiariam' *PL*.

1225 **Here they** 'Audiant' *PL*. 'Let those who trust in their riches, who stir God into wrath by the aridity of their covetousness, hear what judgement God sent . . .'

1275 **I telle too me** 'adoptavi' *PL*.

1297–9 **by whos . . . Amen** not *PL*.

1455 **this gloryows** MS 'this and gloryows'. Either the 'and' has been added or, more probably, a preceding adjective has been omitted.

30. ST AUGUSTINE OF CANTERBURY 2

1–6 **Seynt . . . were** Sentence structures are often difficult to determine, and when we have no source to serve as a guide we leave them as they appear in the MS.

12 **O** See *OED O* int. 2.

21 **Andegauensy** Angers. The text requires a phrase like 'at a place'.

105 **Dorroburnence that now is clepid Canturbury** Its Latin name was *Durovernum*.

130 **desirynge** The sense here requires *to be*.

131 **York** The form of 'York' in this MS seems to depend on the source. In *Oswald* (MSS A2LS) 13.57, 92, 107, pp. 176–8, for instance, York appears as 'Euerwyk(e', while *Chad* (MSS A1A2L) 19.3–4, p. 215, refers to 'Euerwike, that nowe is called Yorke'.

138 **Swale** The river Swale flows into the Ouse, on which York is situated. However, according to Bede *HE* (II,xiv) it was Paulinus, who came to Canterbury with Mellitus in 601, that baptised in the Swale near Catterick.

152 **Coniton** 'In comitatu Oxonia . . . Cumpton,' Brompton.

161 **entent** In Brompton's version, Augustine excommunicates him.

167 **chirche** The sense requires 'chircheyarde'. Brompton adds that Augustine went outside, preceded by a processional cross and a bearer of holy water.

177 **we haue nede of the** 'opus enim de te habemus,' Brompton.

185 **toke . . . rodde** gave the priest a rod, 'Tradidit illi flagellum,' Brompton; cf. *Edmund of Abingdon*, 6.21, 27, 96, pp. 131, 133. For this sense of 'toke' see *MED taken* 31 (b).

210 **kast vpon hym** fastened onto him, 'appendisse', Goscelin; 'affigerent', William of Malmesbury. *MED casten* v. 15(c) gives only 'put a garment on somebody.'

216–17 **the pot . . . brennynge** Jer. 1:13.

246 **desolate** The sense here must be unruly, unrestrained, not given in *MED*. It is presumably an error for *dissolut(e* adj. 1(c). For a similar instance see *What the church betokeneth*, 5.181–3, p. 92.

248 **hauntyd** visited. *MED haunten* v. (1) does not record this sense in the context of illness.

320–22 **prophecie . . . God** Luke 1:64.

331 **tryars** refiners, not recorded in *MED*, but see *trien* v. 1(c), to refine.

352 **schewyd** performed, *MED sheuen* v.(1) 11(a)

358 **Adelstanus** Athelstan was king of Wessex c. 895–939, so cannot have visited Augustine, who died in 604.

378–88 **And whan . . . hole** There were at least eight tumuli in and around Canterbury, evidently Roman burial mounds. This story may have some foundation in fact. See Urry (1967), pp. 199–200.

379 **Chele Hill** possibly St Martin's Hill, Canterbury. Goscelin has 'locum Ciolum nominatum' with the same geographical location.

390–91 *Dominus . . . Syon* Ps. 128:4–5.

425 **angelly** befitting an angel, *MED a(u)ngellich* adj., but this spelling not given.

433 **wille** The sense requires addition of 'he appeared'.

31. ST BARBARA

10 'Trademini autem a parentibus et fratribus et cognatis et amicis, et morte afficient ex vobis.' Luke 21:16.

22–4 **Pope Vrbans tyme . . . suffryd martirdome hymselfe** Pope Urban I, elected 220, died c. 230. Butler throws doubt on the martyrdom of this pope, about whom little is known. The notice in the Martyrology is, according to Butler, 'mainly apocryphal.' Urban may have been martyred, but he may have been confused with another Urban, a martyr buried nearby.

39 **mordrement** murder, *MED murtherment* n.

56–8 **Ioseph . . . byrthe** Matt. 2:13–14.

58–60 **cite . . . chapitre** Is. 19:18.

159–66 **First . . . Neptunus** It has not been possible to elucidate all the references in this passage, the Latin for which is on Br f. 14r. Names of places in the Latin appear as the names of their inhabitants in the English, and both texts have misreadings, *e.g.* 184 Nemyns, Latin 'veninos'; Iraxyns, Latin 'yraxos' (for Thrace?).

159 **Egipt . . . Vsis** Isis was the national deity of Egypt.

161 **Romaynes Quyrynus** Quirinus was the local deity of Rome.
    Mawrynce Iuba 'apud mauros iuba' Br. Iuba II, king of Mauretania, was of great learning and culture.

162 **Latynes Faunus** 'apud latinos fanus' Br. Latins are the inhabitants of Latium, Faunus the god of herdsmen.
    Atthenys Mynerva 'apud athenas minerua' Br. The Italian goddess Minerva was identified with Athena, patron goddess of Athens.

163 **Sames Iuno** 'apud sanium Iuno' Br. Samos was the site of the temple of Hera, identified with Juno.
    Paphyns Clitera 'apud paphos hiaterea' Br. Paphos was the site of the famous temple of Aphrodite, patroness of 'hetairai' or prostitutes.

164 **Nemyns Volcanus** 'apud veninos vulcanus' Br. Volcanus, ancient Italian fire-god, was worshipped at Puteoli (Pozzuoli).
    Iraxyns Liber 'apud yraxos liber' Br. Liber, Italian god of fertility and wine, was commonly identified with Dionysus, widely worshipped in Thrace.

165 **Epiromis Ceres** 'apud epyron seres' Br. Ceres, the Italian corn goddess, was identified with Demeter.
    Lyddyns Apollo 'apud ledos apollo' Br. Apollo was the principal deity of Lycia.

165–6 **Eristans in Troy Neptunus** 'apud eristam troiani neptunus' Br. Neptune was the Roman god of the sea and waters.

225 **as it ys** The meaning of these words is unclear, and the Latin they are paraphrasing (f. 15r) gives no help.

281–2 **Iubiter . . . Saturne** a mistranslation of the Latin: 'Iupiter autem fuit Saturni patricida.' Br f. 16v.

334 **commandyd** The sense is that Origen dominated the argument. This is an example of the translator's elaboration; the Latin reads: 'quod ei in facie nullus philosoforum stoicorum vel peripateticorum resistere posset: qui certis inditiis commendaret veram diuinitatem ac ydolorum confunderet vanitatem.' Br f. 18r.

346 **oone . . . Veste** Co tries to improve the sense by adding a phrase. The Latin reads: 'Nam eum feruere circa deos videbat quia deuota erat ei veluti vinca in perhenne dearum obsequium: specialiter tamen dee veste: cui ipse eam deuouerat castam perpetuo confernari.' Br f. 18r.

355–421 Rhymes and repetitions of sound in this letter include: 355 **name, fame**; 363–4 **many oone, everichone**; 365–6 **beholde, golde**; 373–4 **reverence, evidence**; 381–2 **expressed, gessyd**; 387–9 **tyme is, he is, amysse**; 390–1 **mynde, eende**; 392–3 **dovte, aboute**; 393–4 **wonder, asondre**; 395–6 **supersticion, season**; 402–3 **name, fame, frame**; 404–6 **lettre, bettyr**; 413–5 **fayne, tweyne**.

359 **fadirhode** *MED faderhode* 3 (b)(c), see also l. 1114.

379 **strangely** vehemently, *MED strongli* adv.

400 **leen** The Latin reads: 'Huic me semper deuoui a quo sum id quod sum: nisi me sententia fallat cuius spiritum me animatam sentio: vt non desistam donec ad eum pertingam.' Br f. 19v.

404 **lothesom** disgusted. *MED lothsom* does not record this sense; *OED* records it for 1577.

425–6 **Alisaunder and Nichomede were right ferre in sondre** de Gaiffier points out that Greek and Syriac passions of Barbara, as well as early Latin versions, localise the story to Heliopolis in Syria, but later Latin texts place it in Nicomedia. Our author has chosen to locate the story in Egypt, perhaps because he had heard of the relics of Barbara, widely believed in the fourteenth and fifteenth centuries to be in Cairo, and to identify Heliopolis with Nicomedia (**thys duke dwellyd in a city of Egipt clepyd Solys** 55). The long distance here survives from Wackerzeele's source, which according to de Gaiffier (p. 22) is Peter the Deacon.

486–597 Rhymes and repetitions of sound in this letter include: 492–4 **gladnes, swetnesse**; 494–7 **trewe, sue**; 495–500 **grace, case, grace, trace**; 509–11 **substaunce, avaunce**; 513–14 **se, degree, be**; 524–5 **moo, doo**; 540–1 **majeste, dyvynyte**; 550–1 **oone, alone**; 553–7 **mynde, fynde, kynde, ende**.

The highly mannered style of the Latin may be seen in the following typical selection: 'deus enim si **tempora** facta sunt vt michi videtur ante **tempora** fuit a quo **tempora** sunt homo autem sit in **tempore**. Quo igitur aut **temporale intemporaliter** aut **intemporale** solum **temporaliter** esset? Non ergo vniquam deos credere **potui**: quos homines mortales **cognoui**. In multis tum motibus animi posita perpendi deum proculdubio nobis ignotum esse: qui solus **intemporaliter temporalia** per **tempora** fecit in quibus sunt homines: quos prophana superstitio putat deos [f.19v] hunc quamuis me latentem semper amaui. Huic me semper deuoui a **quo sum** id **quod sum**: nisi me **sententia** fallat cuius spiritu me animatam **sentio**: vt non **desistam** donec ad eum **pertingam**'. Br f. 19r-v.

524 **and so but he may be no moo** This whole passage is a loose and rather unsatisfactory paraphrase of the Latin, and these words represent '(omnia) vt motu suo essentialiter subsistant,' so that all things essentially subsist by his movement.

526 **presencial** Not in *MED*, first recorded in *OED* for 1635.

680 **qvene . . . wordes** 3 Kgs. 10:3.

711–13 **Hester . . . palyce** Esther 5:1–2.

748 **distempered** rendered intemperate. This sense not recorded in *MED*, cf. *distemperen* v. 5(a).

800–1 **purpose . . . trowest** The sense requires a verb meaning 'intend' or 'have in mind' for **trowest**. *MED trouen* 5 indicates the diminished force of the word. The Latin is no help as Dioscorus replies with a single interrogative.

819–20 **bathes . . . wyse** an example of the exuberance of the translator; the Latin reads: 'in ea balneandi causa lauacharum opere nobilissimo circumtexturum.' Br f. 29r.

846 **lavatory** bath. *MED lavatori(e* n. does not record this sense.

892–3 'Specie tua et pulcritudine tua intende, prospere procede et regna' Ps. 44:5.

908–9 'Nostra autem conversacio in celis est' Phil. 3:20.

909 **conversacion** *MED conversacioun* n. 3, the place where one lives or dwells, whether physically or spiritually.

966–7 **ponde . . . palsey** John 5:2–9.

967–8 **fresshe . . . Samarie** John 4:15.

969 **wasschyng . . . Syloe** John 9:7.

986 **scripulnes** scrupulosity, not in *MED*; *OED* scrupulenes, Caxton 1489.

1004–5 **title** 'pudicitie titulus' Br f. 33v; not in *MED*, but see *OED title* sb. II.6.

1039 'Beatus qui intelligit super egenum et pauperem' Ps. 40:2.

1040 'Et dispersit dedit pauperibus iusticia eius manet in seculum seculi.' Ps. 111:9.

1048–9 'Benedicam dominum in omni tempore semper laus eius in ore meo.' Ps. 33:2.

1144 **ever the** The text seems corrupt. Perhaps *the* Co should have read *ye*.

1150 **ieberdye** dangerous situation. *MED juparti(e* n. does not record this spelling.

1204–5 'Adhesit anima mea post te, me suscepit dextera tua.' Ps. 62:9.

1225 **an happe and** a stroke of good luck if . . . The Latin reads: 'aut vix aut numquam curatur' Br f. 38v.

1255 **brasen** Not in *MED* in this sense, which is first recorded in *OED* for 1573.

1275 **knowe . . . wene** Barbara is asserting that she knows something for a certainty and is not merely supposing it to be the case. *OED ween* v.1.

1278–9 **Turne . . . turne** convert, change one's mind. *MED turnen* v. 27 (a).

1310–11 'Benedictus Deus qui non amouit orationem meam et misericordiam suam a me.' Ps. 65:20.

1333 'Ego sum Deus et non est alius preter me.' This is a conflation of biblical texts rather than a quotation, cf. Ex. 20:2–3 and Deut. 5:6–7.

1340–1 'Os habent et non loquentur, oculos habent et non videbunt. Aures habent et non audient, nares habent et non odorabunt. Manus habent et non palpabunt, pedes habent et non ambulabunt.' Ps. 113 (B):5–7.

1438 **rakked thorough** pierced. *MED raken* v.(2) records this sense only for ppl. as adj.

1471 **lay** see *MED lei* n. 2(c), religious practice, custom.

1528–30 **flowres . . . they** Luke 12:27.

1548–9 **Iudith . . . body** Judith 13:10.

1555 **certeyne . . . Thaslasser** 'per quendam in eadem vrbe vicum qui thalassis vocabatur' Br f. 45v.

1654–5 'Veni electa mea, veni sponsa mea formosa, veni coronaberis aureola quam tibi ab eterno preparaui in regno meo.' (The Tract for the Common of the mass for Virgin Martyrs.)

1716 **lay** see *MED lei* n 2(a), religion, faith, creed.

1743–4 'Quamobrem elegit suspendium anima mea, et mortem ossa mea' Job 7:15.

1745 **hevenlynes** not in *MED*, earliest citation in *OED* is 1530, state or quality of being heavenly in origin, nature or character.

1813 *danti . . . gloriam* Sirach 51:23.

1921 **preciosite** i.e. splendour, veneration. The word is from the Latin text and metaphorical uses are not common in Latin or in English. See du Cange s.v. 'pretiositas' for two Latin examples; the instance cited in *MED*, from Wycl. Ser. shows the same tendency.

1980 **from Rome . . . Italye** Rome was not in the Kingdom of Italy in the time of Charlemagne but was part of the Papal States, sometimes called the Patrimony of Peter. Piacenza is in Lombardy, part of the Kingdom of Italy annexed by Charlemagne in 774. The author's geography is as dubious as his chronology, as is clear from the reference in l. 1990 to Honorius the First, who was pope from 625–638. The Latin of this passage reads: 'Ita tribus vicibus ipsam de loco ad locum voluit translatari. A loco scilicet prime quietis primo: deinde in sanctam vt prenotatum est vrbem Romanam. Denuo itaque tertio sequitur quod Karolus ille qui Karolus Magnus dicitur Romanorum imperator Francorumque rex existens deuotam valde habuit vxorem nomine Angisbergam; que apud Italiam in ciuitate dicta Placentia monachorum ordinis sancti Benedicti fundauerat monasterium quod vulgariter monasterium beati Sixti est nuncupatum.' Br f. 56r. ('vxorem' is an error; **sustir** l. 1984 is correct, and the MS for l. 2015 correctly reads 'soror'. Charlemagne's wife was Hildegard of Swabia.)

1996 **in processyon wyse** *OED wise* sb.1 II, 3.

1999 **save the hede** Brewyn (1933), p. 30, claimed that St Barbara's head was in the chapel of the Saviour in the church of St John Lateran in 1470.

2015 **monasterye . . . Sixte** This monastery was founded in 874 by Angelberge, wife of the emperor Louis II.

2021–3 **Iewes . . . peple** Esther 8:17.

2026 *Venerunt . . . illa* Wisdom 7:11.

2030 **cronycle** This Chronicle is not mentioned in the Latin, 57r–57v.

2051 **thykke and threfolde** The sense is clear, the people came in great numbers. This may be an unrecorded idiom or it may be that the scribe was distracted while writing **thikkefolde**. **Threfolde** seems always to have a sense of triple aspect in *MED*.

2087–8 'Imitatores mei estote, sicut et ego Christi.' 1 Cor. 11:1.

2104–5 *Laus . . . glorie* The response used in the Office of the Church from Septuagesima until the Vigil of Easter in the place of *Alleluia*.

2166–8 **racke, whele, whele** The author writes as if these were synonymous, and may have thought that they were. Both involved a frame upon which the victim was stretched. *MED rak* n.(2) 2b, instrument of torture; *OED wheel* sb. II, 2.

2178 **cherefully** comfortingly; this adverb is not in *MED*, though the adj. is given with this sense. In *OED cheerfully* is first recorded for 1553, and with this sense for 1599.

2188–9 'Iudica me, Domine, quoniam ego in innocentia mea ingressus sum, et in Domino sperans non infirmabor.' Ps. 25:1.

2192 **putte hym to his iewes** see *MED juwis(e* n., judicial sentence, punishment, *ben put to i-*, suffer a penalty, be punished.

2213 **streyte** adv., directly. *MED streight* adv. does not record this spelling.

2230–1 **Braban . . . Parke** 'Parc (abbaye norbertine pres de Louvain),' de Gaiffier (1959), p. 8, note 2.

2242 **smylyngly** with a smile; this sense not recorded in *MED*.

2249 **place and monasterie** This may be a scribal correction, writing **place** and then correcting it. The Latin reads: 'vt postmodum abbas in monasterio eodem factus' Br f. 63v.

2263–4 'In sole posuit tabernaculum suum, et ipse tamquam sponsus procedens de thalamo suo exultavit ut gigas ad currendam viam. A summo caelo egressio eius, et occursus eius usque ad summum eius; nec est qui se abscondat a calore eius.' Ps. 18:6–7.

2264–5 **toke flessh and blode of** i.e. was born of. The 'gigas' quoted in the psalm here was taken by early commentators as a figure of Christ, and this added clause is intended to draw attention to this signification.

2310 *Sabatum sanctifices* 'Observa diem sabbati ut sanctifices eum.' Deut. 5:12, 'Memento ut diem sabbati sanctifices.' Ex. 20:8.

2338–9 'Beati mortui qui in Domino moriuntur' Apoc. 14:13.

2356 *Perdes . . . mendacium* Ps. 5:7. 'Odisti omnes qui operantur iniquitatem, perdes omnes qui loquuntur mendacium; virum sanguinum et dolosum abominabitur Dominus.' Ps. 5:7.

2364–5 **prynce called Raynolde Selrye** 'duce gelrie Reynaldo' Br f. 67r., Reynald, duke of Geldern.

2377–8 'Ergo, dum tempus habemus, operemur bonum ad omnes, maxime autem ad domesticos fidei.' Gal. 6:10.

2399–400 **Take hede . . . hymselfe** 'Curam domini vestri habete potius: semet interfecit,' which seems to mean 'Pay attention rather to your lord; he has killed himself.' The English translator has apparently attached 'potior' to the slaying, using 'anaunter' with the sense 'in case'.

2421–2 **Ioseph . . . grace** Gen. 43.

2460 **dreder of God** God-fearing man; this word is not in *MED*, *OED* records *dreader* 1556.

2637 **Wolflaghen** 'apud Almannia partibus hassie in opido vulgariter dicto Wolphagen' Br f. 74v.

2959 **drede of his frendes whom he hadde so slayn.** i.e. for fear of the friends of the slain man.

2985 **Gilrens** 'Gelrensi' Br f. 85r.

3030 **fasten** *MED fasten* v.1 3(b), to land a blow. The Latin reads: 'precepit vt ille gladio supradicto qui in famulum gloriose virginis Barbare scindere nequit decollaretur' Br f. 86r.

3041 **symple poore womman** 'quedam beghina' Br f. 86v. Presumably the translator did not expect his readers to understand beguine, the first citation for which in *OED* is Caxton 1483.

3043 **before or** 'antequam'.

3200 **abated** removed, not in *MED* in this sense.

SELECT GLOSSARY

The glossary contains only obsolete words and those whose senses are not easily recognisable in modern English. For words with a range of meanings, only those differing from modern English or likely to cause difficulty are recorded. References are usually given only to the first occurrence of a word in a particular sense within a text. Cross references are given only for words not easily referable to a head word.

In the alphabetical arrangement, both *i* and *y* are treated as *i* when they represent a vowel and as *j* when they represent a consonant; *y* representing a semi-vowel is treated as *y*; *v* representing a vowel is treated as *u*; and *u* representing a consonant is treated as *v*. Words beginning with *sch-* and *sh-* are combined under *sh-*. In the forms supplied, *ow* and *aw* are not distinguished from *ou* and *au*; variations between endings *-s*, *-es*, *-is*, in plurals, and *ed*, *-id*, *-ied* in past forms are also ignored.

Abbreviations: adj(ective), adv(erb), conj(unction), comp(arative), fig(urative), imp(erative), impers(onal), interj(ection), lit(eral), n(oun), num(eral), ord(inal, p(articiple), ppl. = participial, pa(st, pl(ural), poss(essive), prep(osition), pr(esent), pron(oun), refl(exive), sg. = singular, subj(unctive), superl(ative), v(erb), vbl. = verbal.

a *v.* have 28.1143 (*note*), 31.1408

a *prep.* in the process of, *a smytyng* 18.74, *a cuttynge* 31.1479; with, *a blode* 31.1441

abak *adv.* put a- set aside 3.47

abas(s)hid *v.pa.p.* upset 1.1202, perplexed 25.18, surprised 28.346

abate *v.* strike down 28.387; **abated** *pa.p.* reduced 31.2725, removed 31.3200 (*note*)

abide *v.* await 1.476, 3.245, 28.598, 29.233, remain 1.941, 6.308, 16.164, 19.39, 28.81, 29.148, 31.3056, live 2.73, 29.63; *imp.* wait 6.199, 29.577; **abydyng** *pr.p.* awaiting 1.822, remaining 29.267, attending to 31.822; **abode** *pa.* remained 2.17, 6.204, 13.61, 19.36 etc., dwelt 9.58, delayed 29.838, awaited 7.51, 31.2906; *pa.p.* remained 29.275; **abiden** awaited 31.1312

abydyng *vbl.n.* dwelling place 5.489

abyte *n.* habit, religious dress 28.1129

abought, aboute *prep.* surrounding 1.832, 21.45, around 3.167, 26.78, 27.58, 29.324, 30.36, throughout 31.24

abowtewarde *adj.* busy 31.2350

abrod(e *adv.* wide 31.1631, scattered widely 31.1688

accedentalle *adj.* incidental, secondary 31.536

accomptis *n.pl.* accounts 7.64

ac(c)ord(e *n.* agreement 28.915, 31.1831, correlation 31.227

accorde *v.* correspond with 3.81; **accordith** *pr.3sg.* is appropriate 3.658; **ac(c)ordyd** *pa.* agreed 29.705, 31.616; *pa.p.* 18.34, 28.856; **accordyng** *ppl.adj.* appropriate 1.276, 3.189, 31.1112, consistent with 1.419, comparable 31.809

ac(c)urse *v.* excommunicate 28.945; **acursid** *pa.* 28.1047, 30.170; *pa.p.* 1.539, 28.277, 30.155

ado(o) *n.* concern 15.11; *have a-* have sexual intercourse 9.38

adrad *ppl.adj.* frightened 1.714; **adred(de** 26.115, 31.928

advaile *n., v. see* avayle

advise *n.* opinion 31.834

a(d)vowe *n.sg.* solemn promise 1.255, 31.400; **avowes** *pl.* 31.3038

afer *adj.* far 26.176

aferd(e *v.pa.p.* frightened 21.14, 29.746, 31.592

affeccion *n.* emotion 1.1261, inclination 28.15, thoughts 29.243, 30.233; *pl.* love 5.31

afore *prep.* earlier than 1.811, 5.368, 18.2, in the presence of 4.333, 28.178

afraye *n.* attack (of illness) 3.540 (*note*)

after, aftir *prep.* according to 1.653, 5.105, 13.23, 14.80, etc., depending upon 5.693; *askyd a-* enquired about 8.14

after *adv.* afterwards 1.32, 7.29, 8.19, etc.

agast *v.pa.p.* frightened 6.197, 7.37, 19.20, 26.113, etc.

agon *v.pa.p.* past 1.851; **agoo** gone 29.1174

aleyged *v.pa.* a- *an auctoryte* cited a text 29.1239

alene *n.* foreigner 3.806 (*note*)

algates *adv.* in any case 31.3082

alleredy *adv.* willingly 1.1085

almesdede *n.* charitable act 6.171, good deed 28.661; **almysdede** *pl.* 6.250

almesse *n.* charitable gift 31.2260; **almis** 30.430

alonge *adv.* at full length 3.599

alowid *v.pa.p.* praised (?) 1.1130 (*note*)

als(o) *adv.* as 24.23, 29.736

alther *gen. of* al *oure* a- of us all 31.1650

amasid *v.pa.p.* bewildered 1.335, frightened 3.419, 30.270

ambycyon *n.* arrogance 29.1163

amende *v.* repair 17.21, improve 3.447, 28.171; **amendide** *pa.* restored 17.27; *pa.p.* improved in spirit 31.684

amerveiled *v.pa.p.* astonished 31.2277

amevid *v.pa.p.* angry 1.1203

amyte *n.* eucharistic vestment, amice 5.171

amoste *adv.* almost 3.619

anaunter *conj.* lest 31.2400 (*note*)

and *conj.* if 1.659, 5.721, 12.13, 16.147, etc.

angelly *adj.* befitting an angel 30.425 (*note*)

anker *n.*[1] anchor 29.1105; **ankyr** 26.183

anker *n.*[2] hermit 1.412; **ankres** *pl.* 26.252

ankres *n.* anchoress 30.415

anone *adv., conj.* at once 1.117, 3.514, 9.27, 11.17 etc., soon 1.118, 11.74, 13.16; **anoon** at once 16.148

apechid *v.pa.p.* accused 16.36

appareylde *v.pa.p.* arrayed 5.1382

appetyte *n.* inclination 29.401

applye *v.* comply 1.206, 31.1592

applys *n.pl.* apples 22.79, 26.533; **appollys** 23.74; **appullys** 23.85

appropr(i)ed *v.pa.p.* attributed 5.910, characteristic 31.2172

apreved *v.pa.* confirmed 29.82

apte *adj.* fit 3.484

ar *see* or *prep.*

ar *conj.* or 29.1094

araye *n.* magnificence 1.731

araye *v.* adorn 2.24; **arayeth** *pr.3sg.* gets dressed 5.170; **araiying** *pr.p.* arranging 29.149; **araied** *pa.* dressed 28.1126; *pa.p.* prepared 1.788, provided 29.200,

adorned 29.1095; **araied** *ppl.adj.* dressed 1.73, 3.795, 30.422, 31.1538

arayment *n.* clothing 31.2869; **araymentys** *pl.* 31.804

arere *v.* build 1.376; **areryd** *pa.p.* raised 29.579

arewe *adv.* in a row 26.199

argentere *n.* silversmith 3.586; **argentoures** *pl.* 30.355

armure *n.* armour 28.466, 31.1246

aromatike *adj. as n.* fragrant substance 1.1167

artificer *n.* tradesman 30.429; *pl.* 3.79

as(s)chis *n.pl.* ashes produced during metal refining 30.331

ascryvid *v.pa.* attributed 30.270

asownyng *v.pr.p.* swooning 28.47

aspye *v.* discover 31.130; **aspied** *pa.* watched unobserved 20.71; *pa.p.* caught sight of 2.28, 3.550

as(s)ay(e *v.* try, test 1.934, 29.763, 31.1294

assayled *v.pa.* attacked 30.282

assoyle *v.* absolve of sin 5.1007, free from excommunication 28.997; **assoyling** *pr.p.* releasing from ecclesiastical obligation 1.373; **assoyl(l)yd** *pa.* forgave 14.118; *pa.p.* forgiven 3.936, 28.319, 31.2442, freed from excommunication 28.1003, 30.171

astates *see* **estate**

astony(e)d *v.pa.p.* amazed 1.77, 29.195, 31.2402

astronomyar *n.* one versed in astronomy/astrology 31.253

astronomye *n.* astronomy together with astrology (the terms are interchangeable) 5.1480, 31.252

atachyd *v.pa.p.* taken into custody 30.336

athurste *adj.* thirsty 18.129

at(t)empte *v.* test 1.934, 31.788; **attemptid** *pa.* 1.699

auctoryte *n.* text 29.1239; *pl.* 3.284

audience *n. in* a- *of* in the hearing of 31.2873

aurealle *n.* crown 29.380

auter(e *n.* altar 1.295, 3.870, 4.11, 5.110

avayle *n.* advantage 28.276, 30.94, 333; **advayle** 31.82

avayle *v.* help 3.176, 5.482; **avayleth** *pr.3sg.* 29.1157; **advaile** to be of advantage 31.2352

auaunsyd *v.pa.p.* enhanced 24.20

avauntith *v.pr.3sg.* speaks proudly about 5.765

aventure *n.* occurrence 30.281

avisement *n.* *by goode a-* with careful consideration 31.664

avoide *v.* leave 28.884; avoyded *pa.* sent away 31.635

avowe *n. see* a(d)vowe

avowed *v.pa.p.* made a vow of 31.808

avowry *n.* protector, patron saint 1.768

awbe *n.* white ecclesiastical vestment, alb 5.181

awmener *n.* one who distributes alms for another 1.772

awne *adj.* own 6.125, 10.5, 29.38

awondred *ppl.adj.* astonished 31.1859

awreke *ppl.adj.* avenged 28.367

axe tre *n.* axle 3.119

axe *v.* ask 3.361; axeth *pr.3sg.* requires 31.1345; axid *pa.* asked 1.433, 30.289

axyng *vbl.n.* request 28.310

axys *n.* fever 3.841 (*note*)

ayenst(e *prep.* towards 2.20, 3.816, 5.761, 6.142 etc., in honour of 18.138, in contrast to 31.656

aye(y)n *prep.* back 1.480, 3.165, 6.256, 9.65, etc.; ayeen 31.1556; *a- by* redeem 5.344

ayenward *adv.* conversely 29.1426

backebiter *n.* one who slanders another behind his back 27.206

bacbytingis *n.* slanderous statements behind someone's back 5.1138

bade *see* bidde

bayly *n.* bailiff 6.252; *pl.* 28.281

balled *adj.* bald 27.204

banke *n.* seashore 31.2605

bannyd *ppl.adj.* outlawed 28.607

barne *n.* child 18.103

barre *n.* railing in front of judge's seat 31.1243

ba(w)me *n.* aromatic balsam 3.136, 4.142, 22.28, 23.31

bare *see* bere

be *v.* exist 31.1106(1); *pr.pl.* are 31.144; ben 3.144, 5.71, 26.216; byn 26.219, 27.8; beth(e 7.11, 27.120, 29.449

because *conj.* in order that 31.451, 629, 1410

bechosen *ppl.adj.* chosen 31.988

beclippe *v.* envelop 27.228; beclypped *pa.* embraced 31.813

becovered *ppl.adj.* covered 31.1030

bedampnyd *ppl.adj.* subject to damnation 27.8

bedis *n.* prayers 6.170

bedmen *n.pl.* those who pray for others 28.309

bedrede *adj.* bedridden 5.697

be(e)st(e *n.* farm animal 6.253, animal 30.406, 31.1471; *pl.* cattle 18.89, animals 3.123, 22.139, 24.236, etc.

before, byfore *prep.* in the presence of 7.109, 21.50; *adv.* in front 3.826, 5.242, 26.456, 28.1233, 30.174; *b- goyng* previously mentioned 5.1201

behapned *v.pa.p.* happened to 31.1219

behe(e)st *n.* promise 5.660; *Londe of B-* Promised Land 3.203, 26.56; *pl.* promises 6.17, 24.48, requests 31.802

behight *see* byhote

behofe *n.* benefit 6.260

behouyth *v.pr.3sg.* is appropriate, follows 5.1091 (*note*)

behouefulle *adj.* necessary 31.913

belded *v.pa.* built 31.62

bele(e)ue, bileve *n.* belief 21.16, 30.194, doctrine 31.474; *the trew b-* the Christian faith 31.1421; *owte of the b-* unconverted 31.1821

beleve *v.pr.sg.* believe 31.1232

belongeth *v.impers.pr.sg.* is incumbent 31.922; belongyng *ppl.adj.* appertaining 1.344

bemente *v.pa.* signified 31.2283

benefe(e)te *n.* benefit 1.33; *pl.* 31.1430

benefice *n.* favour 31.1862

benynge *adj.* benign 31.1650

bere *n.* bier 3.210, 31.1704

bere *v.pr.* carry 3.178, 28.472, 31.2386; berith *pr.3sg.* *b- wrath* is angry 27.203; bereth carries 31.251; bare *pa.* 3.210, 16.25, wore 29.364; *b- the maistry* had pre-eminence 31.1003; *b- recorde of* spread abroad 31.2885; bere carried 3.153, 16.91; beryn *pa.pl.* 25.32; bore *pa.p.* 3.167, 6.9, 18.70, born 1.32, 6.2, 7.1, 9.1, etc.; ibore 29.726; borne held 31.3116

beriel(e)s *n.* tomb 3.318, 17.57, cemetery 18.84

beryng *n.* conduct 28.962; *hie b-* arrogant behaviour 5.775, 27.208

besech(e *v.* pray 31.489; beseke entreat 1.130, 3.190; besyke 28.349; besekith *pr.3sg.* prays 5.614; **besekyng** *pr.p.* entreating 29.1184; **besechyng** 3.482; **besought** *pa.* prayed 1.67, entreated 1.330, begged 31.3008; **bysought** entreated 28.489

besecher *n.* suppliant 31.2935

besely *adv.* urgently 31.2471; **besyly(e** diligently 31.222

besemed *v.pa.* was fitting 31.1895

besett(e *ppl.adj.* studded 31.1893, surrounded 31.2100

besy *adj.* intent on 1.186, 31.3002, diligent 3.101, persistent 29.887

besyed *v.pa.* *b- hym* made it his business 29.884

besynes(se *n.* activity 3.50, 5.48, 29.1144

besought *see* **besech(e**

besprent *ppl.adj.* sprinkled 23.108

best *see* **be(e)st(e**

betoke *see* **bytake**

bette *v.pa.* beat 31.1193

better *comp.adj.* *had the b-* had the advantage 13.6

betyme *adv.* early 26.439; **bytymes** 26.156, in advance 31.2376

beutevous *adj.* beautiful 31.1657

bewepte *v.pa.p.* drowned in tears 29.22

bewreyed *v.pa.* revealed 31.2673

by and by(e *conj.* one by one 31.767, 2552, close together 31.1572

bycome *v.pa.* went 26.345

bidde *v.* command 28.1039; **biddyst** *pr.2sg.* 16.22; **byd** *imp.* 1.494; **bad(e** *pa.* 1.491, 3.510, 6.50, 11.63 etc.; **bode** *pa.p.* 29.105; **bodyn** 5.763

byddyng *vbl.n.* praying 6.170; *pl.* commands 12.11

byde *v.* stay 31.829; **bode** *pa.* 1.646, 3.470, 6.298

bydis *n.pl.* commands 26.552 (*note*)

bygate *v.pa.* begot 26.378; **bygotyn** *pa.p.* 28.70

byhe(e)ste *see* **behe(e)ste**

byhight *see* **byhote**

byholde *v.* look at 16.87, 30.425; **beholde** 31.517; **byhilde** *pa.* 26.236, **behilde** 31.276, watched 3.437

byhote *v.* promise 29.685; **behightist** *pa.2sg.* 5.662; **behotyng** *pr.p.* 23.21, 24.41; **byhotyng** 29.767; **byhight** *pa.* 18.32, 22.18

bynde *v.* impose penance on 5.1007

bynym *v.* deprive of 28.1068

bystade *ppl.adj.* circumstanced 28.900

bytake *v.pr.* *b- me to þe* put myself in your charge 16.22; **betoke** *pa.* entrusted 1.935, 2.98, 3.90, gave 31.601, commended 31.2335; **bytake** *pa.p.* handed over 16.54; **betaken** 31.2645

bythynke *v.imp.* consider 29.739

bytymes *see* **betyme**

blamyd *v.pa.* rebuked 6.121, 29.820

blesse *v.refl.* make the sign of the cross 6.51; **blessyd** *pa.* 13.49, 26.352

blisse *v.imp.* bless 31.949

blondyryng *vbl.n.* disturbance 27.129 (*note*)

bloode *n.* lineage 31.1321

bode *see* **byde**

bodely *adv.* bodily 5.64

boystous *adj.* awkward 27.195, turbulent 31.1631

bollys *n.pl.* layers of embryo 27.215 (*note*)

bolnyngis *n.pl.* swellings of the heart (with wrath) 5.788

bondys *see* **bo(u)ndys** *n.pl.²*

bondship *n.* servitude 1.897

bone *n.* petition 22.109, 31.1625

book *n.* nave 5.62 (*note*)

bo(o)rdes *n.pl.* planks 31.743, ships' timbers 31.2320

boost *n.* boasting 5.764

bore *see* **bere**

borowys *n.pl.* guarantors 28.278, 30.342

boster *n.* boaster 27.206

boteler *n.* butler 10.26

botyr *n.* butter 7.61

bouchis *n.pl.* boils 1.452 (*note*)

bownde *v.pa.p.* obliged 6.262, 26.39, 28.398

boundis *n.pl.¹* bonds 12.10

bo(u)ndys *n.pl.²* limits of control 27.44, 31.245

bowe *v.* bend 6.94, 28.1091; *b- the browes* frown 31.651; *imp. b- thyn eeres* condescend to listen 31.1464; **bowyng** *pr.p.adj.* flexible 1.1171; **bowed** *pa.* bent 31.3004; *pa.p.* swayed (*fig.*) 1.196; *ppl.adj.* bent 27.230, curved 27.231

brasen *adj.* shameless 31.1255 (*note*)

brast(e *v.pa.* broke down 27.147

breche *n.* underpants 6.91, 28.1186

brede *n.* breadth 3.755

breest *n.* *with an hole b-* wholeheartedly 1.843 (*note*)

breke *v.* give expression to 28.474 (*note*);

brekyng *v.pr.p.* breaking 3.914; **breke** pa. broke 17.30, 28.957; **brake** 3.431, 7.133, 11.72; *b- vp* burst into speech, cried out 3.909 (*note*); *b- owte* 23.119; **brokyn** *pa.p.* *b- the pryson* escaped 3.381; **broken** 1.286 (*note*)

brenne *v.* burn 1.41, 3.418, *lete b-* commanded to burn 16.84; *pr.pl.* 26.232; **brennyng** *pr.p.* 18.40, 26.239; *ppl.adj.* 3.437, 30.227; **brend(e** *pa.* 8.13, 18.39; **brent(e** 1.18, 3.405, 11.25, 14.7 etc.; **brende** *pa.p.* 7.38; **brente** 3.402

brere *n.* prickly bush 3.20; *pl.* 31.113

bretelle *adj.* brittle 1.252

brether *n.pl.* brothers 31.2481

brethyng *vbl.n.* vaporisation 27.157 (*note*)

brid *n.* bird 18.45, 26.126; **briddes** *pl.* 26.131

brondes *n.pl.* firebrands 24.116

buffettes *n.pl.* buffets, blows 24.155

burgeys *n.* freeman, citizen 31.2366

burthyn *n.* responsibility 1.1082, load 3.273; **byrthen** 31.252

but *conj.* except 1.126, 27.136, 29.161, merely 3.748, only 1.12, 10.2, 13.24, 26.401; **but for** but because 3.848, if it were not for 3.849; **but yf** unless 4.361, 5.126, 22.36, 27.37 etc.; **but yiff** 23.39

caytyfe *n.* prisoner 3.379

caytyfe *adj.* miserable 5.1227

can *v.pr.* knows how to 5.903, *pl.* know (by heart) 5.1520

Capitle *n.* chapter, meeting of ecclesiastics 28.812

care *n.* distress 31.1524

cardynal vertues *n.pl.* chief virtues 5.1029

caryon *n.* walking corpse 30.173

carle *n.* knave 14.43

carnalle *adj.* *c- affeccion* personal friendship 29.351

cas(s)e *n.* coffin 3.587, 596

cast(e *v.pa.* threw 1.684, 11.67, 18.73, 21.30, tossed 3.346, 6.105; *did c- downe* caused to be demolished 1.521; **caste** *pa.p.* *c- ayenst* denounced 28.648

casuellye *adv.* by chance 31.3064

catelle *n.* chattels 5.781

cater *n.* buyer of provisions for lord's household 28.714

caught *v.pa.* pilfered 7.106

celle *n.* subordinate monastic house 20.47; **selle** 19.14, monastic cell 29.186

cenacle *n.* dining room 1.788

chapyter *n.* chapter house 29.1177

chare *n.* wheeled vehicle 3.105

charge *v.pr.* load 26.545; *imp.* take care 5.1278

charmes *n.* magic spells 31.1581

chaunselle *n.* chancel 5.58

cheffe *n.* chief 13.2

chepyng *vbl.n.* market-place 5.1290

chere *n.* welcome, greeting 1.1305, 26.82, 28.591; facial expression, mood, demeanour 1.649, 14.34, 16.62, 24.143, 27.196, 28.31, 30.390, reception 28.624; **chyere** 29.143; **shere** 21.34

cherefully *adv.* comfortingly 31.2178

chereue *n.* sheriff 28.1000

cheryd *ppl.adj.* cheerful 31.682, healthy 31.1558

chese *v.* choose 6.177, 14.75, 15.12, 28.831, 29.609; **chase** *pa.* 1.400, 3.49

chesiple *n.* eucharistic vestment, chasuble 5.213, 15.18, 28.770; **chisiple** 2.85, 28.464

chyne *n.* backbone 31.2167

chippys *n.pl.* splinters 3.110

chisiple *see* **chesiple**

chorylle *n.* rustic, peasant 1.1202; **chorles** *pl.* 1.1199

churcheyerth(e *n.* churchyard 6.194, 10.52; **churcheyearth** 10.57

clause *n.* text 30.323

clene *adj.* righteous 5.114, chaste 6.73(2), 29.491, 31.1061, cured 7.125

clene *adv.* completely 5.98, 6.73(1), 28.419, 31.325

clepe *v.* call 27.40, 29.353; name 27.23; **clepith** *pr.3sg.* 27.46; **clepyng(e** *pr.p.* calling upon 29.835, 31.2609; **clepid** *pa.* called out 15.36, summoned 1.657, 28.217, called 26.38; *pa.p.* 29.142, named 1.20, 2.4, 3.97, 4.136 etc. called to 29.142

clere *adj.* unconditional 1.373, 28.414, bright 27.68

clerely *adv.* brightly 31.1728

clerenes(se *n.* moral purity 1.960, serenity 5.45

clerk(e *n.* secular cleric 1.231, 6.177, 16.1, 28.139, theologian 31.331; *pl.* clerics 27.107, 29.34, 30.20

cleve *v.* adhere 6.93, 29.109; **clevith**

pr.3sg. 5.1302; **clevyd** *pa.* 9.74, 30.286, joined 1.430

clippid *v.pa.* grasped 1.446, embraced 28.152

clippyng *vbl.n.* embracing 1.285

clonkyn *ppl.adj.* shrivelled up, wasted away 1.979 *(note)*

close *v.* enclose 29.206; **closith** *pr.3sg.* 5.218; **closyd** *pa.* 30.416, 31.1165

clotte *n.* human body 29.185 *(note)*

clove *v.pa.* split 3.427, 26.310

clowis *n.pl.* claws 26.483

cognycion *n.* knowledge 31.408

collacyon *n.* evening gathering of members of monastic house for devotion or devotional readings 29.1340

collecteralye *adv.* *error for* **collaterally** slantwise 4.98

collet *n.* prayer for a specific purpose, collect 5.352

collyke *n.* spasmodic pain 3.471 *(note)*

colour *n.* *under c- of* on the strength of 24.39

combered *ppl.adj.* confused 31.186

comenyd *v.pa.* discussed 1.316

comfortably *adv.* reassuringly 31.2087

comfortyd *v.pa.* encouraged 13.32; *pa.p.* 13.10

comyn *adj.* *c- people* freemen, not nobility or clergy 1.158; *c- woman* prostitute 5.646, 9.54

comyn *v.*[1] *pa.p.* came, arrived 31.2486

comyn *v.*[2] administer holy communion 31.2408; have dealings with 5.484; **comened** *pa.p.* administered holy communion 24.239

comynalte *n.* common people 31.302; **comynte** 1.112

comyns *n.pl.* House of Commons 1.147; **comynis** common people 1.203; **comons** common soldiers 31.1847

commodytees *n.pl* benefits 5.1461

communed *v.pa.* discussed 29.42

comons *see* **comyns**

compas *n.* dimension 27.60

compassith *v.pr.3sg.* surrounds 26.15, 27.58

compleynt *n.* lament 31.3079

Complyn *n.* Compline, the final Hour of the daily Office 5.532

compuncte *ppl.adj.* remorseful 31.885

comunly *adv.* usually 31.1787

conceyt(e *n.* mind 28.76, favour 1.701; **conseyte** 1.280

conceyuid *v.pa.* learned 3.91, thought 3.434

concupiscible *adj.* strongly desirous 5.1412

condicion *n.* disposition 3.280, 16.123; *pl.* 1.88, natures, qualities 1.278, 31.108

condytes *n.* conduits for fresh water 31.819

conditour *n.* guide 31.1967

confermed *v.pa.* strengthened 31.476; *pa.p.* administered sacrament of confirmation *or* strengthened 30.146

confesse *v.* hear someone's confession 28.1174; **confessid** *pa.p.* 16.210, *ppl.adj.* absolved 31.2083

confesso(u)r(e *n.* christian who is persecuted but not martyred 3.476, 15.1; *pl.* 29.322

confortable *adj.* agreeable 30.78

confortith *v.pr.3sg.* refreshes 27.169

confusyd *ppl.adj.* perplexed 31.1351

congellacion *n.* clotting 1.1333

coniurid *v.pa.* charged, urged 16.140

connyng *n.* knowledge 6.132; **cunnyng** 1.603, 3.90, 5.346; **kunnynge** 31.2893; **cunnyng** learning 1.1070; **kunnyng** 16.217, 29.287; **konnyng** 16.3, skill 14.106

connyng *ppl.adj.* clever, knowledgeable 3.235, 31.655; **cunnyng** skilful 1.1189, 31.2669; **kunnyngeste** *superl.adj.* 31.732

consubstanciall *adj.* of the same essence 23.132

consubstantly *adv.* with the same essence 24.245

consume *v.* destroy 1.1026; **consumyd** *pa.* 31.1685

consumpcion *n.* wasting away 31.3147

contynuance *n.* perseverance 31.897

contre *n.* district 1.212, area 18.144, county 19.2, 30.203, region 19.16, 26.313, 28.902; **cuntre** county 8.8; **countre** country 7.6; **cuntre** 12.4; **contrey** countryside 21.37; **cuntre** 1.1200; **cuntray** region 3.37; **contray** 31.604; *owne cuntraye* homeland 5.246; **contreys** *pl.* counties 18.13

convenience *n.* compatibility 31.1831

convenient(e *adj.* opportune 31.843, appropriate 31.1112, favorable 31.2929

conuenyentlye *adv.* appropriately 5.122

conuersacion *n.* manner of living 1.403, 2.75, 14.18, 26.245, dwelling place 31.909 *(note)*

conuersaunt *ppl.adj.* intimate 1.847

co(o)lys *n.pl.* cinders 3.438, embers 6.23

coostys *n.pl.* coasts 30.72

cope *n.* ecclesiastical vestment 28.464, cloak 28.581; *pl.* 26.195 *(note)*

corious *adj.* sumptuous 31.1721

corne *n.* cereal crop 30.54, grain 30.58, 31.99; *pl.* cereal crops 30.52

correccion *n.* punishment 28.183, correction 31.1346

correcte(d *v.pa.p.* punished 3.861, 13.22, 28.184

corse *n.* corpse 31.1706

cosyns *n.pl.* relations 1.956

coste *n.*[1] expense 3.463, 15.6, 28.784, 31.62; *pl.* 6.27, 28.498, 30.436

costys *n.*[2] pl. borders, bounds 30.244, 31.606

costelewe *adj.* expensive 6.220, magnificent 31.738

coude *v.pa.* knew 3.240, 28.36, 29.151, was able 11.43; *c- thonke* was grateful 28.495

covenaunte *n.* agreement 31.735; **coue-nandys** *pl.* 16.23

covent *n.* community of monks 6.224, 26.202, 28.1270, 31.2058

covetyse *n.* avarice 5.759, strong desire 31.772

craft(e *n.* skill 2.43, 14.32, trickery 31.317

creature *n.* person 3.736, 6.35, 19.24; *pl.* created things 31.228

credence *n. letter of c-* letter certifying validity of information 28.688

cressettes *n.pl.* metal vessels containing oil or fat, used as lamps 31.1439

cryeng *v.pr.p. c- vpon* calling upon 29.1129; **crying** crying out 1.655; **cryeng** objecting 30.404; **cried** *pa.* entreated 1.207, 30.345, shouted 1.656, 13.99; *c- on* called out to 16.127, 31.1562

crying *vbl.n.* shouting 1.656; **cryenge** 29.887

crispe *adj.* curly 22.115, 23.107, 27.197

crolled *ppl.adj.* curly 24.199

crome *n.* fragment 31.1686

croser *n.* prelate's crozier-bearer 28.1085

crosser *n.* one who receives vows of those who wish to go on crusade and invests them with the insignia of a crusader 6.176 *(note)*

crossid *v.pa.* made sign of the cross over 31.1539

crowne *n.* top of skull 28.844, 1084

cunnyng *see* **connyng**

cunnyngly *adv.* skilfully 3.722

cuntre *see* **contre**

curat(e *n.* parish priest 5.132, 30.153

cure *n.* care 2.99, 13.79, 31.1535; *pl.* cares, responsibilities 3.50; *do c-*, considered carefully 29.1347

curiously *adv.* exquisitely 26.237, 31.849

curse *n.* course 27.64

cursyd *v.pa.* excommunicated 6.282

cursyng *vbl.n.* excommunication 28.1064

curteys *adj.* courteous 26.539

curtil *n.* tunic 28.582

custumably *adv.* habitually 31.722

custume *n.* habit 31.973

d[enarius] *n.* penny 30.340

Day(e *n.* feast day 1.1195, 3.764, 4.42, 6.4 etc.

dam(y)selle *n.* young woman 1.1186, 3.38, 31.2694; **dameselle** 5.738

dampned *v.pa.p.* condemned 29.1092, damned 31.2293

darst *v.pr.2sg.* dare 26.431; **durst(e** *v.pa.sg.* dared 1.50, 3.245, 9.34, 16.9, 18.83 etc.

daunger *n.* power 3.180, 31.3027

debate *n.* dispute, disagreement 6.268, 28.176, 31.2150

debonayre *adj.* courteous 1.183, 5.1375

declaracion *n.* explanation 5.1431; *to the d-* as a public statement 3.572

declarith *v.pr.* explains 5.*rubric*; **declar-yng** *pr.p.* 29.149, 31.332; **declared** *pa.* showed 29.759; *pa.p.* made known 3.775

declyne *v.* turn away 31.1331

ded(e)ly *adj.* mortal 29.732, 31.390

deed *adj.* dead 30.69

defaute *n.* want 3.290, lack 28.802

defende *v.pr.* forbid 6.262, 28.422

defensour *n.* protector 29.1356

defoile *v.* rape 31.288

deformyd *v.pa.p.* disfigured 29.48

defoule *v.* seduce 2.18; rape 9.54; **defou-lith** *pr.3sg.* makes foul 5.1396, seduces 29.965; **defoulid** *pa.p.* defiled 1.882 *(note)*, 3.32

degre *n.* social status 1.165, 5.703, 31.1322

deynte *n.* esteem 31.810; *pl.* delicacies 1.788

deyry *n.* dairy 7.64
dele *v.* give 16.202
dele *n.* part 29.1369
deliberacion *n. with a gode d-* after much thought 3.337
delve *v.imp.* dig 31.2848; **delvid** *pa.* 31.2273; **dolven** *pa.p.* buried 31.3185
delvyng(e *vbl.n.* digging 31.2847
deme *v.* think 1.714, judge 5.948; **demeste** *pr.2sg.* 31.1495; **demyng** *pr.p.* 29.727; **demyd** *pa.* judged 3.710, condemned 29.1093; *pa.p.* 31.3028
demerytis *n.pl.* offences 3.355, crimes 31.3173
demewre *adj.* calm 28.187; demure quiet 1.297
demewrely *adv.* in a dignified way 27.263
denye *v.* refuse 1.254, 16.60; **denyed** *pa.* 1.437, 6.236, 22.20, 28.267
denounce *v.* announce publicly 28.981
departable *adj.* distinguishable 31.1121
departith *v.pr.3sg.* divides 26.548; **departid** *pa.* 3.519; 28.973, *pa.p.* 5.1291, 18.17, separated 5.63, 8.46, 29.710, 31.561
departyng *vbl.n.* separating 29.693
deposicion *n.* interment 3.662
depped *v.pa.* dipped 31.982
derogacyon *n.* disparagement 29.419; **dirogacion** 3.603
deseyued *see* **dysseyue**
desese *see* **dissese** *n.*
desiderable *adj.* desirable 29.1449
desire *n.* pleasure 16.98 (*note*)
desyrous *adj.* desirable (?) 31.637
desyrously *adv.* fervently 29.357
desolat(e *adj.*[1] deserted 10.30, 27.188
desolate *adj.*[2] religiously or morally lax 5.182 (*note*), unruly, unrestrained 30.246 (*note*)
despyte *see* **dispite**
desseyte *n.* deceit 31.1268
determinacion *n.* dispute 23.23
determyne *v.* define 31.572, bring about 31.1511
dettis *n.pl.* sinful acts 5.1166
dettours *n.pl.* offenders 5.1168
devetelyer *comp.adv.* more devoutly 31.3062; **devotelyer** 31.2455
devoure *n.* duty 31.222
devourid *v.pa.* consumed 3.409
dewte *n.* tax, fee, rent 28.269, 413
dichers *n.pl.* ditch diggers 31.2273

did *see* **do**
diffyne *v.* declare 3.263
dyffuselye *adv.* in detail 31.18
dyght *v.* prepare 26.110; **dight** *pa.* 30.277
diligence *n. do d-* make an effort 1.323
dynte *n.* stroke 1.757
direccion *n.* directive 28.694
dirogacion *see* **derogacyon**
discesse *v.* die 4.350
disce(y)ue *see* **dysseyue**
disclandre *v.imp.* slander 28.1081; **disclandride** *pa.p.* 28.629
disclaundyr *n.* defamation 22.98
discordyng *ppl.adj.* differing from 29.341; **descordyng** 29.919
discover *v.* reveal 31.1176
discresith *v.pr.2sg.* belittles 5.770 (*note*)
discrete *adj.* wise 1.191, 31.355
discryve *v.* ascribe 1.458 (*note*); **dyscryvid** *pa.* 1.888
dyshoneste *n.* shame 29.929
dishonestid *ppl.adj.* disgraced 1.195
dismembre *v.* rend the body of 16.291
disperpelyd *ppl.adj.* dispersed 29.145
dispite *n.* contempt 1.861, 3.275, 5.769, 13.23, 25.42; **despyte** disgrace 29.944
dispitously *adv.* cruelly 16.288
displesaunce *n.* displeasure 31.2760
dispoyle *v.* ransack 31.1849; *pr.* deprive 3.171; *pa.* dispoyled plundered 28.343
dispose *v.* prepare 31.881; *pr.pl.* 31.1423; **disposeth** *pr.3sg.* directs 31.1968; *imp.* make provision for 31.2766; **disposyng** *pr.p.* arranging 29.148; **disposid** *pa.* got ready 1.421; *pa.p.* directed 31.46, inclined 28.727
dyspoused *v.pa.* betrothed 24.52 (*note*)
dispute *v.* engage in formal debate 29.810
dysseyue *v.* deceive 9.28; **disceyue** 5.627; **disceue** 24.140; **disseyuid** *pa.p.* mistaken 1.1097; **disceyuid** 3.745; **deseyved** disappointed 31.2118
dyssernith *v.pr.3sg.* recognises 29.343
dissese *n.* infirmity 1.971, injury 22.58; **desese** suffering 3.493; **dissesis** *pl.* afflictions 1.601, misfortunes 1.761
dissese *v.* torment 11.69; **dissesid** *ppl.adj.* unwell 2.16
dissoluyd *v.pa.* wasted 3.620; *pa.p.* separated 29.199
distemperate *adj.* inclement 31.755
distempered *pa.p.* rendered intemperate 31.748 (*note*)

distrouble *v.* impede 6.200
disworschip *n.* dishonour 31.1792
dyuers *adj.* of various kinds 31.238; *adj. as n.pl.* various persons 3.863
do *v. followed by inf.* cause to, **do make** 4.89, **do synge** 4.234, **do slee** 1.12, **do spende** 1.220, **do to wete** 28.205; **dydde do bylde** 30.49; **dyd do make** 26.565; **had do make** 2.1, 30.297; *followed by pa.p.* **had do brought** 3.785
doest *v.pr.2sg.* do 29.501; **doyst** 28.882; **doyth** *pr.3sg.* 28.898; **done** *pr.pl.* 5.517, 7.32, 28.437; **dyd(de** *pa.* behaved 6.270, 29.924; **do** *pa.p.* done 28.1269; **doo** 31.2708; **doon** 28.1193
do of *v.* take off 21.27; **dyed of** *pa.* took off 29.184 *(note);* **doone of** 31.1354; **dide on** put on 28.464; **dydde appon** 29.36; **done vpon** *pa.p.* placed upon 31.2166; **did grete coste** paid heavy expenses 3.463
doare *n.* offender 29.1443
docto(u)r *n.* doctor of the Church 29.92 *(note),* theologian 29.1323, learned man 31.330; *pl.* Church Fathers 5.24, 29.387, 31.879
dolven *see* delve
dombe *adj.* mute 3.334, 30.245; **dome** 31.1715
dome *n.* judgement 5.167, 19.23, 28.682, 29.452; *pl.* 31.2280, Judgement Seat 29.9; *domes man* judge 28.507
dominacion *n.* rule 31.798; *pl.* powers 31.777
downe n. treeless upland 10.18
dowte n. uncertainty 5.1427
dowte *v.imp.* *d- not* have no fear 31.2183; **doubtid** *v.pa.* were afraid of 11.76
dowtefulle *adj.* to be dreaded 3.543, hesitant 31.2131
drad *see* drede
drawe *v.* convert 12.14, move 31.338, *d-after* follow 29.296; **drawyng(e** *pr.p.* coming 3.298, 31.2801, **drewe** *pa.* came 11.75, turned 14.22, 28.89, tugged 1.1112, stretched 3.84, went 3.229, led 9.6, dragged 18.71; **drowe** moved 14.39; **drawe(n** *pa.p.* dragged 16.37, 31.1243, *d- away* removed from 31.1491
drawyng(e *vbl.n.* pulling 10.73, *d-out,* tearing off 31.1485
drawyng *ppl.adj.* spiritually attracted 3.132

drede *v.* honour 1.89; **drad** *pa.* feared 1.36, 3.240, 26.306; **dredde** 31.1034; **dradde** *pa.p.* 19.22; **dredde** honoured 29.114
dredeful(le *adj.* afraid 1.363, awesome 31.3010
dreder *n. d- of God* God-fearing man 31.2460 *(note)*
dresse *v.* raise 5.87, prepare 31.743; **dressid** *pa. d- her downe* sat 31.3050; *pa.p.* addressed 5.359
dreve *v.pa.p.* driven 26.266
drewe *see* drawe
drynesse *n.* greed (fig.) 29.1226
droppist *v.pr.2sg. d- wordes* speak 29.226
dubitacions *n.pl.* hesitations 31.2054
ducherie *n.* duchy 31.2985
duras *n.* imprisonment 30.357
durst *see* darst
dwelle *v.pr.* remain 5.1257

easely *adv.* gently, quietly 31.2178
easid *see* esyd
edefyed *v.pa.* improved 6.174, strengthened 29.150; *pa.p.* uplifted 31.2524
eftesones *adv.* at once 31.2134, afterwards 31.2585
eggyng *vbl.n.* incitement 5.718
eyen, eeyen, eyzen, eyhen *see* ye
eyled *v.pa. what her e-* what was the matter with her 29.890
eyrys *n.pl.* heirs 29.1413, 31.1950
either *conj.* or 1.1305(2), 5.775, 27.74; **ether** 5.917
elacion *n.* inordinate self-esteem 5.775
eluys *n.pl.* elves 27.33 *(note)*
enbrowdre *v.* embroider 1.1189
enclyne *v.* bow 5.472, dispose one's mind favorably 31.581, deviate 31.1620; **enclyned** *pa. e- to* favoured 31.1994
encombred *v.pa.p.* ensnared 31.501
encresid *v.pa.* made progress 28.89; *pa.p.* improved 29.880
endewe *v.* endow 1.378; **endewyng** *pr.p.* 31.466; **endewid** *pa.* 3.62, 31.88, provided 11.9; *pa.p.* endowed 3.883
endowance *n.* dowry 24.44 *(note)*
endure *v.* continue 34.241; **endurid** *pa.* 1.19, 29.813
enflawme *v.* inspire 30.108; **enflawmed** *pa.* 30.119; *pa.p.* 31.1100; **enflamyd** *ppl.adj.* 2.13

enformacion, enforme *see* **informacion, informe**

enforsid *v.pa.* constrained 31.2835

enhaunce *v.* exalt 29.494; **enhaunsed** *pa.p.* 29.197

enioyne *v.pr.* prescribe 28.1168; **enioyned** *pa.* charged 29.460; *pa.p.* 1.408; **inioyned** *ppl.adj.* prescribed 4.7

enlumyned *ppl.adj.* enlightened 5.623

ensa(u)mple *n.* example 2.102, 5.117, 19.10, 20.77, 30.69, 31.474, precedent 6.288; **ensamplis** *pl.* examples 3.284

ensuraunce *n.* promise 31.823

entende *v.* devote (oneself) to 14.80, strive to go 31.582; **intendeth** *pr.3sg.* strives 24.29; **entendyng** *pr.p.* devoting themselves to 29.301; **entendid** *pa.* 29.132, hoped for 31.2266

entent(e *n.* purpose 13.60, 18.30, 28.209, 30.19, 31.146

ent(i)erly *adv.* wholeheartedly 31.2370, 2409

entyre *v.* enter 29.1364

entredited *v.pa.* put under an interdict 28.947

entrete *v.* deal with 21.15; **entretid** *pa.p.* 28.378, 31.1228, persuaded 31.1369

entretyng *vbl.n.* negotiation 6.274

entryng *n.* entrance 4.38

eqvyte *n.* rectitude 31.287

er *conj.* or 29.49

erand *adj.* e- *theffe* notorious thief 28.260

erbe *n.* shrub 26.35; *pl.* plants 26.33, 27.170, vegetables 26.204

erely *adj.* early 11.65

errable *adj.* arable 30.54

erthe *n. brought on e-* buried 15.49 (*note*)

eschewe *v.* shun 27.85

esyd *v.pa.* eased 26.420; **easid** 26.421

estate *n.* rank 1.276, 28.495; *pl.* 17.25, 28.130, 31.23, 31.2453; **astates** 31.84; *in his e-* in a manner fitting his rank 1.295 (*note*)

esteme *v.* estimate 29.692

ether *see* **either**

etyr *n.* eater 6.218

Even *n.* the Eve of a festival 31.2522; **Yevyn** 1.814; **evyn** evening 26.424, 29.1040

even, evyn *adj.* equal 29.340, on the same level 31.1753; *e- crysten* fellow christian 4.366, 5.468; *pl.* 31.476

euen, euyn *adv.* exactly 5.512, 7.133, 26.119, 27.56; *e- after* immediately 5.434; *e- plat est* due east 26.76; *e-sodeynly* at once 31.1163; *e- to* right up to 19.19

evenyng *v.pr.p.* equating 29.413

euerychone *pron.* each, every one 17.35, 26.80, 31.364

evydently *adv.* clearly 29.192

except *v.pr.* accepts 5.105

excite *v.pr.* prevail upon 28.502; **excyting** *pr.p.* 3.188; **excited** *pa.* prompted 31.2723

excludith *v.pr.* eliminates 5.1012

expownyd *v.pa.p.* described 1.350, interpreted 1.619, 5.1277

expressyd *v.pa.p.* set forth 29.772

ex(s)ample *n.* illustration 29.715, 31.1111

fables *n.pl.* fictitious stories 31.269

fadirhode *n. your f-* address to a father 31.359 (*note*); **faderhode** 31.1114; **faderhede** 28.687

fadred vppon *v.pa.* represented as belonging to 29.815

fayn, feyn *v.* feign 31.450; **feynid** *v.pa.refl.* 2.24, 31.648; *ppl.adj.* 31.269

fayne *adj.* desirous of 7.6, 28.819

fayne *adv.* willingly 6.190, 28.353, gladly 26.494, 31.173

falle *v.* happen 29.1040; *f- in* come to 31.1587; **fal** *pa. f- to* became 30.188; **felle** *pa.* happened 3.743; **fillen** *pa.pl.* fell 27.21; **falle** *pa.p.* become desirous 5.1149 (*note*); *f- in* failed in 1.374(*note*)

fals(e *adj. f- fame* untrue rumour, false reputation 23.92; *f- stok* unreliable ancestry 1.289 (*note*)

fame *n.* reputation 5.779, 23.93

famyliarite *n.* fellowship 31.419

famulyer *adj.* close 31.3069; **famylier** kindly 1.182, friendly 28.17, 30.231

fanon *n.* eucharistic vestment, maniple 5.205

fantasie *n.* apparition 31.2133, illusion 31.2623; **fantesye** 1.889

fare *n.* behaviour 5.835

fare *v.* behave 3.369, 7.4, be provided with food 28.144; **faryng** *pr.p.* behaving 31.1598; **ferde** *pa.* 9.51, 21.25, 28.531; **fared** 31.1458; **feerde** 29.836; **ferde** *pa.pl.* were provided with food 28.17

faste *adj.* firm 1.1179

fast(e *adv.* closely 1.1004, persistently 3.873, 9.83, 26.326, quickly 7.62, 8.9, intently 16.233, 26.174; **fast by** nearby 29.1085; **faster** *comp.* more firmly 1.1112

fasten *v.* inflict suffering 31.3030 (*note*); **festned** *pa.p.* fixed 29.654

favowrer *n.* follower 31.67

fecch(e *v.* bring 7.70, 9.38, 10.25, fetch 9.69, 26.408, procure 21.26

fedyrd *ppl.adj.* fettered 15.50

fee *n.* *lay f-* estate held in tenure to feudal or royal superior 28.257

feer *v. see* **fere**

feest *n.* patronal festival 4.127

feyn *v. see* **fayn**

feyntid *v.pa.* became enfeebled 3.620

feyrenes(se *n.* courtesy 21.15, beauty 29.1279

feith(e *n.* belief 5.592; *yeve f- to* believe 29.807

felawe, felowe *n.* associate 1.1197, companion 3.9, 16.149, 29.53; **felew** equal 27.252; **felowis** *pl.* associates 1.858, companions 12.3, 28.17

felawed *ppl.adj.* accompanied 29.230

felowship *n.* companions 6.37, 26.18; **felowschip** 30.88; **felouship** company 1.639; **felawship** 18.92; **felyshyp** 24.8; **felischyp** 30.25

fe(e)le *v.pr.* understand 31.437, 506

felle *v.* fell, cut down 9.73; **felde** *pa.* 18.42; **fel** *pa.p.* 18.43

felte *v.pa.* smelt 1.1165, 3.135; **felyd** *pa.p.* 29.202

fendes *n.pl.* devils 21.26, 23.41

ferde *see* **fare**

fere *v.* frighten 1.934; **feer** 13.39

ferefulle *adj.* awe-inspiring 29.544, 31.3010

fer(e)fully *adv.* in fear 29.547, terrifyingly 29.986

ferforth *adv.* forthrightly 29.1411

ferme *v.* let out for rent 28.1050

fermours *n.pl.* those who rent or lease land 28.323

ferthyng *n.* farthing, quarter of a penny (as type of smallest unit of money) 4.356

ferre *comp.adv.* farther 10.28

ferser *comp.adj.* more impetuous 30.28

ferslye *adv.* ferociously 31.46

fe(e)rsnes(se *n.* ferocity 3.793, 31.38

feruent *adj.* fiery 21.41, severe 22.132

(*note*), 27.165, 29.7, burning 23.28, ardent 25.7; **vervent** 31.1510

feruently *adv.* fiercely 3.409, 24.60, severely 3.471, ardently 31.343, enthusiastically 31.2895

festenyng *v.pr.p.* fixing 29.552

festfully *adv.* with due ceremony, solemnly 29.315

fet *v.* take away 28.262; **fette** bring 1.1109, fetch 18.83; **fet** *pa.* carried away 21.64; **fette** fetched 6.252, 31.1706, brought 9.13; *pa.p.* 1.1183, 31.1228

feters *n.pl.* fetters 30.338; **fetyrs** 30.347

feuer quarten *n.* intermittent fever, with attacks recurring every three days 1.1231

fidil *n.* fiddle 26.133

fyel fallible (?) 1.1096 (*note*)

fygere *n.* prefiguration 5.1335

figures *n.pl.* statues 31.365, constellations 31.852

fynde *v.pr.* maintain, support 28.92 (*note*); **founde** *pa.* 28.851

firmament *n.* sky, heavens 26.175, 29.207; *pl.* 27.70

flambes *n.pl.* flames 29.665

flatlyng *adv.* prostrate 31.1946

fle *v.* flee 1.65, fly 26.131; **fleeth** *pr.3sg.* flies 26.73; **fle(e** *pr.pl.* flee 5.252, 255; **fleyng** *pr.p.* fleeing 3.344; **fle** *pa.* flew 18.54; **fly** 18.45, 26.152; **fled** shunned 29.124

fleyng *vbl.n.* fleeing 13.7

fles(sc)h(e *n.* flesh of mammals and birds 5.582, meat 5.583, 6.220, 28.718; *f-hookis* *n.pl.* meat hooks 31.1438

flesshly *adv.* carnally 9.38

fleshlynes *n.* carnality 5.828

flode *n.* river 3.490; **flo(o)des** *pl.* 31.957, ocean waves 31.1630

flotered *v.pa.* floated 31.2320

flowme *n.* flame 29.1329

flowyng *v.pr.p.* streaming 3.828, 29.1260; *ppl.adj.* abounding 3.351

flum *n.* river 31.960

folyly *adv.* stupidly 5.1313

foller *n.* fuller 28.565

fondament *see* **foundement**

fon(n)de *adj.* foolish 31.1226, 31.1898

fonnednes *n.* foolishness 31.1294

foo *n.* foe 28.1021; **foon** *pl.* 28.433

for *prep.* on account of 1.81, 10.37, 18.84(1)

fordo *v.* destroy 28.204; **furdo** 28.863

forme *n.* model 31.1004

forsweryngis *n.pl.* perjuries 5.794

forsworne *ppl.adj.* perjured 28.493

forthy *conj.* f- *that* in order that 29.285

fortune *n.* by f- by chance 3.810

fortunyd *v.pa.* happened by chance 2.16, 3.118

foryetyng *vbl.n.* forgetting 5.1368

foryeve *v.* forgive 5.19; *pa.p.* foryovyn 5.1514

foryevenes *n.* forgiveness 5.18

foule *see* fowle *n.*

founde *see* fynde

foundement *n.* foundation 31.2690; fondament 5.30; fundament 31.744

fourme *n.* burrow of a hare 27.230

fourmer *n.* creator 5.1342

fowle *n.* bird 8.29; foule 18.44; fowlys *pl.* 6.104

fowle *adv.* badly 7.4, wickedly 28.629

fowlid *v.pa.* defecated 1.16

frame *n.* literary composition 31.403

franchis(e, fraunchyes *n.* freedom of action 6.275, 28.646, independence 28.195, territory under jurisdiction of a city or town 31.2688

fraytour(e *n.* refectory of a religious house 1.1356, 26.201

free *adj.* generous 31.1750

fre *adv.* generously 28.518

fretyng *v.pr.p.* vexing 24.151

fro *prep.* f- *themselfe* out of their minds 3.414

frowarde *adj.* stubborn 3.285

frowardnes *n.* contrariness 1.1205, 3.670; frowardnys disobedience 3.271

fulfylle *v.* carry out 26.476, fill up 27.19; fulfylled *pa.* gratified 6.31; *pa.p.* filled 1.32, 3.917, 12.21, 16.85, 17.36 etc., satisfied 5.516, 31.2836, implemented 13.76, 30.303, elapsed 26.250

fulle *v.* fill 27.14

fulle *adv.* completely 31.1015

fully *adv.* foully 18.52

fundament *see* foundement

furdo *see* fordo

gad(e)rid *v.pa.* collected 1.203, 30.358; *pa.p.* 1.204

gaf *see* yeve

gay *adj.* richly attired 17.23, 28.107

gallous *n.pl.* gallows 24.112

garnementis *n.pl.* garments 1.1190

gastful(l *adj.* frightening 6.120, 26.355, 27.148

gate *see* gete

gefe *see* yeue

geydyng *n.* behaviour 27.83 *(note)*

gendre *v.* produce 31.986

gendryng *vbl.n.* engendering 27.228

generacion *n.* sexual intercourse 1.290 *(note)*, procreating 5.1013, origin 29.269, 31.579

gentilnes *n.* generosity 1.543

gentyls *n.pl.* gentry 1.815; non-christians, pagans 31.127, 1913

gessyd *v.pa.* guessed 31.382

gete *v.* obtain 1.607, 6.214, 28.715, 29.251; gate *pa.* 1.653, 3.253, 14.85, 30.340, 31.2777, took possession of 11.42; gette obtained 15.9; gete *pa.p.* 1.634, 15.13, 31.2864; goten 31.1844

gibette *n.* gallows 31.1436; iebet(t) 22.37, 23.41; gebet 24.112

gylte *v.pa.p.* gilded 3.587

gnawe *v.pr.* tear with the teeth 31.1499; gnawest *pr.2sg.* tear with sharp instruments 31.1481

go(o) *v.* walk 1.429, 2.62, 3.639, 20.34, 25.9, etc.; gon *pr.pl.* go 26.16

gobettes *n.pl.* small pieces 24.235, 28.1244, 31.1038

goddas *n.* goddess 31.1323

go(o)de *n.* alms 7.85; godis *pl.* possessions, property 7.102, 30.406; goode *pl.* provisions 16.159 *(note)*, 28.798 *(note)*, possessions 31.1849

godely *adj.* handsome 9.18

godenes *n.* praise 13.71

goydid(e *v.pa.* directed 14.71 *(note)*, 17.26; goyded *pa.p.* 26.248

goydyng *vbl.n.* guidance 14.74 *(note)*, 28.115

gospelles *n.pl.* passages from the gospels to be read at mass 29.80

gost(e)ly *adj.* spiritual 3.104, 28.379, 31.986; g- *fader/fadyr* confessor 1.564, 30.308

gostely(e *adv.* spiritually 5.713, 31.596

gowte *n.* gout 20.32

grace *n.* providence 5.778; *toke them to* g- received them with favour 31.2422

graciously *adv.* by God's grace 31.15, 1250

grayle *n.* Gradual, versicle and response sung at mass 5.386

gramarcy *n. & interj.* many thanks 31.1387

graunte *n.* guarantee 30.66
grave *v.* decorate with carvings 31.734; **graven** *pa.p.* carved 31.849
grenes *n.* greenness 1.903
grennyng *v.pr.p.* grimacing 24.152, 27.267; **grennyd** *pa.* 21.9, snarled 31.1574
grese *n.* grease 21.30
grete *adj.* numerous 9.80, 11.76, of high estate, rich 31.2568; *alle in g-* all together 31.834; **gretter** *comp.* higher 31.1017; **grettist** *superl.* largest 5.455
grete *v.pr.* greet 1.795; **gret** *pa.* 28.1059
greue *v.* distress 27.24; **greuyn** *pr.pl.* 27.25; **grevyd** *pa.* bothered 6.18; *pa.p.* weighed down 29.915; *ppl.adj.* obstructed 1.871
grevons *n.* burden 29.346 (*note*)
grevous *adj.* burdensome 1.146, 29.382, 30.99
Grewe *n.* Greek language 1.508, 29.2
grewe *v.pa.* increased 29.928
grynde *n.* groin 1.1043
gripe *n.* fabulous beast, gryphon 26.325
grisely(s)che *adj.* horrible 26.305, 315
gryses *n.pl.* steps 5.373
grownde *n.* foundation 5.30
growndly *adv.* thoroughly 29.484 (*note*)
grucchid *v.pa.* found fault 1.287, grumbled 28.789
grucchyng *n.* complaint 1.169

habitudis *n.pl.* bodily constitutions 31.578
hafte *n.* handle 31.2388
hayres *see* heyre *n.*²
haled *v.pa.p.* hauled 31.1243
halowe *v.* consecrate 1.472, celebrate 3.271; **halowyn** *pr.pl.* commemorate 23.90; **halowe** *imp.* bless 31.950; **halo-wynge** *pr.p.* celebrating 31.2117; **halo-wid** *pa.* consecrated 1.402, 4.135, 28.172, 30.51; *pa.p.* celebrated 1.1337, 16.92, consecrated 1.813, 4.28, 17.22, blessed 5.598
halowyng(e *vbl.n.* blessing 5.597, consecration 4.57, 30.51
halte *adj. as n.* lame 31.1714
haltid *v.pa.* limped 3.885; **haltynge** *pr.p.* 29.1340; *vbl.n.* 3.886
ham *see* hem
hammys *n.pl.* part of leg behind knee 1.979
handel *v.* touch, feel 31.311; **handelyst**

pr.2sg. caress 5.1151; **handelyng** *pr.p.* touching 5.1151; **hondelyng** 5.1132
hap *v.pr.* happen 5.544; **happid** *pa.* 28.160; **hapned** 31.827; *impers.pa. h-me* fell to my lot 29.593
happe *n.* stroke of luck 31.1225; *pl.* 5.696; *in h-* perhaps 29.463, 1181
harde *adj.* harsh 29.550; **herde** hard, painful 21.29, 28.778
hardely *adv.* resolutely 31.1489
hardenesse *n.* obduracy 29.1191; **hard-nysse** austerity 13.56; **herdenes** 28.1240
hardy *adj.* foolhardy 27.206
harmeles *adj.* unharmed 3.445, 16.113; **hermeles** 28.536
hastely *adv.* eagerly 28.143, soon 29.789
haunte *v.pr.* frequent 5.695; **hauntyng** *pr.p.* 1.122; **hauntyd** *pa.* visited 30.248 (*note*)
haue *v. h- awey* take away 31.2698, *h-ayene into* bring back into 28.689; *h-owt* remove 28.1267; **hauye** *pr.* have 26.397; **had** *pa.* took 6.240 (*note*); **hadde** remembered 31.265
hauye *see* haue
hauyn *n.* harbour 26.80, 30.359
hede *n. toke none h-* paid no attention 11.36; *take h-* pay attention 31.2399
heddis *n.pl.* head coverings 3.420 (*note*)
hed(d)yd *v.pa.p.* beheaded 23.89, 29.841, 31.1604
hedynesse *n.* obstinacy 5.799
hedyr *adv.* to this place 31.1228
heer *see* he(e)r(e *n.*
heggis *n.pl.* pools formed by blocking river 11.56
heyneth *v.pr.3sg.* exalts 29.355
heyre *n.*¹ heir 9.3, 11.2, 17.11; *pl.* 31.2844
heyre *n.*² haircloth 4.78, 28.1110, 31.1357; garment of haircloth 6.19, 28.136; **hayres** *pl.* 6.28
helid *v.*¹ *pa.p.* healed 3.764, 5.958, 17.67
helyd *v.*² *pa.* covered 29.127; *ppl.adj.* concealed 5.135
helyng *vbl.n.* covering 5.143
help(e)ly *adj.* kindly 31.2135, 2151
hem *pron.* them 14.87, 31.1873; **ham** 29.844
her(e *poss.pron.* their 3.142, 14.87, 23.67, 29.432
herber *n.* pleasure garden 29.1132
herbore *n.* place to stay 5.1052
herborowe *v.* give shelter to 5.1052

herde, herdenes *see* **harde, hardenesse**
here *v.* hear 28.969; **her** 31.2345; **hyre** 6.204; **here** *imp.* 31.1635; **heryng** *pr.p.* 22.19; **hyryng** 6.280, 23.23
harde *pa.* 31.494
he(e)r(e *n.* hair 1.684, 3.420 (*note*), 22.115, 26.191, 31.2275; **herre** 27.197; *pl.* **heris** 23.107
herefore *adv.* because of this 5.150
heryng *n.* praise 5.1225 (*note*)
heryott *n.* payment by heirs to lord of manor on death of tenant 6.253
herita(i)ge *n.* inheritance 3.60, 9.14, 28.20, spiritual inheritance 5.249
herken *v.* listen attentively 31.2476
hermeles *see* **harmeles**
herryd *adj.* haired 27.201
hertely *adj.* heartfelt 31.3059
hervest *n.* autumn 31.245
hette *v.pa.* heated 16.104
heueryth *v.pr.3sg.* hangs in the air 27.163
hevenlynes *n.* state of being heavenly 31.1745(*note*)
hevy(e *adj.* sorrowful 1.816, 3.887, 16.158, 18.43, 28.33, troubled 7.64, 26.121, 28.896, troublesome 28.606, 30.100, grievous 31.1218
hevynes(se *n.* sorrow, anxiety 1.245, 2.48, 3.751, 10.46, 16.242, 20.9, 29.1282, 30.307, 31.426
hevynnes *n.pl.* heavens 29.101, 164, 232
hewe *v.* cut into shape 31.734
hyder *adv.* to the present time 31.1637
hydly *adv.* secretly 3.728
hydousness *n.* horror 5.800
hye *adj.* an *h-* on high 16.117
hye *v.* hasten 5.490; *imp.* 3.852, 26.545; **highed** *pa.* 26.114; *pa.p.* paid attention 3.369
hight *v.pa.* was named 1.8, 3.468, 7.2, 9.2, 10.4, etc.
hilde *see* **holde**
hynder *adj.* rear 26.482
hyng *see* **hong**
hyre *see* **here** *v.*
hoke *n.* hook 14.109; *pl.* 3.416, 733, 22.53, 23.55
holde *v.* detain 29.473; *h- with* be loyal to 28.610; **holdeste** *pr.2sg.* consider 28.724, 31.1407; **holdist** 26.467; **holdyn** *pr.pl.* hold, sponsor 5.968 (*note*); **helde** *pa.* were loyal to 31.1774; **hilde** 28.483, 28.1223, held 1.996, 3.350, 14.40, main-

tained 28.302; **holde** *pa.p.* 5.661; obeyed 28.359, considered 29.1193, held 31.1444; **holden for** regarded as 31.274
ho(o)l(l)e *adj.* whole, sound 17.35, 20.42, 29.1157; *made h-* cured 30.246, healthy 31.1848
hole *adv.* wholly 6.172, 31.1015
ho(o)l(l)y *adv.* wholly 1.1359, 28.1223, 29.1019
holpist *pa.2sg.* helped 1.131; **holpe** *pa.* 3.493, 6.250, 11.62, 15.55; *pa.p.* 1.1252, 29.848; **holpyn** 1.971, 3.815; **holpen** 31.999
holsom(e *adj.* beneficial 3.133, 30.395, 31.1319
holsomly *adv.* safely 3.2
hondelyng *see* **handel**
honest *adj.* virtuous 29.1153, honourable 31.2366
honestly(e *adv.* richly 1.788, reverently 5.932, respectfully 31.1537
hong *v.pr.* hang 26.417; **heng** *pa.* 7.73; **hyng(e** 14.108, 15.18, 26.411, 31.3086; **hong(e** *pa.p.* 3.567, 7.72; **hongen** 31.3099; **hanged** 31.3092
ho(o)r(e *adj.* white 1.1177, 26.191, 26.458, 27.172
hoost *n.* eucharistic wafer 5.454
hope *v.pr.* expect 5.900, believe 29.580
horryd *v.pa.* abhorred 29.1170
hoste *see* **oste** *n*[1], *n*[2]
hosteler *n.* person in charge of guests 20.47
hovyd *v.pa.* waited 31.2476
howge *adj.* huge 31.2689
howselid *v.pa.p.* given the eucharist 4.272, 16.96
howsylle *n.* the holy communion, eucharist 31.2223
humors *n.pl.* fluids 1.573
husbondeman *n.* householder, head of family 3.922
huswyfe *n.* woman in charge of household 31.769

ibore *see* **bere** *v.*
idelle *adj.* foolish 29.136, lazy 29.137
ydilnes *n.* laziness 14.28; *in y-*, useless 6.169
ye *n.* eye 29.208; **yene** *pl.* 7.114; **eyen** 1.550, 29.201; **eien** 31.1525; **eeyen** 31.126; **ey3en** 31.714; **eyhen** 31.771; **yehen** 31.803; **iyen** 31.1337

ylle *adj.* wicked, sinful 31.51
illudid *ppl.adj.* deceived 1.448
illumyned *pa.p.* spiritually enlightened 5.272
ymage *n.* effigy 1.1233, 24.190, statue 4.262, 6.60, 16.49, 31.1183
ymaginacions *n.pl.* fancies 27.40
ympne *n.* hymn 5.324; **ympnus** *pl.* 3.738
importable *adj.* difficult or impossible to pay 1.112 (*note*)
impressyd *pa.p.* fixed 29.772
impressyon *n.* picture 24.155
impropred *pa.p.* assigned 31.537
inclynyng *vbl.n.* bowing in worship 5.266
indignacion *n.* displeasure 28.223
indurate *adj.* obdurate 1.871
infect *v.pa.* afflicted 30.247
infyrmyte *n.* moral weakness 5.1112
inflate *adj.* puffed up, proud 1.195
influence *n.* power of stars and planets over earthly bodies 31.853
informacion *n.* teaching 31.340, 1970; **enformacion** advice 31.773
info(u)rme *v.* instruct, teach 1.863, 2.76, 3.236, 5.1006; **enforme** tell 1.528, instruct 31.447; **informyd** *pa.* 3.90; **enformyd** 2.11, 30.128, told 28.630
infortune *n.* bad luck 31.427
inioyned *see* **enioyne**
inowh *adj.* enough 31.807
inow *adv.* enough 31.1240
inquyraunce *n.* inquiry 3.330
insensible *adj.* incapable of sensation 31.310, 1289
ynsolent *adj.* disreputable 29.1437
instaunce *n.* insistence 29.597, 31.2406, entreaty 31.3187
intysingis *n.pl.* enticings 3.36
invencyon *n.* finding, discovery 31.2066, 2070
yrked *v.impers.pa.* wearied 29.459
ironge *v.pa.p.* rung 3.326
islayne *see* **sle(e**
ysope *n.* hyssop 5.1333

iangle *v.* gossip 3.589
iangelynge *vbl.n.* chattering 30.247, 31.1344
ieberdye *n.* dangerous situation 31.1150; **ieopardy** 1.354, 3.340
iebet(t) *see* **gibette**
iewes *n.* punishment, judicial sentence

putte hym to his i- sentenced him 31.2192 (*note*)
iocunde *adj.* joyful 31.685; *as n.* pleasant 31.2731
yoye *n.* joy 29.656
ioy(e *v.* rejoice 24.148, 30.236, 31.3095; *pr.pl.* 29.188; **ioieth** *imp.* 29.844; **io(i)yng** *pr.p.* 23.30, 29.320; **ioyed** *pa.* 6.35
ioyned *v.pa.* enjoined 1.375; **iunyng** *pr.p.* joining 1.916
iowelle *n.* jewel 31.1698
iuged *v.pa.p.* condemned 31.2646
iugement *n.* punishment 3.384, assessment 28.258
iunctures *n.pl.* joints 31.3148
iunyng *see* **ioyned**
iuse *n.* sap 20.40
iustelye *adv.* righteously 3.92
iustice *n.* punishment 31.2906; **iustise** judge 21.4
iuuent *adj.* young 24.32 (*note*)

kalender *n.* model 5.128
karres *n.pl.* wagons 31.2698
karyon *n.* rotten flesh 31.1500
kast *v.pa.* *k- vpon* put on 30.210 (*note*)
kendelid *v.pa.p.* set alight 1.34; **kyndelid** 1.157, 3.404
kepe *n.* *nought take k-* paid no attention 29.836; *take not k-* am not careful, do not bother 29.916
kepe *v.* observe 3.280, 26.104, care for 20.28, 29.684, remain in 26.221, withhold 31.610, preserve 31.1692, guard 31.2170, uphold 31.2424; **kepith** *pr.3sg.* preserves 5.975; **keping(e** *pr.p.* watching over 31.1169, observing 31.2117; **kept(e** *pa.* observed 3.288, attended 13.103, guarded 8.29, 31.2169, watched over 16.260, cared for 20.25, 31.2793, preserved 29.1136, provided for 30.429; *pa.p.* preserved 16.116, 22.103
keper *n.* custodian 3.708, 31.2529, gatekeeper 29.1217 (*note*), attendant 31.2383; *k- vp* sustainer 31.770; *pl.* attendants 3.632, custodians 30.277; gaolers 29.1139; **kepars** 31.1199
kerchyr *n.* woman's headcloth 16.111, handkerchief 28.731
kernels *n.pl.* pathological lumps, tumours 1.452; **kyrnels** 1.572
kynde *n.* nature 5.777, 27.255, 29.158,

31.239, sort 5.582, natural behaviour 31.74; *pl.* sexes 31.1106
kynd(e *adj.* natural 27.141, 29.208
kyndely *adv.* naturally 5.918, 31.2684
kyndelid *see* **kendelid**
kyne *n.pl.* cows 7.22
kynred(e *n.* family 11.2, race 31.2256; **kynraddis** *n.pl.* tribes 5.1072 (*note*)
kyrnels *see* **kernels**
kytte *v.pa.p.* cut 25.15, 31.2276
knytteth *v.pr.* unites 31.569; **knyt(te** *pa.p.* 31.560, 1206; **knette** linked 6.89
knowe *v.* acknowledge 28.479
knowlech(e *v.* acknowledge 29.417, confess 29.1091, 31.2646; **knowlyche** reveal 29.164; **knoleched** *pa.* professed 21.54; **knowlechid** declared 22.21, 23.25, admitted 31.2589
konnyng *see* **connyng** *n.*
kunne *v.* know by heart 5.437 (*note*)
kunnyngeste *see* **connyng** *ppl.adj.*

laborious *adj.* burdensome 31.2082
laboure *v.* work 13.44; **labouryd** *pa.* 10.7, 18.25, urged 6.64
lad *v.pa.* *l- lyff* lived 6.19, 9.89, 11.11; **ladde** led 11.48
lade *v.pa.p.* laden 29.1382
lay *n.* religious practice 31.1471 (*note*), religion 31.1716 (*note*)
lay(e *adj.* non clerical 1.342, 3.195, 5.118, 28.189
layser *see* **leyser**
lake *v.* lack 6.30; **lakkyd** *pa.* 16.137, 31.2550
langage *n.* discussion 24.59
lappid *v.pa.p.* wrapped 1.1184
large *adj.* generous 1.184, 3.519, 31.531; *at more l-* freer to move 31.1492
largely(e *adv.* liberally 1.963, 5.914, 16.212, 28.707, 31.466
largenesse *n.* liberality 5.840
lasseth *v.pr.3sg.* reduces 29.297
lat(e *see* **let**
late *adv.* recently 13.24, 28.74; *l- afore* shortly before 1.353
laude *n.* praise 1.357, 3.222, 5.91 etc. *pl.* 31.1046
Laudes *n.pl.* Lauds, the second Hour of the daily Office 5.565
lavatory(e *n.* washbasin 4.124, bath 31.846 (*note*), 31.940
lave *v.* bale 13.114

lavours *n.pl.* washbasins 31.819
lawghyng *ppl.adj.* laughing, cheerful 31.2243; **lawhyng** 27.201; **lough** *pa.* 1.448
lazar *n.* leper, diseased person 7.121
leche *n.* physician 3.610, 5.858
lecherous *adj.* dissolute 5.1138 (*note*)
lectrine *n.* lectern 5.372
lecture *n.* knowledge from books 29.142; **letture** 31.124
lede *v.pa.p.* laid 21.28
leene *v.* incline 31.1319
lefe *n.* permission 31.507
left(e *see* **leve** *v.²*
le(e)ful(le *adj.* legitimate 3.42, 28.525, 29.118, 31.288
legat(e *n.* ecclesiastic invested with papal authority 28.667
legende *n.* account of a saint's life 4.233
leyged *v.pa.* cited 29.814
leyne *see* **lithe**
leyser *n.* opportunity 29.177; **leysor** 31.662; **layser** *be long l-* taking plenty of time 31.1473
leke as *adv.* in the way that 6.270
leke *v.pr.* like 12.13
lekenes *n.* likeness 11.51
lemman *n.* lover 9.22
lene *v.pr.* lend 6.259
lenger *comp.adj.* longer 3.747, 13.47; *comp. adv.* 1.1345, 7.5, 26.51 etc.
lentis *n.pl.* forty-day indulgences 4.17
lernyd *v.pa.p.* taught 5.129, 29.192
lese *v.* lose 1.37, 6.288, 7.110, 13.75 etc. *to l- hymselfe* to be damned 3.618; **lesith** *pr.3sg.* loses 31.593; **lesyng** *vbl.n.* losing 24.184
lesyng(e *n.* lie, falsehood 5.673, 31.2355; **lesyngis** *pl.* idle tales 31.270
leste *superl.adj.* smallest 31.259, lowest in rank 31.2571
let(te *v.¹* hinder 1.934, 3.725, stop 5.104, 28.275, 29.207, prevent 15.11, 28.102, deprive 31.753, restrain 31.1786; **let(t** hinder 5.1040, 26.428, 31.1093; **lettyn** *pr.pl.* 5.869; **let** *imp.* stop 1.434; **lette** *pa.* restrained 6.184; **lettid** prevented 3.496, 5.330; **let** *pa.p.* 30.17; **lette** 1.685; **lettyd** 7.95
let(e *v.²* allow 1.438, 28.520, 31.2055; **lat** *imp.* let 31.986; **let(e** 10.38, 19.26, 31.987; *pa.* caused to, ordered to 1.106, 2.7, 6.263, 12.29, 13.133 etc., **late** 14.40;

lettyth goo by dismisses from his thoughts 31.396

letewse *n.* lettuce 5.633

letture *see* **lecture**

levacion *n.* elevation of the consecrated host at mass 1.296

leve *v.*[1] live 1.15, 5.547, 6.22, 9.8, 13.75; *to l- by* to subsist on 6.215; **leuest** *pr.2sg.* live 6.48; **levid** *pa.* 2.59, 9.15, 20.73, 26.66, 29.22

leve *v.*[2] leave 14.90, leave off 3.672, 29.776, abandon 31.317; **levyth** *pr.3sg.* 29.844; **levyng** *pr.p.* setting aside 29.708, departing from 29.996; **left(e** *pa.* gave up 3.260, remained 31.1686, *l- of* desisted 6.72; *l- not* did not desist from 25.6; *pa.p.* disregarded 28.296

leuer *comp.adv.* had *l-* would rather 5.1283, 7.110, 28.364, 29.1192, 31.1330

levyd *v.*[3] *pa.* believed 11.53

leuyng *vbl.n.* living 6.88, 13.57, 14.11, 17.16

levys *n.pl.* leaves 11.90, 18.67, 26.259

lewde *adj.* lay 28.268

lewdenes *n.* wickedness 31.1600

li(bra *n.* pound sterling 28.398; pound weight of 12 ounces 6.21

licence *n.* permission 30.103, 31.659; **lysens** 16.131, 26.189; **lycens** 26.209, 28.256

lyfelode *n.* property, rent, income 1.378, 3.63, property 5.780, living 27.200

light *adj.*[1] *makith l-* heals 5.1024

light *adj.*[2] bright 26.258 (*note*)

light *v.* dismount 16.183; *pa.* 1.766, 10.74, 30.362, 31.2992, mounted 28.533

light(e)ly(e *adv.* easily 1.1285, 3.92, carelessly 5.1313

lightnes *v.pr.2sg.* enlightens 31.436; **lyghten** *imp.* 3.360; **lightned** *pa.p.* 31.126

lyke *adj.* similar 11.79, 27.7

lyke *adv.* equally 7.134, similarly 27.238; **lyche** alike 29.362

liked *v.pa.* licked 20.66

lykyng *vbl.n.* delight 5.1434 (*note*)

likyth *v.impers.pr.3sg.* pleases 31.236; **lyke** 31.1125; **liked** *pa.* 31.962; *refl.pa.* 31.1876

lymmes *n.pl.* arms of the sea 27.176, bodily organs 27.217

lypsyng *adj.* lisping 29.100

lystis *n.pl.* desires 3.616

lyst(e *v.pr.* choose 29.443, 31.286; **lystyst** *pr.2sg.* 3.280

lithe *v.pr.3sg.* lies 17.57, 18.103, 27.229; **leyne** *pa.p.* lain 30.190

lyve *n. on l-* alive 6.313

lyvarys *n.pl.* those who live 29.1433

lyuer *n.* liver 27.217

lofe *n.* love 5.799

logge *v.* accommodate 28.1265; **logged** *pa.p.* housed for the night 29.1041, 31.2521

loggyng *n.* lodging 28.427

lokid *v.pa. l- aftir* looked towards 26.174

lollardys *n.* heretics 29.1434

longe *v.* pertain 31.530; **longyth** *pr.3sg.* belongs 5.1486, 28.212, pertains 15.37; *pl.* 29.80; **longyng** *pr.p.* affiliated with, belonging to the household of 3.183, 28.915; **longed** *pa.* pertained 31.2625

lo(o)re *n.* teaching 3.102, 31.483

lordiship *n.* authority 14.93 (*note*)

lose *n.* loss 1.197

lose *v.* release 1.408; **loseth** *pr.imp.* 31.2941; **losid** *pa.* 1.424, 3.126; *pa.p.* 4.345; **lousyd** 4.350; **losyng** *vbl.n.* 3.370

lothe *adj.* reluctant 16.138, 31.1161; **lother** *comp.* 31.987

lothesom *adj.* disgusted 31.404 (*note*)

lough *see* **lawghyng**

lousyd *see* **lose** *v.*

lovers *n.pl.* friends 1.956, followers 31.472

lovly *see* **lowlye**

lowe *adj.* weak 5.738, 28.137

lowlye *adv.* humbly 1.774; **lovly** 31.410

lust(e *n.* desire 5.684, 6.72, 9.63, 14.44, 27.199; *pl.* 6.71, 27.48, 29.943, 31.326

lusty *adj.* pleasure-loving 31.322

mageste *n.* power 31.1585

magnefie *v.* praise 1.966; **magnyfied** *pa.* 31.471; *pa.p.* made famous 31.2447, praised 31.1024

mayne *see* **meyne**

maister *n.* teacher 3.256, 16.14, 31.499, one who has control over another 16.38; *pl.* teachers 3.94, master craftsmen 31.834

maystres *n.* female patron saint 31.3046

maistry *n.* pre-eminence 31.1003

man *n.* servant 7.10

manaclis *n.pl.* handcuffs 30.347

maner *n.* manor 28.221, 31.3132; *pl.* tenanted farms 28.322
manerly *adv.* politely 31.2243
manhode *n.* manly virtue 31.73
manyplis *n.pl.* eucharistic vestments worn over priests' arms, maniples 5.205
manly *adv.* resolutely 30.233
manqueller *n.* murderer 31.49
mansleer *n.* murderer 16.121
mansleyng *n.* murder 5.714
mantelle *n.* sleeveless overgarment 1.261, 2.86; *pl.* 29.365
mare *n.* incubus 27.23
maryed *v.pa.p.* given in marriage 3.33, 7.108, 22.22
mased *ppl.adj.* bewildered 31.1561
mater *n.* pus 1.1348, 28.779, import 29.1159, physical substance 31.369, story 31.2278; **matir** subject of dispute 28.309; *pl.* subjects of discussion 31.698, subjects of dispute 28.367; *m- of suspesyon* occasions of, causes of wrongdoing 30.335
Matyns *n.* the first Hour of the daily Office, usually including Lauds 5.549
maunde *n.* basket 22.116
mawme(n)t *n.* representation of pagan deity, idol 24.103; **mawmetes** *pl.* 31.134; **mawmettys** 31.336
mawmetrie *n.* worship of pagan deities 31.1267; **mawmetry** 24.7
meane *n.* method 3.843, 31.223, intercessor 31.2376; *pl.* intercessions 31.20, representations 31.765, methods 3.545, 31.1069; *made meanys* interceded 1.279
meche *adj.* many 11.27, 28.1000, much 14.114, 26.400, 27.110, 28.1021; **myche** 27.101, many 30.113; **moche** 1.40, 3.228, 28.1264
mede *n.*[1] reward 5.693, 15.52, 16.39, 21.66, 28.898 etc.
mede *n.*[2] meadow 3.214, 28.953
medlid *v.pa.* mixed 3.786, 27.213, 28.1095; **medelid** *ppl.adj.* 1.191
meyne *n.* retinue 1.767, 30.128, 31.2486, religious community 1.1300 (*note*), company 9.19, household 31.469; **mayne** 31.807; **meny** retinue 18.127
meke *adj.* unaggressive 27.199, 30.75
mekyth *v.pr.3sg.refl.* humbles 4.364; **mekid** *pa.p.* chastened 5.1218
membre *n.* limb 5.417; **membris** *pl.* 1.1209, 3.569, 27.30, 31.2702

memorie *n.* renown 31.1953
menable *adj.* moderate 26.536
mende *n.* mind 6.164
mene *n.* intermediate state 31.244
menydde *v.pa.* meant 7.43
merchandyse *n.* possessions 9.14
merciable *adj.* merciful 3.122
merely *adv.* joyfully 6.241, pleasantly 26.90; **meryly** joyfully 26.137
merke *v. refl.* cross oneself 5.451
mesel *n.* person afflicted with disfiguring skin disease 28.1242
mesylle *adj. m- man* someone suffering from leprosy or other disfiguring skin disease 9.82
mesurably *adv.* moderately 4.368
mesure *n.* moderation 5.845, prudence 5.1044
mete *n.* food 3.535, 4.368, 5.517, 6.220, 18.92 etc. *pl.* 5.631; *angels m-* manna 4.66; *Lente m-* food prescribed for any period of fasting 6.222; *went to m-* went to eat 14.108
meteles *adj.* without food 24.78
mevable *adj.* changing 31.237
meue *v.* move 26.113; **meove** 26.509; **me(e)vid** *pa.* urged 3.607; *pa.p.* moved 30.10
myche *see* **meche**
mydmorowe *n.* mid-morning 29.588
myght(e)ly *adv.* strongly 28.362, 31.1589
mylche *adj. m- kyne* cows providing milk 7.60
mynde *n.* remembrance 5.999, 29.438, mind 5.1028, 29.772, mention 29.776; *oute of m-* from time immemorial 28.864; *haue m- to* remember 5.676, 29.242
mynysh *v.* diminish 1.1181
myre *n.* swamp 11.58, 18.143; *pl.* 11.56
myryer *comp.adj.* merrier 26.134
myschef(f)(e *n.* trouble 16.42, wickedness 18.82, misfortune 27.152, 29.1220, 31.1867; *bringe to m-* bring to ruin 28.486
myschevous *adj.* painful 31.50
mysdo *v.pa.p.* done wrong or harm to 28.587
misdoer *n.* malefactor 28.182
myslyvarys *n.pl.* those leading an evil life 29.1446
mysrulid *ppl.adj.* badly-behaved 3.594
mysse *n.* exception 31.547
mysterye *n.* hidden religious symbolism

31.1074, hidden spiritual significance 31.2280

mo(o *comp.adj.* more 2.47, 3.801, 23.127, 27.116, 28.302 etc.

moyster *n.* bodily fluid 27.191

mordrement *n.* murder 31.39

mordryd *v.pa.p.* murdered 10.33

more *comp. adj.* greater 5.1431, 6.18, 27.60, 29.336; *adv.* again 9.34; **moor** *n.* more 26.543

moreyn *n.* murrain, cattle disease 1.744

moryn *n.* morning 23.58

moryng *n.* increase 29.233

morne *v.* mourn 1.737

mornyng *n.* mourning 5.397, 16.11 (*note*), lamentation 8.41, 26.13, anxiety 9.77

mornyng *adj.* sorrowful 28.77, 30.390

mornyngly *adv.* regretfully 30.121

morowe *n.* morning 1.501, 3.239, 11.65, 29.487

mo(o)st(e *superl.adj.* greatest 1.129, 5.546, 16.192, 28.383, 31.38, *as n.* highest in rank 31.2571

motes *n.pl.* specks of dust 31.1688

mowe *v.* be able to 29.210; *pr.2sg.* maiste may 5.880, 31.1405; *pr.sg.* may 28.478, 31.206; myght 31.1420

mowes *n.pl.* grimaces 29.1197

mowyng *v.pr.p.* grimacing 27.267

mowly *adj.* mouldy 28.1053

muse *v.pr.* ponder 31.176; *pa.* musyd 31.185; *vbl.n.* musynge 31.183

nas *v.pa.* was not 30.54

nat *n.* nothing 29.562

nature *n.* natural law 31.74

naville *n.* navel 31.955

neder *see* nether

nedid *v.impers.pa.* was necessary 6.30

neyburgh *n.* neighbour 31.1063

neyde *n.* compulsory tax 1.204 (*note*)

neighed *v.pa.* approached 31.2128; neyhed 29.1310

nerehand *adv.* almost, nearly 31.955

nerre *adv.* nearer 29.1035

neshe *adj.* soft 27.201

netheles *adv.* nevertheless 31.51

nether *adj.* lower 5.192; **neder** 5.184; *n-ende* anus 30.212

newe *adv.* newly 28.219

next(e *superl.adj.* nearest 27.77, 30.299, 31.3121

ny(e *adv.* almost 3.785, 25.8, 26.112, 28.29, closely 30.29

nye *adj.* close 26.107, 30.37; *n- kynne* close relative 1.172

nye, nygh *prep.* near 31.613, 3090

nyl *v.imp. negative* (= ne wyl) do not 5.1179

nyse *adj.* foolish 14.36

noble *adj. as n.* nobility 5.777 (*note*)

nobley *n.* nobility of nature, dignity 5.1340

noyce *n.* outcry 31.2553

noye *v.* harm 5.733, 16.199, 26.435; *pr.pl.* noyen afflict 5.8; *pr.p.* noiyng 31.1498

nombrid *v.pa.p.* counted 4.52

nonys *n. for the n-* for the occasion 28.441

noote *v.pr.* do not know 29.792

norysshid *v.pa.p.* consumed 1.1254 (*note*), brought up, raised 3.11

norsher *n.* provider of nourishment 27.155 (*note*)

not *pron.* nought, nothing 31.804

notable *adj.* noteworthy 3.332, 28.1282

notably *adv.* in noteworthy manner 30.88

notefied *ppl.adj.* made known 31.2236

nothyng *adv.* not at all 3.442, 6.230

notis *n.pl.* nuts 28.591

nought *adv.* not 31.2426

o(o *num.* one 5.1349, 7.24, 28.249, 31.1345

obedience *n.* submission 30.126

obey *v.refl.* submit 28.672

obyte *n.* death 3.472

occian *n.* the sea surrounding the world 26.14, 27.174

office *n.* required duty 5.1003, 25.26, 29.1352

officers *n.pl.* officials 30.336, 31.1579

oyselle *n.* vinegar 4.140 (*note*)

olde *adj.* former 1.1121

on *num.* one 15.41, 20.40, 26.69, 27.8, 28.189

on *pron.* a person 14.63, 17.67, 26.202, a certain 28.618

oneth *see* vnneth(es

onys *adv.* once 6.29, 9.29; *at o-* simultaneously 14.4, 18.141

onware *see* vnware(s

oon(e)ly *adv.* exclusively 31.95

open *v.* reveal 31.350; opyn 1.1175; opened *pa.* 24.40, 31.353; opnyd 28.551 (*note*); openyd *pa.p.* 3.683

openyng *vbl.n.* revealing 5.1534

opyn *adj.* known 3.39, 28.482, notorious 5.774
oppresse *v.* rape 2.23; **oppressid** *pa.* 31.2642; *ppl.adj.* smothered 31.2697
oppression *n.* smothering 31.2703
opteynid *v.pa.* captured, intercepted (?) 1.1020 (*note*)
or *prep.* before 1.119, 3.68, 5.517, 6.118, 9.92 etc.; **ar** 6.72, 13.53, 20.52, 27.128
ordeyne *v.* provide 26.214, 29.73; **ordeynid** *pa.* allotted 1.7, 26.89, 31.184, destined 1.133, 26.84, 31.240, established, instituted 2.2, 3.52, 27.55, 29.78 etc., provided 3.76, 26.299, 29.79, gave orders 3.512, 4.271, 29.536, invested with holy orders 5.1003, commanded 31.1084, prepared 31.1658; **ordeigned** *pa.p.* prepared 11.71
ordinaunce *n.* ordering 29.347, establishment 31.178
ordir *n.* priestly orders 5.1002; **ordre** 28.186; *by o-* in sequence 9.50, 30.389
ordrid *v.pa.p.* invested with holy orders 5.1003
orisons *n.pl.* prayers 14.31
orphalyns *n.pl.* orphans 1.352 (*note*)
osprynge *n.* progeny 26.48
oste *n.*[1] army, troops 1.694, 31.1772; **hoste** 11.34
oste *n.*[2] lodgings 28.429; **hoste** 28.400, 716
oste *n.*[3] host (of lodgings) 6.64
ostr(y)e *n.* inn 31.2521, 31.2535
other *conj.* either 1.695, or 24.35, 27.205, 28.280
otyr *n.* otter 26.482; *pl.* 20.66
outerage *adj.* violent 1.167
outeragyous *adj.* very dangerous 3.454
ouerchargid *v.pa.p.* overburdened 1.710
ouergylte *ppl.adj.* gilded 4.263
ouerhelyng *vbl.n.* covering 5.1330 (*note*)
ouerkeueryd *v.pa.* overshadowed 26.29
ouerled *v.* defeat 28.1035
overpassed *ppl.adj.* past 31.1679
ouerplewse *n.* surplus 6.24 (*note*)
ouerpressyng *vbl.n.* oppression 1.59
ouerseen *v.pa.p.* *were o-* were mistaken 3.80
ouersprad *v.pa.* overshadowed 24.26
overswomen *v.pa.p.* swum across 31.270
ovyn *n.* oven 16.104
owches *n.pl.* pins, necklaces, buckles, clasps 31.805
owest *v.pr.2sg.* ought 24.142, 29.617;

owist 5.656; **oweth** *pr.3sg.* 31.259; **owith** 3.668, 5.669; **owe** *pr.pl.* 5.61; **owyd** *pa.* *o- but little favour* had only little goodwill 30.334

paynid *v.pa.* *p- hymselfe* mortified himself 1.1340
paynym(e *n.* non-christian, pagan 3.5, 31.54; *pl.* 1.755, 13.4, 22.29, 24.70
palfray *n.* fine riding-horse (as opposed to war-horse) 28.1228; **palfrey** 28.534
palle *n.* archiepiscopal vestment, *pallium* 28.132, altar cloth 30.284; *pl.* shrouds 1.961
palme *n.* palm leaf, emblem of victory 31.2091
pals(e)y *n.* paralysis, shaking palsy 31.967
pament(e *n.* paved or tiled floor 3.430, 5.29, 31.1461
panyer *n.* basket 23.108
pappis *n.pl.* breasts 31.1482
paramour *n.* lover 31.870
parauenture *adv.* perhaps 1.1216, 28.961, 31.1227
pardon *n.* indulgence 4.*rubric*; *gret p-* plenary indulgence 28.1260
paryl *n.* peril 26.323; **parellys** *pl.* 23.98; **perellys** 23.101
partide *v.pa.* departed 26.344
partye *n.* region 8.1; *pl.* 3.39; *in p-* in a manner (?) 31.862
partyners *n.pl.* sharers 31.2110
partyng *vbl.n.* division 7.132
pas *n.* speed 28.583; **pace** 16.182
pascalle *n.* paschal candle 5.597
passand *adv.* exceedingly 31.293; **passyng** 31.64
passed *v.pa.* died 31.2226; **passith** *pr.3sg.* surpasses 5.1171, 31.538
passion *n.* pain, suffering 16.238; *pl.* 31.1451
pax(e *n.* plaque kissed by the priest and congregation during celebration of mass 5.466, 28.970
peas(e *n.* peace 1.2, 31.1064
pe(a)sible *adj.* peace-loving 1.7, 5.829, at peace with 31.1062
pece *n.* wine cup 31.2590; *pl.* fragments 31.1038
peyne *n.* suffering 5.1025, penalty 5.1167
pelers *n.pl.* supporters 3.237, pillars 4.70; **pylers** 31.942

pensiful *adj.* thoughtful 27.195
percels *n.pl.* payments 1.218
perylous *adj.* spiritually dangerous 1.1196
perypatetykis *n.pl.* sect of philosophers following the teaching of Aristotle 31.334
person(e *n.* parson, parish priest 14.75, 28.293, 31.3048; *pl.* 5.1243, 13.74
personage *n.* parsonage 14.76
pertable *adj.* *p- of* able to share in 3.125 (*note*)
pesibly *adv.* peacefully 1.103, 3.494
pestylence *n.* bubonic plague 1.1042
petye *n.* piety 5.862
picche *v.* drive (a stake) 18.63; **pyght** *pa.* drove 11.87, 18.66; thrust 28.1099
pilgrymaigis *n.pl.* places to which pilgrimages are made 3.475
pynyth *v.pr.* endure pain 27.31
pystelle *n.* letter 29.189, treatise 29.808; **pistles** *pl.* passages from the epistles to be read at mass 29.79
pyte *n.* piety 3.235
pytefulle *adj.* merciful 29.524
pitevous *adj.* pitiable 1.353, compassionate 31.77
pitevously *adv.* pitiably 16.131, 31.1513
pytuoslye *adv.* in a manner arousing pity 11.68
pytte *n.* underground chamber 4.162, well 4.294, abyss 16.26, 25.47, 31.1601, hole in ground 18.60, 31.3202; *pl.* caves 21.37
place *n.* house 3.142, 16.60, manor house 31.2123, location 31.2126
play *n.* game 31.1477; **pleys** *pl.* 20.7
playne *adj.* full 4.154
plat *adv.* *p- est* due east 26.76
ple(e *n.* lawsuit 28.271, 288
pledid(e *v.pa.* litigated, brought suit 14.86, 28.268; *pa.p.* 28.272
pleyn(e *adj.*[1] level 3.408, 30.53
pleyn *adj.*[2] explicit 31.1
pleynly *adv.* certainly, 29.171, 31.1888, explicitly 30.16, **playnly** certainly 28.521
plener *adj.* *p- remyssyon* complete forgiveness 24.186
plentefulle *adv.* abundantly 1.97
plentevous *adj.* generous 3.519, 31.1475
plentevously *adv.* plentifully 31.1969
plesaunce *n.* gratification 3.48, 6.171
plesaunte *adj.* pleasing 31.710

plesyng *vbl.n.* satisfaction 21.12, pleasure 21.17, 28.913
plesure *n.* *do hym p-* do him a service 18.85
plite *n.* condition, plight 18.96
plited *v.pa.p.* pledged 31.2742
pollutyd *v.pa.p.* desecrated 3.314
poste *n.* authority 31.551
postome *n.* festering sore 1.1333; **postym** 5.849
potacions *n.pl.* drinks 31.1582
power *n.* capacity 2.62, ability 16.87; *be of p-* can afford 5.691; *was not of p-* could not afford *or* had not authority 15.38 (*note*)
praty *adj.* charming, pleasant 31.1710
prebendis *n.pl.* estates from which the stipends of cathedral officials are provided 6.226
precepte *n.* commandment 5.1364
preciosite *n.* reverence 31.1921 (*note*), 31.2048
preysable *adj.* good 29.831, 31.329
prese *n.* crowd, throng 3.724, 28.1266
presencial *adj.* being present 31.526 (*note*)
prevay(l)le *v.* succeed 1.1179, 3.418; **prevaylid** *pa.* proved superior 1.3
preve *v.* test 1.209, 31.788, prove by test 31.1296; **preveth** *pr.3sg.* proves 31.1666; **preved** *pa.p.* investigated 31.415
prevely *adv.* secretly 6.295, 31.276; **previlye** 3.27; **pryvely** 28.332, 31.76; **pryueleche** 28.556; **pryuyly** 24.72
prev(e)y *adj.* secret, private 1.1040, 28.1105, 31.342
previlegid *ppl.adj.* endowed with special rights or immunities 4.2
previlegis *n.pl.* special rights or immunities 1.536; **priueleges** 15.10
prevyte(e *n.* divine secret 6.145; **pryvite** 26.463; *pl.* 26.544, mysteries 29.149
prykkes *n.pl.* spikes 24.89; **pryckis** prickles 8.22
prise *n.* value 28.1067; *litel p-* slight honour 17.42; *settist no p- of* despise 28.1067
processe *n.* *in p-* in the course of time 31.2035
procuratour *n.* provider 26.521
professyd *v.pa.* *was p-* made vows for entry into religious order 7.117
profite *n.* spiritual benefit 3.375

promytte *v.* hold out hope of 30.296; *pa.* promised 31.2148

promote *v.* advance 29.526 (*note*)

prophite *n.* benefit 31.83

proporcion *n.* shape, likeness 31.175; *pl.* 31.167

proposicion *n.* *brede of p-* shewbread of the Temple 4.67

propre *adj.* own 1.876, 28.299; **propyr** specific 29.78; *his p- persone* himself 1.393; *p- place* allotted position 3.81

propurly *adv.* intrinsically 31.220, correctly 31.511, in strict terms 31.535

propurte *n.* nature 31.107, *after his p-* according to his nature 31.241

prosperyte *n.* well-being 29.971

prothonary *n.* (for prothonotary) principal notary 24.168

provided *v.pa.* planned 31.935

provision *n.* providence 3.18

publican *n.* tax collector 5.277

puyssaunce *n.* force 31.2594

purchased *v.pa.p.* obtained 31.2937

purgid *v.pa.p.* vindicated 1.1140, purified 29.458

purpour *n.* garment of royal purple 31.1152

purpur(e *adj.* purple 5.227, 23.107, 24.199; **purpil** 22.115

pursuer *n.* persecutor 31.64; *pl.* 29.523

pursuynge *vbl.n.* persecution 31.73

purtreyed *ppl.adj.* portrayed 31.128

puruey(e *v.* provide 1.83, 26.190, 30.436; make arrangements 10.83, 26.63; **purveyst** *pr.2sg.* provide 28.835; **purveyed** *pa.* made preparations 31.2376; provided 1.467; **purueyd** *pa.p.* 26.321

purvia(u)nce *n.* providence 2.83, 7.113, 10.49, 11.84, 14.7, 16.106 etc.

put *v.pa.* *p- theym vp* sheathed them 29.1063

qualite *n.* attribute, character 27.84

quarten *see* **feuer**

quenche *v.* extinguish 27.154; **quenchid** *pa.* 3.453, 31.325; **qwenchyd** *pa.p.* 30.228; **quenched** 26.240

quere, queer *n.* chancel, part of chancel where choir sings 3.706, 5.62, 26.221, 28.1088, choir 5.494, 28.1157

quyck(e *adj.* living 3.483, 26.252, 27.120, 28.1115 etc.; **qwycke** 31.2168; *adj. as n.* the living 5.948

quytte *v.* acquit 28.506; **quyte** pay 1.476; *q- hym ayene* pay him back 14.44; *pr.subj.* give 15.52, 21.65; **quitte** *pa.p.* released 28.111, acquitted 28.278; *ppl.adj.* free 28.415

quod *v.pa.* said 31.142 etc.

racke *n.* instrument of torture 31.2166 (*note*)

rad(de *see* **rede** *v.*¹

rakked¹ *v.pa.p.* tortured on a rack 31.2218

rakked² *v.pa.p.* pierced, injured 31.1438 (*note*)

rampyng *v.pr.p.* roaring 29.833 (*note*)

rather *comp. adv.* sooner, more quickly 1.737, 3.49, 5.459, etc., more willingly 6.287, 28.438, 29.902

ravisshid *v.pa.p.* raped 1.60, transported 1.832

ravynours *n.pl.* robbers 3.171; **ravenours** 3.176

ravysschynge *adj.* rapacious 29.804

reame *see* **reme**

rebelle *adj.* rebellious 30.368

recchid *v.pa.p.* stretched 1.451 (*note*)

recheles *adj.* reckless 17.30

recke *v.* care about 28.185; **rought** *v.pa.* 26.179

reclusyd *ppl.adj.* confined 23.34

recommendacion *n.* praise 31.1970

rede *adj.* red, purple 31.1152

rede *v.*¹ advise 28.473; **rad(de** *pa.* lectured 6.133, read 16.81, 18.142, 22.102, 28.541; *pa.p.* 1.567

rede *v.*² *pa.sg.* rode 16.187; **rydde** 30.378; **reden** *pa.pl.* 16.181

redely *adv.* certainly 31.1861

reende *v.* tear 29.773

refo(u)rme *v.* restore 3.294, 5.1309; **refourmed** *pa.p.* 1.93, corrected 3.286

refresshid *v.pa.* provided shelter and refreshment for 13.118

refusyd *v.pa.* rejected 30.206

refute *n.* refuge 3.359, 29.937

reherse *v.* recite 3.240; **reherce** reiterate 28.971; **rehersid** *pa.* told 3.284, 31.1634; *pa.p.* mentioned 1.668, 28.343; *ppl.adj.* 31.454

rehersynge *vbl.n.* repetition 31.3087

reynes *n.pl.* kidneys 3.506

reyne *v.* rule 25.49; **reynid** *pa.* 3.415

reken *v.* enumerate 31.156; **rekened** *pa.p.* counted 31.1634

rekenyng *vbl.n.* financial records 7.61, 28.94, settlement of account 28.387, account 28.405

rekyd *v.pa.* covered over, buried 6.23

relacyon *n.* report, account 29.176, relationship 31.579

religion *n.* religious life 31.2826; *woman of r-* nun 3.10

relygious *adj.* belonging to a religious order 6.136, 10.81, 13.29, 29.29; **relygeous** 2.51

reme *n.* realm 28.193; **reame** 1.80; **rewme** 28.118

renteste *v.pr.2sg.* tear 31.1482; **rente** *pa.p.* 31.1354

replenysshed *ppl.adj.* filled 24.22

repre(e)f(e *n.* complaint 3.287, shame 30.213, 31.1465, insult 29.1182; **reprofe** shame 1.578; **repreves** *pl.* insults 29.904

repreve *v.pr.* revile 30.219, rebuke, reproach 1.1093, 29.811; **reprevid** *pa.* accused 2.64; **reprovyd** censured 11.86; **repreved** 31.277

rere *v.imp.* raise 28.1108

reserue *v.* retain 3.476; **reserveth** *pr.3sg.* 31.1683

resigne *v.* give back 1.1132

reson *n.* reasoning 29.454; *pl.* 31.264

resonable *adj.* fitting, suitable 31.758, capable of reasoning 29.103, 31.1751

resorte *v.* go 3.29; **resortyng(e** *pr.p.* 3.327, 30.139; **resortid** *pa.* 3.731, 30.51

responde *n.* responsory, anthem consisting of versicles and responses 5.395

restyn *v.¹ pr.pl.* lie 4.112

reste *v.²* remain 30.207

reule *see* **rewle** *v.*

revolued *v.pa.* pondered 31.912

rewe *n.* by *r-* in turn 26.539; *by rowe* 26.200

rewle *n.* rule 28.124

rewle *v.* rule, govern 13.25, 28.117; **reule** 27.85; **rewlith** *pr.* 31.526; **rewlyd** *pa.* 6.266, 28.148; *pa.p.* 13.23

rewler *n.* leader 6.213, prominent person 16.31; **ruler** tutor 18.31 (*note*)

rewme *see* **reme**

rewthe *n.* *see* **ruthe** *n.*

rial *adj.* sumptuous 26.195; **r(o)yalle** magnificent 3.423, 31.738

ryally *adv.* sumptuously 3.499, 30.422

rialte *n.* elaborate ceremony 28.942, royalty 31.759

ribalde *n.* wicked person 31.2348

rychesses *n.pl.* possessions 24.10

right *adv.* *r- est* due East 26.102; **ri3t** very 31.1282

righted *v.pa.* straightened 31.3022

rightfulle *adj.* pious, virtuous 1.1125, just 29.744

rightis *n.pl.* last rites of the church 31.2404

rightwys(se *adj.* just 29.616, 30.392

rightwysly *adv.* justly 29.614

rightwysnes *n.* holiness 1.1126, 31.1330

roche *n.* rock 21.46

rode *n.* crucifix, rood 6.81, 14.88, 16.233; *r- lofte* gallery above chancel arch giving access to the rood 5.413

rootyd *v.pa.* rotted 28.1242

rote *n.* root 3.103; *pl.* 26.204

rotid *ppl.adj.* rooted 5.1219

rought *see* **recke**

rowe *see* **rewe**

rubbers *n.pl.* plunderers 1.859

rubbyd *v.pa.* plundered 8.13

ruddier *comp.adj.* fresher complexioned 31.1558

ruel *n.* pattern 31.1004

ruler *see* **rewler**

ruthe *adj.* pitiful 26.445

ruthe *n.* compassion 28.485, 31.1190; **rewthe**, calamity 28.680, pity 31.1403

ruthefully *adv.* sorrowfully 26.437

sacryd *v.pa.p.* consecrated 13.59, 19.5, 28.128

sacryng *vbl.n.* consecration of the host at mass 16.282

sadde *adj.* serious 1.191, 31.296, dignified 31.86, wise 31.481; **sadder** *comp.* steadier 1.707

sadly *adv.* resolutely 2.35, 3.249, 22.38, 23.41, certainly 31.423

sadnes *n.* seriousness 1.199

safe *prep.* except 29.1269, 31.83; **save** 31.677; **sauf** 31.53

saide *v.pa.p.* named 4.61

satisfaccion *n.* penance, reparation 4.362, 5.280

save *adj.* safe 31.1387

savegarde *n.* safety 31.1498

saverist *v.pr.2sg.* understand 5.1352; **saverith** *pr.3sg.* 5.1350; **saveryd** *pa.* pleased 29.5

savour(e *n.* smell 3.442, 5.1145, 17.64, 20.57, 29.202

sawte *n.* raid 3.718

sch- *see* **sh-**

science *n.* knowledge 31.2894; *lyberalle scyens* liberal art 29.151

sclowe *adj.* sluggish 27.194

scorned *v.pa.* deceived 29.407, disdained 30.25

scornynge *vbl.n.* mockery 30.24

scourfe *n.* scaly skin disease 3.928; **scurvis** *n.pl.* scabs 1.453

scripture *n.* inscription 6.81, 30.46, the bible 31.1783

scripulnes *n.* scrupulosity 31.986 (*note*)

seche *v.imp.* seek 29.220

se *v.* see 1.95; **seyng** *pr.p.* 13.9; **se(e** *pa.* 1.101, 7.41, 10.47, 13.14, 14.100, etc.; **seigh** 21.47; **sye** 16.130, 28.1182; **seyn** 16.278 *pa.p.* **seyen** 31.140

sekirlye *adv.* certainly 5.168

selde *adv.* seldom 6.220, 10.7, 27.138

seldyn *adv.* seldom 28.14

selle *n.*[1] saddle 30.286

selle *n.*[2] *see* **celle**

selle *v.* *to s-* for sale 28.739

semblant *n.* facial expression 22.76, 27.267; **sembland** 27.202

semely *adj.* honourable 30.341, good-looking 31.86

semyng *v.pr.p.* fitting, proper 29.1007; *to his s-* to his mind 26.28

sensible *adj.* capable of sensation 31.308

sensour *n.* censer 5.284

sentence *n.* opinion 1.1092, 29.603, verdict 1.1137, 5.1073, judicial sentence 31.1584, penalty 28.950, 29.1200, 30.66, doctrine 31.214, verdict 31.1137, 5.1073; *gret s-* sentence of excommunication 28.437; *pl.* judgements 1.1130

sepulture *n.* tomb 3.301, burial 29.777

sequence *n.* a nonscriptural text sung after the Alleluia or Tract during mass on important liturgical days 5.403

sercher *n.* examiner 31.2053

serchynge *vbl.n.* inspection 31.2065

seruyle *adj.* laborious 3.312

sese *v.*[1] cause to cease 3.197, cease 31.131; **sease** 31.1307; **sesyd** *pa.* 31.20

sese *v.*[2] seize 28.323; **sesid** *pa.p.* 28.372

sethe *v.* bake, roast 30.218; *imp.* boil 20.41; **sode** *pa.* 26.486; **soden** *pa.p.* 26.112, **soth** 29.53

sett *n.* dwelling-place 29.167 (*note*); **setys** *pl.* seats 26.238

set(t)(e *v.pa.* sat 16.186, 29.938, 31.1396

sette *v.* establish 29.73; **settyng** *pr.p.* *s-littelle by* caring little about 31.1681; **set(te** *pa.p.* put 7.21, 9.4, established 29.71; *pa.* *s-* *not* cared nothing 28.968

sewe *v.pr.* follow 5.950; **sue** 31.497; **sewid** *pa.p.* 5.1070

schappe *n.* shape 31.1133

schare *n.* groin 27.232

scharpe *adj.* severe 31.1320

scharpely *adv.* severely 31.1228

scharpnes *n.* austerity 29.121

scheder *n.* *s-* *of mannes blode* murderer 31.1396

sherewd *see* **schrewed**

scherdis *n.pl.* potsherds 31.1366

S(c)here Thursday(e *adj.,n.* day before Good Friday 4.63, 26.272

shere *see* **chere**

schethe *n.* sheath 31.1191

schetith *v.pr.3sg.* shoots 27.132

shette *see* **shittist**

s(c)hewe *v.* reveal 14.101; **schewynge** *pr.p.* 30.76; **schewed** *pa.* demonstrated 31.226, revealed 4.155, 16.247, performed 30.352 (*note*)

schewer *n.* revealer, teacher 31.358

ship *n.* incense boat 5.286

schyryne n. shrine 15.57

shittist *v.pr.2sg.* shut 1.1253; **shette** *pa.* 3.870; *pa.p.* 22.31; **shytt** 5.153; **schitte** 31.2551; *ppl.adj.* 3.732

shoryn *v.pa.p.* shorn 4.83; **schorne** *ppl.adj.* *of s-* cut off 18.103

shorte *n.* garment worn next to skin 28.779; **schurte** 28.1229

schortyd *v.pa.p.* shortened 31.2201

schreven *v.pa.p.* received absolution 16.152, 31.2332

schrewed *adj.* wicked 16.149, malicious 31.2721; **sherewd** ill-behaved 28.40; **shrewde** evil 5.789

schrewedly *adv.* wickedly 31.1599

schryfte *n.* confession to a priest 31.2223; **shryfte** 4.362

schryned *v.pa.p.* enshrined 28.1255, 31.1695; **shyrrynyd** 28.174

schuldres *n.pl.* shoulders 31.1234

syder *n.* strong drink 29.124

sides *n.pl.* times 27.107

syeyeng *v.pr.p.* sighing 29.1097

syker *adj.* certain 5.1446, 31.2241, secure 16.27 .

sykerly *adv.* certainly 29.171
sykylle *n.* sickle 31.3004
synguler *adj.* specific 31.509; **singler** 24.26
syngulerly *adv.* uniquely 31.515
synnys *adv.* afterwards 9.64
sith *conj.* since, because 19.29, 29.55, 31.920, after 29.1049; *adv.* afterwards 29.43
sythe *n.* scythe 31.3004
sythen *adj.* ago 31.2490; *conj.* since 31.3105
sythes *n.pl.* times 5.1338
sittyng(e *ppl.adj.* fitting, suitable 3.189, 30.13
skabby *adj.* rough 1.447
skille *n.* reason 31.1091; *pl.* 5.1449
skyrte *n.* lower part of gown 1.996
skrowe *n.* scroll 18.100
slaked *v.pa.* ceased 28.1008
sle(e *v.* overcome 14.28, kill 1.12, 2.31, 18.33 etc., **slowe** *pa.* 11.46, 26.329, 28.1235 etc.; **slewe** 13.6; **slayne** *pa.p.* 1.55, 7.94, 14.96; **islayne** 29.951; **sleynge** *vbl.n.* killing 31.2587
slym *n.* slime 23.24
slode *v.pa.* slid, fell 14.96
slouth(e *n.* indolence 3.869, 5.207
slowe *see* sle
slowfulle *adj.* slothful 29.411
sluggisch *adj.* lazy 31.1898; **slouggishe** 5.685
smale *adj.* small 20.40, of low estate 31.2568
smartnes *n.* anguish 31.1230
smylyngly *adv.* with a smile 31.2242 (*note*)
smyte *v.* strike 26.483, 29.850, 31.1233; *s- of* cut off 24.143, 29.851; *pa.* 18.69; **smete** *s- down* felled 18.53; struck 26.485; **smyte** penetrated 25.42; **smote** pricked 30.385, struck 1.707, 3.660, 31.1668; **smot** 29.1388; **smyten** *pa.p.* 31.1548; **smeytn** afflicted 3.604; **smytte** 29.740; **smete** 29.532; **smytyng** *vbl.n.* striking off 8.46, 18.74
socour(e *v.* support 1.710, 31.1420
socour(e *n.* support 3.482, 6.246, 30.107; soker 31.3176; *doo thowe s-* give help 29.847
sode(y)n *adj.* unexpected 3.735, 30.281, 31.428; **sodayne** 23.99
soden *see* sethe
sodenly *adv.* unexpectedly 31.2541

soget(t) *adj.* submissive 4.367, 5.853
sogettis *n.pl.* subjects 1.862; **subgettis** servants 7.16
soiernyd *v.pa.* stayed 3.644
solde *v.pa. s- faste away* sold off 7.62
sompnyd *v.pa.p.* summoned 28.633
sonde *n.* sand 1.507
sondre *adv. in s-* apart 31.426
sonyst *superl.adj.* foremost 5.1393
soper *n.* supper 26.154
sore *adv.* intensely 3.303, 29.1359, grievously 3.363, 13.45, 19.20, 21.36, 31.592
sory *adj.* poor 31.1715
soryly *adv.* sorrowfully 29.1363
soth *see* sethe
sothe *n.* truth 29.12
sothely *adv.* truly 29.58, 31.3182
sothefastnes *n.* certainty 31.2270
sotil *adj.* ingenious 27.40
sotylly *adv.* secretly 1.119, 29.266
souerayn *adj.* excellent 23.100; **soueryne** 22.106; **souereyn** supreme 27.94
so(u)fte *adj.* mild, restrained 1.297 (*note*), 3.101
sowe *v.* scatter 31.2721
sowke *v.* suck 31.1488
sowne *n.* sound 3.331, noise 3.393
sowneth *v.pr.3sg. s- to* pertains to 31.1506; **sownyd** *pa.* sounded 14.111, 29.204, resounded 29.305
sownyng *v.pr.p.* noisy, resounding 5.216
space *n.* period of time 1.140
sparyth *v.pr.3sg.* hesitates 29.865; **spare** *imp.* 31.1489; **sparyd** *pa.* 25.12
spede *n.* progress 5.1455
spede *v.* prosper 1.800, succeed 28.698; **sped(de** *pa.p.* accomplished their purpose 1.382, 28.133, prospered 31.626
spent *pa.p.* used up 26.316
sper(r)yd *v.pa.* barred 2.26; *pa.p.* enclosed 29.213 (*note*)
spice *n.* sub-class or branch of sin 5.764(*note*)
spyed *v.pa.p.* noticed 3.380
spiritualte *n.* body of spiritual or ecclesiastical persons, clergy 5.63, 28.460
spytte *v.pa.* spat 31.1035
spoyled *pa.p.* stripped of clothing 31.2201
sporis *n.pl.* spurs 30.385
sporyd *v.pa.* spurred 10.28
sporte *v.refl.* enjoy oneself 18.57, 28.708
spowsed *v.pa.* betrothed 31.2367
spousesse *n.* wife 24.53

spoushed *n.* marriage 1.284
sprynge *v.* sprinkle 5.1333, sprout 27.243; **spryngynge** *pr.p.* growing 16.227; **sprang(e** *pa.* became known 1.170, 21.2; **sponge** grew 16.224, sprang up 30.239
spryngyng *vbl.n.* sprinkling 5.229
squames *n.pl.* films, scales on eyes 1.676
stale *v.pa.* stole 1.243, 29.1361, 30.284
stallyd *v.pa.p.* enthroned 6.248
stappes *n.pl.* footsteps 29.292
stature *n.* height 30.298
staues *n.pl.* clubs 24.155, 29.1271
stede *n.* place 13.58, 16.192, 30.90; *pl.* 13.78
sted(e)fastly(e *adv.* firmly 5.900, 30.146
stekyd *v.pa.* stuck 6.89, stabbed 31.2390; **styked** stuck 1.1100, 3.650, 28.1131; **styckyd** 30.33
steppe *n.* footprint 20.55; *pl.* 4.247; soles of feet 9.25, footsteps 9.32
ster(e *v.* move 3.307, 27.246, 29.900; **sterith** *pr.3sg.* 27.20; **steryng** *pr.p.* persuading 29.668; **sterid** *pa.* stirred up, moved 3.23, 31.1766, stirred (lit.) 28.844, 1100; exhorted 29.536, 31.475, incited 16.143, provoked 29.674; **ster(r)ed** 23.20, 24.37; *pa.p.* exhorted 31.299
steryng(e *vbl.n.* provocation 5.103, 28.382, persuasion 28.1257; *s- of the flessche* bodily temptations 31.326
steryn *adj.* loud 22.129
sterke *adv.* completely 9.47
stewes *n.pl.* bathhouses 31.819
stye *v.* ascend 5.945
styed *ppl.adj.* restraiined 27.36 *(note)*
styked *see* **stekyd**
stylle *adj.* silent 29.103, quiet 31.2926
stylle *adv.* continuously 1.337, 6.264, 13.94, without moving 3.872, 6.199, without speaking 9.85, 31.3054
stylly *adv.* privately 28.1111
stynche *n.* stench 9.33, 26.372
stoble *n.* stubble 3.410
stoburne *adj.* stubborn 30.368
Stoykis *n.pl.* Stoics 31.333
stok(k)(e *n.* descent, ancestry 1.289 *(note)*, 3.21, 31.79; block of wood 31.1155, base of tree 1.875, 31.2480; *pl.* blocks of wood 31.303
stole *n.*[1] stool 1.429
sto(o)le *n.*[2] ecclesiastical vestment, stole 5.196, 5.404

storye *n.* history 31.987; *pl.* 3.760
storyns *n.pl.* historians 31.56
strayte *see* **streite** *adv.*[1]
strangely *adv.* vehemently 31.379 *(note)*
strangelyd *v.pa.* killed 25.45
straunge *adj.* foreign 7.7, 31.92, aloof 31.93, unusual 31.150
straunger *n.* foreigner 31.650; *pl.* 4.31
stree *n.* straw 29.1118
streyte *adj.* strict 5.1140, austere 17.9, 26.3, 28.145, 31.1810, narrow 26.183, tight 30.337; **strayter** *comp. adj.* more austere 2.102
streite *adv.*[1] austerely 28.108, tightly 28.780; **strayte** 6.93
streyte *adv.*[2] directly 31.2213 *(note)*
streytenes *n.* constriction 1.1334; **straytenesse** austerity 31.1010
stryves *n.pl.* conflicts 5.788
stroke *v.pa.* stabbed 31.2358, spurred 31.2469, struck 31.2491; **streken** *pa.p.* 31.3002; **stryken** 31.1587
strokes *n.pl.* blows 31.1959
stronkyn *ppl.adj.* tightly drawn up 1.979 *(note)*
stuffe *n.* supplies 26.557
sturdy *adj.* rebellious 6.271, 28.351
sturnely *adv.* frighteningly 26.512
subgettis *see* **sogettis**
substaunce *n.* being 31.509
sudary(e *n.* cloth to wipe sweat from face; cloth of St Veronica 4.12
sue *see* **sewe**
sufferaunce *n.* permission 1.852, 31.2135; **suffrauns** 31.2053
suffise *v.* be capable of 3.802
suffragies *n.pl.* prayers for the dead 5.1501
suffre *v.* allow 1.392, 3.31, 7.5, 18.85, 28.471 etc., bear 1.1028, endure 5.874, 21.21; *imp.* allow 5.1169; **suffrid** *pa.* allowed 3.418, 12.6
suyr *see* **sure**
sumdele *adj.* somewhat 27.202
sumtyme *adv.* once 26.470, 28.500, 31.142
sure *adj.* secure 3.741; **suyr** free from danger 31.2241
surete(e *n.* protection 28.549, money or property offered as guarantee 28.1013; *pl.* 30.340
suspesyon *n. matyrs of s-* grounds for suspicion 30.336
suspecious *adj.* ill-famed 5.696
susteyne *v.* bear the weight of 24.39,

continue 24.157; **susteyned** *pa.p.* bore the weight of 31.3116; **susteynyng** *pr.p.* tolerating 23.18

swage *v.imp.* relieve 3.830; **swaged** *pa.p.* subsided 28.543, reduced 3.417

sware *v.pa.sg.* swore, vowed to carry out 31.1238; **sworne** *pa.pl.* 21.4

swownyd *v.pa.* swooned 28.1140

table *n.* retable 4.84; **tablis** *pl.* tablets 4.65

take *v.* give 30.431; *t- ayen* give back 1.796; **toke** *pa.* gave 6.21 (*note*), 7.83, 28.1104(2), 30.185 (*note*), arrested 29.1086, received 5.300, 31.2422; *t- the crosse* 6.182 (*note*), 28.3; **take** *pa.p.* arrested 31.2586; *t- with* caught in 28.300

talage *n.* forced levy 1.228

tale *n.* time 31.243

taper *n.* candle 14.6, **tapre** 14.8; *pl.* **tapers** 3.167, 5.588, 16.261; **tapurs** 26.256

tawe *v.* prepare animal skins for dressing 3.664

telle *v.* consider 29.118(2), 29.1275

tellyng *vbl.n.* counting 31.2550

temporalte *n.* laity as opposed to clergy 28.461

tempre *v.* moderate 1.874; **temperith** *pr.3sg.* combines with 27.210

temptacion *n.* testing 3.847

tempte *v.* test 30.65; **temptid** *pa.* attempted 3.416

tende *v.pa.* lit 14.8

tenour *n.* meaning, purport 31.665

teraundis see **tyra(u)nd**

tetys *n.pl.* teats, *from hys moder t-* from early childhood 29.142

theraftir *adv.* accordingly 27.83

ther(e *poss.pron.* their 5.157, 6.224, 9.49, 27.83, 30.115, 31.1868

thyes *n.pl.* thighs 31.2902

thykke *adv.* in great numbers 31.2051 (*note*)

tho *adv.* then 1.1067, 4.268, 13.4, 18.124, etc.

tho(o *pron.* those 1.810, 5.131, 6.282, 9.20, etc.

thof(f)(e *conj.* though 31.188, 312, 488; **thow(h** 31.1001, 1477; **thouh** 29.836

thral *adj.* in servitude 28.189

thraldom(e *n.* state of subjection 1.147, 28.202, 29.867, 31.672

threes *adv. see* **thryes**

threfolde *adv.* in threes (?) 31.2051 (*note*)

thretyd *v.pa.* accused 29.856

threxholde *n.* threshold 7.24

thrid(d)e *ord.num.* third 27.261, 31.2012

thryes *adv.* thrice 31.2876; **threes** 5.311

thrust(e *n.* thirst 31.1056

thrustelewe *adj.* thirsty (fig.) 31.972

þurst *v.pa.3sg.* dared 29.1364

tyde *n.* *.xij.th t-* twelfth day after Christmas, Epiphany 26.267 (*note*)

tye dogge *n.* tethered dog 27.37

tylle *v.*[1] cultivate 30.159

tyllyd *v.*[2] *pa.* reached 26.455

tyra(u)nd *n.* tyrant 8.25, 21.3, 25.2; **tyraunte** 31.1448; **teraundis** *pl.* 8.5; **tyra(u)ndys** 21.8, 25.8; **tyrauntis** 28.457

tysyng *vbl.n.* enticement 5.718, 10.14

tythyng *vbl.n.* paying of tithe 17.20

tiþis *n.pl.* tithes, tenth part of goods/income given to church as religious obligation 30.154

tytle *n.* descriptive appellation 1.260, name 31.1004 (*note*)

tobete *v.pa.* beat severely 1.1204, 3.876; *pa.p.* 31.1354; **tobetyn** 22.81, 24.115

tobrake *v.pa.* broke apart 3.393, 30.347; **tobreke** broke to pieces 31.1836; **tobroke** *ppl.adj.* damaged 6.96

tobraste *v.pa.* shattered 13.9

tobrent(e *pa.p.* burned up 31.2841; *ppl.adj.* singed 29.46

tocrussched *pa.p.* entirely crushed 31.2703

todrawe *v.pa.p.* dismembered 22.53; **todrawyn** 23.55

todyr *pron.* the other 26.186

tofore *adv.* previously 13.14, 29.25

tofore *prep.* in front of 13.54, 29.19, above, better than 29.318, previous to 14.108

tohewen *pa.p.* cut up 24.234

tokyn *n.* sign 1.810, 3.191, 17.56; *pl.* 27.263, 31.941

torente *ppl.adj.* lacerated 24.114

toschake *ppl.adj.* shaken forcefully 30.348

toslytte *v.pa.* split open 10.27

totoryn *v.pa.p.* torn to shreds 6.105

touchid *v.pa.p. not t-* untouched sexually 1.286 (*note*)

towarde and frowarde *advs.* forwards and backwards 3.346

towe *n.* raw flax used for kindling 3.410

trace *n.* track 31.500

tracte *n.* choral chant sung in place of

Alleluia at mass during penitential season 5.396

trad *v.pa.* trod 30.52; **trodyn** *pa.p.* trodden 30.59

traitourly *adv.* surreptitiously 28.602

translacion *n.* disinterment of body or relics of saint and removal to shrine 3.727, 28.1261, 30.260

translate *v.pa.p.* disinterred and removed to a (new) shrine 3.730; **translatyd(e** 10.93, 15.56, 17.44, 20.78 etc., removed 1.850

trauaylous *adj.* full of suffering, *t-bataylles* path of martyrdom 23.81

traveyle *v.* strive 29.916; **travayle** *imp.* 29.219; **trauayled** *pa.* took pains 29.66, laboured 29.879; **traveilde** *pa.p* 5.1328

traveyle *n.* hard labour 29.918

trauelyng *vbl.n.* childbirth 24.188

tre(e *n.* wood 3.412, 4.147, 31.366, cross of the crucifixion 4.310

treen *adj.* wooden 4.149

trespas *n.* sin, transgression 3.608, 16.210, 27.15, 28.190, 30.200; **trespasse** *pl.* 5.20; **trespace** crimes 31.3019

trespasid *v.pa.* sinned 5.1110

trespassour *n.* criminal 31.2902

tretice *n.* treatise 31.988; **tretys(e** 5.*rubric*, 29.188

tretyng *v.pr.p.* discussing terms 1.250

tryars *n.pl.* refiners 30.331 (*note*)

tryffuls *n.pl.* ribald anecdotes 14.36

trompe *n.* trumpet 29.1331

trouble *n.* turbulence 28.579

troublis *adj.* turbulent 5.389; **trowbles** 31.641

trouthe *n.* betrothal vow 31.2742

trowble *v.imp.* disturb 30.195; **troubled** *pa.* oppressed 28.323, afflicted 30.206; **troubelid** *ppl.adj.* perturbed 3.345; **trowblid** 31.1564

trowbles *adj. see* **troublis**

trowest *v.pr.2sg.* believe 29.205, 31.800 (*note*); **trowed** *pa.* 31.2804

truste *v.imp.* be assured 2.37

turne *v.* change 30.161, *imp.* convert 31.1278 (*note*); t-(d ayen(e return 3.165, 28.331, 29.765, 30.388; **turned** *pa.* turned over 21.32; *pa.p.* converted 1.868; **tornyd** 24.128

twey *num.* two 29.362; **tweyn(e** 7.11, 29.365, 31.2315; **twayne** 29.782

tweys *adv.* twice 6.29, 28.190; **twyes** 31.2473

vnbodely *adj.* spiritual 29.716

vnbrent *adj.* not burned up 6.98

vnchaunce *n.* misfortune 31.2839

vnclene *adj.* sinful 24.47

vnclennes *n.* sinfulness 29.55

vncorupte *ppl.adj.* pure 3.43

vncunnyng *n.* lack of learning 1.1082; **vnkonnyng** ignorance 29.352

vncunnyng *adj.* uneducated 5.1101

vndedelynesse *n.* immortality 29.186

vndedly *adj.* immortal 29.231

vndefouled *adj.* unharmed 29.505

vndepartable *adj.* indivisible 31.1120

vndernyme *v.* rebuke 5.1107

vndevoute *adj.* irreverent 3.272

vndiscretely *adv.* imprudently 31.2860

vngoodely *adv.* rudely 30.369

vngracious *adj.* displeasing 31.1222

vngreve *adj.* not distressing, benign 29.466

vnhappy *adj.* ill-fated 31.1223

vnharde *adj.* unheard 29.202

vnhoneste *adj.* physically unpleasant 31.1506

vnkynde *adj.* unnatural 16.246; **vnkyndely** 31.748

vnle(y)ful(le illicit 1.700, 5.792, 24.38, 31.180

vnneth(es *adv.* scarcely 1.56, 28.216, 29.50, 31.3148, with difficulty 3.550, 25.21, 26.127; **vnnethis** 26.183; **onethe** scarcely 29.117

vnqvyet *v.* disturb 31.3074

vnresonable *adj.* lacking the power of reason 5.760, 29.103, 30.406

vnright *n.* wrongdoing 6.283, 28.651

vnrightwysse *adj.* unrighteous 31.1336

vnshamefastenesse *n.* shamelessness 5.773

vnsittyng *adj.* unfitting 5.796, 28.394

vnspecable *adj.* indescribable, ineffable 5.390; **vnspekable** 29.113

vnstableness *n.* inconstancy 5.798

vnthrifte *n.* shiftless, dissolute person 31.2348

vnware(s *adv.* without warning 8.11, 31.2991; **onware** unsuspectingly 18.29

vnwarly *adv.* without warning 31.2234, carelessly 31.2781

vnwemmyd *ppl.adj.* uninjured 24.67

vnwildeful *adj.* not wilful 27.196 (*note*)

vnwonte *adj.* unusual 29.114
vnworthy *adj.* unwarranted 31.751, undeserving 31.1827
vrchyn *n.* hedgehog 8.22
vsage *n.* custom 31.304
vse *n.* custom 3.149, 26.223
vsid *v.pa.* was in habit of 1.125, 31.2115; *v-* . . . *lyfe* lived 1.122
vtas *n.* ecclesiastical Octave, the eight days after a church festival or any one of them 4.27
vttirmur *comp.adj.* farther away 27.186
vttirst *superl.adj. as n.* utmost 28.304; **vttrest** *superl.adj.* extreme 29.126

vayle *n.* curtain hung between altar and choir during Lent 5.133, veil 4.76
valure *n.* value 1.1183
vanyte(e) *n.* foolishness 29.1073; *pl.* 3.57, 5.12
variaunce *n.* difference of opinion 15.26; *pl.* differences 31.242
vawte *n.* vault 3.427
veer *n.* Spring 31.245
veyn(e *adj.* worthless 5.695, 17.24, 20.7
veynes *n.pl.* channels 27.177
vengeaunce *n.* retribution 3.605
very(e *adj.* genuine 1.46, 5.55, properly so-called 5.19, real 29.383; **ver(r)ay** true 31.96, faithful 31.108
veryly, verely *adv.* certainly 1.512, 3.313, 9.27, 14.92, 16.186 etc., truly 6.61
vertues *adj.* vertuous 1.178, 2.94, 3.21, 28.165
vervent *see* **feruent**
vesture *n.* royal apparel 31.1529
vexid *v.pa.p.* afflicted 1.1284, 3.768
vitayled *v.pa* supplied with food 26.64; **vityllyd** 26.162
viteyle *n.* food, provisions 26.316; **vytayle** 26.300
voyde *adj.* without its bishop or abbot 28.284, empty-handed 31.822
voyde *v.* avoid 5.1446
vomyd *v.pa.* foamed 1.1207
vouchesa(u)f(e *v.* grant 3.124, 26.40, 31.2414; **vouched safe** *pa.* 31.2158

wacche *v.* keep under surveillance 31.1199; **wacchydde** *pa.* kept vigil 30.318; **wecchid** 16.277, 30.410, kept guard 3.717; **wacched** *pa.p.* kept under surveillance 31.2169

wacchynge *vbl.n.* vigil 30.309; *pl.* 3.73; **wecchyngis** 3.901
waye *n.* road 3.159, 4.212, 10.65; *fowle w-*muddy path 26.421; **wey(e** road 28.429, 30.147, 31.429, direction 31.799, route 31.837, journey 29.1099
waynes *n.pl.* wagons 31.2695
wais(s)h *v.* wash 1.581; **weish** 1.671; **wesshe** *pa.* 5.524; **wissh(e** 1.587, 26.200; **wysh** 1.612; **wais(s)h** *pa.p.* 1.608; **waisshyn** 1.972; **wassched** 31.673; **wasschen** 31.980; **wesshe** 7.28
wake *v.* stay awake 27.209; *imp.* 5.209; **wakyng** *ppl.adj.* awake 29.1176; **woke** *pa.* 29.130
wakyng *vbl.n.* keeping vigils 29.783
wantone *adj.* unruly, undisciplined 30.247
warde *n. to w-* in custody 28.391
ware *adj.* cautious 5.845, aware 31.557
warely *adv.* prudently 31.130
warre *n.* enmity 31.2150
wastid *v.pa.* diminished 1.201, 3.411, 26.257
waters *n.* rivers 18.6
wawis *n.pl.* waves 2.87, 3.347, 26.389
wax(e *v.* become 3.104; **waxith** *pr3sg.* 27.165; **wax** *pa.* 6.186, 30.246; **waxyd** grew 18.67, became 3.46, 6.301, 14.116, 26.562; **wexe** 29.84; **wexid** 7.33, 19.31, 28.250
wecchid *see* **wacche**
wecchyngis *see* **wacchynge**
weder *n.* weather 3.215, 6.196, 19.19; **wedyr** 18.124, 26.228, 27.78; **wed(d)yrs** 19.21, 27.159; **wether** storm 6.211
wey *see* **waye**
weyefaryng *ppl.adj. w- men* travellers 29.1043
weytyd *v.pa.p. w- on* laid in wait for 16.144
wele *n.* welfare 14.80
welfare *n.* wellbeing 1.792, 31.595; **wilfare** 26.6; *pl.* 28.153
welle *n.* spring 2.41, 9.70, 10.55, 18.118, 26.125 etc.
welle *adj. not w- with thyselfe* not of sound mind 3.282
welthe *n.* well-being 1.826, 10.12, 31.1715
wel-willed *adj.* well disposed 1.323
wem(m)e *n.* blemish 17.59, 24.161
wene *v.* think 29.39; suppose 31.1275; *pr.2sg.* **wenyst(e** 31.1273, 29.206; **wene** *imp.* 29.159; **wenyng(e** *pr.p.* thinking

1.232, 7.38, 29.38, expecting 16.105, believing 16.186; **wend(e** *pa.* expected 26.326, thought 3.592, 7.36, 21.46, 28.344, 29.894; **wente** 3.458

werche *v.* work 14.28

were *v.* wear 6.29, 28.136; **weryd** *pa.* 4.78, 6.32, 28.138

werker *n.* producer, creator 31.1952

wesshe *see* wais(s)h

wet(t)e *v.* know 3.299, 15.36, 26.167, 28.205, 29.704; **wyt(t)e** 29.250; **wote** *pr.sg.* 3.363, 7.90, 28.317, 31.291; **woste** *pr.2sg.* 29.371; **wete** *pr.pl.* 28.681; **wote** 29.617; **wyttyng** *pr.p.* 29.566; **wetyng** 29.896; **wiste** *pa.* 16.43, 26.74, 28.333, 31.321; **wyst(e** 1.254, 3.343, 6.156, 7.3, 11.40, 13.53, 29.196

wether *see* weder

wetyn *v.pr.p.* wetting 3.212

wexe *see* wax(e

wheder *adv.* whither 5.898, 16.178; **whether** 29.1134, 30.355; whence 31.1240

whele *n.* instrument of torture 31.2168 (*note*)

where as *prep.* where 31.966

whete *adj.* white 29.366

while *adv.* one *w-* . . . *anoþer w-* at one time . . . at another time 3.348-9; *other whyle* at another time 29.407

wil *see* wylle *v.*

wildefyre *n.* lightning 31.1684

wilful(le *adj.* purposeful 5.1069, willing 5.1143

perverse 31.395

wylfully *adv.* willingly 4.365, 31.479

wylle *n.* wish 5.1175, requirement 5.1176 (*note*), desire 9.53, 29.250

wylle *v.* intend 9.52, desire 29.254(3), *pr.* 31.520; **wylte** *pr.2sg.* wish 1.1100, 7.88, 29.249, 30.192; **wil** *pr.3sg.* wishes 18.62; **wol(l)e** *pr.* 3.147, 5.1321, 10.38, 12.13, 13.46, etc., demands 28.683; **woldyst** *pr.subj.2sg.* 16.194; **wyllyng(e** *pr.p.* wishing 29.900, 31.2845; **wolde** *pa.* wanted 1.114, 3.129, 9.43, 10.16, 13.29, etc.

wynde *v.* hoist with a pulley or winch 13.91; *made w- up* ordered to hoist; *w-awey (fig.)* move away 31.306; **wonde** *pa.* winched up 13.86; **wounde** 26.119

wynnyng *n.* monetary gain, profit 3.666; *pl.* 30.334

wynnyng *vbl.m.* acquisition 1.198

wyse *n.* manner 24.100, 31.1996 (*note*)

wysely *adv.* prudently 31.1860, carefully 31.2425

wiste *see* wet(t)e

without(e *adv.* outside 1.470, 4.37, 5.176, 7.25, 8.17 etc.

withowte *conj.* unless 31.2452

witnessith *v.pr.pl.* attest 5.973

wytte *n.* intelligence 5.777, 31.190; *pl.* 29.713, 31.273; senses 3.547, 5.11

wytte *v. see* wet(t)e

wittely *adv.* wisely 31.482

wytty *adj.* wise 31.262

wode *n.* forest 10.17, 18.88

wo(o)d(e *adj.* insane 2.29, 9.51, 11.41, 24.151, 27.208 etc., fierce 31.1353, angry 31.1574; *w- beste* wild animal 31.1601; *w- thyngis* inanimate things 3.123 (*note*); **wooder** *comp.* more furious 31.36

wo(o)d(e)nes *n.* fury 23.27, 31.1155; recklessness 28.996, ferocity 1.84, 31.46

woke *n.* week 5.384

wolde *adj.* old 5.126

wolde, wolle *v. see* wylle *v.*

wollemen *n.pl.* wool merchants 31.2307

wombe *n.* membrane 27.228 (*note*); stomach 31.2834

wonde *v. see* wynde

wonder *v. w- vpon* marvel 31.1516; **wondryng** *pr.p.* 28.40; **woundrid** *pa.* 3.380, 4.278, 6.219

wonderfulle *adv.* marvellously 5.913 (*note*)

wondyr *adv.* exceedingly 23.4

wonte *adj.* customary 29.199

wonte *v.pa.p.* accustomed 29.36

woo *n.* grief 21.56 (*note*)

worchyng *vbl.n.* carrying out 5.1492

worschip *v.pr.* honour 31.1643; **wurshipped** *pa.p.* 3.776

worschip(pe *n.* honour 31.1546; **wurship** 1.159, 3.733, renown 1.1139, 3.726

worshipful(le *adj.* imposing 9.97, 10.96, 11.98 12.31 14.122 etc.; **worschipful** honourable 16.215, 31.25; **wurshipfulle** 13.134

worshipfully *adv.* with honour 13.132, 28.61

wote *see* wet(t)e

wothe *n.* oath 1.31

wounderly *adv.* extraordinarily 3.731

wracke *n.* destruction; *went to w-* broke up and sank 31.2319

wrecche *n.* despicable person 31.51; *pl.* poor, miserable people 1.184

wrestelle *v.* struggle 31.307; **wrestelyd** *pa.* 17.30

wreth(e *n.* wrath 1.196, 3.174, 24.151, 28.207, 29.1223; **wreythe** 7.94

wretyng *vbl.n.* *by w-* from books 27.112; **writtyng** writ 28.751

wryttis *n.pl.* documents 28.1105

wronge *n.* *doone theym w-* spoken unjustly about them 31.1406

wroth(e *adj.* angry 7.3, 28.933

wrought *v.pa.* worked 1.1197, 3.722, 31.2483; *pa.p.* made 26.238

wurship *see* worschip(pe

yate *n.* gate 17.28, 30.235, 31.631; *pl.* 26.57, 27.147; **yeatis** 4.37

yefte *n.* gift 1.196, *pl.* 3.382; 5.27, 6.16

yerde *n.* rod 18.63

yere daye *n.* anniversary of death 3.472 (*note*)

yerthe *n.* ground 10.89, 11.88

yeue *v.* give 2.5, 3.478, 4.268, 29.414; **gefe** *g- the batelle* grant victory 31.1785; **yevith** *pr.3sg.* gives 29.343; **yeve** *imp.* 1.1100; **yeuyng** *pr.p.* giving 2.102, 5.72, 19.10, 20.77; **yeavist** *pa.2sg.* gave 1.1094; **yeaf(f)e** *pa.* 1.773, 3.21, 6.76, 7.62, 9.88; **gaf** 31.462; **yafe** gave 14.29, yielded 18.94; **yave** gave 29.521; **yeve** *pa.p.* given 3.102, 7.92; **geve** 16.37; **yove** 29.750; **yeve** 29.504; **yovyn** 1.678, 3.359, committed 3.14; **yoven** *ppl.adj.* given 5.554, 28.263

Yevyn *n.* *see* **Even**

INDEX OF PROPER NAMES

This list does not include references in the texts to Christ, the Virgin Mary, saints' names within the text devoted to their life, ecclesiastical offices, feasts, seasons, sacraments, prayers or hymns, book titles, books of the bible, religious orders, unidentified emperors, kings, ecclesiastical office holders or bearers of titles of nobility. Spellings given are those of the scribes, with Latin source and or modern English in brackets where confusion might arise. The following abbreviations are used: ap(ostle, archbp. archbishop, bp. bishop, ch(urch, emp(erour, ev(angelist, k(ing, m(artyr, r(iver, v(irgin, w(ife.

INDEX OF BIBLICAL QUOTATIONS
AND REFERENCES